Stan Roger
603-626-715

Real Estate Valuation in Litigation

Readers of this text may be interested in the following related materials:

The Appraisal of Real Estate, tenth edition
The Dictionary of Real Estate Appraisal, third edition
Environmental Site Assessments and Their Impact on Property Value: The Appraiser's Role
and *The Appraiser as Expert Witness* videotape

For a catalog of Appraisal Institute publications, contact the Publications Department of the Appraisal Institute, 875 North Michigan Avenue, Chicago, Illinois 60611-1980

Real Estate Valuation in Litigation

Second Edition

J. D. Eaton, MAI, SRA

Appraisal Institute
875 North Michigan Avenue
Chicago, Illinois 60611-1980

APPRAISAL INSTITUTE®

Reviewers: Howard C. Gelbtuch, MAI
John H. Love, SRA
Thomas A. Motta, MAI, SRA
George F. Silver, MAI, SRA
Janice F. Young, MAI, RM

Senior Vice President, Communications: Christopher Bettin
Manager, Book Development: Michael R. Milgrim, PhD
Senior Editor/Writer: Stephanie Shea-Joyce
Manager, Design/Production: Julie B. Beich

Printed in the United States of America

Library of Congress Cataloging-in-Publication Data
Eaton, J.D. (James D.)
Real estate valuation in litigation / J.D. Eaton.–2nd ed.
p. cm.
Includes bibliographical references and index.
ISBN 0-922154-20-1
1. Eminent domain–United States. 2. Real property–Valuation–United States. 3. Actions and defenses–United States. I. Title.
KF5599.E25 1995
346.7304'37–dc20
[347.306437] 95-17958
CIP

Table of Contents

Foreword

As real estate appraisers face the challenges of the 1990s, they need to embrace new information and disciplines. Some appraisers are looking to the area of real estate law as a new arena for their expertise and a new potential market for their services. These practitioners and those already doing litigation work will find this updated text to be an invaluable resource.

Real Estate Valuation in Litigation, second edition, is written for both appraisers and attorneys, opening up the channels of communication between these often adversarial professionals. It examines the relationships among appraisers, attorneys, and clients and the courts' attitude toward appraisal testimony. The text provides a comprehensive overview of real estate law with special emphasis on condemnation appraisal assignments, which form the bulk of appraisers' litigation work. Common pitfalls encountered in court are discussed and potential strategies for valuation experts are explored.

Appraisers who can prepare appraisal reports for litigation and present valuation testimony convincingly are in great demand. With the general information and specific instructions provided here, appraisers will have the tools they need to carve out a niche for themselves in a new, exciting area of endeavor.

Richard C. Sorenson, MAI
1995 President
Appraisal Institute

Epigraph

"Nothing that I [will hereafter say] should be construed to place the appraiser in the role of the advocate. However, much as the expert appraiser trains his lawyer, it is the lawyer who must lead in the courtroom; it is the lawyer who has the ultimate responsibility to his client. Therefore, the determinations as to the variant and proper legal approaches are his alone to make. They are never the responsibility of the appraiser. The worst thing an appraiser can do is to become an advocate except for his opinion, for, if he does, his bias and his prejudice will show through. He must stick to the fundamental facts."

Sidney Z. Searles
Examination and Cross-Examination
of Appraiser in Eminent Domain

Preface

This second edition of *Real Estate Valuation in Litigation*, like the first edition, is directed to real estate appraisers who have a basic understanding of real estate valuation principles and techniques and to attorneys who are interested in the valuation techniques applied by appraisers in forensic appraising. It has been written in light of the changes that are occurring in the real estate appraisal industry. With the demand for professional appraisal services in the lending industry on the decline, appraisers are turning their attention toward other areas where appraisal services are needed. Many appraisers with superior expertise in appraising for mortgage loan purposes are turning to litigation valuation as an alternative source of business.

Appraisers new to this field may find the atmosphere somewhat disconcerting. Presenting a written appraisal report to a client is not the same as presenting an appraisal verbally to a trier of fact in what is often a hostile environment. It is for this reason that a new chapter on the litigation environment has been added to the text. While their background in general appraisal practice may be good, appraisers entering the legal arena have a professional responsibility to develop the necessary understanding of the unique characteristics of litigation valuation. One purpose of this text is to help appraisers acquire the knowledge they need to perform competently in the litigation environment and make the transition into the field as painless as possible.

Valuation procedures and applicable laws are so interrelated that a thorough study of one cannot be made without a general understanding of the other. Although this text is not a law book, applicable law and court rulings have been cited throughout. Because laws and court rulings vary from jurisdiction to jurisdiction, no attempt has been made to cover all applicable laws in each jurisdiction. The cases cited were selected to illustrate a general rule or, on occasion, an exception to a general rule. Readers are encouraged to research the applicable law in their jurisdictions.

Much has changed in real estate litigation since the first edition of this work was published in 1982. None of these changes has made the real estate valuation expert's job easier. Some of these changes are discussed as "advanced problems" in a number of chapters. In many instances a valuation problem is described, but a definitive solution is not provided. Instead, alternative solutions are presented because, given the state of the law, a single, universal solution does not exist. Often the solution to such a problem will depend on the specific facts of the case and be determined by the court or other trier of fact. The problems are presented to alert readers to their existence and to demonstrate that issues are often not black and white in the field of litigation valuation

The author is currently employed by the U.S. Department of Justice, but the opinions and statements in this text are his alone and do not necessarily represent the viewpoint of the Department of Justice. In fact, no member of the Department of Justice reviewed any part of this work prior to its publication, and those familiar with the viewpoint of the Department will find that some of the opinions expressed here are in obvious conflict with the Department's positions. Appraisers who work with the Department of Justice should, therefore, not be surprised if they receive instructions contrary to the information contained in this work.

The preface to the first edition of this book stated, "current trends indicate that our society is *litigation happy*." If anything, that trend has escalated in the past 13 years. Further escalation can be anticipated, particularly in the field of property litigation. Government agencies are acquiring vast amounts of land for conservation purposes, with each acquisition requiring an appraisal and, sometimes, condemnation action. Property rights advocates are pushing for the easing of environmental regulations. Legislation has been introduced in a number of state legislatures and in Congress calling for the payment of compensation when property value is diminished by government regulation. The number of inverse condemnation cases filed has grown exponentially, prompting attempts to establish new rules of valuation and compensation. These activities have necessitated the addition of a new chapter titled, "Inverse Condemnation and Regulatory Takings."

To address these issues and provide appropriate professional services, real estate appraisers must have a general understanding of the laws that apply to real estate valuation and the methodology for presenting valuation evidence to a trier of fact. The underlying purpose of this text is to provide this necessary information to the appraisal community.

About the Author

J.D. Eaton, MAI, SRA, has been involved in the appraisal of all types of property since 1961, specializing in forensic appraising and consulting. As an independent fee appraiser in Longview, Washington, until 1991, he testified in a number of state and federal courts. Mr. Eaton is currently Assistant Chief Appraiser for the U.S. Department of Justice in Washington, D.C.

J.D. Eaton has been active in real estate education, serving as a trustee on the Washington Real Estate Education Foundation for six years and as its president. He has written several articles on litigation valuation for *The Appraisal Journal*, is co-author of the 1992 edition of the *Uniform Appraisal Standards for Federal Land Acquisitions*, and is a recipient of the Percy and Betty Wagner Award for his contributions to the advancement of appraisal knowledge. Mr. Eaton has been a frequent speaker and consultant to legal and appraisal organizations on forensic appraisal topics.

Acknowledgments

Many have contributed to the second edition of *Real Estate Valuation in Litigation* since work on the project began in 1990. I would like to thank my current employer, which allowed me a five-month leave of absence in 1992 during which I was able to complete most of the work necessary for this second edition.

Other important contributions came from readers of the first edition. The many comments and questions I have received over the past 13 years have brought to my attention material in the first text that was confusing, inadequately covered, and, on occasion, simply wrong. The comments received from Appraisal Institute reviewers were also appreciated, especially the insightful comments of George Silver, MAI, SRA. The Appraisal Institute's Publications staff has been extremely helpful throughout the development of the text.

As this second edition illustrates, much has changed in the past 13 years but, fortunately for me, one thing has not. My in-house paralegal, proofreader, best friend, and wife, Carol, has remained the same. Although she says this is the last time, she has offered her continuing assistance and support throughout the project without complaint. Thanks, Sam.

J. D. Eaton, MAI, SRA
Arlington, Virginia
March 1995

CHAPTER 1

The Litigation Environment

Ordinarily an appraiser learns how to perform a specialized type of appraisal and then worries about the appraiser-client relationship. Because of the unique appraiser-client relationship in litigation valuation, however, it is wise to discuss the appraiser's role first. Then the appraiser will know what he or she is getting into in accepting a litigation valuation assignment.

Adversarial Atmosphere

The typical appraisal assignment is not conducted in an adversarial atmosphere. When an appraiser conducts an appraisal for sale purposes, the buyer wants to buy, the seller wants to sell, the mortgage lender wants to make the loan, and the broker wants the sale to close. Everyone involved is working towards a common goal. Even if the appraiser's value conclusion is at odds with the agreed-upon sale price, there is still a common interest to consummate the transaction.

This is not the case in litigation. The parties involved are always adversarial and, more often than not, hostile and antagonistic. It is under these circumstances that the appraiser must perform his or her work in a professional manner and, at all costs, remain objective. That may sound simpler than it is. Being chased off a property by an owner with a shotgun does not encourage appraiser objectivity. The appraiser who finds that a mattress stamped "state property" has been used to plug a drainage culvert and flood the property on the day before a scheduled jury view may have trouble remaining unbiased.

In some parts of the country, real estate valuation trials have historically been known as *trials by ambush*. In most areas of the law, pre-trial discovery has been used for years and there are no "Perry Mason"-type surprises. All documents to be presented at trial have been examined by all parties and all witnesses have been deposed prior to trial. This has not been the case, however, in real estate valuation cases. Valuation witnesses have not been deposed and appraisal reports have not been provided to opposing parties. The market data relied on by appraisers were not known prior to their testimony and appraisal reports could be written on the back of an envelope, often in the back of the courtroom, while the opposing party's appraiser was testifying.

Fortunately, this atmosphere is changing. Pre-trial discovery and the deposing of appraisal witnesses prior to trial are becoming commonplace. All the appraisal techniques used and the market data relied on by appraisers are now known well in advance of the trial. It is no longer necessary for lawyers to extemporize during cross-examination. They now have the means to determine what an appraiser's testimony will be long before trial. Thus, they have adequate time to prepare for an in-depth cross-examination of the witness, or they have learned enough to know that they should simply get the well-prepared appraiser off the witness stand as quickly as possible to minimize the damage to their case.

Uniform Standards of Professional Appraisal Practice

One recent development which has the potential to promote discovery and improve the quality of appraisal witnesses is the adoption of Title XI of the Financial Institutions Reform, Recovery and Enforcement Act of 1989, as amended,[1] which requires the states to establish programs for the licensing and certification of appraisers. Implementation of state programs was required prior to December 31, 1992. As part of their licensing/certification programs, the states were required to adopt the Uniform Standards of Professional Appraisal Practice (USPAP), developed by The Appraisal Foundation. These standards include specific minimum appraisal report content requirements, which will ultimately prevent attorneys and appraisers from avoiding discovery by preparing abbreviated appraisal reports at the last minute. It should also eliminate the hiring and testimony of the *local broker* appraiser.

Nichols' describes the types of appraisers available for eminent domain actions as follows:

> Basically, there are two types of appraisers—professionals and so-called "local broker" appraisers. Most frequently, the local broker type of appraiser is the individual whose primary occupation is real estate brokerage; he is an appraiser without specialized formal education in the professional art of appraising.[2]

1. P.L. 101-73, 103 Stat. 183, 511 (Aug. 9, 1989).

2. *Nichols' The Law of Eminent Domain*, rev. 3d ed. (New York: Matthew Bender Co., Inc., 1992), vol. 7, §4.02.

The practice of retaining the local "real estate man" for some types of litigation rather than a professional appraiser[3] will surely die out, not necessarily because such individuals cannot meet the licensing/certification requirements,[4] but because they will be under the same requirements for appraisal competency and appraisal report content as the professional appraiser. If an appraiser's report and testimony do not meet the requirements of USPAP, he or she will be subject to disciplinary action by the state licensing authority. Uniform state licensing procedures will have the added benefit of allowing courts to be more discriminatory in determining who may testify as a real estate valuation expert.

A further benefit of the adoption of USPAP by the states is that it will end, or at least alleviate, disparate discovery practices regarding the exchange of appraisal reports. Most condemning agencies have detailed appraisal reporting requirements,[5] but property owners do not. In the past some attorneys and appraisers have taken advantage of this disparity and have purposely corrupted the discovery process. Adoption of the USPAP standards by the states and the courts should curtail this activity.

EMINENT DOMAIN VALUATION RULES AS A GUIDE

As this text will demonstrate, most real estate valuations involving litigation follow the valuation guidelines established in eminent domain cases. An appraisal for divorce proceedings or a tax appeal is no different than the total taking of a property by eminent domain. A fraud case is no different than a partial taking condemnation case. In the fraud case the *before* situation is "as the property was represented" and the *after* situation is "as the property actually exists." The difference is the damage resulting from the fraudulent representation. The solution to nearly every real estate valuation question encountered in litigation can be found in a corollary eminent domain valuation problem. Thus confronted with a litigation valuation problem that seems to have no rational solution, the appraiser is advised to look for comparable eminent domain situations. "It is . . . established that the United States may elect to condemn whatever interest it deems necessary whether or not the state [in which the property is located] recognizes the definition of the interest selected."[6] The United States has created some unique, even bizarre, situations from which an appraiser confronted with an unusual valuation problem can draw experience and, at times, market data.

3. Henry J. Kaltenbach, *Master Guide to The Successful Handling of Condemnation Valuation* (Englewood Cliffs, N.J.: Executive Reports Corporation, 1978), 1705.

4. Typical licensing/certification requirements for a general appraiser call for 165 hours of real estate appraisal education (at least 15 hours of which must relate to the Uniform Standards of Professional Appraisal Practice), two full years of real estate appraisal experience, and successful completion of an examination conducted by the licensing/certifying agency.

5. For example, see *Uniform Appraisal Standards for Federal Land Acquisitions* (Washington, D.C.: U.S. Government Printing Office, 1992) and U.S. Department of Transportation, Federal Highway Administration, *The Appraisal Guide* (Washington, D.C.: U.S. Government Printing Office, 1990).

6. *Uniform Appraisal Standards for Federal Land Acquisitions*, §A-1, 3.

APPRAISER'S RESPONSIBILITY

There is one feature of forensic appraisal assignments that distinguishes them from typical appraisal assignments. When, in the typical appraisal assignment, the appraisal report has been delivered to the client, the appraiser's professional and contractual obligation to that client is finished, subject, of course, to the correction of any deficiencies found in review. Such is not the case in litigation appraising. When appraisers accept a litigation appraisal assignment, they are committed, ethically if not contractually, to update or revise, as necessary, the appraisal report for trial purposes, assist legal counsel in preparing for trial, prepare themselves for trial, and make themselves available for depositions and the trial. To refuse to fulfill these subsequent obligations is a serious breach of the appraiser's professional responsibilities. If the appraiser is not prepared to fulfill these subsequent obligations to the greatest extent possible, recognizing that they can continue for 10 years or more in some instances, he or she must reject the initial appraisal assignment. The courts have a tendency to set trial dates, and attorneys have a tendency to agree to them, without consulting the appraiser involved. This displays some disrespect for the appraiser and the appraisal profession as a whole, but it does not relieve the appraiser of professional responsibility.

In accepting a litigation valuation assignment, the appraiser takes on responsibilities beyond the time commitments noted above. As will be discussed throughout this text, there are many legal rules of valuation applicable in litigation appraising. Moreover, each rule has exceptions, and the application of the rules often becomes clouded when the appraiser attempts to apply them to specific factual situations. In some instances the rules themselves are not clear.[7] Appraisers must have a general understanding of the legal rules of valuation to perform their professional duties competently. While they need not comprehend all of the nuances of these rules, the appraiser must have sufficient understanding of them to know when a specific rule is being encountered and when to ask legal counsel for assistance or interpretation.

One excellent tool that is used too infrequently in litigation valuation cases, by both appraisers and attorneys, is the *multi-premise* appraisal. Because some of the rules of valuation are vague or become clouded when applied to specific factual situations, it is often impossible to determine with any certainty how the court will ultimately interpret a given rule. For instance, it is not always possible to determine whether the diminution in the value of a remainder property in a partial taking condemnation case was caused by *compensable* or *noncompensable* damage. In such a case the appraiser can make a *double premise appraisal* of the remainder property, taking the damage into consideration under the first premise and excluding consideration of the damage under the second. Irrespective of the court's ultimate ruling, the appraiser will have a creditable appraisal report from which to testify. This procedure has the added advantage of allowing the attorney to determine the importance of this particular element of damage to the overall

7. One reason for this is that the parties directly involved in this type of litigation do not want the rules clarified. They prefer to operate with these clouded rules, interpreting them in the lower courts to the best advantage of their respective clients. If their interpretation does not prevail, the case is not appealed for fear that the higher court decision will be adverse and bar them from using their current interpretation of the rule in future cases.

case. This determination can have a bearing on future negotiations and on the attorney's decision whether or not to submit a pre-trial motion asking the court to make a ruling regarding the compensability of the damage item prior to trial.

The effective use of multi-premise appraisals is not limited to issues relating to the compensability of damages. They can also be used in cases involving disputes concerning the proper date of value, the probability of rezoning or obtaining a permit, alternative highest and best uses, and questions concerning *scope of the project* or the *larger parcel*. (See Chapters 5 and 6 for discussion of these terms.)

Court decisions regarding the amount of compensation due in a land value litigation case are typically final. Therefore, many assumptions that may be appropriate for other types of appraisals are not acceptable in litigation appraisals. Any assumption that results in a *limited appraisal*[8] is unacceptable for trial purposes.[9] For instance, an assumption that a property is free from contamination, when evidence indicates that it is not or may not be free of contamination, *may* be acceptable under certain circumstances. However, such an assumption results in a limited appraisal and thus is not acceptable for trial purposes.[10]

Because of the adversarial nature of litigation appraisal work, the appraiser-client relationship is atypical. Sometimes an appraiser is employed directly by a condemning authority in the early stages of the acquisition process, but often attorneys have been retained and a lawsuit has been filed before an appraiser is even contacted. In fact, in many instances negotiations have already failed and both of the parties have already determined the amount of compensation they feel should be paid. What they are looking for is not the opinion of an unbiased appraiser, but an appraiser who agrees with their previously drawn conclusions and can reasonably support, and testify to, those conclusions. In nearly all of these situations, the appraiser will be dealing with the attorney, rather than directly with the client. If the appraiser is retained under such circumstances and, after preliminary investigation and analysis, finds that his or her ultimate opinion of value will not be favorable to the client, it is the appraiser's responsibility to advise the client of this fact, rather than to proceed with preparation of an appraisal report that will be of no use to the client. (See Chapter 20 for information on preparation for trial.)

GOVERNMENT CLIENTS

When, as mentioned earlier, the appraiser has been retained directly by a condemnor in the early stages of the acquisition process, a different atmosphere is created. First, most condemnors have very specific procedures for awarding appraisal contracts and very exacting appraisal reporting requirements. (See Chapter 19 for appraisal report content requirements.) Most condemnors will award appraisal contracts to the *lowest bidder* from a list of appraisers who meet or exceed some preset *minimal qualifications*, rather than awarding a contract to the best appraiser available. This is usually in direct contradiction to the advice of the

8. A *limited appraisal* is one that is developed from an "assignment that calls for something less than, or different from, the work that would otherwise be required by the specific guidelines." The Appraisal Foundation, *Uniform Standards of Professional Appraisal Practice* (USPAP), 1994 ed., p. 5.

9. *Uniform Appraisal Standards for Federal Land Acquisitions*, §B-1-7, 67.

10. Ibid., §C-9, 96.

condemnor's legal counsel.[11] Many condemnors commission and approve appraisal reports knowing that they are insufficient for trial purposes because they recognize that only a very small percentage of their acquisitions will actually end up in condemnation. The ramifications of this practice are discussed more fully in Chapter 19.

Knowing of this condemnor practice, appraisers must not assume that their appraisal reports are suitable for trial purposes just because they have been approved by a condemning agency. In fact, experience shows that more than 75% of the appraisal reports submitted by agencies for condemnation action are *not* acceptable for trial purposes.

One advantage of working directly for a condemning agency in the early stages of the acquisition program is that the appraiser does not have the agency's attorney looking over his or her shoulder throughout the appraisal process. The appraiser is generally free to complete the appraisal assignment with a minimum of interference. On the other hand, it can sometimes be difficult to obtain needed legal guidance from the agency's legal counsel at this point in the acquisition process.

When entering into a contract with a condemning agency, appraisers must be sure they can complete the terms of the contract without violating the standards of the professional organizations to which they belong, the standards required by state licensing/certification agencies, or their own personal ethics. For example, the minimum appraisal reporting requirements set forth in the Uniform Relocation Assistance and Real Property Acquisition Policies Act of 1970[12] do not meet the minimum reporting requirements of The Appraisal Foundation.[13] While the Federal Highway Administration may consider the reporting provisions of the Relocation Act as a jurisdictional exception to the Uniform Standards, or consider them to fall under the Departure Provision of the standards, and The Appraisal Foundation may concur with that interpretation, various state licensing agencies and/or professional appraisal organizations may not adopt the same interpretation.

Another potential conflict concerns the disclosure of appraisal reports. The Uniform Standards provide that "[a]n appraiser must not disclose confidential factual data obtained from a client or the results of an assignment prepared for a client to anyone other than: 1) the client and persons specifically authorized by the client; 2) such third parties as may be authorized by due process of law; and 3) a duly authorized peer review committee."[14] Many state licensing/certification laws provide that the state may audit an appraiser's files at random. However, the U.S. Department of Justice, which represents all federal agencies in condemnation matters, takes the position that "the appraiser shall not divulge his or her findings and opinions to *anyone*."[15]

---

11. The *Uniform Appraisal Standards for Federal Land Acquisitions*, §C-6, states that "[w]hile price [of appraisal services] is certainly a consideration, more important factors involve appraisal experience, education, professional reputation, court experience and demonstrated competency."
12. P.L. 91-646, January 2, 1971, §301 and §302 (42 U.S.C. §4651 and §4652), as amended by P.L. 100-17, April 2, 1987, Title IV, Uniform Relocation Act Amendments of 1987, and Title 49 CFR Part 24.
13. Consequently, they do not meet the minimum reporting requirements of the state licensing/certification agencies.
14. USPAP, 1994 ed., p. 3.
15. *Uniform Appraisal Standards for Federal Land Acquisitions*, §C-7, 94 (emphasis is added).

> It is the policy of the Department of Justice that this prohibition against disclosure during pendency of litigation without written authorization from the government's legal counsel extends to professional peer review committees and to the state and local appraiser licensing and/or certifying agencies. This policy is considered a "jurisdictional exception" to the *Uniform Standards of Professional Appraisal Practice* (The Appraisal Foundation, 1990).[16]

A third potential conflict is exemplified by condemnation appraisals in the State of Georgia where federal matching funds are involved. "The general rule is that any enhancement in value that is brought about in anticipation of, and by reason of, a proposed improvement, is to be excluded in determining the market value of the land."[17] This rule has been adopted by the Federal Highway Administration[18] and federal matching funds are established based on this rule. The Georgia legislature enacted a statute to enforce the rule in 1966.[19] However, the Georgia Supreme Court later found this statute unconstitutional as a violation of the separation of powers doctrine.[20] Therefore, the law in Georgia now holds:

> Where there is general knowledge that a public improvement will be constructed in the area of the property to be condemned and this knowledge enhances the value of the property, the jury is entitled to award compensation based on the enhanced value even though the public improvement is to be made by the condemnor . . . . The court should allow evidence of any element, including the announcement of the pending public improvement, that affects the fair market value right up to the time the property is taken.[21]

Nevertheless, for some time the Georgia Department of Transportation continued to require that all appraisals prepared for it include a "certification of appraiser" in which the appraiser certified that the appraisal was made in conformity with appropriate state laws, and that any decrease or increase in the fair market value of real property prior to the date of valuation caused by the public improvement for which the property was acquired, or by the likelihood that the property would be acquired for such improvement, other than that due to physical deterioration within the reasonable care of the owner, was disregarded in determining compensation for the property.

These two certifications were, of course, in conflict. Georgia law clearly states that project enhancement must be considered up to the date of taking, yet the "certification of appraiser" statement requires its exclusion. This conflict forced some appraisers to decline any appraisal assignment from the Georgia Department of Transportation.

An additional conflict can arise when a condemnor client insists that the appraiser certify that the estimate of market value, or the difference between the market value before and after a partial taking, is *just compensation* when, as a mat-

16. Ibid., fn. 280. This policy is not in conflict with the Appraisal Institute's peer review process because the Appraisal Institute suspends all peer review until any pending litigation is completed.
17. *Nichols'*, vol. 4, §12.B.17[1] (1990).
18. U.S. Department of Transportation, Federal Highway Administration, *The Appraisal Guide* (Washington, D.C.: U.S. Government Printing Office, 1990), 8.
19. Ga. Code Ann., §§ 36-617a, 36-117, 36-1312.
20. *Calhoun v. State Hwy. Dep't.*, 153 S.E.2d 418 (Ga. 1967).
21. Charles N. Pursley, Jr., *Georgia Eminent Domain* (Norcross, Georgia: The Harrison Company, 1982), §6-4, p. 150 (citations omitted).

ter of law, *market value* and *just compensation* are not always synonymous. (See Chapter 2 for further discussion of this issue.) If the appraiser cannot persuade the agency to remove this requirement, a possible solution is for the appraiser to state in the limiting conditions of the appraisal report that the just compensation reported was based on the assumption that, as a matter of law, just compensation is the mathematical equivalent of the market value of the property (or the difference in the market value of the property before and after a partial taking) and that if that assumption is incorrect, the appraisal must be considered invalid.

APPRAISER/ATTORNEY RELATIONS

Any discussion of the environment in which appraisers involved in litigation find themselves must address the relationship between the appraiser and the attorney. While it cannot be said that they are always mortal enemies, it must be acknowledged that their interests are often not in harmony. "This has led to an attitude currently in vogue among many in [the appraisal] business, which can be expressed as, 'say no to lawyers.'"[22]

The attorney is a sworn advocate for the client's interest and wants to obtain the highest (or lowest) award that is reasonably possible. The appraiser advocates only his or her unbiased estimate of value. The attorney's purpose in a valuation litigation trial is to present the strongest case possible and procure the most advantageous award for the client. The appraiser's purpose is to present the opinion of value in an unbiased, yet persuasive, manner and to come down off the witness stand with his or her integrity and professional reputation intact. These conflicting purposes obviously lead to friction.

Some attorneys take their role as advocate as a license to screen the information they provide to their own appraisers, providing information advantageous to their client's interest and withholding disadvantageous information. Therefore, appraisers must often extend their investigation to supplement and verify attorney-supplied information. If an attorney cites a specific case in a legal instruction as support for a certain proposition, the appraiser should read the case to confirm that it does, in fact, support the proposition being advanced.

In this same regard, appraisers should consider the source when reading any article or text concerning forensic real estate valuation. Articles in law journals, like articles in other professional journals, express the opinions of the author and should be viewed as such. Unfortunately, some lawyers cannot seem to get out of their advocacy mode, even when writing supposedly objective reports or treatises. An article that should be an objective report of the law sometimes becomes a vehicle to advocate a personal point of view. This has led, particularly in recent years, to the presentation of questionable interpretations of case law and, in some instances, flagrant misinterpretation of case law. Some publications which for

22. Ted C. Slack, "The Lawyer, The Appraiser, and Inverse Condemnation," ALI-ABA course of study materials, Inverse Condemnation and Related Government Liability (Atlanta: November 1-3, 1990), 157.

years were viewed as authoritative, objective treatises on eminent domain law are becoming slanted and less reliable than they were in the past. For these reasons, appraisers should consider the source, even when reading publications that have historically been considered authoritative, objective, and balanced.

Some attorneys try to intimidate their own appraisers by becoming belligerent and aggressive. They attempt to persuade their appraisers to change value estimates; to exclude statements or data from the appraisal report that they perceive as weakening their case; or to include statements or data in the appraisal report that they perceive will bolster their case. They will cajole, threaten, and wheedle. On the other hand, appraisers can also become belligerent when questioned about the reasoning or support for their opinions. They may refuse to discuss the basis of their opinions, to assist in pre-trial preparation, or, worst of all, to correct obvious errors in their reports.

Whatever the environment, the appraiser must maintain a balance, keeping an open mind, but not wavering from his or her own opinions. The appraiser's function at trial is to assist the trier of fact by expressing an unbiased opinion of value, not the attorney's opinion of value or an opinion of value that has been modified by the attorney. Nevertheless, appraisers should remember that they can sometimes learn from attorneys. Many attorneys have been specializing in real estate valuation litigation for years and have a wealth of experience that can be invaluable. These attorneys may have the ability to identify flaws in an appraiser's logic and reasoning that, if not corrected, could result in an appraiser's destruction under cross-examination.

When appraisers are employed by private litigants, they should seriously consider requiring that their appraisal fee be paid up front, before the assignment is begun, or suggest that the fee be placed in escrow. If this is done, the appraiser is assured of receiving the fee earned, even if the client is not satisfied with the appraiser's ultimate opinion of value. A third alternative is to obtain a guarantee from the client's attorney that the fee will be paid, regardless of the ultimate value conclusion.

In establishing fees for their appraisal services, appraisers should recognize that the complexity of real estate valuations, particularly for litigation purposes, has increased substantially over the years. Because the litigation appraiser cannot assume away anything that would result in a *limited* appraisal, it is often necessary for the appraiser to retain the services of subsidiary consultants or make provisions for the client to provide for consultants' services. The types of consultants required might include civil engineers, environmental engineers and auditors, cost estimators or contractors, mining experts, timber cruisers or foresters, architects, and hydrologists, just to name a few. The fees for these subsidiary consultants can often run considerably more than the appraisal fee itself, so the client needs to be forewarned. Moreover, appraisers cannot merely accept consultants' reports as accurate. The appraiser must review the reports and adopt them only if they appear reasonable and adequately supported.[23]

23. See Guide Note 6 to the Appraisal Institute's Standards of Professional Appraisal Practice, "Reliance on Reports Prepared by Others," 1994 ed.

Some attorneys, and some clients, routinely request that the appraiser submit a draft report for their review prior to preparation of the final appraisal report. This practice has both advantages and disadvantages. Obviously, in reviewing the draft report the attorney should identify any improper interpretations or applications of the law as it relates to the case. These flaws can then be corrected prior to preparation of the final report. The attorney or client can also identify areas within the report that are weak, thus giving the appraiser the opportunity to include additional market data or reasoning to support the conclusions. However, the review process can also be used by the attorney to try to get the appraiser to change his or her value estimate, or to include or exclude specific data or statements from the final report that were included in the draft. Some attorneys believe that appraisers will be more willing to change their opinions of value if they are approached before the final report is completed. An appraiser who submits a draft report should be prepared to be subjected to pressure to change the final report in ways that may, in the appraiser's opinion, corrupt the objectivity of the report. The appraiser must be prepared to resist such pressure.

Another disadvantage of submitting a draft report is that the appraiser may be asked on cross-examination whether a draft report was submitted and what changes, if any, were made in the final report. If significant changes were made, opposing counsel may suggest to the trier of fact that the appraiser's final report was dictated by the client.

It is the *appraiser's opinion* that must ultimately prevail. Appraisers must keep an open mind in the pre-trial process, but the opinion to which they testify must be theirs, and theirs alone. During the pre-trial process, appraisers can sometimes become confused as to whether an attorney is explaining a legal principle or expressing an opinion in regard to the valuation. "Instructions by the attorney to the appraiser on a matter of law are certainly a proper element to be expressed in the attorney-appraiser relationship, but instructions to the appraiser on valuation are another matter. The appraiser has the choice of accepting or rejecting the attorney's [valuation] premise. Once accepted without reservation, the premise becomes the appraiser's responsibility."[24] "Opinions expressed by an attorney that are not valid and are without foundation should be disregarded by an appraiser."[25]

The appraiser must insist that any legal instruction by the attorney be put in writing and contain a proper foundation. This practice avoids confusion because attorneys are typically willing to put a valid legal instruction in writing, but they will be unwilling to put their opinions concerning a valuation premise in the form of a written instruction to the appraiser. *If it is not in writing, it's not a legal instruction*. This practice has the added advantage of forcing attorneys to prepare written legal instructions and to develop, and cite, the supporting legal authority for them. Experience indicates that a legal premise or instruction that is presented verbally to an appraiser as "cast in stone" is often not quite as clear cut when it has to be stated, and supported, in writing.

24. *Divergences in Right-of-Way Valuations*, National Cooperative Highway Research Program Report No. 126 (Washington, D.C.: Highway Research Board, 1971), 10.

25. Ibid., 16.

In reviewing a written legal instruction, it is important to remember that the appraiser does not have to be convinced that the legal instruction expresses the correct interpretation of the law. To accept a legal instruction, the appraiser merely has to believe that the attorney's interpretation of the law, as expressed in the legal instruction, is not unreasonable and is adequately supported. Most written legal instructions will meet this test. Because such instructions "are generally based on accepted procedures or standards and represent informed opinions on matters beyond the appraiser's expertise . . . . [a]bsent reasonable doubt, these reports usually can be accepted..."[26]

SUMMARY

In conducting a litigation valuation assignment, appraisers must keep in mind that they are involved in an adversarial proceeding and they may be pressured to be something less than objective. Nevertheless, they must perform the assignment with complete objectivity and utmost care, ensuring that their reports and testimony conform to the Uniform Standards in each and every respect.[27]

Before accepting a litigation valuation assignment, appraisers must confirm that they will be allowed, under the terms of their engagement, to develop a completely objective appraisal report that meets all applicable standards of professional appraisal practice. They must also be satisfied that they will not be forced to prepare a limited appraisal because of a lack of information from necessary subsidiary consultants. Appraisers must recognize that their professional responsibility does not end with the delivery of the appraisal report; it continues until the trial has been completed or the case has been settled.

Appraisers should look to the rules of eminent domain valuation to find solutions to other types of valuation problems in litigation. They must also have a general understanding of the rules of valuation applicable in litigation appraising and be prepared to develop multi-premise appraisals when circumstances warrant.

While appraisers should keep an open mind in discussing their appraisals with clients and their attorneys, be willing to correct errors and strengthen weaknesses in their reports, and accept properly supported written legal instructions, they must remain absolutely objective in arriving at their final opinions of value and preparing their reports. To avoid confusion as to whether an attorney is explaining a point of law or expressing an opinion regarding a valuation premise, the appraiser must insist that all instructions from the attorney be submitted in writing and contain adequate support.

As a final note, appraisers who abhor confrontation or feel uneasy when their opinions are questioned are well advised to avoid litigation valuation assignments. However, an appraiser who can continue to function in an unbiased, professional manner in a confrontational environment will find the work both challenging and rewarding.

26. Guide Note 6 to the the Appraisal Institute's Standards of Professional Appraisal Practice, "Reliance on Reports or Information Prepared by Others," 1994 ed.

27. USPAP, 1994 ed.

CHAPTER 2

Origin of Eminent Domain and Just Compensation

E*minent domain* is the right of the sovereign government to take private property for public use upon payment of just compensation. This right can be, and has been, conveyed to other public and quasi-public bodies such as public utility districts, development commissions, and railroad companies.[1] *Condemnation* refers to the taking of private property for public use by the government or an authorized public or quasi-public agency upon payment of just compensation to the owner of the property.[2]

The distinction between the two terms is quite simple. Eminent domain is the *right* of government to take private property for public use upon payment of just compensation, while condemnation is the *act* of doing so.

It is not absolutely necessary that real estate appraisers have any more understanding of sovereign's right of eminent domain and the act of condemnation than is expressed above. However, a deeper understanding of these terms will lead to better comprehension of the reasoning behind many court decisions relating to eminent domain valuation and facilitate effective communication with members of the law profession and others involved in eminent domain and condemnation. Some appraisers feel that meaningful communication between appraisers and attorneys is almost impossible under the best of circumstances. Thus it behooves appraisers to acquire a thorough understanding of legal terms so that they do not compound the confusion and miscommunication in the already complex field of eminent domain litigation.

1. *Black's Law Dictionary*, abr. 6th ed., s.v. "eminent domain."

2. *The Dictionary of Real Estate Appraisal*, 2d ed. (Chicago: American Institute of Real Estate Appraisers, 1989).

EMINENT DOMAIN

The origin of the concept of eminent domain is lost in history, but the sovereign's right of eminent domain has long been acknowledged. The first recorded condemnation action occurred in 871 B.C.[3] The condemnor, King Ahab, attempted to acquire Naboth's vineyard. Naboth refused to sell the vineyard voluntarily, and King Ahab exercised the right of eminent domain. Jezebel became, in effect, the trier of fact. The decision at the end of the trial was that King Ahab did, in fact, have the right of eminent domain and title to the vineyard was transferred to him. By way of compensation for the taking, Naboth was stoned to death for his refusal to sell the land voluntarily. There was no appeal.

The definition of eminent domain presented here could be termed a modern definition inasmuch as it includes a provision for the payment of just compensation. Many early definitions of eminent domain, including those applied in the United States, did not include a provision for just compensation. Until after the Civil War, several states exercised the power of eminent domain without paying compensation. It is now well established, however, that the right of eminent domain cannot be exercised in this country without the payment of just compensation.

Although many believe that the government's right of eminent domain comes from the U.S. Constitution, it does not.[4] The sovereign has always had the right of eminent domain. Some theorize that this right originates with the principle that the sovereign owns all of the property within its boundaries, and that private ownership and possession of property is always subject to reversion or repossession by the sovereign. In some jurisdictions, such as Louisiana, the term *expropriation* has the same meaning as eminent domain.[5]

Expropriation has been defined as a "Canadian and British term representing the act of a sovereign in reclaiming its inherent ownership in real estate which in law was never given up. It is similar to the taking of private property under the law of eminent domain in the United States."[6] However, expropriation was later defined as "[a] British or Canadian term synonymous with *eminent domain* as used in the United States."[7] Obviously, these two definitions conflict; the first indicates that *expropriation* is synonymous with *condemnation*, while the second indicates that the term is synonymous with *eminent domain*. Most legal literature would suggest that the second definition is in error.[8]

Some disagree with the idea that the power of eminent domain comes from the sovereign's inherent ownership in real estate, which was never given up. They theorize that two sovereignties cannot hold ultimate title to the land at the same time, and both the state and the U.S. Government have the right of eminent domain. Not until 1875 was it clearly established that the federal government does, indeed, have the power of eminent domain.[9]

It is now generally acknowledged that the power of eminent domain is not a property right, but an attribute of sovereignty.[10] The powers of the sovereign are

3. *Holy Bible*, rev. standard version, 1 Kings 21.
4. *Kohl v. United States*, 91 U.S. 367, 371 (1876).
5. *Tennessee Gas Transmission Co. v. Violet Trapping Co.*, 200 So. 2d 428 (La. 1967).
6. American Institute of Real Estate Appraisers and the Society of Real Estate Appraisers, *Real Estate Appraisal Terminology*, rev. ed., Byrl N. Boyce, ed. (Cambridge, Mass.: Ballinger Publishing Co., 1981), 96.
7. *The Dictionary of Real Estate Appraisal*, 3d ed. (Chicago: Appraisal Institute, 1993), 127.
8. See *Black's*, s.v. "eminent domain"; *Nichols' The Law of Eminent Domain*, rev. 3d ed. (New York: Mathew Bender Co., Inc., 1992), vol. 1, §1.12 (1992).
9. *Kohl v. United States*, 91 U.S. 367 (1876).
10. *Shoemaker v. United States*, 147 U.S. 282, 299–300 (1893); *Jockheck v. Shawnee Cty.*, 37 P. 621 (Kan. 1894).

broad enough to include the power of eminent domain, so the right does not specifically have to be granted to the sovereign by its constitution. Moreover, the states are not prohibited from exercising their powers of eminent domain by the U.S. Constitution.

The power of eminent domain is limited by its very definition. It cannot be exercised unless the proposed taking is for a public use. For example, a public agency could not invoke its power of eminent domain to take a property from one individual for the sole benefit of another individual. However, recent trends indicate that the courts interpret *public use* quite liberally. Thus, takings for scenic easements, golf courses, and open space have been held to be for *public use.* In 1984 the U.S. Supreme Court used the public use requirement to uphold the Hawaiian Land Reform Act of 1967.[11] Ninety-two percent of the privately owned land in Hawaii is owned by only 72 landowners. The state perceived this land oligopoly to be a social and economical evil and adopted the Hawaiian Land Reform Act, which allows lessees living on single-family lots in developments of at least five acres to ask the state to condemn the leased fee estate in the lot and resell it to the lessee. The constitutionality of the act was challenged in federal district court[12] on the grounds that the taking was not for a public use. The district court found the act to be constitutional, but the federal 9th circuit court held that the act did not meet the public use requirements of the Fifth Amendment and characterized it as "a naked attempt on the part of the State of Hawaii to take the private property of A and transfer it to B solely for B's private use and benefit."[13]

The Supreme Court overturned the 9th circuit,[14] finding that the act met the public use requirement of the Fifth Amendment of the U.S. Constitution because the state legislature determined that the act would serve a public purpose and "deference [by the courts] to the legislature's 'public use' determination is required 'until it is shown to involve an impossibility.'"[15] In support of its decision, the court said that "[t]he Act advances its purposes without the State's taking actual possession of the land. In such cases, government does not itself have to use property to legitimate the taking; it is only the taking's purpose and not its mechanics, that must pass scrutiny under the Public Use Clause."[16]

This case demonstrates that as long as a proposed taking accomplishes a public purpose, as determined by the legislature, it will meet the public use requirements of the Fifth Amendment to the U.S. Constitution. This decision does not, however, affect the meaning of *public use* as it may be used in various state constitutions; an act similar to Hawaii's may be found unconstitutional in other states.[17]

Insofar as eminent domain is an inherent right of the sovereign, the right cannot be limited by the legislature. The power of eminent domain will exist, in unlimited form, as long as the sovereign itself exists.[18] The only way the power can be limited is through the sovereign's constitution. The U.S. Constitution states "[n]o person shall be deprived of life, liberty, or property without due process of

11. Haw. Rev. Stat., Ch. 516 (1967).
12. *Midkiff v. Tom*, 483 F. Supp. 62 (Haw. 1979).
13. *Midkiff v. Tom*, 702 F.2d 788, 798 (9th Cir. 1983).
14. *Hawaii Housing Authority v. Midkiff*, 467 U.S. 229 (1984).
15. Ibid., at 240.
16. Ibid., at 244.
17. For further discussion and analysis of this case, see J. D. Eaton, "A Decade of U.S. Supreme Court Decisions—An Appraiser's View," Part 3, *The Appraisal Journal* (January 1990), 29; Sidney Z. Searles, "The Right To Take After the Midkiff Case," ALI-ABA course of study materials; and *Eminent Domain and Land Valuation Litigation* (West Palm Beach, Florida: January 1986), 189.
18. *Kohl v. United States*, 91 U.S. 367 (1876).

law, nor shall private property be taken for public use without just compensation."[19] This provision of the constitution does not grant the U.S. Government the right of eminent domain, but it does limit the sovereign's inherent power by providing that it cannot be exercised without payment of just compensation to the owner of the property taken.

This provision of the U.S. Constitution has no effect on the powers of the states. However, Section 1 of the Fourteenth Amendment of the U.S. Constitution reads in part, "nor shall any state deprive any person of life, liberty, or property without due process of law." This due process of law provision of the amendment has been interpreted as requiring payment of just compensation for the taking of property.[20] In fact, every state in the Union, except North Carolina[21], has a provision in its constitution for the payment of compensation to the owner of property acquired through eminent domain.[22]

JUST COMPENSATION

> [T]he individual has a fundamental right to compensation when his land is taken for the public use and...the legislature is bound by unwritten restrictions to respect this right. Disregard of this right has been held to be a violation of the "unwritten law," of the "spirit of the Constitution," and of "common law principles," against "natural equity," and a travesty of "natural justice."[23] [Citations omitted]

Not all state constitutions refer to *just compensation*. Terms such as *adequate, reasonable,* and *due* are used in some constitutions in conjunction with *compensation*. The adjectives used to describe compensation do not alter its meaning, but rather emphasize it. It has been said that it is difficult to imagine *unjust compensation*. About half of the state constitutions provide for compensation to be paid for the taking of, *or damage to*, private property by the sovereign.[24]

Even in jurisdictions that do not have a constitutional provision that includes damages, it has been universally held that damages to a remainder parcel in a partial taking case are part and parcel of just compensation in a constitutional sense. The basic premise is that the owner must be compensated for the taking of the land, as opposed to being compensated for the land taken.[25] It is also generally recognized that property encompasses the entire bundle of rights inherent in the ownership of the real estate and that the taking or infringement on these rights often constitutes a taking, even if no part of the physical real estate is taken. The taking of all access rights is an example of such a taking. "Clearly an owner of land abutting on a street or highway cannot constitutionally be deprived of all access to his premises without compensation...total deprivation of access is equivalent to a taking requiring compensation..."[26]

19. U. S. Const. amend. V.
20. *De Salvo v. Arkansas Louisiana Gas Co.*, 239 F. Supp. 312 (E.D. Ark. 1965).
21. *Nichols'*, vol. 1A, §4.8 (1990).
22. "North Carolina recognizes this fundamental right to just compensation as so grounded in natural law and justice that it is part of the fundamental law of the State." *Debruhl v. State Highway & Public Works Comm.*, 102 S.E.2d 229, 232 (N.C. 1958).
23. *Nichols'*, vol. 1A, §4.8 (1990).
24. *Nichols'*, vol. 2, §6.01[3] (1990).
25. *Bauman v. Ross*, 167 U.S. 548 (1897)
26. 26 Am. Jur. 2d. *Eminent Domain* §200.

It is imperative that the appraiser be aware of the damage provision specified in the constitution, or adopted by statute, in the jurisdiction where the property being appraised is located. A list of the constitutional and statutory provisions applicable to eminent domain in each jurisdiction is provided in the addenda. In many jurisdictions that have no damage provision, there must be an actual taking before damages can be recovered; thus in these jurisdictions damages are only recoverable in partial taking cases. The importance of this provision is further discussed and demonstrated in Chapter 14.

Just compensation is defined as "...the amount of loss for which a property owner is compensated when his or her property is taken; should put the owner in as good a position pecuniarily as he or she would be if the property had not been taken; generally held to be market value, but courts have refused to rule that it is always equivalent to market value."[27] Another definition follows:

> Compensation which is fair to both the owner and the public when property is taken for public use through condemnation (eminent domain). Consideration is taken of such criteria as the cost of reproducing the property, its market value, and the resulting damage to the remaining property of the owner. The Fifth Amendment to the U.S. Constitution provides that no private property shall be taken for public use without "just compensation." Within the Fifth Amendment provision that private property shall not be taken for public use without just compensation, "just compensation" means the full monetary equivalent of the property taken.
>
> As regards property taken for public use, the term is comprehensive and includes all elements. It means a settlement which leaves one no poorer or richer than he was before the property was taken. It requires that the owner be put in as good position pecuniarily as he would otherwise have been if the property had not been taken.[28]

The term *just compensation* is not defined in the U.S. Constitution or in any state constitution. It has been up to the courts to interpret and define the term, and they have generally held that just compensation is measured by market value.[29] Infrequently, the courts have deviated from this concept, most notably when the property has no ascertainable market value. *Nichols'* defines market value as:

> The term "fair market value" means the amount of money which a purchaser willing, but not obligated, to buy the property would pay to an owner willing, but not obligated, to sell it, taking into consideration all uses for which the land was suited and might be applied.[30] [Citations omitted]

The *Uniform Appraisal Standards for Federal Land Acquisitions* includes the following statement concerning market value:

> "Fair market value" is defined as the amount in cash, or on terms reasonably equivalent to cash, for which in all probability the property would be sold to a

27. *The Dictionary of Real Estate Appraisal*, 3d ed., 194.
28. *Black's*, s.v. "just compensation."
29. *Nichols'* vol. 4, §12.01 (1990); *Harwell v. United States*, 316 F.2d 791 (10th Cir. 1963); *United States v. Miller*, 317 U.S. 369 (1943).
30. *Nichols*, vol. 4, §12.02 (1990).

> knowledgeable owner willing but not obligated to sell to a knowledgeable purchaser who desired but is not obligated to buy. In ascertaining that figure, consideration should be given to all matters that might be brought forward and reasonably be given substantial weight in bargaining by persons of ordinary prudence, but no consideration whatever should be given to matters not affecting market value.[31] [Citations omitted]

A definition of market value currently in wide use in the appraisal industry is:

> The most probable price which a property should bring in a competitive and open market under all conditions requisite to a fair sale, the buyer and seller each acting prudently and knowledgeably, and assuming the price is not affected by undue stimulus. Implicit in this definition is the consummation of a sale as of a specified date and the passing of title from seller to buyer under conditions whereby:
>
> 1. buyer and seller are typically motivated;
> 2. both parties are well informed or well advised, and acting in what they consider their best interests;
> 3. a reasonable time is allowed for exposure in the open market;
> 4. payment is made in terms of cash in United States dollars or in terms of financial arrangements comparable thereto; and
> 5. the price represents the normal consideration for the property sold unaffected by special or creative financing or sales concessions granted by anyone associated with the sale. . . .
>
> Persons performing appraisal services that may be subject to litigation are cautioned to seek the exact legal definition of market value in the jurisdiction in which the services are being performed.[32]

Various jurisdictions have different definitions of market value. These definitions assume a cash sale or its equivalent. It has long been recognized by the courts that market value need not be estimated in strict terms of cash as long as the terms upon which the value is estimated are equivalent to cash.[33]

It is important to remember that the definition of market value assumes that "a reasonable time is allowed for exposure in the open market" to find a buyer ready, willing, and able to purchase the property for its highest and best use, and that, on the date of valuation, that reasonable exposure time has already transpired. In other words, it is assumed that the property under appraisal has already been exposed on the market for an adequate amount of time to find a buyer who is willing to purchase the property and that such a buyer is, in fact, standing there with cash (or its equivalent) in hand ready to close the sale. This assumption is pointed out because of the savings and loan debacle, which has caused federal and state regulators, the savings and loan institutions, and the appraisal industry to review, and perhaps modify, the assumptions built into the definition of market value.

---

31. *Uniform Appraisal Standards for Federal Land Acquisitions* (Washington, D.C.: U.S. Government Printing Office, 1992), §A-2, pp. 3–4.
32. The Appraisal Foundation, *Uniform Standards of Professional Appraisal Practice* (USPAP), 1994 ed., p. 8.
33. For example, see *Kerr v. South Park Commissioners*, 117 U.S. 379, 386–387 (1886) and *Baucum v. Arkansas Power & Light Co.*, 15 S.W.2d 399, 401 (1929).

Many lending institutions are now requiring appraisers to estimate, in their appraisal reports, the exposure time and marketing time for the property being appraised. The Appraisal Foundation has recently defined *exposure time* as the amount of time that the property would have had to be on the open market, prior to the date of appraisal, to find a buyer.[34] *Marketing time* is defined as the amount of time it would take to find a buyer ready, willing, and able to purchase the property for the appraised value if the property were placed on the open market on the date of appraisal.[35] Therefore, exposure time is historical (prior to the effective date of the appraisal) and marketing time is in the future (after the effective date of the appraisal).

Neither of these time estimates are relevant to an estimate of market value for eminent domain purposes, therefore, no such estimates should be included in an appraisal report made for eminent domain purposes. To do so is to invite cross-examination on issues that have no bearing on the matter at hand.

Because of the recent turmoil in the financial market and the appraisal industry, appraisers and real estate valuation litigators should use extreme care in adopting newly revised real estate appraisal definitions or appraisal methodologies that have been developed to address specific problems in a specific area of the real estate market. Some believe that little thought has been given to the impact these revisions will have on appraisals for other purposes. There is no evidence to indicate that the courts are going to accept these new concepts and apply them to eminent domain valuations.

If an appraisal is to be valid for condemnation purposes, the appraiser must use a definition of market value that is acceptable to the courts where the condemnation trial on the property will be held. Thus it is imperative that the real estate appraiser be aware of the applicable market value definition and include it in the appraisal report; otherwise, the entire appraisal report and/or the appraiser's testimony may be rejected. If the appraiser is in doubt as to the proper definition of market value in the jurisdiction, the safest procedure is to request the applicable market value definition and supporting authority from legal counsel.

Market value is not an end in itself, but merely a means to an end. The ultimate objective of a condemnation trial is the ascertainment of just compensation, but this determination is not made by the appraiser. An appraiser is allowed to express an opinion, rather than testify only to factual matters, because the appraiser is an *expert*.[36] Both the appraiser and the lawyer must recognize that appraisers are experts in estimating value, not just compensation. Among the many educational opportunities available to appraisers, there are no courses offered in estimating just compensation.

"'Market value' is not necessarily the equivalent of just compensation but rather a useful and generally sufficient tool for arriving at this."[37] Moreover, market value is not the only value which the trier of fact may consider in arriving at a determination of just compensation.

34. USPAP, 1994 ed., Statement on Appraisal Standards No. 6, adopted Sept. 16, 1992.

35. USPAP, 1994 ed., Advisory Opinion G-7, adopted Sept. 16, 1992.

36. An expert is "[o]ne who is presumed to have special knowledge of, or skill in, a particular field due to education, experience, or study." *The Dictionary of Real Estate Appraisal*, 3d ed., 126.

37. *United States v. Certain Property*, 306 F.2d 439, 477 (2nd Cir. 1962).

While some condemning agencies make provision for the estimation of just compensation when it is not considered equivalent to market value, such estimates are not made by appraisers.[38] However, many condemning agencies refuse to acknowledge that there may ever be a difference between market value and just compensation.[39] Often appraisal contracts call for the estimation of market value and, at the same time, require that the estimate be called *just compensation*.

At the other end of the spectrum, there are some private attorneys who advocate the proposition that market value is frequently not the measure of just compensation and that appraisers should directly estimate just compensation by whatever means they can, with the assistance of the attorney, conjure up. Those who wish to deviate from the generally applicable market value standard will most often quote the *Cors*[40] case, which reads as follows:

> The Court in its construction of the constitutional provision has been careful not to reduce the concept of "just compensation" to a formula. The political ethics reflected in the Fifth Amendment reject confiscation as a measure of justice. But the Amendment does not contain any definite standards of fairness by which the measure of "just compensation" is to be determined. The Court in an endeavor to find working rules that will do substantial justice has adopted practical standards, including that of market value. But it has refused to make a fetish even of market value, since that may not be the best measure of value in some cases.[41] [Citations omitted]

While appraisers should recognize that there are occasions when market value is not the best measure of just compensation, those occasions are rare. The burden of determining whether there is a better measure of just compensation than market value should not be placed on the appraiser by the client or the client's attorney. If the client's attorney suggests that a value other than market value would be a more accurate measure of just compensation under the circumstances of the case, the appraiser should reject the suggestion, unless it is converted into a written legal instruction with adequate supporting authority. (See Chapter 1 for a discussion of legal instructions.) Even under these circumstances, it is recommended that the appraiser estimate both the property's market value and the value specified in the attorney's instructions. Then, if the court ultimately rejects the alternative definition, the appraiser will still be able to testify to market value.

The appraiser who attempts to determine just compensation, instead of estimating value, is usurping the right and responsibility of the trier of fact. The appraiser should make it clear that his or her estimate is of market value only. If the value estimate is of an instructed value, rather than market value, the appraiser must make that clear in both the appraisal report and in testimony[42] and specifically define that value.[43] To do otherwise would be misleading and violate the professional standards of appraisal practice.

38. U.S. Department of Transportation, Federal Highway Administration, *The Appraisal Guide* (Washington, D.C.: U.S. Government Printing Office, 1990), 58–60.
39. See *Uniform Appraisal Standards for Federal Land Acquisitions*.
40. *United States v. Cors*, 337 U.S. 325 (1949).
41. Ibid. at 332. This case dealt with the government's requisition of a tug boat during World War II and the enhancement of the value of the boat due to the government's special need for it.
42. USPAP, 1994 ed., p. 1.
43. Ibid., S.R. 1-2(b) and S.R. 2-2(d).

The foregoing discussion is not meant to suggest that the appraiser should doggedly estimate market value, and exclude consideration of other forms of value, irrespective of the circumstances of the case. If, after initial investigation, the appraiser concludes that estimating another value would result in a more accurate measure of just compensation under the circumstances of the case, he or she should suggest the alternative to the client's legal counsel. It is then up to legal counsel to determine whether the alternative methodology can be supported as a matter of law. If the alternative can be supported, the attorney should provide the appraiser with a legal instruction to estimate the alternative value. A casual comment from the attorney such as, "Sounds good to me. Go ahead and appraise it that way," is not sufficient. The instruction must be in writing, it must be explicit, and it must contain reasonable supporting authority.

The term *just compensation* has been determined to mean compensation that is just not only to the person whose property is being taken, but also to the condemnor, who is in essence the general public or society as a whole. Thus, just compensation is "[r]easonable compensation" and "compensation which is just, not merely to the individual whose property is taken, but to the public which is to pay for it."[44]

Also, while the price paid for the property may have a bearing on its market value, "[i]t is not the investment, but the 'value of the interest' in land taken by eminent domain that is guaranteed to the owner; the government may neither confiscate the owner's bargain, nor be required to assume his loss."[45]

Generally, market value is the measure of just compensation, but it is often difficult for appraisers to estimate market value while adhering to the specialized rules applicable to eminent domain valuation which have been established by the legislature or handed down by the courts. This is particularly true in partial taking cases, in which the appraiser is burdened with the task of estimating the value of the remainder property as well as the value of the property prior to the government's acquisition. These specialized rules of valuation result in every appraisal conducted for eminent domain purposes being made under hypothetical conditions that do not, in fact, exist in the marketplace.[46]

SUMMARY

Eminent domain is the right of the sovereign to take private property for a public use upon payment of just compensation. The sovereign's act of taking property under its right of eminent domain is called *condemnation*. The appraiser should have a complete understanding of these two terms to communicate effectively with others active in the field of eminent domain litigation.

The sovereign's right of eminent domain is well established as an inherent right; it need not be specifically granted. The right is limited in two ways. First, the use for which the land is being taken must be a *public use*, a term which the courts interpret liberally. Second, the property owner must be justly compensated by

44. *Ballentine's Law Dictionary*, 3d ed., s.v. "just compensation."

45. Ibid.; see also *Kinter v. United States*, 156 F.2d 5 (3rd Cir. 1946).

46. At a minimum, the appraiser must assume that the public project for which the appraised property is being acquired does not exist.

the sovereign for the acquisition. The requirement for the federal government to pay just compensation is specified in the Fifth Amendment to the U.S. Constitution. The requirement that states must pay just compensation when invoking their right of eminent domain is provided in Section 1 of the Fourteenth Amendment to the U.S. Constitution. Also, every state constitution, except one, requires the payment of just compensation for the taking of private property for public use.

Just compensation is not defined in any constitution, but it has generally been held to be market value. The property owner is to be compensated for the taking of his or her property, as opposed to being compensated for the property taken. This provides that an owner must be compensated for damages to the remainder property occasioned by the taking, as well as for the property actually taken. The courts have refused to rule that just compensation is always measured by market value. Other means of measuring value, or just compensation, have upon occasion won court approval.

The appraiser's function is to assist the court in its determination of just compensation by furnishing an opinion of market value, which is one element the court will consider in making its determination. The appraiser may, in certain situations, be asked to estimate a value other than market value to help the court make its determination. Another value should not be estimated without specific legal instructions from the client, or client's legal counsel. Such instructions must be communicated in writing and include supporting authority. The appraiser does not estimate just compensation directly; this is the duty of the trier of fact.

CHAPTER 3

Legal Measurements of Just Compensation

Due to conflicting case law and differing constitutional provisions in various jurisdictions, several different methods of computing just compensation have been promulgated. Although appraisers do not estimate just compensation, they must report their findings of market value and the difference in property value before and after a partial taking in a manner usable to those charged with the responsibility of computing just compensation.

The various condemning agencies have adopted computational rules, often in modified form, to be used by their appraisers in eminent domain valuation. Although the law recognizes that there are exceptions to the general rule that just compensation is equal to market value, the acquisition policies of condemning agencies seldom provide for such exceptions. Therefore, the appraisal forms and guidelines used by many condemning agencies must be modified to ensure that all parties understand that the appraiser's estimate reflects market value, which may or may not represent just compensation within the legal meaning of the term. Condemning agencies use policy statements such as "[u]nder established law the criterion for just compensation is the fair market value of the property at the time of the taking"[1] and "[t]he mathematical difference between the two values (market value "before" minus market value "after") is the just compensation,"[2] which illustrate their reluctance to acknowledge any measure of just compensation other than market value.

The specific rules for computing just compensation are almost as numerous as the states in the Union. Two general rules predominate; others are merely modifications developed to ensure compliance with applicable constitutional and

1. *Uniform Appraisal Standards for Federal Land Acquisitions* (Washington, D.C.: U.S. Government Printing Office, 1992), §A-2, 3-4.

2. Washington State Department of Transportation, *Right of Way Manual*, Chapter 4, Appendix 4-1, "Appraisal Report Guide," Part I, §A-3, p. I-1 (revised August 1991).

statutory provisions. The two general rules are the *before and after rule* (often referred to as the *federal rule*) and the *value of the take plus damages rule* (or the *state rule*).

To understand these rules one must first understand why the different rules were established. The sovereign cannot take private property for public use without the payment of just compensation. Some states have interpreted their constitutions to mean that just compensation must be paid in cash, while others have concluded that just compensation may be paid in a form other than cash, specifically in the form of special benefits bestowed on the remainder property in a partial acquisition. (See Chapter 15 for a discussion of general and special benefits.) In these latter jurisdictions, the special benefits may be offset against the value of the land taken, thereby reducing the amount of cash due the owner (sometimes to zero). This procedure would not meet the constitutional mandate in jurisdictions where compensation for the taking must be in cash. It is for this reason that two general rules have been established. The difference between the rules is generally significant only in partial taking cases in which the remainder property receives a special benefit.

FEDERAL RULE

The federal (before and after) rule is somewhat of a misnomer. This rule is applicable in federal condemnation cases, but it is also applicable in a number of state jurisdictions. In its simplest form, the federal rule is: value before taking minus value after taking equals just compensation. Graphically, this would be shown as:

Value of property before taking	$__________
Value of remainder property after taking	–__________
Difference (just compensation)	$__________

Under the federal rule, no further breakdown is required for trial purposes. However, the Federal Uniform Relocation Assistance and Real Property Acquisition Policy Act of 1970[3] requires the condemnor to furnish the property owner with a written statement summarizing how the figure offered as just compensation was reached. "Where appropriate, damages for the land acquired and consequential damages to the remaining land not taken should be shown separately."[4] The provisions of this act apply not only to federal land acquisitions, but also to acquisitions made by the states and their various subdivisions if federal matching funds are involved in either the land acquisition or construction of the public improvement. Also, it should be noted that the Internal Revenue Service treats the amount paid for the taking differently than the amount paid for damages to the remainder for federal income tax purposes.[5] For these reasons, it is often necessary for the appraiser to present a detailed breakdown of the value estimates in the appraisal report.

3. P.L. 91-646.
4. Ibid., Title III, §301(3).
5. *Nichols' The Law of Eminent Domain*, rev. 3d ed. (New York: Mathew Bender Co., Inc., 1991), vol. 7A, §10.04[3] n.11.

AN EXAMPLE

For purposes of illustration, consider a single property valued under the two different premises. Figure 3.1 shows a single-family property on a site measuring 100 feet by 300 feet, or 30,000 square feet. The site is improved with a 980-sq.-ft., single-family dwelling with an attached 280-sq.-ft. garage and miscellaneous on-site improvements such as trees, landscaping, and a driveway. The site has very poor surface drainage and is zoned for a single-family dwelling with a minimum lot size of 25,000 square feet and a minimum front yard setback of 25 feet.

FIGURE 3.1 PLOT PLAN—PARTIAL TAKING

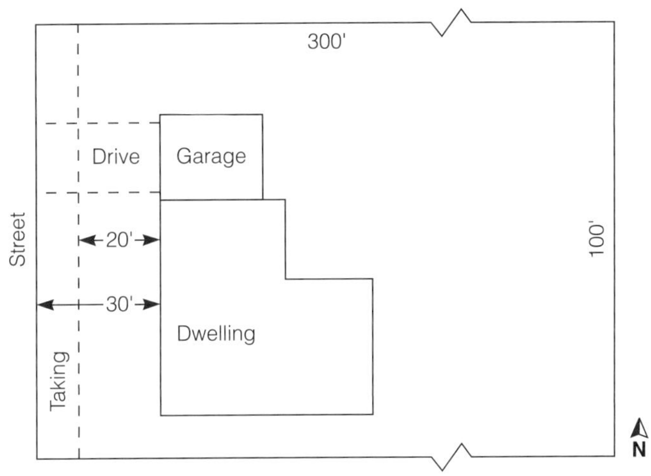

Area before taking	30,000 sq. ft.
Area after taking	29,000 sq. ft.
Area of taking	1,000 sq. ft.

The estimated market value of the property before any acquisition is $47,500, which can be broken down as follows for analytic purposes:

Site (30,000 sq. ft. @ $0.50/sq. ft.)	$15,000
Dwelling	28,800
Garage	1,200
On-site improvements	2,500
Total	$47,500

PREMISE 1

Assume the local municipality will acquire the westerly 10 feet of the site for a road-widening project. Within the area to be taken are two trees and a portion of the driveway. The acquisition will create a nonconforming use because the dwelling and garage will not meet the minimum required front yard setback.

Market analysis indicates that dwellings and garages that do not meet the setback requirement sell for 20% less than comparable, conforming dwellings. The contributory value of the on-site improvements remaining after the taking is estimated at $2,000. The property value before and after the taking under Premise 1 is tabulated in Table 3.1. From the information in Table 3.1, the appraiser draws the following conclusion:

Value of property before taking	$ 47,500
Value of remainder property after taking	-40,500
Difference	$ 7,000

PREMISE 2

Consider the same property described above. Assume that, as part of the road-widening project, the municipality will install storm sewers, which will eliminate the surface drainage problems on the property. Market investigation and analysis indicates that sites with no drainage problems sell for $0.75 per square foot, as compared to $0.50 per square foot for sites with drainage problems. The property's value before and after the taking under this premise is calcuated in Table 3.2.

Using the information in Table 3.2, the appraiser's conclusion is as follows:

Value of property before taking	$ 47,500
Value of remainder property after taking	- 47,750
Difference (just compensation)	$ 0

The difference between the before value and the after value (i.e., just compensation) cannot, of course, be less than zero. The summary of conclusions shown in Tables 3.1 and 3.2 is typical of the type of presentation required by condemnors using the before and after rule.[6] This format satisfies the reporting requirements of condemnors and helps them comply with the Federal Uniform Relocation Assistance and Real Property Acquisition Policies Act of 1970. It should be noted that the phrase, "Accounting tabulation not indicative of appraisal method employed," is printed on the form. This notice is imperative to ensure that the purpose of the summary is not misconstrued. On cross-examination, lawyers tend to dwell on questions such as why an appraiser estimated the contributory value of a tree at $250 instead of $300.

It is advisable that the appraiser include, in the limiting conditions section of the appraisal report, a statement such as the following:

> Where the value of the various components of the property are shown separately, the value of each is segregated only as an aid to better estimating the value of the whole; the independent value of the various components may, or may not, be the market value of the component.

6. Washington State Department of Transportation Form 261-016.

TABLE 3.1 SUMMARY OF CONCLUSIONS

(Accounting tabulation not indicative of appraisal method employed.)					
Indicated value before acquisition:					
Highest and best use: residential					
Land Area		**Unit Value**			
30,000 sq. ft.		$0.50	$15,000		
Total area 30,000 sq. ft.		Total land		$15,000	
Improvements					
Type	**Size**	**Unit Value**			
Dwelling	980 sq. ft.	$ 29.39	$28,800		
Garage	280 sq. ft.	$ 4.29	1,200		
On-site		Lump sum	$ 2,500		
Total improvements				32,500	
Total indicated value					$47,500
Indicated value of remainder:					
Highest and best use: residential					
Land Area		**Unit Value**			
29,000 sq. ft.		$0.50	$14,500		
Total area 29,000 sq. ft.		Total land		$14,500	
Improvements					
Type	**Size**	**Unit Value**			
Dwelling	980 sq. ft.	$23.51	$23,040		
Garage	280 sq. ft.	$ 3.43	960		
On-site		Lump sum	2,000		
Total improvements				26,000	
Total indicated value					40,500
Breakdown of acquisition:					
Land Area		**Unit Value**			
1,000 sq. ft.		$0.50	$ 500		
Total area 1,000 sq. ft.				$ 500	
Improvements					
Type	**Size**	**Unit Value**			
On-site		Lump sum	$ 500		
Total improvements				500	
Damages:					
Item					
Nonconforming house & garage			$ 6,000		
Total damages				6,000	
Subtotal				$ 7,000	
Benefits (subtract):					
Item					
None			$ 0		
Total benefits				0	
Difference between before and after values					$ 7,000

Even in jurisdictions that strongly adhere to the before and after rule, there are generally provisions allowing deviation from the rule under certain circumstances. Such deviation may be necessary when a minimal taking is involved or when a total before and after appraisal would not be economically practical. The formula applied in these instances is generally: the value of the part taken (as a part of the whole), plus damages to the remainder, less special benefits, equals

TABLE 3.2 SUMMARY OF CONCLUSIONS

(Accounting tabulation not indicative of appraisal method employed.)					
Indicated value before acquisition:					
Highest and best use: residential					
Land Area		**Unit Value**			
30,000 sq. ft.		$0.50	$15,000		
Total area 30,000 sq. ft.		Total land		$15,000	
Improvements					
Type	**Size**	**Unit Value**			
Dwelling	980 sq. ft.	$ 29.39	$28,800		
Garage	280 sq. ft.	$ 4.29	1,200		
On-site		Lump sum	$ 2,500		
Total improvements				32,500	
Total indicated value					$47,500
Indicated value of remainder:					
Highest and best use: residential					
Land Area		**Unit Value**			
29,000 sq. ft.		$0.75	$21,750		
Total area 29,000 sq. ft.		Total land		$21,750	
Improvements					
Type	**Size**	**Unit Value**			
Dwelling	980 sq. ft.	$23.51	$23,040		
Garage	280 sq. ft.	$ 3.43	960		
On-site		Lump sum	2,000		
Total improvements				26,000	
Total indicated value					47,750
Breakdown of acquisition:					
Land Area		**Unit Value**			
1,000 sq. ft.		$0.50	$ 500		
Total area 1,000 sq. ft.				$ 500	
Improvements					
Type	**Size**	**Unit Value**			
On-site		Lump sum	500		
Total improvements				500	
Damages:					
Item					
Nonconforming house & garage			$ 6,000		
Total damages				6,000	
Subtotal				$ 7,000	
Benefits (subtract):					
Item					
Improved drainage (29,000 sq. ft. @ $0.25)			$ 7,250		
Total benefits				7,250	
Difference between before and after values					$ 0

difference in value (just compensation). Graphically, this can be shown as:

Value of taking (as part of whole)	$	________
Plus damages	+	________
Less special benefits	-	________
Difference (just compensation)	$	________

As stated in the *Uniform Appraisal Standards for Federal Land Acquisitions*:

> Another approach [besides the before and after approach] is to find the value of the part taken on the date of taking; and to add to or subtract from that figure an allowance for diminution or enhancement in value of the remainder. This method may or may not be more complicated. It usually is more subject to error, however, and is more apt to result in duplication.
>
> It should be borne in mind that there are situations in which insistence upon strict adherence to the "before-and-after" rule would impose costly and sometimes nearly impossible burdens upon the appraisers and the courts. Examples of such situations, in which the...method discussed above would generally be applicable, are minor easement takings (for flowage, roads, pipelines, transmissions lines, etc.) from large ranches, industrial complexes, etc., where the cost of valuing the whole unit before and after the taking is simply unwarranted in view of the minor easement being acquired.
>
> In short, where its application would be logical, practical, and capable of understanding, the 'before and after' method of determining compensation in partial taking cases is preferred. Fortunately, this method is generally applicable and it is the exceptional case where the cost of valuing the whole is unreasonable.[7]

The alternative approach, sometimes called a *strip appraisal*, is seldom used to appraise a property that may be subject to damages and/or special benefits due to the proposed acquisition.

Although the before and after rule is also known as the *federal rule*, the rule is not even applied universally in federal acquisitions. Only the 5th Circuit Court of Appeals of the United States has definitively ruled that the before and after rule is the only acceptable rule to be used in determining just compensation.[8] The 4th Circuit Court has ruled that estimating the value of the taking plus damages is an acceptable method of determining just compensation in federal eminent domain actions,[9] not to the exclusion of the before and after rule, but as an alternative to it. The balance of the federal circuits appear to prefer the before and after rule, but they have not ruled, as a matter of law, that other methods are inadmissible.

As noted earlier, strip appraisals are most often used in nominal taking cases in which the remainder property is neither damaged nor benefitted by the government's project. Many condemning agencies have provisions for abbreviated value estimates when the anticipated compensation is below a certain dollar amount.[10] Such reports are not generally detailed enough for trial purposes, so it

7. *Uniform Appraisal Standards for Federal Land Acquisitions*, §A-11, 34-35.
8. *United States v. 8.41 Acres*, 680 F.2d 388, 392 n. 5 (5th Cir. 1982).
9. *United States v. 97.19 Acres*, 582 F.2d 878, 883 (4th Cir. 1977).
10. For example, the Federal Highway Administration provides for a "low value appraisal waiver" ($2,500 or less), a "value finding appraisal" ($5,000 or less), and a "short form appraisal," in addition to a narrative "detailed appraisal." U.S. Department of Transportation, Federal Highway Administration, *The Appraisal Guide* (Washington, D.C.: U.S. Government Printing Office, 1990).

is often necessary for an appraiser to convert a strip appraisal into a complete before and after appraisal prior to trial.

Regardless of the reporting requirements, it is generally advisable for appraisers to break down their value estimates in a manner similar to that shown in Tables 3.1 and 3.2. Such a breakdown allows for easier and more accurate comparative analysis of the appraised property and comparable properties and will often reveal any flaw in the logic the appraiser applied in reaching the value estimates. If the appraiser's analysis is flawed, it is much more comfortable for the appraiser to discover it in the privacy of his or her own office than on the witness stand under cross-examination.

STATE RULE

The state rule requires more in-depth analysis than the before and after rule. The nine procedural steps followed in applying the state rule are:

1. Value before taking	$	______
2. Value of part taken (as part of whole)	–	______
3. Remainder value before taking	= $	______
4. Remainder value after taking	–	______
5. Damages to remainder	= $	______
6. Special benefits to remainder	–	______
7. Net damage to remainder	= $	______
8. Value of part taken (as part of whole)	+	______
9. Total difference (just compensation)	= $	______

The results of the computations made in Step 5 (damages) and Step 7 (net damages) cannot be less than zero. It should be noted that Steps 3, 5, 7, and 9 are *not* estimates of value; they are merely intermediate mathematical calculations.[11]

Step 1 (value before taking) is the same as the first step in applying the before and after rule. In Step 2 the appraiser estimates the *contributory* value of the property within the area of the taking. This contributory value may be greater or less than its pro rata value, depending on the physical characteristics and utility of the part to be taken, as compared to the property as a whole.

Step 4 is an estimate of the value of the remainder property, considering damages and special benefits to the remainder property by reason of the taking and construction of the public improvement. This is the same value estimated in the second step of the before and after rule. Step 6 is an estimate of the special benefits accruing to the remainder property due to the taking and construction of the public improvement.[12] Step 8 is merely a *carry-down*, a repetition of the estimate made in Step 2.

Returning to the example presented earlier, the state formula is applied to the circumstances described as Premise 1. The calculations follow.

11. Step 3 = Step 1 – Step 2; Step 5 = Step 3 – Step 4; Step 7 = Step 5 – Step 6; Step 9 = Step 7 + Step 8.

12. Note that the state formula does not specifically require an estimate of the value of the remainder excluding benefits. However, the appraiser would be unable to complete Step 6 (special benefits to remainder) without such an estimate.

1. Value before taking	$ 47,500
2. Value of part taken (as part of whole)	– 1,000 *
3. Remainder value before taking	= $ 46,500
4. Remainder value after taking	–40,500 †
5. Damages to remainder	$ 6,000
6. Special benefits to remainder	– 0
7. Net damage to remainder	= $ 6,000
8. Value of part taken (as part of whole)	+ 1,000
9. Total difference (just compensation)	= $ 7,000

* 1,000 sq. ft. of land @ $0.50 ($500) + on-site improvements.

† 29,000 sq. ft. of land @ $0.50 ($14,500) + the value of the dwelling ($28,800) and garage ($1,200) discounted 20% ($6,000) for damage + on-site improvement value ($2,000).

Under Premise 2 the computations would be:

1. Value before taking	$ 47,500
2. Value of part taken (as part of whole)	– 1,000
3. Remainder value before taking	= $ 46,500
4. Remainder value after taking	– 47,750 *
5. Damages to remainder	= $ 0
6. Special benefits to remainder	– 7,250 †
7. Net damage to remainder	= $ 0
8. Value of part taken (as part of whole)	+ 1,000
9. Total difference (just compensation)	= $ 1,000

* 29,000 sq. ft. of land @ $0.75 ($21,750) + the value of the dwelling ($28,800) and garage ($1,200) discounted by 20% ($6,000) + on-site improvements ($2,000).

† 29,000 sq. ft. of land @ $0.25.

Note. The amounts shown in Steps 5 and 7 cannot be less than zero.

There are a number of variations on this formula. In a few jurisdictions, the basic state rule must be modified because the jurisdiction does not allow benefits to be offset against the value of the taking or damages to the remainder. This modified formula eliminates Steps 6 and 7 from the basic state formula, as shown below:

1. Value before taking	$ ________
2. Value of part taken (as part of whole)	– ________
3. Remainder value before taking	= $ ________
4. Remainder value after taking (before benefits)	– ________
5. Damages to remainder	= $ ________
6. Value of part taken (as part of whole)	+ ________
7. Total difference (just compensation)	= $ ________

When this formula is used, the amount shown in Step 4 (remainder value after taking) is always the value of the remainder *excluding* consideration of any benefits.

Applying this formula to the sample property under Premise 1 results in the following calculations:

1. Value before taking	$47,500
2. Value of part taken (as part of whole)	− 1,000
3. Remainder value before taking	= $46,500
4. Remainder value after taking (before benefits)	−40,500
5. Damages to remainder	= $ 6,000
6. Value of part taken (as part of whole)	+ 1,000
7. Total difference (just compensation)	= $ 7,000

Under Premise 2, the computations are:

1. Value before taking	$47,500
2. Value of part taken (as part of whole)	− 1,000
3. Remainder value before taking	= $46,500
4. Remainder value after taking (before benefits)	−40,500
5. Damages to remainder	= $ 6,000
6. Value of part taken (as part of whole)	+ 1,000
7. Total difference (just compensation)	= $ 7,000

When this formula is applied the results under Premise 1 and Premise 2 are identical. In the standard formula, Step 5 (damages) can never be less than zero; under this modified rule, Step 4 (remainder value after taking) can never be greater than Step 3 (remainder value before taking) because the appraiser is prohibited from considering any benefits in estimating the value of the remainder after the taking. Thus it is impossible for the value of the remainder after the taking to be greater than the remainder value before the taking.

Many of these rules of compensation have been developed to avoid a chronic and dangerous problem—*double damage*, i.e., the duplication of just compensation. To illustrate how easy it is to double damage using the taking plus damages (state) rule, consider the situation depicted in Figure 3.2. Assume that the property's annual economic rent prior to the taking is $20,000 net to the lessor, and the applicable overall capitalization rate is 10.5%. The indicated before value is therefore $190,500 ($20,000/0.105), rounded. Market evidence indicates that the land has a value of $10 per square foot, or $60,000. Thus, the before value can be allocated as follows for analytical purposes:

Land	$ 60,000
Improvements	130,500
Total	$190,500

Now, assume that the municipality takes a 10-ft. strip from the westerly side of the property, which eliminates five parking stalls. Analysis indicates that the economic rent after the taking is $15,000 per year. Under the state, or taking plus damages, rule the uninitiated appraiser might make the following calculations:

FIGURE 3.2 PLOT PLAN—PARTIAL TAKING

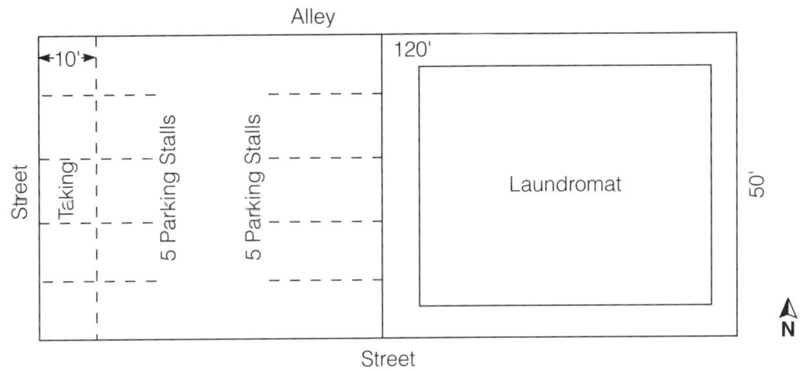

Area before taking	6,000 sq. ft.
Area after taking	5,500 sq. ft.
Area of taking	500 sq. ft.

Value of taking (500 sq. ft. @ $10.00)	$ 5,000
Damages ($5,000 rent loss ÷ 0.105)	47,619
Total difference (just compensation)	$52,619
Rounded	$52,500

When this procedure is applied, the landowner is compensated for the taking twice. Use of the correct state rule formula would result in the following:

1. Value before taking	$190,500
2. Value of part taken (500 sq. ft. @ $10.00)	− 5,000
3. Remainder value before taking	= $185,500
4. Remainder value after taking ($15,000 income ÷ 0.105)	− 142,857
5. Damages to remainder	= $ 42,643
6. Special benefits to remainder	− 0
7. Net damage to remainder	= $ 42,643
8. Value of part taken (as part of whole)	+ 5,000
9. Total difference (just compensation)	= $ 47,643
Rounded	$ 47,500

Comparison of these calculations illustrates the importance of following a set formula when using the state rule. The courts are plagued with appraisals in which damage to the property is doubled when the state rule is applied.

When applying the state rule, the part taken generally is valued as a part of the whole property prior to the taking.[13] There have been court rulings that conflict with this position, however. If the part taken has an independent economic use and its market value as a separate entity is greater than its value as a part of the whole, it has been held proper to value the part taken as a separate tract, not

13. *Department of Public Works and Bldngs. v. Oberlaender*, 235 N.E.2d 3 (Ill. 1969).

as a part of the whole.[14] There is a considerable amount of case law on this point. Analysis of this case law clearly illustrates that these conflicting rulings are not due to differing constitutional and/or statutory provisions in the various jurisdictions. Rather, they result from insufficient or improper analysis on the part of the appraiser in arriving at a conclusion of highest and best use and/or a determination of the *larger parcel*. (See Chapters 5 and 6 for information on highest and best use and determination of the larger parcel.)

If, as the court rulings assert, the part taken has an independent economic use and its market value as a separate entity is greater than its value as a part of the whole, the appraiser must have erred in determining the larger parcel and/or highest and best use because the area taken and the remainder parcel had no unity of highest and best use prior to the taking. Therefore, the larger parcel to be appraised in the before situation is the taken area itself, and there is no after situation because the taking was, in effect, a *total taking* of the larger parcel.

This situation is illustrated in a Louisiana decision in which the court said the following:

> A landowner is always entitled to the fair market value of the land actually taken.
>
> The fair market value of the front land in certain situations is higher than the average unit price of the tract. The fact that adjacent areas of land which have different highest and best uses are all under the same ownership, and together compose a large ownership tract, does not presuppose that they would be developed or marketed as a single tract. In fact, market realities dictate otherwise. An owner ordinarily will sell a portion of his property for the highest price the market will deliver so long as that use does not damage the value of the remainder. This jurisdiction has long recognized that different portions of an ownership tract may have different highest and best uses and, thus, different per unit values.[15]

When appraising property for partial taking purposes, an appraiser must often make more in-depth value estimates than would be called for by other types of appraisal assignments. In a typical appraisal assignment, the appraiser's only concern is the market value of the property as a whole. The contributory value of the components that make up the whole are of no concern. However, when valuing a part taken as a part of the whole, the appraiser must carefully determine whether the area taken contributes an equal pro rata value to the whole or an amount greater or less than its pro rata value. The courts have ruled that it is improper to use an average unit value (e.g., per square foot, per acre) as developed for the whole tract in valuing the part taken unless each unit in the tract has the same value.[16] As one court applying the state rule of measuring compensation put it:

> The landowner is thus to be awarded the actual market value of the particular portion of the property taken, valued according to its highest and best use. He is

14. *People ex rel. Dept. of Pub. Works v. Corp. of Pres. of Church of Latter Day Saints*, 91 Cal. Rptr. 532,537 (Cal. 1970).
15. *State Dept. of H'wys. v. Stegemann, La.*, 269 So.2d 480 (La. 1973).
16. *Los Angeles County Flood Control Dist. v. McNulty*, 379 P.2d 493 (Cal. 1963).

> not limited to its average per acre value as a pro rata portion of the parent tract where the front portion has a different highest and best value.
>
> ...[W]here the evidence shows that the front portion of the tract taken has a higher value than the rear portion not taken, the landowner must be awarded the higher value for the land actually taken rather than an average value based on its proportionate portion of the land-area of the parent tract.[17] [Citations omitted]

AN EXAMPLE

Considerable case law has developed over the use of a valuation procedure variously referred to as the *backland theory*, the *slide back theory*, or the *front land-rear land concept*. Figures 3.3 and 3.4 illustrate a situation in which this theory might be applicable.

FIGURE 3.3 PLOT PLAN—BEFORE PARTIAL TAKING

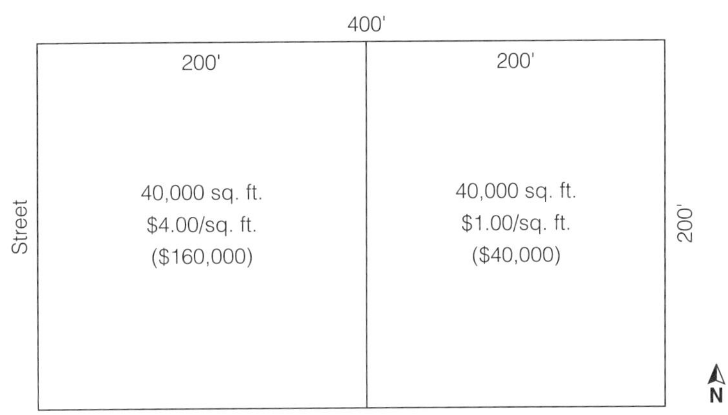

Assume that market evidence indicates that the highest and best use of the property shown in Figure 3.3 is for commercial development. Analysis indicates that tracts 200 feet wide and 200 feet deep can be sold for $4.00 per square foot, or $160,000, on the open market; a tract 200 feet wide and 400 feet deep will bring a price of $200,000. It can be assumed then that the front 200 feet of the tract has a value of $4.00 per square foot, while the land beyond 200 feet has a value of $1.00 per square foot. As shown in Figure 3.4, the front 40 feet of the tract will be acquired for road widening. Two diametrically opposed approaches to such a situation have been developed by the courts in two jurisdictions using the state (taking plus damages) rule. These two different approaches are exemplified by a California case and a Louisiana case.

The California court cited *City of Los Angeles v. Allen*[18] and stated:

17. *State, through Department of Highways v. Hoyt, La.*, 284 So.2d 763, 764 (La. 1973).

18. *City of Los Angeles v. Allen*, 36 P.2d 611 (Cal. 1934).

FIGURE 3.4 PLOT PLAN—AFTER PARTIAL TAKING

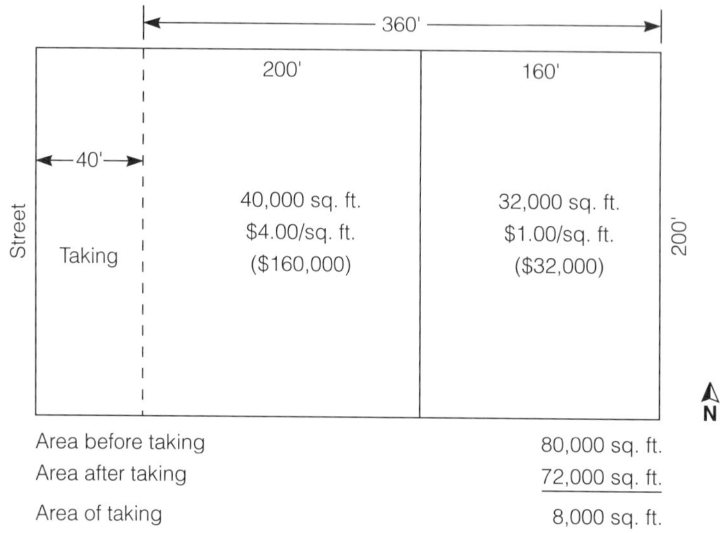

> On appeal, the condemnee contended that the strip taken was frontage and that he should have been allowed the commercial value. The Supreme Court disagreed. It reasoned that if to widen the public highway, a strip of land is taken from a larger parcel under one ownership and if it is clear that the main parcel has more than one theoretical zone of value, not because of any unique characteristic in the land itself, but rather because of the proximity of the theoretical zones to the public highway or similar factors affecting property values, and if it is also clear that the same zones may be immediately reestablished after the "take," the owner is unjustly enriched if he is compensated on the basis of the highest zone of value; under these circumstances, the strip must be treated as an integral part of the whole and not as a separate piece of property having an independent value.[19]

On the other hand, the Louisiana court stated:

> We consider the Louisiana jurisprudence to be settled, therefore, that generally the market value of the particular part of the tract expropriated is determined by the actual market value of the portion taken, and not by its average per acre or per square foot value as a pro rata portion of the parent tract. Also, a landowner is entitled to receive the full and actual market value of highway frontage expropriated for further highway purposes, without deduction therefrom because of the fact that by reason of the taking a new highway frontage will be provided for the formerly rear portions of the parent tract.[20]

---

19. *City of Fresno v. Cloud*, 102 Cal. Rptr. 874 (Cal. 1972).

20. *State, Dept. of H'ways v. LeDoux, La.*, 184 So.2d 604 (La. 1966).

In the *Allen* case cited by the California court, the trial judge used a weighted average in determining just compensation. Applying this procedure to the above circumstances would result in the following computations:

1. Value before taking (40,000 sq. ft. @ $4.00 + 40,000 sq. ft. @ $1.00)	$200,000
2. Value of taking ($200,000 ÷ 80,000 sq. ft. = $2.50)	
(8,000 sq. ft. @ $2.50)	– 20,000
3. Remainder value before taking	$180,000
4. Remainder value after taking	
(40,000 sq. ft. @ $4.00 + 32,000 sq. ft. @ $1.00)	192,000
5. Damages	$ 0
6. Special benefits ($192,000 – $180,000)*	– 12,000
7. Net damages	$ 0
8. Value of part taken	+ 20,000
9. Total difference (just compensation)	$ 20,000

* This benefit is created because 8,000 square feet of land that was worth $1.00 per sq. ft. before the taking will be worth $4.00 per sq. ft. after the taking because it will front the widened roadway.

Under the Louisiana rule, just compensation would be calculated as follows:

1. Value before taking (40,000 sq. ft. @ $4.00 + 40,000 sq. ft. @ $1.00)	$200,000
2. Value of taking (8,000 sq. ft. @ $4.00)	– 32,000
3. Remainder value before taking	$168,000
4. Remainder value after taking	
(40,000 sq. ft. @ $4.00 + 32,000 sq. ft. @ $1.00)	–192,000
5. Damages	$ 0
6. Special benefits	0
7. Net damages	$ 0
8. Value of part taken	+ 32,000
9. Total difference (just compensation)	$ 32,000

Applying the before and after rule, compensation would be:

Value before taking (40,000 sq. ft. @ $4.00 + 40,000 sq. ft. @ $1.00)	$200,000
Value after take	
(40,000 sq. ft. @ $4.00 + 32,000 sq. ft. @ $1.00)	–192,000
Total difference (just compensation)	$ 8,000

The U.S. Supreme Court has justified use of the before and after rule by explaining its logic as follows:

> If, for example, by the widening of a street, the part which lies next [to] the street, being the most valuable part of the land, is taken for the public use, and what was before in the rear becomes the front part, and upon a wider street, and thereby of greater value than the whole was before, it is neither just in itself, nor required by the Constitution, that the owner should be entitled both to receive the full value

> of the part taken, considered as front land, and to retain the increase in value of the back land, which has been made front land by the same taking.[21]

The differing rulings may be caused as much by confusion on the part of the courts as by differences in constitutions and their construction. Nevertheless, these differences are understandable when it is recognized that just compensation is defined as "[T]he full monetary equivalent of the property taken [and] market value at time of taking"..., but the same definition states that just compensation

> requires that the owner be put in as good position pecuniarily as he would otherwise have been if the property had not been taken [and] a settlement which leaves one no poorer or richer than he was before the property was taken.[22]

The Louisiana rule is based on the proposition that if an individual wanted to acquire 8,000 square feet of frontage out of the parcel depicted in Figure 3.3, he or she would have to pay $4.00 per square foot, or $32,000, for it. Thus, it can be argued that the state should pay the same amount. It is the monetary equivalent of the property taken—i.e., the land's market value.

However, the Louisiana ruling certainly leaves the property owner in a far better position pecuniarily than if the property had not been taken. Prior to the taking, the owner had a tract of land that could have been sold for $200,000. After the taking, the owner had $32,000 in cash plus a tract of land that could have been sold for $192,000, for a total of $224,000. It would appear that the before and after rule would more closely approximate just compensation from the standpoint of placing the owner in the same, but no better, position pecuniarily that he was in prior to the taking.

Although either of these positions, or rules of compensation, could legitimately be argued, it is not the appraiser's job to argue them, but rather to apply them. Comparing the results of these computations highlights the need for appraisers to be fully familiar with the rules of eminent domain valuation applicable in the jurisdiction.

All that can be said about the California ruling in the *Allen* case is that it is wrong whatever rule of compensation, or for that matter appraisal theory, is applied to it. However, given other California rulings in the field of eminent domain, particularly in the area of inverse condemnation, the ruling is not surprising. (For more on inverse condemnation, see Chapter 17.)

Nichols' explains that concepts such as the slide back theory had to be created to avoid the errors of percentage valuation, the technique applied in the *Allen* case. *Nichols'* goes on to explain:

> Under this theory, the pre-taking parcel is divided into zones of value from the point of moving backward through the property to its rear-most point from the point of take. Thus the value of the portion taken, even as a part of the whole, is considered only in its value zone. This kind of scientific analysis of market conditions is not representative of what occurs in the market and begins to drift so far

21. *Bauman v. Ross*, 167 U.S. 548, 574–575 (1897).

22. *Black's Law Dictionary*, abr. 6th ed., s.v. "just compensation."

away from reality to be an exercise in abstract philosophy rather than attainment of damage value.

Nichols' concludes:

> Many courts have avoided this problem [of applying the slide back theory] by actually defining a portion of the property, even though contiguous and uniformly held by the condemnee pre-taking as a separate and distinct parcel. Such definition eliminates any applicability of damage to that part of the owner's property remaining, which was not a part of the separate use parcel pre-taking. In applying the "before and after rule" however, the same result is readily attained since the property not effected (sic) by the taking would have essentially the same value both before and after and thus produce no differential in the final ascertainment of damage.[23]

This conclusion is incorrect. Consider the property depicted in Figure 3.3. If the westerly 200 feet of the tract did not have the same, or a unified, highest and best use as the easterly portion of the tract, the easterly portion of the tract should have been excluded from consideration in both the before and after appraisals, irrespective of whether the state rule or the before and after rule was applicable. If the two tracts of land had no unity of use, the easterly portion of the tract would not be a part of the larger parcel. It could be argued, however, that the larger parcel would include the westerly 200 feet of the remainder ownership in the after situation. (See Chapter 5 for related discussion.) With no unity of use, the compensation would be the same ($4.00 per square foot, or $32,000), regardless of whether the state or before and after rule was applied.

On the other hand, if there was unity of highest and best use within the entire ownership, the results would have varied considerably. As the earlier computations demonstrated, if the westerly 200 feet of the tract was considered a separate and distinct parcel under the state rule the compensation would be $4.00 per square foot, or $32,000. However, the premise in *Nichols'* that "the property not affected by the taking would have essentially the same value both before and after and thus produce no differential in the final ascertainment of damage" is flawed. A portion of the remainder is, in fact, affected by the taking; it is specially benefitted. Because the roadway is reconstructed 40 feet east of its former location, the zone worth $4.00 per square foot also shifts 40 feet to the east, reducing the depth of the $1.00 per square foot land to 160 feet (see Figure 3.4). It is for this reason that the before and after rule results in an indicated compensation of $8,000.

Nichols' analysis demonstrates once again the confusion that exists concerning the effect, and the importance, of the correct determination of the larger parcel. This issue is discussed in detail in Chapter 5.

---

23. *Nichols'*, vol. 4A, §14.02[2] (1992).

COMPARISON OF RULES

The two rules of computing just compensation have evolved because judicial attitudes differ as to whether the benefits created by a project can be offset against the value of the taking and/or any damages caused by the taking. (The rules relating to benefits are covered at length in Chapter 15.) Generally jurisdictions that use the state rule do not allow benefits to be offset against the value of the part taken. Some, in fact, will not allow a project benefit to be set off against either the part taken or the damages caused by the taking. The before and after rule is generally applied in jurisdictions that allow benefits to be offset against both the value of the taking and the damages.

Experience suggests that condemning agencies in some jurisdictions do not know which rule to use. Their appraisal reporting requirements are a hybrid, requiring the appraiser to estimate the before and after values of the property under appraisal and then to break down the value using the state rule. Confusion in these jurisdictions results from the fact that state courts require the state rule to be used in eminent domain cases, but federal matching funds for state projects are awarded based on the federal measure of just compensation. This has caused many state agencies to attempt to acquire property using the before and after rule, even though they know that the state rule will apply if the parcel must be condemned.[24]

The rule of compensation used in each state is indicated in the following list compiled by George Schmutz:[25]

Before and After (Federal) Rule

Alabama	Minnesota	Pennsylvania
Arkansas	Mississippi	Rhode Island
Connecticut	Missouri	South Dakota
Delaware	North Carolina	Tennessee
Hawaii	New Hampshire	Virginia
Iowa	New Jersey	Washington
Maine	New Mexico	Wisconsin
Maryland	Ohio	Wyoming
Michigan	Oklahoma	

Taking Plus Damages (State) Rule

Arizona	Kansas	North Dakota
California	Kentucky	Oregon
Colorado	Louisiana	South Carolina
Florida	Massachusetts	Texas
Georgia	Montana	Utah
Idaho	Nebraska	Virginia
Illinois	Nevada	Vermont
Indiana	New York	West Virginia

24. Appraisers must be cautious in these jurisdictions to ensure that they will be able to sign a required statement that the property was valued in accordance with applicable state law. See Chapter 1, "The Litigation Environment."

25. George L. Schmutz, *Condemnation Appraisal Handbook*, rev., Edwin M. Rams, ed. (Englewood Cliffs, N.J.: Prentice-Hall, 1963), 97–98.

Both Rules Held Acceptable

Alabama	New York	United States
Connecticut	North Carolina	Vermont
Mississippi	Rhode Island	Wisconsin
New Jersey		

The two primary weaknesses of the before and after rule are: 1) It does not provide a mechanism to exclude benefits from the after value. 2) It does not provide a mechanism to exclude noncompensable damages from the after value. (See Chapter 14 for a discussion of damages.) However, most authorities argue that the complexity of the state rule and its potential for double damages are so great that the before and after rule should be adopted despite its perceived weaknesses. Lewis Orgel advocates

> ...the abandonment of the attempt to find the separate value of the part taken, in favor of the rule that recovery should be based on the difference between the value of the whole before-and-after the taking. The adoption by all courts of the latter rule should be far less confusing to a jury and would probably avoid a very practical objection that may be urged against the more popular rule of "value of part taken plus damages to the remainder"—the objection that a jury may include in "damages to the remainder" a part of the very injury which it incorporates in "value of the part taken."[26]

Nichols' states

> The before-and-after evaluation approach "is generally the simplest and perhaps the most widely used approach in severance damage determinations. This approach also serves to lessen the problems that arise where a series of factors affecting value are added together to arrive at a total severance damage determination.
>
> ...Under [the part taken plus damages] attempt to evaluate compensation, the trier seeks to value the number of acres in fact taken, including such improvements as they existed in the pre-taking condition as part of an entire tract and then adding to that, those specific, provable damages occasioned to the remainder by the taking, again treating the remainder as it existed prior to the taking, i.e., as part of an entire tract. This results more in sophistry than equity.
>
> The valuation of the part taken plus severance damage has been criticized as tending to allow for duplication of damages and overpayment to the condemnee.[27]
>
> [T]he "before and after rule"...is preferred by most authorities, since it eliminates the difficulty of trying to evaluate a separate piece of land.[28]

The *Model Code on Eminent Domain* provides that

> [j]ust compensation shall consist of the difference between the full market value of the condemnee's entire property interest immediately before condemnation and as unaffected thereby and the full market value of his property interest remaining immediately after such condemnation and as affected thereby ...[29]

26. Lewis Orgel, *Valuation Under the Law of Eminent Domain*, 2d ed. (Charlottesville, Va.: The Michie Co., 1953), vol. 1, §52, 238.
27. *Nichols'*, vol. 4A, §14.02[1] (1992).
28. Ibid., vol. 8A, §16.02[4] (1992).
29. *Model Code on Eminent Domain*, §602.

The *Uniform Eminent Domain Code* provides that

> the measure of compensation is the greater of (1) the value of the property taken...or (2) the amount by which the fair market value of the entire property immediately before the taking exceeds the fair market value of the remainder immediately after the taking.[30]
>
> The principal difference between the rule expressed [above] and the conventional "before and after" approach followed in several states and in federal condemnation practice is that the latter can sometimes result in a zero award (if the remainder after the taking is more valuable than the entire property before the taking), while under the present section, the award cannot be less than the value of the "take."
>
> A different approach, something referred to as the "value plus damage" rule, appears to be followed in one of several variant formulations in a majority of states. Under this rule, briefly stated, compensation in partial taking cases generally consists of the sum of the value of the property taken and of any net damages to the remainder after offsetting benefits. Text writers and commentators, however, are in substantial agreement that the "before and after" rule is preferable to the "value plus damage" approach, since it avoids confusing artificialities inherent in the latter approach, is more consistent with realistic market valuation and appraisal techniques, and reduces the risk of inequitable windfall recoveries by property owners that may unnecessarily increase the cost of public improvements...
>
> The present section takes an intermediate position between these two views, requiring the compensation to be measured by the "before and after" rule, except that the award cannot be less than the value of the "take."[31]

The complexity and confusion that can result when using the state rule is demonstrated by the comments of Judge Hall, who offered a dissenting opinion in a case in which the majority of the court concluded that the lower court had awarded an owner double damages by using the state rule. He said "I am filled with a sense of frustration because of my inability to make my brothers of the majority understand what is so clear to me."[32]

SUMMARY

Two general rules have been developed to measure just compensation in eminent domain litigation. These rules are the before and after rule, often referred to as the *federal rule*, and the value of the part taken plus damages rule, often referred to as the *state rule*.[33] The federal rule is generally used in jurisdictions that allow benefits created by the public improvement to be set off against the value of the property taken and damages to the remainder land resulting from the taking and construction of the public improvement. The federal rule has two perceived weak-

30. *Uniform Eminent Domain Code*, §1002.
31. Ibid., "Official Comment."
32. *United States v. 2.33 Acres of Land, More or Less*, 704 F.2d 728, 732 (4th Cir. 1983) (dissenting opinion).
33. Referred to in recent editions of *Nichols' on Eminent Domain* as the "severance damage rule."

nesses: there are no procedures inherent in the application of the rule to exclude benefits (for those jurisdictions that do not allow benefits to be set off in the after valuation) or to exclude noncompensable damages in the after value of the property. These perceived weaknesses can be overcome by the appraiser, however, by analyzing the remainder property's value properly, without resorting to the convoluted, complex, and confusing hypothetical valuations required by the state rule. When the federal rule is applied, the after value of the property can be equal to, or greater than, its before value, resulting in zero compensation, if the benefits created are equal to or greater than the aggregate amount of the value of the part taken plus damages.

The state rule is generally used in jurisdictions that do not allow benefits to be set off against the value of the part taken and/or damages. Because the state rule is more hypothetical and complex than the federal rule, there is considerable danger that the unwary appraiser, or jury, could double the damages to the property and compensate the owner twice for the taking—once for the value of the taking and again for damages to the remainder. Because of this potential for double damaging, it is essential that the appraiser use a standard formula in making the value computations. Applying the state rule will never result in a difference in value (i.e., just compensation) that is less than the value of the part taken.

There is a considerable amount of conflicting case law with regard to whether the value of the part taken should be valued as a part of the whole property or as a separate entity. If the appraiser carefully analyzes the highest and best use of the property and properly identifies the larger parcel, most inconsistencies can be alleviated.

"Although the two methods differ, it is important to note that, in any given case, if both methods are applied correctly, they will yield the same result"[34] if benefits do not exceed damages. The appraiser must know which rule is applicable in the jurisdiction where a trial on the condemned property may be held. Using the wrong rule will often result in rejection of the appraiser's report and/or appraisal testimony. It is also essential that the appraiser investigate the applicable rule in the jurisdiction to determine whether the rule has been modified from the standard rule applicable in other jurisdictions.

Regardless of the rule applied, the appraiser must guard against double damages and errors in logic by allocating all value estimates systematically (see Tables 3.1 and 3.2). If the figures in the allocation will not balance, the appraiser's analysis is in error and must be corrected.

Although most authorities consider the before and after rule the preferred methodology, case law favoring the taking plus damages rule is so strong in some jurisdictions that nothing short of legislation will alter it (assuming such legislation would not be ruled unconstitutional).

34. *United States v. 2.33 Acres of Land, More or Less*, 704 F.2d 728, 732 (4th Cir. 1983) (dissenting opinion).

CHAPTER 4

Property Rights

DEFINITIONS

In appraisal terminology, *real estate* refers to "the physical land and appurtenances affixed to the land, *e.g.*, structures."; *real property* refers to "all interests, benefits, and rights inherent in the ownership of physical real estate."[1] The appraiser must use these terms carefully because many states regard them as synonymous by statute.[2]

Property is defined "[a]s the term appears in constitutional provisions respecting taking of property: a word of general import, extending to every species of right and interest, capable of being enjoyed as such, upon which it is practicable to place a money value."[3] *Property rights* are "[e]conomic interests supported by the law."[4] In real estate, these property rights are referred to as the *bundle of rights* because "[o]wnership of a parcel of real estate may embrace a great many rights, such as the right to its occupancy and use; the right to sell it in whole or in part; the right to bequeath; the right to transfer, by contract, for specified periods of time, the benefits to be derived by occupancy and use of the real estate. These rights of occupancy and use are called beneficial interests."[5] "The degree, quantity, nature, and extent of interest which a person has in real and personal property"[6] is called an *estate*.

1. *The Appraisal of Real Estate*, 10th ed. (Chicago: Appraisal Institute, 1992), 6.
2. *Black's Law Dictionary*, abr. 6th ed., s.v. "real estate."
3. *Ballentine's Law Dictionary*, 3d ed., s.v. "property."
4. Ibid., s.v. "property rights."
5. American Institute of Real Estate Appraisers and the Society of Real Estate Appraisers, *Real Estate Appraisal Terminology*, rev. ed., Byrl N. Boyce, ed. (Cambridge, Mass.: Ballinger Publishing Company, 1981), 35–36.
6. *Black's*, s.v. "estate."

BUNDLE OF RIGHTS

The bundle of rights inherent in the ownership of real estate has often been likened to a bundle of sticks because, like a bundle of sticks, the various rights may be separated and held by a number of individuals or entities. When an individual is in full possession of all property rights, he is said to have fee (meaning title) simple (meaning unencumbered) ownership, which represents maximum value. Originally, this term meant absolute ownership from the center of the earth, through the earth's surface, and upward to infinity. From a theoretical standpoint, real estate owned absolutely takes the form of an inverted pyramid.

Absolute ownership has been limited, however, by the sovereign's inherent rights, constitutional provisions, and legislative actions. For example, the Air Commerce Act of 1926, the Civil Aeronautics Act of 1938, and the Federal Aviation Act of 1958[7] limit air rights to the height necessary for the full enjoyment of the property. Later legislation and court rulings further defined the real estate owner's rights to air space above the ground. (Aviation easements, and other forms of easements are covered in Chapter 16.)

As stated in Chapter 2, the sovereign has the inherent power of eminent domain, the power of taxation, police power, and the power of escheat, all of which limit property rights. The appraiser must be aware of the existence of escheat, although detailed treatment of this subject is beyond the scope of this work.[8] (Appraising in conjunction with the sovereign's power of taxation is discussed in Chapter 22.)

POLICE POWER

In regard to police power, one court has held "An attempt to define its reach or trace its outer limits is fruitless."[9] Historically, the police power of government has been clearly distinguished from its power of eminent domain by determining whether the government's action required compensation to be paid. When a regulatory action of the government became unreasonable, or went too far, it ceased being a police power action and became a taking under the government's power of eminent domain.

> Police power should not be confused with eminent domain, in that the former controls the use of property by the owner for the public good, authorizing its regulation and destruction without compensation, whereas the latter takes property for public use and compensation is given for property taken, damaged or destroyed.[10] [Citations omitted]

> Care must be taken...to distinguish between the power of the community to zone and the power to condemn.[11]

Both powers have their source in the authority of the community to act in the public interest, but the nature of the public interest is considered differently de-

7. 49 U.S.C. §401.

8. "Escheat is the right of government that gives the state titular ownership of a property when its owner dies without a will or any ascertainable heirs." *The Appraisal of Real Estate*, 10th ed., 7. See also *Black's*, s.v. "escheat."

9. *Berman v. Parker*, 348 U.S. 26, 32 (1954).

10. *Lamm v. Volpe*, 449 F.2d 1202, 1203 (10th Cir. 1971).

11. *Nichols' The Law of Eminent Domain*, rev. 3rd ed. (New York: Matthew Bender Co., 1992), vol. 3, §8.01 [4] 6 (citation omitted).

pending upon which of the two powers the public authority is purporting to exercise. Distinguishing between the exercise of the two powers is not always easy. Indeed, even the Supreme Court can be confused.

Real Estate Appraisal Terminology, published in 1981, defined police power as "[t]he right of the government to limit the exercise of property rights in real estate, *without compensation*,..."[12]

More recent case law suggests that the police power of government and its power of eminent domain are not exclusive of one another, but can co-exist. In these more recent cases, the fact that government undertakes an action under its police power does not mean that compensation is not due for property taken or damaged. For instance, the U.S. Supreme Court clearly found that the State of Hawaii's legislation "to reduce the perceived social and economic evils of a land oligopoly" by use of its eminent domain powers was ". . . a classic exercise of the state's police powers."[13]

In keeping with this trend, current appraisal publications have eliminated the phrase *without compensation* from definitions of the sovereign's police power.[14] For these reasons, appraisers, and others, should use care in attempting to differentiate between actions of the government that are compensable and those that are not compensable by use of the terms power of *eminent domain* (compensable) and *police power* (noncompensable). If the term *police power* is being used in an historical context to connote a noncompensable action, as it is in the balance of this chapter, such use must be explained.

Since the U.S. Supreme Court ruled in 1926 that the zoning of land was a legitimate police power of the government,[15] the noncompensable police powers of government have been broadened by new legislation and legal interpretation. Actions which had historically been viewed as eminent domain powers, requiring the payment of compensation, increasingly were interpreted by government as noncompensable police power actions. The distinction between a *taking*, in a constitutional sense, and the proper use of the government's police power is often unclear. As one court put it:

> Plaintiffs have presented this court with an issue that commonly arises when governmental activity benefits the public generally at the expense of private interests: when does a publicly inflicted private injury rise to the level of a "taking," for which the Constitutions requires payment of compensation? The general question admits of no easy answer, for the courts in grappling with this issue have produced decisions as diverse as the factual situations that called for judicial decision-making.[16]

Justice Holmes explained:

> The general rule, at least, is that while property may be regulated to a certain extent, if regulation goes too far it will be recognized as a taking. . . . We are in danger of forgetting that a strong public desire to improve the public condition is

12. *Real Estate Appraisal Terminology*, rev. ed., 188 (emphasis added).
13. *Hawaii Housing Authority v. Midkiff*, 467 U.S. 229, 241–242 (1984).
14. See *The Appraisal of Real Estate*, 10th ed., 7 and *The Dictionary of Real Estate Appraisal*, 3d ed. (Chicago: Appraisal Institute, 1993), 271.
15. *Village of Euclid v. Ambler Realty Company*, 272 U.S. 365 (1926).
16. *Shrader v. Horton*, 471 F. Supp. 1236 (W.D. Va. 1979).

> not enough to warrant achieving the desire by a shorter cut than the constitutional way of paying for the change. As we already have said, this is a question of degree—and therefore cannot be disposed of by general propositions.[17]

Today there are no clear rules of law by which a government action can be measured. Whether a government action results in a constitutional taking remains an "ad hoc, factual inquir[y]"[18] which "ultimately calls as much for the exercise of judgment as for the application of logic"[19] because the Court cannot establish a set formula for determining whether a regulatory taking has occurred.[20]

Zoning and other land use regulations play an important role in eminent domain valuations. The applicable case law is extensive. Questions of zoning and other land use regulations have such an important bearing on the appraiser's determination of highest and best use and the estimate of market value that these subjects are treated separately in Chapter 7. The increased legal and appraisal activity in the area of regulatory takings is discussed in Chapter 17.

ACCESS RIGHTS

Access, or abutter's, rights have also been the subject of considerable litigation, much of it relating to right-of-way acquisitions for the interstate highway system. Access rights, which are part of the real estate owner's bundle of rights, include the right of reasonable ingress and egress, the right of reasonable light and air, and the reasonable right to see and be seen. These rights are often referred to as the rights of access, light, view, and air.

Access rights are subject to governmental alteration through police power and eminent domain. The government's use of its police power must, of course, be reasonable. When this power is reasonably applied, the abutting property owner is not entitled to any compensation, even though the government's action may decrease the value of the property. Examples of police power action would be the conversion of a two-way street into a one-way street, the elimination of left turns into or out of a property, and the diversion of street traffic to an alternate route. When the government alters access rights under the power of eminent domain, however, the property owner is entitled to compensation. *Unreasonable* access restrictions fall into this category.

In all jurisdictions the damaging alteration of a street grade is compensable if the alteration involves a partial taking of the property affected. Nevertheless, many jurisdictions have no constitutional or statutory provisions for the payment of damages in addition to compensation for a taking, so a damaging change of street grade that does not involve a physical taking is not compensable.[21] On the other hand, if the property is in a jurisdiction that provides compensation for damages, by its constitution or by statute, the grade change would be a compensable damage.[22]

There is a gray area between police power and the power of eminent domain when it comes to the right of access. For this reason access has been called the

17. *Pennsylvania Coal Co. v. Mahon*, 260 U.S. 393, 415–416 (1922).
18. *Kaiser Aetna v. United States*, 444 U.S. 164, 175 (1979).
19. *Andrus v. Allard*, 444 U.S. 51, 61 (1979).
20. *Goldblatt v. Town of Hempstead*, 369 U.S. 590 (1962).
21. *McGarrity v. Commonwealth*, 166 A. 895 (Pa. 1933), *appeal dismissed* 292 U.S. 19.
22. *Chicago v. Taylor*, 125 U.S. 161 (1888).

elastic right.[23] Although private, adjacent property owners have the right to ingress, egress, and a view from their land onto the public way, these rights are not unlimited. They are subordinate to the public's enjoyment and safe use of the route.[24] Expansion of the road surface within the existing right of way has therefore been ruled a police power action for which no compensation is required.[25]

In defining the limits of a property owner's access rights, the courts have referenced "reasonable access,"[26] "suitable access,"[27] and "free and convenient access"[28] and have stressed the need to obtain a "balance between the public and private interest"[29] in regard to use of the traveled way. It is well settled that abutting owners "are not entitled to access to their properties at any and all points along"[30] the public way. Case law indicates that an abutting owner is entitled to reasonable, convenient, and adequate access for the proper use and enjoyment of his property for its present use and for its reasonable uses in the foreseeable future. For example, consider the property shown in Figure 4.1 If this property's highest and best use is for a single-family dwelling as improved, and there is no likelihood that the highest and best use of the property will change in the foreseeable future, legal access to the subject could be limited to 28 feet (the width of the driveway plus the width of the walk) of the property's 100 feet of frontage without payment of compensation.

When a partial acquisition occurs for the construction of a limited-access highway, the remainder parcel is not considered damaged by its lack of access to the new highway.[31] Figure 4.2 demonstrates this situation. The property owner cannot receive compensation for lack of access to the new facility because the owner had no prior rights of access to the road.

FIGURE 4.1 PLOT PLAN

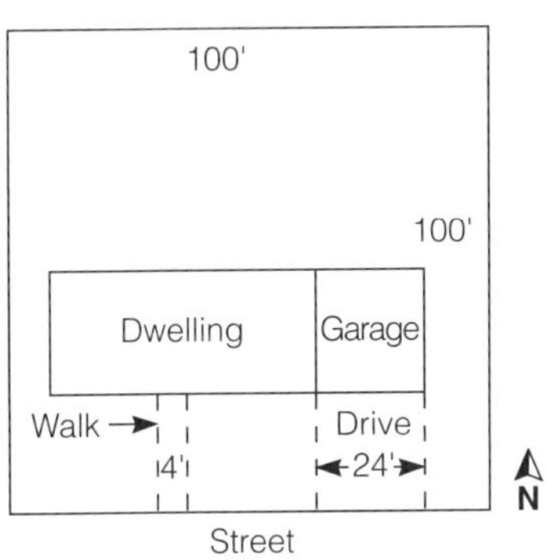

FIGURE 4.2 PLOT PLAN—PARTIAL TAKING

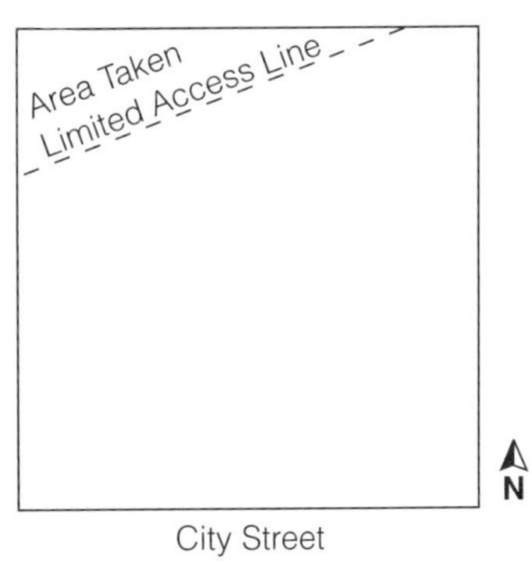

23. Henry J. Kaltenbach, "The Elastic Right–Access," *The Appraisal Journal* (January 1967), 9–16.
24. *State v. Lavasek*, 385 P.2d 361 (N.M. 1963).
25. *Nichols'*, vol. 3, §9.21.
26. *City of Houston v. Fox*, 429 S.W.2d 201, 203 (Tex. 1968) reversed on other grounds 444 S.W.2d 591 (Tex. 1969).
27. *Priestly v. State*, 242 N.E.2d 827, 829 (N.Y. 1968).
28. *Iowa State Highway Comm. v. Smith*, 82 N.W.2d 755, 759 (Iowa 1957).
29. *Wilson v. Iowa State Highway Comm.*, 90 N.W.2d 161, 168 (Iowa 1958).
30. *Iowa State Highway Comm. v. Smith*, 82 N.W.2d 755, 759 (Iowa 1957).
31. *State v. Fonburg*, 328 P.2d 60 (Idaho 1958).

The courts have ruled that an abutting property owner has special rights to the abutting roadway, beyond the rights of the public at large, and that these special rights take the form of an easement in the roadway.[32] Nevertheless, alteration of a formerly unlimited access road into a partially limited, or even fully limited, access facility does not necessarily mean that damages are due the abutting owner.

Figure 4.3 illustrates a property before and after a taking. The easterly 450 feet of the property's frontage becomes limited access in the after situation, leaving only the westerly 50 feet as accessible frontage. A similar situation is depicted in Figure 4.4, but here the property is in a corner location and access to and from the frontage road is totally restricted in the after situation.

FIGURE 4.3 ACCESS TAKING

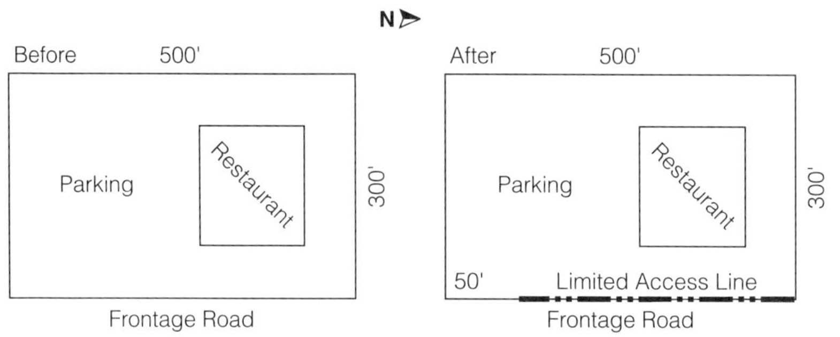

FIGURE 4.4 ACCESS TAKING

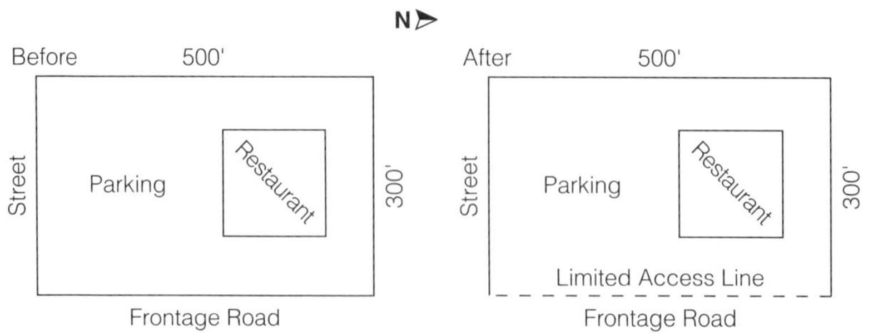

If, in either of these situations, the highest and best use of the property is for a restaurant, and the property has reasonable access and can continue to operate as a restaurant after the taking, it is probable that no compensable damage has accrued to the property by reason of the access limitation. If, however, the prop-

32. *State v. Wilson*, 420 P.2d 992 (Ariz. 1966).

erty becomes a second-rate highway retail location because its access has become unreasonably restricted, remote, and congested, substantial compensable damage may result.

There is some inconsistency in case law with regard to replacing access with substitute access to a frontage or service road. Consider the taking depicted in Figure 4.5. In this type of situation, some courts have ruled that the access to the new frontage road may partially mitigate the damages for the loss of access to the main highway.[33] Other courts have ruled that the access along the new frontage road totally replaces the access lost, so there can be no compensable damages.[34]

FIGURE 4.5 ACCESS TAKING

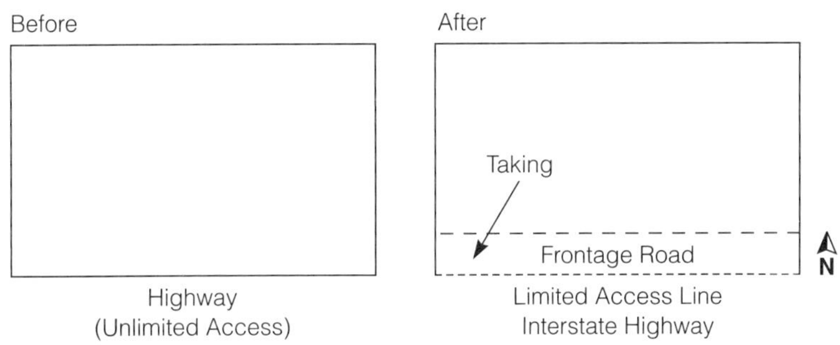

Certain elements of damage have universally been held noncompensable in relation to access and abutter's rights. Four noncompensable elements of damage are discussed below.

Increases,[35] *decreases,*[36] *or diversions*[37] *of traffic on the roadway.* The abutting owner retains rights of access to and from the highway, but has no right to the traffic that uses the highway.

Circuity of travel[38] *caused by government exercise of police power.* It must be kept in mind, however, that the property owner is entitled to *suitable* access.

> "Circuitous," in its commonly accepted understanding, indicates that which is round-about and indirect but which nevertheless leads to the same destination. "Suitable," in its commonly accepted understanding, describes that which is adequate to the requirements of or answers the needs of a particular object. The concepts are not mutually exclusive and, therefore, a finding that a means of access is indeed circuitous does not eliminate the possibility that same means of access might also be unsuitable in that it is inadequate to the access needs inherent in the highest and best use of the property involved.[39]

33. *Balog v. State, Dep't of Roads,* 131 N.W.2d 402 (Neb. 1964).
34. *State, Commissioner of Transportation v. Charles Investment Corp.,* 363 A.2d 944 (N.J. 1976).
35. *State Highway Comm. v. Chatham,* 161 So. 674 (Miss. 1935).
36. *Mabe v. State,* 360 P.2d 799 (Idaho 1961).
37. *People v. Sayig,* 226 P.2d 702 (Cal. 1951).
38. *State, ex rel. Merritt v. Linzell,* 126 N.E.2d 53. (Ohio 1955).
39. *Priestly v. State,* 242 N.E.2d 827, 829–830 (N.Y. 1968).

At least one court has ruled that although an abutting property owner has an inherent right of access to the abutting street, the right extends only to those lanes of travel that actually abut the property. This situation is depicted in Figure 4.6. The jury that heard this case was instructed:

> [Y]ou may allow such compensation to respondents as you find is established by the evidence because the owners or others must take a more circuitous route in going to or leaving their remaining property as a result of the loss of direct access for northbound traffic only.[40]

On appeal, this instruction was upheld as proper. Note that this ruling is in keeping with other rulings that the government may construct a median barrier, separating lanes of traffic, or prohibit left turns into or out of a property under its police power without the payment of compensation.

FIGURE 4.6 LIMITS OF ACCESS RIGHTS

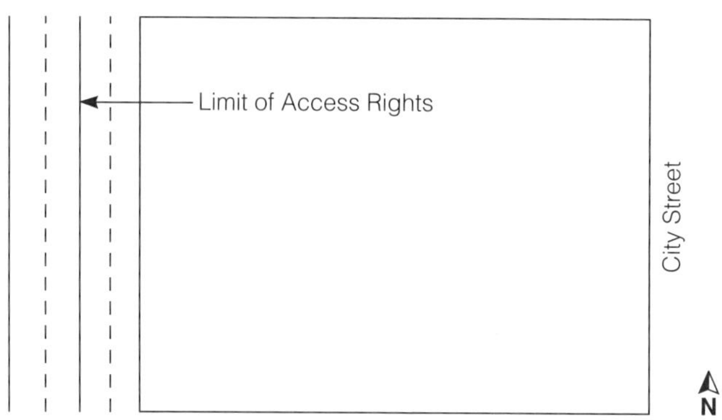

Relocation of highways. The government has no obligation to maintain the location of a street right of way, nor does it have any obligation to continue to lead customers past a retail location. The desires, convenience, and safety of the general public has greater weight than the desires of retail street merchants. If a through street is converted into a dead end, however, the resultant traffic diversion has been held to be compensable as an unreasonable limitation of access rights.[41] The discontinuance, abandonment, or obstruction of a highway has also been held to be compensable[42] but the loss of value must be specific to the property in question because losses common to the general public are noncompensable.[43] The temporary closure of a highway is generally noncompensable,[44] but there is case law in some jurisdictions to the contrary.[45]

Changes in highway width. As previously noted, the widening of a highway within the existing right of way has universally been held to be noncompensable. On

40. *State v. Wineberg*, 444 P.2d 787, 789–790 (Wash. 1968).
41. *O'Brien v. Central Iron & Steel Co.*, 63 N.E. 302 (Ind. 1972).
42. *Wolfe v. City of Providence*, 74 A.2d 843 (R.I. 1950).
43. *Department of Public Works & Buildings v. Hubbard*, 1 N.E.2d 383 (Ill. 1936).
44. *Commonwealth Dept. of H'ways v. Sherrod*, 367 S.W.2d 844 (Ky. 1963).
45. *State v. Widen*, 128 N.W.2d 755 (Minn. 1964).

the other hand, the narrowing of a highway has been considered a *partial street closing* and, therefore, compensable.[46] The damage resulting from the narrowing of a highway is usually not as great as that which results from the dead-ending or total abandonment of a highway.

MULTIPLE ESTATES

Real estate may be divided into more than one estate, and these various estates are often owned by different individuals or entities. Nevertheless, a condemnor generally instructs its appraiser to value the property as if the title were held by a single entity. This procedure has won court approval[47] and is often referred to as the *unit rule*[48] or the *undivided fee rule*.[49]

Condemnors will sometimes make an exception to the unit rule when they condemn less than the fee simple interest in a property. For instance, the estate taken will often be described as "the fee simple estate, excepting therefrom all easements for roadways and utilities." In such an instance, the appraiser's instructions will generally be modified to indicate that the appraisal will be concerned with the estate to be taken. Mineral rights, water rights, and existing mineral leases are other exceptions to the taking of a fee simple estate. Because there are exceptions, the appraiser must obtain a formal description of the estate to be taken, read it carefully, and, most importantly, understand it. Descriptions of the estate to be taken are not always written with the utmost clarity.

The philosophy of the unit rule is described in the *Uniform Appraisal Standards for Federal Land Acquisitions*:

> The unit rule: The fair market value concept which has been adopted by the courts to determine the just compensation required by the Constitution generally requires application of the so-called "unit rule," which is another principle designed to reflect the true situation in the market. The rule has two aspects:
>
> First, the unit rule requires valuing property as a whole rather than by the sum of the values of the various interests into which in may have been carved, such as lessor and lessee, life tenant and remainderman, etc. This is an application of the principle that it is the property, not the various titles, which is being taken. (n. 113. The term "in rem" is used to designate proceedings or actions instituted against the thing, in contradistinction to personal actions, which are said to be in personam. Many cases are illustrative of this principle.) Under this rule, the award for the whole is later apportioned among the claimants (lessor and lessee, life tenant and remainderman, etc.) as a second phase in the proceedings...
>
> If there are several interests or estates in the property, the property should be appraised as a whole, embracing the rights, estates and interests of all who may claim, and as if in one ownership. This is in keeping with the fact that it is the property itself—the thing—rather than the various titles to it which is being ac-

46. *City of Beaumont v. Marks*, 443 S.W.2d 253 (Tex. 1969).
47. *United States v. Dunningham*, 146 U.S. 338 (1892); *Bogart v. United States*, 169 F.2d 210 (10th Cir).
48. *Uniform Appraisal Standards for Federal Land Acquisitions* (Washington, D.C.: U.S. Government Printing Office, 1992), §A-13, pp. 39-42.
49. George L. Schmutz, *Condemnation Appraisal Handbook*, rev., Edwin M. Rams, ed. (Englewood Cliffs, N.J.: Prentice-Hall, Inc., 1963), 75-76; *Nichols'*, vol. 4, §12.05[1] (1990).

> quired. (n. 115. However, the appraiser may be required by the agency to furnish separate valuations of the separate estates or interests for negotiation purposes.)
>
> ...The second aspect of the unit rule is that different elements of a tract of land are not to be separately valued and added together. For example, the value of timber is not added to a value for the house and those, in turn, added to a value for the remainder of the property. The property is to be valued as a whole and its constituent parts considered only in the light of how they enhance or diminish the value of the whole, with care being exercised to avoid so-called "cumulative" appraisals. This is a valid procedure because it is the entire unit which is being hypothetically sold, not the separate parts individually.[50] [Citations omitted]

The *Washington State Department of Transportation Appraisal Report Guide* states: "Basic ground rules of appraising property for WSDOT require the evaluation of all rights of fee ownership because WSDOT assumes the responsibility of clearing all interests presuming the market value or (*sic*) the fee to be equal to the sum of all partial interests."[51]

Therefore, when engaged by a condemnor, the appraiser must often ignore the fact that the property is held by various estates and appraise only the fee simple estate. This is the case even though the knowledgeable appraiser is aware that the value of the various estates, when added together, may or may not equal the value of the fee simple estate. When appraising for the condemnor, the appraiser's assignment is often complete once the market value of the fee simple estate has been estimated. Nevertheless, the condemnor may ask the appraiser to allocate the value of the fee simple estate to the various lesser estates in the property; this allocation can then be used in negotiating settlements with all the parties who hold interests in the property.

When the appraiser's client is not the condemnor, but an individual who holds a lesser estate in the affected property, the appraiser's assignment is often not the simple estimation of the market value of the fee simple estate. Usually, after estimating the market value of the fee simple estate, the appraiser allocates proportionate shares of the total estate value to the various lesser estates. The separation of the fee simple estate most often encountered is its division into the leased fee estate and the leasehold estate. The valuation of these estates is covered in Chapter 18.

A *life estate* in property is also considered on occasion, and the question of its value has been addressed by the courts. The creation of a life estate divides the fee simple estate into two lesser estates held by the *life tenant* and the *remainderman*. The life tenant holds the beneficial interest in the property for his or her life, or the life of a third party, while the remainderman holds all other rights to the fee simple estate, plus the right to the beneficial interest in the property upon death of the life tenant or third party. A life estate has been defined as "[t]otal rights of use, occupancy, and control, limited to the lifetime of a designated party, often known as the *life tenant*."[52] It has been well established that a life tenant is an *owner*

50. *Uniform Appraisal Standards for Federal Land Acquisitions* §A-13, pp. 39–42.

51. Washington State Dept. of Transportation, *Right of Way Manual*, "Appraisal Report Guide," Appendix 4-1, Tab C, p. C-7 (revised August 1991).

52. *The Dictionary of Real Estate Appraisal*, 3d ed., 207–208.

in the constitutional sense and is entitled to compensation in an eminent domain proceeding.[53]

Early English law required that one-third of the fee simple value (or condemnation award or settlement) go to the life tenant, with the balance going to the remainderman. Since the advent of statistically accurate mortality tables, the courts have generally held that proper apportionment can be accomplished by determining the present value of the life estate. The income stream from the property (or the value of the beneficial interest contained therein) over the expected life of the tenant is discounted to present value at an appropriate discount rate.[54] The remainderman is then entitled to the difference between the market value of the fee simple estate and the present value of the life estate.[55]

For example, assume an individual with a remaining life expectancy of 20 years, based on accepted mortality tables, has a life estate in a property under a 25-year absolute net lease with an annual rent of $15,200 per year. The current market value of the undivided fee (fee simple estate) has been estimated at $250,000, and a discount rate of 10% is considered appropriate. The market value of the property would be apportioned as follows:

Market value of unencumbered fee	$250,000
Present value of life estate ($15,200 x 8.513564)*	-129,406
Present value to remainderman	$120,594

* Present value of $1 per period factor for 20 years, discounted at 10%

It is extremely important that the appraiser fully understand two elements of in this procedure. First, the discount rate selected should reflect the risks associated with the future earnings of the real estate (i.e., the quality and durability of the income stream), not the risk of the life tenant living for a shorter or longer period than is indicated by the mortality tables.

Second, although financial tables, financial calculators, and computers are excellent appraisal tools, before using them the appraiser must have a complete understanding of the formula on which the calculations are based. If the appraiser uses the present worth of $1 per year factor, for example, he or she must be prepared to demonstrate, in the presence of a judge and jury, how this factor is computed manually.

In some jurisdictions, the entire condemnation award is placed in a trust and the income from the trust is used by the life tenant until the individual's death, at which time the trust is terminated and the original principal of the award is transferred to the remainderman.[56] This procedure eliminates the need to allocate the award between the life tenant and the remainderman.

Other frequently encountered divisions of the fee simple estate include the restrictive covenant, the reverter, and the condominium form of ownership. These situations are discussed under "advanced problems" later in this chapter.

53. *Stubbs v. United States*, 21 F. Supp. 1007 (D. N.C. 1938); *McGinsey v. Central Neb. P.P. & Irr. Dist.*, 124 F.2d 692 (8th Cir. 1942).

54. *Nichols'*, vol. 4, §12D.10[2] (1990).

55. Ibid., §12.46[2].

56. *Redevelopment Comm. of Greenville v. Capehart*, 150 S.E.2d 62 (N.C. 1966).

Natural Assets

The natural assets of property may include mineral deposits such as gas, oil, gravel, and sand and growing crops, including timber stands. The unit rule has been strictly observed in the valuation of mineral deposits and crops. The rules of evidence and valuation testimony were clearly set forth in *United States v. Land in Drybed of Rosamond Lake*:

> (1) that a landowner in dealing with a parcel of land on which there is a mineral, timber or like substance may not introduce expert testimony by which the expert multiplies the gross material present by the market value per unit thereof and thereby arrive at a figure which purports to be fair market value for the parcel;
>
> (2) that a landowner may not by expert testimony capitalize the present or future value of a business enterprise and thereby arrive at fair market value; that rental value may, however, be capitalized;
>
> (3) that the landowner is entitled to have an expert or lay witness describe the commodity or substance on the land, the quantity thereof, the going price thereof as *factors* only, upon which the expert may in part base his value as to the *fair market value* of the parcel in question; that a landowner is not entitled to present testimony as to the fair market value of the mineral or timber or other substance apart from the value of the land... In other words, a clear distinction must be drawn between what is presented and considered as a *factor* underlying the expert's opinion as contrasted with opinion as to the fair market value of the substance, timber or mineral itself, apart from the land;
>
> (4) that a landowner must make a showing of some sort of market, poor or good, great or small, for the commodity in question before the quantity and price of the commodity or substance may be presented to the jury to be used as a factor in the expert's opinion testimony;
>
> (5) that since the inquiry is essentially one as to what would have been the negotiations between the willing buyer and the willing seller, there may be taken into consideration by the expert only those *factors* which would have been reasonably so considered;
>
> (6) that except in cases where the matter is so clear that it becomes a question of law it is generally a question for the jury to determine whether the proposed *factor* underlying in part the opinion of the expert as to the fair market value, is one which would have reasonably been considered by the willing buyer and the willing seller;
>
> (7) that where the commodity in place on the land has a defect, or is deficient in quality, testimony may be introduced showing that the defect or lack of quality may be remedied or cured by scientific or business methods if the willing buyer and willing seller in the marketplace would have reasonably considered such a *factor*;

(8) that in such instance, unless the matter is so clear that it becomes a question of law, the question is one of fact for the jury to determine whether the commodity could be so remedied or cured and such a factor may only be considered by the jury as supporting the expert's opinion if the commodity could reasonably be corrected or remedied.[57]

These rules are not universal, but they are generally followed in most jurisdictions. They provide excellent guidelines for making an appraisal, writing a report, and testifying in regard to mineral deposits and croplands.

In appraising property that may contain mineral deposits, the appraiser's first step is to determine whether there is a market for the mineral deposits if they do, in fact, exist. If there is no market for the mineral, its presence or absence will have little or no effect on the market value of the property. Without a potential market, the quantity and price of the mineral present lends little, if anything, to the market value estimate of the property and, in accordance with Rule 4 cited above, this information is inadmissible.

In determining whether or not a market exists for mineral deposits, it is improper for the appraiser to consider the government project for which the property is being condemned as a possible market for the minerals.[58] For instance, if a property is being condemned for the construction of a new highway and the property has a gravel deposit on it, the quantity, quality, or price of the gravel cannot be considered by the appraiser in estimating market value if the only present, or reasonably foreseeable future, market for the gravel would be for construction of that new highway.[59]

If there is a market for mineral deposits thought to be on a property, the appraiser should attempt to determine the quantity and quality of the minerals. This is usually accomplished by retaining specialists such as geologists or mining engineers. If the appraiser determines that there is no market for the mineral deposits, he or she can save the client a substantial sum of money: if there is no market, a specialist is not needed.

It is improper to multiply the quantity of mineral deposits or crops present by a price per unit and add the results of this computation to the value of the land to arrive at a market value estimate for the whole property. Again, the unit rule must be followed. It is the enhancement of the land value created by the presence of mineral deposits or crops that must be considered, not the value of the resource estimated mechanically. It is not improper, however, for the appraiser to consider the results of such a mathematical computation as a factor affecting the market value of the property as a whole. It is apparent that the appraiser cannot simply adopt a specialist's estimate of the value of mineral deposits or crops and then add it to his or her own estimate of the land value. Such a procedure even goes beyond the forbidden *summation* or *cumulative* appraisal because the resultant value is not even the opinion of one individual, but of two or more.

57. *United States v. Land in Dry Bed of Rosamond Lake*, 143 F. Supp. 314, 321–322 (S.D. Cal. 1956).

58. *Vobrecht v. State Highway Comm.*, 143 N.W.2d 429 (Wis. 1966); *United States v. Whitehurst*, 337 F.2d 765 (4th Cir. 1964).

59. *United States v. Whitehurst*, 337 F.2d 765 (4th Cir. 1964).

When the income approach to value is applied to property with mineral deposits, it is important to remember that the real estate is to be valued, not the business conducted on the real estate. Thus, it is improper to capitalize the business profits from a mining operation into an indication of value.

> In considering appraisals based on income capitalization, the Court must draw a distinction between the capitalization of income generated by the property itself and income derived from a business conducted on the property. Federal courts have frequently criticized and rejected valuations based on capitalization of profits as being uncertain and speculative.... It is well settled that, at least within the context of an action for just compensation under the fifth amendment, injuries to a landowner's business are not compensable.[60]

The appraiser should capitalize the rental, or *royalty*, income that could be generated by the property, rather than the business income.[61]

> Appraisers are having to rely more and more on consultant's [such an mineral expert's] reports in regard to technical issues. However, the appraiser cannot merely accept such consultant reports as accurate. (n.291. See "Guide Note 6. Reliance on Reports or Information Prepared by Others," The Appraisal Institute, 1991). The appraiser must review such reports and adopt them only if reasonable and adequately documented and supported. The results of secondary valuation reports, such as mineral, equipment or timber valuations, cannot simply be added to the value of the land to arrive at a value of the property as a whole, without proper analysis by the appraiser. To do so is a violation of the unit rule and professional standards. (n. 293. *Uniform Standards of Professional Appraisal Practice*, (The Appraisal Foundation, 1990), Standard Rule 1-4d). The appraiser must consider these components of the property only in light of how they contribute to the value of the property as a whole.[62]

It is extremely important that the appraiser exercise great care in writing appraisal reports and testifying in court. In both instances it must be made clear that the appraiser's final value estimate has not been derived simply by multiplying the number of units of the mineral or crop by a price per unit; such a computation is only one factor the appraiser considers in arriving at the final estimate of value.

When a property being condemned has immature crops growing on it, a specific procedure for valuing the crops has been developed and accorded court approval in some jurisdictions.[63] The procedure has three steps:

1. Estimate the quantity of crops that would be harvested if they were allowed to mature.
2. Estimate the value of the crops if they were mature on the date of the taking (or date of destruction).

---

60. *Cloverport Sand & Gravel Co. v. United States*, 6 Cl. Ct. 178, 191, 193 (1984).

61. *United States v. 103.38 Acres of Land*, 660 F.2d 208 (6th Cir. 1981).

62. *Uniform Appraisal Standards for Federal Land Acquisitions*, §C-10, p. 97.

63. *State v. Dillon*, 121 N.W.2d 798 (Neb. 1953).

3. Deduct all costs of producing, cultivating, harvesting, and marketing the crops from the value of the crops estimated in 2 above.

Again, the value estimated with this procedure is one factor for the appraiser to consider in estimating the market value of the property as a whole. It is not an independent value of the immature crops, to be added to the compensation due for the taking and/or the damage to the land.

In the appraisal of land with mineral deposits or timber, the appraiser must always adhere to the *consistent use theory*, which maintains "that land cannot be valued on the basis of one use while the improvements [or minerals or timber] are valued on the basis of another."[64] Applying this theory to mineral deposits, it would not be proper to value a property for agricultural purposes and then add a substantial value increment for gravel deposits under the surface of the land. If the gravel is mined, the land, in all probability, will have no value for agricultural purposes during or after the mining operation.

The above example is, of course, somewhat oversimplified. To demonstrate the necessity of adhering to the consistent use theory, and the complexity that can be involved, consider a 100- acre tract of land that is being acquired for park purposes. The tract has a lake of 10 acres and the rest of the land is covered with merchantable timber. Market analysis indicates that the property as is, including the area of the lake, would sell for $2,000 per acre for recreational development. A timber cruise of the property indicates there are 810 MBF (thousand board feet) of merchantable timber on the site. The cruiser estimates the timber's value to be $290 per MBF delivered at the mill, with a logging cost of $60 per MBF for clear-cutting (total removal) of the trees. Thus the value of the standing timber (stumpage value) is $230 per MBF ($290 – $60). Using information from the timber cruise, an appraiser unaware of the consistent use theory might value the property as follows:

Land (100 acres @ $2,000)	$200,000
Timber (810 MBF @ 230/MBF)	186,300
Total indicated value	$386,300
Rounded	$386,000

Obviously the two uses, recreational development and clear-cut timber harvesting, are incompatible with one another. The land will lose its aesthetic appeal for recreational use if all of the timber is removed. However, it is not necessarily correct for the appraiser to assume that the highest and best use of the property is limited to only one of the two uses. If market evidence indicates that clear-cut timberland is selling for $300 per acre of usable land area, a value estimate for timber purposes for the property might be developed as follows:

Land (90 acres @ $300)	$ 27,000
Timber (810 MBF @ $230/MBF)	186,300
Total indicated value	$213,300
Rounded	$213,000

64. *The Dictionary of Real Estate Appraisal*, 3d ed., 72.

It might be erroneous for the appraiser to conclude at this point that the highest and best use of the property is exclusively for timber harvesting, simply because the value of the property for this use is $13,000 more than its value exclusively for recreational development ($200,000). Further investigation and analysis may show that a portion of the timber could be harvested through selective cutting without affecting the land's value for recreational development. Assume that 30% of the timber could be removed without affecting the value of the property for recreational purposes or exposing the rest of the trees to blow down. Selective cutting typically increases logging costs, so assume it will cost $10 more per MBF to harvest the timber. Under these circumstances, the value of the property could be computed as follows:

Land (100 acres @ $2,000)	$200,000
Contributory value of timber	53,460 *
Total indicated value	$253,460
Rounded	$253,000

* Timber available for harvesting (810 MBF x 0.30 = 243 MBF). Stumpage value of timber ($290/MBF – $70/MBF = $220/MBF). Timber value (243 MBF x $220/MBF = $53,460.).

This analysis clearly indicates that the two uses are not necessarily mutually exclusive. In fact, it would be prudent for the appraiser to analyze the situation further. If the appraiser discovers that land that was clear-cut 10 years ago has regained all of its recreational value due to new timber growth, and the discount rate used to calculate the present value of the land reversion is 10%, the following analysis might be appropriate:

Timber value (810 MBF @ $230/MBF)	$186,300
Land value (100 acres @ $770*)	77,000
Total indicated value	$263,300
Rounded	$263,000

* Present value of $1 discounted for 10 years at 10% = 0.385543. $2,000/acre value x 0.385543 = $771.09 present value per acre, rounded to a current value of $770/acre.

This computation assumes that natural reseeding of the land would occur after the timber is harvested. If the land would have to be replanted after harvesting, the cost of replanting would have to be deducted from the $263,000 estimate.

To make this type of analysis more understandable to a jury, the appraiser could explain that the acreage value, above the price the land would bring for timber production purposes, is a value increment that reflects the property's potential for future recreational development.

The preceding examples demonstrate various types of analysis that may be applied when valuing land with mineral deposits or crops. The best analysis is the one that most closely replicates the actions of buyers and sellers in the market and results in a final value estimate that reflects the price at which the property, as a single unit, would sell on the open market. If truly comparable sales exist, they are generally considered the best evidence of value. In this case, the types of analysis described above would merely be used to support the value estimate indicated by the comparable sales.

PERSONAL PROPERTY AND FIXTURES

Personal property is defined as:

> Generally, movable items; that is, those not permanently affixed to and a part of real estate. In deciding whether or not a thing is personal property or real estate, usually there must be considered (1) the manner in which it is annexed; (2) the intention of the party who made the annexation (that is, to leave permanently or to remove at some time); (3) the purpose for which the premises are used. Generally, and with exceptions, items remain personal property if they can be removed without serious injury either to the real estate or to the item itself.[65]

Two definitions of *fixture* follow:

> An article that was once personal property, but has since been installed in or attached to the land or building in a rather permanent manner so that it is regarded in law as part of the real estate.[66]

> An article in the nature of personal property which has been so annexed to the realty that it is regarded as a part of the real property. That which is fixed or attached to something permanently as an appendage, and not removable.[67]

Determining whether an item is a fixture or personal property is of the utmost importance to the appraiser because the condemnation of a parcel of real estate does not include the condemnation of personal property on the premises. Thus, personal property used on the real estate taken cannot be considered in the determination of just compensation.[68] If the item in question is identified as a fixture, however, it is part of the real estate taken and compensation must be paid.[69]

A real problem arises in distinguishing between personal property and a fixture because the determination is based, in part on… the intention of the party who made the annexation. In other words, when the annexation was made, did the person making the annexation intend for the item to remain in place as a part of the real estate, or did the individual anticipate removal of the item, as personalty, at some later date?

Often, the final determination of the item's status is a legal question rather than an appraisal matter. It is therefore advisable for the appraiser to obtain legal instruction as to the inclusion or exclusion of questionable items in the value estimate.[70] It is imperative that the appraiser specify in the appraisal report which items have been considered fixtures, and therefore included in the value estimate, and which items have been excluded from the value estimate as personal property. The appraiser should be prepared to extract the contributory value of

65. *Real Estate Appraisal Terminology*, rev. ed., 184.
66. *The Dictionary of Real Estate Appraisal*, 3d ed., 145.
67. *Black's*, s.v. "fixture."
68. *United States v. Certain Lands*, 69 F. Supp. 815 (S.D. N.Y. 1947).
69. *Carmichall v. United States*, 273 F.2d 392 (5th Cir. 1960).
70. *Uniform Appraisal Standards for Federal Land Acquisitions*, §B-1 - 13c, p. 70.

any questionable fixture included in the value estimate, so that testimony can be given as to the market value of the property excluding the item if the court rules it to be personal property.

In a federal condemnation, the court will generally be guided by state law in differentiating between personalty and realty. "This [is] a question of real estate law which must always be determined by the law of the state in which the realty is located."[71] "This does not mean, however, that every local idiosyncracy or artificiality in a state's concepts, or the incidents thereof, necessarily will be accepted."[72]

"In those instances where specialty equipment is encountered, or when the equipment will represent a substantial portion of the property's value, consideration should be given to the retention of an equipment valuation specialist."[73] The value of fixtures is generally based on their depreciated reproduction cost.

It is not proper for the appraiser merely to accept the value estimate of a fixture specialist and add this figure to the estimate of the market value of the balance of the real estate. It is not the value of the fixture alone that is compensable, but rather the enhancement in the value of the whole property because of the fixture's presence. As one court put it:

> To the extent that the value of the real property as a whole is enhanced by the fixtures annexed thereto, the value of the fixtures must be included, in what the city pays, and the tenant is entitled to part of the award, not because the fixtures added to the value of the leasehold, but because they belonged to him and their value enters into the value of what the city has taken.[74]

In this decision the court was applying the *unit rule*, which has already been discussed.

It is a universal rule that fixtures are a part of the real estate and compensation must be paid for them, but the general rule that compensation need not be paid for personal property on the realty being taken does have some exceptions. Michigan allows compensation awards to include personal property.[75] By statute, Iowa courts also grant compensation for personal property.[76] Because of these exceptions to the general rules of compensability, it is always advisable for the appraiser to consult with legal counsel.

ADVANCED PROBLEMS

CONDOMINIUM VALUATION

Appraisers can encounter unique valuation problems when the property being condemned has been divided into various estates, particularly if the appraiser is asked to allocate the value of the property to the different estates. A partial taking from a condominium complex is such a situation.

In most states ownership of the common areas of a condominium complex is held by all of the condominium owners in undivided interests. Thus, theoretically

71. *United States v. Becktold*, 129 F.2d 473, 477 (8th Cir. 1942).
72. *State of Nebraska v. United States*, 164 F.2d 866, 868 (8th Cir. 1947), *cert. denied* 334 U.S. 815.
73. *Uniform Appraisal Standards for Federal Land Acquisitions*, §B-1 – 13c, p. 71.
74. *In re Allen St. & 1st Ave., Borough of Manhattan, City of New York*, 176 N.E. 377, 382 (N.Y. 1931).
75. *City of Fenton v. Lutz*, 250 N.W.2d 579 (Mich. 1977).
76. Iowa Code, §472.14 (1971).

at least, the taking of any part of a condominium project is a partial taking from each of the condominium owners. Each condominium unit in the complex may need to be valued before and after the partial taking of any portion of the complex so as to determine the impact of the taking, if any, on the value of each unit.

However, when a portion of the common area of a condominium complex is acquired, condemnors will typically attempt to value the entire complex before and after the taking as a single unit. This approach is, of course, more cost-effective. They will also attempt to negotiate with the owners' association, rather than with the individual unit owners. The main problem with this approach is that the owners' association does not own anything and often has no authority to negotiate on behalf of the individual owners.

The state condominium statute and the declaration of condominium will often control the valuation methodology to be employed by the appraiser. Most state condominium statutes originally contained no provisions for eminent domain acquisitions. Many second-generation statutes have incorporated provisions of the Uniform Condominium Act[77] or the Uniform Common Interest Ownership Act,[78] both of which provide for the reallocation of common area interests when one or more condominium interests are condemned. They also provide that:

> (c) If part of the common elements is acquired by eminent domain the portion of the award attributable to the common elements taken must be paid to the association. Unless the declaration provides otherwise, any portion of the award attributable to the acquisition of a limited common element must be equally divided among the owners of the units to which that limited common element was allocated at the time of acquisition.[79]

A comment to the act states:

> The provisions of this statute are not intended to supplant the usual rules of eminent domain but merely to supplement the rules to address the unique problems which eminent domain raises in the context of a *condominium*.[80]

The argument for estimating the value of a condominium complex as a single entity stems from the "cardinal principle of eminent domain valuation [that] requires that condemnees receive the fair market value of the property, not the cumulative worth of their various interests therein."[81] However, it would appear more appropriate to view the undivided ownership interest in the common area held by a condominium unit owner in the same manner that an appurtenant easement is viewed.[82] The value of an appurtenant easement is measured by its contribution to the value of the parcel it serves; likewise, the value of an undivided interest in the common area of a condominium project should be measured by its contribution to the value of the condominium unit. If the contributory value of that common area interest is impacted by a partial taking of the common area, the only reasonable means of measuring that impact is by valuing the con-

77. Uniform Condominium Act, 7 U.L.A. (West 1985 & Supp. 1989).

78. Uniform Common Interest Ownership Act, 7 U.L.A. (1985 & Supp. 1989).

79. Uniform Condominium Act, §1-107.

80. Commissioner's Comment to Uniform Condominium Act, § 1-107.

81. *Nichols'*, vol. 4, §12D.06[3][a] (1990).

82. See Chapter 16, "Easements."

dominium unit, together with the undivided interest in the common area, before and after the partial taking.

As of 1992 only one case dealing specifically with the partial taking of a condominium complex had been published.[83] In that case the lower court...

> permitted the parties to introduce expert testimony regarding both the direct and consequential damages to the common elements, as well as any consequential loss to the remaining area of the condominium regime which resulted from the taking, but refused to allow testimony concerning any unit owner's individual loss to his specific unit. At the close of the testimony, the trial judge omitted the specific names of all the unit owners from the inquisition form and instructed the jury to calculate one lump sum to be awarded to the council of unit owners as just compensation for the taking. Thus, as a matter of law, each individual unit owner's separate claim for consequential damages to his respective unit was denied."[84]

On appeal the Maryland State Supreme Court held "that a condominium unit and its respective share of the common elements, within the complex, constitute one parcel. Thus, an individual unit owner may recover consequential damages to his particular unit following an appropriation of the common elements as long as his unit, separate from the whole, is injured."[85]

The Maryland court's view is much more realistic than attempting to value the entire condominium complex as a single entity before and after the taking. However, from a valuation standpoint, the court's decision remains flawed. It essentially provides for the valuation of the common property as common property, and then allows damages to the individual units to be considered to the extent that they exceeded the prorata diminution in value to the common area. For instance, assume that the jury found that $50,000 in compensation was due for the taking of the common area and that Unit 101 of the condominium, with a 1.5% interest in the common area, had a value of $125,000 before the taking and $121,500 after the taking. Compensation to the owner of Unit 101 would then be calculated as follows:

Before value	$125,000
After value	-121,500
Difference	$ 3,500
Unit 101's share of common area award ($50,000 x 0.015)	- 750
Additional damage to individual unit	$ 2,750

The problem with these calculations from a valuation standpoint is that there is no reasonable way to value the common area, as common area, in the first place. Its only utility, or value, is for use in conjunction with the individual condominium units. With no independent value, its value is only the amount it contributes to the individual units. Thus the only way that the diminution in the contributory value of the common area due to a partial taking can accurately be measured is to estimate the market value of each of the condominium units before and after the taking.

83. *Andrews v. City of Greenbelt*, 441 A.2d 1064 (Md. 1982).

84. Ibid., at 1067.

85. Ibid., at 1071.

There could be an instance in which the value of all the units in a condominium complex would be the same before and after the taking of a portion of the common area. In such an instance, the value of the common area taken would be zero. To estimate the value of common area based on the price per square foot being paid for fee simple title to other lands in the neighborhood is to place an artificial value on the property which may or may not bear a relation to its value as common area. (Lands not dedicated to common area use are not comparable because they have a different highest and best use than the subject common area.) The valuation of each condominium unit before and after the partial taking of the common area, on the other hand, measures the contributory value of the common area taken and damages to the remainder properties. This process does not impose an artificial value on the common area as a separate entity.

Figure 4.7 depicts the partial taking of a 100-unit condominium complex. The taking includes 33 condominium units in Building 2, on-site improvements (including a portion of the entrance drive and a swimming pool) and 25,000 square feet of land. Building 1 contains 33 units and Building 3 contains 34 units plus a common recreation room. Unless state law or the declaration of condominium require otherwise, the appraiser would take the following steps and consider the following factors in developing a value estimate.

1. Appraise the 33 individual condominium units in the area to be taken.
2. Appraise the 67 individual condominium units outside of the taking in the before situation.
3. Appraise the 67 individual condominium units outside of the taking in the after situation.
4. Consider these factors after appraising the remainder units:
    - The impact, if any, of the proximity of the public improvement to the various remainder units.
    - The impact of the taking on the monthly maintenance assessments charged against each of the remaining units. This would require an analysis of the historical common area expenses and assessments, a projection of common area expenses in the after situation, and a projection of the assessments charged against each of the remainder units in light of the projected common area expenses and the reallocation of expenses among the remainder units.
    - The methodology of this reallocation may be provided for in the condominium declaration and/or in the condominium bylaws. If not, the appraiser would have to predict how the reallocation would be accomplished and recognize the risk of the prediction in estimating the after value of the remainder units.
    - The impact (i.e., potential benefit) of the greater parking ratio in the after situation.
    - The cost to cure deficiencies (i.e., loss of entrance drive and swimming pool) in the remainder's common area improvements. To analyze this factor, the ap-

Figure 4.7 Partial Taking

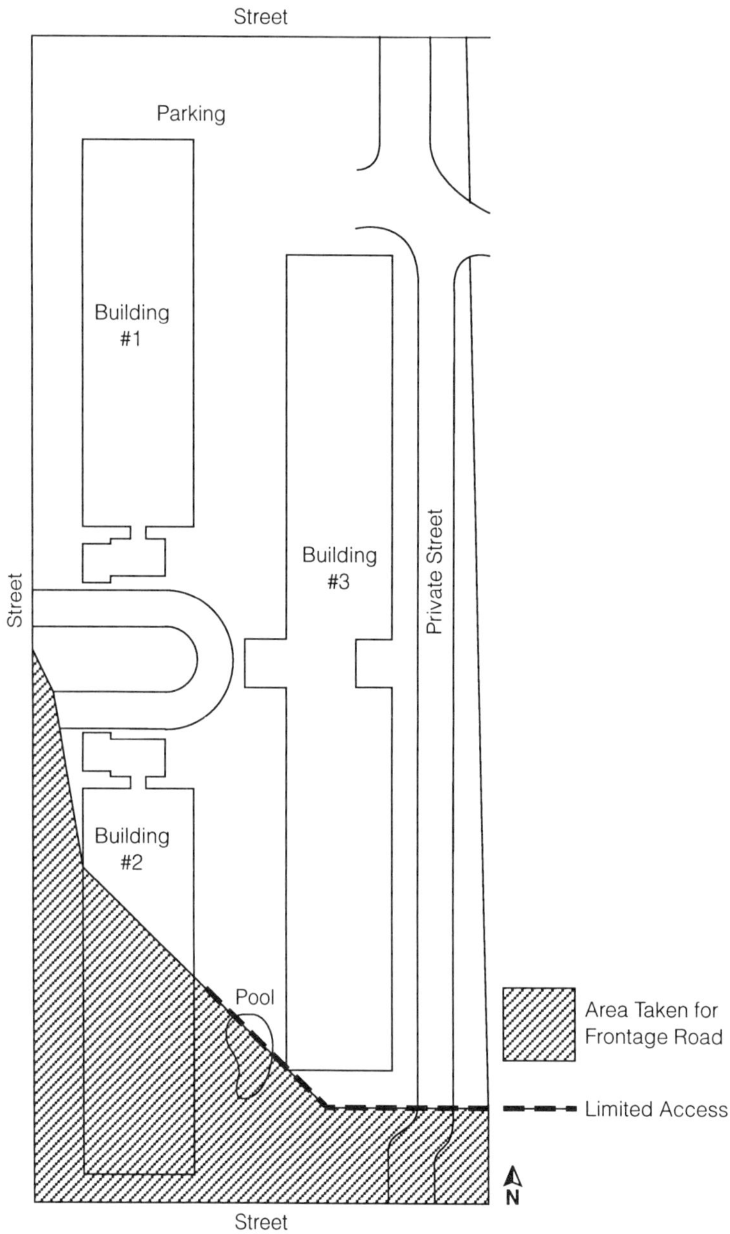

praiser would need to determine how the cost to cure would be allocated to the remainder units and whether the cost to cure would be a reasonable measure of damage. In making this determination, the association's bylaws would have to be examined to determine who has the ability to institute the cure. Could association management do this, or would a vote of the remaining unit owners be required? If a vote were taken, on what basis would the votes be counted? Would each unit have one vote, or would voting strength be based on the newly allocated common area ownership interests?

- The impact of the altered relationship between the common area recreation room and the number of units it serves.

The percentage of common area ownership appurtenant to each unit is often arbitrarily established in the condominium declaration by the original developer. It is usually based on the ratio of the size of each unit to the total square footage of all of the units or on the value of the unit (set by the developer) as it relates to the value of all of the units. Therefore, the altered burden and reallocation of common area maintenance charges will tend to affect each unit differently.

Damages to a single condominium unit resulting from the taking shown in Figure 4.7 might be measured and reported:

- As the rent loss, measured by paired data analysis, multiplied by a gross rent multiplier.
- As the change in the gross rent multiplier due to the decreased ratio of net income to gross income. The taking will decrease gross income, increase vacancy, and increase owners' association dues. The percentage of association expenses assessed to a single unit must increase as the total number of condominium units decreases.
- As the anticipated special assessment charged by the owner's association to cover the cost to cure the deficiencies in the driveway, landscaping, and swimming pool, plus the legal fees associated with the drafting and filing of a new declaration of condominium, which will be required by reason of the taking.

The sum of these estimates would represent the total diminution in value (damages).

VALUE OF REVERTER

Another form of estate is the *reverter*, defined as "[a] possibility of reverter is that species of reversionary interest which exists when the grant is so limited that it may possibly terminate."[86] One of the most common forms of such a reversionary interest is the sale of real estate with the provision that the purchaser can use the property for one purpose only (e.g., single-family use) and if the purchaser violates this provision, ownership of the property reverts to the seller.

There are two valuation questions that arise when property is held subject to such a reversion. First, is the property to be valued for eminent domain purposes subject to its restricted use or as if unrestricted? In a typical appraisal assignment,

86. *Black's*, s.v. "reverter."

an appraiser must "consider... restrictions... reservations, covenants... or other items of a similar nature."[87] For purposes of eminent domain, however, it is the property that is to be acquired, not the individual interests therein.[88] "It appears . . . from an exhaustive review of the writings on the subject that the majority view in the United States where property is held subject to a restriction limiting its use to specific charitable, religious, education, or non-commercial purposes is that the property may be given a value as if it were *un*restricted."[89] There are exceptions to this majority view, however,[90] so the appraiser is advised to seek guidance from legal counsel. If the law is unclear in the jurisdiction, the assignment may warrant a dual-premise appraisal—i.e., an appraisal of the property as if unrestricted and a second appraisal of the property as restricted. The situation becomes even more complex when a partial taking occurs and it is not possible to put the remainder property to the restricted use.

The second question in regard to a reverter relates to allocation of the condemnation award. The majority view is that the grantor (*i.e.*, the owner of the reversionary interest) is not entitled to share in the condemnation award. "When land is held in fee simple but determinable when the land ceases to be devoted to a certain use . . . the rights of the grantor, although enforceable if the land ceased to be used for the designated purpose, are not generally considered an estate or interest in land which is compensable upon a public taking. A mere *possibility of reverter* is not considered property."[91] The denial of compensation to the grantor is often based on the fact that the possibility of actual reversion is "of such a nebulous nature that it [has] no legally estimable market value."[92] However, if it can be shown that a reversion is probable, the grantor may be entitled to share in the award.[93]

It has been recognized that in some instances applying the majority rule, that a grantor is not entitled to share in the condemnation award, results in a windfall for one party. If the property is valued as restricted, the government will receive the windfall because it will pay only the restricted value, but will have unrestricted use of the land. If the property is valued as if unrestricted, the owner of the property will receive a windfall because he or she did not purchase, or own, the unrestricted fee.

For example, assume that an owner proposed developing a residential subdivision on his land and, to prevent this and conserve the land, a nonprofit environmental group purchased the land for $10 million. The environmental group then sold the land for $1 million with the provision that ownership of the land would revert to the group if the land were ever used for any purpose other than agriculture and open space. Now assume that the government subsequently condemns the land for a public airport. If the government pays the $10 million unre-

87. The Appraisal Foundation, *Uniform Standards of Professional Appraisal Practice*, 1994 ed., Standard Rule 1-2(c), p. 10.

88. *Bogart v. United States*, 169 F.2d 210 (10th Cir. 1948).

89. *Legislative Route 1094, Appeal of Commonwealth, Dept. of Transp.*, 352 A.2d 244, 247 (Pa. 1976).

90. *So. Calif. Fisherman's Assn. v. United States*, 174 F.2d 739 (9th Cir. 1949); *Boston Chamber of Commerce v. City of Boston*, 81 N.E. 244 (Mass. 1907), *aff'd* 217 U.S. 189 (1910).

91. *Nichols'*, vol. 2, §5.05 (1990).

92. *People v. City of Fresno*, 26 Cal. Rptr. 853, 862 (Cal. 1962).

93. *United States v. 2184.81 Acres of Land*, 45 F. Supp. 681 (W.D. Ark. 1942).

stricted value of the property and, in accordance with the majority rule, the environmental group is not entitled to share in the award, the grantee will receive a windfall of $9 million. If the land is valued as restricted for $1 million, the government will receive a windfall of $9 million. In either case the environmental group will have expended $9 million for naught and its philanthropic goal of preserving the land will have been thwarted by the taking.

This type of situation has been recognized by the courts. "[I]t seems apparent that, at the very least, the amount, if any, by which the value of an unrestricted fee exceeds the value of the restricted fee, is something that should go to the grantor. ...That difference certainly represents the value of something which the grantor expressly refrained from conveying to the grantee."[94] To address this apparent inequity, it has been suggested that "recent legislation modernizing the attributes of the possibility of reverter... [may] lead to different legal consequences when such interests are appropriated in the exercise of the power of eminent domain."[95]

RESTRICTIVE COVENANTS

Another problem arises when the property to be condemned is subject to restrictive covenants, or plat restrictions. Such restrictions are often encountered in large subdivisions where the developer has restricted the use of all lots to residential use for the benefit of all the lot owners. It is clear that the property to be condemned is to be valued in light of the restrictive covenant, but it is equally clear that the property must be valued in light of the benefit it receives by virtue of the restrictive covenant on all of the other lots in the subdivision. The question is do those in whose favor the restriction exists (*i.e.*, all other lot owners in the subdivision) have a compensable interest in the property condemned. Opinions on this issue are split.

> The federal rule is uncertain... Indeed, the distinction between rights in land and consequential losses has been blurred in restrictive covenant cases by policy considerations other than the need to draw a predictable line between direct and remote interests.

However, the same court went on to say:

> The argument that an impermissible burden is put upon the power of eminent domain by a restrictive covenant is untenable. Why should a party receive compensation for an easement right which enhances the value of his property and yet be denied compensation for a right obtained by restrictive covenant which similarly adds to the value of his holdings? Both interests are directly connected to the land and we are unable to find a distinction between them which will justify dissimilar treatment at the hands of a condemning authority.[96]

Based on this ruling, it is possible that the government's action would equate, at least theoretically, to the total taking of the lot condemned in fee simple plus the partial taking of every other property that is the beneficiary of the restrictive

94. *Ink v. City of Canton*, 212 N.E.2d 574 (Ohio 1965).
95. *Nichols'*, vol. 2, §5.05[1] (1990).
96. *Adaman Mutual Water Co. v. United States*, 278 F.2d 842, 847, 849 (9th Cir. 1960).

covenant. Thus, it is easy to see why the results in restrictive covenant cases have been blurred by "policy considerations."

Because the law in this area is not clear, appraisers are advised to seek guidance from legal counsel before accepting an assignment involving properties that are restricted, or benefitted, by restrictive covenants.

MINERAL VALUATION

It was noted in Chapter 3 that, except in special benefit cases, the amount of compensation will generally be the same regardless of whether the part taken plus damages rule or the before and after rule is applied, as long as the rule is correctly applied. However, it has also been demonstrated that the two rules do not result in the same indicated compensation when the *backland theory* is employed. The two rules also diverge in regard to the partial taking of minerals.

For example, assume that a gravel pit is to be partially taken. There are 10 million cubic yards of minable gravel in the pit prior to the taking and market evidence indicates that there is market demand for one million cubic yards of gravel from the property per year. Further assume that the royalty rate, or rent, being paid for comparable gravel pits is $0.50 per cubic yard net to the property owner, and that the appropriate discount rate to be applied to the income stream generated by the property is 10%. Now assume that the government will condemn a portion of the property and leave 8.5 million cubic yards of minable gravel.[97]

Applying the federal rule to these circumstances, compensation could be computed as follows:

Before value:

Annual income stream (1 million cu. yd. @ $0. 50)	$500,000
Duration of income stream (10 million cu. yd. ÷ 1 million cu. yd. per year)	10 years
Present value of $1 per period for 10 years discounted at 10%	6.144567
Indicated before value ($500,000 x 6.144567)	$3,072,284
Rounded	$3,072,000

After value:

Annual income stream (1 million cu. yd. @ $0.50)	$500,000
Duration of income stream (8.5 million cu.yd. ÷ 1 million cu. yd. per year)	8.5 years
Present value of $1 per period for 8.5 years discounted at 10%	5.552027
Indicated after value ($500,000 x 5.552027)	$2,776,014
Rounded	$2,776,000

97. The computations that follow represent *only one of the factors* that an appraiser would consider in arriving at the final value estimates.

Difference (just compensation):

Before value	$3,072,000
After value	- 2,776,000
Difference (just compensation)	$ 296,000

Under the state rule, compensation might be computed as follows:

Value of taking:

Annual income stream taken (1 million cu. yd. @ $0.50)	$ 500,000
Duration of income stream taken (1.5 million cu. yd. ÷ 1 million cu. yd. per year)	1.5 years
Present value of $1 per period for 1.5 years discounted at 10%	1.332158
Indicated value of taking ($500,000 x 1.332158)	$ 666,079
Rounded	$ 666,000
Damages	0
Value of taking plus damages	$ 666,000

Using the state rule applied by the California court in *City of Los Angeles v. Allen*,[98] just compensation would be computed as follows:

Before value (as computed under before and after rule)	$3,072,000
Value per cu. yd. of gravel ($3,072,000 ÷ 10 million cu. yd.)	$ 0.3072
Value of taking (1.5 million cu. yd. @ $0.3072)	$ 460,800
Rounded	$ 461,000
Damages	0
Value of taking plus damages	$ 461,000

Essentially, the before and after rule incorporates the assumption that the gravel in the taking is the *last* gravel that would be mined. The classic application of the state rule assumes that the gravel in the taking is the *first* gravel that would be mined. Using the average value per cubic yard builds in the assumption that the gravel taken would be mined *midway* in the life of the mining operation.

The appraiser should use the approach that has been adopted in the jurisdiction in which the trial will be held. If the law is unsettled in the jurisdiction, it may be advisable for the appraiser to prepare multiple-premise appraisals. Whatever method of valuation is employed, it is important for the appraiser to understand what assumptions are built into each method and to recognize that the indicated compensation will differ significantly depending on the method of valuation applied.

Although the before and after method of valuation probably reflects the actual diminution in property value by reason of the taking most accurately, it may not meet the definition of just compensation in those states that require that "[a] landowner is always entitled to the fair market value of the land actually taken."[99]

98. *City of Los Angeles v. Allen*, 36 P.2d 611 (Cal. 1934). See Chapter 3 for a detailed discussion of this case.

99. *State Dept. of H'wys. v. Stegemann*, La., 269 So.2d 480, 481 (La. 1972).

SUMMARY

The absolute ownership of real estate is limited by the sovereign's right of taxation, eminent domain, escheat, and police power. The sovereign further limits absolute ownership of real estate by constitutional and statutory provisions. The distinction between the police power of government and its power of eminent domain is often fuzzy and has been the subject of considerable litigation. For example, a fee simple interest in real estate includes an easement in the abutting roadway to provide for ingress and egress, light, view, and air. This easement is subordinate to the public's rights to the roadway, however, and the abutter's rights are subservient to those of the public. The abutter's rights of access, light, view, and air can be limited by the sovereign's police power, without compensation to the abutter, so long as the limitation of these rights is reasonable and the abutter's property retains *adequate* access, light, view, and air.

The bundle of rights also includes crops that grow on the land and mineral deposits under the land as part of the real estate. Therefore, when property with crops or minerals is condemned, these items are included in the valuation of the real estate because they contribute to the value of the whole property as a unit. Fixtures are also included as part of the real estate and must be considered in arriving at a final value estimate. Personal property, on the other hand, is not generally included in valuing real estate. Personal property located on a property being condemned is not considered *taken* or *damaged* in most jurisdictions and, therefore, no compensation is due.

The bundle of rights may also be divided by private action such as the creation of a leasehold estate, a life estate, private easements, reverters, and restrictive covenants. However, appraisers must keep in mind the general rule that the value of the various estates in property cannot, for the purposes of condemnation, exceed the market value of the unencumbered fee to the real estate. When more than one estate exists, the compensation paid for the fee taken is generally "apportioned in accordance with the respective interests of such owners. The matter of such apportionment is of no concern to the condemnor and is a problem in which only the claimants are involved. The compensation that must be paid is for the land, and not for the different interests therein."[100]

As stated in *Lewis on Eminent Domain*, "[w]hen there are different interests or estates in the property the proper course is to ascertain the entire compensation as if the property belonged to one person and then apportion this sum among the different parties according to their respective rights. The value of the property cannot be enhanced by any distribution of the title or estate among different persons or any contract arrangements among the owners of different interests. Whatever advantage is secured by one interest must be taken from another, and the sum of all the parts cannot exceed the whole."[101]

Because various estates may constitute the fee simple estate in a parcel of real estate, and because the courts are inconsistent in their treatment of estates of

100. *Nichols'*, vol. 4, §12D.04[3] (1990).

101. *Lewis on Eminent Domain*, 3rd ed., vol. 2, §716, p. 1253

various natures, the real estate appraiser must insist on reviewing the title report pertaining to any property being appraised for the purpose of litigation. This is the only way that the appraiser can be sure that he or she is aware of all interests of record in the property being appraised. In addition, the appraiser should obtain legal instruction, with documenting citations, as to the proper treatment of the various estates if multiple estates do, indeed, exist.

CHAPTER 5

The Larger Parcel

The appraiser seldom encounters a valuation or analytical premise in condemnation appraising that cannot also be found in general appraisal assignments. The concept of the *larger parcel*, however, is an exception. It is an analytical premise unique to eminent domain valuation and is often misunderstood and/or misapplied by appraisers, condemnors, lawyers, and the courts.

The term *larger parcel* cannot be found in comprehensive appraisal textbooks such as *The Appraisal of Real Estate*,[1] but two definitions are provided in *The Dictionary of Real Estate Appraisal*. One definition of the larger parcel is

> In condemnation, the portion of a property that has unity of ownership, contiguity, and unity of use, the three conditions that establish the larger parcel for the consideration of severance damages in most states. In federal and some state cases, however, contiguity is sometimes subordinated to unitary use.[2]

Black's Law Dictionary defines the larger parcel as:

> A term used in eminent domain proceedings, signifying that the parcel taken is not a complete parcel but part of a "larger parcel"; the owner, therefore is entitled to damages from the severance as well as the value of the parcel taken. Unity of ownership, use, and contiguity must be present, although federal courts and some states do not require contiguity where there is a strong unity of use.[3]

The larger parcel is sometimes referred to as the *parent tract*[4] or the *rule of joinder*.[5]

1. *The Appraisal of Real Estate*, 10th ed. (Chicago: Appraisal Institute, 1992).
2. *The Dictionary of Real Estate Appraisal*, 3d ed. (Chicago: Appraisal Institute, 1993), 202.
3. *Black's Law Dictionary*, abr. 6th ed., s.v. "larger parcel."
4. *United States v. 8.41 Acres of Land*, 783 F.2d 1256 (5th Cir. 1986).
5. *People v. Ocean Shore R.R.*, 196 P.2d 570 (Cal. 1948); *M & R Invest. Co. v. Nevada DOT*, 744 P.2d 531 (Nev. 1987).

A second definition of the larger parcel included in the *Dictionary of Real Estate Appraisal* is more meaningful and useful to appraisers. It reads:

> In condemnation, that tract or tracts of land which are under the beneficial control of a single individual or entity and have the same, or an integrated, highest and best use. Elements for consideration by the appraiser in making a determination in this regard are contiguity, or proximity, as it bears on the highest and best use of the property, unity of ownership, and unity of highest and best use.[6]

Understanding the concept of the larger parcel is vital in condemnation appraisal because the appraiser cannot determine the highest and best use of a property until a conclusion as to the larger parcel is reached. The larger parcel may be all of one parcel, part of a parcel, or several parcels, depending to varying degrees on unity of ownership, unity of use, and contiguity.

In a typical appraisal assignment, an appraiser is retained to estimate the value of a parcel of land which has specific boundaries and the parameters of the property are known before any in-depth appraisal analysis is made. This is not, or should not be, the case in condemnation appraisals.

It is useful to understand how parcel, or right-of-way, maps are developed by a condemnor. If, for example, a roadway is to be constructed or widened, the condemnor's engineers prepare a survey of the proposed right-of-way limits. This survey is then given to the title department within the condemning agency, or to a title company, with instructions to identify all ownerships within the proposed right-of-way and to determine the property boundaries of each parcel. These boundaries include all land that is contiguous and under the same ownership as the land within the proposed right-of-way. A right-of-way map like the one shown in Figure 5.1 is then prepared. Figure 5.2 shows the typical ownership information included on such a map. The right-of-way map is then usually passed on to the appraiser with instructions to appraise a specific parcel identified on the map.

The physical contiguity of land is an engineering question, while unity of ownership is usually a legal question. The right-of-way map is prepared and the boundaries of the properties to be appraised are determined prior to any consideration of unity of use. Therefore, most appraisal contracts between an appraiser and a condemning agency, and most instructions assigning an appraisal to a staff appraiser, specify that the appraiser is to estimate the value of a parcel which may or may not be the "larger parcel." The ultimate determination of the larger parcel must be made by the appraiser. If it is found that the parcel defined by the right-of-way map and the appraisal contract or assignment does not constitute the larger parcel, the appraiser must insist on a revised contract or assignment. As stated in the *Uniform Appraisal Standards for Federal Land Acquisitions*:

6. *The Dictionary of Real Estate Appraisal*, 202.

Figure 5.1 Typical Right-of-Way Map

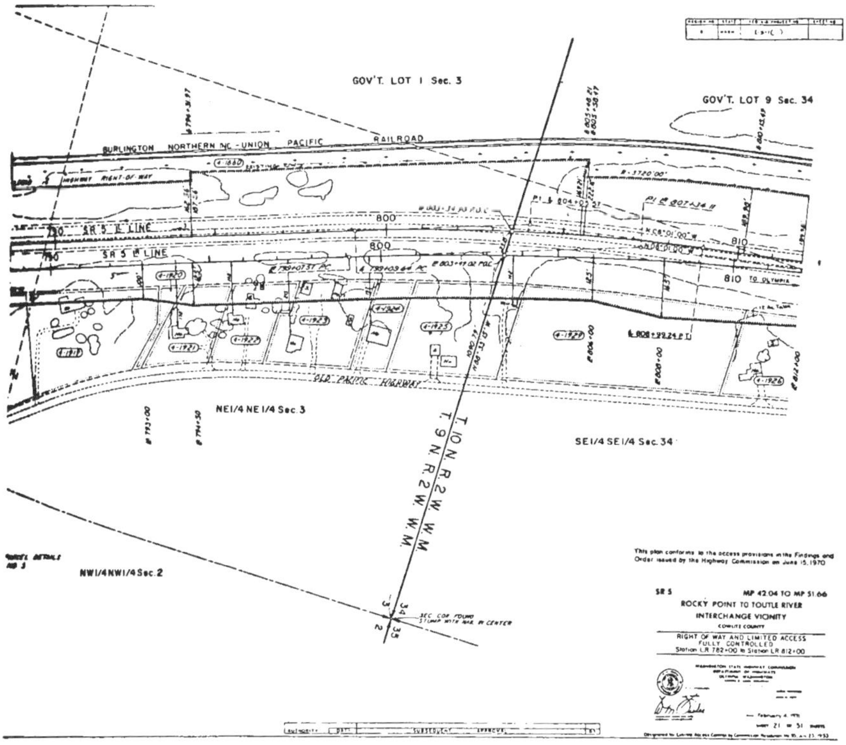

Figure 5.2 Typical Ownership Information

OWNERSHIPS						
PARCEL NO.	NAME	TOTAL AREA	TAKE	LT. REMAINDER	RT.	EASEMENTS
4-1917	J. ALDRICH		SEE	SHEET 20		
4-1918	B. E. TREISCHEL	3.24 AC.	0.32 AC.		2.92 AC.	
4-1919	E. A. SOWERS	2.44 AC.	0.38 AC.		2.06 AC	
4-1920	K. DECKERT	0.20 AC.	0.07 AC.		0.13 AC	
4-1921	R. P. SCHUMACHER	0.86 AC.	0.20 AC.		0.66 AC.	
4-1922	R. L. SNAZA	0.92 AC.	0.28 AC.		0.64 AC.	
4-1923	S. LOCKWOOD	1.39 AC.	0.32 AC.		1.07 AC.	
4-1924	E. C. MORRIS	0.65 AC.	0.15 AC.		0.50 AC.	
4-1925	A. R. JANISCH	1.96 AC.	0.36 AC.		1.60 AC.	
1926	D. D. WALSTON	1.14 AC.	0.13 AC.		1.01 AC.	
4-1929	A. JANISCH	3.88 AC.	0.60 AC.		3.28 AC.	
4-1660	BURLINGTON NORTHERN INC.					

> Often essential in the appraiser's consideration of highest and best use is the conclusion concerning the larger parcel. Because the ultimate determination of highest and best use is the appraiser's to make, and that determination cannot be made until after considerable investigation and analysis has been completed, the appraiser's conclusion as to the larger parcel is sometimes different from the specific parcel he or she was requested to appraise by the agency. In such an instance, the appraiser shall inform the agency of his or her determination of the larger parcel and the agency shall amend the appraisal assignment accordingly.[7]

The determination of the larger parcel is particularly important in partial taking cases, in which compensable damages and/or special benefits accrue to the remainder parcel after the taking. Like many other elements in condemnation appraisal, the tests to determine the larger parcel (i.e., unity of ownership, unity of use, and contiguity) cannot be applied universally and blindly. The federal courts and some state courts have ruled that all three tests need not be met in every instance.

A situation in which a right-of-way map may not correctly depict the larger parcel is illustrated in Figure 5.3. In this case, the entire parcel meets the tests of unity of ownership and contiguity, but it fails the test of unity of use. Therefore, the service station is not a part of the larger parcel[8] and cannot suffer compensable damage or receive a special benefit.

FIGURE 5.3 NO UNITY OF USE

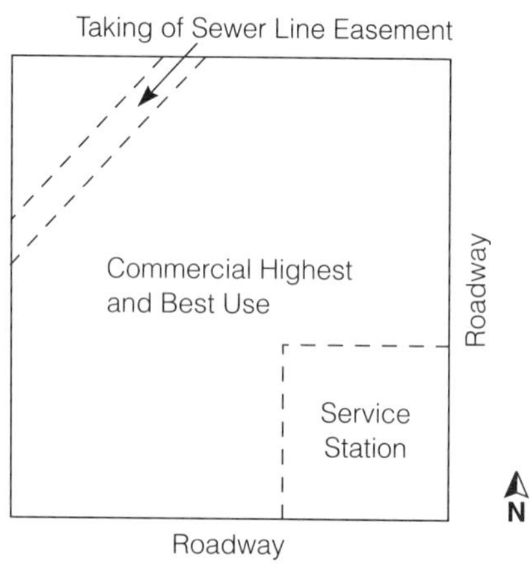

Another situation is depicted in Figure 5.4. In this instance, the two sites have unity of ownership, but they are certainly not contiguous or put to the same use. However, unity of use has often been defined to include an integrated use.[9] The mill may have been constructed for the sole purpose of processing logs harvested from

7. *Uniform Appraisal Standards for Federal Land Acquisitions* (Washington, D.C.: U.S. Government Printing Office, 1992), §B-1 - 14, p. 73.

8. *O'Brien v. City of New York*, 32 A.D.2d 1059 (N.Y. 1969).

9. *United States v. Mattox*, 375 F.2d 461 (4th Cir. 1967).

FIGURE 5.4 NONCONTIGUOUS LARGER PARCEL

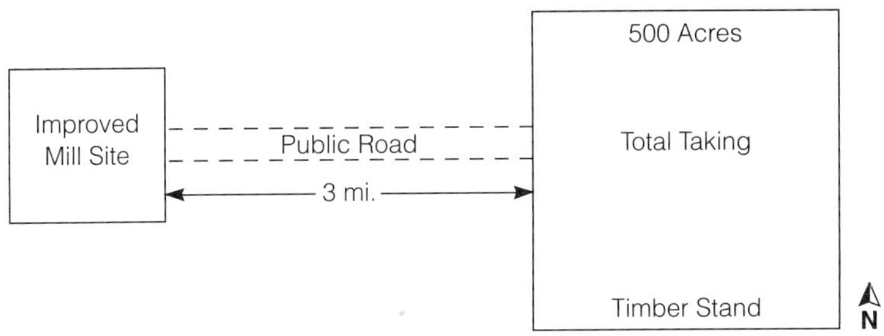

the 500-acre timber stand. Thus, while the two tracts do not have identical uses, they certainly have an integrated use. In some jurisdictions, the larger parcel would be defined as the mill site plus the timber stand. In such a case, damages accruing to the mill site due to the taking of the timber stand would be compensable.

In an often-cited landmark case, a federal court ruled that two parcels located 17 miles apart, on two different islands, constituted a single larger parcel. In this ruling the court said:

> The first question before us here, therefore, and the basic one in all severance damage cases, is what constitutes a "single" tract as distinguished from "separate" ones. The answer does not depend upon artificial things like boundaries between tracts as established in deeds in the owner's chain of title, nor does it depend necessarily upon whether the owner acquired his land in one transaction or even at one time. Neither does it wholly depend upon whether holdings are physically contiguous. Contiguous tracts may be "separate" ones if used separately, and tracts physically separated from one another may constitute a "single" tract if put to an integrated unitary use or even if the possibility of their being so combined in use "in the reasonably near future" "is reasonably sufficient to affect market value."
>
> ...Integrated use, not physical contiguity, therefore, is the test. Physical contiguity is important, however, in that it frequently has great bearing on unity of use... [S]eparation still remains as evidentiary, not an operative, fact.[10] [Citations omitted]

Note that in the above case the court recognized that separate parcels do not have to be put to the same use on the date of valuation; rather, if the highest and best use of the properties requires a unity of use, they constitute a single larger parcel. However, the mere fact that two parcels constitute a single larger parcel does not necessarily mean that the remainder property is damaged. On remand of the above case, the court found that the remaining lands had not suffered any compensable damages.[11]

By defining the larger parcel, the appraiser can confine his or her judgments to those parcels, or parts of a single parcel, that are affected by condemnation.

10. *Baetjer v. United States*, 143 F.2d 391, 394–395 (1st Cir. 1944) *cert. denied* 323 U.S. 772 (1944).

11. *United States v. 7936.6 Acres of Land*, 69 F. Supp. 328 (P.R. 1947).

Figure 5.5 shows a 100-acre farm that is subject to two zoning classifications. The proposed widening of Road A necessitates the acquisition of the easterly 25 feet of the tract. The highest and best use of the property coincides with its current zoning. The property is owned by a single individual and is contiguous, but there is no unity of highest and best use. Thus, the larger parcel in this case is the easterly 500 feet of the ownership and only this part of the tract is subject to compensable damages and/or special benefits.

FIGURE 5.5 NO UNITY OF USE

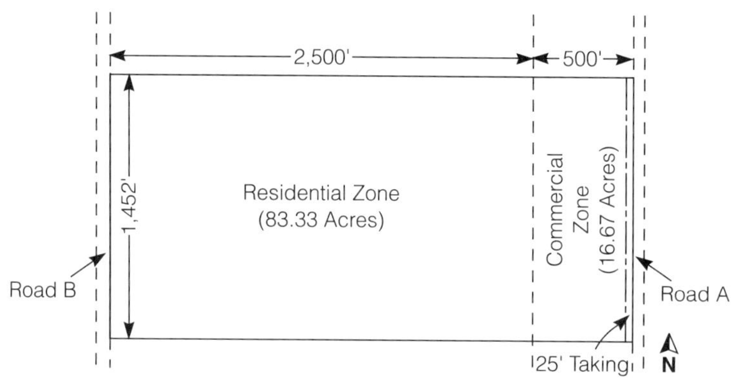

This determination of the larger parcel eliminates the application of the *backland theory* described in Chapter 3. The backland theory would be used, and misused, far less frequently if appraisers and others involved in condemnation proceedings had a better understanding of the larger parcel premise. Once the appraiser has identified the larger parcel, the scope of the analysis required is narrowed substantially. In the above case, only the easterly 500 feet need to be appraised, so only comparable commercial land sales have to be investigated and analyzed. Residential land sales need not be studied.

As the preceding examples illustrate, the appraiser must consider more than single ownership and parcel size to define the scope of the assignment. Because the tests of the larger parcel can be applied in a variety of ways, it is necessary to study each element of this *trinity*—unity of ownership, unity of use, and contiguity—in some depth. Although most of the rulings pertaining to the larger parcel involve the question of compensable damages, the rulings are equally applicable to special benefits.

It generally has been held that determination of the larger parcel is a matter of fact, not a matter of law. Therefore, when a question of the larger parcel arises in a condemnation trial, it is a question to be answered by the jury (or trier of fact), not by the court.[12] However, some confusion exists in this regard in the federal court system because all federal condemnation cases are conducted under

12. *Arkansas State H'way Comm. v. Arkansas Real Estate Co.*, 471 S.W.2d 340 (Ark. 1971); *Sharp v. United States*, 191 U.S. 341 (1903).

the *Federal Rules of Civil Procedure*, which provide that just compensation will be determined by the trier of fact, but that "[t]rial of all issues shall otherwise be by the court."[13] The U.S. Supreme Court has said that "[t]he Rule [71(h)] thus provides that, except for the single issue of just compensation, the trial judge is to decide all issues, legal and factual, that may be presented."[14]

Because determination of the larger parcel is intertwined with the question of highest and best use, strict adherence to the above rule would result in the court, rather than the trier of fact, making the finding of highest and best use. The *Reynolds'* decision quoted above dealt with the issue of the *scope of the project* rather than the question of highest and best use or the larger parcel. (See Chapter 6 for further discussion of the scope of the project rule.) Several federal circuit cases decided after *Reynolds* have interpreted that decision narrowly and have ruled that the question of highest and best use, and thus the larger parcel, rests with the jury.[15]

It is suggested that "it is safe for the practitioner to prepare and present the case upon the assumption that the theory of unity of use [the larger parcel] is a factual question for the trier as it relates to the ultimate issue of value, damage and just compensation. If there is a question, the *Motion in Limine* is available to preliminarily resolve questions, particularly in the federal courts where judges and magistrates have broad powers available to them at the pretrial stage of litigation."[16]

As the examples presented demonstrate, determination of the larger parcel is critical. The appraiser should discuss this issue with legal counsel in the early stages of the appraisal assignment if the larger parcel determination is in question.

UNITY OF TITLE

It is generally held that for one or more parcels to be considered a single larger parcel, it is essential that they be owned by the same individual or group of individuals.[17] In a few cases, however, the courts have held otherwise. In a Kansas case, for instance, the court held that three contiguous parcels of land, owned by three different individuals and being used as one farm operation by mutual agreement, were a single larger parcel and, therefore, "... injury to each [parcel] resulting from the whole taking may be considered."[18] Most cases that have allowed consideration of lands owned by others have done so under the theory of the highest and best use of an assemblage. (The highest and best use of an assemblage is further discussed in Chapter 6.)

On the other side of the coin, there is case law that supports the proposition that the quality of the title to all parcels must be identical for the tract to be

13. *Federal Rules of Civil Procedure*, 71A(h).
14. *United States v. Reynolds*, 397 U.S. 14, 17 (1970).
15. *United States v. 320.0 Acres of Land, More or Less in Cty.*, 605 F.2d 762 (5th Cir. 1979); *United States v. 100 Acres of Land, Etc., Marin Cty., Cal.*, 468 F.2d 1261 (9th Cir, 1972), *cert. den.*, 414 U.S. 822 (1973); *United States v. 341.45 Acres of Land*, 633 F.2d 108 (8th Cir. 1980), *cert. denied* 451 U.S. 938 (1981).
16. *Nichols' The Law of Eminent Domain*, rev. 3d ed. (New York: Mathew Bender Co., Inc., 1992), vol. 4A, §14B.04[2].
17. *Commonwealth, Dept. of Highways v. Dennis*, 409 S.W.2d 292 (Ky. 1966); *United States v. 429.59 Acres of Land*, 612 F.2d 459 9th Cir. (1980).
18. *County of Smith v. Labore*, 15 P. 577 (Kan. 1887).

considered a single larger parcel. For example, if Parcel A in Figure 5.6 is owned by Mrs. Jones, as her sole and separate property, and Parcel B is owned by Mr. and Mrs. Jones jointly, some courts would rule that the larger parcel is Parcel A only and that no compensable damages can accrue to Parcel B, even though the two tracts have contiguity and unity of use.[19] The federal government has historically supported the proposition that the form of title must be identical.

> To satisfy the requirement as to *unity of ownership*, title to all parts of the whole must be vested to the same extent in the same person(s). Unity of ownership is lacking when the owner has different interests in the two or more tracts, as, for example, where he owns one tract in fee simple, has a leasehold interest in another, and owns in entirety the stock of a corporation which owns another tract. Likewise, unity of ownership is lacking between two tracts when one is owned by the husband and the other by the wife, or where one is owned by the father and the other is owned by the son.[20]

FIGURE 5.6 NO UNITY OF TITLE

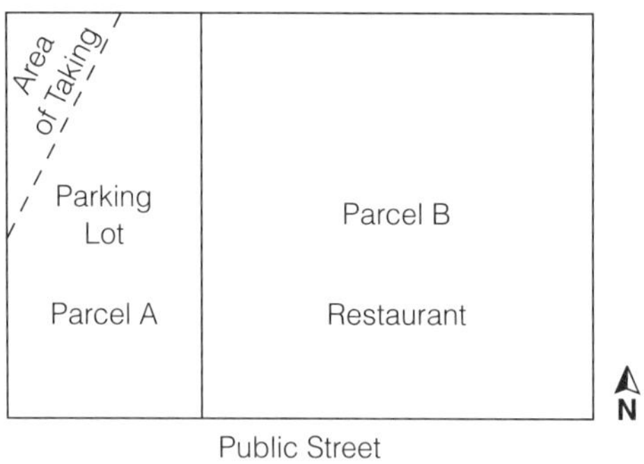

The federal government most often cites *United States v. Honolulu Plantation Co.*[21] in support of identical ownership. The court in that case said (at page 178, 179) "[t]he rule requiring compensation for loss in market value of the remainder of the tract is applied strictly only where there is but a single parcel owned by one party in fee simple. . . . If, therefore, the fee owner of one tract holds a lesser tenure in the tract taken, there can be no additional compensation for this reason. The explanation is that the fee is the integer." However, it is clear that the foregoing is dicta. In introducing this issue the court said (at page 178) "[a]lthough disposition has thus been made of the erroneous claims and theories of the experts, it behooves us to consider whether Plantation is entitled to compensation, without regard to the clauses of the respective leases."

Nevertheless, the same court later ruled in two different cases that identical title was not required to find a single larger parcel. In one case the larger parcel

19. *Glendenning v. Stahley*, 91 N.E. 234 (Ind. 1910).

20. *Uniform Appraisal Standards for Federal Land Acquisitions*, §A-11, p. 29.

21. *United States v. Honolulu Plantation Co.*, 182 F.2d 172 (9th Cir. 1950) *cert. den.*, 340 U.S. 820 (1950) at 178, 179.

was found to be ownership of an easement in one parcel and a leasehold interest in a second parcel. The court said "Honolulu Plantation is inapposite, however, because the party seeking severance damages in that case had no interest whatsoever in the land which had been condemned."[22] In the second case, the court found that three tracts of land constituted a single larger parcel, even though the tracts were owned by three different corporations, because ownership of all three corporations was held by the same individuals. In making this ruling the court said that "[t]he fact that land thus treated [as a single entity] is owned by different entities does not destroy the unity concept."[23] In a footnote the court distinguished this case from *Honolulu Plantation* "because the plaintiff sugar refinery in that case had no compensable interest in sugar cane fields taken from a third party."

These rulings suggest that the policy stated in the *Uniform Appraisal Standards for Federal Land Acquisitions* with regard to unity of ownership is not without its weaknesses. Any appraiser involved in a federal condemnation assignment concerned with multiple tracts that have a unity of highest and best use, but lack identical ownership, should seek the advice of legal counsel, whether the client is the property owner or the government.

In most jurisdictions, unity of ownership does not necessarily mean that the quality of the title is identical. Two parcels, one owned in fee and one owned equitably by a vendee's interest in a real estate contract, could be considered to have unity of title.[24] One California case held that unity of title existed where an individual owned one parcel in fee and was the equitable owner of an abutting parcel because he had exercised an option to purchase the second parcel.[25] In another California case, however, where the interest in the second parcel existed only in the form of an unexpired, but unexercised option, the court held that there was no unity of title.[26]

Unity of title generally requires equal legal control over the ownership and future of the lands in question. Acquisition of the parts of a whole at different times does not destroy unity of title,[27] nor, in some cases, does the fact that one parcel is owned by an individual and the second parcel is owned by a corporation under the control of that individual.[28] Some courts, however, have ruled conversely.[29]

A fee interest in one parcel and a leasehold interest in an abutting parcel, as depicted in Figure 5.7, can operate as one larger parcel for the remaining term of the lease.[30] Similarly, if three individuals independently own separate parcels of land and lease them to a fourth individual, there could be unity of title during the term of the lease of all the parcels,[31] and the compensation would flow to the lessee.

22. *United States v. 57.09 Acres of Land*, 706 F.2d 280, 281 (9th Cir. 1983).
23. *United States v. 429.59 Acres of Land*, 612 F.2d 459, 464 (9th Cir. 1980).
24. *State Highway Comm. v. Miller*, 155 N.W.2d 780 (S.D. 1968).
25. *County of Santa Clara v. Curtner*, 54 Cal. Rptr. 257 (Cal. 1966).
26. *People v. Hemmerling*, 58 Cal. Rptr. 203 (Cal. 1967) reversed on other grounds, *Hemmerling vs. Jombeau* 432 P.2d 697 (Cal. 1967).
27. *Baetjer v. United States*, 143 F.2d 391 (1st. Cir. 1944), *cert. denied* 323 U.S. 772 (1944).
28. *M.T.M. Realty Corp. v. State*, 261 N.Y.S.2d 815 (N.Y. 1965); *United States v. 429.59 Acres of Land*, 612 F.2d 459 (9th Cir. 1980).
29. *Sams v. Redevelopment Authority*, 244 A.2d 779 (Pa. 1968).
30. *Chicago, etc., R. Co. v. Dresel*, 110 Ill. 89 (Ill. 1884).
31. *Berman v. Urban Redevelopment Authority of Pittsburgh*, 324 A.2d 811 (Pa. 1974).

FIGURE 5.7 LEASEHOLD LARGER PARCEL

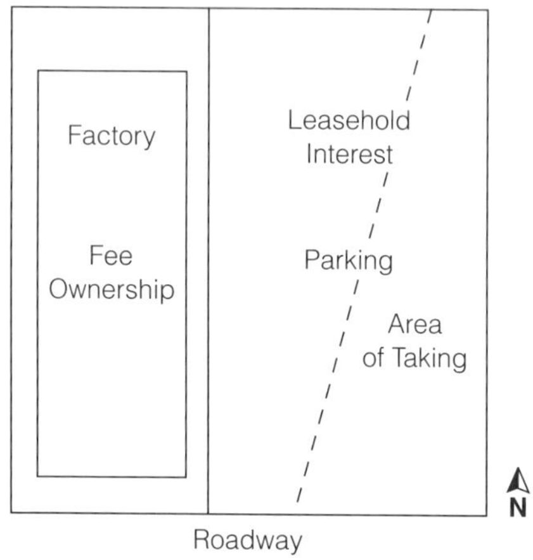

UNITY OF USE

The second test of the larger parcel requires that the parcel or parcels of land can be devoted to the same use as, or an integrated use with, the land from which the taking is made. It is generally not the presence or absence of actual unity of use that is considered; rather the unity of *highest and best use* is the controlling factor.[32] If a property is not being put to its highest and best use, but has a common highest and best use, the current use of the land does not generally destroy the unity of use.[33] Some courts that have ruled conversely, however.[34] These decisions, which seem to contradict the well-established premise that property is appraised at its highest and best use, are generally based on the reasoning that the unity of use has to exist because potential unity of use is too speculative and conjectural to be considered.[35] A careful reading of many of these cases (e.g., the case cited above) suggests that the court may well have found that the proffered highest and best use of the property would have been too conjectural and speculative to be considered by the jury, even if the larger parcel were not at issue.

Appraisers must recognize that stronger proof of unity of use is required when the parcels are not currently being used as a unit, but merely have a common highest and best use. "The question of unity of use of two or more tracts is a question of fact to be determined upon the facts and circumstances of the particular case, and is not to be based upon fanciful claims, speculation or conjecture, and in such cases the burden of proof is upon the landowner to prove his claim."[36]

Political boundaries do not interrupt the continuity of use if the government's land-use controls permit a continuous highest and best use. [37] Moreover, unity of use does not require physical adjacency. There may be physical separation by

32. *Baetjer v. United States*, 143 F.2d 391 (1st Cir. 1944), *cert. denied* 323 U.S. 772 (1944).

33. *United States v. Mattox*, 375 F.2d 461 (4th Cir. 1967).

34. *Cole Investment Co. v. United States*, 258 F.2d 203 (9th Cir. 1958).

35. *City of Washington v. Koch*, 456 S.W.2d 628 (Mo. 1970).

36. *Ives v. Kansas Tpke. Authority*, 334 P.2d 399, 407 (Kan. 1959).

37. *Northeastern, etc., v. Frazier*, 40 N.W. 604 (Neb. 1888).

barriers such as streets, railroads, and creeks, but again this type of separation requires stronger proof of unity.[38]

CONTIGUITY

The third element of the larger parcel trinity, contiguity, normally requires that physical contiguity be present for a larger parcel to exist. However, this condition is not always mandatory and jurisdictions have ruled differently on this issue. Most courts hold unity of title and unity of use as the most important tests of the larger parcel.[39] For this reason, the *Uniform Appraisal Standards for Federal Land Acquisitions* states:

> To constitute a "whole" for purposes of assessing severance damages, the law requires the property to meet *two* tests. First, there must be a unity of ownership in all parts of the whole. Second, there must be a unity of use as to all parts of the whole.[40]

Whether a real estate ownership constitutes a single larger parcel as distinguished from *separate* parcels is best reflected by unity of use, and does not preclude a reasonable separation. Such a separation does, however, require study. The appraiser must be able to answer "yes" to the question: "Is it probable that the separated tracts would sell as an integrated single entity, even with the separation?" Only then can the separated tracts can be considered as a single larger parcel. As a Rhode Island court put it:

> Quite a different situation is presented when, as here, the two parcels in question are unequivocally separated from each other by fixed and definite boundaries, such as a highway. In such a case it is generally held that the two tracts can be considered as one only when they are so inseparably connected in the use to which they are applied that the taking of one *necessarily* and *permanently* injures the other.[41]
>
> An important factor to bear in mind, particularly (but not only) where the taking involves non-contiguous parcels devoted to a unitary use (e.g., a mill site and one or more parcels providing raw material for the mill) is the availability of replacement property for the parcel taken, since a reasonable buyer and seller would consider the availability of a replacement."[42]

The greater the separation between the parcels, the more likely it is that suitable replacement property will be available.

Sometimes a larger parcel exists in the before situation but, in the after situation, the parcel has been severed by the taking and becomes two separate parcels. Such a situation is illustrated in Figure 5.8. Although the property had unity of ownership, unity of use, and contiguity in the before situation, it is no longer contiguous in the after situation. Quite probably, one or both of the tracts will have a different highest and best use after the taking than they did before. It is

---

38. *Tucker v. Massachusetts C.R. Co.*, 118 Mass. 546 (Mass. 1875); *State v. Hoblitt*, 288 P. 181 (Mont. 1930).

39. *Barnes v. North Carolina State Highway Comm.*, 109 S.E. 2d 219 (N.C. 1959); *Baetjer v. United States*, 143 F.2d 391 (1st Cir. 1944), *cert. denied* 323 U.S. 772 (1944).

40. *Uniform Appraisal Standards for Federal Land Acquisitions*, §A-11, pp. 28–29 (emphasis added).

41. *Sasso v. Housing Authority of the City of Providence*, 111 A.2d 226, 230 (R.I. 1955).

42. *Uniform Appraisal Standards for Federal Land Acquisitions*, §A-11, p. 30.

highly unlikely that unity of use, or integrity of use, will exist between the two parcels in the after situation. Thus, it is unlikely they would be sold as a single parcel and, in all probability, they would be considered two separate larger parcels.

FIGURE 5.8 TWO LARGER PARCELS—AFTER SITUATION

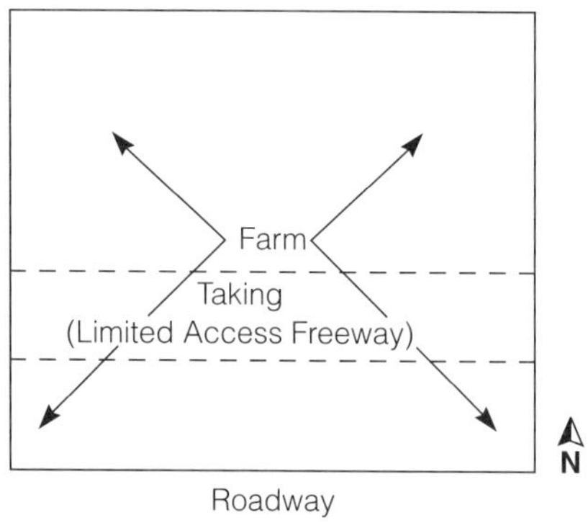

Figure 5.9 illustrates a very different situation in which two tracts that were separate in the before situation could become a single larger parcel in the after situation. If Parcel A could be developed to a greater density in the after situation by using Parcel B for required parking, special benefits could accrue; in those jurisdictions that allow the offsetting of special benefits against both damages and the value of the property taken, the property owner might not be entitled to any monetary compensation. (See Chapter 12 for information on the offsetting of special benefits.)

FIGURE 5.9 ONE LARGER PARCEL—AFTER SITUATION

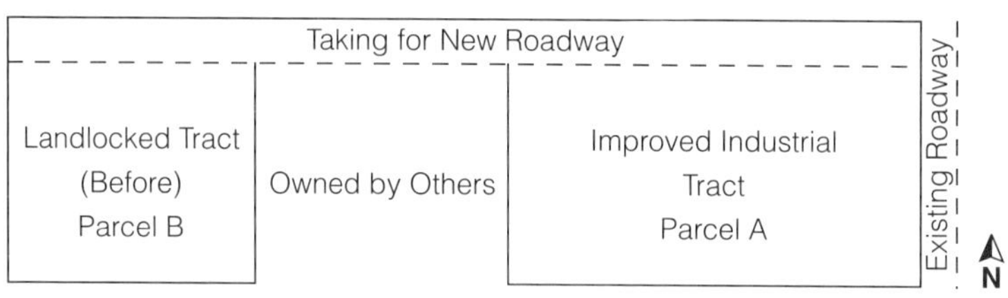

Another problem which the courts have addressed upon occasion is illustrated in Figure 5.10. This could be described as the problem of the *paper plat*. The tract identified as Parcel A, the whole parcel, is, of course, considered the larger parcel and the entire remainder parcel is subject to potential compensable damages by reason of the taking. In regard to Parcel B, however, the determination of the larger parcel will often depend on the specific status of the paper plat.

FIGURE 5.10 PAPER PLATS

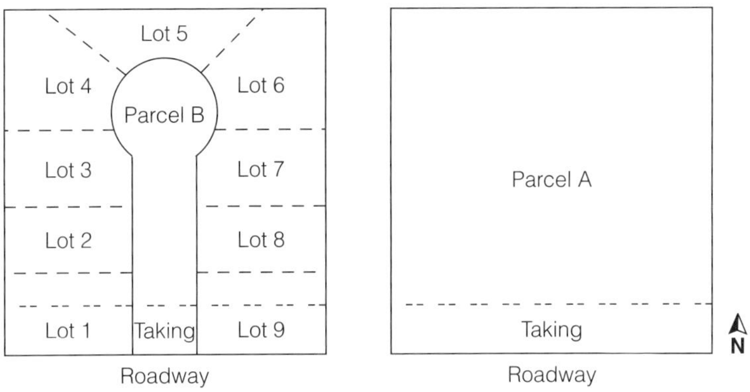

If the property owner has not dedicated the proposed street rights of way, or has only granted easements thereto while retaining the underlying fee, and no lots have been sold, the courts have generally ruled that all of Parcel B constitutes the larger parcel. The current status of the particular paper plat appears to be the key determinant. If the plat processing is beyond its initial stages, there could be two larger parcels (i.e., Lots 1 and 9), with Lots 2 through 8 falling outside the larger parcel and not subject to any compensable damages and/or special benefits.

An Ohio court expressed this situation well:

> As an allotment develops, as it progresses from open land to individual lots, there comes a point where the lots not only can be but must be considered as separate entities. When this point arrives and a part of the allotment only is taken, consisting of a number of lots, the question arises as to what is the remaining land to which damage may occur. Is it the whole remaining subdivision, or is it just the fragment of an individual lot not taken?
>
> Whether certain lots, taken by appropriation proceedings, constitute part of an entire tract so as to entitle the owner of the remaining continuous lots to damages within the rule is principally a question of unity of use and, as such, constitutes a factual matter to be determined by the jury under proper instructions.[43] [Citations omitted]

43. *In re Appropriation For Highway Purposes*, 239 N.E.2d 110, 115 (Ohio 1968).

MYTHS ABOUT THE LARGER PARCEL

As has been demonstrated, nearly all of the court decisions relating to the larger parcel involve either alleged damages or special benefits to the remainder. Two of the definitions of the larger parcel quoted previously specifically relate the term to damages to the remainder property. However, determination of the larger parcel is also important in cases in which damages and/or benefits are not claimed. In nearly all jurisdictions, the value of the land taken is measured as it contributes to the whole (larger parcel), rather than as a separate entity, regardless of whether the before and after or taking plus damages rule is applicable. Thus, appraisers must make a determination of the larger parcel in all cases.

Even when damages or benefits are not alleged, determination of the larger parcel can have a significant impact on the amount of compensation indicated. Two economic factors can come into play in larger parcel valuations: *plottage* (or assemblage) and *size regression*.

> *Plottage* is an increment of value that results when two or more sites are combined to produce greater utility. Sometimes highest and best use results from assembling two or more parcels of land under one ownership. If the combined parcels have a greater unit value than they did separately, plottage value is created.[44]

Size regression is the basic economic principle that as the number of units of a commodity increases, the price per unit paid for the commodity decreases. It is the concept of the bulk sales discount. As applied to land, as the number of units (*e.g.*, acres, square feet) in a tract of land increases, the price, or value, per unit tends to decrease. "Common sense tells us that a larger tract of land, holding other factors equal, would sell for less per unit."[45]

The courts seem to recognize plottage, but fail to acknowledge the effect of size regression. In fact, at least two courts have ruled, *as a matter of law*, that two assembled tracts of land always have a larger square foot value than they would if considered as two separate tracts.[46]

Appraisers are well aware of size regression. In fact, a favorite technique of the biased (and unethical) appraiser who is attempting to support a high value estimate is to compare the prices paid per acre for small tracts against the price of a substantially larger subject parcel, without making a size adjustment. Conversely, the biased appraiser attempting to support a low value will compare the prices paid per acre for large tracts against a small tract under appraisal without making a size adjustment.

The situation shown in Figure 5.11 illustrates the importance of the larger parcel determination even when damages and/or benefits are not at issue. Assume that the physical characteristics of all parts of the 100-acre farm are equal and that sales data show that farms of 75 to 125 acres sell for $2,000 per acre. If no damages or benefits are involved and the entire farm is considered a single larger

44. *The Appraisal of Real Estate*, 10th ed., 211–212.

45. Gene Dillmore, "Size Adjustment Tables," *The Real Estate Appraiser* (May–June 1976), 23.

46. *City of Buffalo v. Goldman*, 406 N.Y.S.2d 407 (N.Y. 1978); *In re Elgart's Appeal*, 149 A.2d 641 (Pa. 1959).

parcel, the indicated compensation for the two-acre taking would be $4,000, regardless of whether the before and after rule or the taking (as a part of the whole) plus damages rule is applied.

FIGURE 5.11 PARTIAL TAKING OF 100-ACRE FARM

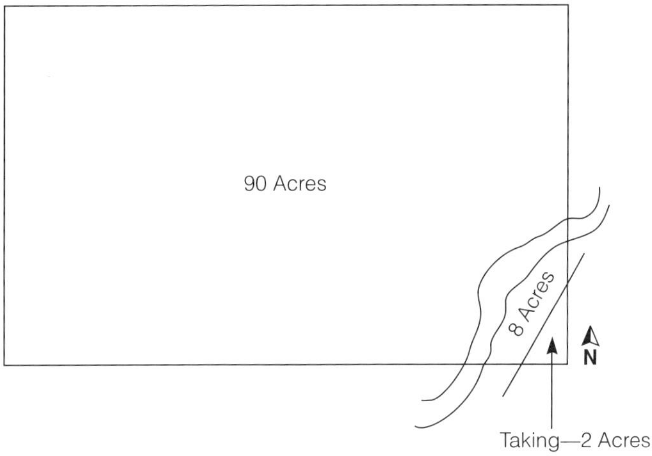

However, the situation might be more complicated. Further assume that small acreage sales in the area, ranging from five to 15 acres, typically sell for $5,000 per acre for use as rural homesites. If the appraiser concluded that the 10-acre parcel separated from the balance of the ownership by the creek had an independent highest and best use as a homesite, and thus a value of $5,000 per acre, the indicated compensation would be $10,000.

Even if the 10-acre tract had the same highest and best use as the 90-acre tract (i.e., farming), the two parcels could constitute separate larger parcels. A conclusion that two larger parcels existed could probably be justified if there were no *actual* unity of use between the parcels and/or no bridge across the creek physically connecting the two parcels. In such a case, it would not be surprising to find that 10-acre tracts were selling for substantially more per acre than 100-acre tracts because of size regression, even though the tracts had the same highest and best use.

Appraisers, whether they are retained by the condemnor or the condemnee, have a tendency to estimate the value of the parcel shown on the condemnor's right-of-way map, often without adequately analyzing the larger parcel. If an appraiser receives an assignment from a condemnor to appraise the property shown in Figure 5.11, and is provided with a right-of-way map depicting the entire 100-acre ownership as the parcel to be appraised, it is the appraiser's obligation to determine whether the larger parcel is, in fact, the 100-acre parcel or the

10-acre parcel. If the appraiser reasonably concludes that the 10-acre parcel is the larger parcel and thus the value of the taking, as a part of the whole, is $10,000, it is possible that he will receive resistance and/or criticism from the client. Nevertheless, the larger parcel determination, as a part of highest and best use analysis, is the appraiser's decision, and it must be made objectively regardless of the desires, or opinions, of the client.

The condemnor may disagree with the appraiser's conclusion as to the larger parcel and reject the appraiser's value conclusion; that is the condemnor's prerogative. However, a distinction must be made between rejection of the appraiser's conclusion and rejection of the appraiser's report. Appraisal reports are rejected for technical deficiencies; conclusions are rejected because of a difference of opinion. If an appraisal report is technically sufficient but the conclusion is rejected, the appraiser has fulfilled his or her obligation under the terms of the appraisal assignment and the appraisal contract. The appraiser has been retained to furnish the client with an adequately supported opinion of value. There is no guarantee that the client is going to like the opinion. As a matter of fact, it is considered a compliment by some appraisers to have their reports approved, but their opinions rejected because appraisal reviewers tend to look harder for technical deficiencies in appraisal reports when they disagree with the appraiser's conclusion. A report must be well supported to pass such scrutiny.

The property owner's appraiser also has an obligation to make a proper analysis of the larger parcel, rather than merely to appraise an entire ownership or the parcel shown on the condemnor's map. Returning to the situation depicted in Figure 5.11, improper analysis of the larger parcel in this case could result in the appraiser's client receiving only 40% of the compensation due.

Figure 5.12 shows the same property shown in Figure 5.11, but in this instance it is assumed that the taking is of the entire frontage of the property. Condemnors would invariably treat this situation as one taking from one parcel, even those condemnors who would be astute enough to recognize that the 10 acres shown in Figure 5.11 might constitute a separate parcel. Nevertheless, the

FIGURE 5.12 TAKING OF FARM FRONTAGE

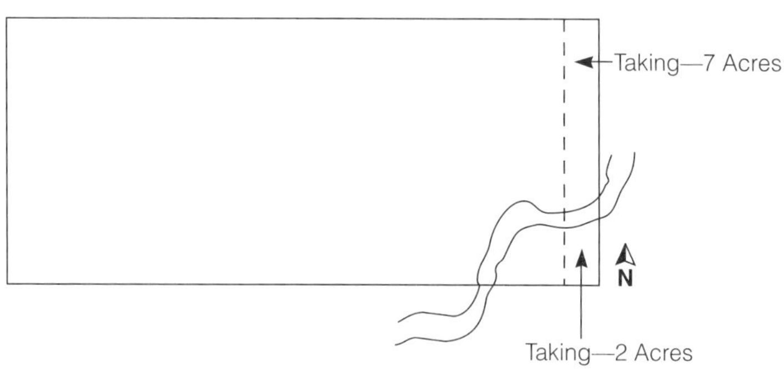

extent or location of the taking should not alter the analysis of the larger parcel in the before situation. The larger parcel determination made under the circumstances shown in Figure 5.11 would be the same under the circumstances shown in Figure 5.12, or under the circumstances of any other taking configuration, including the taking of the entire ownership.

The *Uniform Appraisal Standards for Federal Land Acquisitions* states:

> It should be noted, however, that since unity of use is one of the elements for an integrated unit, it would not necessarily follow that a contiguous body of land in the same ownership constitutes a unit for valuation if the highest and best use for various parts are different. Failure to value the property as an integrated unit should, however, always be explained and supported [in much the same way that highest and best use is supported].[47]

If the appraiser concludes that the 10-acre tract south of the stream is a separate larger parcel, in the situation depicted in Figure 5.12 the appraiser would estimate the values of the 10-acre parcel and the 90-acre parcel as two separate, independent tracts. If the client has requested a single appraisal report, the appraiser can simply include two separate valuations within a single report. In such a report, many of the report sections (e.g., regional data, neighborhood data, assumptions and limiting conditions) will be applicable to both parcels, while other sections (e.g., highest and best use, sales comparison approach to value) will have to be developed separately for each parcel.

If the appraiser is following the before and after rule, the value conclusions might be reported as follows:

Homesite parcel:

Before value (10 acres @ $5,000)	$ 50,000
After value (8 acres @ $5,000)	- 40,000
Difference (just compensation)	$ 10,000

Farm parcel:

Before value (90 acres @ $2,000)	$180,000
After value (83 acres @ $2,000)	- 166,000
Difference (just compensation)	$ 14,000

Note that the before value of the homesite parcel and the before value of the farm parcel are *not* added together and reported as a single figure. Together the value of the farm parcel and the value of the homesite parcel do not equal the value of the two parcels as a single entity. The above value estimates are separate appraisals and should be reported as such. If the client insists that a single figure be reported before and after the takings, this can be done, but it must be shown as the *sum* of the two independent value estimates. Moreover, it must be explained, every time the sum is reported, that the total is the *mathematical sum* of two independent value estimates and does not (or at least may not) represent the value of the properties if sold as a single entity.

47. *Uniform Appraisal Standards for Federal Land Acquisitions*, §A-13, p. 42.

Although the courts seldom address the issue, larger parcel determination can be important in cases that do not involve alleged damages and/or benefits. Because most legal treatises on eminent domain do not recognize this fact, they usually state that property owners often advocate the expanded parcel (so as to claim damages to the remainder), while condemnors advocate the limited larger parcel (to limit the property subject to compensable damage).[48] As the preceding discussion demonstrates, however, reducing the larger parcel can, in some circumstances, substantially increase an owner's claim of compensation.

The myth that the larger parcel determination is only important in damage and/or benefit cases can only be broken if appraisers carefully analyze properties subject to eminent domain action, properly support larger parcel determinations, and properly explain the valuation principles involved.

ADVANCED PROBLEMS

There are a number of larger parcel questions that have not been adequately addressed by the courts and by condemnors and thus no definitive guidance on these matters can be provided to the appraiser. This is not because these problems are rarely encountered; rather, it is because they are frequently unrecognized or ignored. Some of these issues are not really valuation problems, but inequalities in the treatment of property owners.

The best advice for the appraiser in these situations is to remember two things. First, the appraiser is estimating market value, so any approach to value should mirror market realities. Second, the goal is to place the owner in the same position, monetarily, after the taking that he or she was in before the taking.

To demonstrate the potential inequality in the treatment of property owners, assume that all of the property depicted in Figure 5.13 is under the same ownership and that the condemnor is acquiring all of Lot 1. Under these circumstances, the condemnor would undoubtedly treat Lot 1 as a separate parcel, claiming that

FIGURE 5.13 TREATMENT OF PROPERTY OWNERS

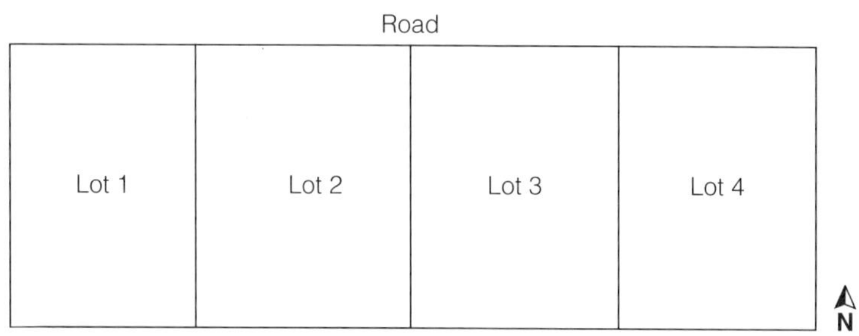

48. *Nichols'*, vol. 4A, §14B.03[2] (1992).

the balance of the property is not part of the larger parcel because it consists of legally platted lots that have separate highest and best uses. Such treatment would deny the owner the right to any damages to the remainder lots. However, if all of the lots were being taken, many condemnors would take the position that all of the lots should be valued as if they were sold as a single parcel because all of the lots are being acquired by the government as a single parcel. Valuing the land as if it would be sold as a single parcel would typically lead to a value estimate lower than the sum of the values of the lots valued individually.

This variation in treatment suggests that many condemnors attempt to apply different standards in larger parcel determination, depending on the extent of the taking. This different treatment appears to have no basis in either the law or market realities. The extent of the taking does not alter the larger parcel in the before situation. If the four lots are considered independent parcels when only Lot 1 is being taken, they should remain independent parcels when all four are taken, and they should be valued as such.

The argument advanced by condemnors that they are acquiring the entire property in one transaction, and therefore the property should be valued on the basis of a single sale, is without merit. The fact that the government is condemning the entire ownership should not preclude the property owner from receiving compensation equal to the market value of the property as if voluntarily marketed in the most advantageous way. The owner should not be forced to take a bulk sales discount when a bulk sale of the property does not produce its highest value, and is therefore not the highest and best use of the property.

Another potential inequity can be demonstrated by referring to Parcel B in Figure 5.10. If Parcel B were fully developed, the courts and condemnors would undoubtedly recognize Lots 1 and 9 as independent parcels. However, they often fail to recognize that the larger parcel in the after situation can include lands that were not part of the larger parcel in the before situation, as was demonstrated in Figure 5.9. This failure can result in overcompensation in some instances. For example, assume that Lots 1, 2, 8, and 9 each contain 12,000 square feet of area in the before situation and that comparable sales indicate that residential lots are selling for $3.00 per square foot. Further assume that the taking from Lots 1 and 9 removes 9,000 square feet of area from each lot and that, in the after situation, the two remainders would be *uneconomic remnants* as independent parcels with only a nominal value of $0.60 per square foot.

If Lots 1 and 9 are treated as two separate larger parcels in both the before and after situations, total compensation might be computed using the before and after rule:

Before value:

Lot 1, as separate parcel (12,000 sq. ft. @ $3.00)	$36,000	
Lot 9, as separate parcel (12,000 sq. ft. @ $3.00)	36,000	
Sum of before values		$ 72,000*

After value:

Lot 1, as separate parcel (3,000 sq. ft. @ $0.60)	$ 1,800	
Lot 9, as separate parcel (3,000 sq. ft. @ $0.60)	1,800	
Sum of after values		3,600*
Difference (indicated compensation)		$ 68,400

* Not indicative of the value of both lots if sold as a single entity.

However, the reality of the situation is that the owner of Lots 1 and 9 also owns Lots 2 and 8. Recognizing this market reality, and the fact that the remnants of Lots 1 and 9 could be merged with Lots 2 and 8 after the taking, compensation could be computed as follows:

Before value:

Lot 1, as separate parcel (12,000 sq. ft. @ $3.00)	$36,000	
Lot 2, as separate parcel (12,000 sq. ft. @ $3.00)	36,000	
Lot 8, as separate parcel (12,000 sq. ft. @ $3.00)	36,000	
Lot 9, as separate parcel (12,000 sq. ft. @ $3.00)	36,000	
Sum of before values		$144,000*

After value:

Lots 1 & 2 merged, as separate parcel (15,000 sq. ft. @ $3.00)	$45,000	
Lots 8 & 9 merged, as separate parcel (15,000 sq. ft. @ $3.00)	45,000	
Sum of after values		90,000*
Difference (indicated compensation)		$ 54,000

* Not indicative of the value of the lots if sold as a single entity.

This second method of analysis produces an indicated compensation amount that is 21% lower than the compensation calculated by the first method. Moreover, this second method mirrors the realities of the marketplace and puts the owner in exactly the same position, pecuniarily, in the after situation as he would have been in had the taking never occurred.

Another inconsistency in the treatment of property owners can be demonstrated by considering Parcel B in Figure 5.10. Assume that all lots in the subdivision are fully developed and all are to be taken. Under Premise 1, each lot is owned by a different party and each, as a independent entity, has a market value of $36,000. The typical condemnor would have each lot valued independently and pay each lot owner $36,000 in compensation; thus the condemnor would pay total compensation of $324,000 (9 lots @ $36,000) for all of the lots.

Now consider the same property under another premise. Under Premise 2, the fully developed lots have not yet been sold and ownership of the lots remains with the developer. In this situation the typical condemnor would attempt to apply a modified development approach to value. (See Chapter 12 for a detailed description of the development approach.) Compensation, under Premise 2, might be computed as follows:

Retail value of lots (9 lots @ $36,000)	$324,000
Less costs:	
Sales costs (10%)	- 32,400
Developer's (entrepreneur's) profit (20%)*	- 64,800
Net sale proceeds	$226,800
Market absorption:	
Absorption rate - 3 lots per year	
Absorption time (9 lots ÷ 3 lots per year)	3 years
Annual net sales income ($226,800 ÷ 3 years)	$ 75,600
Factor to convert 3-year income stream into present value discounted @ 10%†	x 2.486852
Value of property (compensation)	$188,006

* Supported by market data.

† Present worth of $1 per period for 3 years discounted at 10%. (See *The Appraisal of Real Estate*, 10th ed., 710.) Rate supported by market data.

In comparing the results of these two approaches, a number of interesting and perplexing questions arise. First, how can the market value of a property change by more than 40% due to its ownership, particularly when an eminent domain action is *in rem* and not *in personam*. The answer is, of course, it cannot. Therefore, it is necessary to look at the elements, or assumptions, that are built into these two different value indications.

Under Premise 2, sales costs are deducted from the retail value of the lots, but no such deduction is made under Premise 1. Realistically, sales costs would be incurred in both situations. However, it is a long-standing policy in eminent domain valuation, and in estimating market value for other purposes, that sales costs are not deducted from the price at which a property could be sold. No definition of market value in use today suggests that market value is the price that could be received for a property less the costs of sale. Thus, it must be concluded that to penalize a property owner by deducting sales costs from the market value of his lots merely because he owns more than one lot is inappropriate.

The other amount deducted from the retail value of the lots using the modified development method of valuation was identified as developer's, or entrepreneur's, profit. Developer's profit is obviously an appropriate part of any real estate development proposal, be it the subdivision of land or improvement of the land with a building. However, a distinction must be drawn between a proposed development and an existing development. In this instance all of the lots are *fully developed*, not proposed. Therefore, the developer has already designed the development, obtained all necessary permits, procured financing (if necessary), and made all improvements to the land necessary for the sale of the individual lots. This is an existing subdivision, not a proposed subdivision.

Developer's, or entrepreneur's, profit compensates the developer for the time and risks assumed in undertaking the development. In this case the developer has already expended the time and money to develop the land and already assumed the risks associated with the land's development. In other words, the developer has already earned his profit associated with the development. (The risks inherent in the actual sale of the lots is reflected in the discount rate applied to the projected annual net sales income.) This position was supported in a Louisiana case. In fact, the court went beyond allowing developer's profit for fully developed lots, saying:

> Thus, where an owner-developer owns land forming part of a subdivision actually developed and in the process of being sold as individual lots, and where a portion of the tract destined for that use but not actually yet developed is taken, the owner-developer is entitled to receive just and adequate compensation for the tract taken on the basis of the retail value of the lots to individual purchasers (assuming that the evidence shows such sales to be reasonably prospective), rather than artificially limited to a value based upon a hypothetical sale as a single-tract unit to another developer. The owner-developer should not be excluded from the land-profit the evidence shows he was reasonably certain to receive, except that the taking took place.
>
> The owner-developer is entitled to receive as just and adequate compensation the actual pecuniary loss caused by the taking which the evidence shows to be attributable to the loss of the value of the land itself. He should not be deprived of the profit attributable to the retail (as compared with the wholesale) value of the land simply because of some arbitrary formula that bases the market value of the tract, not upon its actually prospective retail sales to lot-purchasers, but instead upon a fictitious, unintended, and unlikely sale of it as a single tract to a nonexisting third person who would himself develop and retail the land (and keep the land-profit), just as the owner-developer was in the process of doing.[49]

However, because this Louisiana case dealt with land that was not fully developed, as is the land in our example, the court added:

> Nevertheless, as the Department correctly contends, an owner of land is not entitled to recover on the basis of its retail value if sold as lots, simply because the land's highest and best use is for subdivision purposes. The evidence must additionally show that it was reasonably certain that the owner could and would have sold them on such basis, had it not been for the intervening expropriation.[50]

The issue of absorption, or marketing time, is more difficult to relate to the factual situation and market realities. First, there must be a clear understanding of the definition of market value. Implicit in all definitions of market value is the presumption that "a reasonable time is allowed for exposure in the open mar-

49. *State, Dept. of Highways v. Terrace Land Co. Inc.*, 298 So.2d 859, 863 (La. 1974).

50. Ibid.

ket."[51] *Exposure time*, as used in the definition, is retrospective, not prospective. It has already occurred on the date of value. If a reasonable exposure time for the property under appraisal is 90 days, the question to be answered by the estimate of market value is "What would the property have sold for today (the date of value) had it been placed on the open market 90 days ago?", not "What would the property sell for within the next 90 days if it were placed on the market today?"

When this definition is applied to an individual lot valued under Premise 1 (with each lot owned by a different party), it is assumed that the exposure time has already occurred. There is no presumption that the other eight, individually owned lots being acquired by the condemnor were placed on the market at the same time, thereby skewing the supply and demand for such lots and resulting in abnormally excessive competition for the lot under appraisal. Yet that is precisely the presumption made under Premise 2.

Under Premise 2 it is assumed that all nine lots will be placed on the market at same time, outstripping the demand for such lots so that they must compete for a limited number of buyers. This is obviously treating, and valuing, the lots differently because of the nature of their ownership, which would appear to violate the *in rem* nature of the condemnation action. It would also appear to violate the definition of market value applied under Premise 1, inasmuch as prospective, rather than retrospective, market exposure time is being assumed.

However, treating the nine lots owned by the developer in exactly the same manner as the lots owned by nine individuals is to ignore the realities of the situation and the market. The nine lots are, in fact, owned by the developer and if he were to sell them individually, it would take him three years to do so.

The source of this apparent conflict is found in the various definitions of *just compensation* handed down by the courts. *Black's Law Dictionary* states that "'just compensation' means the full monetary equivalent of the property taken," but goes on to say that "[i]t means a settlement which leaves one no poorer or richer than he was before the property was taken. It requires that the owner be put in as good position pecuniarily as he would otherwise have been if the property had not been taken."[52]

Applying the first part of this definition to the example would indicate just compensation of $324,000 because the market value of the lots is not altered by the form, or nature, of their ownership. However, applying the second part of the definition (i.e., putting the owner in the same position pecuniarily that he would have been without the take) leads to a different conclusion. Recognizing that sales costs are never deducted from the estimate of market value and that the developer has already earned his profit from developing the land, and further recognizing the market realities of the situation, the developer's "pecuniary position" before the taking is essentially:

51. The Appraisal Foundation, *Uniform Standards of Professional Appraisal Practice*, 1994 ed., p. 8.

52. *Black's*, s.v. "just compensation."

Retail value of lots (9 lots @ $36,000)	$324,000
Absorption rate (9 lots ÷ 3 lots per year)	3 years
Annual income stream ($324,000 ÷ 3)	$108,000
Factor to convert 3-year income stream into present value discounted @ 10%*	x 2.486852
Pecuniary position of owner before taking	$268,580

* Present worth of $1 per period for 3 years discounted at 10%. (See *The Appraisal of Real Estate*, 10th ed., 710.) Rate supported by market data.

Resolving this conflict is ultimately the obligation of the courts, not appraisers. Nevertheless, the appraiser must understand the conflict and why it exists and should make the client aware of the conflict when it is encountered. Until this conflict is settled by the courts, if it ever is, the best policy for appraisers is to estimate the market value of the real estate unaffected by its ownership. While the courts have deviated from the market value standard of measuring just compensation in some instances, for every such instance there are literally hundreds of instances in which the courts have adhered to the market value standard. Thousands of the public acquisitions that occur each year are based on the market value standard. To encourage appraisers to use a different standard of measurement and then proclaim, as some lawyers do, that "[a]n appraiser's mission in a condemnation case is to estimate 'just compensation'"[53] is misleading. Accepting such advice places a burden on appraisers that even the U.S. Supreme Court has found difficult to shoulder. The appraiser should never deviate from estimating market value without clearly written legal instructions that are reasonable and adequately supported.

If the appraiser's condemnor client wants to argue to the court that the Premise 2 method of valuation results in just compensation, rather than the Premise 1 valuation, the appraiser can, upon receipt of proper legal instructions, prepare a double-premise appraisal and report both value estimates. It will then be up to the court, or trier of fact, to determine whether just compensation requires payment of the market value of the individual lots (Premise 1) or whether the owner should merely be put back in the same pecuniary position enjoyed before the taking (Premise 2).

Although one of the rules of the larger parcel specifies that for two or more parcels to be considered part of a single larger parcel, there must be unity of ownership, there is no inverse rule. There is no rule that prescribes that two or more tracts under the same ownership must be treated as a single larger parcel. With regard to subdivided lots, or legally separate parcels, case law supports the conclusion that they are separate larger parcels and should be treated as such:

> In the case now before the court there is no evidence whatsoever as to the adaptability of the plaintiff's land for any purpose other than building lots, and therefore each lot, *prima facie*, is a separate and distinct entity. . . . Where the entire tract has no adaptability peculiar to itself as an entity, and can be subdivided without

53. Jay Dushoff and Denise Henslee, "When Eminent Domain 'Working Rules' Don't Work," *The Appraisal Journal* (July 1991), 429.

> injury to its adaptability for use as an entire tract, and the value of a particular subdivision thereof is not dependent upon being incorporated in the tract as a part of the entity, as where the entire tract has been subdivided and plotted into building lots, and the value of no individual lot is dependent upon its relationship to the entire tract, each lot, for the purpose of assessment of damages... may be regarded as a separate distinct tract.[54]

It is clear that the nine lots used in our example are separate and distinct parcels, each with their own highest and best use, and therefore should be valued independent of one another.

The example above referred to nine subdivided lots, but lands under the same ownership do not necessarily have to be subdivided for the appraiser to conclude that they constitute two or more separate and distinct larger parcels. If there are two or more distinct highest and best uses in geographically different portions of the property, the ownership may consist of two or more larger parcels, and each larger parcel should be treated and valued as a separate and distinct entity. In fact, it has been ruled that they *must* be valued as separate parcels.[55]

If a client requests that the value of an entire ownership be reported as a single figure, the appraiser can comply with such request, but only if the single figure is identified as the mathematical sum of the two or more estimates of market value, which is not or may not be indicative of the market value of the entire ownership as a single entity.

SUMMARY

The larger parcel is a premise unique to eminent domain valuation. The premise asserts that it is the larger parcel which is considered in condemnation valuation, and that the larger parcel must generally possess unity of title, unity of use, and contiguity. Court rulings clearly indicate that all three of these elements need not be present in every case. The courts have been most lax in requiring physical contiguity, but unity of use and unity of title have been almost universally held to be prerequisites of the larger parcel.

The courts in the various jurisdictions disagree as to whether unity of use must be an existing unity, or a highest and best unity, of use. The latter view appears to be prevalent in the majority of jurisdictions. In many of the cases in which the courts have ruled that unity of use must be existing, it appears that the alleged highest and best use would have been ruled so remote and speculative as to merit no consideration, even if the larger parcel were not in question.

Unity of title is generally a legal question. The quality of title to the various tracts making up the larger parcel need not be identical; as a general rule, if the same individual or group of individuals control the title and future use of all of the tracts, unity of title is considered to be present. Physical contiguity, which is generally an engineering matter, is not always necessary, nor does it follow that a whole parcel constitutes the larger parcel just because it possesses contiguity and

54. *Gains v. City of Calhoun*, 42 Ga.App. 89 (Ga. 1931).

55. *Foster v. Sanders*, 557 S.W.2d 205 (Ky. 1977).

unity of ownership. Right-of-way maps do not control the determination of the larger parcel and, in fact, may have no bearing on the question. The same is true of appraisal contracts or assignments.

Unity of use is an appraisal question, and the ultimate determination of the larger parcel is typically in the strict purview of the appraiser. This is strongly supported by two court rulings. First:

> The method of valuation of the parcels taken, whether as a separate entity or in a relationship to the whole tract, then becomes a matter of opinion of appraisers to be weighed by the jury.... We conclude that in this case the use of either method of valuation by the expert witnesses was proper and their testimony admissible, subject only to the inherent risk of nonpersuasion.[56]

And second:

> Where the property taken is less than the entire tract, other considerations arise. The highest and best use of the part taken may be as a separate and distinct piece of property unrelated to the entire property endowing such part with a fair cash market value. On the other hand the highest and best use of the part taken may be so related to the entire property that the value of the part taken for its highest and best use is dependent upon the value of the entire tract. Such a relation or dependence may present an issue of fact and either party is entitled to present his theory of independent or dependent valuation.[57]

It is commonly believed that determination of the larger parcel is only important in cases in which damages and/or special benefits are alleged. This belief is false. Due to the effects of size regression and plottage, determination of the larger parcel can have a significant effect on the indicated compensation in cases in which neither damages nor benefits are claimed.

Because of the importance of the appraiser's determination of the larger parcel and its potential effect on value, the appraiser should exercise the same care in developing the larger parcel determination as is exercised in developing highest and best use conclusions and value estimates. A complete description of the analysis of the larger parcel and the reasoning on which the appraiser's conclusion is based should be included in the appraisal report.

The extent of a condemnor's taking does not alter the standards under which the larger parcel is determined. A larger parcel determination made prior to the government's taking should be made without any reference whatsoever to the taking. The appraiser should only be concerned with contiguity, or proximity, as it relates to highest and best use, unity of ownership, and unity of highest and best use.

"It should be noted...that since unity of use is one of the elements for an integrated unit, it would not necessarily follow that a contiguous body of land in the same ownership constitutes a unit for valuation if the highest and best use for various parts are different."[58] Thus, parcels that are contiguous and under the same ownership may have independent highest and best uses. Those highest and

56. *Territory of Hawaii v. Adelmeyer*, 363 P.2d 979, 986 (Haw. 1961).

57. *Department of Public Works & Buildings v. Oberlaender*, 235 N.E.2d 3, 9 (Ill. 1968), Aff'd 247 N.E.2d 888 (1969).

58. *Uniform Appraisal Standards for Federal Land Acquisitions*, §A-13, p. 42.

best uses may be identical (e.g., single-family homesite), but if the highest and best uses of the tracts do not require a common, or integrated use, they are separate larger parcels and should be valued as such.

Proper application of the larger parcel premise can reduce the scope and complexity of the appraisal assignment. Moreover, it will often prevent misapplication of the backland theory.

Court applications of the larger parcel premise can be quite contradictory. Therefore, it is important that the appraiser fully understand the court's application of this premise in the jurisdiction where the property being appraised is located. If, after proper analysis, the appraiser concludes that the larger parcel is unquestionably that tract or tracts that are physically contiguous, are under the same ownership, and have the same existing, and highest and best, use, it is usually safe to complete the appraisal assignment without legal guidance. Under any other circumstance, however, the legal permissibility of the appraiser's larger parcel determination should be reviewed by legal counsel.

If there is a question as to the legal acceptability of the appraiser's determination of the larger parcel, the appraiser must obtain legal instructions from the appropriate attorney, with supporting citations as to the legal acceptability of such a determination. If these instructions are contrary to the appraiser's determination of the larger parcel, and the legal instructions are reasonable and supported by applicable citations, the appraiser must alter his or her determination to conform with jurisdictional law. This is the only way appraisers can fully comply with their professional obligations. The inclusion of such legal instructions in the appraiser's report is a prudent appraisal practice and is required by professional and technical appraisal standards.[59]

59. USPAP, 1994 ed., Ethics Provision (Conduct), p. 2 and *Uniform Appraisal Standards for Federal Land Acquisitions*, §C-9, pp. 95–97.

CHAPTER 6

Highest and Best Use

"When the purpose of an appraisal is to estimate market value, highest and best use analysis identifies the most profitable, competitive use to which the property can be put."[1] This statement holds true in condemnation appraisal. The courts have universally held that property acquired under the sovereign's power of eminent domain is to be valued in recognition of its highest and best use.[2] A number of different definitions of highest and best use have been developed. Two of these definitions follow:

> The reasonably probable and legal use of vacant land or an improved property, which is physically possible, appropriately supported, financially feasible, and that results in the highest value. The four criteria the highest and best use must meet are legal permissibility, physical possibility, financial feasibility, and maximum profitability.[3]

> In real estate valuation (e.g., in condemnation proceedings) the use of land or buildings which will bring the greatest economic return over a given time. This method of valuation requires the expert to determine what the condemned property's fair market value would realistically be if the owner were hypothetically allowed to adapt his property to its most advantageous and valuable use.[4]

In the early 1980s one definition of highest and best use that was advocated, and published, asserted that "[i]mplied within these definitions is recognition of the contribution of that specific use to community environment or to community

1. *The Appraisal of Real Estate*, 10th ed. (Chicago: Appraisal Institute, 1992), 275.
2. *Mississippi and Rum River Boom Co. v. Patterson*, 98 U.S. 403 (1879).
3. *The Dictionary of Real Estate Appraisal*, 3d ed. (Chicago: Appraisal Institute, 1993), 171.
4. *Black's Law Dictionary*, abr. 6th ed., s.v. "highest and best use."

development goals in addition to wealth maximization of individual property owners."[5] This provision was immediately recognized as inappropriate for eminent domain valuations. It is now recognized, in all forms of highest and best use analysis, that "[t]he benefit a real estate development produces for a community or the amenity contribution provided by a planned project (i.e., the public space in a park-like area) are not considered in the appraiser's analysis of highest and best use."[6]

When an appraisal involves a partial acquisition, the appraiser must make two separate and distinct highest and best use estimates. In determining a property's highest and best use in the before situation, any special influences of the proposed project are generally disregarded. To estimate the highest and best use of a property in the after situation is often more difficult because it is necessary to study the impacts of the proposed project—e.g., zone changes to be made by reason of the project, the conformance of the remainder property to existing zoning and setback requirements, and general changes in the neighborhood. The appraiser must realize that, in the after situation, an entirely new real estate environment has been created by reason of the project.

The analysis of the property's highest and best use in the after situation is a totally independent study of the property, not a modification of the study of the property's highest and best use in the before situation. If the appraiser does not estimate the property's highest and best use correctly in both the before and after situations, it will be impossible to estimate the property's value correctly.

In condemnation appraisal there is a presumption that the existing use of a property is its highest and best use.[7] Therefore, when the highest and best use of a property is determined to be other than its existing use, the burden of proof falls on the party who claims the different use.[8]

> Elements affecting value that depend upon events or combinations of occurrences which, while within the realm of possibility, are not fairly shown to be reasonably probable, should be excluded from consideration, for that would be to allow mere speculation and conjecture to become a guide for the ascertainment of value—a thing to be condemned in business transactions as well as in judicial ascertainment of truth.[9]

This is not to say that a highest and best use *"to hold for a speculative rise in market value"* is not a proper determination of highest and best use; the courts have allowed testimony of such use. In the words of the court, such a use "... is a matter of such common knowledge that argument to the contrary is unrealistic."[10] The appraiser who uses the word *speculative* or *speculation* in the description of highest and best use should exercise great care to ensure that the court or the trier of fact does not misunderstand the term. For instance, when two witnesses testified that

---

5. American Institute of Real Estate Appraisers and the Society of Real Estate Appraisers, *Real Estate Appraisal Terminology*, rev. ed., Byrl N. Boyce, ed. (Cambridge, Mass.: Ballinger Publishing Company, 1981), 127.
6. *The Appraisal of Real Estate*, 10th ed., 276, n.1.
7. *United States v. 8.41 Acres of Land, Etc.*, 680 F.2d 388, 394 (5th Cir. 1982).
8. Ibid.
9. *Olson v. United States*, 292 U.S. 246, 257 (1934).
10. *State v. Whitlow*, 52 Cal. Rptr. 336, 342 (Cal. 1966).

the highest and best use of a property was "holding for future development" an Illinois court said: "In our opinion this was an improper element—it was not a use at all and was highly speculative."[11]

Use of the term *reasonably probable* in regard to highest and best use has been widely accepted by the courts. "[T]he fact that the property is merely adaptable to a different use is not in itself a sufficient showing in law to consider such different use as a basis for compensation. It must be shown that such use of the property is so reasonably probable as to have an effect on the present value of the land."[12] [Citations omitted]

THE FOUR TESTS OF HIGHEST AND BEST USE

There are four tests that a property must meet before its highest and best use can be determined. The use must be physically possible, legally permissible, financially feasible, and maximally profitable (i.e., create the highest economic value). The appraiser must apply each of these tests and discuss each in the appraisal report to justify the ultimate opinion of highest and best use.

While the four criteria are interrelated, the tests are often applied sequentially. The tests of physical possibility and legal permissibility *must* be applied before the tests of financial feasibility and maximum profitability. There is little to be learned from analyzing the financial feasibility of an illegal, or physically impossible, use.

Land use regulations play an important role in the appraiser's determination of a highest and best use. The appraiser cannot, of course, conclude a highest and best use that is illegal under applicable land use regulations unless there is a reasonable probability that the regulations will be changed to allow this use within the foreseeable future. The effect of land use regulations on highest and best use, and on the value of property, is discussed in detail in Chapter 7.

The physical factors to be considered by an appraiser in determining the highest and best use of a parcel being appraised for eminent domain purposes are no different than those that would be considered in any other appraisal assignment. Size, shape, the availability of utilities, topography, soils, access, and environmental influences (e.g., floodplain areas, frost damage in agricultural areas) all must be studied to assess the physical adaptability of a property to its legally allowable uses.

Once the appraiser has identified those uses of the land that are legally permissible and physically possible, the test of financial feasibility is applied. First supply and demand in the general location of the subject property must be analyzed. Often the appraiser needs to estimate the cost of various types of improvements and the amount of net income that could be generated from each. The appraiser then determines the amount of net income needed to provide an adequate return on the improvement cost so as to determine if there remains ad-

11. *Dept. of Transportation v. Janssen*, 339 N.E.2d 359, 361 (Ill. 1975).

12. *Dep't of Transportation v. Great Southern Enterprises*, 225 S.E.2d 80, 83 (Ga. 1976).

equate net income to support a reasonable land value. If the remaining income is sufficient, the use is considered financially feasible.

Finally the appraiser performs a comparative analysis of the financially feasible uses of the property to determine which use will be maximally profitable—i.e., produce the highest economic land value. This last step is typically accomplished through the use of a land residual technique.[13] Appraisers must recognize that this procedure is used merely to determine highest and best use; it is not generally considered an acceptable method for estimating land value for eminent domain purposes. Although the land residual technique is recognized as a proper land valuation method in the appraisal industry,[14] it is generally rejected by the courts as too speculative. As a New York court in the *Blackwell's Island* case stated:

> In regard to the vacant lots, parcel No. 31, a witness was asked what would be the best use to which these lots could be put. He replied: "The erection of three apartment houses, 33 front each." He was then allowed to testify, over objections and exceptions, that the cost of constructing three such buildings would be $75,000, and that the rental value of such buildings would be between $14,000 and $15,000 a year. This is clear error. It involved so much of the elements of uncertainty and speculation as to be inadmissible as proof of any fact. As said in the case of *Tallman v. Met. El. R. R. Co.* (121 N.Y. 119): "There can be no certainty that the plaintiff would ever have erected dwelling houses upon the lot, and there could be no certainty as to the rents which could have been obtained from them."[15] [Citations omitted]

Because of rulings such as this, the appraiser is generally well advised to testify under direct examination only as to the analytical methodology used in determining highest and best use, without specificity. Specific details are typically not admitted on direct examination. If the appraiser's estimate of highest and best use is questioned under cross-examination, however, the appraiser is often allowed to explain, in detail and with specificity, the process employed to arrive at the highest and best use conclusion.

In cases in which the question of highest and best use is crucial and/or complex, the appraiser may find it necessary, or advisable, to retain the services of a consultant such as a contractor or marketing consultant.

Highest and Best Use as Improved

The original concept of highest and best use called only for an estimate of the highest and best use of the land as though vacant. The concept of highest and best use as improved "was developed to answer an important question that the original concept does not address. How should the property as improved be used?"[16] Recognition of this concept is extremely important in eminent domain

13. *The Appraisal of Real Estate*, 10th ed., 474–475.

14. Ibid., 307–308.

15. *Matter of City of New York (Blackwell's Island Bridge)*, 103 N.Y.S. 441, 443–444 (N.Y. 1907).

16. *The Appraisal of Real Estate*, 10th ed., 277.

valuation; if it is ignored, the appraiser may very well analyze himself into an extremely uncomfortable position on the witness stand.

A tract of land considered as though vacant may have a highest and best use different than that of the whole property as improved. Classic appraisal theory requires that "[t]he value of land is generally estimated as though vacant."[17] Adoption of this procedure in eminent domain valuation would result in an accurate conclusion, but one that may be totally unbelievable to the court because of the procedure used to develop it. Figure 6.1 illustrates a situation in which the appraiser may be well advised to deviate from standard appraisal procedure.

Assume that the appraiser has developed the following conclusions after investigating and analyzing the property depicted in Figure 6.1.

FIGURE 6.1 HIGHEST AND BEST USE AS IF VACANT

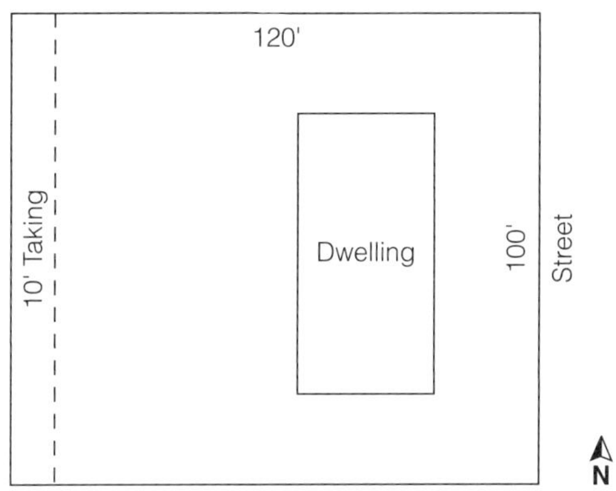

Highest and best use of site, as if vacant	multifamily
Before value of site as if vacant: $3.00/sq. ft.	$ 36,000
After value of site as if vacant: $3.00/sq. ft.	$ 33,000
Highest and best use of property, as improved	single-family
Before value of property, as improved	$119,000
After value of property, as improved	$118,000
Before value of site for single-family purposes: $1.00/sq. ft.	$ 12,000
After value of site for single-family purposes: $1.00/sq. ft.	$ 11,000

If the appraiser were allowed to report and testify only on the value conclusions before and after, no problems would arise. The conclusions would be simply:

Before value	$119,000
After value	-118,000
Difference between before and after values	$ 1,000

17. *The Appraisal of Real Estate*, 10th ed., 279; see also The Appraisal Foundation, *Uniform Standards of Professional Appraisal Practice* (USPAP), 1994 ed., Standards Rule 1-3(b), p. 11.

However, the appraiser is seldom allowed to report on or testify to only the conclusions, particularly when an experienced and knowledgeable attorney is conducting the appraiser's cross-examination. As one court said:

> When a witness, having qualified, gives his opinion as to the value of the land sought to be condemned, he may properly give his reasons upon direct examination for his conclusions. As the element of highest and best use is an important factor to be considered in reaching a conclusion in respect to value it would seem clear that one who is entitled to give an opinion as to the value of real property should necessarily be in a position to give an opinion also with respect to its highest and best use.[18] [Citations omitted]

Using classic appraisal methodology, the appraiser's before value computations, or allocation of component values, might look like this:

Land value (12,000 sq. ft. @ $3.00)	$ 36,000
Value of dwelling	81,500
On-site improvements	1,500
Total before value	$119,000

Using the cost approach, the appraiser's value computations in the before situation might take this form:

Reproduction cost of dwelling (2,200 sq. ft. @ $60.00)		$132,000
Less depreciation:		
Physical deterioration	$26,500	
External obsolescence (misplaced improvement)	24,000	
Total depreciation		- 50,500
Value of dwelling		$ 81,500
Contributory value of on-site improvements		1,500
Total improvement value		$ 83,000
Land value (12,000 sq. ft. @ $3.00)		36,000
Total property value		$119,000

The appraiser's after value computations would be:

Land value (11,000 sq. ft. @ $3.00)	$ 33,000
Value of dwelling	83,500
On-site improvements	1,500
Total	$118,000

The appraiser's cost approach computations of value in the after situation follow:

Reproduction cost of dwelling (2,200 sq. ft. @ $60.00)		$132,000
Less depreciation:		
Physical deterioration	$26,500	
External obsolescence (misplaced improvement)	22,000	
Total depreciation		- 48,500

18. *People v. Alexander*, 27 Cal. Rptr. 720, 723 (Cal. 1963).

Value of dwelling	$ 83,500
Contributory value of on-site improvements	1,500
Total improvement value	$ 85,000
Land value (12,000 sq. ft. @ $3.00)	33,000
Total property value	$118,000

In these calculations the external obsolescence of the dwelling is reduced by $2,000 in the after situation because the ratio of land to building value has been redistributed. However, it would take an unusually persuasive appraiser to convince a client, or a jury, that the value of the dwelling has increased $2,000 due to the taking of a 10-foot strip from the rear of the site. The appraiser could, of course, protect himself by including in the appraisal report a statement such as:

> Where the value of the land and improvements are shown separately, the value of each is segregated as only an aid to better estimating the value of the whole; and the value shown for either may, or may not, be its fair market value.

Unfortunately, such a statement is usually forgotten or ignored by the reader of the appraisal report and the trier of fact.

Under the circumstances shown in Figure 6.1, the appraiser should consider the advisability of abandoning standard appraisal methodology and appraising the land at the highest and best use of the property as improved, rather than as though vacant. The propriety of using such a procedure under certain circumstances is acknowledged in current professional appraisal standards. The "guideline [that land is appraised as though vacant and available for development to its highest and best use] may be modified to reflect the fact that, in various legal and practical situations, a site may have a contributory value that differs from the value as if vacant."[19]

Application of this modified procedure would result in the following before value computations:

Land value (12,000 sq. ft. @ $1.00)	$ 12,000
Value of dwelling	105,500
On-site improvements	1,500
Total	$119,000

If the cost approach is applied, the before value would be calculated:

Reproduction cost of dwelling (2,200 sq. ft. @ $60.00)	$132,000
Depreciation (physical deterioration)	- 26,500
Value of dwelling	$105,500
Contributory value of on-site improvements	1,500
Total improvement value	$107,000
Land value	12,000
Total	$119,000

19. USPAP, 1994 ed., Comment to Standards Rule 1-3(b), p. 11. See also *The Appraisal of Real Estate*, 279, n. 2.

The after value computations would then be:

Land value (11,000 sq. ft. @ $1.00)	$ 11,000
Value of dwelling	105,500
On-site improvements	1,500
Total	$118,000

Computations of value in the after situation using the cost approach would be:

Reproduction cost of dwelling (2,200 sq. ft. @ $60.00)	$132,000
Depreciation (physical deterioration)	- 26,500
Value of dwelling	$105,500
Contributory value of on-site improvements	1,500
Total improvement value	$107,000
Land value	11,000
Total	$118,000

Adopting this modified procedure does not alter the appraiser's conclusion. It merely presents a computational process that is more persuasive and believable to those not familiar with real estate valuation techniques. Nevertheless, use of this procedure leaves the appraiser open to questions about multifamily residential land sales in the area transacted at $3.00 per square foot. This argument can be derailed with a simple explanation of the consistent use theory, which is described later in this chapter.

It is advisable for the appraiser to include both the classic appraisal computations and the computations based on the highest and best use as improved in the report. This serves two purposes. First, if the appraisal report is reviewed by a person who is knowledgeable in real estate valuation (e.g., the condemnor's review appraiser), he or she cannot criticize the appraiser for abandoning the classic appraisal methodology. Second, providing both sets of computations demonstrates that the results are identical and shows legal counsel how and why the appraiser has deviated from classic appraisal methodology. This will enable the attorney to better prepare for trial.

ALL AVAILABLE USES

As previously mentioned, the courts have universally acknowledged the concept of highest and best use. An appraiser may take the position that the property has been appraised for a specific use (i.e., the appraiser's estimate of highest and best use), but the courts have rejected this position. Most of the courts that have addressed this question have ruled that a property is not to be valued for a specific use, but rather in light of all available uses to which the property might, in reason, be applied.

A Tennessee court clearly defined its position on this matter:

> In this State we have adopted the view that "value in view of all available uses" is the proper phrase to use in valuation as against the phrase "value for the best use" as is used by the minority of the States. We are bound by the majority view, that is that we consider the "value in view of all available uses." It is well said that we use this phrase to warn the jury against awarding the "value for a particular use."[20] [Citations omitted]

A Massachusetts court used the same reasoning when it ruled:

> The sum to be awarded for real estate taken is the fair market value of the property, having reference to all the uses to which it is adapted. Its value for any special purpose is not the test, although it may be considered, with a view of ascertaining what the property is worth in the market for any use for which it would bring the most.[21]

At first glance, these rulings may appear to contradict the appraiser's concept of highest and best use. This is not the case, however, because the courts recognize the concept of highest and best use and its importance in determining market value. The courts have adopted the *all available uses* concept in an attempt to avoid receiving testimony from various witnesses as to the value of the property for different specific uses,

> for such evidence opens wide the door to unlimited vagaries and speculations concerning problematical prices which might under possible contingencies be paid for the land, and distracts the mind of the jury from the single question—that of market value—the highest sum which the property is worth to persons generally, purchasing in the open market in consideration of the land's adaptability for any proven use."[22]

The distinction between highest and best use and all allowable uses may appear to be merely a question of semantics and of little concern to appraisers, but this distinction may ultimately determine whether an appraiser's testimony is ruled to be admissible or excluded from consideration by the courts. As stated by a Nebraska court:

> The power company also asserts that the trial court erred in permitting, over objection, the testimony of witnesses as to their opinions as to the value of the property for use as a filling station. In this respect one witness was permitted to testify that the corner was worth $14,000 as a filling station site. Sump [another witness] was permitted to state that the corner was worth $15,000 as a filling station site. The evidence was erroneously admitted. The rule is: Witnesses should not be allowed to give their opinion as to the value of property for a particular purpose, but should state its market value in view of any purpose to which it is adapted. The condition of the property and all its surroundings may be shown as well as its availability for any particular use. If it has a peculiar adaptation for certain uses, this may likewise be shown, and if such peculiar adaptation adds to its value the owner is entitled to the benefit of it. Where these facts and circum-

20. *Davidson County Bd. of Ed. v. First American Nat. Bank*, 301 S.W.2d 905, 907 (Tenn. 1957).
21. *Conness v. Commonwealth*, 69 N.E. 341, 341 (Mass. 1904).
22. *Sacramento Southern R. Co. v. Heilbron*, 104 P. 979, 981 (Cal. 1909).

> stances are shown, the only question as to value that is properly in issue is the reasonable market value at the time the property is taken or damaged. We conclude that the trial court erred in admitting the evidence as to the value of the property for use as a filling station.[23] [Citations omitted]

It can be seen that there is no conceptual conflict between the appraiser's highest and best use and the court's all available uses. The appraiser who concludes that the highest and best use of a site is for a service station site, and values the property being condemned using sales of comparable service station sites, is not in conflict with the all available uses concept. Such a valuation procedure automatically incorporates the fact that all of the sites analyzed, the one being appraised as well as any comparable sale sites, have potential for uses other than their highest and best use as service station sites. Thus, appraisers must simply be cautious in their use of terminology when testifying in jurisdictions that have adopted the concept of all available uses.

The all available uses concept does not generally include the use for which the property is being condemned. In other words, it is the value of the land taken which is to be estimated, not the value of the land to the *taker*. This distinction is illustrated by a case in which the government condemned land to improve and maintain a natural earthen dam. The property owner did not prevail when he claimed that his land was worth a substantial sum because it dammed a lake created by the eruption of Mt. St. Helens, thereby preventing the flooding of communities downstream.

Following this same logic, it has recently been suggested that lands being acquired by the government and conservation groups must have a highest and best use for preservation purposes; if not, why would the government acquire them? There are a number of problems with this logic. First, the term *value*, as used in eminent domain context, must be capable of quantification in money. Second, the preservation of land falls outside the scope of the definition of highest and best use used by the courts which require an economic use.[24] The U.S. Supreme Court has defined highest and best use for eminent domain valuation purposes as "the highest and *most profitable* use for which the property is adaptable and needed or likely to be needed in the reasonably near future."[25]

The market for lands acquired for purposes of preservation "involves public agencies (federal, state, or municipal), environmental or conservation organizations like The Nature Conservancy and The Trust for Public Lands, and numerous smaller land trusts as acquirers."[26] However, any sale to a government agency with the power of eminent domain must be viewed with skepticism because such transactions are in the nature of compromises made to avoid litigation. There is no actual *competitive* market for lands for preservation purposes. The Nature Conservancy, The Trust for Public Lands, and the U.S. Fish and Wildlife Service are not out in the open market bidding against one another. "These are not competitors;

23. *Petition of Omaha Public Power Dist.*, 95 N.W.2d 209, 213–214 (Neb. 1959).

24. The concept of preservation or conservation as a use and its relevance to value was recently studied and debated by various interested appraisal bodies.

25. *Olson v. United States*, 292 U.S. 246, 255 (1934) (emphasis added).

26. Victoria Adams and Bill Mundy, "The Valuation of High-Amenity Natural Land," *The Appraisal Journal* (January 1991), 48, 49.

they are acting with a common purpose."[27] In fact, conservation groups would prefer a government acquisition of the lands and many groups actually acquire these lands for the sole purpose of holding them until a governmental agency can procure funding and buy the lands from the conservation group at its cost. Such transactions clearly do not meet the criteria for an open-market transaction reflecting market value.

Neither government agencies nor conservation groups base their purchase price of a property on its value for preservation purposes. The price is based on the highest and best *economic* use of the property. Therefore, although the property was purchased for preservation purposes, the price paid was based on the *economic* value of the property, not some esoteric noneconomic or non-use value, which the courts have shown no inclination to accept in the context of eminent domain.

> The very purpose of reserving in the people the power of eminent domain is to prevent an owner of a site especially available for a public work [*e.g.*, preservation], but not of great value for other purposes, from trading upon the necessities of the public when it is sought to acquire his land for public use, and from compelling the public to pay for his land whatever figure he may name, and it seems clear that the owner has no such power."[28]

For these reasons, appraisers must reject a highest and best use for preservation or conservation unless, or until, there is clear evidence that a competitive private market for such lands exist.

This prohibition does not preclude a highest and best use of "mitigation lands," which are typically lands that have suffered from environmental degradation and are purchased and environmentally restored in return for "mitigation credits" on other lands to be developed. In some parts of the country, most notably California, an active, private market exists for such lands. Nor does this prohibition exclude a highest and best use as a private hunting preserve, a duck club, or the like because, again, an active private market for such lands exists in some regions.

Sometimes, however, the highest and best use of the property is, in fact, the use to which the condemnor will put the land. This type of situation often arises in the acquisition of recreational properties such as golf courses. When the property's highest and best use and the use for which the property is being taken are identical, the appraiser could properly estimate property value for this use. This practice is not inconsistent with court rulings that land should not be valued for the use to which the condemnor will put it. As explained by the court:

> [I]t is the "no value attributable to Government demand" principle that informs those decisions which hold that in determining the fair market value of condemned property, the use to which the Government proposes to devote the property should not be considered *unless private owners could also reasonably devote the property to that use.*[29]

27. Parker Reynolds, "Letters to the Editor," *The Appraisal Journal* (July 1992), 438.
28. *Nichols' The Law of Eminent Domain*, rev. 3d ed. (New York: Mathew Bender Co., Inc., 1990), vol. 4, §12B.16.
29. *United States v. 320.0 Acres of Land*, 605 F.2d 762, 783 n.26 (5th Cir. 1979) (emphasis added).

CONSISTENT USE THEORY

Consistent use is "[t]he concept that land cannot be valued on the basis of one use while the improvements are valued on the basis of another." [30] The consistent use theory was discussed in relation to the valuation of mineral deposits and timberland in Chapter 3.

The consistent use theory seems straightforward, but a review of appraisal reports, appraisal testimony, and court rulings indicates otherwise. The consistent use theory is often misapplied when the cost approach is used. Consider once again the property shown in Figure 6.1. In this situation it would be a violation of the consistent use theory for the appraiser to value the land for multifamily purposes, and then value the improvements for single-family purposes, without deducting the external obsolescence present in the dwelling.

This error can be carried through to the sales comparison approach by analyzing comparable sales improperly. For instance, assume the appraiser has valued the subject land for multifamily purposes at $36,000 and then makes the following analysis of the sale of a comparable dwelling on a residential site:

Sale price	$130,000
Land value (12,000 sq. ft. @ $1.00)	– 12,000
Value of improvements	$118,000
Value of on-site improvements	3,500
Value of dwelling	$114,500

The appraiser then compares the subject property to the sale property as follows:

Land—subject is superior ($36,000 – $12,000)	$ 24,000
On-site improvements—subject property is inferior ($3,500 – $1,500)	– 2,000
Dwelling—properties are physically equal	0
Net adjustment	$ 22,000
Sale price of comparable	130,000
Indicated value of subject property	$152,000

Note that a substantial error results when the consistent use theory is misapplied by valuing land for multifamily purposes and improvements for single-family purposes. The New York court addressed a similar situation when it said:

> The claimant was awarded $55,500 for the entire taking of her property. It was conceded that the highest and best use for this property was commercial. At the time of the appropriation there was a dwelling house and combination garage and work shop on the property. The trial court awarded $40,850 as the market value of the land and $14,700 for the value of the buildings. The expert for the claimant as well as the State testified the buildings would of necessity have to be removed from the property to permit its use for commercial purposes. It was error, therefore, to award anything for the value of the buildings while at the same time fixing the land value for commercial usage since the two bases [sic] are

30. *The Appraisal of Real Estate*, 10th ed., 46; *The Dictionary of Real Estate Appraisal*, 3d ed., 72.

> entirely inconsistent. Under the facts here the commercial value of the land was in no way enhanced by the value of the buildings.[31] [Citations omitted]

Although it is relatively easy for appraisers to understand and properly apply the consistent use theory, it is often difficult to explain its application persuasively to a jury. It may be difficult for the average person to accept the fact that a large, well-kept, single-family dwelling has no value, particularly when the property owner is living in the house and had no intention of tearing it down and constructing a commercial building. In fact, the courts have, on occasion, refused to accept the consistent use theory and made erroneous rulings.[32]

Although it is a violation of the consistent use theory to value a parcel for two uses that are mutually exclusive, it is permissible to value a parcel for two uses that are not incompatible and can take place simultaneously. A potato farm that attracts a great number of waterfowl can have a highest and best use for both farming and recreational hunting, because neither use is necessarily mutually exclusive.

INTERIM USE

An *interim use,* which is also referred to as a *transitional use,* is "[t]hat existing and relatively temporary use where the transition to highest and best use is deferred. A building or other improvement may have a number of years of remaining life yet may not enhance the value of the land which has a higher use, except as an interim-use taxpayer while the land is in transition."[33]

One property may, in effect, have two highest and best uses—one for a relatively short period and one as a deferred highest and best use. Developing a property to its ultimate highest and best use may be inadvisable at the time of the appraisal because of market conditions or other factors, such as the unavailability of mortgage money. The property owner can choose to either let the property lie fallow until it is ripe for development to its ultimate highest and best use, or put it to an interim use and at least receive some benefit from the property until its ultimate highest and best use is realized. An example of an interim use would be the utilization of potential subdivision land for agricultural purposes. Courts have ruled that such an analysis is proper.

> In the case at bar, witness Barnes substantiated his estimates with competent testimony as to the value, nature and use of the property as a dairy farm and also ...sufficiently demonstrated an increasing demand for the property as a residential development site. Certainly a future purchaser of the Wallace property might well desire to continue the interim use of the dairy operation to offset any costs and interest charges that might exist during the piece-meal process of a housing development. There is nothing incompatible about or inconsistent in these two uses of the property.[34]

---

31. *Spano v. State of New York,* 253 N.Y.S.2d 730, 730–731 (N.Y. 1964).
32. *State, Dep't. of Highways v. Luster,* 277 So.2d 181 (La. 1973).
33. *Real Estate Appraisal Terminology,* rev. ed., 137.
34. *Arkansas State Highway Comm. v. Wallace,* 459 S.W.2d 812, 814 (Ark. 1970).

The best way to determine whether interim improvements (i.e., those incompatible with the land's ultimate highest and best use) actually contribute any value to the property as a whole is to analyze sales of comparable properties in the same economic position. Because such sales are sometimes unavailable, however, various methods of estimating an improvement's interim contributory value have been developed.

To apply one of these methods the appraiser values the income that can be realized during the interim period as if it were income from a lease and values the land as if it were a leased fee reversion. For example, assume a 50-acre farm that has an ultimate highest and best use for subdivision purposes can be leased for $5,000 net per year for an estimated interim period of three years, at which time the land will be ready for development. Similar land currently ready for development is selling for $6,000 per acre. Therefore, the subject property would have a value of $300,000 if it were ready for development. The proper discount rate applicable to this type of investment is 10%. The value of the property can be estimated by computing the present value of the income stream and the present value of the reversion as follows:

Value of income stream:	
$5,000 income x 2.486852*	$ 12,434
Value of reversion:	
$300,000 x 0.751315†	225,395
Present value of property	$237,829
Rounded	$238,000

* Present worth of $1 per period for 3 years discounted at 10%.

† Present value of $1 in 3 years discounted at 10%.

Another way to estimate the contributory value of interim improvements is to use the building residual technique of capitalization. Consider a lot improved with a single-family dwelling that has commercial potential and a current value of $30,000 in light of this potential. The property will rent for $300 net per month, or $3,600 per year. Recognizing the lot's commercial potential, the appraiser estimates that the improvements have a remaining economic life of only five years. An appropriate return rate is 8%. With this information, the contributory value of the improvements can be computed:

Annual net income	$ 3,600
Income imputable to land ($30,000 x 0.08)	- 2,400
Income residual to improvements	$ 1,200
Value of improvements ($1,200 ÷ 0.28)*	$ 4,286
Land value	30,000
Total indicated property value	$34,286
Rounded	$34,300

* 8% interest rate plus 20% recapture rate to reflect 5-year life.

Although this methodology is widely applied, it contains a flaw. Assume that the current value of the land, recognizing its commercial potential, is $60,000, not $30,000. The contributory improvement value would then be calculated as follows:

Annual net income	$ 3,600
Income imputable to land ($60,000 x 0.08)	– 4,800
Income residual to improvements	$ 0
Contributory value of improvements	$ 0
Land value	60,000
Total property value	$60,000

It is quite probable that the land, if it were vacant, could not be rented during the interim period. In this case the property is capable of producing $300 per month in net income because of the existing dwelling. However, the above computations indicate that the improvements add nothing to the value of the property as a whole.

To correct this type of error, another method of estimating the contributory value of interim improvements has been developed.[35] To apply this procedure the appraiser adds the present value of the interim income stream created by the improvements to the current land value. The computations follow:

Annual net income from property, as is	$ 3,600
Annual net income from property, as if vacant	0
Income imputable to improvements	$ 3,600
Indicated present worth of improvements	
($3,600 x 3.992710)*	$14,374
Land value	60,000
Total property value	$74,374
Rounded	$74,500

* Present worth of $1 per period for 5 years discounted at 8%.

In estimating the net income imputable to the improvements on the site, the appraiser should determine what portion of the real estate tax burden and other expenses are attributable to the improvements and deduct that portion of the tax from the gross income attributable to the improvement. If the land if vacant could be rented to produce a net income, that income would be deducted from the net income produced by the property as improved. In the above example, assume that the land if it were vacant could be leased as a parking lot during the interim period for a net rental of $1,000 per year. Then the income imputable to the improvements would be $2,600 ($3,600 – $1,000) and the indicated contributory value of the interim improvements would be $10,381 ($2,600 x 3.992710).

Appraisers who estimate the contributory value of interim improvements must remember to consider the demolition cost of any improvements that will have to be removed from the site before it can be put to its ultimate highest and

35. Laurence Sando, "Theories of Valuation for Interim Use," *The Appraisal Journal* (January 1964), 29–34.

best use. This can be a substantial amount, especially if the improvements are contaminated with asbestos or other hazardous materials. If demolition is anticipated at the end of the interim life of the improvements, it is appropriate to discount the anticipated cost of demolition to its present worth.

Lengthening the estimated interim time period diminishes the validity of this estimating procedure. To estimate an interim use period longer than five years can be considered speculation and conjecture. Because the property owner is not receiving any return on the land, this valuation method should be applied only when the interim period is relatively short and, perhaps, when the land is appreciating relatively rapidly. The appraiser should not use this valuation procedure if comparable sales exist; the procedure is not intended to eliminate the need for market research. Moreover, the results of this procedure should not be accepted blindly, but must be correlated with the realities of the marketplace. Due to the simplicity of this procedure, it is often misused by uninitiated appraisers and advocates.

At times, interim improvements can have a contributory value beyond the value created by their income-producing capabilities. Many real estate lenders will not make loans on unimproved properties as a matter of policy, but they will lend on improved properties regardless of the ratio of land-to-building value. This fact can sometimes affect market value, as can the fact that the existence of the improvements may produce an income-tax advantage.

In arriving at an estimate of highest and best use, the appraiser must remember the doctrine of reasonable probability. If the amount of time between the effective date of the appraisal and the time when the property is expected to reach its ultimate highest and best use is too great, the appraiser's conclusion of highest and best use becomes remote and speculative and will be rejected by the courts.

ENHANCEMENT AND BLIGHT

Condemnation blight is a diminution in the market value of a property due to pending condemnation action; *project enhancement* is an increase in a property's market value in anticipation of a public project requiring condemnation action. As a general rule, the appraiser cannot properly consider either of these factors in the before situation when estimating highest and best use or value. "The United States cannot be charged in condemnation proceedings for values which it has created in constructing the project for which the property is taken; nor can the owner be charged for any diminution in value attributable to the project."[36] The appraiser "shall disregard any decrease or increase in the fair market value of real property, prior to the date of valuation, caused by the project for which the property is to be acquired, or by the likelihood that the property would be acquired for the project other than that due to physical deterioration within the reasonable control of the owner."[37]

36. *Uniform Appraisal Standards for Federal Land Acquisitions* (Washington, D.C.: U.S. Government Printing Office, 1992), §A-10, pp. 26-27.

37. Uniform Relocation Assistance and Real Property Acquisition Policy Act of 1970 (P.L. 91-646) §42.11(c)(1).

There are exceptions to this rule however.

> In 1966, the Georgia legislature enacted a statute providing that any increase or decrease in the value of the property caused by the knowledge of the public project could not be considered in assessing just and adequate compensation [Ga. Code Ann., §§ 36-617a, 36-1117, 36-1312]. The [State] Supreme Court declared this statute unconstitutional on the grounds that the legislature was attempting to interpret the constitutional requirement of just and adequate compensation in violation of the separation of powers doctrine [*Calhoun v. State Hwy. Dep't* 153 S.E.2d 418 (Ga. 1967)].[38]

Thus, in Georgia, both increases and decreases in value that have occurred prior to the date of taking are properly considered. There appear to be other jurisdictions that also allow consideration of value enhancement and/or diminution by reason of the government's project. [39] Therefore, appraisers should consult legal counsel as to the applicable rule in the jurisdiction.

Condemnation blight, which decreases property values, most often occurs when public projects are announced long before property acquisition begins or when the acquisition program is not completed in a timely manner. Urban renewal projects are a classic example. Once an urban renewal project is announced, tenants tend to vacate buildings, vacancy rates escalate, property maintenance is often ignored, and vandalism tends to increase; these factors have a depressing effect on property values within the area. All of these conditions, except for physical deterioration within the reasonable control of the owner, must be disregarded by the appraiser in estimating the property's highest and best use and its market value.

The owner of a property located within a designated urban renewal area is well advised to retain the services of an appraiser well before the actual appraisal will be required. If this is done, the appraiser can analyze and inspect the property and neighborhood before the negative impact of the urban renewal designation has had a chance to distort the actual before situation. Condemnation blight can be so severe at times that property owners may claim a *de facto taking*.

The distinction between condemnation blight and a de facto taking has been described as follows:

> The concept of a de facto appropriation is limited to situations in which there has been a *direct* invasion by the condemning authority upon the property of the condemnee or some *direct* legal restraint upon the use of such property. Condemnation blight, on the other hand, properly refers to the diminution in value of the property of the condemnee, caused by acts of the condemning authority between the time of the announcement of the projected taking and the *de jure* vesting of title.[40] [Citations omitted]

38. Charles N. Pursley, Jr., *Georgia Eminent Domain* (Norcross, Georgia: The Harrison Company, 1982), §6-4, 151.
39. *Anderson v. State Road Dept.*, 204 So. 2d 899 (Fla. 1967); *Prudential Insurance v. Central Neb. Pub. P.&I. Dist.*, 296 N.W. 752 (Neb. 1941).
40. *Beaux Arts Prop., Inc. v. United Nations Dev. Corp.*, 328 N.Y.S.2d 16, 22 (N.Y. 1972).

The distinction between these terms is important to appraisers because the date of value is affected. If a de facto taking has occurred, the date of value is the date of the de facto taking and interest must usually be paid on the condemnation award from the date of the de facto taking to the date the award is received by the condemnee. If only condemnation blight has occurred, the valuation date usually is the date of actual vesting of title in the condemnor, and the appraiser does not consider any diminution in value by reason of the proposed taking. To assume a de facto taking, the appraiser must have adequately supported written legal instructions from legal counsel. Because of the complex distinction between a condemnation blight case and a de facto taking case, and the significant implications involved, legal counsel will often request a dual-premise appraisal, one assuming a de facto taking and one assuming condemnation blight.

Project enhancement can also have a dramatic effect on property values. Zoning may be changed to accommodate a pending public project, which will require all or part of the rezoned property to be acquired. The appraiser must decide whether the property in question was rezoned because of the pending project or not. This determination will have a substantial impact on the appraiser's estimate of highest and best use and market value in the before and/or after situations.

If the rezoning is a result of the proposed public project, under the premise of project enhancement the appraiser must ignore the rezoning in the before situation. On the other hand, if the appraiser concludes that the property would have been rezoned anyway, the conclusion of highest and best use in both the before and after situations should be made in light of the rezoning. The proper treatment of this appraisal problem is demonstrated in the next chapter.

If the highest and best use of the property changes to a more valuable use immediately before the announcement of a public project and the date of valuation, project enhancement may be indicated. In such a case it is the responsibility of the appraiser to investigate the possibility and determine whether project enhancement has actually occurred. One of the most difficult determinations to be made in such an investigation is the *scope of the project.*

As a classic example of project enhancement, consider a property that contains a gravel deposit. Before the announcement of a road project requiring acquisition of the property for right-of-way purposes, there was no foreseeable market demand for the gravel. However, the pending project will create a demand for the material and the condemnor's contractor may, in fact, use the gravel for construction of the new roadway. Nevertheless, the appraiser must not consider the demand for the gravel in the before situation because the demand was created by the project itself and is therefore project enhancement.

Scope of the Project Rule

In addressing enhancement and blight, as well as highest and best use and value, the appraiser must adhere to the scope of the project rule. The scope of the project rule essentially holds that the effects of a proposed project *cannot* be considered in valuing a property to be acquired for the project when it was clear that the parcel under appraisal would, or probably would, be acquired in whole or in part for the project. Conversely, the effects of a project on a parcel under appraisal *must* be considered when the parcel was not included in the area to be acquired for the initial project, but the project is later expanded to include acquisition of the parcel in whole or in part for the expanded project. The scope of the project rule can best be demonstrated by analysis of an actual case.

United States v. Miller[41] concerned the construction of the Shasta Dam and Reservoir in northern California. Congress authorized the project in 1937 and property values escalated in proximity of the proposed project. Alternative routes for the relocation of a railroad right-of-way that would be flooded by construction of the dam and reservoir were surveyed and staked in 1936. One of these routes passed through the Miller property. The federal district court ruled that the appraisers had to estimate the value of the property excluding any enhancement in value from the proposed project after its date of authorization in 1937. The Supreme Court upheld the lower court, stating:

> If a distinct tract is condemned, in whole or in part, other lands in the neighborhood may increase in market value due to the proximity of the public improvement erected on the land taken. Should the Government, at a later date, determine to take these other lands, it must pay their market value as enhanced by this factor of proximity. If however, the public project from the beginning included the taking of certain tracts but only one of them is taken in the first instance, the owner of the other tracts should not be allowed an increased value for his lands which are ultimately to be taken....
>
> The question then is whether the respondent's lands were probably within the scope of the project from the time the Government was committed to it. If they were not, but were merely adjacent lands, the subsequent enlargement of the project to include them ought not to deprive the respondents of the value added in the meantime by the proximity of the improvement. If, on the other hand, they were, the Government ought not to pay any increase in value arising from the known fact that the lands probably would be condemned....
>
> If [the lands] were within the area where they were likely to be taken for the project, but might not be, the owners were not entitled, if [the lands] were ultimately taken, to an increment of value calculated on the theory that if they had not been taken they would have been more valuable by reason of their proximity to the land taken.[42]

Application of the scope of the project rule can be difficult. The two most problematic questions that arise are: When was the government committed to the project? Was it probable that the parcel under appraisal would be acquired, in whole or in part, for the project? As one court stated:

41. *United States v. Miller*, 317 U.S. 369 (1943).

42. Ibid., at 376–377, 379.

> As with any test that deals in probabilities, its application to any particular set of facts requires discriminating judgment. The rule does not require a showing that the land ultimately taken was actually specified in the original plans for the project. It need only be shown that during the course of the planning or original construction it became evident that land so situated would probably be needed for the public use.[43]

In the same case it was noted at page 18 that in the federal courts "it is for the judge and not the jury to decide whether the property condemned was probably within the project's original scope." Thus it may be advisable to obtain a ruling from the court in this regard prior to trial. "If there is any real question whether the property under appraisement meets the 'scope of the project' test, the appraiser should confer...with the responsible trial attorney."[44]

It is also possible that a property under appraisal could be subject to two takings at, or near, the same time for two different projects or for different elements of a joint project. For example, consider the situation depicted in Figure 6.2. Taking A is for the construction of a dam and reservoir, which will flood the state highway that serves much of the remainder property. This acquisition is being funded by the state. Taking B is for the construction of a new highway. The acquisition of property for this new highway right-of-way is being funded by the federal government. The acquisitions for both projects will be made by the state. From an appraiser's standpoint, the most logical approach to this valuation problem would be to treat the two projects as one. This, however, would require agreement between the condemnee and the condemnor, which is not always possible. Even if such an agreement can be reached, it may be necessary for the appraisers, or at least the condemnor's appraiser, to allocate the total compensation between the two projects because of their different funding.

Even if the two projects must be viewed independently, the appraiser's approach to the appraisal problem must not be unreasonable. In this case it would not be reasonable to estimate the value of the property remaining after Taking A as if the remainder would be without access forever. Nor would it be reasonable to claim that the value of the taking and damages caused by Taking B would be totally offset by the benefits of the new highway because, without it, the property would have inadequate access. The only reasonable approach would be for the appraiser, when valuing the property in conjunction with Taking A, to estimate the property's after value in light of the *probability* that Taking B will occur and that the new highway will be constructed. In appraising the property in conjunction with Taking B, the appraiser would estimate the after value of the remainder in light of the *probability* of Taking A and the probable construction of the dam and reservoir. If the probability of both projects coming to fruition is at, or near, 100%, there would be little or no difference in the total compensation due the owner if the projects were treated as one consolidated project or two separate projects.

43. *United States v. Reynolds*, 397 U.S. 14, 18 (1970).

44. *Uniform Appraisal Standards for Federal Land Acquisitions*, §A-10, pp. 27-28.

In such a situation, a determination must be made as to which of the two takings will occur first. The dates of takings for the two projects, if they differ, will decide this matter. If the two takings are simultaneous, the appraiser will have to determine which is to be considered first. When the appraiser has been retained by the condemnor, it is probable that the condemnor will instruct the appraiser as to which taking to consider first; in that way the condemnor can have some control over the attribution of damages. For instance, if it is found that the remainder area identified in Figure 6.2 as "isolated lands" is damaged due to the isolation, the condemnor (the state) would probably instruct its appraiser to treat Taking B as the second taking. Then the damages attributable to the isolation would be chargeable against Taking B, which is being funded by the federal government, rather than against the acquisition cost of Taking A, which is state funded.

FIGURE 6.2 SIMULTANEOUS TAKINGS

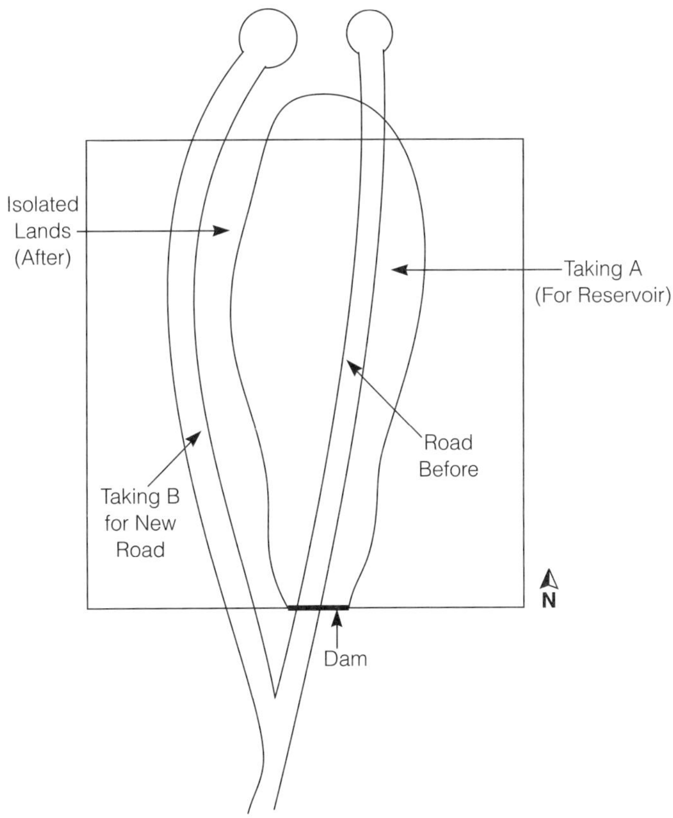

There is some precedence for this approach. In 1978 the Washington Metropolitan Area Transit Authority (WMATA), as part of its expansion of the Washington area subway system, decided that it would acquire land from Old Georgetown for the construction of a parking lot to serve transit system users. As a part of that decision, Montgomery County agreed to extend roads into the parking lot; these road extensions required the acquisition of a portion of Old Georgetown's property. The county acquired the new right-of-way from Old Georgetown by negotiation. The remainder of Old Georgetown's property was split into three tracts by the county's acquisitions. When WMATA condemned 2.52 acres of Old Georgetown's property, it claimed that compensation for the taking was nominal because the remainder of Old Georgetown's property was specially benefitted by its proximity to the transit facility. Old Georgetown claimed that the 2.52 acres formed a separate larger parcel because it was severed from the balance of its ownership by the rights-of-way acquired by the county, and there was no contiguity or unity of use between the parcels. The court found that the entire ownership constituted a single larger parcel, stating:

> We think that the impact of the planned road extensions should not be taken into account, and therefore that there is a potential unity of use between the taken land and the retained land. If, with no advance warning, the same governmental entity has simultaneously condemned both the 2.6 acres needed for the rights-of-way for the planned road extensions and the 2.52 acres needed for the parking lot, there would be no doubt that the compensation should be reduced by the amount of the special benefit to be conferred, and increased by the amount of the damage to be inflicted, by the taking on the land retained by the landowner. We think for practical purposes that this is that case. Both takings—the taking of land for the rights-of-way, achieved by purchase rather than condemnation, and the taking for the parking lot—were for the same basic purpose—the extension of the Washington mass transit system into the surrounding area in Maryland. The final decisions to take both were reached contemporaneously, if not simultaneously, in 1978. Both takings were contemporaneous with each other. The only distinction between this case and that posited is that in the instant case, the acquiring authorities were two separate governmental entities. Yet they were working in a cooperative effort to accomplish a single objective so that we think the distinction is without real difference. Stated otherwise, we do not think that there should be a different result in the present case simply because it was necessary that the mass transit project be undertaken by an alliance of various governmental entities formulating, announcing and carrying out their plans at different speeds.[45]

As with the scope of the project rule, the appraiser is well advised to seek legal advice if the property under appraisal is subject to contemporaneous takings.

45. *Washington Metropolitan Area v. One Parcel of Land*, 691 F.2d 702, 705 (4th Cir. 1982).

ADVANCED PROBLEMS

ASSEMBLAGE

At times appraisers conclude that the highest and best use of a specific parcel of land is to assemble it with other ownerships. Historically, definitions of highest and best use have included the provision that "if the intended use is dependent on an uncertain act of another person, the intention cannot be considered."[46] This provision is considered overly restrictive in some jurisdictions. The courts have generally reverted back to *reasonable probability* in such instances. One court stated:

> Proof of use of lands in combination with other lands [not owned by the condemnee] is not excluded from [consideration in] a condemnation case, "if the possibility of such connection is reasonably sufficient to affect market value."
>
> This is part of the question of the highest and best use. "Value may be determined in light of the special or higher use of the land when combined with other parcels."
>
> It is elemental that the burden of proof of the highest and best use contended by the defendant-landowners, as well as the burden of proof of fair market value is upon the defendant-landowners. Accordingly, if they contend for a use involving utilization or combination with other lands they have the burden of showing "the reasonable probability" of such use.[47] [Citations omitted]

When assemblage is considered, the appraiser must be cautious in writing the appraisal report and in testifying because the question of *reasonable probability* is generally considered a preliminary question for the court, not a question for the appraiser. In the case quoted above, the court went on to say:

> In determining the question of law as to whether a sufficient showing is made of the "reasonable probability" the court will want to hear *facts* and not some expert's ultimate opinion about the very problem the court is to decide. An expert, of course, may be used to present factual matters. Nor are we stating that expert testimony may not be offered on technical problems such as the adequacy of a sewer line. What we are stating is that we will not hear experts give their opinion that there is or is not the required "reasonable probability."[48]

The fact that the appraiser can consider the probability of assemblage in estimating highest and best use introduces some interesting valuation problems. First, the appraiser cannot assume that the assemblage has occurred in estimating the value of the property under appraisal. Only the *probability* of such an assemblage can be considered. Therefore, the estimated value of the property has to be something less than it would be if it were part of an assembled tract. Second, the appraiser must address which property is to be the beneficiary of the plottage factor.

46. *Appraisal Terminology and Handbook*, 4th ed. (Chicago: American Institute of Real Estate Appraisers, 1962), 92.

47. *United States v. 70.39 Acres of Land*, 164 F.Supp. 451, 476 (S.D. Cal. 1958).

48. Ibid.

For example, consider two parcels (A and B), each with 12,000 square feet of area. Each parcel would have a value of $5.00 per square foot individually, but if they were assembled under one ownership they would have a higher and better use and a value of $8.00 per square foot.

Forgetting for a moment the discount in value that must be applied because the tracts are not, in fact, assembled, there are several arguments that can be made regarding how Parcel A and Parcel B should be valued. From the condemnor's viewpoint it could be argued that Parcel A is not, in fact, assembled and that if the owner of Parcel B wanted to acquire Parcel A for purposes of assemblage he or she would pay no more than the market value of Parcel A as a separate entity. On the other hand, the condemnee might take the position that if Parcel B has a value of only $5.00 per square foot, or $60,000 (12,000 x $5.00) as a separate entity and the total value of the tracts if assembled would be $192,000 (24,000 sq. ft. x $8.00), Parcel A must be worth $132,000 ($192,000 – $60,000). Of course, neither of these positions is reasonable.

To value the parcels accurately the appraiser would probably have to know, or assume, who the assembler would be—the owner of Parcel A or the owner of Parcel B? Of course, working in the hypothetical field of eminent domain valuation, the answer to this question can never be determined with any degree of certainty. Therefore, the only practical solution is for the appraiser to allocate the beneficial effect of the plottage over both of the tracts that are to be assembled on a pro rata basis. To do otherwise would indicate appraiser advocacy and result in an unjust award for either the condemnor or condemnee.

To illustrate the condemnor's and the condemnee's positions, assume that both Parcels A and B are being condemned. If the condemnor's argument were accepted by the trier of fact, total compensation for both parcels would be $120,000. If the condemnee's argument were accepted, the total compensation paid would be $264,000. Neither of these results is reasonable. The only reasonable solution is for the condemnor to pay total compensation of $192,000, less a discount for the fact that the two tracts are not, if fact, assembled.

To make and support an adjustment for the probability of an assemblage is most difficult. As the number of parcels in the anticipated assemblage increases, the amount of risk, and thus the amount of discount, tends to increase. The appraiser can ask the owner of Parcel A, "If this condemnation action had not been pending for 3 years, do you think that you and the owner of Parcel B would have assembled your ownerships?" but an objective response cannot be expected. The property owner has been negotiating with the government for the sale of his land for 3 years. With substantial money at stake, his answer is obviously going to be the one that is to his economic advantage.

An appraiser can attempt to develop some indication of an appropriate probability of assemblage discount by thoroughly investigating similar land assemblages and interviewing the parties involved. If other parcels of land have been assembled and resold, the price differential between the assembler's cost of the assemblage and the resale price of the assembled parcel can give some indication of the profit such land assemblers demand in the marketplace. Interviews with the assembler are essential. What the assembler wanted, or anticipated, as a profit before the assemblage began may be entirely different from the profit actually realized. It is the former that is important to the appraiser. Because land assemblages are seldom similar in the types of land, the number of parcels to be assembled, and the value increment created by the plottage, however, the proper adjustment is often up to the judgment of the appraiser. In any case, the adjustment must be well reasoned and thoroughly explained in the appraisal report.

One other factor must be considered in the assemblage of grazing land.

> A ranch owner is not entitled to compensation for any value added to fee lands as a result of their actual or potential use in combination with Taylor Grazing Act permit lands, as these permits to use the public domain for grazing are revocable and create no property rights in the holder (n. 193; *United States v. Fuller*, 409 U.S. 488 (1973)). To require the United States to pay for this value would be to create private claims in the public domain. This same principle should apply to situations involving federal grazing permit lands held under permit authority other than the Taylor Grazing Act, where the permit is revocable and creates no property rights in the holder, such as permits issued by the U.S. Forest Service under 16 U.S.C. 580(L), for example.[49]

However, value added to fee land as a result of their actual or potential use in combination with grazing permits issued from parties other than the federal government can be considered in valuing the fee land for federal condemnation purposes.[50]

UNDIVIDED FEE RULE

In estimating highest and best use, appraisers are typically advised to consider the legal restrictions on the property being appraised, including private limitations such as deed restrictions and leases.[51] Highest and best use estimation for eminent domain is different from other types of appraisal analysis in this regard because of the *undivided fee*, or *unit*, rule. (This rule was introduced in Chapter 4.) "[T]he unit rule requires valuing property as a whole rather than by the sum of the values of the various interests into which it may have been carved, such as lessor and lessee, life tenant and remainderman, etc.. This is an application of the principle that it is the property, not the various titles, which is being taken."[52] Because the various estates in the property must be disregarded in the valuation process, they must also be disregarded in estimating the property's highest and best use.

This can lead to some rather unique results. For example, assume that a 20,000-sq. ft. site with a highest and best use for an office building would have a value of $100 per square foot, or $2,000,000, for this use. However, the property is under a long-term lease, with 15 years remaining, for specific and restricted use as a parking lot. The rental specified in the lease is $40,000 per year, net to the

49. *Uniform Appraisal Standards for Federal Land Acquisitions*, §A-24, p. 62.
50. *United States v. 27,223.21 Acres of Land, Las Animas County*, 589 F. Supp. 1121 (Colo. 1984).
51. *The Appraisal of Real Estate*, 10th ed., 280–281.
52. *Uniform Appraisal Standards for Federal Land Acquisitions*, §A-13, p. 39.

lessor, which is equivalent to the economic, or market, rent for the land for parking lot purposes. Therefore, the lessee's interest in the property is neither positive nor negative. In a typical appraisal assignment, the appraiser might conclude that 10% is an appropriate rate to be applied to the lessor's interest and that the value of the leased fee could be computed as follows:

Value of income stream ($40,000 x 7.606080)*	$304,243
Value of reversion ($2,000,000 x 0.239392)†	478,784
Total value of leased fee estate	$783,027

* Present worth of $1 per period for 15 years discounted at 10%.

† Present worth of $1 in 15 years discounted at 10% per annum.

Thus, the value of the lessor's interest plus the value of the lessee's interest in the property would be $783,027 ($783,027 + $0). (The value of these interests could change if there was *reasonable probability* that the lessor could buy out the lessee's interest in the property.)

Under the *unit rule* applicable in eminent domain valuation, however, the condemnor must pay the market value of the undivided fee interest in the property, which is $2,000,000. The allocation of condemnation awards between lessors and lessees is discussed in Chapter 17.

An opposite situation could also result. Consider a parcel that is leased for $60,000 per year, but has a market, or economic, rent of only $40,000 per year. The value of the property under the undivided fee rule would be based on its market rent of $40,000; the contract rent of $60,000 would have no influence on the property's market value.

CONTAMINATED PROPERTY

Highest and best use estimation has been further complicated by the recent adoption of environmental regulations concerning hazardous waste. In the analysis of a site, the appraiser must make a reasonable effort to determine whether it is contaminated and, if so, the impact of that contamination on the property's highest and best use and value.[53]

Disregarding the contamination issue, an appraiser might make the following highest and best use analysis of a property under appraisal:

Highest and best use, if vacant	Office building
Value of site as if vacant	$300,000
Demolition cost of building	– 45,000
As is value of site for office building	$255,000
Value as improved with industrial building	$175,000

From these calculations, the appraiser would conclude that the highest and best use of the property would be to demolish the industrial building and convert the site to office building use.

53. *Uniform Appraisal Standards for Federal Land Acquisitions*, §B-1 - 13a, fn. 206, p. 70.

However, if the site or building were contaminated, the cost of cleaning up the site to make it suitable for office building purposes might change the highest and best use of the property. For example, assume that the industrial building is contaminated with asbestos. Then the highest and best use analysis might be:

Highest and best use, if vacant	Office building
Value of site as if vacant	$300,000
Demolition cost of building (including asbestos removal)	-190,000
As is value of site for office building	$110,000
Value as improved with contaminated industrial building	$145,000

Under these circumstances, the highest and best use of the property would be for its continued use as improved. This situation could occur if the asbestos in the building were nonfriable and the industrial building could continue to function in its existing condition. The cost of the asbestos removal would be delayed, and therefore discounted to present value.

Some environmental agencies have established different standards of clean-up of sites, depending upon their intended use. The problem then becomes, *how clean is clean?* The existence of such regulations can also have an impact on highest and best use. A site located in an industrial area may have a highest and best use, if clean, as a day-care facility to accommodate the children of industrial workers in the area. However, the standards for cleaning up the site for day-care use may be so much stricter than the standards for use as an industrial site that the highest and best use of the site may be for industrial purposes when the comparative costs of cleanup are considered.

SUMMARY

Highest and best use is the most profitable, likely use to which a property can be put. The appraiser's estimate of highest and best use is an integral part of the appraisal process because, without an accurate estimate, the appraiser cannot accurately estimate the market value of the property being appraised. In appraising a property subject to a partial acquisition, two independent highest and best use estimates are made—one in the before situation and one in the after situation.

Many definitions of highest and best use have been promulgated over the years. The appraiser must take care to use the definition applicable in the specific jurisdiction where the property being appraised is located. The courts have adopted economic highest and best use definitions exclusively, rejecting noneconomic definitions and the considerations of community development goals.

The highest and best use of a site as though vacant may be different from the highest and best use of the property as improved. In such instances, the appraiser may wish to include two sets of computations: the classic appraisal computations, which reflect the obsolescence present in the improvements due to their lack of conformity to the highest and best use of the land as though vacant, and another set computing the land value for the property's highest and best use as improved.

Most courts have held that a property should be valued for *all available uses*, rather than for a specific use. This concept in not in conflict with the appraiser's interpretation of highest and best use. Rather, it is an attempt on the part of the courts to eliminate the possibility that the trier of fact will add together the values of the property for several specific uses to arrive at a conclusion of just compensation.

It is improper to value the land for one use and the improvements for another. This practice violates the consistent use theory and has been soundly rejected by the courts. Several methods can be used to estimate the value of improvements on properties that are in transition from one use to another. The appraiser should be familiar with all applicable procedures and adopt the methodology that best reflects the actions of buyer and sellers in the market.

As a general rule, an estimate of market value should

> not include an increase or decrease in value before the date of valuation that is caused by (1) the proposed improvement or project for which the property is taken; (2) the reasonable likelihood that the property would be acquired for the improvement or project; or (3) the condemnation action in which the property is taken.[54]

Because there are some exceptions to this general rule, the appraiser must confirm which rule is applicable in the specific jurisdiction.

A change in the highest and best use of a property immediately before the announcement of a public project and the date of valuation may indicate that condemnation blight or project enhancement has occurred. It is sometimes difficult to make a conclusive determination in this regard. Appraisers often reach different conclusions concerning the existence of condemnation blight and/or project enhancement, and this determination can have a material impact on their value estimates.

In estimating a property's highest and best use, the appraiser may usually consider the probability of assembling the property with lands owned by others if such probability affects the current market value of the property being appraised.

The appraiser must follow the undivided fee, or unit, rule in estimating the highest and best use of property in an eminent domain valuation. Private land use restrictions, leases, and other divisions of the fee simple estate are to be disregarded.

In estimating highest of best use, appraisers must consider the impact of environmental regulations and land use regulations that affect the utility of the property. The presence of hazardous materials on a site and the regulations governing its removal may have a bearing on the property's highest and best use.

It is implicit in all definitions of highest and best use that the use must be legal. Any estimate of highest and best use must be reasonably probable on the

54. *Uniform Eminent Domain Code*, 1974. §1005, p. 10.9.

date of the appraisal or in the reasonably near future. There is a presumption in eminent domain cases that the existing use of a property is its highest and best use. The burden of proving that the highest and best use of a property is something other than its existing use is upon the party advocating the different use. An estimate of highest and best use cannot be remote, speculative, or conjectural in nature. The key to determining whether a specific highest and best use can be considered by the appraiser is whether the potential for that use has an effect on the property's market value as of the effective date of the appraisal. If the potential use of the property has a recognized effect in the marketplace, the appraiser not only may, but must, acknowledge that effect and consider it in estimating market value.

CHAPTER 7

Land Use Regulations

A property's highest and best use must be a *legal use*, so zoning and other land use regulations are of utmost importance in determining highest and best use and estimating value. Market value is not inherent in the tangible real estate; value flows from the utility the real estate offers. Thus, it can be said that market value is nothing more than a measure of utility.

Value is created by utility, scarcity, demand, and purchasing power, all of which are influenced by zoning and other land use regulations. It is imperative that the appraiser be completely familiar with the applicable land use regulations and their impact on the utility, and therefore value, of the property under appraisal. Land use regulations are part of the sovereign's police power and, over the past few years, they have multiplied almost geometrically. A partial list of land use regulations follows:

- Building codes, including structural codes, fire codes, electrical codes, plumbing codes, health codes, and earthquake codes
- Comprehensive plans
- Zoning ordinances
- Off-street parking ordinances
- Mining regulations
- Development moratoriums
- Environmental impact statement regulations
- Shorelines management ordinances

- Floodplain management ordinances
- Platting ordinances
- Shortplat ordinances
- Open space ordinances
- Rent controls
- Timber harvesting controls
- Air, water, and noise pollution controls
- Wetlands regulations
- Endangered species regulations
- Solid waste ordinances

Because some of these land use ordinances are quite recent, the courts have not yet addressed their impact on properties subject to eminent domain proceedings. However, those few cases involving environmental permits that have been reported indicate the impact of these additional requirements on market value will be treated in an appraisal in much the same way as more classic land use regulations such as zoning. Some jurisdictions have ruled that a land use designated in a comprehensive plan takes precedence over the land use designated in a zoning ordinance if there is a conflict between the two. Historically, however, comprehensive plans have been considered planning tools rather than enforceable ordinances. Some municipalities have denied development permits based on their comprehensive plans, even though they have no ordinances to implement the plan.

It is becoming increasingly complicated and risky to obtain all but the most basic development permits, so most recent land sales have been contingent on the purchaser's ability to obtain the permits needed to proceed with the contemplated development. This trend has added a new dimension to the appraisal of developable land in eminent domain proceedings.

Typically, the sale of a developable tract of land is closed only after the purchaser has procured all necessary permits for development. Thus, the purchaser incurs no risk as to whether development permits will be available. But a property being appraised for eminent domain purposes is without any development permits and is, therefore, in a different economic position than the typical sale property. Developable land sales without "subject to procurement of permits" clauses are often unavailable, so the appraiser must adjust the price of any comparable sale property to reflect its superior economic position, as of the date of closing, compared to the property being appraised.

In analyzing comparable sales, it is important for the appraiser to determine the date when an agreement was reached between the buyer and the seller. Sales of this nature often do not close and become a matter of public record until months, and even years, after the buyer and seller have agreed on the price and the other terms of the sale. By the time it is recorded, the sale may actually be several months old and the appraiser must consider an adjustment for its date of sale.

Due to the complexity of the development permit process, some investor/developers who acquire raw land by purchase or option are processing all necessary development permits to approval and then reselling the land. They make a profit, not on the actual development, but on the incremental value produced by the existence of the development permits. An analysis of such sales and resales can help the appraiser determine the proper adjustment to make when comparing properties sold *subject to the procurement of permits* with properties sold (or appraised) without permits or such clauses.

Each additional permit required to develop a tract of land to its physical and economic highest and best use increases the risk that the site cannot be developed for that use. Potential purchasers in the marketplace consider this added risk in determining the price they are willing to pay for the land. When the risk increases, the potential purchaser wants a greater return, which often results in a diminution of raw land value. The land's physical limitations are set by nature, but land use regulations are written and interpreted by individuals. They can be revised, but many individuals tend to resist change. In some cases regulations that define the legally permitted uses of property may seem irrational to the appraiser, but they are the law within which the real estate market must function and within which the appraiser must estimate value. They cannot be ignored simply because the appraiser disagrees with them or because they do not serve the client's interest. "The concept of highest and best use is applicable in determining fair market value in appropriation cases. It is not a concept to be considered in determining the constitutionality of a zoning ordinance."[1]

In recent years, property rights advocates have made some inroads against the overregulation of land use. However, it has generally been held that a condemnation trial is not the proper forum for challenging a land use regulation.[2] As discussed in Chapter 17, such challenges are generally conducted by separate action.

NONCONFORMING USE

Some properties are classified as pre-existing nonconforming uses under existing zoning. This situation can result when the improvement of a property predates the applicable zoning ordinance or when the ordinance has been changed since the improvements were constructed. A nonconforming use is defined as:

> A structure the size, dimension or location of which was lawful prior to the adoption, revision, or amendment of a zoning ordinance, but now fails to conform to the requirements of the zoning district in which it is located by reasons of such adoption, revision or amendment. A use which does not comply with present zoning provisions but which existed lawfully and was created in good faith prior to the enactment of the zoning provision.
>
> Uses permitted by zoning statutes or ordinances to continue notwithstanding that similar uses are no longer permitted in area in which they are located.[3]

1. *Flair Corp. v. City of Brecksville*, 359 N.E.2d 459, 466 (Ohio 1976).
2. *Robinson v. Commonwealth*, 141 N.E.2d 727 (Mass. 1957).
3. *Black's Law Dictionary*, abr. 6th ed., s.v. "nonconforming use."

Zoning nonconformity may have a detrimental or beneficial effect on a property's market value. If a nonconforming use exists on the property being appraised, the appraiser must extensively investigate and analyze the specific ordinance provisions governing nonconforming uses and determine how the nonconformity affects the market value of the property.

Some zoning ordinances require that a nonconforming use be terminated when the property is sold or transferred. Others preclude the use of the property for a nonconforming activity if it has been vacant for a specific period of time—e.g., one year. Some ordinances preclude the enlargement or repair of a nonconforming use and may not allow the improvement to be rebuilt if it is even partially destroyed by a disaster such as a fire or flood. For example, in some jurisdictions the owner of a property valued at $100,000 would be unable to restore the improvement if it were 50% destroyed by fire. He might receive an insurance settlement for the physical loss sustained, but would not be able to recover the additional loss of market value. A provision that forbids the repair or structural alteration of nonconforming improvements will often decrease the remaining economic life of the improvements. Some ordinances provide for an automatic phasing out, or amortization, of nonconforming uses, which establishes the maximum economic life of the nonconforming use.[4]

The appraiser must analyze these factors to determine whether they have any effect on the market value of the nonconforming property being appraised. In verifying sales of nonconforming properties, it is important for the appraiser to establish whether the buyer was aware of the nonconformity at the time of purchase and, if so, whether he or she understood the implications of the nonconformity. If a value penalty or benefit due to the nonconformity is reflected in the market, the appraiser must reflect it in the estimate of value.[5] If, on the other hand, market analysis indicates that no change in market value can be attributed to the nonconformity, the appraiser must report this fact too. The appraiser cannot report a value differential merely because he or she believes there should be one.

In addition to determining whether a nonconforming use exists prior to an acquisition under the power of eminent domain, the appraiser should recognize that a partial acquisition may result in the remainder property becoming a nonconforming use. If this is the case, the appraiser must make the same type of investigation and analysis outlined above in the after situation. The definition of nonconforming use presented earlier relates only to uses that predate the zoning ordinance, not to uses that became nonconforming after the effective date of the ordinance. For this reason, the appraiser will have to make a specific determination as to how the zoning authority will treat the post-ordinance nonconforming use. Because such post-ordinance nonconforming uses are not supposed to exist, there may be no provision for their treatment in the zoning ordinance. The appraiser will have to assess the options available to the owner of such a property, e.g., the probability of obtaining a variance to the ordinance.

Some zoning ordinances provide that a property that becomes nonconforming due to a partial acquisition by a governmental agency will continue to be

4. William R. Theiss, ed., "The Appraisal Docket," *The Appraisal Journal* (January 1966), 123.

5. *Gebrian v. Bristol Redevelopment Agency*, 370 A.2d 1055 (Conn. 1976).

treated as a conforming use. In this instance, the appraiser need not be concerned with the penalty provisions for nonconforming uses within the ordinance, e.g., the inability to renovate or rebuild if the improvements are destroyed by fire. The appraiser need only be concerned with the property's physical nonconformity to surrounding properties and its potential effect on value, not with the any legal nonconformity.

A property can benefit from a pre-existing nonconformity, particularly in regard to density and occupancy. For example, consider a 6,000-sq.-ft. site improved with a 10-unit apartment structure. The property is now subject to a zoning ordinance that requires 1,000 square feet of land area for each dwelling unit. Vacant land in the neighborhood under the same zone classification is selling for $8,000 per allowable unit. However, other land that is similar to the site being appraised, but subject to zoning that requires only 600 square feet of land area per unit, is selling for $6,000 per allowable unit. Based on these data, it appears that the subject site enjoys a value enhancement, or bonus, due to its nonconformity.

Value of site as nonconforming use (10 units @ $6,000)	$60,000
Value of site as though vacant (6 units @ $8,000)	48,000
Value enhancement due to pre-existing nonconformity	$12,000

Note that this value bonus is created by the existence of the building, not because of some special characteristic of the land. Therefore, under classic appraisal methodology, the bonus is attributable to the building; the land value for its highest and best use as though vacant remains at $48,000. As demonstrated in Chapter 6, however, the appraiser may find it advisable under certain circumstances to value the land for its existing use rather than its highest and best use as though vacant. "The appraiser may find it helpful to allocate value separately to the nonconforming improvements and the bonus created by the nonconforming use."[6] The courts have recognized and approved consideration of an increment in value created by a nonconforming use.[7]

VARIANCES

Most zoning ordinances provide for variances, or special-use permits, in some instances. These variances may, for example, reduce setback requirements, allow a preschool facility to locate in a residential area, or modify building density requirements. A *zoning variance* is:

> A legally authorized modification in the use of property at a particular location that does not conform to the regulated use set forth in the zoning ordinance for the surrounding area; not an exception or change in the legally applicable zoning.[8]

6. *The Appraisal of Real Estate*, 10th ed. (Chicago: Appraisal Institute, 1992), 292. See also George A. Cuddleback, "Allocating Added Value from Nonconforming Uses," *The Appraisal Journal* (October 1989), 492–497.

7. *Gebrian v. Bristol Redev. Agency*, 370 A.2d 1055 (Conn. 1976).

8. *The Appraisal of Real Estate*, 10th ed., 330.

To consider the variance's effect on property value, the appraiser must confirm that the variance is transferable and runs with the land, rather than the owner of the land. It is generally the market value of the property that is to be estimated, not the value of the property for a specific use or to a specific user. If the variance is nontransferable, legal counsel should be consulted to determine the advisability of preparing a dual-premise appraisal to estimate the market value and the value in use of the property. This latter value estimate can usually be made by simply assuming that the variance would be transferable to a new buyer of the property. A dual-premise appraisal should not be undertaken without written legal instruction. It is then up to legal counsel to convince the court of the appropriate measure of just compensation, given the facts of the case.

The possible impact on value attributable to an existing variance is analyzed and assessed in the same way that a nonconformity's effects are investigated. In the case of a partial acquisition, the appraiser must determine whether a variance will automatically be extinguished or continued. On some occasions it will be necessary to obtain a variance to develop the remainder land to its highest and best use. In such a case, the appraiser must determine whether there is a reasonable probability of obtaining the variance and what effect this probability may have on the market value of the remainder parcel. Care must be exercised, however, because many zoning ordinances provide for variances for new construction only. They make no provision to allow a variance for a nonconformity that occurs after initial construction, which may be the case in a partial acquisition.

ZONING IN ANTICIPATION OF A PROJECT

It has generally been held to be improper for a government entity to zone or refuse to rezone a property in an attempt to depress the property's value so it can be acquired for a lower price in a future eminent domain proceeding. "Where the real purpose of the enactment [of an ordinance] was to depress or limit property values in order to minimize the costs of acquisition of such property in anticipated condemnation proceedings the courts have not been reluctant to declare such ordinances unconstitutional and void."[9] "Zoning cannot be used as a substitute for eminent domain proceedings to defeat the payment of just compensation by depressing values and so reducing the amount of damages to be paid when private property is to be taken for public use."[10]

In fact, it has been ruled that any government action or inaction intended solely to depress the value of property to be condemned is improper.

> An easement, which otherwise would have been extinguished upon request of the landowner, may not be used by a government to diminish the value of the fee simple interest in the land in order to allow that government or other public agency to acquire said fee simple interest by eminent domain at a lesser cost for a purpose entirely different from that for which the easement originally existed.

9. *Dept. of Public Works & Bldgs. v. Exchange Nat'l. Bank*, 334 N.E.2d 810, 819 (Ill. 1975).

10. *Symonds v. Bucklin*, 197 F.Supp. 682, 685 (D. Md. 1961).

> Such action would be an abuse of governmental authority, resulting in a denial of due process, no different in principal [sic] than using the zoning process for the purpose of depressing values in eminent domain proceedings."[11]

It is incumbent upon the appraiser to investigate any government action concerning the allowable uses of the property being appraised that occurred within a reasonable length of time preceding the condemnation action. The period of time to be investigated will depend on how long the project for which the property is being acquired has been contemplated. Interviews with the property owner can help determine whether there has been any change in zoning or any refusal to rezone by the government. If a hearing on rezoning the property has been held, the appraiser must review the minutes of the hearing and establish the reasons for any legislative action taken.

If the appraiser concludes that a zoning action was taken in anticipation of the property's acquisition by a government body, this fact must be considered in the estimates of highest and best use and market value. The appraiser may reach one of three conclusions:

1. The action taken would have been the same if the acquisition were not pending.
2. There is a reasonable probability that the action taken would have been different if an acquisition were not anticipated.
3. The action taken would definitely have been different had there been no anticipation of an acquisition.

If it is concluded that the action would have been the same with or without the anticipated acquisition, the appraiser need only report the zoning activity. If, however, the appraiser concludes that the zoning action was affected, or there is a reasonable probability that it was affected, by the anticipated acquisition of the property in question, the matter must be specifically addressed in the appraisal report. If the action has had a depressing effect on the property's value, this effect must be disregarded.

At times the record so clearly indicates that the condemning agency has taken a zoning action, or influenced a zoning action by another governmental entity, because of the pending acquisition of property that it can be concluded that, except for the pending acquisition, the action would have been different. For example, in one case the appraiser discovered that the state department of transportation had sent a letter to a county planning commission which included the following statements:

> ...we feel that if this change in zoning was approved, it would increase the value of the property and represent an undue expenditure of public funds.
>
> We would like to urge that the planning commission refuse this zone change in light of the forthcoming purchase.

11. *Washington Metropolitan Area Transit Authority v. One Parcel of Land*, 413 F.Supp. 102, 106 (D. Md. 1976).

In this case the appraiser refused to accept a legal instruction from his condemnor-client that he appraise the property under its current zoning. The appraiser found this instruction to be unreasonable and unsupported and included the following statement in his appraisal report:

> It is specifically called to the client's attention that Subject has been appraised as if it had been rezoned to general manufacturing on [the date of the planning commission hearing]—not as if a reasonable probability exists for such rezoning as of the effective date of this appraisal.

The appraiser concluded that the property would have been rezoned had it not been for the state's interference with the zoning application and the planning commission's improper consideration of how the rezoning would affect the cost of acquisition of the property by the state. Under these circumstances, the appraiser's approach was warranted.

Most active condemnors are aware of the hazards of interfering with requests to rezone property they plan to acquire and do not interfere with such requests, or at least show a greater degree of subtlety in their dealings. Appraisers should also be aware that an opposite situation has been known to occur—i.e., a property is rezoned for a higher use at the request of the property owner and the planning commission agrees with the rezoning for the specific purpose of assisting the property owner to achieve a larger award. This type of scenario generally occurs in smaller communities and is referred to by some condemnors as being *home-towned*.

An appraiser who encounters zoning actions that were taken in response to pending governmental acquisition of the property under appraisal is well advised to seek appropriate legal counsel before preparing an appraisal report. There are some legal intricacies that need to be addressed in such situations. For instance, a California court ruled:

> The distinction between the governmental entity imposing the improper restrictions in the guise of zoning and the governmental unit taking property for which the constitution demands it pay just compensation creates the critical problem in case at bench. A zoning restriction imposed to depress value with a view to future eminent domain proceedings itself creates a cause of action in inverse condemnation against the governmental unit enacting the zoning ordinance.[12] [Citations omitted]

In establishing this rule, however, the court limited its applicability to instances in which the condemnor and the zoning authority were the same government entity.

It is not improper for a zoning authority to base its decisions, in part, on a proposed project that will involve government acquisition of real estate. It is improper, however, for the zoning authority to take action purposefully to depress the value of the property to be acquired. Zoning agencies cannot be estopped from incorporating consideration of proposed public projects into their

12. *People, Dep't of Public Works v. Southern Pacific Transp. Co.*, 109 Cal. Rptr. 525, 528–529 (Cal. 1973).

planning and land use documents. However, if the zoning authority takes action, the proximate cause of which is the proposed public project, the appraiser must disregard the zoning action in appraising the property in the before situation. On the other hand, if the eminent domain proceedings involve only a partial acquisition, the appraiser must consider the zoning action in estimating the value of the property in the after situation.

For example, consider the partial taking shown in Figure 7.1. The property consisted of 50 acres of land before the taking and was zoned for its highest and best use for single-family residential development. The condemnor proposed acquisition of 20 acres of the property for the construction of a new, limited-access highway. The county planning commission rezoned the property for multifamily residential use, primarily so that the remaining area could act as a buffer zone between the proposed highway and the surrounding single-family residential areas. Thus, after the rezoning the subject property had a highest and best use for multifamily residential use.

FIGURE 7.1 REZONING DUE TO PENDING PUBLIC PROJECT

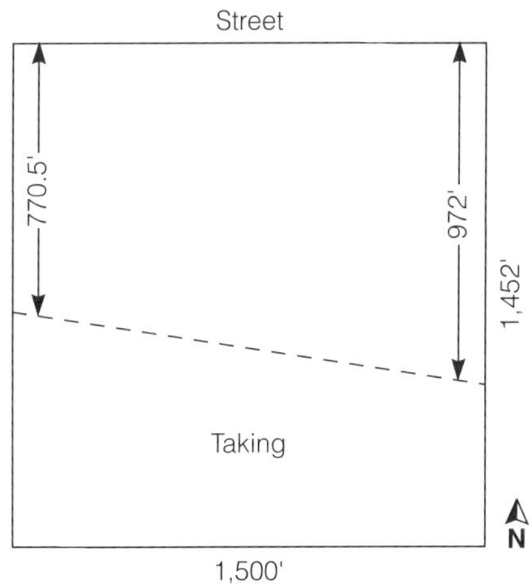

Area Before Taking	50 Acres
Area After Taking	30 Acres
Area Taken	20 Acres

The rezoning to multifamily use cannot be considered in the appraiser's before valuation because it was predicated on the proposed highway project. The before value must be based on single-family zoning and highest and best use. In the after situation, however, the appraiser must estimate value based on multifamily residential zoning and highest and best use because the zoning change was a direct result of the proposed highway project.

If land with a highest and best use for single-family residential development is selling for $10,000 per acre, and land with a highest and best use for multifamily residential development is selling for $15,000 per acre, the before and after values might be computed as follows in jurisdictions that allow the offsetting of special benefits against the taking:

Before value (50 acres @ $10,000)	$500,000
After value (30 acres @ $15,000)	–450,000
Difference between before and after values	$ 50,000

In jurisdictions that do not allow special benefits to be offset against the taking, the computations would be:

Value before taking (50 acres @ $10,000)	$500,000
Value of part taken (20 acres @ $10,000)	–200,000
Remainder value before taking	$300,000
Remainder value after taking (30 acres @ $15,000)	–450,000
Damages	$ 0
Special benefits (30 acres @ $5,000)	–150,000
Net damages	$ 0
Value of part taken	200,000
Total difference	$200,000

Special benefits are discussed in Chapter 15.

Now assume that the rezoning would have occurred regardless of the proposed project. In this case, the property would be valued under its multifamily residential zoning and highest and best use in both the before and after situations. The benefit offset rule would make no difference in these calculations:

Before value (50 acres @ $15,000)	$750,000
After value (30 acres @ $15,000)	–450,000
Difference between before and after values	$300,000

PROBABILITY OF REZONING

The general rule is that present market value must ordinarily be determined by consideration only of the uses for which the land "is adapted and for which it is available." The exception to this general rule is that if the land is not presently available for a particular use by reason of a zoning ordinance or other restriction imposed by law, but the evidence tends to show a "reasonable probability" of a change "in the near future" in the zoning ordinance or other restriction, then the effect of such probability upon the minds of purchasers generally may be taken into consideration in fixing present market value.[13]

13. *Martens v. State*, 554 P.2d 407, 409 (Alaska 1976).

Because probability of rezoning is fertile ground for the unscrupulous, the naive, and the dreamer, there is a considerable amount of case law on the subject. Some appraisers always seem to conclude that a reasonable probability of rezoning exists, while others never conclude that this probability exists. Even though "[a]n appraiser is reasonably expected to possess the special knowledge of the factors which bear upon market value [and o]ne such factor is a study of the reasonable probability of a change in a zoning restriction due to trends of which he is cognizant,"[14] few appraisers adequately support their conclusion on this matter in their appraisal reports. Most court rulings on the subject state that an appraiser *may* consider reasonably probable zone changes, but, ethically and professionally, the appraiser *must* consider reasonably probable zoning changes.[15]

The ultimate judge of whether rezoning is reasonably probable is not the appraiser or even the court, but buyers and sellers in the marketplace. For example, assume Lot 7 in Figure 7.2 is being appraised. The entire neighborhood is

FIGURE 7.2 PROBABILITY OF REZONING

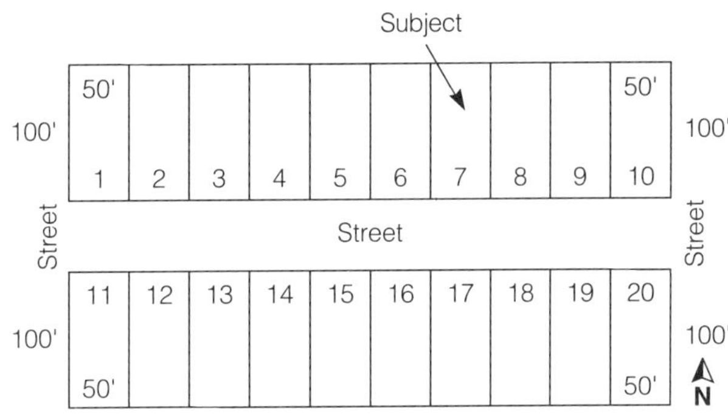

currently zoned for single-family residential purposes. A search of public records discloses the following lot sales, all transacted in the past six months.

Lot No.	Price	Price/Sq. Ft.
1	$30,000	$6.00
3	$32,000	$6.40
4	$27,500	$5.50
6	$34,000	$6.80
9	$30,000	$6.00

Three other lots were also sold in the last six months:

Lot No.	Price	Price/Sq. Ft.
11	$7,500	$1.50
16	$8,000	$1.60
18	$8,250	$1.65

14. *Nichols' The Law of Eminent Domain*, rev. 3d ed. (New York: Mathew Bender Co., Inc., 1990), vol. 4, §12C.03[3].

15. The Appraisal Foundation, *Uniform Standards of Professional Appraisal Practice* (USPAP), 1994 ed., Standards Rule 1-3, p. 11.

These last three lots, which are located on the south side of the street, have been developed with single-family homes since their purchase. Lots 1, 3, 4, 6, and 9, which are on the north side of the street, remain undeveloped. Verification of the sales with the purchasers indicates that the lots were purchased for commercial development in anticipation of rezoning.

Under these circumstances it makes no difference what the appraiser thinks about the chances of having the area rezoned. Buyers and sellers speak louder than appraisers in such instances because they are talking with money. Even if the purchasers were overenthusiastic about the potential for rezoning, the evidence indicates that there are enough overenthusiastic buyers to create a market value of $5.50 to $6.40 per square foot for the property being appraised.

Appraisers do not determine what constitutes a good buy or a bad buy; they only estimate the price at which a property can be sold on the open market. Authoritative texts and courts have recognized this fact. As one court put it:

> The test, of course, is not either possibly (sic) or probability of rezoning in absolute terms, but the fair market value of the locus in the light of the chances as they would appear to the hypothetical willing buyer and seller...
>
> We think that the "market effect" principle...is the crux of the test to be applied. The ultimate enquiry in any condemnation case is the market value of the condemnee's land. Evidence which has a material bearing on market value should be admissible, without regard to whether it relates to an eventuality that might or might not occur in the "near" or more "distant" future, as long as the prospect of the event has substantial present influence on market value. It seems to us that the real purpose of the "near future" and anti-"remote or speculative" qualifications of the rule...is to exclude consideration of an asserted prospective rezoning which is nothing much more than a figment of a bullish owner's imagination.[16]
>
> It should be noted that some courts have used the phrase "reasonable probability" of rezone, while others have used the phrase "reasonable possibility" of rezone, while still others have used the phrases interchangeably. The appraiser should utilize the phrase applicable in the circuit [or jurisdiction] in which the property is located. If "reasonable possibility" is the test to be used, the USPAP Jurisdictional Exception would apply.[17]

However, the appraiser should remember,

> The difference between the "reasonable probability" standard and the "any possibility sufficiently substantial to affect market value" standard urged in the *Moschetti* and *Wolff* cases should not, in our opinion, be exaggerated. They are but different expressions of the requirement that evidence must be relevant and material to be admissible. It is the effect, if any, upon the fair market value on the date of taking which makes relevant the evidence of a possible rezoning of the property. A prospect of rezoning, no matter how imminent, is irrelevant if it has no effect upon such fair market value; and, on the other hand, a prospect of rezoning which may appear to be somewhat remote should, nevertheless, be considered

16. *Moschetti v. City of Tucson*, 449 P.2d 945, 950 (Ariz. 1969).

17. *Uniform Appraisal Standards for Federal Land Acquisitions* (Washington, D.C.: U.S. Government Printing Office, 1992), §B-3, p. 85.

by the court if it affects the fair market value of the property on the date of taking.[18] [Citations omitted]

It should be noted that the U.S. Court of Federal Claims, in a recent decision,[19] introduced the question of "How *knowledgeable* is *knowledgeable?*" as the term is used in the definition of market value. The court found that there was no viable market for the property that was the subject of the lawsuit, even though some 240 purchases of similar land nearby had occurred in the 1970s and 1980s and the owners of the property in question had rejected a cash offer of $3.5 million for the property. In the court's view, none of the purchasers were "knowledgeable" concerning land use regulations that might impede development of the lands. The court substituted its judgment regarding the value and potential use of the lands for the judgment of actual market participants.

While the U.S. Court of Federal Claims may feel that it can substitute its judgment for that of actual market participants in regard to the degree of knowledge that is or is not required to constitute a prudent investment, appraisers do not have the same luxury. If there is an adequate number of "typically informed" buyers to constitute a viable market, the prices that these buyers are paying is *market value* and cannot be ignored by appraisers. Sellers of real estate seldom reject offers because they feel the buyers did not have sufficient knowledge to make an informed purchase. The government appealed this decision to the United States Court of Appeals for the Fifth Circuit.[20] In considering this appeal, the court noted, at pages 1565–66, that

> The Court of Federal Claims rejected the testimony of [the government's appraiser]—the same testimony which we had noted with approval in *Florida Rock II*—solely because [the government's appraiser] with little exception, assumed sufficient knowledge on the part of the purchasers. (*Florida Rock II*, 21 Cl. Ct. at 172.) Instead, the court accepted the testimony of Florida Rock's assessor, which rejected all of the comparable sales values on the principle that none of the purchasers were sufficiently sophisticated and knowledgeable. That was error—contrary to our instruction in *Florida Rock II*, contrary to generally accepted understandings of market valuation, and finally, contrary to the working assumptions of a free market.

In a footnote, the court said "[t]he market from which a fair market value may be ascertained need not contain only legally trained (or advised) persons who fully investigate current land use regulations; *ignorance of the law is every buyer's right*" (emphasis added), and added, at page 1567, "[w]hen the market provides a well-substantiated value for a property, a court may not substitute its own judgment as to what is a wise investment." The court then vacated the judgment of the Court of Federal Claims and remanded the case back to that court, stating, at page 1568, that "[t]he Court of Federal Claims must reconsider the assessments [i.e., appeals] proffered by the parties and other evidence in the record, and determine a fair market value accordingly."

18. *Nashville Housing Authority v. Cohen*, 541 S.W.2d 947, 951–952 (Tenn. 1976).

19. *Florida Rock Industries, Inc. v. United States*, 21 Cl. Ct. 161 (1990) *cert. denied* 115 S.Ct. 898 (1995).

20. *Florida Rock Industries, Inc. v. United States*, 18F. 3d 1560 (Fed. Cir. 1994).

The Appellate Court denied both the government's and Florida Rock's petitions for a "rehearing and suggestion for rehearing in Banc." As long as this case remains open, appraisers who are verifying sales should pay particular attention to what knowledge buyers had. Appraisers should also be prepared to see surveys made by pollsters introduced in an attempt to discredit the validity of an entire segment of the real estate market.

Market evidence that there is, or is not, an increment in value attributable to the probability of rezoning is not, unfortunately, always clear. As the possibility that an area will be rezoned for a more intensive use begins to develop, prices in the neighborhood begin to rise. Property owners in the area withhold their properties from the market in hopes of receiving ever-higher prices as the potential rezoning moves closer toward becoming a reality. The relationship between sales activity, values, and the possibility of rezoning is graphically illustrated in Figure 7.3. When potential sellers hold onto their properties, market activity decreases and an appraiser using the sales comparison approach to value is faced with two choices. He or she may use residential sales with no rezoning potential and develop a reliable increment of value for the property's commercial potential or use commercial sales and develop a reliable discount to reflect the fact that the property being appraised is not, in fact, zoned for commercial purposes.

FIGURE 7.3 RELATIONSHIP BETWEEN MARKET ACTIVITY AND REZONING PROBABILITY

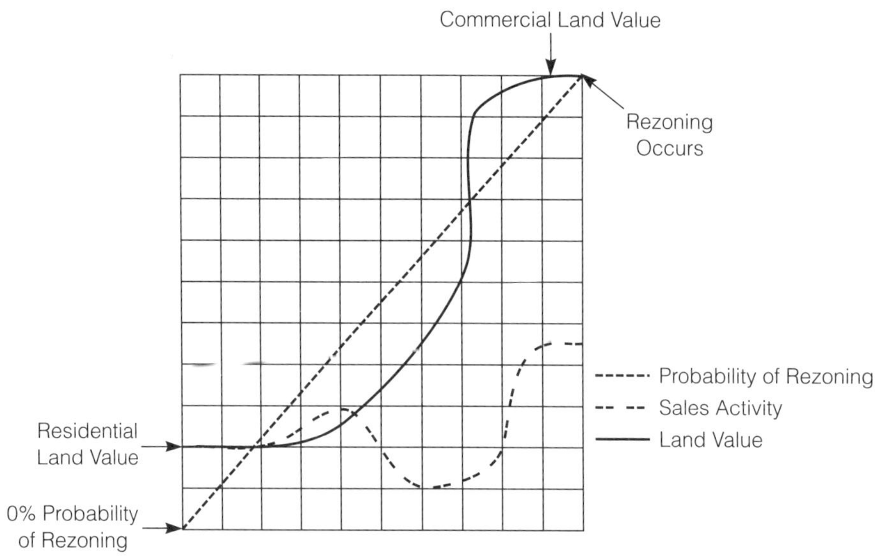

Under the doctrine of reasonable probability, a property cannot be valued as if it were already rezoned for a higher use. As a New Jersey court stated:

> The important *caveat* is that the true issue is not the value of the property for the use which would be permitted if the amendment were adopted. . . . A purchaser in a voluntary transaction would rarely pay the price the property would be worth if the amendment were an accomplished fact. No matter how probable an amendment may seem, an element of uncertainty remains and has its impact upon the selling price. At most a buyer would pay a premium for that probability in addition to what the property is worth under the restrictions of the existing ordinance. In permitting proof of a probable amendment, the law merely seeks to recognize a fact, if it does exist. In short if the parties to a voluntary transaction would as of the date of taking give recognition to the probability of a zoning amendment in agreeing upon the value, the law will recognize the truth.[21]

The courts have recognized that "the fact that the rezoning had not actually been accomplished would call for at least some discount"[22] and that the burdens of obtaining rezoning must be considered. For instance, if rezoning would require the property owner to dedicate additional land for a right-of-way, this fact would have to be considered.[23] The probability of rezoning a remainder property may be considered in a partial taking for the purpose of estimating special benefits.[24]

The courts appear to favor the practice of analyzing comparable sales with the same zoning as the existing zoning on the property being appraised, rather than using higher-zoned sale properties and discounting their values. Ultimately, however, the choice of methodology is generally left to the judgment of the appraiser. If there is little doubt that the property will be rezoned, and the discount applicable to the higher-zoned sales would be comparatively small, it may be advisable to use sales of higher-zoned property. On the other hand, if only a marginal increment in value is attributable to the probability of rezoning, it is generally best to analyze sale properties that have the same zoning as the property being appraised and adjust the values upward. In either case, it is often advisable for the appraiser to include and discuss both lower-zoned and higher-zoned sales in the appraisal report to establish minimum and maximum values for the property being appraised.[25]

If the appraiser concludes that the property being valued has a highest and best use that is physically and economically contrary to its existing zoning, an exhaustive analysis of the possibility of having the property rezoned must be undertaken. Factors to be considered in this analysis include:

- Rezoning applications and the government's reaction to rezoning in the neighborhood
- Actual rezonings after the date of taking (to demonstrate probability on the date of taking)
- Community growth patterns
- Changes in use patterns and the character of the neighborhood
- Demand for certain types of land use in the area

21. *State v. Gorga*, 138 A.2d 833, 835 (N.J. 1958).
22. *City of New York v. Nelkin*, 415 N.E.2d 970, 970 (N.Y. 1980).
23. *City of Fresno v. Cloud*, 102 Cal. Rptr 874 (Cal. 1972).
24. *Dept. of Public Works & Bldgs. v. Exchange Nat'l Bank*, 334 N.E.2d 810 (Ill. 1975).
25. William B. (Trey) Knipe III, "Valuing the Probability of Rezoning," *The Appraisal Journal* (April 1988), 217–222.

- Provisions of applicable comprehensive land use plans
- Age of the zoning ordinance
- Sales of similar properties at prices that reflect anticipated rezoning
- Physical characteristics of subject and surrounding properties
- Attitudes and opinions of zoning officials
- Traffic patterns and volume
- Condition of improvements in the neighborhood
- Activities and attitudes of community groups in regard to past zoning matters

Many courts will not admit the opinion testimony of a *zoning expert* because "[t]he difficulty of anticipating what any legislative body is going to do is obvious, and the practice of permitting prognostication on legislative policy...should not be encouraged."[26]

These rulings do not, of course, preclude the appraiser from interviewing zoning officials and members of the legislative body that would ultimately rule on a rezoning request. In fact, this should be done if it is at all possible. Sometimes an appraiser can obtain a commitment from the zoning administrator as to whether he or she would make a favorable or unfavorable recommendation to the legislative body on a particular rezoning request. Then the appraiser should determine whether the legislative body routinely follows the administrator's recommendation or often overrides it. Appraisers and lawyers should be aware, however, that planners and zoning officials have a habit of being much less decisive on the witness stand than they are in their offices.

It has become increasingly difficult for appraisers to obtain opinions regarding potential rezoning or permit approvals from members of legislative bodies and zoning officials for two reasons. First, the appearance of fairness doctrine is applicable in many jurisdictions. This doctrine holds that it would be unfair, or at least appear unfair, for a public official to offer an opinion on the advisability of proposed legislative action before all interested parties have had a chance to be heard. It has also been held, under this doctrine, that it is improper for a public official to meet and discuss proposed legislative action without inviting all interested parties to the discussion, i.e., a public hearing. Thus, a member of a legislative body cannot, at least theoretically, decide on the advisability of proposed legislative action until all public hearings have been held and all interested parties have had an opportunity to express their views. For this reason it is often impossible for an appraiser to have a meaningful discussion with a member of a legislative body, a zoning official, or a land use permit official about the possibility of rezoning.

A second impediment arises from the recent increase in inverse, or regulatory, taking cases being filed, which have made many governmental officials reluctant to express their opinions on the probability of obtaining a rezoning or a permit. In fact, many agencies have adopted policies that prohibit their employees from expressing their opinions on such matters, even to employees of other

26. *Park Dist. of Highland Park v. Becher*, 208 N.E.2d 621, 623–624 (Ill. 1965).

agencies within the same government entity. Often appraisers are simply told that the zoning official has absolutely no idea whether rezoning will be granted and that the only way to find out is to submit a formal application for rezoning. Such responses are not terribly enlightening and have made quantifying the probability of rezoning (or permit issuance) even more difficult for appraisers.

The courts have expanded the concept of *reasonable probability* beyond the question of rezoning. They have referred to reasonable probability in the context of a "zoning ordinance or other restriction,"[27] extending the concept to the reasonable probability of an annexation,[28] a zoning variance,[29] and issuance of environmental permits,[30] including "the reasonable probability of obtaining an EPA permit for the operation of a sanitary landfill."[31]

ADVANCED PROBLEMS

"In developing a real property appraisal, an appraiser must...consider the effect on use and value of the...existing land use regulations [and the] reasonably probable modifications of such land use regulations."[32] Historically that has meant zoning, but this is no longer true. Although the federal government does not have the power to zone land, it has in recent years issued more than 70,000 pages of environmental laws and regulations that impact land use. State and local governments have added their own environmental regulations. Some of the most significant regulations relate to hazardous contaminants.

Because the field of hazardous waste is so technical, appraisers have tended to ignore it. If their shoes didn't melt while making their property inspection, they assumed the property was free from contamination. Such an assumption can lead to a limited appraisal, which is unacceptable for eminent domain purposes. "For example, it is improper to estimate the market value of a property assuming it is free of contamination when there is evidence, by the past use of the property or the appraiser's inspection thereof, that contamination may exist."[33]

Appraisers *must* take all reasonable steps to determine whether the property under appraisal is or is not contaminated. If there is any suspicion whatsoever that a property may be contaminated, the procurement of an environmental audit is generally required. Procurement of such an audit can create problems for the appraiser because 1) audits are often time consuming; 2) audits are expensive; and 3) the EPA has refused to identify the specific investigation that should be undertaken in conducting an environmental audit.

Many condemning agencies are required, by their policies or regulations, to determine whether property is contaminated before they acquire it. They will, therefore, undertake an environmental investigation before an appraisal of the property is conducted, but these same agencies fail to provide their appraisers

27. *Martens v. State*, 554 P.2d 407, 409 (Alaska, 1976).
28. *Lake County Forest Preserve District v. Reliance Standard Life Ins. Co.*, 329 N.E.2d 344 (Ill. 1975).
29. *Redevelopment Agency v. Contra Costa Theatre*, 185 Cal. Rptr. 159 (Cal. 1982).
30. *Laurel, Inc. v. State*, 362 A.2d 1383 (Conn. 1975).
31. *Lake County Forest Preserve Dist. v. Petersen*, 417 N.E.2d 862, 864 (Ill. 1981).
32. USPAP, 1994 ed., Standards Rule 1-3(a), p. 11.
33. *Uniform Appraisal Standards for Federal Land Acquisitions*, §C-9, p. 96.

with the results of their investigation. Appraisers should always determine what property investigations the condemning agency has already made and procure copies of all reports pertinent to the appraisal of the property.

If no environmental audit has been conducted and the appraiser suspects that the property under appraisal may be contaminated, he or she must do everything possible to procure such an audit. The appraiser must explain to the client that any appraisal report prepared without an audit, under the assumption that the property is free of contamination, will be absolutely meaningless for eminent domain purposes. If the client agrees that an audit is required, the next question is who will select and retain the auditor.

It has been "[s]uggested that the client choose and hire any qualified environmental professionals."[34] It may be assumed that this recommendation was made in an attempt to reduce the appraiser's liability. While such a practice may have that effect, appraisers must remember that they are eventually going to be asked to accept the environmental professional's report and adopt the findings it contains. Thus, irrespective of who selects or retains the consultant, the appraiser must be sure that the individual is qualified and has been requested to provide answers to the questions the appraiser needs answered. The appraiser must have enough confidence in the consultant to adopt his findings.

Extreme care must be exercised in reviewing the qualifications of any environmental consultant. Instant experts have appeared in the marketplace. Environmental associations have sprung up which offer designations in environmental inspection to those with little or no qualifications, beyond the ability to pay the membership fee. Environmental audits are generally conducted in three phases. Phase 1 establishes whether a property is contaminated; Phase 2 determines the extent of contamination; and Phase 3 includes development of a mitigation or cleanup plan and estimation of its cost. In reviewing the qualifications of any auditor, even for a simple Phase 1 audit, it is important to confirm that the auditor has the qualifications to conduct Phase 2 and Phase 3 audits if they become necessary.

Until recently there was no industry standard for the activities that should be undertaken in an environmental audit. In May of 1993 the American Society for Testing and Materials (ASTM) published standards for a Phase I environmental site assessment and a transaction screen.[35] ASTM is a respected, non-profit, standard-setting organization well known in the engineering profession. The transaction screen could become the recognized industry standard, through legislative action or approval by environmental regulatory agencies. Note, however, that the appraisal profession has objected to ASTM's transaction screen and to other environmental checklists for use by appraisers because these forms require knowledge beyond the expertise of the typical real estate appraiser.

In 1995 the Appraisal Institute developed and adopted its own Property Observation Checklist. This checklist provides appraisers with useful guidelines for recording observations about the possible presence of environmental contami-

34. Guide Note 8 to the Standards of Professional Appraisal Practice of the Appraisal Institute, 1991 ed.

35. *Standard Practice for Environmental Site Assessments: Phase 1 Environmental Site Assessment. Process* (Practice E 1527-93); *Standard Practice for Environmental Site Assessments: Transaction Screen Process* (Practice E 1528-93).

nants. The checklist was not developed to be used in the inspection of single-family or agricultural properties. Use of the checklist is voluntary.

It is important to determine the extent of the investigation and reporting planned by an environmental auditor and to describe it in any contract for professional services. ASTM's "Recommended Table of Contents and Report Format" in its Standard E 1527-93 for Phase I assessments can be used as a starting point, or even referenced in the contract.

Because the area of hazardous waste cleanup is new and still evolving, cost estimates for mitigation prepared by even the most qualified consultants can be in substantial error. For instance, a site cleanup was conducted by a property owner and the site was "certified as clean" by the state environmental agency before it was acquired by the condemnor. While constructing the public improvement, however, the condemnor unearthed some buried drums and caused a release of hazardous material. The cost of environmental cleanup, at last count, was $350 million. In another case, an appraiser had two environmental audits conducted on a site. One auditor estimated the cleanup cost at $3.5 million, while the second estimated a cost of $5 million. The condemnor took possession of the property and cleaned up the contamination prior to trial for less than $500,000.

These examples demonstrate that, even though hazardous waste cleanup costs can be estimated, substantial risk remains for a purchaser of a contaminated property. The appraiser must take this factor into consideration when estimating the market value of a contaminated property.

Some agencies ask appraisers to estimate the value of a contaminated site as if it were uncontaminated. The agency then deducts the estimated cost of cleanup from the appraiser's estimated value to arrive at the agency's determination of just compensation. This procedure is obviously flawed. First, market evidence shows that at times the presence of contamination on a property, even when known, does not affect its market value. Second, deducting the basic estimated cost of cleanup from the "as clean" value of the property does not account for the risks that a potential purchaser of a contaminated property assumes, or the entrepreneurial profit that such a purchaser may demand. Third, the procedure does not take into account any diminution in the property's value that may remain after the contamination has been eradicated or mitigated. This last factor has been dubbed by some as *stigma*.

It might be argued that a property that has been thoroughly audited and cleaned up could have an enhanced value, rather than a diminished value, as compared to a typical property that has not been audited and thus could contain environmental hazards. There seems to be a misconception in the appraisal industry that the typical real estate appraiser is not competent to appraise a contaminated property. This belief may rise from the fact that the typical real estate appraiser is not competent to appraise a contaminated property without the assistance of an environmental consultant or it may be promulgated by the pseudo-experts on contaminated property valuation who have miraculously emerged. In any case, the conception is false.

For years appraisers have used the services of specialized consultants such as general contractors, marketing experts, civil engineers, geologists, hydrologists, and structural engineers. An environmental consultant is no different. If it is assumed that the typical appraiser is not competent to appraise contaminated property because it might be suffering from so-called *stigma*, that assumption is also incorrect. Many different types of properties can suffer from stigma. Properties that have historically flooded or have been damaged by fire, earthquake, or landslide can suffer from a diminution in value after the physical damage has been repaired. Properties where a violent crime has been committed can also be stigmatized. Appraisers with average experience in the real estate market have encountered and solved these types of valuation problems in the past. There is nothing mystical about a contaminated property that makes it any different.

Another approach suggested is to have the local appraiser estimate the value of a contaminated property as if uncontaminated and then call in a national expert to apply a magical *contamination adjustment* to the local appraiser's value estimate. A value estimate developed with such a procedure would be considered incompetent evidence of value for eminent domain purposes. The local appraiser cannot attest to the accuracy of the national expert's adjustment and the national expert cannot attest to the accuracy of the local appraiser's value estimate. Thus no one can testify to an independent opinion of the market value of the subject property in its as is condition.

An appraiser with typical field experience is competent and qualified to estimate the market value of a contaminated property, providing the appraiser has sound environmental consulting services and adheres to the Appraisal Institute's Guide Note 6 and Guide Note 8.[36]

The relationship between hazardous waste laws and eminent domain valuation has not yet been addressed by the courts, so situations will arise for which there are no definitive answers. Under the Comprehensive Environmental Response, Compensation, and Liability Act of 1980, "the adjudication of liability is strict, joint, several, and retroactive. *Strict liability* refers to the assigning of liability without regard to intentional fault or proof of negligence. *Joint and several liability* means that if several persons or entities have contributed hazardous waste to a site, each (several) and any (joint) is liable for the cost of assessing the damage, cleaning it up, and restoring the environment to an uncontaminated condition."[37] This liability extends to past, present, and future owners of the property, except in limited circumstances.[38]

Under these circumstances, it has been found that some contaminated real estate has no market value, as that term is defined customarily and in the area of eminent domain. Yet the usual measure of just compensation in an eminent domain action is market value. A property may serve the needs of its current owner and have the ability to continue to do so for some time, yet have no market value. A suggested solution to this dilemma is discussed in Chapter 11 of this text.

36. Guide Note 6, "Reliance on Reports Prepared by Others," and Guide Note 8, "The Consideration of Hazardous Substances in the Appraisal Process," to the Standards of Professional Appraisal Practice of the Appraisal Institute, 1994 ed.

37. *The Appraisal of Real Estate*, 10th ed., 181–182.

38. Under the Superfund Amendments and Reauthorization Act (SARA), an "innocent purchaser" of the property has no such liability. An "innocent purchaser" is one who "did not know and had no reason to know that any hazardous substance was disposed of on, in, or at the facility."

Ownership of contaminated land can result in a financial liability for cleanup that is greater than the value of the uncontaminated land. In other words, ownership of the land creates a negative value. The condemnor's assumption of that liability is essentially a form of compensation. For example, consider a 50-acre tract of uncontaminated land that has a market value of $1,000 per acre. If 20 acres of the land is condemned, with no damages or benefits to the remainder, compensation would be calculated:

Before value (50 acres @ $1,000)	$50,000
After value (30 acres @ $1,000)	-30,000
Difference between before and after values	$20,000

Now assume that 20 acres of the 50-acre tract is contaminated and that the cleanup cost is $30,000. Ten acres of the contaminated land is within the condemnnor's area of acquisition. Compensation would be calculated as follows:

Before value		
30 acres @ $1,000	$30,000	
20 acres @ $1,000 – $30,000	-10,000	
Total before value		$20,000
After value		
20 acres @ $1,000	$20,000	
10 acres @ $1,000 – $15,000	- 5,000	
Total after value		-15,000
Difference between before and after values		$ 5,000

The owner's compensation could be viewed as

Cash	$ 5,000
Assumption of owner's liability by condemnor	15,000
Total compensation	$20,000

Now assume that the cleanup cost is $60,000 rather than $30,000

Before value		
30 acres @ $1,000	$30,000	
20 acres @ $1,000 – $60,000	-40,000	
Total before value		-$10,000
After value		
20 acres @ $1,000	$20,000	
10 acres @ $1,000 – $30,000	-20,000	
Total after value		0
Total compensation		-$10,000

The owner's compensation could be viewed as

Cash	-$10,000
Assumption of owner's liability by condemnor	30,000
Total compensation	$20,000

It will be interesting to see how the courts address such problems, particularly the situation described in the last example. Will the courts accept the position, demonstrated in the before situation, that property can have a negative value because of the cleanup liability associated with its ownership? Also, will the court allow for *negative just compensation*? Under the above scenario, the property owner would owe the condemnor $10,000. Will the court require the property owner to pay? If the assumption of liability is viewed in the same light as a special benefit, the answer is no. Some constitutions have been interpreted to mean that just compensation must be paid in cash. Obviously, the assumption of liability is not cash. Of course, these questions can only be answered definitively by the courts. Until they are, appraisers will have to approach problematic situations armed with common sense and well-reasoned, written legal instructions.

Another problem in this same area arises when contaminated property does not reflect a diminution in market value because of its contamination. In such a situation, the appraiser who is estimating market value would report the contamination, but make no deduction for it. However, the condemnor may take the position that the owner of the property is legally responsible for its cleanup and, therefore, as a matter of law (or of public policy) the cost of the cleanup must be deducted from the value of the property. If an appraiser received an adequately supported written legal instruction to that effect, it would have to be accepted. Under such a circumstance, however, it would not be proper to add an entrepreneurial profit factor onto the cost of cleanup.

SUMMARY

Market value is measured utility and the utility of property is directly affected by a variety of land use ordinances. The number of land use ordinances and other regulations that affect the use of land has risen sharply over the past few years, and appraisers must be thoroughly familiar with them and their potential impact on the value of the property being appraised.

Because of the promulgation of land use ordinances, particularly the ordinances requiring development permits, many sales of developable land now occur only after the purchaser has procured all necessary development permits. These sales reflect properties in a better economic position than the typical property being appraised for eminent domain purposes, for which development permits seldom exist. Therefore, it is often necessary for the appraiser to adjust the sale prices downward to reflect the risk inherent in a property without development permits.

Zoning ordinances are the most common type of land use regulation. Nearly all zoning ordinances have provisions for pre-existing nonconforming uses and for the issuance of variances. In investigating a property under appraisal, the appraiser must determine if its use is nonconforming to the zoning ordinance and whether a variance exists. If either of these factors is found, the appraiser must analyze its impact on the market value of the property.

The appraiser must also determine whether a zoning action has taken place or been denied and how this has affected the property being appraised. The appraiser must determine whether the zoning decision was influenced by the anticipated acquisition of the property in an attempt to depress its value or was made in light of the proposed public improvement for which the property is being condemned. If the latter circumstance applies, the appraiser must not consider the zoning decision in estimating the market value of the property prior to the taking. However, if the property being appraised is subject to a partial acquisition, the zoning decision must be considered in appraising the remainder parcel.

If the appraiser finds that a government action was taken in an attempt to depress the value of the property so that it could be acquired by the condemning agency at a lower price, he or she is well advised to seek legal counsel in regard to the specific procedure to be used in appraising the property. It is well established that governmental action taken to depress property values in anticipation of an eminent domain proceeding is in violation of the provision requiring the payment of *just compensation*; the appraiser must therefore disregard this governmental action.

When a question concerning the probability of rezoning arises, it is generally a question of law to be determined by the court. If the court finds that a probability of rezoning exists as a matter of law, the probability of rezoning is then to be determined by the trier of fact. The question is immaterial unless the existence of such probability has an influence on the value of the property being appraised.

It is not the appraiser's opinion of the probability of rezoning that is important, but rather the actions of buyers and sellers in the marketplace. If it is concluded that rezoning is probable or imminent, the property being appraised is not valued as if the rezoning has occurred, but rather in recognition of the probability that it may occur. Thus, the value of the property will be less than it would be if the property were rezoned. The difference reflects the risk, time, and cost involved in actually obtaining the rezoning.

The factors to be considered in determining the probablility of rezoning are varied and extensive. Many appraisal reports are deficient in their coverage of this topic. The appraiser should address each of the factors considered in determining the probability of rezoning and provide the support and reasoning leading to the appraiser's ultimate conclusion. Not all jurisdictions accept, or place the same importance on, the various factors considered in this regard. Henry J. Kaltenbach's *Just Compensation Resume* summarizes the probability of rezoning issue in this way:

> In considering this question, courts of different jurisdictions appear to emphasize different factors. In some cases, weight has been given to the fact that an application for rezoning has been made, and weight has also been given to the opinions of the officials on the zoning board. In other cases the emphasis has been upon the physical aspects of the matter, such as the location of the property, the use made of properties nearby, the traffic on the streets, and other physical factors. Some courts state that the physical factors without more are sufficient to indicate the probability of a change, while others require that applications to the zoning board shall have been made, and that there be some showing that there is a reasonable probability that the application will be granted. The probability of a change in some jurisdictions is regarded as a question of law, while in others it is regarded as a question of fact. In one case when a change in zoning was made after the taking it was held that evidence of this change might be proper at the retrial of the case.[39]

Not only *may* appraisers consider the probability of rezoning and its effect on market value, they *must*, from a professional and ethical standpoint, consider such a reasonable probability and its impact on market value.

In recent years substantial environmental regulations that affect land use have been added to the classic land use regulations that appraisers must consider. Among the most significant concerns are hazardous waste regulations and the potential liability associated with them. Because many of these regulations are recent, their impact on market value in eminent domain valuations has not been established by the courts. For this reason, the solution to some of the valuation problems created by these new environmental laws remains unclear. Nevertheless, with adequate support from environmental consultants and legal counsel, appraisers with eminent domain valuation training and experience should be able to provide reasonable value estimates, provided they adhere to the professional standards of the industry.

39. Henry J. Kaltenbach, *Just Compensation Resume* (Warrenton, Va.: Right of Way Consultants, Inc., 1969), §1-4-7.1, pp. 9–10.

CHAPTER 8

Cost Approach to Value

The cost approach to value is

> A set of procedures through which a value indication is derived for the fee simple interest in a property by estimating the current cost to construct a reproduction of, or replacement for, the existing structure; deducting accrued depreciation from the reproduction or replacement cost; and adding the estimated land value plus an entrepreneurial profit.[1]

According to one text

> This approach is particularly useful in valuing new or nearly new improvements and properties that are not frequently exchanged in the market. Cost approach techniques can also be employed to derive information needed in the sales comparison and income capitalization approaches to value.[2]

The major steps in applying the cost approach are: 1) estimate the reproduction (or replacement) cost of the improvements as of the date of appraisal, 2) estimate the amount of depreciation present in the improvements, 3) deduct total depreciation from the estimated reproduction cost to arrive at an indicated value of the improvements as of the date of appraisal, and 4) add the estimated value of the land to the indicated improvement value to arrive at an indication of total market value.

The appraiser is advised to explain the appraisal process to the trier of fact in some detail before testifying to the value of a specific property. The appraiser should emphasize that the three approaches to value are not independent of one

1. *The Dictionary of Real Estate Appraisal*, 3d ed. (Chicago: Appraisal Institute, 1993), 81.

2. *The Appraisal of Real Estate*, 10th ed. (Chicago: Appraisal Institute, 1992), 80.

another and that appraisers do not use the single most applicable approach. Rather, all three approaches are used if possible because they are all integral parts of the appraisal process. The indicated values derived by the various approaches are then correlated into a final estimate of property value, giving consideration to the relative strengths and weaknesses of each approach in relation to the specific property being appraised.

Most courts do not seem to understand that each of the three approaches to value is an integral part of the valuation process. Many court rulings appear to be based on the assumption that the three approaches to value are totally independent of one another and that only the most applicable approach is used in the appraisal of a specific property.

A Washington court has recognized the relationship between the three approaches to value. Citing *The Appraisal of Real Estate*, fifth edition, as its authority, the court described the cost, income capitalization, and sales comparison approaches as follows:

> 1. The current cost of reproducing a property less depreciation from deterioration and functional and economic obsolescence.
> 2. The value which the property's net earning power will support, based upon a capitalization of net income.
> 3. The value indicated by recent sales of comparable properties in the market.[3]

Citing the Washington case, however, a Massachusetts court held:

> Whatever the relative importance or usefulness of the three methods to the real estate profession, however, they have not been viewed as equally applicable or as interchangeable under the law of eminent domain as it has developed in our cases. More specifically, the introduction of evidence concerning value based upon DCR [depreciated reproduction cost] computations has been limited to special situations in which data cannot be reliably computed under the other two methods.[4]

To say that the cost approach is generally disliked by the courts is an understatement. Another court has stated:

> A third method of appraisal is somewhat tentatively and timidly put forward by the claimant, namely, the reproduction method. Here an expert is called upon to give his version of the sound value of the building by estimating what it would cost to reproduce it, and then deducting a fair amount for depreciation. This "method" is perhaps the most excellent example conceivable to demonstrate that none of such abstractions ought to have a place in the search for market value, generally speaking....[I]gnoring the fact that on the figures an absurd result is reached, it is apparent that the reproduction method is in itself absurd in the ordinary case, because even in ordinary times it is ridiculous to suppose that anyone would think of reproducing this or any like property, and that same thing would be true in the vast majority of cases, I should think.[5]

3. *State v. Wilson*, 493 P.2d 1252, 1256 (Wash. 1972).
4. *Correia v. New Bedford Redevelopment Authority*, 377 N.E.2d 909, 911 (Mass. 1978).
5. *United States v. 49,375 Square Feet of Land in Borough of Manhattan*, 92 F. Supp. 384, 387–388 (S.D. N.Y. 1950), *affirmed per curiam sub. nom. United States v. Tishman Realty & Constr. Co.*, 193 F.2d 180 (2d Cir. 1952), *cert. denied*, 343 U.S. 928 (1952) (Footnote omitted).

Despite such pronouncements, most courts allow the cost approach into evidence as long as the improvements enhance the value of the land for its highest and best use and proper deductions are made for depreciation of the improvements. The minority rule, which excludes consideration of cost data, has evolved for a number of reasons. The cost approach has been viewed by some courts as a violation of the unit rule. (See Chapter 4 for a discussion of multiple estates and Chapter 6 for coverage of the undivided fee rule.) Other courts have referred to the cost approach as a *summation* appraisal,[6] which is typically forbidden. The cost approach, as applied, has also been seen as a violation of the consistent use theory. (See Chapter 6.) Another reason the courts may hesitate to allow reproduction cost testimony stems from a weakness in human nature, not a deficiency in the cost approach. Federal Judge James Carter described this weakness:

> No matter how carefully a judge attempts to instruct a jury that certain evidence is only background material or not direct evidence of value, there is no assurance that he can, in a complicated case, put that over to a jury; and the impact of direct testimony of dollars and cents of "reproduction cost less depreciation," will tend to mislead a jury in fixing, as they should, what the willing buyer and willing seller would arrive at in the market place, and would divert them from their consideration of comparable sales as to the best evidence of value and from properly considering all the factors that an expert would consider, i.e., whether the comparable sales, were sufficiently close in time, size, description; and the various other factors underlying the expert's opinion.[7]

Authoritative texts also warn of the dangers of using the cost approach to value in eminent domain cases. Lewis Orgel makes these suggestions:

> In the first place, reproduction cost should be regarded as setting the upper limit upon a valuation derived by any other method.... In the second place, structural cost should be recognized as an inferior measure of value, to be given weight only in those cases where more satisfactory evidence based on actual sales or on earning power is not available. In the third place, whenever reproduction cost is offered as evidence, the court should make every effort to assure a full deduction for those elusive forms of depreciation, obsolescence and inadequacy, that are so often disregarded by all but the most careful appraisers.[8]

A reading of pertinent cases indicates that the courts' lack of confidence in the cost approach is caused not because of some weakness in the approach itself, but by flagrant misuse of the approach by appraisers. Some errors may result from a lack of knowledge, but more often practitioners use the cost approach to intentionally exaggerate the market value of property to benefit their clients' interests.

The usefulness of the cost approach is discounted in many condemnor appraisal guidelines.

---

6. *In re Park Street, Vicinity of Bay Land*, 325 N.Y.S.2d 555 (N.Y. 1971).
7. *United States v. 70.39 Acres of Land*, 164 F.Supp. 451, 489 (S.D. Cal. 1958).
8. Lewis Orgel, *Valuation Under the Law of Eminent Domain*, 2d ed. (Charlottesville, Va.: The Michie Co., 1953), vol. 2, §199, p. 57.

> The cost approach is generally recognized as the least reliable method of valuation. The courts have made clear that this approach should never be used "when no one would think of reproducing the property" or when no prudent investor would reproduce it for the figure or amount given as replacement or reproduction cost.[9]

The fact that the courts seem to distrust the cost approach and will sometimes exclude testimony based on this approach does not, of course, restrict the appraiser from using it in arriving at a final estimate of value. The appraiser has an ethical and professional obligation to develop a cost approach to value whenever the results of the approach will assist in estimating the value of the property.[10] In an attempt to reduce appraisal fees, some condemnors will offer appraisal contracts with the provision that the appraiser need only apply the sales comparison approach to value. An appraiser must reject such a contract unless the cost and income approaches will be of no assistance whatsoever in estimating the value of the property or the appraiser is prepared to apply *all applicable approaches* for the appraisal fee offered despite the contract provisions.

Note that the appraisal guidelines developed by the Federal Highway Administration (FHWA), in implementation of the Uniform Relocation Assistance and Real Property Acquisition Policies Act of 1970,[11] provide for appraisals that exclude both the cost and income capitalization approaches to value. At the request of FHWA, The Appraisal Foundation ruled these guidelines to be in accordance with its Uniform Standards of Professional Appraisal Practice and determined that the exclusion of the cost and income capitalization approaches would fall within USPAP's departure provisions. This ruling was obviously based on political considerations, rather than professional or technical considerations. Appraisers are cautioned that the Appraisal Institute has not formally ruled that the FHWA guidelines are a jurisdictional exception to its Standards of Professional Appraisal Practice, nor have the individual state appraiser licensing/certification agencies. As stated by the Federal Highway Administration itself, some of these appraisal reports:

> May not meet current minimum requirements of some state and local agencies.
>
> May necessitate expanded appraisal if litigation is necessary.
>
> May not reflect "before" and "after" values.
>
> Appraiser might tend to "bend" the situation to permit use of this [abbreviated appraisal] format.[12]

While the FHWA guidelines were established to "save time and costs," they also appear to result in less careful estimates of just compensation for owners who choose to accept settlements rather than litigate the issue.

The appraiser who does not use all applicable approaches to value has sim-

9. *Uniform Appraisal Standards for Federal Land Acquisitions* (Washington, D.C.: U.S. Government Printing Office, 1992), §A-6, p. 17.
10. The Appraisal Foundation, *Uniform Standards of Professional Appraisal Practice*, 1994 ed., Standards Rule 1-4(b), p. 11; see also Standards Rule 2-2(j), p. 16.
11. Public Law 91-646.
12. U.S. Department of Transportation, Federal Highway Administration, *The Appraisal Guide* (Washington, D.C.: U.S. Government Printing Office, 1990), 14.

ply not made an analysis that is thorough enough for trial purposes. "Even though the cost approach...is often maligned by the courts it can be a useful analytical tool in allocating the contributory value of various elements of the property in partial taking appraisals. Therefore, the indicated value of the property by the cost approach should be developed with care."[13]

REPRODUCTION COST

In appraisal the distinction between reproduction cost and replacement cost is quite clear. *Reproduction cost* is the current cost to reconstruct the improvements physically using the same or very similar materials; *replacement cost* is the cost of constructing improvements equal in utility to those being appraised.

For example, consider a lumber mill constructed in 1920 that is a 4-in.-by-4-in., wood-frame structure with a sawtooth roof and 3-in.-thick wood decks over 18-in.-by-18-in. floor framing. If reproduction cost is to be estimated, the cost estimate will represent the cost of reconstructing these facilities using the same or similar materials. If replacement cost is to be used, however, the appraiser may estimate the cost of a steel-frame structure with steel skin, concrete floors, and a gable roof, which has the same utility as the existing facility. Replacement cost is differentiated from reproduction cost by the removal of many, if not all, items of construction excess. Although there is a clear distinction between replacement cost and reproduction cost in appraisal, these terms are not clearly distinguished by the courts in most jurisdictions. Most court opinions use the term *reproduction cost*, but many others use the terms *reproduction cost* and *replacement cost* interchangeably.

Because many courts fail to distinguish between reproduction and replacement costs, appraisers must be careful in using these terms on the witness stand. When the terms are used, the appraiser must explain their precise meanings in an appraisal context. It is generally permissible for an appraiser to estimate either reproduction cost or replacement cost as long as all forms of depreciation are accounted for in a manner consistent with the cost estimate used.

There are three standard methods for estimating reproduction or replacement cost: the quantity survey method, the unit-in-place method, and the comparative-unit method.[14] The quantity survey method is generally considered the most accurate, while the comparative unit method is the least reliable. Whichever method is used by the appraiser, it is important that all indirect costs be included in the cost estimate and that entrepreneurial profit be considered as an element of cost.

The appraiser must, of course, make an accurate, detailed property inspection before a cost estimate can be developed. Many of the computations can be made after the appraiser's field inspection, especially if a detailed field inspection checklist is used in the physical inspection of the property. This practice is highly recommended because it obviates multiple trips to the property to obtain data over-

13. *Uniform Appraisal Standards for Federal Land Acquisitions*, §B-1 - 16, p. 75.

14. For examples illustrating how reproduction cost estimates are developed by these methods, see *The Appraisal of Real Estate*, 10th ed., 330-339.

looked during the first inspection and, more importantly, prevents embarrassing situations on the witness stand. The appraiser will not have to answer inquiries about construction details by saying "I don't know," "I didn't notice," or worse, "No, that item of cost is not included in my reproduction cost estimate."

When an appraiser cannot testify to the size of the hot water tank in the single-family dwelling being appraised, typical jurors often forget that they do not know the size of the hot water tank in their own home. Instead, the juror may wonder how the appraiser was able to estimate the reproduction cost of the hot water tank without knowing its size. The juror may also speculate that if the appraiser missed this item of reproduction cost, he may have missed others and made significant errors in the appraisal.

Although experienced appraisers often develop their own field inspection checklists, a number of excellent published forms are available. Whether the appraiser uses the quantity survey, unit-in-place, or comparative-unit method of estimating reproduction cost, a detailed field inspection sheet is essential. Even if an independent cost estimator is retained to arrive at a reproduction cost estimate, a detailed field inspection form can help the appraiser describe the improvements in the appraisal report and on the witness stand.

Appraisers must avoid representing themselves to the trier of fact as both *expert appraisers* and *expert cost estimators*. In a Rhode Island case an appraiser was precluded from testifying to the cost of replacing a portion of a fence taken in an eminent domain action when the court ruled that being an expert appraiser does not necessarily qualify the appraiser as an expert fence builder.[15]

If the cost approach is important to the appraiser's value conclusion, the appraiser is well advised to obtain a reproduction or replacement cost estimate from at least one contractor. To supplement the contractor's cost estimate, the appraiser should develop at least one other cost estimate or use one developed by a cost service. If the appraiser adopts the contractor's estimate with no other evidence, the estimate is not the opinion of the appraiser, but of the contractor. In such a circumstance, the appraiser could be excluded from testifying in regard to the cost of the improvements because the estimate is not the appraiser's opinion and, therefore, is hearsay evidence. A simple solution to this problem is for the appraiser to obtain two independent cost estimates, using two different contractors or two different methods. Then the appraiser can consider both cost estimates and arrive at a final opinion as to the reproduction or replacement cost of the improvements.

The problem of hearsay can also arise if an appraiser uses a published cost service as the sole source of data. Aside from the hearsay rule, using a cost service as the sole source of data in estimating reproduction cost has been viewed with skepticism by some courts.

> They [the appraisers] relied largely upon reproduction costs calculated on a rule of thumb cubic footage basis, less depreciation.... [T]he rule of thumb basis for estimating cost of reproduction, used by the Agency appraisers, has been de-

15. *Palazzolo v. Rayhill*, 394 A.2d 690 (R.I. 1978).

scribed as being "not even approximately accurate, except for a few highly standardized types of structures." There is no showing that this was such a standardized structure. Accordingly, if such testimony is repeated on a new trial the jury should be cautioned . . . that the cubic foot cost method of computing reproduction cost is not entitled to great weight in such a case as this even in arriving at reproduction cost.[16]

DEPRECIATION

Depreciation is a loss in the value of improvements from any cause; it is the difference between the current cost of reproducing or replacing the improvements, new, and the dollar amount they add to the value of the land as of the date of appraisal. Whenever the courts have considered reproduction cost in eminent domain proceedings, they have universally recognized that depreciated reproduction cost rather than reproduction cost new is the proper measure of value.[17] Most courts have also recognized the various forms of depreciation—i.e., obsolescence as well as physical deterioration.[18]

In the analytic process, the appraiser will often break down the estimate of depreciation into these categories: physical deterioration—curable and incurable; functional obsolescence—curable and incurable; and external obsolescence—incurable.[19] (In the past, external obsolescence has also been referred to as *environmental obsolescence* or *economic obsolescence*.)[20] Each of these forms of depreciation is measured by different means. Some forms of depreciation are curable and can be measured by the cost to cure, while others are incurable and are measured by capitalizing the rent loss attributable to the depreciated item.[21]

Depreciation analysis is a valuable appraisal tool, but presenting it to a judge or jury may lead to confusion. Phrases such as *curable physical deterioration* or *incurable functional obsolescence caused by a superadequacy* may have precise meanings in the real estate appraisal profession, but they are meaningless to most jurors. If the appraiser uses such terms on the witness stand, the jury may be confused or, even worse, they may feel patronized or manipulated. Any appraiser who uses a detailed breakdown method to estimate the depreciation present in a property being appraised is advised to find a way to explain the methodology in simple terms before taking the witness stand.

Four methods of estimating accrued depreciation are used in the appraisal industry. They are the economic age-life method, the modified economic age-life method, the breakdown method, and the sales comparison method, which is also referred to as the *abstraction method*.

16. *Riley v. District of Columbia Redevelopment Land Agency*, 246 F.2d 641, 644 (D.C. Cir. 1957) (citations omitted).
17. *Commonwealth, Dep't of Highways v. Gibson*, 523 S.W.2d 885 (Ky. 1975); *Hickey v. United States*, 208 F.2d 269 (3rd Cir. 1953) *cert. denied*, 347 U.S. 919 (1954).
18. *Harvey School v. State of New York*, 180 N.Y.S.2d 724 (N.Y. 1958); *In re U.S. Comm. to Appraise Washington Market Co. Prop.*, 295 F. 950 (D.C. Cir 1924).
19. *The Appraisal of Real Estate*, 10th ed., 347.
20. *The Appraisal of Real Estate*, 7th ed. (Chicago: Appraisal Institute, 1978).
21. *The Appraisal of Real Estate*, 10th ed., 347.

The economic age-life method is based on the ratio between the effective age of the improvement and its total economic life. The formula is (effective age/total economic life) x cost new = accrued depreciation. The modified economic age-life method employs the same formula, but it is applied only after separate adjustments are made to the reproduction or replacement cost for items of curable physical deterioration (deferred maintenance) and curable functional obsolescence. The formula for the modified economic age-life method is (effective age/ total economic life) x (cost new - cost of physical and functional curable items) + cost of physical and functional curable items = accrued depreciation.[22]

The breakdown method of estimating depreciation includes the consideration, and separate estimation, of physical deterioration (curable and incurable), functional obsolescence (curable and incurable), and external obsolescence. This is the most thorough and complex method of estimating accrued depreciation.[23]

If adequate market data are available, the fourth method of estimating depreciation, the sales comparison technique, is an excellent appraisal tool that is ideal for jury presentation. For example, assume that a 12-unit apartment building with an effective age of 12 years is being appraised. Further assume that the appraiser's preliminary analysis indicates that 1) the land value is $48,000, 2) the garage facilities have a contributory value of $15,000, 3) the on-site improvements have a contributory value of $9,600, and 4) the estimated reproduction cost of the apartment structure itself is $530,400. Market investigation reveals four recent comparable sales, which are analyzed in Table 8.1. By analyzing the comparable sales, the depreciation present in the property being appraised can be estimated in six steps:

1. Estimate the reproduction cost of each comparable improvement in the same way that the reproduction cost of the property being appraised was estimated.
2. Compute the price paid for each comparable improvement by deducting the estimated land value and the contributory value of the secondary improvements not included in the reproduction cost estimate (e.g., garage, on-site improvements) from the total sale price.
3. Deduct the price paid for the improvement from its reproduction cost, which indicates the total depreciation in the comparable improvement.
4. Divide the total depreciation indicated in each comparable by the effective age of the comparable to obtain the average annual depreciation suffered.
5. Divide the average annual depreciation in the improvement by its reproduction cost to obtain an annual rate of depreciation.
6. Multiply the annual rate of depreciation by 100 to convert it to an annual percentage of depreciation.

For purposes of illustration, assume that Step 1 indicates that the estimated reproduction cost of the apartment structure in Sale 1 is $48 per square foot, or

22. For sample applications of the economic age-life method and the modified age-life method, see *The Appraisal of Real Estate*, 10th ed., 345-346.

23. For an explanation and illustration of this method, see *The Appraisal of Real Estate*, 10th ed., 346-361.

TABLE 8.1 COMPARABLE SALES

	Sale 1	Sale 2	Sale 3	Sale 4
Price	$480,000	$510,000	$432,000	$550,000
No. of units	12	12	10	14
Building size (in sq. ft.)	10,200	10,400	8,000	12,250
Building age (effective)	7	15	14	12
Contributory value of garages	0	$24,000	$20,000	0
Contributory value of on-site improvements	$7,200	$9,000	$10,000	$8,400
Estimated land value	$48,000	$48,000	$42,000	$50,000

$489,600. When Step 2 is applied to Sale 1, the appraiser concludes that $424,800 was paid for the apartment structure, computed as follows:

Sale price		$480,000
Less:		
Garage value	$ 0	
On-site improvement value	7,200	
Land value	48,000	
Total deductions		- 55,200
Sale price of apartment structure		$424,800

Step 3 indicates the total depreciation present in Sale 1.

Reproduction cost	$489,600
Indicated price of improvement	-424,800
Total depreciation present	$ 64,800

The annual depreciation computed in Step 4 is therefore $64,800 (total depreciation) divided by 7 years (effective age), or $9,257. The annual rate of depreciation is developed in Step 5 by dividing $9,257 (annual depreciation) by $489,600 (reproduction cost of the improvement), which results in an annual depreciation rate of 0.0189. This figure is multiplied by 100 in Step 6 to indicate 1.89% depreciation per year.

In Table 8.2 the six-step process is applied to derive the annual rate of depreciation for each of the comparables. The comparables indicate that an annual depreciation rate from 1.77% to 1.89% per year is applicable to the property under appraisal. Applying this range to the 12-year effective age of the subject property suggests a range of depreciation from 21.24% (1.77% x 12 years) to 22.68% (1.89% x 12 years), or $112,657 ($530,400 x 0.2124) to $120,295 ($530,400 x 0.2268).

From this cost approach analysis, the appraiser arrives at the following conclusions regarding the subject apartment building:

TABLE 8.2 COMPARABLE SALES TECHNIQUE FOR ESTIMATING DEPRECIATION

	Sale 1	Sale 2	Sale 3	Sale 4
Price	$480,000	$510,000	$432,000	$550,000
Less garage value	0	24,000	20,000	0
Less on-site improvement value	– 7,200	– 9,000	– 10,000	– 8,400
Less land value	– 48,000	– 48,000	– 42,000	– 50,000
Improvement value	$424,800	$429,000	$360,000	$491,600
Reproduction cost	$489,600	$598,000	$483,000	$624,500
Less improvement value	– 424,800	– 429,000	– 360,000	– 491,600
Improvement depreciation	$ 64,800	$169,000	$123,000	$132,900
Effective age	7 years	15 years	14 years	12 years
Depreciation per year	$9,257	$11,267	$8,786	$11,075
% depreciation per year	1.89%	1.88%	1.82%	1.77%

Reproduction cost of apartment building	$530,400
Less depreciation (22.5%)	–119,340
Indicated value of apartment building	$411,060
Contributory value of garage	15,000
Contributory value of on-site improvements	9,600
Total indicated improvement value	$435,660
Estimated land value	48,000
Total indicated property value by cost approach	$483,660
Rounded	$484,000

This type of analysis can be clearly and convincingly presented to a jury, particularly when the appraiser uses charts like those shown in Tables 8.1 and 8.2.

When the sales comparison technique is applied to estimate depreciation, it is sometimes advisable to estimate the reproduction cost of secondary improvements (e.g., the garages and on-site improvements in the foregoing example) and include them in the total reproduction cost. If this is done, the contributory value of the secondary improvements is not extracted from the sale price of each comparable property and the indicated rate of depreciation is applicable to the reproduction cost of all the improvements. Including the reproduction cost of secondary improvements in the total reproduction cost is particularly advantageous when the ratios between the values of the primary and secondary improvements are similar in the comparable sale properties and the property under appraisal.

For condemnation appraisals, "[t]he preferred methods of estimating depreciation are the breakdown method and the abstraction, or sales comparison, method. The estimating of depreciation by the use of published tables or age-life computations is to be avoided whenever possible."[24]

24. *Uniform Appraisal Standards for Federal Land Acquisitions*, §B-1 - 16, p. 75.

Land Value

Six methods of land valuation are recognized in the appraisal industry: sales comparison, ground rent capitalization, subdivision development, allocation, extraction, and land residual.

If the appraiser does not employ the cost approach to value, estimating the value of the land separately is not technically required in a typical appraisal assignment. However, in eminent domain valuation a separate land value estimate is often required, even if the cost approach is not applied. There are two reasons for this requirement. First, a partial taking requires a separate land value estimate because without it the value of the part taken cannot be accurately estimated; if the before and after rule is applied, the before and after values of the property cannot be properly analyzed without a separate land value estimate. Second, many condemnors require a separate estimate of land value.[25]

The sales comparison approach is the preferred method of land valuation. It is the only method of land valuation recognized by some condemnors when the estimate is being used in the cost approach to value. "[T]he value of the land bare and subject to improvement is always estimated by a study of comparable sales."[26]

The technique applied to value land using comparable sales is the same as that used to value whole properties in the sales comparison approach to value. The technique is described in Chapter 10. Similarly, to value land with the ground rent capitalization technique, the appraiser applies the same procedures employed to value improved properties by the income capitalization approach, which are covered in Chapter 9. The subdivision development methodology, or development approach, to value is described in Chapter 12.

Attempts to value vacant land using improved property sales, as prescribed in the allocation and extraction methods, have generally been rejected by the courts. The single exception to this rule is the use of the extraction method when the improvements constitute a comparative small percentage of the total sale price of the comparable. The procedure used to estimate land value by extraction, is similar to the procedure applied to estimate the amount of depreciation in the improvements, which was demonstrated previously. In this case, however, the residual value is the land value rather than the depreciated value of the improvement. In other words, the depreciated, or contributory, value of all of the improvements on a sale property are deducted from the sale price of the property and the remaining portion of the sale price represents the land value.

The methodology and acceptability of the land residual technique of estimating land value was discussed in Chapter 6. This method of land valuation is, to say the least, looked upon with disfavor by the courts. As one court put it:

> Such a method of evaluation of vacant, unimproved land is completely unprecedented. There is no authority cited by claimants in support of it and none is to be found, for how can income be capitalized to produce a residual land value when

25. Ibid., §B-1 - 15, p. 74.

26. Ibid., §A-6, p. 17.

the appropriated land is neither producing income nor equipped to produce such income.[27]

All six methods of land valuation are discussed in detail in *The Appraisal of Real Estate*.[28] In general, valuation of land using the extraction, allocation, or land residual method is not well received by the courts and may be inadmissible in some jurisdictions. The land residual technique of land valuation, which involves projecting income from a hypothetical improvement, would appear to have no place in the courtroom or in eminent domain valuation.[29]

Appraisers who are forced to estimate land value with a method other than the sales comparison approach should expect to receive strong criticism from the courts and their clients.

ADVANCED PROBLEMS

Entrepreneurial profit is a relatively new concept, at least as a separate item of cost in the cost approach. It was not mentioned as a separate item of cost in *The Appraisal of Real Estate* until the eighth edition of that textbook was published in 1983. As yet, the courts have not adequately addressed the issue sufficiently to determine its place in eminent domain valuation.

Although entrepreneurial profit has only recently been formally recognized as a separate item of cost in the cost approach, it is evident that it has been recognized by appraisers in developing their reproduction or replacement cost estimates. If appraisers had historically omitted this important element of cost, their estimates of market value developed by the cost approach would have been consistently lower than their estimates of market value by the sales comparison and income capitalization approaches to value. This has not been the case. The only logical explanation is that appraisers have incorporated entrepreneurial profit into their cost approach estimates by either including it in their reproduction cost estimates or underestimating depreciation to account for it. Either way, it has been included in their estimates. If it had not, their value estimates by the cost approach would have always been low, which is certainly not the case.

Including a separate cost item for entrepreneurial profit is obviously a more desirable, and technically correct, methodology. However, appraisers must recognize that, historically, they may have built this cost factor into their estimates of value by the cost approach. Thus, they may need to adjust their methods of estimating reproduction cost and/or depreciation so as not to count this item of cost twice.

"Entrepreneurial profit is a market-derived figure that reflects the amount an entrepreneur expects to receive for his or her contribution. It represents the degree of risk and expertise associated with the development of a project."[30] It must be remembered that an entrepreneur is not guaranteed a profit. The entrepreneurial profit in a project may be totally eradicated by poor project management or unfavorable market events or conditions. If this is the case, it would be proper

27. *Levitin v. State of New York*, 207 N.Y.S.2d 798, 799 (N.Y. 1960).
28. *The Appraisal of Real Estate*, 10th ed., 299–310.
29. *United States v. 75.13 Acres of Land, etc.*, 693 F.2d 813, 816 (8th Cir. 1982).
30. *The Appraisal of Real Estate*, 10th ed., 327.

to include entrepreneurial profit in the reproduction cost estimate, but then deduct it from the indicated market value of the property by increasing depreciation.

> Potential entrepreneurial profit should be derived from market analysis and through interviews with developers to determine the expectations of profit required as motivation or incentive to undertake a particular development.
>
> Less emphasis should be given to historical profit margins. Historical profits are records of results and often differ from the anticipated profit which originally motivated the entrepreneur to proceed with the project. Estimating an appropriate amount of entrepreneurial profit is a continued challenge for appraisers because expectations of profit vary with different market conditions and property types and typical relationships between profit and other costs are difficult to establish.[31]

In estimating entrepreneurial profit the appraiser must rely on indirect evidence (i.e., opinions expressed by developers) more than direct evidence (i.e., factual market data), so it is very important that the appraiser's estimate of depreciation be market-derived. The sales comparison, or abstraction, method of estimating depreciation is particularly reliable. The appraiser must include an appropriate entrepreneurial profit in the reproduction cost estimates of the comparables. By deducting the extracted price of the improvements from their estimated reproduction or replacement cost, which includes entrepreneurial profit, the amount of depreciation applicable to the entrepreneurial profit is automatically reflected.

It has been said that "[s]ince [the cost] approach almost invariably tends to result in the highest possible valuation and thus to implant in the minds of the factfinding body inflated figures which are difficult to erase, it should not be used even as a check upon more reliable methods without a showing that a reasonably prudent person would consider reproduction of the property involved."[32] With historical statements such as this endorsed by a number of courts, appraisers will have difficulty convincing the courts of the propriety of including a separate entrepreneurial profit factor in the cost approach unless they have very strong market evidence to support it.

According to one source, "[e]ntrepreneurial profit can take the form of profit on a sale, additional return on an investment in an operating property, or use value to the entrepreneur."[33]

Nevertheless, including entrepreneurial profit in the reproduction cost of a structure built for nonprofit purposes such as a church, school, or public utility would appear questionable, as would its inclusion in the reproduction cost estimate of a special-purpose structure. This is not the case, however, in the appraisal of owner-occupied property. Appraisal clients such as mortgage lenders sometimes object to the inclusion of entrepreneurial profit in the appraisal of an owner-occupied property because they fear the owner will have no cash invested in the property. However, an eminent domain case is an action *in rem* (i.e., against the

---

31. Ibid., 10th ed., 328.
32. *A Procedural Guide for the Acquisition of Real Property by Governmental Agencies*, Department of Justice, Land and Natural Resources Division (1972), p. 12, citing *United States v. Certain Interest in Property in the Borough of Brooklyn (Fort Hamilton)*, 326 F.2d 109, 115 (2d Cir. 1964) *cert. den.* 377 U.S. 978 (1964).
33. *The Appraisal of Real Estate*, 10th ed., 327.

property rather than against the property owner) and the form of ownership is not a consideration. The fact that a property is owner-occupied or tenant-occupied does not change its market value. Therefore, the validity of including entrepreneurial profit in an estimate of reproduction or replacement cost is not altered by the type of occupation of the property.

Summary

There is substantial disagreement among the courts regarding the competency of cost approach evidence in an eminent domain action, but most courts will accept such evidence as long as it is established that the improvements contribute value to the land. The appraiser should be aware of the court's attitude toward the cost approach and the admissibility of reproduction cost estimates before attempting to testify. A jury will not be impressed with an appraiser who testifies that his conclusion of value is based primarily on an approach that the court subsequently rules inadmissible. Although a majority of the courts allow evidence on reproduction cost and the cost approach, most have developed safeguards in regard to its admission. Many courts have expressed the opinion that the cost approach will often produce an exaggerated indication of market value.

The courts universally agree that if reproduction cost evidence is admissible, the cost estimate must be reduced by the depreciation present in the property, which includes physical deterioration, functional obsolescence, and external obsolescence.

Even in jurisdictions that do not allow testimony in regard to reproduction cost or the cost approach, the appraiser is ethically and professionally obligated to use this approach in the appraisal process if it will assist in developing a more accurate and reliable value conclusion. Whether the data developed in the approach is admissible or not, it can be of invaluable assistance to the appraiser in allocating the elements of value and damages in partial taking cases. In all cases the appraiser must make a detailed inspection of the improvements noting all material construction details. An extensive field inspection checklist is very useful in documenting necessary physical data.

No matter how the cost approach was applied in the appraisal process, the appraiser should present the data to the trier of fact as clearly and simply as possible. The actual, recent costs of comparable improvements are excellent data upon which to base a reproduction cost estimate. Because such costs represent identifiable market data, they are more likely to be accepted by the courts. Similarly, the sales comparison, or abstraction, method of estimating depreciation can generally be presented most clearly and convincingly, thus it is most likely to gain the acceptance of the court and the review appraiser.

An appraiser who plans to testify to reproduction cost should avoid claiming expertise in cost estimating. Rather, he or she should use direct market data to estimate reproduction cost whenever possible or obtain cost data from two independent sources to ensure that the testimony will not be considered hearsay.

The appraiser must always consider entrepreneurial profit as an element of reproduction cost. The estimate of entrepreneurial profit should be market-derived. Appraisers must recognize that entrepreneurial profit, like any other element of reproduction cost, is subject to depreciation.

Despite the skepticism of some courts, the cost approach is an integral part of the appraisal process. It does not always produce the highest indication of value among the three standard approaches. If properly developed, the cost approach can produce a reliable indication of *market value* comparable to the market value estimates derived by the sales comparison and income capitalization approaches to value.

CHAPTER 9

Income Capitalization Approach to Value

The income capitalization approach to value has been defined as follows:

> A set of procedures through which an appraiser derives a value indication for an income-producing property by converting its anticipated benefits (cash flows and reversions) into property value. This conversion can be accomplished in two ways. One year's income expectancy can be capitalized at a market-derived capitalization rate or a capitalization rate that reflects a specified income pattern, return on investment, and change in the value of the investment. Alternatively, the annual cash flows for the holding period and the reversion can be discounted at a specified yield rate.[1]

In the past 25 years, the income capitalization approach has been modified and expanded more dramatically than any other procedure in real estate appraisal. The fourth edition of *The Appraisal of Real Estate*, published in 1964, devoted 89 pages to the development and application of the income capitalization approach; the tenth edition of the same text, published in 1992, has approximately 60% more material on the approach. Educational offerings as well as the educational requirements for a general appraisal designation from professional real estate appraisal organizations have been expanded substantially over this same time period.

The income capitalization approach began its transition in 1959 with the publication of *The Ellwood Tables*.[2] Before that time the income capitalization approach was dominated by application of residual techniques, which emphasized

1. *The Dictionary of Real Estate Appraisal*, 3d ed. (Chicago: Appraisal Institute, 1993), 178.
2. See *Ellwood Tables for Real Estate Appraising and Financing* (Ridgewood, N.J.: L.W. Ellwood, 1959).

the physical components of property (land and improvements) with provisions for depreciation (or recapture) of the improvements. The Ellwood technique mirrored the realities of the marketplace by analyzing investment property, like investors do, in terms of its economic components (mortgage and equity) rather than its physical components. The Ellwood formula also incorporated consideration of typical holding, or investment, periods (rather than the remaining economic life of the improvements), the effects of anticipated appreciation or depreciation over the holding period, and the effect of mortgage amortization over the ownership term.

To address the increasing complexity of real estate investment and financing, and the inflationary and recessionary trends of the 1970s and 1980s, more sophisticated investment analysis was developed. New techniques of analysis probably contributed in some degree to the financial woes of the banking industry, not because these techniques are flawed, but because they can easily be misused and manipulated.

In general appraisal practice, "[t]he methods that are most useful today include direct capitalization based on equity capitalization rates derived from comparable sales and yield capitalization that employs DCF [discounted cash flow] analysis."[3] Because of the relatively recent introduction of Ellwood and DCF analysis into the income capitalization approach, there is little case law reflecting the courts' attitude toward these techniques.

Courts differ in their willingness to accept the income capitalization approach to value in eminent domain cases. In all jurisdictions the courts appear to accept evidence developed through the income capitalization approach when the property in question is income-producing and sufficient market data to develop the sales comparison approach are not available. In general the courts seem to view the income capitalization approach as superior to the cost approach, but inferior to the sales comparison approach.[4]

The various courts differ greatly in their attitudes toward income capitalization approach evidence. The Uniform Eminent Domain Code states:

> A valuation witness...may consider, as a basis for an opinion of value, the actual or reasonable net rental income attributable to the property when used for its highest and best use, capitalized at a fair and reasonable interest rate.[5]

Although the code allows the expert to *consider* the income capitalization approach to value, it does not necessarily allow for testimony in this regard. By way of explanation, the code states "[a] valuation witness...may consider as the basis for his opinion of value any nonconjectural matters ordinarily relied upon by experts in forming opinions as to the fair market value of property, whether or not they are admissible in evidence."[6]

Condemnors' attitudes toward the income capitalization approach mirror those of the courts.

3. *The Appraisal of Real Estate*, 10th ed. (Chicago: Appraisal Institute, 1992), 424.
4. *United States v. Certain Interest in Prop.*, 271 F.2d 379 (7th Cir. 1959), *cert. denied* 362 U.S. 974 (1960); *United States v. 47.14 Acres*, 674 F.2d 722 (8th Cir. 1982).
5. Uniform Eminent Domain Code, 1974, §1110, p. 11.10.
6. Ibid., §11.06, p. 11.7.

> Initially, use of the income approach frequently consumes a disproportionate amount of time, and, as a result, it receives unmerited emphasis to the detriment of the sales evidence which demonstrates what buyers and sellers are paying on the market for comparable income producing properties. Also, the myriad factors and great variables involved in the capitalization process (capitalization rates, Inwood factors, gross income, effective gross income, net income before recapture, net income after all depreciation, residual techniques, etc.) preclude it from being a readily understandable approach in any event.[7]

It is essential that the appraiser assess the court's attitude toward the income capitalization approach in the jurisdiction in which a case is to be heard before testifying. In light of the general attitude of the courts, "reliance upon a valuation approach other that the comparable sales approach should be given careful consideration."[8]

There are two basic types of capitalization rates that can be used in the income capitalization approach to value: income rates and yield rates. "[T]he rates are not conceptually the same, nor are they interchangeable. An income rate is the ratio of one year's income to value; a yield rate is applied to a series of individual incomes to obtain the present value of each."[9] Because of this conceptual difference, the following discussion of income, vacancy, and expense estimation would be applicable to a single year when an income rate is to be used and to each year of the projection or ownership term if yield capitalization is to be employed.

GROSS INCOME ESTIMATE

The first step in the income capitalization approach is to estimate the annual gross rental income the property being appraised would produce if it were 100% occupied. To accomplish this, the appraiser usually investigates and analyzes the actual rent schedule of the property, if there is one, and compares it with the rent schedules of similar properties. From this analysis the appraiser estimates the economic, or market, rent applicable to the property under appraisal.

> As with a recent and unforced sale of the property under appraisal, if the property is actually rented its current rent is often the best evidence of its economic, or market, rent and should be given appropriate consideration by the appraiser in estimating the gross economic rent of the property.[10]

If the property being appraised is rented and the appraiser's conclusion of economic rent deviates from the actual rent schedule, the appraiser is professionally and ethically obligated to present strong market support for the deviation.[11] The courts have adopted this position.

7. *Uniform Appraisal Standards for Federal Land Acquisitions* (Washington, D.C.: U.S. Government Printing Office, 1992) §A-7, 20.

8. Ibid.

9. *The Appraisal of Real Estate*, 10th ed., 414–415.

10. *Uniform Appraisal Standards for Federal Land Acquisitions*, §B-1 - 18, p. 77.

11. The Appraisal Foundation, *Uniform Standards of Professional Appraisal Practice* (USPAP), 1994 ed., Standards Rule 1-4(c), p. 12.

> Estimates of earnings out of conformity with actual earnings should, in the main, be disregarded except when accompanied by some convincing proof as to why they form a more reasonable basis for valuation than actual earnings.[12]

Some courts have rejected income capitalization approach testimony because the property under appraisal was not actually rented. In *City of Chicago v. Giedratis* the court said

> We know of no instance in which speculative or future anticipated rentals were held to be competent valuation factors...Since the Giedraitis property was owner occupied and no actual rental had been made or was even anticipated, it is clear that the trial court did not err in striking testimony based upon such improper elements.[13]

However, an Alabama court took an opposite view when it held that evidence of rental value is admissible even where the owner occupied the property himself and did not actually rent it.[14] As noted in Chapter 8, value estimates based on income from hypothetical improvements are generally rejected by the courts.

In estimating the gross income attributable to a property, the appraiser must exclude any income that would be considered business income, rather than real estate rental income. It is the real estate, not the business, that is generally being acquired under the sovereign's power of eminent domain.[15]

> Textbook writers, as well as judicial dicta, often state as a general rule that neither the realized nor the estimated future profits of a business are admissible evidence of the value of the land on which the business is, or may be, located.[16]

Evidence of business volume may be admitted, however, when it can be shown that this is the basis of market value and/or economic rent within the industry. For example, a Missouri court ruled it an error to instruct the jury to consider the amount of fuel being pumped by a service station that was being condemned only to indicate the property's highest and best use. Evidence showed that service station properties were sold and rented on a dollar amount per gallon of gasoline pumped. The higher court ruled that "[i]n view of the evidence offered and received, we think the instruction was erroneous and misleading and particularly prejudicial to respondent."[17]

Note that there are exceptions to the general rule that a business located on property being condemned is not to be valued and compensation is not to be paid for the taking of the business. A number of states have made specific statutory provisions allowing payment for the taking or destruction of businesses under certain circumstances. For instance Florida, Vermont, and California have adopted such statutes.[18] Other states (e.g., New York, Pennsylvania, Louisiana, Georgia) have permitted compensation for business losses under certain circumstances.[19]

---

12. *Matter of City of New York*, 82 N.Y.S.2d 55, 70 (N.Y. 1948).
13. *City of Chicago v. Giedraitis*, 150 N.E.2d 577, 580, 581 (Ill. 1958).
14. *Kayo Oil Co. v. State*, 340 So.2d 756 (Ala. 1976).
15. *Arkansas State Hwy. Comm. v. Wilmans*, 370 S.W.2d 802 (Ark. 1963); *United States v. General Motors Corp.*, 323 U.S. 373 (1945).
16. Lewis Orgel, *Valuation Under the Law of Eminent Domain*, 2d ed., (Charlottesville, Va.: The Michie Co., 1953), vol. 1, §162, 655.
17. *St. Louis Housing Authority v. Bainter*, 297 S.W.2d 529, 533 (Mo. 1957).
18. Florida Statutes §73.10(4); 19 Vermont Stat. Ann. §212(2), No. 242 of Acts of 1957; California Code of Civil Procedure §1263.
19. See *Application of Huie*, 202 N.Y.S.2d 954 (N.Y. 1960), Administrative Code, City of New York, §K41-44.0; *Redevelopment Auth. of City of Chester v. Swagger*, 316 A.2d 136 (Pa. 1974); La. Const. art. I, §4; *De Kalb County v. Cowan*, 261 S.E.2d 478 (Ga. 1979).

Compensation for business loss has been found to be due when the government actually takes over a business located on a condemned property. This most commonly occurs when the government condemns a public utility such as a water company and continues its operation. This situation also arises in federal condemnations. For example, the federal government condemned a commercial laundry during World War II and continued to operate the facility, retaining many of the condemnee's 180 employees. In this case the court ruled that the business itself had been condemned and, in addition to the real estate, compensation was due for the business.[20] This line of reasoning was followed recently in a case in which the National Park Service condemned a canoe livery facility and planned to operate a canoe livery service.[21]

The appraiser is cautioned that compensation for business loss is generally due only in unique and legally complex circumstances. Appraisers should never assume that business loss is compensable without properly supported, written legal instruction.

Proper professional practice requires that the appraiser use rent comparables in estimating the economic rent of the property being appraised, whether or not the conclusion conforms to the property's actual rent schedule. A few courts exclude testimony on comparable rentals, but most follow the same rules adopted in regard to the admissibility of comparable sales. (See Chapter 10.)

Vacancy and Collection Loss

The second step in the income capitalization approach is to estimate the vacancy and collection loss applicable to the property under appraisal and deduct this amount from the property's gross income to produce an estimate of the effective gross income of the property.

> In considering income for capitalization purposes, it is usually essential to deduct (in most cases) a normal reserve for vacancies...Thus the resultant capitalization figure is based on normal earnings and does not excessively penalize property in "bad times" nor inflate its value in "boom times." It is axiomatic that a reasonably prudent investor will provide such a safety margin in his calculations in weighing the relative attractiveness of a new investment.[22]

An appraiser usually estimates a property's the vacancy rate by analyzing the quality and durability of the projected income and the vacancy levels of comparable properties under similar circumstances. At times, however, courts have held that it is not improper to exclude a vacancy factor.[23] This practice may become more prevalent as the courts begin to rule on cases involving income projections over a typical ownership term, rather than over the economic life of the improvements. A vacancy factor may be unnecessary if the projected ownership term is equal to or less than the existing lease term and the lease is held by a high-quality tenant.

20. *Kimball Laundry Co. v. United States*, 338 U.S. 1 (1949).
21. *United States v. 0.88 Acres of Land*, 670 F.Supp. 210 (W.D. Mich. 1987).
22. *Matter of City of New York*, 82 N.Y.S.2d 55, 70, 71 (N.Y. 1948).
23. *In re Lincoln Square Slum Clearance Project*, 222 N.Y.S.2d 786 (N.Y. 1961).

EXPENSES

According to one source,

> In considering evidence of existing rents as an element in the determination of market value, care must be taken to distinguish between gross rentals and net rentals. It is the latter which is ordinarily considered as an evidentiary factor in the valuation process. Thus, rentals may be considered as evidence of value only after expenses such as light and heat have been deducted from gross rentals."[24]

Expenses must be deducted from the effective gross income of property. Fixed expenses, operating expenses, and a reserve for replacement of short-lived items are estimated by the appraiser and deducted from the effective gross income of the property to arrive at an estimate of net income.

Many appraisers are using a projected ownership term, rather than the property's economic life, and are not establishing specific reserves for replacements. Instead, they include some of these items in their estimate of annual repairs and maintenance and/or consider the probable condition of these short-lived items in terms of their effect on the probable resale price of the property at the end of the projected ownership term. This procedure tends to produce a more accurate cash flow projection, which can be useful to an appraiser who wishes to make a cash flow analysis as part of the appraisal process.

In estimating the expenses applicable to the property being appraised, the appraiser should be aware of expense trends as well as the historical expenses of the property. The actual expenses incurred by comparable properties can also be used to make accurate expense projections. For example, persuasive evidence will result if the appraiser can testify that estimated expenses are 30% of the property's effective gross income and that comparable rental properties (or comparable sales used in the sales comparison approach) are experiencing expenses ranging from 28% to 32% of their effective gross incomes.

> It is important to carefully scrutinize "actual" operating expenses, since in any one year they are apt to include either a substantial capital investment or at least disbursements which are more properly spread or prorated over a number of years, depending upon the life of the particular improvements.[25]

The appraiser is therefore required to develop a *stabilized* estimate of expenses. A *stabilized expense* is "[a] projected expense that is subject to change, but has been adjusted to reflect an equivalent, stable annual expense."[26]

NET INCOME

Once gross income, vacancy, and expenses are estimated, the appraiser can compute the estimated net income for the property being appraised in two steps.

---

24. *Nichols' The Law of Eminent Domain*, rev. 3rd ed. (New York: Mathew Bender Co., Inc., 1991), vol. 5, §19.03.

25. Ibid.

26. *The Dictionary of Real Estate Appraisal*, 3d ed., 344.

Gross income - vacancy and collection loss = effective gross income
Effective gross income - expenses = net income

The appraiser should prepare a clear, detailed stabilized income and expense statement for presentation to the trier of fact and inclusion in the appraisal report. Table 9.1 illustrates an effective format for presenting a stabilized, or reconstructed, operating statement. To support the appraiser's estimate, information on comparable properties can be presented using the format shown in Table 9.2 or the simpler presentation shown in Table 9.3. If the situation demands it, the figures may be expressed both as a percentage of gross income and in dollars per

TABLE 9.1 RECONSTRUCTED OPERATING STATEMENT OF 14-UNIT APARTMENT BUILDING (SUBJECT PROPERTY)

	3 Years Ago	2 Years Ago	Last Year	Projected Stabilized
Gross income:				
Scheduled rent	$31,080	$33,600	$35,280	$35,280
Less vacancy and collection loss	- 1,243	- 3,380	- 2,470	- 2,822
Subtotal	$29,837	$30,220	$32,810	$32,458
Laundry income	1,260	1,580	1,848	1,750
Other income	0	300	50	0
Effective gross income	$31,097	$32,100	$34,708	$34,208
Less expenses:				
Fixed:				
Real estate taxes	$ 2,100	$ 2,400	$ 2,500	$ 2,600
Insurance	0	0	520	175
Total fixed expenses	$ 2,100	$ 2,400	$ 3,020	$ 2,775
Operating:				
Utilities	$ 1,848	$ 1,830	$ 1,950	$ 1,900
Advertising	820	830	858	840
Office expenses	137	140	142	150
Professional management	2,089	2,115	2,297	2,272
Resident manager	840	840	840	840
Professional fees	300	50	320	300
Repairs and maintenance	2,675	1,850	4,032	1,850
Cleaning	324	375	309	350
Yard and ground care	240	280	280	280
Miscellaneous expenses	0	40	100	50
Total operating expenses	$ 9,273	$ 8,350	$11,128	$ 8,832
Reserves:				
Drapes and carpets	$ 0	$ 0	$ 0	$ 560
Appliances	0	0	0	1,680
Roof	0	0	0	230
Total reserves	$ 0	$ 0	$ 0	$ 2,470
Total expenses	$11,373	$10,750	$14,148	$14,077
Net income	$19,724	$21,350	$20,560	$20,131

TABLE 9.2 INCOME AND EXPENSE COMPARISON PER UNIT

	Rental 1	Rental 2	Rental 3	Subject Stabilized
Gross income:				
Scheduled rent	$2,400	$3,120	$2,340	$2,520
Less vacancy and collection loss	– 96	– 250	– 164	– 202
Subtotal	$2,304	$2,870	$2,176	$2,318
Laundry income	112	128	120	125
Other income	8	0	0	0
Effective gross income	$2,424	$2,998	$2,296	$2,443
Less expenses:				
Fixed:				
Real estate taxes	$ 175	$ 190	$ 172	$ 186
Insurance	12	15	14	13
Total fixed expenses	$ 187	$ 205	$ 186	$ 199
Operating:				
Utilities	$ 132	$ 140	$ 128	$ 136
Advertising	62	60	56	60
Office expenses	8	10	12	11
Professional management	170	210	161	162
Resident manager	60	61	48	60
Professional fees	0	25	12	21
Repairs and maintenance	128	140	113	132
Cleaning	28	30	27	25
Yard and ground care	18	23	22	20
Miscellaneous expenses	0	8	0	4
Total operating expenses	$ 606	$ 707	$ 579	$ 631
Reserves:				
Drapes and carpets	$ 35	$ 44	$ 32	$ 40
Appliances	115	130	117	120
Roof	15	20	16	16
Total reserves	$ 165	$ 194	$ 165	$ 176
Total expenses	$ 958	$1,106	$ 930	$1,006
Net income	$1,466	$1,892	$1,366	$1,437

TABLE 9.3 INCOME AND EXPENSE COMPARISON PER UNIT

	Rental 1	Rental 2	Rental 3	Subject Stabilized
Effective gross income	$2,424	$2,998	$2,296	$2,443
Expenses:				
Fixed	187	205	186	199
Operating	606	707	579	631
Reserves	165	194	165	176
Total expenses	$ 958	$1,106	$ 930	$1,006
Net income	$1,466	$1,892	$1,366	$1,437

applicable unit of comparison (e.g., per apartment unit, per room, per square foot). (See Table 9.4.) Regardless of how the information is presented to the trier of fact, a detailed reporting of historical and projected income and expenses similar to that shown in Table 9.1 should be included in the appraisal report.[27]

TABLE 9.4 RECONSTRUCTED OPERATING STATEMENT OF 14-UNIT APARTMENT HOUSE (SUBJECT PROPERTY)

	Total	Percent of Scheduled Gross Rent	Per Unit
Gross income:			
Scheduled rent	$35,280	1000	$2,520
Less vacancy and collection loss	– 2,822	– 80	– 202
Subtotal	$32,458	920	$2,318
Laundry income	1,750	50	125
Other income	0	0	0
Effective gross income	$34,208	970	$2,443
Less expenses:			
Fixed:			
Real estate taxes	$ 2,600	74	$ 186
Insurance	175	5	13
Total fixed expenses	$ 2,775	79	$ 199
Operating:			
Utilities	$ 1,900	54	$ 136
Advertising	840	24	60
Office expense	150	4	11
Professional management	2,272	64	162
Resident manager	840	24	60
Professional fees	300	9	21
Repairs and maintenance	1,850	52	132
Cleaning	350	10	25
Yard and ground care	280	8	20
Miscellaneous expenses	50	1	4
Total operating expenses	$ 8,832	250	$ 631
Reserves:			
Drapes and carpets	$ 560	16	$ 40
Appliances	1,680	47	120
Roof	230	7	16
Total reserves	$ 2,470	70	$ 176
Total expenses	$14,077	399	$1,006
Net income	$20,131	571	$1,437

The appraiser must convince the trier of fact and the reader of the appraisal report of the accuracy of the net income estimate. If he does not, the development of an appropriate capitalization rate will be of little interest or value, however clearly and convincingly it is presented.

27. *Uniform Appraisal Standards for Federal Land Acquisitions*, §B-1 18, p. 77.

CAPITALIZATION PROCESS

The mathematics of direct capitalization are quite simple. The process is based on the fact that there is a direct relationship between the value of a property and the net income it can produce. All appraisers, even those inexperienced in the appraisal of income-producing properties, are aware of this relationship and of the formulas $I \div R = V$ and $F \times I = V$. The factor F is simply the reciprocal of the rate R. Thus, the reciprocal of 5% is 20 (1/0.05) and the reciprocal of 20 is 0.05 (1/20), or 5%.

It can be seen that if any two elements of the formula are known, the third can be computed with the proper formula. For example, if a property sold for $100,000 ($V$) and had a net income of $9,000 ($I$) per year, the unknown element in the formula is the rate (R) and applying the formula $I \div V = R$ produces $9,000 ÷ $100,000 = 9%. If this 9% rate is considered applicable to a property under appraisal, which has a net income of $12,000, the value of the property could be computed as follows:

$$I/R = V$$

$$\$12{,}000/0.09 = \$133{,}333$$

Although the relationship between value, income, and rate of return is ingrained in the appraiser's mind, it is less apparent to the typical juror or lawyer. Therefore, the appraiser must explain this relationship or a good portion, if not all, of the jury will not follow the appraiser's testimony regarding the capitalization process. The appraiser must educate the jury in the matter carefully, striking a delicate balance. The appraiser's explanation must be so clear and precise that it cannot be misunderstood, but it must not appear condescending. The appraiser can impress upon the jurors that they are not expected to have this knowledge because they are not experts in the field of valuation or finance, but they must acquire a general understanding of the capitalization process to fulfill their duties as jurors in the case under consideration. The appraiser's explanation will be most effective if it is presented to a jury in both written and oral form. It might be wise to illustrate the relationship between value, income, and rate of return with something familiar to most jurors, such as the operation of a savings account.

If the trier of fact is not a jury, but a judge or commission, the appraiser's task may be simplified or obviated. The appraiser should follow the advice of legal counsel in this regard. Attorneys typically know the level of experience and understanding of the judge or commission hearing the case.

The degree to which the trier of fact must be educated on the capitalization process depends on the complexity of the appraiser's testimony. If the appraiser will testify on developing an applicable overall capitalization rate from market sales, the jury need only understand two relationships:

Comparable property's income/comparable property's price = rate

Subject property's income/rate = subject property's value.

On the other hand, if the appraiser's testimony will involve concepts such as the band-of-investment method of rate selection, equity capitalization, one of the residual techniques, or yield capitalization, the jury must understand these more complex techniques.

It must be remembered, however, that the appraiser's job is not to conduct a capitalization seminar, but to give the jurors enough information to understand the income approach testimony. The application of a capitalization rate is a simple mathematical process. It is the selection and/or development of a proper rate that appears complex to the uninitiated. If residual techniques, equity yield rates, discount rates, equity capitalization rates, and the like can confuse appraisers and the attorneys who are not continually involved in income-producing property valuations, imagine their effect on a trier of fact. Practicing appraisers or attorneys who have not continued their professional education can also find themselves woefully behind the times. Unfortunately this deficiency is often brought to light under cross-examination, much to the chagrin of the appraiser.

Each method of capitalization rate selection or development has built-in assumptions regarding the nature of the income stream, the income projection term, the form of the investment yield rate, the amount of money recaptured over the projection period, the recapture term, and the recapture rate. It is not enough for the appraiser simply to understand and utilize the appropriate method of capitalization rate selection. He or she must fully understand all methods of rate selection, be able to describe them, and be prepared to explain why they are not as reliable or applicable to the property under appraisal.

When the appraiser has employed direct capitalization using an overall capitalization rate extracted directly from comparable sales, the resulting value indication is often difficult to attack effectively on cross examination. In such circumstances, some attorneys try to confuse the trier of fact about the entire capitalization process, rather than directly attack the appraiser's income capitalization approach valuation. By displaying a complete understanding of all facets of the income capitalization approach, the appraiser can often derail this line of questioning. For this reason the appraiser should understand all the methodologies and techniques available for use in the income capitalization approach and be able to explain them in a manner that will not confuse the trier of fact.

These methodologies are described in detail in *The Appraisal of Real Estate*.[28] A reading of *Burritt Mutual Savings Bank v. City of New Briton*[29] could prove interesting for comparison. Although this tax review case was heard in 1958, does not address the more recent techniques of capitalization, and was subsequently set aside, it is one of the most detailed descriptions of the income capitalization approach laid down by any court.

In selecting the method of capitalization to be applied to a specific property, the appraiser must ensure that the assumptions built into the method apply to the property being appraised and that the method of analysis that would be employed by typical buyers and sellers of such properties. "[O]ne of the principal keys in the capitalization of income process is determination of the capitalization

28. *The Appraisal of Real Estate*, 10th ed., 409–551.

29. *Burritt Mutual Savings Bank v. City of New Briton*, 140 A.2d 324 (Conn. 1958); set aside 154 A.2d 608 (1959).

rate, i.e., that percentage which will provide for the recapture or amortization of the value of the investment in the improvements, plus a reasonable and proper rate of return to the investor."[30]

Time and time again, the courts have recognized the importance of selecting the proper capitalization rate to be applied to the net income of the property being valued. One court has stated, "[i]n this whole process the vital factor is the capitalization rate"[31] and another held that "[p]erhaps the most vital factor in the process of capitalization of income is the determination of the capitalization rate."[32] According to a third court, "The capitalization or interest rate selected and applied to the formula used here reflects the degree of risk in the undertaking involved. It is an extremely important figure in the computation because a change of even a fraction of one percent will produce a surprisingly material change in the result."[33]

Because the courts recognize the importance of the capitalization rate, they often insist that the rates selected be supported by market data.

> Market value is ascertained by the income approach by the mathematical process of dividing the estimated annual income from the highest use of the property by a capitalization rate appropriate to the type of investment risk involved. A slight variation in the capitalization rate profoundly affects the value to be attributed to the property. Accordingly, unless the components of the formula, the annual income and the capitalization rate, are determined with reasonable certainty, the resulting value is speculative, and of little use to the trier of fact...
>
> Absent foundation information about the relevant capitalization rate the witness should not be permitted to express an opinion on market value by use of the income approach to value.[34]

Condemnors have also been critical of appraisers who do not support selected capitalization rates with sound market data.

> Too often appraisal witnesses select a capitalization rate "on the basis of my own judgment and experience." This is not substantial support for the rate used. As has been indicated, support from the market place is vital.
>
> The most effective guide to the proper rate at which the net income should be capitalized is the ratio of net income to sale prices in similar transactions.[35]

The most easily understood method of rate selection is direct sales comparison. On several occasions the federal court has approved the admission of comparable sales, even when their sole purpose was to establish the ratio between income and sale price (overall rate).[36] Table 9.5 illustrates how overall capitalization rates can be developed from comparable sales; these rates can then be directly applied to the net income of the property being appraised. This form of analysis, presented graphically to the trier of fact, is convincing evidence. Although the appraiser may have to analyze such data further in the appraisal report or in later testimony, its preliminary presentation to the trier of fact in the

30. *Sill Corp. v. United States*, 343 F.2d 411, 417 (10th Cir. 1965).

31. *Burritt Mutual Savings Bank v. City of New Briton*, 140 A.2d 324, 329 (Conn. 1958); set aside 154 A.2d 608 (1959).

32. *United States v. Tampa Bay Garden Apartments, Inc.*, 294 F.2d 598, 607 (5th Cir. 1961).

33. *United States v. Whitehurst*, 337 F.2d 765, 772 (4th Cir. 1964).

34. *Eikelberger v. State, Dep't of Highways*, 429 P.2d 555, 557 (Nev. 1967).

35. *Uniform Appraisal Standards for Federal Land Acquisitions*, §A-7, pp. 20–21.

36. *United States v. Certain Interest in Property*, 239 F.Supp. 822 (D. Colo. 1965); *Linkins-Foster Monterey Corp. v. United States*, 308 F.2d 595, (9th Cir. 1962).

TABLE 9.5 RATE SELECTION BY DIRECT COMPARISON

	Sale 1	Sale 2	Sale 3	Subject
1. Confirmed sale price	$147,500	$237,500	$225,000	N/A
2. Effective gross income	$ 24,240	$ 35,976	$ 36,736	$34,208
3. Less expenses	– 9,850	– 13,272	– 14,880	–14,077
4. Net income (2 - 3)	$ 14,390	$ 22,704	$ 21,856	$20,131
5. Overall rate (4/1)	0.097559	0.095596	0.097138	N/A
Rounded	9.75%	9.56%	9.71%	

format shown in Table 9.5 is generally most persuasive. The appraiser may subsequently break down the overall rate into components of return on investment and recapture, or into debt service and equity capitalization rates; the trier of fact will be better able to follow the appraiser's analysis if a clear understanding of how the overall rate was developed has been established.

For example, assume the appraiser has chosen to use a mortgage-equity, band-of-investment method of capitalization rate selection, rather than an overall rate developed by direct comparison because of the variations in the financing of the comparable sales. To describe this procedure, the analysis of the comparable sales could be expanded and presented as shown in Table 9.6.

TABLE 9.6 RATE SELECTION BY BAND OF INVESTMENT

	Sale 1	Sale 2	Sale 3
1. Confirmed sale price	$147,500	$237,500	$225,000
2. Mortgage amount	–118,000	–178,125	–180,000
3. Equity (1 - 2)	$ 29,500	$ 59,375	$ 45,000
4. Net income	$ 14,390	$ 22,704	$ 21,856
5. Annual debt service	– 10,929	– 15,313	– 16,315
6. Equity capitalization (4 - 5)	3,461	$ 7,391	$ 5,541
7. Equity capitalization rate (6/3)	0.117322	0.124480	0.123133
Rounded	11.73%	12.45%	12.31%

From the information developed in Table 9.6, the appraiser could reasonably conclude that the appropriate equity capitalization rate for the property under appraisal would be 12%. If the property under appraisal could be financed on the date of valuation with a 75% loan with a 25-year amortization term and an 8.25% interest rate, an overall capitalization rate applicable to the property could be developed with the calculations demonstrated in Table 9.7.

TABLE 9.7 MORTGAGE-EQUITY, BAND-OF-INVESTMENT RATE SELECTION

	% of Total Investment		Rate		Weighted Rate
Mortgage	0.75	x	0.094614*	=	0.070961
Equity	0.25	x	0.12	=	0.030000
Totals	1.00				0.100961
Overall rate (rounded)					10%

* Annual mortgage constant for 25-year loan with 8.25% interest. For example see *The Appraisal of Real Estate*, 10th ed. (Chicago: Appraisal Institute, 1992), 731.

Appraisers who choose to use annuity or mortgage-equity methods of rate selection must fully understand the construction of the rates or constants used and be able to demonstrate the methods in court. Furthermore, they must be able to distinguish how the adopted rates relate to the real estate market and to competitive investments. As one court put it:

> ...Capitalization of income comprehends the use of a rate of return in comparable investments.... There was no testimony whatsoever about comparable investments. [The appraiser] merely used a formula from a handbook of factors for present value of an annuity of $1.00 per year.[37]

The construction of an annuity factor can be demonstrated to a jury, or to another trier of fact, by describing the accumulation of interest in a savings account. The jury could be asked to assume that they are depositing $100 in a savings account today, at 6% interest compounded annually, and want to know what the account balance would be at the end of two years. The computation shown below uses a deposit of $1.00 for convenience.

Deposit	$ 1.00
Interest for Year 1 ($1.00 x 0.06)	0.06
Balance at end of Year 1	$ 1.06
Interest for Year 2 ($1.06 x 0.06)	0.0636
Balance at end of Year 2	$1.1236

Thus, the balance for a $100 deposit at the end of two years would be $112.36 ($100 x 1.1236).

The appraiser can then ask the jurors to assume that they want to end up with a $100 balance in their savings account at the end of two years. How much will they need to deposit today to accumulate this amount? The answer can be calculated by dividing the factor of 1.1236 into one, which results in a factor of 0.889996. This factor is applied to $100 to indicate a required deposit of approximately $89 ($100 x. 0.889996). The accuracy of this factor can be demonstrated as follows:

37. *United States v. 158.76 Acres of Land, etc.*, 298 F.2d 559, 561 (2nd Cir. 1962).

Deposit	$0.889996
Interest in Year 1 (0.889996 x 0.06)	0.053400
Balance at end of Year 1	$0.943396
Interest in Year 2 (0.943396 x 0.06)	0.056604
Balance at end of Year 2	$1.000000

Therefore, the right to receive $100 two years from now is currently worth $89 today. What if $100 is to be received each year for two years? What is that right currently worth? This can be determined by adding the factors for Years 1 and 2 together:

Factor for payment deferred 1 year	0.943396
Factor for payment deferred 2 years	0.889996
Present worth of right to receive $1.00 per year for two years	$1.833392

Thus, the current value of the right to receive $100 per year for two years is $183.34 ($100 x 1.833392). The right to receive $100 one year from today is currently worth $94.34 ($100 x 0.943396), and the right to receive $100 two years from today is currently worth $89 ($100 x 0.889996). So the total current value of the two payments is $183.34 ($94.34 + $89).

To demonstrate the construction of an annual mortgage constant, the factor used to develop an overall rate by mortgage-equity analysis in Table 9.7, the sample calculations can be expanded one more step. If the factor for the present value of a 2-year annuity at 6% is divided into 1, the result is the annual constant, or the installment to amortize. Therefore, the factor to amortize $1.00 over two years at 6% would be 0.545437 (1 ÷ 1.833392) and the annual payment to amortize $100 over 2 years would be $54.54($100 x 0.545437). The proof is demonstrated as follows:

Loan beginning of Year 1	$100.00
Interest during Year 1 ($100 x 0.06)	6.00
Balance before Year 1 payment	$106.00
Year 1 payment	- 54.54
Balance at end of Year 1	$ 51.46
Interest during Year 2 ($51.46 x 0.06)	3.09
Balance before Year 2 payment	$ 54.55
Year 2 payment	- 54.54
Balance	$ 0.01 *

* Balance caused by rounding.

These sample calculations may seem rather simplistic to experienced appraisers and unnecessary because financial calculators are commonly used by appraisers, investors, and mortgage lenders. However, eminent domain juries are seldom made up of appraisers, investors, and mortgage lenders and may not have these experts' confidence in the results shown on a calculator. If an appraiser cannot clearly and simply explain the construction of a financial factor, he or she should not testify to it.

CAPITALIZED VALUE OF RENT COMPARABLES

On occasion, appraisers have attempted to testify to the value of rental properties, other than the property being appraised, by capitalizing their rental incomes. Such testimony has been excluded because "A witness cannot state his opinion of value of neighboring land."[38] As stated by a Missouri court:

> There is no merit to the defendant's contention that the court erred in refusing to allow their witnesses to testify as to the market value of comparable real property computed from the witnesses' knowledge of the lease on the property and its terms. The capitalization of rentals may tend to show the value of the particular property under lease, but an expert witness cannot give an opinion of the value of similar land in support of his opinion of the value of the land in question.[39]

The procedure used by appraisers who have attempted to introduce this methodology is described in the following example.

Step 1. The appraiser locates a comparable rental property that has a gross annual income of $50,000 per year.

Step 2. The appraiser estimates the vacancy and collection loss for the comparable at, say, 7% ($3,500) and calculates its effective gross income to be $46,500 ($50,000 - $3,500).

Step 3. The appraiser next estimates the expenses of the comparable at 35% of effective gross income, or $16,275 ($46,500 x 0.35).

Step 4. Next the appraiser computes the net income of the comparable to be $30,225 ($46,500 - $16,275).

Step 5. Then the appraiser estimates the capitalization rate applicable to the comparable to be 10.5%.

Step 6. The appraiser computes the indicated value of the comparable at approximately $288,000 ($30,225 ÷ 0.105).

Step 7. Finally the appraiser treats the $288,000 indicated value as if it were the bona fide sale price of the comparable and compares the comparable and the property being appraised—the normal procedure in applying the sales comparison approach to value.

In all but the most unusual circumstances, the courts have rejected this procedure, and rightfully so. In at least one case, the appraiser failed to inform the court and the trier of fact that the *comparables* to which he was testifying were developed by the above procedure and were not, in fact, bona fide sales. This was discovered only during cross-examination. The appraiser deceived the court with statements such as "My next comparable, after adjustment for time, indicates a price of X dollars." The appraiser then described the *comparable* as if it were a bona fide sale and made a comparative analysis of the comparable and the property under appraisal.

---

38. *Nichols'*, vol. 5, §23.08[1] (1991).

39. *State v. Vorhof-Duenke Co.*, 366 S.W.2d 329, 340 (Mo. 1963).

This type of conduct, on the part of appraisers, has prompted the courts to make statements such as "in any case where opinion evidence is admissible the particular kind of an opinion desired by any party to the investigation can be readily procured by paying the market price therefor,"[40] and "[i]f I were to give my interpretation of an expert witness, you wouldn't like it, and the lawyers wouldn't like it..."[41]

ADVANCED PROBLEMS

Discounted cash flow analysis is often employed in the income capitalization approach to value.

> Discounted cash flow (DCF) analysis is an accepted analytical tool and method of valuation within the income capitalization approach to value. DCF is not a new method, but it did not enjoy widespread use until modern computer technology enabled appraisers to automate the process. Because DCF analysis is profit oriented and dependent upon the analysis of uncertain future events, it is vulnerable to misuse...
>
> The acceptance of DCF analysis as a method of valuation began in the institutional real estate market and has spread to investment real estate in the general real estate market. DCF techniques may be applied in the valuation or analysis of proposed construction; land development; condominium development or conversion; rehabilitation development; and income-producing real estate of various types. DCF analysis is becoming a requirement of advisors, asset managers, fiduciaries, portfolio managers, syndicators, underwriters and others dealing in investment grade real estate. These users of appraisal services favor the inclusion of DCF analysis as a management tool in projecting cash flow and return expectations, capital requirements, refinancing opportunities and timing of future property dispositions. DCF analysis is regarded as one of the best methods of replicating steps taken to reach investor buy/sell/hold decisions, and is often a part of the exercise of due diligence in the evaluation of an investment.[42]

The benefits of discounted cash flow (DCF) analysis for the *evaluation*[43] of real estate is not particularly pertinent to eminent domain appraisal. Condemnors and the courts would probably like to eliminate the use of DCF analysis in eminent domain cases, not because the methodology is flawed, but because it can be so easily, and convincingly, misused. DCF analysis cannot be eliminated, however, because it can be an extremely valuable appraisal tool when used correctly. It is especially useful in certain partial taking, and temporary taking, cases in which the government's action will result in a temporary interruption of a property's income stream.

---

40. *Roberts v. New York El. R. Co.*, 128 N.Y. 455, 28 N.E. 486, 487 (N.Y. 1891).

41. *Brown & Vaughn Dev. Co. v. Commonwealth*, 143 A.2d 815, 818 (Pa. 1958).

42. USPAP, 1994 ed., Statement on Appraisal Standards No. 2.

43. *Evaluation*, which is distinct from *valuation*, is defined as "[a] study of the nature, quality, or utility of a parcel of real estate or interests in, or aspects of, real property, in which a value estimate is not necessarily required." *The Dictionary of Real Estate Appraisal*, 3d ed., 123.

The advantage of applying direct capitalization with overall capitalization rates extracted from comparable sales is that every component of the analysis is directly supported by actual market data. Income, vacancy, and expense estimates can be supported by the historical income, vacancy rates, and expenses of the property being appraised and by the current incomes, vacancy rates, and expenses of comparable properties. Capitalization rates can be developed directly from market data.

Another advantage of direct capitalization is that it is not the income stream that is actually being valued; rather, it is the relationship, or ratio, of the net income to value that is being measured. Thus, it is not important that the appraiser's estimated net income for the property being appraised mirrors the net income that the property will actually produce. What is important is that the net income from the subject property be estimated in precisely the same manner as the net income from each of the comparables used to develop an applicable capitalization rate.

For example, as noted previously, some appraisers include reserves for the replacement of short-lived items in their expense estimates while other appraisers omit this item from their expense analysis. Whether or not these reserves are included in the expense estimate makes no difference in the final result, (i.e., the indicated market value of the property) as long as both the subject property and the comparables are treated in the same manner. For instance, assume the appraiser analyzes a comparable sale as follows:

Sale price	$100,000
Net income before replacement reserves	8,000
Replacement reserves	– 250
Net income after replacement reserves	$ 7,750

Now assume that the appraiser estimates the net income for the subject property to be $12,800 without any replacement reserve and $12,400 after consideration of a replacement reserve. If the appraiser does not wish to include a replacement reserve in the reconstructed operating statement of the property under appraisal, value would be computed as follows:

Capitalization rate indicated by comparable ($8,000/$100,000)	8.00%
Indicated value of subject property ($12,800/0.08)	$160,000

If the appraiser includes a replacement reserve in the reconstructed operating statement of the property under appraisal, the value would be:

Capitalization rate indicated by comparable ($7,750/$100,000)	7.75%
Indicated value of subject property ($12,400/0.0775)	$160,000

The indicated value remains the same as long as the comparable and the property under appraisal are analyzed consistently. This holds true for income, vacancy, and expense estimates. For example, if an appraiser interprets the market incorrectly and estimates the management expense for the subject property to be 3% of effective gross income when it should have been 7%, the indicated value of the property will be correct as long as the appraiser applies the same incorrect 3% management expense to the comparables before computing the indicated capitalization rate. In essence, the appraiser will commit compensating errors.

DCF analysis does not have the advantages of direct capitalization. It does not measure the ratio of income to value, but the present value of future income streams. For the resulting value to be correct, each of the projected income streams must be correct. Moreover, there is little solid market data that an appraiser can present to support the many conclusions reached in a DCF analysis.

It has been stated that "DCF analysis reflects investment criteria and requires the appraiser to make empirical and subjective assumptions."[44] If this statement were entirely true, DCF analysis would have no place in an eminent domain case because an *assumption* is a "statement accepted or supposed true without proof or demonstration."[45] Appraisers should not base their value estimates on *assumptions*, but rather on well-reasoned conclusions. Application of DCF analysis typically requires the appraiser to reach conclusions in regard to the following items:

- Typical ownership term (forecast period)
- Typical lease term
- Anticipated tenant turnover
- Tenant improvement costs (for both new tenants and existing tenants)
- Current market rent
- Market rent growth or contraction rate
- Typical vacancy, plus vacancy on rollover of tenants
- Current expenses
- Expense growth or contraction rate (which may vary for different expenses)
- Lease commissions (for new leases and lease renewals)
- Selling expenses at end of ownership term
- Selling price of property at end of ownership term (usually based on projected income capitalized at a terminal capitalization rate)
- Discount rate to be applied to income streams

If an appraiser were to testify that he made *assumptions* in regard to each of these items in the appraisal, his testimony would surely be rejected by the trier of fact, if not by the court itself. Many of these factors are forecasts into the future, so they cannot be proven or supported with factual market data. However, the conclusions reached by the appraiser in regard to these items do not necessarily

44. USPAP, 1994 ed., Statement on Appraisal Standards No. 2.

45. William Morse, ed., *The American Heritage Dictionary* (Boston: Houghton Mifflin Co., 1976), 80.

represent his own forecasts of the future; rather these conclusions represent factors currently being used by investors in developing their own forecasts.

Computer-generated DCF analyses can look very impressive, which is one of the major weaknesses of DCF analysis. "Appraisals using the DCF method in the income capitalization approach may contain computerized projections of itemized future cash flow supported by exhaustive printouts that can be misleading. The seeming precision of computer generated projections may give the appearance of certainty to projections that are actually variable within a wide range."[46] It is not always readers of appraisal reports with DCF analysis who are misled; appraisers themselves are sometimes misled. Appraisers cannot abdicate responsibility for their analyses by claiming computer error.

In one case an appraiser was advocating the use of a property that was the subject of the lawsuit as an oyster farm. He projected the number of oysters that would be grown, harvested, and sold each year over a 10-year projection term. In the first year of ownership, the appraiser estimated that the cost to clean each oyster would be 0.5 cent. However, when he entered the formula into his computer spreadsheet, he entered 0.0005 instead of 0.005. He then replicated the same formula (with the same error) for each of the 10 years of the projection term. This was not pointed out to the appraiser until his cross-examination, when he was invited to recompute the estimated value of the property. The recomputed value of what became known as the "digital oyster farm" was several hundred thousand dollars less than appraiser's original value estimate.

"[T]he appraiser is responsible for the entire analysis including the controlling input, the calculations, and the resulting output."[47] Much of the DCF computer software available has been found to contain technical flaws. Some software was developed in such a manner that the user cannot alter some of the assumptions built into it. Appraisers are responsible for the errors and assumptions contained in any software they use.

No cases have been found that address the acceptability of DCF analysis as a valuation method for eminent domain purposes. There are probably several reasons for this, including these facts:

- Only recently has DCF analysis been widely used in real estate valuation.
- DCF analysis has limited applicability in eminent domain appraisals.
- DCF analysis is so complex, compared to other methods of valuation, that it is not understood by attorneys. Thus, they do not know what they should object to about it.
- Because of the complexity of the approach, the courts do not understand it either. When it is objected to, they are inclined to admit it and rule that it is a question of how much weight should be given to the evidence, not the technique's admissibility.
- When DCF analysis is appropriate to an eminent domain appraisal, it is often recognized and used by both the condemnor's and condemnee's appraisers. Thus neither party can object to its admission.

46. USPAP, 1994 ed., Statement on Appraisal Standards No. 2.

47. Ibid.

The courts have historically favored the sales comparison approach to value, often to the exclusion of the cost and income capitalization approaches, and preferred valuation opinions that can be supported by solid market data. Therefore, it is probable that the use of DCF analysis in eminent domain cases will not be warmly received. When an appraiser testifies about how much a property is going to sell for in 10 years, or speculates about whether a nonexistent tenant is going to renew his nonexistent lease in seven years and at what rent, the courts will probably reject, with some justification, the testimony as being speculative and conjectural.

It might be argued that DCF analysis in the context of eminent domain valuation is not entirely new. DCF analysis has been used and approved by a number of courts in the valuation of mineral deposits.[48] However, mineral valuation using DCF analysis is relatively simple compared to the DCF analysis of a shopping center or a multistory, multitenanted office building. Moreover, there do not appear to be any mineral cases in which an appraiser attempted to project increasing or decreasing prices for the minerals over the projection term in developing a value indication by DCF analysis.

Because of the drawbacks in DCF analysis and the danger of its misuse, its applicability in eminent domain valuation is severely limited. The warning that DCF analysis should not be the only method of valuation employed,[49] is especially relevant to eminent domain valuation. DCF analysis was misused in one case in which an appraiser applied the method to an office building and concluded that the typical ownership (or projection) term should be 10 years, typical leases would have 5-year terms, and that there would be a six-month vacancy at the time of lease rollover. The appraiser then computed the resale price of the property at the end of the projection term by capitalizing the projected net income in year 11 by a terminal capitalization rate. However, the eleventh year of the projection just happened to be the year when all of the leases in the building expired, so the projected gross income from the property was only 50% of the typical annual income. Due to the projected six-month vacancy at lease rollover, net income was reduced to only about 20% of its typical level.

Another method of yield capitalization is accomplished with the *mortgage-equity formula*, which is also referred to as the *Ellwood equation*. While this method of capitalization certainly has its place, its place is not in the courtroom. The Ellwood equation is expressed as:

$$R_o = \frac{Y_E - M\,(Y_E + P1/S_n - R_m) - \Delta_o 1/S_n}{1 + \Delta_I J}$$

The equation is explained in detail in *The Appraisal of Real Estate*.[50]

The mortgage-equity method of capitalization has some of the same problems as DCF analysis. To use the mortgage-equity method, the appraiser must project the property's net income over the entire projection term and estimate

48. *United States v. 47.14 Acres of Land*, 674 F.2d 722 (8th Cir. 1982).

49. USPAP, 1994 ed., Statement on Appraisal Standards No. 2.

50. *The Appraisal of Real Estate*, 10th ed., 517–529.

what the sale price of the property (as a percentage of present value) will be at the end of the projection period. This method of rate selection will probably be as poorly received by the courts as DCF analysis.

An additional problem with the mortgage-equity method is the complexity of the formula. Placing the Ellwood equation on an exhibit board is a sure way to lose the trier of fact.

SUMMARY

The income capitalization approach is a procedure that appraisers use to develop an indication of market value by applying a rate or factor to the anticipated net income from a property. This process, which is known as capitalization, acknowledges that a relationship exists between the amount of net income a property can produce and its market value. Over the past several years, capitalization theory has been modified and expanded more than any other concept within the appraisal process. Our highest courts have not yet ruled upon the admissibility of much of this new theory.

Testimony pertaining to the income capitalization approach to value will generally be admitted by the courts as long as the property under appraisal is income-producing in nature and market support is presented for the estimates made by the appraiser in applying this approach. The rental income from the property is to be used in the income capitalization approach, not the profits realized from the business conducted on the property. Business volume may be admitted into evidence only when it can be shown that such volume is the basis of market value and/or market rent in the industry.

The income to be considered by the appraiser is the net rental income from the property, after allowances have been made for vacancy and collection loss and for property expenses. Estimates of gross rents, vacancy rates, and expenses should be supported by the historical income and expenses of the property under appraisal and by the current income and expenses of comparable properties.

The appraiser develops an indication of market value by the income capitalization approach in seven steps:

1. Estimate gross income.
2. Estimate vacancy and collection loss.
3. Compute effective gross income (1. minus 2.).
4. Estimate fixed and operating expenses and reserves for replacement of short-lived items.
5. Deduct expenses from effective gross income to arrived at an estimate of net income.
6. Select an applicable capitalization rate.
7. Apply the capitalization rate to net income to arrive at an indication of the market value of the property being appraised.

When a yield capitalization rate is used, the appraiser must perform Steps 1 through 5 for each year of the projection, or ownership, term. Each annual income stream as well as the sale proceeds at the end of the projection period are discounted to a present value.

The various steps and methodologies of the income capitalization approach are discussed in detail in *The Appraisal of Real Estate.*

> Deriving capitalization rates from comparable sales is preferred when sufficient data on sales of similar, competitive properties are available...This simple technique for estimating overall capitalization rates is preferred and will produce a reliable indication of value by the income capitalization approach if three conditions are met.
>
> 1. Income and expenses must be estimated on the same basis for the subject property and all comparable properties.
> 2. Market expectations concerning resale prices, tax benefits, and holding periods must be similar for all the properties.
> 3. The financing terms and market conditions that affect the comparables must be similar to those affecting the subject property or an adjustment must be made for dissimilarities.[51]

Explaining the income capitalization approach in a courtroom can present special challenges.

> This approach to the valuation of property is, at best, complicated. Should the condemnation get to trial, the clarity with which the appraiser can explain the computations which have been made and the assumptions on which they are based will determine the impact that his conclusion of value based on this approach will have. Unlike the comparable-sales approach, for example, which is based on evidence easily understandable by jurors, the capitalization-of-income approach is based on mathematical computations and assumptions, and is a method of determining value to which most jurors will never have been exposed. Failure to adequately convince a jury that each step in the capitalization-of-income process has been accurately applied to the particular valuation will lessen or even eliminate any effectiveness that the approach and its conclusion might otherwise have.[52]

In 1953, Lewis Orgel wrote:

> Our discussion of rents as evidence of market value is extremely unsatisfactory. This inadequacy is due to the fact that many of the questions that might be raised are not even mentioned in the cases. Beyond stating that evidence of rents is admissible and should be considered, the courts fail to resolve many ambiguities to which the mere statement of the rule gives rise. The major difficulties center around the concept of rental value and the rate of capitalization...
>
> The important problem of discounting future expectations is left completely in the dark. How are we to take account of the likelihood that rental value will

51. Ibid., 468–469.

52. *Nichols'*, vol. 7, §4.04[3] (1992).

> increase in the future? What allowance is to be made for the fact that the community is decadent? And what weight is to be given, in the case of property that is rented piecemeal, such as apartment houses and office buildings, to the extent of future vacancies? The cases yield no answer to these questions and the courts appear content to leave the matter to the judgment of the appraisers.[53]

This argument is more true today than it was in 1953. Not only do Orgel's questions remain unanswered by the courts, but modifications of the income capitalization approach over the years have added a whole myriad of new problems. The best advice for appraisers who must testify to the income capitalization approach is to keep it as simple as possible within the parameters of existing market data and market realities.

53. Orgel, *Valuation Under the Law of Eminent Domain*, 2d ed., vol. 1, §187, 721.

CHAPTER 10

Sales Comparison Approach to Value

The sales comparison approach is

> A set of procedures in which a value indication is derived by comparing the property being appraised to similar properties that have been sold recently, applying appropriate units of comparison and making adjustments to the sale prices of the comparables based on the elements of comparison.[1]

Once referred to as the *market data approach*, this approach to value has more fully been defined as:

> [T]raditionally, an appraisal procedure in which the market value estimate is predicated upon prices paid in actual market transactions and current listings, the former fixing the lower limit of value in a static or advancing market (price wise), and fixing the higher limit of value in a declining market; and the latter fixing the higher limit in any market. It is a process of analyzing sales of similar recently sold properties in order to derive an indication of the most probable sales price of the property being appraised. The reliability of this technique is dependent upon (a) the availability of comparable sales data, (b) the verification of the sales data, (c) the degree of comparability or extent of adjustment necessary for time differences, and (d) the absence of non-typical conditions affecting the sales price.[2]

Over the years, the term *market data approach* was criticized as misleading because all approaches to value require the use of market data. "Estimates of market rent, cost, depreciation, and other value parameters may be derived in the other

1. *The Dictionary of Real Estate Appraisal*, 3d ed. (Chicago: Appraisal Institute, 1993), 318.
2. American Institute of Real Estate Appraisers and the Society of Real Estate Appraisers, *Real Estate Appraisal Terminology*, rev. ed., Byrl N. Boyce, ed. (Cambridge, Mass.: Ballinger Publishing Company, 1981), 160.

approaches to value using [market data] comparative techniques."[3] The approach is now referred to as the *sales comparison approach* in the real estate appraisal community. Hopefully, this change in terminology will help the courts recognize that, like the sales comparison approach, the income capitalization and cost approaches are based on market data and result in indications of *market value*.

The courts appear to prefer the sales comparison approach to value overwhelmingly. "Ordinarily, if there are sales of comparable property at or near the time the condemned property is taken, evidence in regard to such sales would be more appropriate than any other method in determining the market value of the property taken."[4] In a few jurisdictions, this preference has caused courts to exclude any other approach to value when comparable sales are available. One court stated, "[t]o be consistent with our many decisions holding the omission of evidence as to capitalization of revenue or cost of reproduction to be proper because of the nonavailability of evidence of comparable sales of similar lands, we hold the availability of evidence of comparable sales of similar lands operates to exclude from evidence testimony as to other methods for determining the fair market value."[5]

Comments by condemnors support the courts' preference for the sales comparison approach. "Arm's length transactions in lands in the vicinity of and comparable to the land under appraisement, reasonably near the time of taking, are the best evidence of market value."[6] "The most reliable evidence of the value of the site is recent sales of similar sites."[7] "The comparative method of presenting market value evidence is the method most acceptable to WSDOT [Washington State Department of Transportation] and to the courts and juries; consequently, the greatest reliance is usually placed upon market comparison."[8] "The sales comparison approach should be developed and relied upon whenever there is adequate market data."[9]

ADMISSIBILITY OF COMPARABLE SALES DATA

Evidence of comparable sales has been admitted in nearly all jurisdictions, but the reasons for admitting such evidence vary.

> Evidence of sales of comparable property may be offered under three conditions: (I) on direct examination of expert or lay witnesses as independent substantive evidence of the value of the property to which the comparison relates, or (II) on direct examination of the value-witness to give an account of the factual basis upon which he founds his opinion on the issue of value of the real estate in controversy, or (III) on cross-examination of the value-witness to test his knowledge, experience and investigation and thus affect the weight to be given to his opinions.[10]

3. *The Appraisal of Real Estate*, 10th ed. (Chicago: Appraisal Institute, 1992), 367.
4. *United States v. 100 Acres in Marin County*, 468 F.2d 1261, 1265 (9th Cir. 1972) *cert denied*, 414 U.S. 822 (1973); see also *United States v. 24.48 Acres*, 812 F.2d 216 (5th Cir. 1987).
5. *Lataille v. Housing Authority of City of Woonsocket*, 280 A.2d 98, 100 (R.I. 1971).
6. *Uniform Appraisal Standards for Federal Land Acquisitions* (Washington, D.C.: U.S. Government Printing Office, 1992), §A-4, p. 11.
7. Washington State Dept. of Transportation, *Right of Way Manual*, Chapter 4, Appendix 4-1, Tab C, Item 4A, p. C-11 (revised August 1991).
8. Ibid., Item 4B, p. C-12.
9. U.S. Department of Transportation, Federal Highway Administration, *The Appraisal Guide* (Washington, D.C.: U.S. Government Printing Office, 1990), 43.
10. *Hays v. State*, 342 S.W.2d 167, 170–171 (Tex. 1960).

The minority position is that sales may only be admitted on cross-examination. The reasoning for the exclusion of sales data on direct examination is twofold. First, it has been argued that the admission of such testimony opens up too many collateral issues and "...proves nothing. It is therefore irrelevant, improper, and dangerous."[11] Second, testimony by an appraiser in reference to the price, terms, and conditions surrounding a sale is hearsay evidence because the witness was not a party to the transaction and was not present at the time of the closing.[12] Despite these arguments, the trend is to allow direct evidence of comparable sales on direct examination.[13] "Actual experience in the trial of land damage cases in states in which evidence of this character is admitted does not show the objections mentioned above to be as formidable as supposed. If the admission of such evidence is regulated with reasonable judgment by the presiding justice, it throws light upon the issue before the jury as nothing else can."[14] Some jurisdictions have, in fact, enacted legislative exception to the hearsay rule so as to allow evidence of comparable sales on direct examination.[15]

An exception to the hearsay rule is allowed in federal courts under the Federal Rules of Evidence, which allow an expert to testify to the factors upon which his opinion is based, as long as the facts or data are "of a type reasonably relied upon by experts in the particular field in forming opinions or inferences upon the subject."[16]

It is probably of little concern to the appraiser whether the sale price of a comparable is admitted as direct evidence of the value of the property being appraised or as support for the appraiser's opinion of market value. It may be significant, however, insofar as a sale presented as direct evidence of the market value of the property under appraisal must generally have a higher degree of comparability than a sale submitted as support for the appraiser's opinion of market value. In fact, a court will often rule on the comparability of a sale, as a matter of law, before the appraiser is allowed to testify to the price of the comparable.[17]

Most jurisdictions allow the price of comparable land to be admitted as direct, or independent, evidence of the market value of the property in dispute.[18] Under such circumstances, the rule of admissibility is an exception to the hearsay and best evidence rules.[19] The reasoning behind this exclusion from the rules is well stated in a Montana case:

> All expert opinion is based on "hearsay" to a great extent and much of what is presented by such witnesses is "secondary" evidence. We feel we can achieve speedy litigation and still preserve the truth by the rule adopted here. It must be shown that the witness is expert and that the sales are comparable and recent. With these safeguards plus the fact that the witness has his professional reputation riding on his testimony we feel that the repugnancy of this line of testimony is reduced, if

11. *East Pennsylvania R. Co. v. Hiester*, 40 Pa. 53 (Pa. 1861). Comparable sales are now admissible on direct examination in Pennsylvania under Act of June 22, 1964, P.L. 84 §705(2)(i).
12. *National Bank of Commerce v. City of New Bedford*, 56 N.E. 288 (Mass. 1900).
13. *Pipeline v. O'Brian*, 418 F.2d 15 (5th Cir. 1969); *State v. Johnson*, 191 S.E.2d 641 (N.C. 1972).
14. *Nichols' The Law of Eminent Domain*, rev. 3d ed. (New York: Mathew Bender Co., Inc., 1991), vol. 5, §21.3[1].
15. Colorado, §38-1-118, C.R.S., 1973; New York, see *Lawrence v. Greenwood*, 90 N.E.2d 53 (N.Y. 1949) for statutory citings; Pennsylvania, Public Law 84 (1964) (Eminent Domain Code), §705(2)(i); California Evidence Code, §816.
16. Federal Rule of Evidence 703.
17. *People v. Murata*, 326 P.2d 947 (Cal. 1958).
18. *Jones v. United States*, 258 U.S. 40 (1922).
19. *United States v. 18.46 Acres of Land*, 312 F.2d 287 (2d Cir. 1963).

> not eliminated altogether. The development of a value pattern by one experienced in the business and knowledgeable as to the area involved will best bring uniformity to the market value determination in the most efficient manner.[20]

In discussing the expert's reliance on hearsay evidence, it has been said that "[t]he physician makes life-and-death decisions in reliance upon [hearsay evidence]. His validation, expertly performed and subject to cross-examination, ought to suffice for judicial purposes."[21]

When a comparable sale is admitted only in support of the appraiser's opinion, it generally does not have to possess the same high degree of comparability as does the sale submitted as direct evidence of value. In such a case, "there is less reason for being strict in regard to similarity, because the evidence serves the purpose only of supporting the credibility of the estimate of value given by the witness."[22] When such support testimony is given, it is not usually necessary for the court to rule on its comparability before admitting the sale price of the comparable property. The price is not admitted as direct evidence of value but, rather, to assist the jury in measuring the reliability of the expert's ultimate opinion of value.[23]

Sale of Subject

"Since compensation is measured by market value, prior sales of the same property, reasonably recent and not forced, are extremely probative evidence of market value. Accordingly, the appraiser has an obligation to determine what the owner paid for the property."[24] It is for this reason that appraisers are required to consider and report recent sales of the property under appraisal. Federal standards require the following:

> **Sales history.** Include a ten-year record of all sales and, if possible, offers to buy or sell, the property under appraisal. If no sale of the property has occurred in the past ten years, include a report of the last sale.
>
> Information to be reported shall include, name of the seller, name of the buyer, date of sale, price, terms and conditions of sale, and the appraiser's opinion as to whether the sale price represented market value at the time, and, if not, the reasons for the appraiser's conclusion.[25]

According to the Uniform Standards of Professional Appraisal Practice,

> In developing a real property appraisal, an appraiser must:
>
> (a) consider and analyze any current Agreement of Sale, option, or listing of the property being appraised, if such information is available to the appraiser in the normal course of business;
>
> (b) consider and analyze any prior sales of the property being appraised that occurred within the following time periods:

20. *State v. Greenfield*, 399 P.2d 989, 992 (Mont. 1964).
21. Federal Rule of Evidence 703, "Notes of Advisory Committee on 1972 Proposed Rules."
22. *West Kentucky Coal Co. v. Commonwealth*, 368 S.W.2d 738, 741 (Ky. 1963).
23. *Bowers v. Fulton County*, 176 S.E.2d 219 (Ga. 1970).
24. *Uniform Appraisal Standards for Federal Land Acquisitions*, §A-5, p. 16.
25. Ibid., §B-1 - 13e, p. 71.

(i) one year for one-to-four family residential property; and

(ii) three years for all other property types.[26]

The Federal Highway Administration's appraisal guide states,

> Short form appraisal must contain...[t]itle information, including a five year sales history of the subject property.

and

> Minimum requirements for a detailed appraisal are set forth in 49 CFR [Code of Federal Regulations] Part 24 and include...title information, including 5-year sales history.[27]

A historical sale of the property in dispute is universally admitted as direct evidence of the value of the property as long as the sale was recent and voluntary, there were no changes in the property's condition, and no material fluctuations have occurred in the property's value since the date of sale.[28] No rule has been set down as to what constitutes *recent*; whether the sale of a property is recent enough to allow it into evidence is generally within the discretion of the court.[29]

For instance, a federal district court excluded from evidence a sale that occurred two years prior to the date of valuation for being too remote in time,[30] but in another case the federal court of appeals approved the admission into evidence of the purchase price of the property in dispute, although the sale occurred 14 years prior to the date of valuation.[31] A Michigan court ruled that "[a] nine year interval between the purchase of the land and its condemnation does not render the purchase price patently inadmissible."[32] Of course, evidence explaining the circumstances of such a sale may be admitted, and it has been held that consideration must be given to any appreciation between the date of sale and the date of condemnation.[33] Therefore, the appraiser must make an adjustment for the date of sale if it is warranted.

The rules regarding the admission of a prior sale of the property in dispute were laid down by the North Carolina court as follows:

> In general, purchase price is admissible if it is relevant to the value of the land at the time of condemnation. This rule was stated by this Court in *Board of Transportation v. Revis*, 40 N.C.App. 182, 252 S.E.2d 262, *review denied*, 297 N.C. 452, 256 S.E.2d 805 (1979).
>
> We review the established rules in North Carolina governing the competency and admissibility of evidence of purchase price paid by a condemnee for land later appropriated for public use, in a proceeding to establish just compensation for the taking:
>
> (1) It is competent as evidence of market value to show the price at which the property was bought if the sale was voluntary and not too remote in point of time.

26. The Appraisal Foundation, *Uniform Standards of Professional Appraisal Practice* (USPAP), 1994 ed., Standards Rule 1-5, p. 13.

27. *The Appraisal Guide*, 29, 37.

28. *Commonwealth of Kentucky, Dept. of Highways v. Whitledge*, 406 S.W.2d 833 (Ky. 1966).

29. *Lembo v. Town of Farmingham*, 115 N.E.2d 370 (Mass. 1953).

30. *United States v. 765.56 Acres of Land*, 174 F.Supp. 1 (E.D. N.Y. 1959).

31. *United States v. Becktold Co.*, 129 F.2d 473 (8th Cir. 1942).

32. *Petition of Michigan State Highway Comm. v. McGuire*, 185 N.W.2d 187, 188 (Mich. 1970).

33. *Virgin Islands Housing Authority v. 15.5521 Acres of Land*, 230 F.Supp. 845 (D. V.I. 1964).

(2) When land is taken by condemnation, evidence of its value within a reasonable time before the taking is competent on the question of its value at the time of the taking.
(3) Such evidence must relate to the value of the property sufficiently near the time of taking as to have a reasonable tendency to show its value at the time of its taking.
(4) The reasonableness of the time is dependent upon the nature of the property, its location, and the surrounding circumstances. Some of the circumstances to be considered are the changes, if any, which have occurred between the time of purchase by the condemnee and the time of the taking by the State, including physical changes in the property taken, changes in its availability for valuable uses, and changes in the vicinity of the property which might have affected its value.
(5) The fact that some changes have taken place does not *per se* render the evidence incompetent. If the changes have been so extensive that the purchase price does not reasonably point to, or furnish a fair criterion for determining value at the time of the taking, when purchase price is considered with other evidence affecting value, the evidence of purchase price should be excluded.
(6) The ultimate criterion is whether, under all the circumstances, the purchase price fairly points to the value of the property at the time of the taking.[34]

A number of courts have held that a prior sale price of the property being condemned is the best evidence of value. It is imperative, therefore, that the appraiser investigate and thoroughly analyze any fairly recent sale of the property being appraised. Although the appraiser may conclude that comparable sales more than two years old are too remote in time to be meaningful, this would not necessarily apply to an earlier sale of the property being appraised.

It is not sufficient simply to report a prior sale of the property in question; the sale must be analyzed to determine its relevancy. If the appraiser finds that the sale did not represent market value and was not an arms-length transaction, that conclusion and the reasoning behind it should also be reported. It is not enough to state, "Based upon my analysis of the sale of the subject property, which occurred six months ago, I am of the opinion that the sale did not represent market value." Why didn't it represent market value? If changes in the property since the date of sale—e.g., rezoning, improvement, destruction—render the prior sale meaningless as a reference to current value, these factors must be reported and explained. For example:

> Following each sale [of the property under appraisal], state an opinion on whether the sale can be considered as evidence of value. Any physical changes to the property made after each such sale are briefly described, such as additional construction remodeling, etc. Also indicate the probable effect of remodeling, etc., upon market value. If more than one sale has occurred, an explanation is given

34. *City of Winston-Salem v. Davis*, 296 S.E.2d 21, 23–24 (N.C. 1982).

> for any change in price which could not be equated to physical changes, such as: contract sales vs. cash sale, change in neighborhood development, changes in general economics, etc. If the sale can be considered as evidence of value, the sale information and the appraiser's analysis thereof are reported on a Market Data Form...and included in the report. If the sale cannot be considered as evidence of value, the appraiser inserts a brief narrative instead of a Market Data Form giving the details of the sale, any physical changes subsequent thereto and an explanation of why the sale cannot be considered as evidence of value.[35]

If it is determined that a prior sale of the property is, in fact, relevant to its current value, this sale should be analyzed like any other comparable sale. Often, but not always, the only adjustment needed is for the date of sale. It is extremely important to verify any sale of the subject property. If the appraiser cannot make a reliable verification of the sale of the property under appraisal, it may be necessary to ask legal counsel to help verify the sale, possibly through the discovery process.

The appraiser may justifiably conclude that the prior sale of the subject should be given greater weight in the final estimate of value due to the lack of adjustments required for physical differences. However, this is not necessarily true as a matter of law. The prior sale price of the property in question is only one of many factors to be considered in arriving at a final estimate of value. As stated by the federal court, "[w]e reject the conception that a prior sale or sales of condemned property must always, as a matter of law, be given more weight in condemnation proceedings than sales of comparable property. Recent sales of the very property condemned are entitled to considerable weight, but sales of similar property are entitled to weight also; and the relative importance of the two is dependent upon the facts in the particular condemnation proceedings."[36]

If the appraiser has made a *time increment* or *market conditions* study, applying the results of this study to the prior sale price of the property should serve to support the final value estimate of the property. If it does not, a clear explanation of the divergence must be included in the appraisal report.

Any question concerning the appreciation/depreciation rate posed during cross-examination must be answered with great care. Opposing counsel may try to apply the appraiser's casual reply regarding general property appreciation/depreciation rates to a prior sale of the property in dispute, which may undermine the appraiser's testimony and final estimate of value. A leading question should never be answered with a simple *yes* or *no*. For example, the examiner may ask, "Do you agree with the article in the local paper last week which stated that property values in this county have increased 15% over the last year?" The appraiser must first determine whether such an article did appear in the local paper and, if so, whether it was accurately represented by counsel's question. Then the appraiser must let it be known that appreciation (and depreciation) rates fluctuate, depending on a number of variables such as property location, property type, property size, price ranges, and available financing. Although 15% might be

35. Washington State Dept. of Transportation, *Right of Way Manual*, Chapter 4, Appendix 4-2, Appraisal Report Guide, Part IIC, Item 4, pp. 8-9 (revised 11/10/76).

36. *Hickey v. United States*, 208 F.2d 269, 273 (3rd Cir. 1953) *cert denied*, 347 U.S. 919 (1954).

an average rate of appreciation for a large geographical area, it would not necessarily be correct to apply this rate to a specific property.

COMPARABLE SALES

An appraiser will generally investigate, analyze, and consider many sales before selecting those that are the most pertinent to valuation of the property being appraised. Because the appraiser is usually attempting to estimate market value and "[t]he best evidence of such value is like and comparable sales within a reasonable time preceding the condemnation,"[37] it is imperative that all relevant factors be considered in the selection process.

The comparables selected must be the best from an appraisal standpoint and, whenever possible, there should be no question as to their admissibility. If the appraiser feels that a comparable sale may be inadmissible, but it is absolutely necessary for the proper estimation and support of value, the sale may be included, but its questionable admissibility should be pointed out, either in the appraisal report or separately, depending on the discovery rules within the jurisdiction. (For further information on the items included in the appraisal report, see Chapter 19.)

The best comparable sales, from both an appraisal standpoint and legal standpoint, are those that are most similar. To the appraiser this means the properties requiring the fewest adjustments to equalize them to the property under appraisal. The courts recognize "...that 'similar' does not mean 'identical,' but means having a resemblance, and that property may be similar in the sense in which the word is here used though each possess various points of difference."[38] The degree of similarity varies from case to case, so neither appraisers nor the courts can arrive at a formula to test comparability or similarity. In one instance adjustments totaling 15% of the sale price may indicate that the property is, in fact, not a *comparable sale*, but in another instance a sale with total adjustments equaling 15% of the sale price might turn out to be the most comparable sale available.

Before a property can be considered a comparable, the appraiser must ensure that the sale was an *open market transaction*. In other words, did the sale occur under the conditions commensurate with market value? (See Chapter 2 for a discussion of market value.)

1. Did the sale convey unencumbered fee simple title or its equivalent?
2. Were both the buyer and seller typically motivated?
3. Were both parties well informed or well advised and each acting in what they considered their own best interests?
4. Was the property allowed exposure in the open market for a reasonable length of time?
5. Was payment made in cash or its equivalent?
6. Was financing, if any, on terms generally available in the community at the time of sale and typical for the property type in its locale?

37. *Onego Corporation v. United States*, 295 F.2d 461, 463 (10th Cir. 1961).

38. *City of Chicago v. Vaccaro*, 97 N.E.2d 766, 773 (Ill. 1951).

7. Did the price represent normal consideration for the property sold unaffected by special financing amounts and/or terms, services, fees, costs, or other credits incurred in the transaction?

If these questions can all be answered affirmatively, the sale probably meets the criteria for an arm's-length transaction. A negative answer to Question 1 does not necessarily eliminate the sale as a comparable, however. For instance, if a leased fee estate was conveyed, it may be possible to adjust the sale price of the property to reflect the impact of the leasehold interest held therein. An affirmative answer to Question 2 eliminates all *forced sales* and all sales in which the price paid was affected by a personal relationship between the parties. A positive answer to Question 5 will eliminate sales involving trades or exchanges for other real or personal property.

A negative answer to some of the questions listed above does not necessarily mean the sale was not an open market, arm's-length transaction. For example, a seller may have paid a portion of the purchaser's financing fees. If the fees actually paid by the seller can be determined, this amount may be used as the basis for an adjustment to the indicated sale price. If the sale was actually a contract sale, it may or may not be admissible as evidence, depending on the jurisdiction and the specific terms and conditions of the transaction.

To determine whether a contract sale is admissible within a specific jurisdiction, applicable case law must be carefully analyzed. A distinction must be made between a *contract of sale* (real estate contract) and a *contract to sell* (e.g., an earnest money contract). A contract to sell is sometimes referred to as a *sale contract*[39] and this can cause confusion. Case law is divided on the admissibility of installment sales. Most jurisdictions appear to allow their admissibility, taking the position that if the offered sale is a contract of sale, this fact affects the weight of the evidence, not its admissibility. As *Nichols'* has stated, "[i]f evidence were to be excluded of all sales every cent of which was not cash, the door would practically be closed as to the evidence of other sales."[40] The admission of evidence in regard to contracts to sell, such as earnest money contracts, has met with mixed reactions. As a general rule, unexercised options are not admissible. [41] Similarly, sales which involve the exchange of property are generally inadmissible.[42]

The appraiser should personally verify sales with either the buyer or seller. If neither is available, the verification of a participating broker or attorney who handled the transaction is generally satisfactory. Verification of a sale with the broker or attorney *and* the buyer or seller will usually produce the greatest amount of useful, reliable information.

Many real estate appraisers employ research assistants or associate appraisers, who do much of the field research required for an appraisal and, at times, verify sales. This practice may be perfectly adequate for an appraisal report, but it is unacceptable for trial purposes. "Verification must be by competent and reliable personnel, and if the property goes into condemnation the sale must be personally verified by the appraiser who will testify."[43] As a Colorado court put it:

39. *State v. Bowling*, 414 S.W.2d 551 (Mo. 1967).
40. *Nichols'*, vol. 5, §21.3[1] (1991).
41. *Phillips Petroleum Co. v. City of Omaha*, 106 N.W.2d 727 (Neb. 1960).
42. *Nichols'*, vol. 5, §21.3[1] (1991).
43. *Uniform Appraisal Standards for Federal Land Acquisitions*, §A-4, p. 12.

> By this statute [¶38-1-118, C.R.S. 1973] a legislative exception to the hearsay rule was created, but it is limited in its application. The use in this statute of the terms "personally" and "communicated directly" do not mean by or through someone other than the witness.[44]

By statute, the New Jersey courts allow testimony as to comparable sale prices so long as the appraiser has verified the sales with the buyer, the seller, or the broker.[45] This provision has been expanded by New Jersey case law to include attorneys as well.[46]

The weight of authority holds that sales to a purchaser with the power of eminent domain are not admissible.[47] However, there have been exceptions to this rule.[48] It has been stated that "...the burden is upon the party who offers such evidence to establish as a preliminary fact that the purchase, concerning which evidence is offered, was made without compulsion, coercion or compromise."[49] If the appraiser is to use such a sale, he or she must verify it with all the parties involved and explain the results of such verification explicitly in the appraisal report and in testimony.

If the seller made the initial contact and offered the property to the purchaser, there is strong evidence of no unusual compulsion. Also, a historical review of the number of parcels acquired versus the number condemned by the purchaser over a period of time can give some insight into any possible undue compulsion to buy or sell. Sales to purchasers with the power of eminent domain do not necessarily demonstrate a pattern of being either above or below the market value of the property. "A company condemning land might be willing to give more than it was worth, and the owner of the land might be willing to take less than it is worth, that is, less than its market value, rather than have a lawsuit."[50] The procedure recommended for reliable verification of sales to the government is discussed later in this chapter in the section titled "Advanced Problems."

The appraisal profession recognizes that accurate adjustments can sometimes be made for atypical financing and conditions of sale.[51] Adjustments for these factors can be made within the adjustment process. For example, an FHA discount paid by a seller to obtain a purchaser's financing can generally be accurately quantified by proper sales verification. The discount can then be deducted from the gross sale price of the property to determine the effective price the seller actually received for the property. In the same way, an atypical contract of sale may be accurately converted to a cash equivalent price.

COMPARABILITY

As is the case with sales to an entity with the power of eminent domain, "[t]he party offering the sales claimed to be comparable has the burden of proving, as a preliminary to the introduction of the prices involved in such sales, that they are

44. *Denver Urban Renewal Authority v. Hayutin*, 583 P.2d 296, 299 (Colo. 1978).
45. N.J.Stat. Ann. §2A:83-1.
46. *New Jersey Sports and Exposition Authority v. Cariddi*, 395 A.2d 895 (N.J. 1978).
47. *United States ex rel. T.V.A. v. Bailey*, 115 F.2d 433 (5th Cir. 1940).
48. *United States v. 10.48 Acres of Land*, 621 F.2d 338 (9th Cir. 1980).
49. *Hannan v. United States*, 131 F.2d 441, 442 (D.C. Cir. 1942).
50. *Yonts v. Public Service Co.*, 17 S.W.2d 886, 887 (Ark. 1929).
51. *The Appraisal of Real Estate*, 10th ed., 376-381.

similar both in character and locality to the land being condemned."[52] "[N]o fixed or general rule has or could be laid down which governs the degree of similarity that must exist between the properties sold and that condemned to make evidence of the sale or sales admissible...."[53] However, it is universally recognized that to be valid, a comparable sale must have the same economic highest and best use as the property being appraised.

> Appraisers have a special responsibility to consider carefully the comparability of all data used in a valuation assignment. They must fully understand the concept of comparability and should avoid comparing properties with different highest and best uses....[54]

Various lists of the typical adjustments to be considered have been developed. For instance, *The Appraisal of Real Estate* lists nine basic elements of comparison.[55]

1. Real property rights conveyed
2. Financing terms
3. Conditions of sale
4. Market conditions
5. Location
6. Physical characteristics
7. Economic characteristics
8. Use
9. Non-realty components of value

The *Uniform Appraisal Standards for Federal Land Acquisitions* lists the following factors of adjustment:[56]

- Property rights conveyed
- Financing terms
- Conditions of sale
- Market conditions (also know as "time of sale")
- Location
- Physical characteristics

These two lists are not substantially different. Economic characteristics, Item 7 in the first list, are considered in the second list under property rights conveyed and physical characteristics. Sales that have a different highest and best use are generally not considered comparable for eminent domain valuation purposes, and thus are rejected. The same is true of sales that include non-realty items in the sale price.

The date of sale (i.e., market conditions) of a comparable property is most important in a rapidly changing market.[57] At times an appraiser may be allowed to testify in regard to sales used in a time increment or market condition study to

52. *Dep't. of Public Works & Buildings v. Exchange Nat. Bank*, 356 N.E.2d 376, 383 (Ill. 1976).
53. *City of Evanston v. Piotrowiez*, 170 N.E.2d 569, 575 (Ill. 1960).
54. *The Appraisal of Real Estate*, 10th ed., 153.
55. Ibid., 373.
56. *Uniform Appraisal Standards for Federal Land Acquisitions*, §A-4, pp. 11–12.
57. *City of St. Louis v. Vasquez*, 341 S.W.2d 839 (Mo. 1960).

support an adjustment for this factor, even though the sale properties used in the study are not *comparable*.[58] Whether or not the specific data used in such a study are admissible, a time increment study should be undertaken by the appraiser, even if the appraiser makes no time, or market conditions, adjustments. Although the appraiser may not be able to testify to the specifics of the study, he or she will generally be allowed to testify that the time adjustment, or lack of an adjustment, was based on such a study.

Sales occurring after the date of taking have met with mixed reactions. The use of these sales falls under what is often termed the *hindsight rule*. It has long been argued that sales transacted subsequent to the date of taking should not be submitted as evidence, or considered by the appraiser, for two reasons. First, such sales represent information that would not have been available to the hypothetical purchaser on the date of taking; thus the appraiser would be considering market factors unknown as of the date of value. Second, subsequent sales may reflect *project enhancement*, which the appraiser must generally disregard in estimating the value of a property at the time of taking.

"Sales after the date of taking are not inadmissible *per se* (contrary to popular belief) and with appropriate caution and restraint may be utilized by the appraiser if they meet the usual standards of comparability and are not otherwise incompetent as evidence of value."[59] As a general rule "[s]ales occurring after the date of taking can be used to show the value of the subject property in the 'before' situation. It is also the general rule that comparable sales which reflect an enhanced value brought about by the making of the improvement are not admissible."[60] Sales occurring subsequent to the date of taking have generally met with greater acceptance when used to estimate a property's after value in a partial taking case rather than to value the property in the before situation. Such sales will often demonstrate damages or special benefits accruing to a remainder parcel.

Both appraisers and attorneys must be aware of the applicable law in the jurisdiction regarding the admissibility of sales subsequent to the date of taking. This information is essential even if the appraiser does not anticipate using such sales because the appraisers testifying for the opposing party may. If the admissibility of such sales is not clear in the specific jurisdiction, the appraiser should have available alternative sales to which he or she can testify if sales subsequent to the date of taking are ruled inadmissible. "Sales transacted on or before the date of taking are the preferred basis for an appraisal and if there are adequate such sales available there is little justification for using post-taking sales."[61]

The degree of proximity required of any specific sale property will vary with the type of property being appraised and sales activity in the area. The courts have, on many occasions, recognized this fact. "[N]o general rules can be laid down as to the distance at which other land ceases to be similar enough in location to the land in question so that evidence as to its sale price is admissible to

58. *City of Los Angeles v. Retlaw Enterprises, Inc.*, 546 P.2d 1380 (Cal. 1976).

59. *Uniform Appraisal Standards for Federal Land Acquisitions*, §A-4, pp. 13–14, citing *United States v. 312.50 Acres, Prince William County, Va.*, 812 F.2d 156, 157 n.3 (4th Cir. 1987); *United States v. 320.0 Acres of Land, More or Less, Etc.*, 605 F.2d 762, 799–803 (5th Cir. 1979).

60. *City of Tucson v. Ruelas*, 508 P.2d 1174, 1176 (Ariz. 1973) [citations omitted].

61. *Uniform Appraisal Standards for Federal Land Acquisitions*, §A-4, p. 14.

prove the value of the latter land. The determination of this question depends upon the character of the land involved and the facts and circumstances of a particular case."[62]

If an appraisal involves a single-family dwelling located within a subdivision, it will probably not be necessary for the appraiser to look outside that subdivision for comparable sales. If, however, the property under appraisal is a commercial site on an interstate freeway, properties 100 miles away could be termed *comparable* insofar as comparables are not always found in the immediate vicinity of the property being appraised and the properties would very probably be competing for the same customers—interstate highway users.

The test of comparability in terms of location is not the physical distance between properties, but whether the properties are within *economic proximity*. As stated by a Texas court:

> The distance between the condemned property and the property involved in an alleged comparable sale is important in determining whether both are in the same economic use area.[63]

A property's unique physical features can also expand the geographical area from which comparable sales may be drawn.

> We also reject the condemnor's contention that the trial court erred in admitting into evidence sales of property located in the Old Creek area, 30 to 50 miles from the Bailey land. The county apparently claims that all four of these sales were "noncomparable" as a matter of law, because the lands involved in these sales were "too remote" from the property which was the subject of the eminent domain proceeding. The 30 to 50 miles distance alone, it is suggested, required the exclusion of this evidence....
>
> In the instant case defendants' appraisal witness explained that because of the rather distinctive terrain of the Bailey property there were few sales of "comparable property" within the immediate vicinity. He testified that he searched for sales of properties which were similar to the condemned property in "size, character, topography, suitability for recreational use, access to creeks and access to roads," and on that basis, chose the Old Creek sales which plaintiff now claims are too distant to be "comparable." Given the great variety of factors of "comparability" to be considered, and the relative scarcity of similar property in the immediate vicinity, we cannot find that the trial judge abused his discretion in admitting the challenged sales....[64]

Nevertheless, the best rule of thumb for the appraiser is that, all else being equal, the best comparables are those located closest to the property being appraised. If the appraiser retained by one party in a dispute must go far afield to find truly comparable properties, it is likely that the appraiser retained by the opposing party will have to do the same. However, the appraiser must be cautious. One condemnor's attorney has been known to display an 8-ft.-by-10-ft.

62. *Chicago v. Harbecke*, 100 N.E.2d 616, 619 (Ill. 1951).
63. *Hays v. State*, 342 S.W.2d 167, 172 (Tex. 1960).
64. *County of San Luis Obispo v. Bailey*, 483 P.2d 27, 32–33 (Cal. 1971).

map of the United States in closing arguments to point out the location of the comparable sales used by the opposing party's appraiser.

A comparison of the physical characteristics of two properties can, of course, cover many items. The specific characteristics that require adjustment, or at least consideration, will vary with the type of property being appraised. An extensive list of the different physical characteristics of the properties can be developed, but the appraiser should only consider and include in the appraisal report those differences that are reflected in the marketplace. All such differences should be recorded in the appraiser's notes, whether or not an actual adjustment is called for, to help the appraiser testify competently on cross-examination.

Many appraisers have found that approximately one-third of the typical adjustments to a comparable sale applied in the appraisal of a single-family dwelling will represent 85% to 90% of the difference in value between the two properties. The mere existence of physical differences between two properties does not mean adjustments are required. An adjustment is necessary only if the difference is reflected in the price at which sellers are willing to sell and buyers are willing to buy.

In comparing the physical characteristics of properties, it is often desirable, and sometimes absolutely necessary, to apply a common unit of measure. The common units of measure for comparing vacant land are price per square foot, price per acre, price per front foot, price per whole site and in some instances price per developable (or typical) unit. This last unit of measure is often applied to land that has a highest and best use for multifamily dwellings. A common unit of measure for urban commercial sites is the allowable floor area ratio (FAR). The appraiser should use the unit of comparison that is common in the area and produces the most reliable range of values for the property being appraised. An appropriate unit of comparison generally establishes a much clearer pattern or trend of values than an inappropriate unit of comparison.

The units of comparison applied to improved properties are as varied as the number of uses to which property can be put. In appraising a unique or specialty property, the appraiser may spend as much time determining the common denominator as is spent performing the rest of the appraisal. Applicable units of comparison for typical property types are listed below.

Property Type	Unit of Measurement
Single-family dwellings	Per sq. ft. or per room
Motels/hotels	Per room, gross income multiplier (*GIM*)
Apartments	Per sq. ft., per room, per unit, gross rent multiplier (*GRM*)
Retail	Per sq. ft. or per front foot
Warehouse	Per sq. ft.
Theaters	Per seat
Dairy or beef farms	Per head per acre
Parking garages	Per stall
Gasoline service stations	Per gallon pumped

Mineral deposits	Per unit of reserve
Office buildings	Per sq. ft. of net rentable area
Mobile home parks	Per pad
Auto repair shops	Per bay
Marinas	Per slip

The adjustment of comparable sales is discussed in detail in *The Appraisal of Real Estate*.[65] In selecting a method of adjusting comparables in an eminent domain appraisal, it is most important that the method be consistent, logical, and easy to present and explain.

PRESENTATION OF COMPARABLE DATA

Appraisers can choose from several options for presenting comparable sales data and analysis in the appraisal report and in appraisal testimony. In some instances, however, a condemning agency will specify the format in which the adjustment process should be presented in the appraisal report. According to one source "each significant element of difference between the comparable and the subject is explained separately on its own particular merits, with an indication as to its value differential made either on a dollar or percentage basis"[66] and to another "[s]imilarities or dissimilarities of each comparable used to compare to the subject shall be discussed and individually adjusted in dollars or percentage."[67] The *Uniform Appraisal Standards for Federal Land Acquisitions* leaves the specific presentation of the comparative process applied to the discretion of the appraiser:

> A narrative comparative analysis of each comparable sale shall be made explaining how the sale relates to the property under appraisal in respect to those features which have an effect on market value. The comparative weight given to each comparable sale by the appraiser in developing a final value estimate by this approach will be explained. A comparative adjustment chart, or grid, may assist the appraiser in explaining his or her analysis in this regard.[68]

It is interesting to note that *The Appraisal Guide*, which is published by the Federal Highway Administration to explain the appraisal process under the Uniform Relocation Assistance and Real Property Acquisition Policies Act,[69] states that sales *shall* be adjusted for each item of difference in dollar or percentage amounts, while the *Uniform Appraisal Standards for Federal Land Acquisitions* leaves the adjustment process to the discretion of the appraiser. A review of numerous appraisal reports prepared for state and federal condemnors suggests that some follow *The Appraisal Guide*, but most condemnors seem to allow the appraiser the flexibility described in the *Uniform Appraisal Standards for Federal Land Acquisitions*. *The Appraisal Guide* is just that—a *guide*; it does not establish standards or require-

65. *The Appraisal of Real Estate*, 10th ed., 371–402.
66. Washington State Dept. of Transportation, *Right of Way Manual*, Chapter 4, Appendix 4-1, Tab C, Item 4A1b, p. C-12.
67. U.S. Department of Transportation, Federal Highway Administration, *The Appraisal Guide* (Washington, D.C.: U.S. Government Printing Office, 1990), 39.
68. *Uniform Appraisal Standards for Federal Land Acquisitions*, §B-1 16, p. 76.
69. Uniform Relocation Assistance and Real Property Acquisition Policies Act of 1970, P.L. 91-646, as amended, 42 U.S.C. §4601, *et seq*.

ments. Some condemnors have incorporated the provisions of *The Appraisal Guide* into their appraisal standards or requirements, but most have chosen to retain flexibility in the comparable sales adjustment process. Appraisers are, therefore, advised to determine the reporting requirements of the specific agencies that have retained them.

A detailed comparative analysis, using dollar adjustments might follow the form shown in Table 10.1. Regardless of the reporting requirements, the appraiser must have detailed and accurate notes on the comparable analysis and the adjustments made. Also, a format for presentation of the comparable sales data and analysis to the trier of fact must be selected, generally in conjunction with legal counsel. In all but the simplest cases, a verbal presentation of sales data and anal-

TABLE 10.1 COMPARISON CHART—SINGLE-FAMILY DWELLING: DOLLAR ADJUSTMENTS

Item	Subject	Sale 1	Sale 2	Sale 3	Sale 4
Sale price	N.A.	$75,000	$85,000	$82,500	$78,500
Sale terms	Cash	Equal, Cash	-$1,700 Loan fee	-$1,650 Contract	Equal Cash Equivalent
Adjusted price	N.A.	$75,000	$83,300	$80,850	$78,500
Sale date (market conditions)	N.A.	Equal 2 months	+$5,000 1 year	+$4,850 1 year	+$2,350 6 months
Adjusted price	N.A.	$75,000	$88,300	$85,700	$80,850
Site value	$12,000	+$2,000 $10,000	-$750 $12,750	Equal $12,000	+$800 $11,200
Design/appeal	Average	Equal	Equal	Superior -$1,700	Equal
Quality/condition	Good	Equal	Equal	Equal	Equal
Age	1968	Equal 1970	-$1,700 1975	Equal 1968	Equal 1970
Size	1,450 sq. ft.	+$1,250 1,400 sq. ft.	-$1,750 1,520 sq. ft.	-$1,700 1,500 sq. ft.	Equal 1,450 sq. ft.
Bedrooms/baths	3/2	Equal 3/2	-$1,000 4/2.5	Equal 4/2	Equal 3/2
Utility	Average	Equal	Equal	Equal	Equal
Auto storage	600 sq. ft. garage	Equal 560 sq. ft. garage	Equal 540 sq. ft. garage	Equal 620 sq. ft. garage	Equal 600 sq. ft. garage
Other	N.A.	Equal	-$1,000 Superior built-ins	Equal	Equal
Net location/physical adjustments	N.A.	+$3,250	-$6,200	-$3,400	+$800
Indicated value of subject		$78,250	$82,100	$82,300	$81,650

ysis is inadequate. To supplement the verbal testimony, the appraiser should submit sales data and analysis in table form.

There are several ways to present data for trial purposes, and each has its advantages and disadvantages. The format shown in Table 10.1 has the advantage of appearing detailed, well thought out, and mathematically correct. If the trier of fact disagrees with a specific adjustment made by the appraiser, it can be replaced and the indicated value of the subject property can be mathematically recomputed. The danger of using this type of presentation is that it invites questions upon cross-examination as to why each adjustment was made or not made. When this type of presentation is employed, the appraiser should be prepared to admit freely the possibility that a $500 adjustment could just as easily have been estimated at $400 or $600.

Table 10.2 illustrates the presentation of adjustment factors calculated by per-

TABLE 10.2 COMPARISON CHART—SINGLE-FAMILY DWELLING: PERCENTAGE ADJUSTMENTS

Item	Subject	Sale 1	Sale 2	Sale 3	Sale 4
Sale price	N.A.	$75,000	$85,000	$82,500	$78,500
Sale terms	Cash	Equal, Cash	-2% Loan fee	-2% Contract	Equal Cash Equivalent
Adjusted price	N.A.	$75,000	$83,300	$80,850	$78,500
Sale date (market conditions)	N.A.	Equal 2 months	+6% 1 year	+6% 1 year	+3% 6 months
Adjusted price	N.A.	$75,000	$88,300	$85,700	$80,850
Site value	$12,000	+3% $10,000	-1% $12,750	Equal $12,000	+1% $11,200
Design/appeal	Average	Equal	Equal	-2% Superior	Equal
Quality/condition	Good	Equal	Equal	Equal	Equal
Age	1968	Equal 1970	-2% 1975	Equal 1968	Equal 1970
Size	1,450 sq. ft.	+2% 1,400 sq. ft.	-2% 1,520 sq. ft.	-2% 1,500 sq. ft.	Equal 1,450 sq. ft.
Bedrooms/baths	3/2	Equal 3/2	-1% 4/2.5	Equal 4/2	Equal 3/2
Utility	Average	Equal	Equal	Equal	Equal
Auto storage	600 sq. ft. garage	Equal 560 sq. ft. garage	Equal 540 sq. ft. garage	Equal 620 sq. ft. garage	Equal 600 sq. ft. garage
Other	N.A.	Equal	-1% Superior built-ins	Equal	Equal
Net location/physical adjustment	N.A.	+5% +$3,750	-7% -$6,181	-4% -$3,428	+1% +$809
Indicated value of subject (rounded)		$78,250	$82,100	$82,300	$81,650

centages. This method of presentation has the same advantages and disadvantages as the presentation in Table 10.1. Note that the sale prices are first adjusted for financing and date of sale (market conditions), and the resulting adjusted sale price is used as the basis for location and physical difference adjustments. (If adjustments were required for the property rights conveyed or conditions of sale, these adjustments would also be made before the adjustments for location and physical differences.) The financing adjustment must be made before the location and physical difference adjustments because if it is not, the appraiser will be working with dollars that are not cash equivalent. The same is true with the market conditions adjustment. If the date of sale adjustment is not made first, the appraiser will be working with historical dollars as of the date of sale, rather than current dollars as of the date of valuation.

For example, consider a parcel of vacant land which sold for $7.50 per square foot. The property is comparable to the property being appraised, except that its location is 10% inferior. The adjustment would be calculated as follows:

Sale price	$7.50
Location adjustment (10%)	+0.75
Indicated value of subject	$8.25

Now assume that the sale was not recent, but two years old, and the sale price was $6.52 per square foot. Assume also that, in addition to the location adjustment, a 15% upward adjustment is required for time. The adjustment process might be

Sale price		$6.52
Adjustments:		
Time	+15%	
Location	+10%	
Net adjustment	+25%	+1.63
Indicated value of subject		$8.15

There should be no difference between the indicated values produced by these two processes. The reason there is a difference is that the location adjustment in the latter instance was not $0.75, as it was in the first scenario, but $0.65 ($6.52 x 0.10) because the 10% adjustment was applied to the historical sale price. This error could be corrected by applying a time adjustment to both the location and physical adjustments. The calculations are

Sale price		$6.52
Adjustments:		
Time	+15.0%	
Location (10% x 1.15)	+11.5%	
Net adjustment	+26.5%	1.73
Indicated value of subject		$8.25

For simplicity and clarity in trial presentations, adjusting the sale price for the date of sale and for financing prior to other adjustments is preferable. This process is shown as follows:

Sale price	$6.52
Time adjustment (15%)	0.98
Time adjusted price	$7.50
Location adjustment (10%)	0.75
Indicated value of subject	$8.25

It has been said that the use of "[s]ome adjustment techniques tend to exaggerate results, particularly if all are subtractions, and others to minimize, if all [are] additions. For example, a +20% [adjustment] for location versus a $5.00 sale would suggest a +$1 [adjustment]. But if the $5 sale were first...[adjusted upward] 45% for other elements, reflecting $7.25, a +20% [adjustment] would be $1.45.... To level these variations or to expand them appropriately, each adjustment may be multiplied by the product of previous adjustments."[70]

Some appraisers use a factoring technique to make adjustments. For example, equality between the comparable property and the property being appraised would indicate a factor of 1.00, a 10% superiority of the property being appraised would result in a factor of 1.10, and a 5% inferiority of the property being appraised would indicate a factor of .95. When this procedure is applied to the preceding example, the adjustment for the date of sale is automatically applied to the location adjustment.

Sale price		$ 6.52
Adjustments:		
Time	+10%	
Location	+15%	
Net adjustment (1.15 x 1.10)		x1.265
Indicated value of subject		$ 8.25

However, this is not the case with multiple adjustments. To illustrate, consider the comparative adjustments shown in Table 10.3. It can be seen that a time

TABLE 10.3 COMPARATIVE ANALYSIS OF VACANT LAND—PERCENTAGE ADJUSTMENTS

Sale price per square foot		$ 6.52
Time adjustment (15%)		0.98
Time-adjusted sale price per square foot		$ 7.50
Other adjustments:		
Topography	+20%	
Location	+15%	
Shape	- 5%	
Utilities	+25%	
Access	+10%	
Net adjustment	+65%	4.88
Indicated value per square foot		$12.38

70. John Cotton, "Market Data: Adjustment Techniques," *Condemnation Appraisal Practice*, vol. II (Chicago: American Institute of Real Estate Appraisers, 1973), 107.

adjustment of +15% was applied before any of the other adjustments were made. Adding the adjustments together indicates a total net adjustment of 65% and a final value indication of $12.38 per square foot for the property being appraised. Applying the factoring system of adjustment to the same circumstances, however, results in the value indication shown in Table 10.4. There is a substantial difference in the results produced by the two techniques, nearly 10%.

TABLE 10.4 COMPARATIVE ANALYSIS OF VACANT LAND—FACTORING ADJUSTMENTS

1.15 (Time) x 1.20 (Topography) x 1.15 (Location) x .95 (Shape) x
1.25 (Utilities) x 1.10 (Access) = 2.08
Indicated value per square foot ($6.52 x 2.08) = $13.56

The factoring technique was taught to appraisal students in the 1960s. Its use was encouraged because "[t]he comparison process cannot be reduced to an exact mathematical formula [and this factoring method of comparison]...is an example of the orderly mental process through which an appraiser might go in weighing the plus and minus items as between two properties."[71] Although the factoring technique was dropped from subsequent appraisal texts,[72] it has been reincorporated into more recent publications.[73]

Appraisers are particularly discouraged from using the factoring technique when presenting comparable sales data and analysis to a trier of fact. This process complicates an otherwise easily understood method of estimating market value. The main problem with using this technique is that the appraiser cannot testify on cross-examination as to the actual dollar adjustment made for any individual item. Moreover, the attorney representing the opposing party can take a composite factor developed by the appraiser and convert it into a net adjustment by adding and subtracting the percentage adjustments. Using this figure, he can then demonstrate to the trier of fact that the appraiser's analysis results in a totally different indication of value than the one to which the appraiser has testified.

For example, assume an appraiser is testifying on behalf of a property owner who owns 35,000 square feet of land. The appraiser uses the composite factor developed in Table 10.4 and presents an indicated value for the subject property of $475,000 (35,000 sq. ft. @ $13.56, rounded). The attorney representing the condemnor could then ask the appraiser on cross-examination to add and subtract the percentage adjustments shown in Table 10.3 and develop the indicated value of the property based upon these assumptions. The result would be $433,000 (35,000 sq. ft. @ $12.38, rounded), $42,000 less than the appraiser's original figure. It is more likely that the attorney would not ask the appraiser to make this computation, but instead do it for the jury himself during final argument. By then the appraiser will be off the witness stand and unable to defend his original estimate. Because the adding and subtracting of percentage adjustments is easier to under-

71. *The Appraisal of Real Estate*, 4th ed. (Chicago: American Institute of Real Estate Appraisers, 1964), 355.

72. *The Appraisal of Real Estate*, 7th ed. (Chicago: American Institute of Real Estate Appraisers, 1978), 59.

73. *The Appraisal of Real Estate*, 10th ed. (Chicago: Appraisal Institute, 1992), 392.

stand, the trier of fact may very well accept these later calculations rather than those originally presented. In this case the condemnor's counsel would be delighted because the newly computed value indication of $433,000 may be closer to the condemnor's indication of value than the condemnee's.

It is important for appraisers to recognize that dollar and percentage adjustments can, and sometimes should, be used together in the comparative analysis. For instance, percentage adjustments may be most appropriate for location and date of sale adjustments while other adjustments are better calculated in dollar amounts. If all of the comparables have sewer service, for example, and it would cost $5,000 to extend sewer service to the property being appraised, this adjustment should be made in dollars. If a percentage were applied, the sewer adjustment would vary depending upon the price of each comparable, and this would not reflect the real situation. A dollar adjustment should be made for any deficiency in the subject property that can be economically corrected. A dollar adjustment is also appropriate when the property under appraisal has a valuable attribute that can be assigned a dollar amount (e.g., merchantable timber) and is not present on the comparable sale property.

An appraiser may employ the comparative analysis techniques demonstrated in Tables 10.1 and 10.2, but elect to present the comparable sales data and comparative analysis in the manner shown in Table 10.5. This method can be altered

TABLE 10.5 COMPARISON CHART—SINGLE-FAMILY DWELLING

Item	Subject	Sale 1	Sale 2	Sale 3	Sale 4
Sale price	N.A.	$75,000	$85,000	$82,500	$78,500
Sale terms		=	–	–	=
	Cash	Cash	Loan fee	Contract	Cash Equivalent
Sale date	N.A.	=	+	+	+
		2 months	1 year	1 year	6 months
Site value		+	–	=	+
	$12,000	$10,000	$12,500	$12,000	$11,000
Design/appeal	Average	=	=	–	=
				Superior	
Quality/condition	Good	=	=	=	=
Age	1968	=	–	=	=
		1970	1975	1968	1970
Size		+	–	–	=
	1,450 sq. ft.	1,400 sq. ft.	1,520 sq. ft.	1,500 sq. ft.	1,450 sq. ft.
Bedrooms/baths		=	–	=	=
	3/2	3/2	4/2.5	4/2	3/2
Utility	Average	=	=	=	=
Auto storage		=	=	=	=
	600 sq. ft. garage	560 sq. ft. garage	540 sq. ft. garage	620 sq. ft. garage	600 sq. ft. garage
Other	N.A.	=	–	=	=
			Superior built-ins		
Net adjustment	N.A.	+$3,250	-$2,900	-$200	+$3,150
Indicated value of subject		$78,250	$82,100	$82,300	$81,650

slightly by eliminating the specifics of the property being appraised and each comparable and simply indicating whether the comparable analysis suggests that the value of the property under appraisal is above or below the sale price of the comparable. Applying this technique to the data shown in Table 10.5 would change the last line in the table to:

	Sale 1	Sale 2	Sale 3	Sale 4
Indicated value of subject	$75,000+	$85,000-	$82,500+	$78,500+

Both the method illustrated in Table 10.5 and the suggested variation have an advantage in that they avoid showing specific adjustments for each item of dissimilarity in the properties.

Properly presented, these methods can show the trier of fact that appraisal is not an exact science and that adjustments are not merely mathematical calculations or formulas. Rather, the adjustment process is a subjective comparison in which the appraiser's experience and judgment are more important than arithmetic computations. On the other hand, these methods of presentation open the appraiser to intense cross-examination in regard to specific itemized adjustments. Also, in the opposition's final argument it is often alleged that the appraiser's work was sloppy and the final estimate of value is only a guess.

Regardless of the method of sales presentation, some appraisers prefer to testify to one sale that is clearly superior to the property under appraisal and one that is clearly inferior to the property, providing no adjustments, to establish a minimum and maximum value for the property in question. Sometimes this procedure can be quite effective, especially when the highest and best use of the property is not being disputed. On occasion, however, it has been ruled that the trial court has the right to limit the number of sales that can be admitted by each appraiser or each party to the lawsuit.[74] In such an instance, the appraiser should carefully consider whether it is worthwhile to use some of the allocated number of sales for this purpose.

It is not necessary in all jurisdictions for the appraiser to testify to comparable sales. In fact, one court has said "... these witnesses were testifying as expert land appraisers, and that having so qualified, their opinion evidence, within the bounds of their expertise, would be acceptable in evidence even without giving the basis for the opinion."[75] Another court put it this way: "On direct examination [the appraiser] stated in general terms that his estimates of value were based on his experience in dealing with coal properties and on comparable sales. He was not asked to identify any particular sale he relied on. It was not necessary, in order for his testimony to have probative value, that he identify the comparable sales."[76]

When testifying in a jurisdiction where the appraiser may, but is not required to, justify the opinion of value presented, it is essential that the appraiser support

74. *United States v. 1,053.27 Acres of Land in Osage Co., Kan.*, 446 F.2d 1234 (10th Cir. 1971).

75. *Arkansas State H'way Comm. v. Hartsfield*, 454 S.W.2d 82, 84 (Ark. 1970).

76. *West Kentucky Coal Co. v. Commonwealth*, 368 S.W.2d 738, 741 (Ky. 1963).

his or her opinion on direct examination, by comparable sales as well as by other means. If this is not done, a prudent opposing counsel will probably not ask for the appraiser's comparables on cross-examination or may decline to cross-examine the witness altogether, particularly if the appraiser is well qualified and has a reputation as a good expert witness. This leaves the appraiser's opinion unsupported before the trier of fact, a circumstance which opposing counsel will be sure to point out during final argument. The argument will probably be, "Who are you going to believe? My appraiser, who testified to all of these comparable sales in the area, or the other appraiser, who testified to a totally unsupported guess?" Such a final argument is generally very persuasive.

Most jurisdictions require that an expert explain and support his or her opinion of value before the court will allow the opinion to be considered by the trier of fact. The Oregon court has said "[t]he witness testified that, taking into consideration adjustments, two parcels were comparable; but he failed to state what the adjustments were. It would have been improper for the court to admit the sale price until the adjustments were explained."[77] In Rhode Island, the court said:

> In the L'Etoile case [*L'Etoile v. Director of Pub. Works*, 89 R.I. 394, 402, 153 A.2d 173] the opinion of an admitted real estate expert as to the fair market value, based solely on his long experience, was held to have been properly excluded for the reason that to have admitted it without supporting data would have denied the opposite party an opportunity to conduct an intelligent cross-examination.[78]

In a later case, the same court said "[a]n expert may not give an opinion without describing the foundation on which his opinion rests."[79]

An extreme example of this requirement for justification and support of opinion evidence is illustrated by a New York case in which the court said:

> The claimant's appraiser did not give a dollars and cents adjustment in any instance between the comparable and the subject land; neither did he give a breakdown percentage-wise nor state the factors which entered into his judgment. His failure to do so affords no basis for review of his testimony and it is insufficient to justify an award.[80]

When testifying in a jurisdiction that has a propensity to favor specific supporting data, analysis, and documentation, the appraiser might be wise to use the method shown in Table 10.1 or 10.2 to present sales data and analysis.

ADVANCED PROBLEMS

CASH EQUIVALENCY SALES

The courts have universally acknowledged that market value is to be measured in terms of cash or its equivalent. However, most of the cases reported have dealt with comparable sales that involved property exchanges or other non-cash considerations, not sales on installment terms or other seller financing. When market

77. *State H'way Comm. v. Callahan*, 410 P.2d 818, 819 (Ore. 1966).

78. *Hunt v. Director of Pub. Works*, 206 A.2d 91, 94 (R.I. 1965).

79. *Nasco, Inc. v. Director of Public Works*, 360 A.2d 871, 876 (R.I. 1976).

80. *Geffen Motors, Inc. v. State*, 307 N.Y.S.2d 389, 389 (N.Y. 1970).

value is defined in terms of cash or its equivalent, appraisers now recognize that comparable sales sold on terms other than cash must be analyzed to determine whether the price paid was affected by the non-cash nature of the transaction.

> The appraiser shall analyze and make appropriate adjustments to any comparable sale that included favorable or unfavorable financing terms as of the date of sale, when comparing the sale to the property being appraised. Such adjustment must reflect the difference between what the comparable sold for with the favorable or unfavorable financing and the price at which it would have sold for cash or its equivalent.[81]

In one of the few reported cases that has addressed this issue, the court's ruling supports the appraisal requirement quoted above. In this case the property being appraised was purchased three years before the date of value. The purchaser made a down payment and was paying the balance of the purchase price, which was secured by notes, plus interest to the seller through monthly payments. The court ruled that the lower court should have given the jury a definition for the phrase "terms equivalent to cash." The court said:

> [M]arket value may be either what the property would sell for in cash or on terms equivalent to cash. These are alternative criteria for establishing the fair market value. [Citations omitted]
>
> The terms are equivalent to cash if the deferred purchase money notes are such that under normal conditions the notes can be turned into cash at their face amount. Thus, the principal of the notes is not increased by the addition thereto of a charge for credit. The rate of interest earned by the notes and their underlying security are factors to be considered in determining their cash value.[82]

Appraisers use a number of methods to adjust non-cash sales to a cash equivalent price.[83] However, "[w]hile cash equivalency of favorable or unfavorable financing can be estimated by discounting the contractual terms at current market or yield rates for the same type of property and loan term over the expected holding period of the property, the preferred method of estimating a proper cash equivalency adjustment is by the analysis of actual market data, if such data is available."[84] Because the courts have not addressed the appropriate methodology for adjusting non-cash sale prices to a cash equivalency value, the appraiser must be prepared to demonstrate the reasonableness of any cash equivalency adjustment made with market data.

If paired sales data are not available and the appraiser is forced to use a discounting process to equate the actual terms of the sale to typical financing terms, the appraiser should be prepared to demonstrate, with factual market data, the typical financing terms available at the time of the sale and how the typical holding period of the property was determined. The appraiser should also be ready to demonstrate the mathematics of the discounting process.

81. *Uniform Appraisal Standards for Federal Land Acquisitions*, §B-1 17, p. 76.

82. *Riley v. District of Columbia Redevelop. Land Agency*, 246 F.2d 641, 643 (D.C. Cir. 1957); see also, *Surfside of Brevard, Inc. v. United States*, 414 F.2d 915 (5th Cir. 1969). For a discussion of these cases, see Stanley J. Fineman, "Law and the Appraiser – Cash Equivalency: A Problem for Courts as Well as Appraisers," *The Appraisal Journal* (October 1985), 617–620.

83. For examples, see *The Appraisal of Real Estate*, 10th ed., 376–380, and the *Appraisal Journal* articles cited in the footnote on p. 377 of that text.

84. *Uniform Appraisal Standards for Federal Land Acquisitions*, §B-1 – 17, p. 77.

SALES TO ENVIRONMENTAL ORGANIZATIONS

It has been noted that sales to government agencies are usually not admissible as comparable sales. What about sales to a party that does not have the right of condemnation, but is acquiring the land for the purpose of transferring its ownership to a condemnor? This question has not yet been addressed by the courts. Such situations often arise when a public project (e.g., a wildlife refuge) is authorized, but the acquisition has not been funded. An environmental organization might acquire lands within a project area for the sole purpose of transferring those lands, at the organization's cost, to the government when funding becomes available.

At times the relationship between the government agency and the environmental group is so close that the environmental group almost seems to act as an agent of the government. Appraisal reports commissioned by an environmental group for purposes of acquisition are prepared in accordance with the government agency's requirements and guidelines and, on occasion, may even be reviewed and approved by the government agency before the environmental organization makes the purchase.

Sales to environmental groups, under the conditions described, are obviously *project influenced*. It is not unheard-of for sellers of such lands to take (or attempt to take) a tax write-off for a contribution to the environmental group and claim its value in excess of the actual purchase price of the property. In many instances the property owners know that if they do not sell to the environmental group, they will be unable to sell their land on the open market because it has been designated as being within the government's authorized, but as yet unfunded, project area and is scheduled for government acquisition in the future. The motivation behind purchases by environmental groups, i.e., transfer to the government, is certainly not the motivation behind most market transactions, i.e., purchase to put the land to its highest and best economic use.

Because of these complications, appraisers should avoid using such sales if at all possible. If they must be used, objections should be anticipated, so careful verification is essential. The appraiser should determine whether the purchases were made based on competent appraisals and whether the appraisers' instructions, if any, specified that the market value of the property for its highest and best use be estimated. The appraiser's investigation should determine whether the environmental group's appraisal was written in accordance with government guidelines and whether the report was reviewed and approved by the government agency. If a tax write-off was claimed by the seller, an adjustment for this factor should be considered by the appraiser.

Even with verification of this additional information, some courts may exclude evidence of such sales. They are often so much a part of the government project for which the property is being acquired that no amount of verification or adjustment can totally remove the blemish from the sale.

Sales to the Government

In a perfect world appraisers would always find an abundance of comparable market data and there would never be a need to even consider using a sale to the government as a comparable. Some governmental agencies have historically prohibited the use of sales to the government as comparables in their appraisals, while others merely discourage it. This position is somewhat justified because government purchases generally fail at least two of the seven tests used to determine whether a sale was an open-market transaction. When a government purchase occurs, the buyer and seller are not "typically motivated" and the property sold was not typically exposed in the open market.

But, because of the unique needs of some government agencies, there is sometimes an inadequacy of private market data with which to develop a reliable indication of market value. Indeed, without resorting to sales to the government as comparables, it would be impossible to develop an indication of market value by the sales comparison approach at all. The one positive aspect of this situation is that, unlike most private purchases, a government purchase and the decision-making process that led to it are usually well documented. The appraiser can take advantage of that documentation in the sales verification process. In fact, the appraiser *must* take advantage of it.

The legislation which authorized, or mandated, the purchase is, of course, available for inspection. It should be studied carefully to ensure that the purchase was not authorized for a price other than market value. Many acquiring agencies are required by law to release the information and data they relied on in making land purchases once the transactions are consummated. This information can include appraisal reports, appraisal reviews, the report or diary of the negotiator, correspondence relating to the acquisition, internal memoranda justifying the final acquisition price, and copies of all conveyance and closing documents. The type of information available and the difficulty encountered in obtaining it will vary from agency to agency. If adequate information is not willingly provided and a sale is critical to the appraisal, the appraiser may want to consider filing a formal request under the federal Freedom of Information Act or a similar state law.

Equally important is thorough verification of the sale with the seller. This can lead to additional information, such as whether the seller had the property appraised. Also sellers will sometimes sell at prices that they believe are below market value if they support the government's project, are simply tired of the protracted government negotiations (which in some circumstances go on for years), or want to avoid litigation.

The whole purpose of collecting this information is to ensure that any sale used as a comparable is a true representation of market value and that the price paid by the government is equivalent to the price that would have been paid for the property had it been sold to a private party. However, the fact that the price paid by the government was different from the value estimated in its approved appraisal or was influenced by nonmarket factors does not necessarily invalidate the transaction as a reliable comparable sale. The government's appraisal is not the last word; it is not necessarily the only reasonable estimate of market value. Sales to the government at prices that are 10% to 15% above the appraised value should not necessarily be rejected as invalid comparable sales. Sales that are substantially higher than the government's appraised value do, however, require close scrutiny.

Some sales that have been affected by nonmarket factors can be adjusted and used as comparable sales. For example, if a fee simple estate was appraised and the government paid the appraised value, but as part of the negotiations the property owner retained a life estate in the property, the sale can be adjusted for the present value of the life estate, if such an adjustment is justified. Similarly, if an internal memorandum in the government's file indicates that the government agreed to pay a price higher than market value because the excess was less than the cost of a condemnation trial, a reasonable adjustment can be made for this factor.

If a sale to the government is used as a comparable, the appraiser must fully report the investigation and analysis that were undertaken to verify the sale. Because sales to the government are generally considered inadmissible, it is incumbent upon the appraiser to convince the reader of the appraisal report of the reliability of the sale as a valid and admissible indication of market value.

Summary

The sales comparison approach is widely accepted by the courts, at times to the exclusion of any other approach to value. Most courts will allow testimony regarding sales of similar property on direct examination in technical violation of the hearsay rule. In some jurisdictions these sale data are admitted as direct evidence of the market value of the property being appraised, while in others the evidence is admitted only in support of the expert's opinion. Jurisdictions that do not admit comparable sales data into evidence on direct examination will generally allow it on cross-examination, to test a witness's opinion.

A prior sale price of the property being appraised is admissible if the transaction was proximate to the date of valuation or taking, and no major physical changes to the property have taken place between the sale date and the date of valuation. It has been said that the prior sale of a property is the best evidence of its value. The appraiser has a professional obligation to consider and report any recent sale of the property being appraised, regardless of whether the price paid was market value and whether or not that price supports the appraiser's estimate of the property's value.

The selection of comparable sales is of utmost importance. Forced sales and sales to purchasers with the power of eminent domain generally do not meet the criteria of an arm's-length transaction and will often not be admitted as comparable sales. If an appraiser is forced to use sales to the government as comparables because of a lack of private market transactions, the terms and conditions of the sales and the circumstances surrounding them should be extensively investigated and reported. The burden of demonstrating that such sales are not tainted is on the appraiser who uses them.

While the courts have not specifically ruled on the issue, sales to environmental groups for the purpose of ultimately transferring ownership of the property to the government may be viewed as tainted sales. In addition, sales in which the consideration included non-cash items such as property exchanges or personal property are also usually not considered *comparable*. Real estate contracts, or contract sales, have been admitted, but the price paid in such transactions must be converted to a cash or cash equivalency basis. Adjustments to sale prices should be supported by market data. The fact that a sale does not meet all the criteria of an open market transaction does not mean the appraiser cannot consider it, only that he or she cannot testify in regard to the sale.

Once an appraiser learns the price and terms of a nonmarket sale, how can he or she avoid considering it? A bell cannot be unrung and an appraiser cannot totally erase knowledge of the nonmarket sale from his mind. However, considering a sale, or any other factor, does not mean that it has influenced the appraiser's final value estimate. The appraiser certainly may and, in fact, should consider all sales with which he is familiar. Nevertheless, the appraiser should be prepared to testify, "I considered that sale, but gave it no weight because..."

A federal court has ruled on whether an expert witness's testimony should be allowed to stand after it appeared that the witness had based his appraisal, in part, on sales made to the United States under the shadow of condemnation. The judge said:

> Be that as it may, it would be absurd to exclude a qualified expert's appraisal because he had considered such evidence; indeed he ought to consider it; it is part of the data on which his opinion should rest. It is just because he is an expert, and for that reason able to give its proper weight to all data, that he is allowed to appraise the property at all. No court has held, so far as we can find, that his opinion shall not be received because it is so based in part; and we should not follow its ruling, if there were one, unless we had no escape.[85]

When Justice Holmes was serving as Chief Justice of the Supreme Judicial Court of Massachusetts, he also addressed this issue: "An expert may testify to value, although his knowledge of details is chiefly derived from inadmissible sources, because he gives the sanction of his general experience. But the fact that an expert may use hearsay as a ground of opinion does not make the hearsay admissible."[86]

This is not to say that an appraiser's opinion will be admitted if his value estimate is based entirely on sales that do not meet the criteria of market value. "Where a witness testifies as to value and bases his opinion entirely upon im-

85. *United States v. Delano Park Homes*, 146 F.2d 473, 475 (2d Cir. 1944).

86. *National Bank of Commerce v. City of New Bedford*, 56 N.E. 288, 290 (Mass. 1900).

proper considerations or incompetent and inadmissible matters, his testimony may be properly stricken from the record."[87] [Citations omitted]

If verification of a sale indicates that the price was representative of market value, the appraiser should determine the overall comparability of the sale property. In verifying a comparable sale the appraiser must take care to confirm that the parties to the transaction were *knowledgeable*. The appraiser must consider how that term has been defined by the courts in the jurisdiction where any dispute concerning the value of the property under appraisal will be heard. If the sale property being appraised could have fairly competed with the sale property for a buyer, had it then been competitively offered, the sale can generally be considered, from a physical, locational, and economic standpoint, to be a comparable sale. If the property meets this test of comparability, the appraiser may then make a comparative analysis of this property and the property being appraised.

Adjustments are made to the sale price of a comparable property for property rights conveyed, financing terms, market conditions, location, and physical characteristics. On occasion, an additional adjustment is required for conditions of sale. The indicated values developed in the comparative analysis of the sale properties are then correlated into a final value estimate for the property being appraised. This correlated value is *not* an average of the various value indications developed. It has been ruled on several occasions that to average the comparable sales prices is a faulty procedure.[88]

Appraisers often have several options for presenting comparable sales data and analysis in an appraisal report. Appraisal reporting standards or requirements may limit these options. Appraisers can also choose from several formats when presenting sales data and analysis to the trier of fact. However, this selection should never be made by the appraiser alone, but by mutual agreement between the appraiser and legal counsel. The presentation format selected should be simple, clear, and logical. Applicable case law concerning the amount of reasoning required to support an opinion of value may also influence the manner in which the appraiser presents sales data and analysis.

87. *City of Gilroy v. Filice*, 34 Cal. Rptr. 368, 375 (Cal. 1963).

88. *Latham Holding Co. v. State of New York*, 209 N.E.2d 542 (N.Y. 1965).

CHAPTER 11

Special-Purpose Properties

A special-purpose property is "[a] property devoted to or available for utilization for a special purpose, such as a clubhouse, a church property, a public museum, a public school, and so on. It also includes other buildings having value, such as hospitals, theaters, breweries, etc., which cannot be converted to other uses without large capital investment."[1] The identifying features of a special-purpose property are:

1. The property has physical design features peculiar to a specific use.
2. The property has no apparent market other than to an owner-user.
3. The property has no feasible economic alternate use.[2]

Special-purpose properties, referred to as *specialties*[3] in some jurisdictions and as *limited market properties*[4] in some appraisal literature, have caused the courts to avoid adopting market value as the exclusive test of just compensation. Determining whether a property is a special-purpose property is important to its appraisal:

> In summary, the rule to be followed is that cost, as evidence of market value, should be restricted to those cases where:
>
> 1. The property involved is unique.
>
> 2. Or, it is a specialty.
>
> 3. Or, there is competent proof of an absence of market data.[5]

---

1. American Institute of Real Estate Appraisers and the Society of Real Estate Appraisers, *Real Estate Appraisal Terminology*, rev. ed., Byrl N. Boyce, ed. (Cambridge, Mass.: Ballinger Publishing Company, 1981), 226.
2. George L. Schmutz, *Condemnation Appraisal Handbook*, rev., Edwin M. Rams, ed. (Englewood Cliffs, N.J.: Prentice-Hall, Inc., 1963), 163.
3. *In re Lincoln Square Slum Clearance Project*, 222 N.Y.S.2d 786 (N.Y. 1961).
4. *The Appraisal of Real Estate*, 10th ed. (Chicago: Appraisal Institute, 1992), 23.
5. Julius L. Sackman, "The Limitations of the Cost Approach," *The Appraisal Journal* (January 1966), 53, 58.

Some jurisdictions have excluded cost approach testimony unless it can be proven to the court's satisfaction that the property in dispute is a special-purpose property. There is some disagreement as to whether certain property types are, in fact, special-purpose properties. One significant criterion of a special-purpose property is that there is no market for the property, as demonstrated by the lack of comparable sales data.

Identifying a special-purpose property may be problematic. For instance, a church may be classified as a special-purpose property because it is unique, it was built for a specific purpose, and there are no sales of comparable churches; in another location or at another time, however, the same property may not qualify as a special-purpose property for eminent domain valuation because there are comparable sales with which to value the property. The fact that one court classifies a church as a specialty and another refuses to do so does not necessarily mean that these court decisions are in conflict. It may simply mean that market data did not exist in the first instance and they did in the latter. Appraisers and lawyers should not assume that a court that has historically ruled that a specific property type is a specialty will rule this way in every instance. The court's decision will often hinge on the availability of comparable market data.

A uniform method of measuring compensation in the taking of special-use properties has never been developed; thus the potential for widely divergent value testimony is great. Although there is a great deal of case law on the proper methodology to be applied in the valuation of special-use properties, few specific guidelines exist for the appraiser.

The Uniform Eminent Domain Code provides that ". . . the fair market value of property for which there is no relevant market is its value as determined by any method of valuation that is just and equitable."[6] The United States Court of Federal Claims has said that "the fair market value of property, in the absence of an actual market, is the estimated or imputed fair market value based on sufficient evidence which justifies a conclusion as to the fair market value which would be established when an informed seller disposes of his property to an equally informed buyer."[7]

It can be seen that the courts are reluctant to abandon the concept of market value completely. In reference to the market value concept, the courts have recognized that an actual buyer may not exist for the property in question, but note that the estimate of market value is always based on the hypothetical assumption that a willing seller and willing buyer do, in fact, exist.[8] However, to ensure that the owner is fully compensated for the property taken, some courts have used such terms as *value to the owner*, *intrinsic value*, and *value in use*. The condemnation of special-purpose property presents a valuation challenge to the appraiser and a legal challenge to the attorney.

6. Uniform Eminent Domain Code, 1974 §1004(a), p. 10.7.

7. *Tlingit and Haida Indians of Alaska v. United States*, 389 F.2d 778, 782 (Ct. Cl. 1968).

8. *Olson v. United States*, 292 U.S. 246 (1934).

PROPERTY CLASSIFIED AS SPECIAL-PURPOSE

The specific type of property being appraised will influence the valuation approach employed by the appraiser. The following properties have been classified by the courts as special-purpose:[9]

- Amusement parks
- Banks
- Camps
- Car washes
- Cemeteries
- Churches
- Clubhouses
- Dam sites and reservoir sites
- Duck clubs
- Freight terminals
- Golf clubs
- Hospitals
- Mill sites
- Museums
- Nursing homes
- Private lakes
- Public utilities
- Schools
- Specialized industrial uses (i.e., packing plants, laundries, etc.)
- Stadiums
- Theaters

The appraiser must not automatically assume that a property is special-purpose simply because similar properties have been so classified. As stated earlier, to be truly special-purpose, a property must have: 1) physical features peculiar to its specific use, 2) no apparent market other than the current owner-user, and 3) no feasible economic alternate use. The most convincing evidence that a property is, in fact, a special-use property is the absence of sales of similar property. Lack of sales data and the classification of a property as a specialty:

> ...may afford a basis for the application of more liberal rules of evidence or a different measure of value.
>
> Relaxation of rules may take various forms:
>
> 1. Modification of the yardstick of compensation.
>   a. The market value measure applied but rules of evidence relaxed.
>   b. Use of measures other than market value.
> 2. Use of appraisal methods other than the market data [sales comparison] approach.
>   a. Use of the cost approach and evidence of costs allowed.
>   b. Use of the income approach and income data, which may include business done and profits earned, allowed.
> 3. Variations and proof more or less peculiar to special purposes properties.[10]

The traditional approaches to value are sometimes applicable to the valuation of special-purpose properties. The reliability of these approaches often suffers, however, because adequate data on which to base an estimate of value are lacking and the criteria for what are considered acceptable data must be relaxed.

9. For information on the appraisal of specific types of special-purpose properties, see *Encyclopedia of Real Estate Appraising*, Edith J. Friedman, ed. (Englewood Cliffs, N.J.: Prentice-Hall, Inc.), 1959, 1968, and 1978 editions and *Appraisal Reporting Techniques*, vol. 4 (Chicago: American Institute of Real Estate Appraisers, 1954). Also check *Readers' Guide to The Appraisal Journal*, 1970–1980, 1980–1987, and 1988–1993 editions for articles relating to special-purpose properties.

10. Edward E. Level, *Valuation and Condemnation of Special Purpose Properties*, National Cooperative Highway Research Program, Rep. No. 92 (Washington, D.C.: Highway Research Board, 1970), 5.

SALES COMPARISON APPROACH

"One factor that makes a property special purpose is the lack of sales of similar properties. Therefore, little can be said of this approach when discussing special purpose properties."[11] The degree of comparability required between a property under appraisal and a sale property is often relaxed in the appraisal of special-purpose property. This is particularly true in terms of geographic comparability. "[I]f land is not of a character commonly bought and sold, [the court] should allow evidence of the sales of similar land located at some distance from the land taken."[12]

When comparable sales are available, the most perplexing task facing the appraiser is often finding the proper unit of comparison. This is particularly true in appraising unusual types of special-purpose properties. In valuing unique properties, appraisers may wish to investigate units of comparison that have been applied in the past. The following list may prove instructive:

Property Type	Unit of Measure
Hospital or nursing home	Per bed
Log dumps	Per 1,000 board feet in or out of dump
Chemical waste sites	Per cubic ft. or per drum of storage space
Theaters/churches	Per seat
Freight terminals	Per door
Duck clubs	Per gun
Cemeteries	Per plot
Funeral homes	Per case
Campgrounds	Per campsite

This list is not complete, but it does illustrate the diverse units of measurement which the appraiser may employ to value special-purpose properties with market data techniques.

INCOME CAPITALIZATION APPROACH

The income capitalization approach is applicable to special-purpose properties that have rental income potential, but not, of course, to properties such as churches and municipal buildings. Several problems are typically encountered in applying the income capitalization approach to special-purpose properties.

Most special-purpose properties are owner-occupied and it is therefore difficult, if not impossible, to find sufficient comparable rental data from which to develop an accurate and reliable estimate of the property's economic rent. Another problem is that the only income data available may be the net income from the property owner's business, which will include both business profit and a return on the real estate. Therefore, "[t]he appraiser of special-use properties requires a closer familiarity with the particular type of operation or business conducted than in evaluation of properties suitable for a variety of uses."[13]

11. Ibid., 13.

12. *United States v. 84.4 Acres of Land*, 224 F.Supp. 1017, 1022 (W.D. Pa. 1963), *rev'd on other grounds*, 348 F.2d 117 (3rd Cir. 1965).

13. *Encyclopedia of Real Estate Appraising*, 767.

Often the appraiser must develop a stabilized net income from the business operation and the return on the real estate. After developing this estimate, the appraiser is faced with two choices. He must either extract the net income attributable to the business from the total net income, so the residual net income attributable to the real estate can be capitalized into an indication of value, or develop a capitalization rate high enough to reflect the value of the real estate only when it is applied to the total stabilized net income from both the business and the real estate.

Developing and supporting a capitalization rate applicable to the special-use property being appraised presents further problems. Because sales and rental data for such property are not available, a capitalization rate cannot generally be developed directly from market data. An appropriate capitalization rate must be developed by indirect methods, analyzing the attributes of the property being appraised as a real estate investment and comparing it with other real estate and non-real estate investments available in the marketplace.

Normally the profits from a business operated on a site to be acquired by eminent domain are not admissible in court. It is generally held that "[e]vidence of profits derived from a *commercial* business upon land taken for public use is ordinarily inadmissible as a basis upon which to ascertain market value in condemnation proceedings because it is too speculative, remote and uncertain."[14] While it is well established that business profits are inadmissible in an ordinary eminent domain action, this general rule may not apply when the subject of the condemnation action is a special-purpose property. "In some jurisdictions and situations, the income from the business conducted on the property and values arrived at by using such income may be admissible. This is another area in which the courts have, of necessity, been more liberal in the allowance of proof when dealing with special purpose properties."[15]

The courts' reasons for admitting evidence of business profits seem mixed. Some courts have, in the absence of comparable sales, admitted income data *as a measure of value*, while others have admitted it for the sole purpose of demonstrating the *productivity of the property*. "Although the profits of a business do not determine the value of land, it is proper to show, in arriving at the market value, that it is valuable for certain purposes and productive to the owner."[16] As stated by one court:

> Business profits, it is well recognized, are no sure test of land value for they depend not only on location but on other factors; the same location may be fruitful of profit to one and not so to another. This does not mean, however, that in determining the value of the land no consideration is to be given to its productive capacity which, in such circumstances as are present in this case, has an important bearing on value.
>
> As a practical matter, a prospective purchaser would hardly fail to consider whether or not the business conducted on the premises had proved profitable, for this would be a measure of the desirability of the location, if not to him then to

14. *Shelby County R-IV School District v. Herman*, 392 S.W.2d 609, 613 (Mo. 1965).

15. Level, *Valuation and Condemnation of Special Purpose Properties*, 22.

16. *Sanitary Dist. of Chicago v. Pittsburgh, Ft. W. and C. Ry. Co.*, 75 N.E. 248, 252 (Ill. 1905).

> other purchasers. The precise weight to be accorded to this factor is a matter of judgment on which experts may differ, and of this the jury is the final judge....[17] [Citations omitted]

In light of these differing court rulings, it is incumbent upon the appraiser and the lawyer to determine: 1) whether the property being condemned would be classified as a special-purpose property by the court with jurisdiction; 2) if so, is the net profit from the business operated on the property admissible; and 3) if admissible, for what purpose—as a criterion of value or as evidence of productivity?

COST APPROACH

In valuing a special-purpose property, it has been held that the reproduction cost, or replacement cost minus depreciation, may be considered and "may even be the only method in some situations... Usually, reproduction costs or replacement costs are used as a starting point, *with no recognition being made of the distinction in these two terms*. Some courts have required costs to be those of an identical structure, despite increasing criticism against such an approach."[18] This ruling is apparently based on the proposition that the trier of fact should concern itself with the cost of reproducing the improvements that are actually on the land, rather than some hypothetical structure. Thus, it is critical for the appraiser and the attorney first to determine whether the property being appraised is in a jurisdiction requiring use of the reproduction cost of an identical structure. If this is not required, they then must ascertain whether a reproduction cost estimate or a replacement cost estimate is more appropriate under the circumstances. It is, of course, important that the appraiser clearly identify both in the appraisal report and to the trier of fact whether reproduction or replacement cost has been used. The distinction between these terms must be made clear.

In applying the cost approach to value, the appraiser first estimates the value of the land. The land underlying a special-purpose improvement will often have a different highest and best use as if vacant than it does as improved. If the special-purpose improvement could be located on a different, less valuable, site, the appraiser must choose either to value the site as if vacant and available for its highest and best use or to estimate its value for the existing use. If the former methodology is adopted, the appraiser must compensate for the fact that the improvements could offer equal utility on a less valuable site. This is accomplished by deducting from the reproduction or replacement cost of the improvement the difference between the value of the site for its highest and best use as if vacant and the value of the site for its current use, i.e., the cost of acquiring an equally desirable substitute site. This is essentially a measure of the external, or economic, obsolescence in the improvements.

17. *State Roads Commission v. Novosel*, 102 A.2d 563, 565 (Md. 1954).

18. *Nichols' The Law of Eminent Domain*, rev. 3d. ed. (New York: Matthew Bender Co., Inc., 1990), vol. 4, § 12C.01[3][b]. (Emphasis added.)

FIGURE 11.1 SPECIAL-PURPOSE PROPERTY—EXTERNAL OBSOLESCENCE

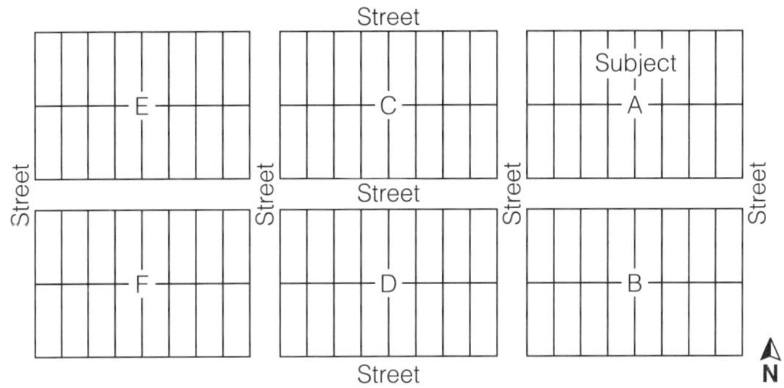

For example, consider a church located on a 200-ft.-by-120-ft. site, as shown in Block A of Figure 11.1. Assume the improvements have a reproduction cost of $500,000 and the underlying land, which is zoned for commercial use, has a value for commercial purposes of $5.00 per square foot, or $120,000. The land in Blocks D and F is zoned for residential use, which permits a church use, and has a value of approximately $1.50 per square foot. If the subject improvements could serve the parishioners equally well on Block D or F as they do on Block A, external obsolescence of the improvements is indicated.

Under these circumstances, the appraiser could value the property as follows (assuming no other forms of depreciation):

Reproduction cost of improvements	$500,000
Value of site for church use	
(24,000 sq. ft. @ $1.50)	36,000
Total indicated value	$536,000

Or the appraiser might choose to value the site for its highest and best use and calculate the external obsolescence in the improvements as follows:

Reproduction cost of improvements	$500,000
Less external obsolescence ($120,000 [value of site for highest and best use] less $36,000 [value of equally desirable substitute site for church purposes])	– 84,000
Indicated improvement value	$416,000
Site value for highest and best use	120,000
Total indicated value	$536,000

Both procedures result in the same conclusion. The procedure selected by the appraiser will depend on the specific circumstances and the availability of market data. It is often advisable to use both procedures in the appraisal report to ensure complete understanding by reviewers and other readers of the report. By discussing both procedures on the witness stand, the appraiser can gain the understanding of the trier of fact and severely limit the effectiveness of any cross-examination intended to confuse the trier of fact or diminish the appraiser's credibility.

The most difficult aspect of applying the cost approach to special-purpose properties is the accurate estimation of depreciation. "Both physical, economic, and functional depreciation must be included. Although physical depreciation, by inspection is not difficult, functional or economic depreciation is much more difficult to determine..."[19] Generally, economic and functional obsolescence are measured using market data, but it is the lack of market data that identifies a property as special-purpose. Therefore, "[i]n assessing the value of a church, for example, the appraiser will have to exercise some effort and ingenuity in determining what elements affecting the utility of the subject church are superior or inferior to similar churches. Each church may have its own needs, however. Ultimate determination of the amount of depreciation will rest on the appraiser's judgment, assuming that the appraiser has made an adequate investigation of the factors that affect the utility and enjoyment of a particular property and that he has attempted to gauge such factors of the subject against what might be considered as the norm in properly improved facilities of the same type."[20]

Because factual data from which to estimate depreciation are lacking, the cost approach has been severely criticized, even though it is sometimes the only reasonable measure of value available. This was the conclusion reached in an extensive research report regarding the valuation and condemnation of special-purpose properties:

> It [the cost approach] is mechanical from its inception. Reproduction costs of a building may have no correlation whatever to value, market or otherwise. If value is to be reached, it is by appropriate allowances for depreciation. The ultimate basis of depreciation is the appraiser's opinion, which is no better than his experience, knowledge, and judgment. As a practical matter, failure to recognize depreciation is to the owner's advantage. Some indefiniteness of depreciation might be avoided if the starting point were replacement cost; i.e., starting with a building functionally equivalent to the subject. Nevertheless, the cost approach is the only method that can be used on some special purpose properties that do not have production of income as their purpose.[21]

SUBSTITUTE FACILITIES

The doctrine of substitute facilities is not a valuation or appraisal technique, but a concept that has evolved from court decisions. Condemnation appraisers and condemnation attorneys should be familiar with this doctrine. The New Jersey court defined the substitute facilities doctrine as follows:

> We think the rule of substitute facilities is a just and sensible one. Henceforth, therefore, when the State or some other condemnor takes property which is al-

19. *Nichols'*, vol. 4, §12C.01[3][b] (1992).
20. Ibid.
21. Level, *Valuation and Condemnation of Special Purpose Properties*, 18.

> ready devoted to some public use by a municipality or other agency of government, the requirement of just compensation will be met by the condemnor furnishing an adequate, substantially equivalent substitute facility, which need not, however, be an exact duplicate of what has been taken. This may either be done by the condemnor actually constructing the replacement facility,... or it may take the form of a monetary award in an amount deemed sufficient to construct an adequate substitute for what has been taken."[22]

Generally the substitute facilities doctrine is applied to publicly owned properties such as public schools, municipal buildings, public streets (which require replacement), and sewer and water treatment plants. The age of the improvement and the depreciation it has suffered are disregarded. The doctrine was established in 1923 by the United States Supreme Court.[23] The doctrine's applicability to publicly used properties owned by nonprofit organizations was not decided until 1979 when the same court ruled that the substitute facilities doctrine did not apply to such property.[24] In that case the Court said, "In light of our disposition of this case, we express no opinion on the appropriate measure of compensation for publicly owned property."[25]

However, in the *Duncanville* case[26] in 1984, the Court found that while the concept of substitute facilities was constitutionally *permissible*, it was not constitutionally *required*. "The text of the Fifth Amendment certainly does not mandate a more favorable rule of compensation for public condemnees than for private parties."[27] Based on this decision, it appears that "[t]he Substitute Facilities Doctrine will not be substituted for market value, as a measure of just compensation, unless it can clearly be proven that to do otherwise would result in manifest injustice. The not insignificant burden of proving such injustice will clearly be on the shoulders of the governmental condemnee."[28]

Application of the substitute facilities doctrine in the federal courts has been severely limited by the *Duncanville* decision. In those rare occasions when it might be applicable, the appraiser estimates the replacement cost of the public improvements taken and adds the value of the land, making no deduction for depreciation. The value of the land should be based on the cost of acquiring a substitute site, not on the value of the site for its highest and best use.

ADVANCED PROBLEMS

CONTAMINATED PROPERTY

Recently situations have arisen in which property found to be contaminated has to be cleaned up, or the contamination mitigated, prior to any sale of the property. Sometimes the cost of mitigation is more than the market value of the prop-

22. *State Commissioner of Transportation v. Township of South Hackensack*, 322 A.2d 818, 823 (N.J. 1974).
23. *Brown v. United States*, 263 U.S. 78 (1923).
24. *United States v. 564.54 Acres of Land*, 441 U.S. 506 (1979).
25. Ibid., 441 U.S. 506, 509 n.3.
26. *United States v. 50 Acres of Land*, 469 U.S. 24 (1984) (*Duncanville*). For a discussion of this case, see J.D. Eaton, "A Decade of U.S. Supreme Court Decisions–An Appraiser's View," *The Appraisal Journal* (January 1990), 33–36.
27. *United States v. 50 Acres of Land*, 469 U.S. 24, 37.
28. Eaton, 36.

erty as if uncontaminated, thus the property can be said to have no market value in its contaminated condition, even though it is providing functional utility to its existing owner. In many instances, owners are not required to clean up their contaminated properties until they are sold.

A review of the criteria for special-purpose property suggests that such a property would qualify as a special-purpose property. The property is unique, it has no apparent market, and there is currently no economic alternative use for the property. Nevertheless, the property can continue to be used by its current owner. To say that such an owner would be due no compensation for the condemnation of his land by a governmental agency would be manifestly unjust. Consequently, a means must be developed to measure the value of such property for eminent domain purposes.

Obviously, the sales comparison approach to value cannot be applied. There are no comparable sales and technically the property has no market value. Application of the cost approach would not be practical either. Elements of the income capitalization approach can be used, however, to measure the present worth of the benefits and liabilities of owning the property under appraisal.

For example, consider a contaminated property that is leased to an industrial tenant for $500,000 per year net to the owner. Assume that 12 years remain on the lease. Further assume that the property would have a market value of $5,000,000 if it were free from contamination and the current cost of cleanup would be $7,500,000. The present value of the property, for eminent domain purposes, might be computed as follows:

Discount rate applicable to real estate	12%
Discount rate applicable to cleanup cost	15%
Value of 12-year income stream ($500,000 x 6.194374)*	$3,097,187
Value of reversion ($5,000,000 x .256675)†	1,283,375
Subtotal	$4,380,562
Less value of cleanup liability ($7,500,000 x .186907)‡	-1,401,803
Present value of property	$2,978,759
Rounded	$3,000,000

* Value of $1 per year for 12 years discounted at 12%.
† Present value of $1 to be received in 12 years discounted at 12%.
‡ Present value of $1 to be received in 12 years discounted at 15%.

Several precautions must be taken in applying this approach. First, the estimate derived is not truly an estimate of *market value* because there would be no buyer for the property. However, as the courts have stated in the past, when valuing special-purpose property for eminent domain purposes it must be assumed that a hypothetical buyer exists. Second, although it was assumed in the example that the property was under lease at economic, or market, rent, special-purpose properties are usually not leased, but owner-occupied. In such a situation, the appraiser will have to estimate economic rent. In doing so, a determination must be made as to whether the contamination will have an impact on its economic rent and/or vacancy level of the property and, if so, to what degree.

In the example a discount rate of 12% was applied to the real estate. The property's rental income of $500,000 and value, if clean, of $5,000,000 would suggest a 10% capitalization rate ($500,000 ÷ $5,000,000). The discount rate is higher to reflect the additional risk involved, especially the possibility that environmental laws may change and require remediation of the contamination prior to the sale of the property.

The discount rate applied to the cleanup cost is different than the rate applied to the real estate. Two factors should be considered in selecting this rate. First, inflation may increase the cost of remediation over the 12-year period, which would justify increasing the estimated cost of cleanup or decreasing the discount rate applied to the present cleanup cost. On the other hand, cleanup costs have been decreasing as new, more efficient means to handle contamination are developed; this would suggest a higher discount rate. The appraiser would have to consider both of these factors in selecting the rate to be applied to the anticipated cost of remediation.

Note that in the example the value of the reversion was estimated based on the current value of the property if clean ($5,000,000). Such an assumption may or may not be appropriate. Consideration would have to be given to a number of factors, including whether the improvements will be at the end of their economic lives at the end of the lease term and whether the improvements might have to be removed from the site as part of the remediation process. In the latter case only the land value would be considered for reversionary purposes. The appraiser would also consider whether the property will suffer from some diminution in value after remediation simply because of its historical contamination; the current buzz word for this effect is *stigma*.

ENTREPRENEURIAL PROFIT

The inclusion of entrepreneurial profit in the estimate of reproduction or replacement cost was discussed in Chapter 8. Including this factor in the estimated reproduction or replacement cost of some special-purpose properties would appear inappropriate. Obviously, application of the substitute facilities doctrine would preclude the use of such a factor. Moreover, entrepreneurial profit would appear to be inappropriate in an estimate of the reproduction or replacement cost of a specialty property devoted to a nonprofit use such as a church, which is not built to produce a profit. While indirect costs such as builder's overhead and profit, bond costs, and architect's fees have been approved by the courts for inclusion in the reproduction cost of a specialty,[29] no published case approving the inclusion of a specific entrepreneurial profit factor has been found.

The courts have a basic mistrust for the cost approach as demonstrated by the following:

29. *In re Washington Market Company Property*, 295 F. 950 (D.C. Cir. 1924) *cert. dismissed*, 265 U.S. 598 (1924).

> ...reproduction cost evidence almost invariably tends to inflate valuation. This is so because the reproduction cost of a structure sets an absolute ceiling on the market price of that structure, a ceiling which may not be, and most frequently is not, even approached in actual market negotiations. When this inherently inflationary attribute of reproduction cost evidence is considered in the light of the misleading exactitude which such evidence almost inevitably imparts to a jury unsophisticated in the niceties of economics, the justification for placing substantial safeguards upon its admission is apparent.[30]

Because this attitude toward the cost approach is shared by most courts, any attempt to include a specific entrepreneurial profit in the reproduction or replacement cost estimate of a special-purpose property will probably not be, and should not be, viewed favorably.

STREETS AND RAILROADS

When functioning streets or railroads, or even utility lines, are taken, the measure of just compensation is usually the *cost to cure*, which could be viewed as an application of the substitute facilities doctrine. If a portion of a railroad right-of-way that was taken had a reproduction cost of $1,000,000 and a depreciated value of $750,000, the conclusions of an appraisal might be:

Reproduction cost of taking	$1,000,000
Less depreciation	– 250,000
Value of taking	$ 750,000
Plus damages to remainder	250,000
Total (just compensation)	$1,000,000

Technically the entire railroad would have to be valued before and after the taking. However, such an undertaking is generally unwarranted from both a time and cost standpoint, thus the appraiser's conclusions are shown simply as the cost to cure or the cost to substitute the facilities taken. This approach is reasonable and will result in the same amount of compensation as long as the balance of the facility (street or railroad) had a before value of not less than the amount of damages, as shown in the foregoing computation. In practice, some condemnors and condemnees agree to base the compensation amount on the cost of a substitute facility without the benefit of an appraisal.

A problem occurs, however, when the property taken is a nonfunctioning rail or street corridor. Many appraisers have estimated the compensation due for the taking of such property by estimating its *at* or *across the fence* (ATF) *value*.[31] This procedure is incorrect. Estimating ATF values is only the first step in a rather complex valuation procedure which includes analysis of the highest and best use of the subject property as well as analysis of the sales of other corridors. Then a factor that reflects the utility of the property must be developed and applied to the ATF value to produce a reasonable estimate of the market value of the corri-

30. *United States v. Benning Housing Corp.*, 276 F.2d 248, 250 (5th Cir. 1960).

31. *Across-the-fence value* is defined as "the estimated sale price based on the unit price of sales of similar land adjoining the subject." Clifford A. Zoll, "Rail Corridor Sales," *The Appraisal Journal* (July 1985), 379, 380. See also *The Dictionary of Real Estate Appraisal*, 3d ed. (Chicago: Appraisal Institute, 1993), 5.

dor under appraisal. One study showed that this factor ranged from 0.18 to 3.73 times the ATF value.[32]

If the appraiser is not familiar with the proper method of corridor valuation and is unwilling to take the time to become familiar with the process and develop a properly documented appraisal, he or she must reject any request for such an appraisal.[33] Otherwise, the appraiser is in jeopardy of violating the competency provision of the Uniform Standards of Professional Appraisal Practice.[34]

In valuing functioning corridors, the appraiser must determine whether there will be a need to replace the facility in the after situation. If so, compensation will typically be computed as demonstrated here. However, "[t]he overwhelming weight of modern authority is to the effect that a municipality, a county, a State, or other public entity is entitled to compensation for the taking of a street, road or other public highway *only to the extent that, as a result of such taking, it is compelled to construct a substitute highway.*"[35] For instance, consider the taking of land for a reservoir as shown in Figure 11.2. The condemnor would be required to pay the condemnee the cost to reconstruct Road 2 around the area taken, creating a substitute facility. However, there would be no (or nominal) compensation due for the taking of Road 1 because there will be no necessity for its replacement.

In might be argued that the condemnor in this situation is getting a portion of the area taken (Road 1) for nothing. However, "[i]t is customary to say that the value of the land in the streets and alleys is 'reflected' in the value of the [abutting lands], and since this value must be paid for upon condemnation, it cannot be said that the condemnor acquires without cost the lands within the lines of the highway."[36] Following this same logic, the rule would apply to the private owner of a street (e.g., a subdivider of the land) inasmuch as the developer received the value of the street to the extent that this value was reflected in the value of the lots sold.

It might also be argued that the condemnee will receive a windfall in regard to Road 2 because the condemnee will receive a new roadway in return for the roadway taken, which was depreciated. The *Duncanville* case[37], which was previously discussed, might be cited in support of this argument. However, the *Duncanville* case would not appear to be on point when it is related to the partial taking of Road 2. It is obvious that the damages to the remainder of Road 2, caused by its severance, will far exceed the excess cost of the replacement facility (i.e., the cost of the substitute facility less the depreciated value of the road taken). Therefore, the measure of compensation would not be premised on the substitute facilities doctrine at all, but rather on the cost to cure measure of damage. This is proper because the cost to cure is less than the damage would be if the cure were not undertaken. (See Chapter 14 for more information on the cost to cure measure of damage.)

32. See Zoll, "Rail Corridor Sales," 379–387.

33. For a discussion of rail corridor valuation, see the following articles in *The Appraisal Journal*: John P. Dolman and Charles F. Seymour, "Valuation of Transportation/Communication Corridors" (October 1978), 509–522; Clifford A. Zoll, "Rail Corridor Sales" (July 1985), 379–387; Zoll, "Rail Corridor Markets and Sale Factors" (October 1991), 504–512; and Frederick D. Mitenberger, "Rail Right-of-Way Valuation" (January 1992), 79–85.

34. The Appraisal Foundation, *Uniform Standards of Professional Appraisal Practice* (USPAP), 1994 ed., p. 4.

35. *State of California v. United States*, 169 F.2d 914, 924 (9th Cir. 1948).

36. *Mayor and City Council of Baltimore v. United States*, 147 F.2d 786, 790 (4th. Cir. 1945).

37. *United States v. 50 Acres of Land*, 469 U.S. 24 (1984) (*Duncanville*).

To demonstrate, assume that Road 2 in Figure 11.2 has a total length (Point A to Point B) of 6,000 feet and that its depreciated reproduction cost (including right-of-way acquisition costs) is $200 per linear foot. Further assume that the taking (Point C to Point D) is 300 feet in length and that the cost (including right-of-way acquisition) of building a new roadway from Point A to Point E, a distance of 750 feet, would be $350 per linear foot.

FIGURE 11.2

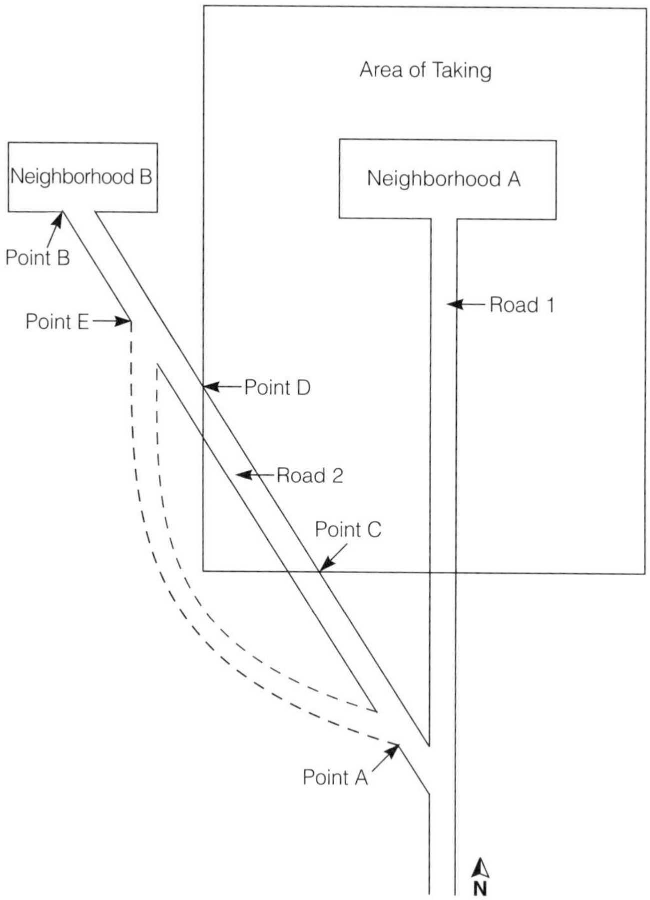

If Road 2 is not reconnected after the taking, it will have no utility and thus no value, or at most a nominal value. If the cost to cure method of measuring damages is not considered, the before and after value of the roadway would be:

Before value (6,000 lin. ft. @ $200)	$1,200,000
After value (nominal 5,700 lin. ft. @ $0)	0
Difference	$1,200,000

Using the state rule, the values would be:

Value before (6,000 lin. ft. @ $200)	$1,200,000
Less value of part taken (300 lin. ft. @ $200)	– 60,000
Remainder value before taking	$1,140,000
Remainder value after taking (nominal 5,700 lin. ft. @ $0)	0
Damages	$1,140,000
Special benefits	0
Net damages	$1,140,000
Plus value of part taken	+ 60,000
Total difference	$1,200,000

However, if the cost to cure measure of damages is used, as it should be, the before and after value of the property using the federal rule would be calculated as follows:

Before value		$1,200,000
After value		
Point A to Point C (abandoned—200 lin. ft. @ $0)	$ 0	
Point D to Point E (abandoned—150 lin. ft. @ $0)	0	
Point A to Point E (750 lin. ft. @ $350 –$132,500)	130,000 *	
Point E to Point B (5,350 lin. ft. @ $200)	1,070,000	
After value after cure	$1,200,000	
Less cost to cure (750 lin. ft. @ $350)	262,500	
Less net after value		– 937,500
Difference		$ 262,500

* The contributory value of this section of road, regardless of its cost, is limited to the contributory value of the roadway it replaces. In this instance, the new roadway replaces the 300 linear feet of road taken, plus the roadway abandoned between Points A and C (200 lin. ft.) and Points D and E (150 lin. ft.). Therefore, the contributory value of the new roadway is limited to ([300 lin. ft. + 200 lin. ft. + 150 lin. ft.] x $200) $130,000.

Using the state rule, the value would be computed as:

Value before taking (6,000 lin. ft. @ $200)		$1,200,000
Less value of part taken (300 lin. ft. @ $200)		- 60,000
Remainder value before taking		$1,140,000
Remainder value after taking after cure		
(Per above computation)	$1,200,000	
Less cost to cure (750 lin. ft. @ $350)	- 262,500	
Less remainder value before cure		- 937,500
Damages		$ 202,500
Special benefits		0
Net damages		$ 202,500
Plus value of part taken		60,000
Total difference		$ 262,500

It might be argued that the condemnee has received a special benefit because a section of the road in the after situation is now a *new* road, rather than a depreciated road. However, the new roadway section did not extend the life of the entire roadway. Thus, the economic life of the new roadway is no longer than that of the old section of roadway. It will lose its utility when the old roadway reaches the end of its useful life.

The principle of roadway replacement was summarized by the Pennsylvania court as follows:

> [I]f it is necessary to provide substitute roads to replace and utilize the uncondemned portion of the viable entity, the federal government, as condemnor, should construct or supply the cost of constructing the necessary substitute roads, regardless of whether that cost be greater or less than the value of the roads taken....
>
> By the same token, however, the federal government as condemnor enjoys the corresponding mitigating principle that it must furnish only substitute facilities that are reasonably necessary in the circumstances.... If none are reasonably necessary, no compensation is allowed.[38] [Citations omitted]

SUMMARY

A special-purpose property is one with a physical design peculiar to a specific use, no apparent market other than sale to an owner-user, and no financially feasible alternative use. The lack of comparable sales data is generally the key in distinguishing a special-purpose property.

The courts have been reluctant to abandon the market value concept totally in the valuation of special-purpose properties; instead, they tend to relax the rules of evidence and comparability in evaluating these properties. The three classic approaches to value used in the appraisal of real estate all have severe limitations when applied to special-purpose properties due to the paucity of market data.

38. *City of Chester v. Commonwealth Dept. of Transp.*, 434 A.2d 695, 703 (Pa. 1981).

Many appraisers apply the cost approach to value in appraising special-purpose properties because of the mechanical nature of this approach. Without adequate market data, however, the required estimates of depreciation, particularly functional and economic obsolescence, generally lack support. The courts are suspicious of the cost approach. There appears to be no published case in which a court has specifically approved the inclusion of entrepreneurial profit in the reproduction or replacement cost of a special-purpose property. Including such a factor in the reproduction or replacement cost estimate of a property used for public purposes and owned by a government entity or nonprofit organization is clearly inappropriate. In fact, appraisers should give serious consideration to excluding entrepreneurial profit in the reproduction or replacement cost estimate of any special-purpose property.

Because the three traditional approaches to value are not reliable, the appraiser is encouraged to use a commonsense approach in estimating the value of special-purpose properties. Some ingenuity is often required on the part of the appraiser. The abandonment or modification of the three approaches to value has, on occasion, been approved by the courts. Due to the unique nature of special-purpose property, the appraiser must often develop a complete understanding of the business operation conducted on the premises.

It appears that a contaminated property that cannot be economically cleaned up on the date of value, but still has substantial utility to its current owner or occupant, meets the definition of a *special-purpose property* used by most courts. The value of such a property, even when there is no market for it, is the present worth of the right of use and occupancy of the property minus the present worth of the anticipated cost of remediating the contamination at the termination of the property's economic life.

Many jurisdictions apply the substitute facilities doctrine to special-purpose properties that are government-owned when there is a duty on the part of the condemnee to replace the property. The substitute facilities doctrine requires that the compensation paid be the replacement cost of the improvements, without depreciation, plus the value of a substitute site. In some jurisdictions, this can be accomplished by the condemnor actually constructing a substitute facility. Because of a recent U.S. Supreme Court ruling, however, the substitute facilities doctrine has extremely limited application in the federal courts.

Special procedures have been developed for the valuation of operating and non-operating rail, roadway, and utility corridors. Any appraiser who accepts an assignment to appraise this type of property has a professional obligation to understand these procedures fully and apply them correctly.

Because of the unique nature of special-purpose properties and the lack of market data pertaining to them, there is considerable divergence in valuation testimony. The following recommendations have been made in regard to the valuation of special-purpose properties for eminent domain purposes:

The extent and nature of the taking, as well as the nature of the specific property involved, can affect the appraisal approach and the proof that would establish value. Factors that it is believed will assist in solving special purpose problems include:

1. Avoid "market value" or qualify the definition of "market value" in takings from special purpose properties of a public or nonprofit owner.
2. Use more extensive consideration of income in valuing income-producing special purpose properties.
3. Allow more leeway as to proof admissible to establish the value of special purpose properties.
4. Avoid the cost approach, if possible, and the confining of proof to this approach. For the approaches used, use reproduction cost rather than replacement cost.
5. Consider extension of allowing the cost of a functionally equivalent substitute as compensation when dealing with other than publicly owned special purpose properties.
6. Value in use for special purposes, which is a form of value to the owner, must be recognized if the owner is to be indemnified for his loss.
7. Exercise a more extensive investigation and ingenuity by appraisers in determining and considering factors that affect the value of special purpose properties, particularly if an attempt is made to measure depreciation....

The more factors that an appraiser can consider and the more reasons that he can use in arriving at his opinion, the more reasonable is his opinion. Opinions of value should be less extreme in either direction, and constitutional compensation should be more likely.[39]

39. Level, *Valuation and Condemnation of Special Purpose Properties*, 47.

CHAPTER 12

Development Approach

The development approach to value can be applied in valuations for eminent domain purposes. According to *Nichols',*

> The best illustration of the rule that market value is not limited to value for the existing use, and the situation in which this rule is most frequently invoked (and also most frequently abused), is where evidence is offered of what the value of a tract of land that is used for agricultural purposes (or is vacant and unused) would be if cut up into house-lots.[1]

The *development approach,* or *anticipated use method* of valuation, is described in another source as

> [a] method of estimating the value of vacant land. The usual application is to [value] raw, unsubdivided land by deducting from the estimated gross selling price, the direct expense of development such as cost of streets, utilities, sales, advertising, and overhead (taxes, carrying charges, inspection). Profit and "time lag" (interest on the money invested for the time needed to complete the project) are also deducted, after which the land value is indicated.[2]

This method of land valuation has also been referred to as the *lot method*[3] and *the developer's residual approach.*[4]

The development approach to value is examined in detail here not because it is widely applied in eminent domain valuation, but for two other reasons. First, there has been a great deal of controversy and confusion among the various

1. *Nichols' The Law of Eminent Domain,* rev. 3d ed. (New York: Mathew Bender Co., Inc., 1990), vol. 4, §12B.14[1][a].
2. American Institute of Real Estate Appraisers and the Society of Real Estate Appraisers, *Real Estate Appraisal Terminology,* rev. ed., Byrl N. Boyce, ed. (Cambridge, Mass.: Ballinger Publishing Company, 1981), 14.
3. *United States v. 47.3096 Acres, etc.,* 583 F.2d 270 (6th Cir. 1978).
4. *United States v. 147.47 Acres of Land,* 352 F.Supp. 1055 (M.D. Pa. 1972).

courts as to the applicability of this approach. Thus a considerable amount of case law has been developed on the subject. Second, in many cases the development approach has been applied under the wrong circumstances or in the wrong way. If all of the land that has been appraised by the development approach were actually subdivided, there would be enough subdivision lots on the market to last hundreds of years and little, if any, farmland left in the United States.

There is no single correct way to apply the development approach to value. In 1978 the American Institute of Real Estate Appraisers published *Subdivision Analysis*, an educational memorandum on subdivision analysis and the development approach to value.[5] Seven different methods of subdivision analysis were demonstrated in this publication. All of the methods are correct, but some are more applicable under certain circumstances. In 1993 the Appraisal Institute published a monograph titled *Subdivision Analysis*,[6] which emphasizes market analysis, forecasting techniques, and financial modeling. The new text delves into the theory and economics of subdivision analysis and contains some excellent discounted cash flow examples. Nevertheless, the 1993 book is not a replacement for the 1978 publication which focuses on the mechanics of the development approach. Both publications are useful to appraisers, but an attorney preparing to present, or rebut, a development approach appraisal to a trier of fact will probably find the 1978 memorandum more helpful.

APPLICABILITY

The development approach is the primary, and sometimes the only, method of valuation in a condemnation case when:

1. The appraiser concludes through proper market analysis that the property in question does, in fact, have a highest and best use for subdivision purposes;
2. Comparable before and/or after sales are lacking, and
3. Sufficient market and technical data are available to estimate the value of the property being appraised reliably using the development approach.

In determining that a property's highest and best use is for subdivision purposes, the appraiser must consider factors such as supply and demand, zoning, the available utilities, the direction of population growth, the physical characteristics of the property being appraised, local land development regulations, and legislative attitudes towards the development of properties in the area. Properties valued with the development approach may range from raw acreage to sites that are nearly 100% developed. With a partially developed site, of course, there is a stronger case for determining that the highest and best use is for subdivision purposes and that the development approach to value is appropriate. If data on recent sales of developed lots that were originally part of the tract being appraised are available, the demand for developed lots can be demonstrated with factual market data. "The bald assertion by the condemnee or his witnesses that such a de-

5. American Institute of Real Estate Appraisers, *Subdivision Analysis* (Chicago: AIREA, 1978).

6. Douglas D. Lovell and Robert S. Martin, *Subdivision Analysis* (Chicago: Appraisal Institute, 1993).

mand exists is not enough. Such a demand must be established by competent proof."[7]

If comparable sales are available, they should be used in evaluating the property under appraisal. "Bona fide sales data provide a better indication of value than a subdivision development prospectus."[8] If the sale property is truly comparable, it will have the same potential as the property being appraised. As one court put it,

> The comparable sales relied upon by both expert witnesses in valuing the subject property involved properties purchased by developers for development purposes and accordingly were sales in which development costs have been considered and were reflected in the sale price. To add an increment to the value established on the basis of these sales is to inflate and distort the market value of the subject property.[9] [Citations omitted]

A New York decision stated,

> [t]he court actually valued the property as having a residential development potential by relying upon the State's comparable sales. In the present case there was no need for a separate increment value to be found by the appraisers or the court because the market data inherently included the value in raw acreage sales.[10]

This is not to say that under such circumstances the development approach should be totally disregarded. Rather, it should be used to support the indicated value of the property developed using comparable sales, if additional support is needed. The procedure applied in the development approach can often give the appraiser greater insight into the relative comparability of the sale property. Although many condemning agencies will not allow the development approach to be used as the only measure of value, they recognize it as supporting evidence. According to a Washington State Department of Transportation rule,

> The employment of the hypothetical subdivision to develop raw land value may be introduced to support the market data and to illustrate the amount of money a prudent purchaser would likely pay for raw subdivision land. However, due to the many variables and speculative elements, the estimate of value is never based solely upon such a hypothesis.[11]

If the appraiser cannot find any raw acreage sales with development potential comparable to the property being appraised, the analysis of supply and demand for developed lots may need to be re-examined as well as the estimate of highest and best use. Similarly, if market data on retail lot prices, development costs, and sellout times in the neighborhood are not available, a review of the supply and demand analysis and estimate of highest and best use may be re-

7. *Shillito v. Metropolitan Edison Co.*, 252 A.2d 650, 651 (Pa. 1969).
8. *The Appraisal of Real Estate*, 10th ed. (Chicago: Appraisal Institute, 1992), 307.
9. *Ridgeway Associates, Inc. v. State*, 300 N.Y.S.2d, 944, 947 (N.Y. 1969).
10. *United Artists Theatre Circuit, Inc. v. State*, 384 N.Y.S.2d 543, 544 (N.Y. 1976).
11. Washington State Dept. of Transportation, *Right of Way Manual*, Chapter 4-1, p. C-11, Tab C, §4A (revised August 1991).

quired. While a lack of sales and/or development activity may indicate an insufficient supply of land suitable for such use, it can also indicate a lack of demand. Any appraiser who uses the development approach to value should confirm that the lack of market data is a result of the first condition, rather than the latter.

Technical data can be obtained from engineering firms involved in plat design and development cost estimating or from contractors who install underground utilities or construct other subdivision improvements. "[T]his approach to value is complex, often requiring the assistance of other experts and always requiring substantial amounts of research, analysis and supporting documentation."[12]

APPRAISAL PROCEDURE

If the development approach is applicable, the appraiser must apply it in a logical sequence. The development approach to value replicates the land residual technique[13] applied to land with a highest and best use for subdivision purposes. In fact, if an owner-developer were planning to develop lots and lease them on a long-term basis rather than sell them, the two procedures would be identical.

The procedure described below is a typical application of the development approach to value. It is not necessarily the only workable procedure nor the most appropriate in every instance.

First, the appraiser determines the number and size of the lots that can be developed. After completing the highest and best use analysis, the appraiser should be totally familiar with the applicable subdivision ordinances regarding minimum lot sizes, widths, and depths; minimum street right-of-way width; pavement width; etc. The appraiser must remember, however, that land often is not developed to its maximum allowable density or to the minimum improvement requirements. Analyzing existing subdivisions and lot sales in the area will help the appraiser determine the typical conditions, as well as the minimums and maximums legally allowed.

It is often advisable, particularly in preparing for trial, to request that an engineering consultant be retained to help lay out the most economical and physically practical plan for subdividing the property. Topographic maps of the property in question can be extremely useful in this process. The appraiser and the engineer should work together to construct a subdivision plan that develops marketable lots and produces the greatest residual value for the raw acreage.

The appraiser will work with a paper plat showing the number, size, and shape of the anticipated lots as well as the proposed street rights-of-way and open space. The retail value of each proposed lot is estimated by comparing it with similar, fully developed lots in the same neighborhood which have been sold recently. If no such lot sales exist, the value of the lots can be estimated using the *abstraction* or *extraction* method of site valuation.[14] However, as mentioned earlier, lack of comparable lot sales in the area might suggest that the estimate of highest and best use should be reconsidered.

---

12. *Uniform Appraisal Standards for Federal Land Acquisitions* (Washington, D.C.: U.S. Government Printing Office, 1992), §B-1 15, p. 74.

13. *The Appraisal of Real Estate*, 10th ed., 307–308.

14. Ibid., 304–305.

It is not always necessary to estimate the retail value of each potential lot within the parent tract; often only the average or typical value of a lot is estimated. From this estimate, the cumulative retail market value of all the proposed lots within the appraised property can be computed.

The next step in the valuation process is to estimate the direct and indirect costs of developing the subject tract into a completed subdivision. Direct development costs include items such as engineering, street construction, installation of underground utilities, street light installation, and construction of sidewalks. Indirect development costs cover items such as the increasing development fees charged by many local municipalities to generate additional revenues or discourage further development within their boundaries. Other indirect costs to be considered include municipal exactions, advertising expenses, sales costs, and administration and overhead expenses incurred during the development and sellout period. Administrative and overhead expenses cover taxes, insurance, interest, financing, and inspection fees. Cost information can be extracted from market data on similar developments; gathered from engineers, contractors, and real estate agents; or obtained from a combination of these sources.

The estimated direct and indirect costs of development are deducted from the cumulative retail value of all the potential lots. Then the appraiser allocates the amount remaining to entrepreneurial (developer's) profit, raw land value, and a discount that reflects the time required for full development and market absorption of the lots.

A profit factor is deducted from the value of the lots to compensate the developer for the time, trouble, and risk incurred in the undertaking. A deduction for time is necessary because, in the construction of any large subdivision, a considerable period could elapse from the beginning of the development process to the sale of the last lot. Thus, the developer could receive net income over a period of years. The income stream from the development must be converted into a current value by discounting it at an appropriate risk rate. The result will be the indicated market value of the property being appraised in its present, undeveloped state.

The steps in the development approach are summarized below.

1. Prepare a subdivision layout to determine the number, typical size, and shape of all potential lots.
2. Estimate the retail value of the lots.
3. Estimate direct development costs.
4. Estimate indirect development costs.
5. Compute the income attributable to developer's profit and land value (Step 2 minus Steps 3 and 4).
6. Deduct developer's profit.
7. Estimate the amount of time required to develop and sell out the subdivision.
8. Discount the anticipated income stream into an indication of the current raw land value.

The federal court has summarized the procedural steps in the development approach as follows:

> In arriving at their values, the owner's witnesses took into consideration the market data of sales of adjacent subdivided lots and made deductions for selling and advertising expenses, engineering and development costs, overhead costs, taxes, buyer's anticipated profits, and for acreage loss for streets, etc., in order to reflect or indicate the value of the property at the time of taking. In this case, the data relied on was derived from the market and facts as had been generated in the development of adjacent land. This method is referred to as the "developer's residual approach."[15]

Figure 12.1 illustrates how a relatively small tract (19.90 acres) might be subdivided into 60 lots. Table 12.1 demonstrates the application of the development approach to this property.

FIGURE 12.1 PROPOSED SUBDIVISION LAYOUT

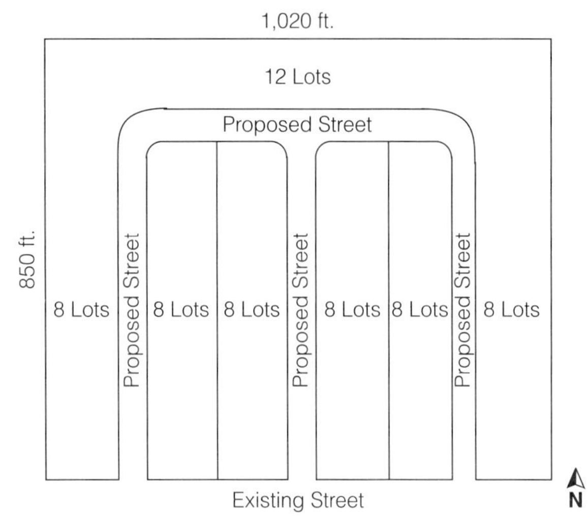

All direct unit costs have been applied to the linear measure of the streets to be developed in the tract (i.e., 2,740 linear feet). This methodology is commonly used in making preliminary estimates of this type and is also employed in some cost manuals.[16]

The costs per linear foot used in Table 12.1 include all engineering, plan, and inspection fees. Direct costs can generally be more accurately estimated with unit costs for various items than with a cost per linear foot of street. Unit costs might include the cost per streetlight, per sewer manhole, or per fire hydrant. Costs per cubic yard of grading or base rock are also generally accurate. The figures used in

15. *United States v. 100 Acres in Marin County*, 468 F.2d 1261, 1266 (9th Cir. 1972) *cert. denied*, 414 U.S. 822 (1973).

16. *Marshall Valuation Service* (Los Angeles: Marshall and Swift Publishing Company, 1979), §66, 1.

Table 12.1 were selected merely to demonstrate the application of the development approach; they should not be construed as typical or all-inclusive. The sellout time, developer's profit, and discount rate shown were also selected for demonstration purposes only.

TABLE 12.1 DEVELOPMENT APPROACH TO VALUE

Step 1.	19.90 acres @ 3.02 lots per acre			60 lots
Step 2.	60 lots @ $17,500			$1,050,000
Step 3.	Direct costs:			
	Grading (2,740 lin. ft. @ $6.72)		$ 18,413	
	Base rock (2,740 lin. ft. @ $8.96)		24,550	
	Paving (2,740 lin. ft. @ $20.14)		55,184	
	Curbs & gutters (2,740 lin. ft. @ $11.10)		30,414	
	Concrete walks (2,740 lin. ft. @ $10.40)		28,496	
	Sewer main (2,740 lin. ft. @ $12.40)		33,976	
	Sewer laterals (2,740 lin. ft. @ $9.50)		26,030	
	Sewer manholes (2,740 lin. ft. @ $2.43		6,658	
	Fire hydrants (2,740 lin. ft. @ $4.27)		11,700	
	Street lighting (2,740 lin. ft. @ $6.50)		17,810	
	Water main (2,740 lin. ft. @ $13.20)		36,168	
	Water laterals (2,740 lin. ft. @ $3.25)		8,905	
	Electric (2,740 lin. ft. @ $7.25)		19,865	
	Total direct costs			–318,169
Step 4.	Indirect costs:			
	Overhead and sales costs ($1,050,000 @ 10%)	$105,000		
	Management and supervision	36,000		
	Taxes and insurance	12,500		
	Total indirect costs			153,500
Step 5.	Developer's profit & raw land value			$ 578,331
Step 6.	Developer's profit ($1,050,000 @ 20%)			210,000
	Net before cost of capital			$ 368,331
Step 7.	Sellout in 3 years @ 20 lots per year.			
Step 8:				
	Annual income stream ($368,331 ÷ 3)			$ 122,777
	Discount rate factor (present worth of one per period, 3 years, 12%)			x 2.401831
	Indicated raw land value			$ 294,890
Indicated value per acre ($294,890 ÷ 19.90)				$ 14,819

Both the appraiser and the attorney should be aware of the basic assumptions built into this methodology. First, it is assumed that the expenses of development will be incurred steadily over the three years of project development, and that sales income will be spread evenly over the life of the project. In this case, it is assumed that exactly 20 lots will be sold each year.

Such assumptions will be true only under the most unusual circumstances. The procedure has merit, however, because it is probably the most easily understood application of the development approach. Also, the actual pattern of development expenses and sales income may approximate the assumptions built into the method enough to warrant its use. After all, the development approach is an appraisal tool, not an exact mathematical formula. In using this methodology, the appraiser should be aware of the value differential that would result if the sales income and expenses were treated as they are actually anticipated to occur, rather than being spread evenly over each year. If the differential is significant, the appraiser may have to use one of the more complex methods of applying the development approach. These methods are demonstrated in the 1978 publication, *Subdivision Analysis*.[17]

PROBLEM AREAS

Much of the data used in applying the development approach can be supported by market evidence, but in two areas the appraiser must reach conclusions that cannot be readily supported. First, the appraiser's estimate of the sellout or market absorption period is affected by so many factors that the appraiser could spend hours answering hypothetical questions about how various economic trends could affect the development's absorption. The appraiser might be asked: "What if mortgage interest rates go up three points? What if the largest employer in the area reduces its workforce by 50%? What if two competing subdivisions opened up directly across the street?" If the cross-examiner has done his homework, he may be able to question the appraiser about absorption rate projections made by the appraiser in prior development approach applications and ask why they did not come to fruition.[18]

To estimate absorption time, the appraiser must be fully familiar with the economic factors affecting the market in which the property being appraised is located. After ascertaining the general economic trends in the area, the appraiser should establish the geographic boundaries of the areas that will compete with the parcel under appraisal. The area of competition may be a neighborhood, a city, or an entire county. After this determination is made, the appraiser should make a physical inventory of the lots in developed subdivisions that could compete with the lots to be developed from the parcel being appraised. The appraiser should also investigate whether any preliminary plats have been submitted for projects that could foreseeably compete with the property being appraised.

Next, the appraiser should ascertain the number of dwellings constructed annually in the neighborhood over the past several years. Under normal circumstances, this will indicate how many lots can be absorbed each year within the subject's market area. Based on this local economic information, the appraiser can logically estimate the absorption time required to sell the lots to be developed from the property under appraisal. The appraiser must make this estimate carefully. If the appraiser testifies that a hypothetical subdivision of 400 lots can be sold out

17. *Subdivision Analysis* (1978).

18. In responding to such questions, the appraiser may properly state that the absorption projection made in the approach is an attempt to mirror developer/purchaser attitudes at the time of the appraisal.

within two years, when historically only 150 lots have been absorbed each year in the entire area of competition, the court or trier of fact will be skeptical.

The appraiser's estimate of sellout time can be supported by some historical data, but the second problem area requires more pure judgment. The appraiser must estimate the developer's profit to be deducted from the retail price of the developed lots. In Table 12.1 a developer's profit equal to 20% of the retail value of the lots is indicated for purposes of illustration. Many developers estimate potential profit as a percentage of gross retail sales, so the procedure used to compute developer's profit in the table is representative of the thinking and actions of typical buyers in the marketplace.

However, the appraiser should recognize that not all developers estimate profit as a percentage of gross retail sales. Some developers estimate profit at a certain dollar amount per lot; others project profit as a percentage of raw land costs; and still others calculate profit as a percentage of raw land costs plus development costs. No matter which method is used by the developer, the question for the appraiser remains: How much should be allowed for developer's profit in applying the development approach to value?

One way to select an appropriate profit factor is to examine the actual profit earned by developers of completed subdivisions similar to the one contemplated for the property being appraised. Table 12.2 illustrates how a developer's profit can be extracted from sales data. It concerns a 22-acre parcel purchased for $286,000 and subdivided into 66 lots that sold for an average price of $14,500 each. In actual practice, of course, several subdivisions would be analyzed in this manner to establish a pattern of the net profit realized by developers.

The problem with this procedure is that the computations are based on the amount of money the developer ended up with after the development was completed, and that amount is not of concern to the appraiser. Rather, the appraiser wants to know what the developer envisioned when the raw acreage was purchased. Unless the 27.3% profit factor computed is the amount of profit the developer anticipated when the land was purchased, it is of little or no use to the appraiser in estimating an appropriate profit factor for the property being appraised.

The computations shown in Table 12.2 may support the appraiser's estimate

TABLE 12.2 ABSTRACTION OF DEVELOPER'S PROFIT

Gross retail price (66 lots @ $14,500)		$957,000
Direct costs	$270,000	
Indirect costs	140,000	
Less total development costs	410,000	
Profit and land cost		$547,000
Less land cost		286,000
Profit		$261,000
Percent of profit ($261,000 ÷ $957,000)		27.3%

Note. All figures were verified by the developer.

of developer's profit, but this estimate must be based on the developer's expectations going into the project, not the profit eventually gotten out of it. Extremely careful and extensive sales verification is required. It may also be helpful for the appraiser to determine whether developers active in the area have any rules of thumb for anticipated profit that they use when purchasing raw acreage for subdivision purposes.

THE COURT'S VIEW

In an all too infrequent moment of lucidity and comprehension, one court said:

> It is significant that the method of valuation used [by the appraiser] has been recognized by the American Institute of Real Estate Appraisers. Indeed, income capitalization in general and the anticipated use or development method in particular are standard appraisal practices. It would be unwise for us to require exclusion of such a widely recognized method of valuation through unduly rigid evidentiary rules.[19]

However, "[t]here is some authority for the proposition that valuation evidence based on the lot method of appraisal should never be admitted in condemnation cases involving unimproved raw land."[20] Nor is the development approach necessarily applicable because a legal plat of the property being appraised has been recorded. "[T]he fallacy of treating land as subdivision land or as farm land depending upon whether or not a plat thereof had been recorded, is the conclusion that there is magic in the recording of a subdivision plat. Obviously the highest and best use of the land is not transformed from one thing into another by that ministerial act."[21]

This is not to say that the subdivision plan of a tract of land is inadmissible. These plans generally are admissible, but often only in support of a witness's opinion as to the highest and best use of the land.[22] Thus it is often good trial strategy for a condemnor to stipulate that the highest and best use of the land is for subdivision purposes, if the question of highest and best use is not contested. This stipulation will often preclude the submission of any specific development plan, which can severely restrict the effective presentation of the condemnee's case. "Where both parties have conceded or agreed upon adaptability to the highest and best use of the land in question, the introduction of a plat showing the land as subdivided lots is merely cumulative and is subject to misconception by the jury, and should therefore be excluded by the trial court."[23] [Citations omitted]

As a general rule, it can be said that as a tract of land physically and legally progresses from a state of raw acreage to a completed subdivision, the development approach also progresses from inadmissibility to admissibility. The two extremes were discussed in a federal case.

> It may well be that even though the highest and best use of a property is for a residential subdivision, if no meaningful steps have been taken in that direction,

19. *Dash v. State*, 491 P.2d 1069, 1075 (Ak. 1971).
20. *United States v. 47.3096 Acres*, 583 F.2d 270, 271 (6th Cir. 1978).
21. *State v. Maplewood Heights Corp.*, 302 N.E.2d 782, 785 (Ind. 1973).
22. *Southern Indiana Gas and Electric Co. v. Riley*, 299 N.E.2d 173 (Ind. 1973).
23. *City of Lafayette v. Beeler*, 381 N.E.2d 1287, 1291 (Ind. 1978).

> viz., construction expenses and actual lot sales, then a "lot method" appraisal or a "developer's residual" approach, as it is also known, would be inappropriate. But that is not the situation here. The status of the subdivision and its availability for sale within the reasonably foreseeable future was an actual and real one, certainly not hypothetical, remote or speculative. Someone about to purchase the property on... the date of condemnation, would have to regard it as having a highest and best use as a subdivision and, in determining what purchase price he would be willing to pay, would have to consider all factors, including sales price for individual lots and additional expense of development, in arriving at his decision.... This is not a case where a landowner dreamily contemplates the use to which his property may be put at some undefined future time but rather one where the property is geographically suited for development; is located in a booming developmental area; has been subdivided into lots according to a duly certified map; has been cleared and graded and improved with the creation of a spring-fed lake, the construction of access roads, and the digging of a deep well sufficient to supply water to 150 homes; and where actual sales of lots as identified on the map have taken place, the deeds of which contain building restrictions compatible only with a residential real estate development.[24]

According to another source,

> The First, Sixth and Ninth [federal] Circuits have indicated that [the development approach] is a permissible approach to valuation, but only if the costs of subdivision are taken into account; the rationale is that the potential value of land if subdivided could be considered by a willing buyer and a willing seller where subdivision is a reasonable possibility and the costs of subdivision are not speculative or uncertain.[25]

Nichols' also addresses the admissibility of the development approach:

> It is well settled that if land is so situated that it is actually available for building purposes, its value for such purposes may be considered, even if it is used as a farm or is covered with brush and boulders.
>
> In some case[s], however, condemnees have attempted to go so far as to show the number of lots into which a tract is divisible, estimate sales prices per lot and sales prices of comparable sales in the vicinity. In most cases, however, the courts have adopted the approach that raw land as such, with little or no improvements or preparation for subdivision may not be valued as if the land were in fact a subdivision. Thus, the "lot method" approach to valuation may not be used.
>
> In the case of land that has actually been fully subdivided, or nearly so, the courts are in agreement that the "lot method" or "developer's residual approach" valuation is proper. The problems involved in the partially developed subdivision have evaporated. The costs to the developer are no longer speculative, the value of the individual lots in the market may be ascertained with as much certainty as in any other condemnation proceeding, and the possibility of such a use is no longer remote.[26]

24. *United States v. 147.47 Acres of Land*, 352 F.Supp. 1055, 1060 (M.D. Pa. 1972).
25. Jacques B. Gelin and David W. Miller, "The Federal Law of Eminent Domain" (Charlottesville, Virginia: The Michie Company, 1982), §4.2, p. 344, citing *United States v. 125.07 Acres of Land*, 667 F.2d 243, 245, 246, 251 (1st. Cir. 1981); *United States v. 47.3096 Acres*, 583 F.2d 270, 272 (6th Cir. 1978); *United States v. 100 Acres*, 468 F.2d 1261, 1266, 1267 (9th Cir. 1972), *cert. denied*, 414 U.S. 822, 864 (1973).
26. *Nichols*, vol. 4, §12B.14[1][a] and [d] (1990).

Thus, the admissibility of the development approach is not questioned in most jurisdictions when the property being appraised is either raw land or fully subdivided land. In the latter circumstance, the appraiser should carefully analyze the determination of the larger parcel (see Chapter 5). If the lots affected by the taking are fully developed and salable as separate entities, it is possible that each individual lot represents a separate larger parcel and each should be appraised independently.

A problem arises when the land being appraised is neither raw acreage nor a fully developed subdivision, but falls somewhere in between. There is no clear-cut rule applicable to such properties. For one property, a legal plat may have been filed, while on another a portion of the property may have been physically and legally subdivided. There is simply no uniform rule as to what point the development process must reach before the development approach is admissible.[27]

The weight of authority, however, appears to favor starting with raw acreage value and adding incremental upward adjustments for subdivision potential as well as the legal and physical steps taken towards actual subdivision development.

> The actual market value of the lots insofar as that value is presently enhanced by the property's availability for subdivision may be shown, but the possible future value if subdivision were made may not be shown.[28]

> There being no dispute that the most advantageous use of claimants' property at the time of taking was as a potential residential subdivision, the correct rule to be applied "was to treat the premises not as raw acreage nor as part of the completed development but as a potential subdivision site giving the acreage an increment in value because of that potential use."[29] [Citations omitted]

> Whenever such an increment must be added to the raw acreage value to reflect a property's subdivision potential, then the specific increment which is selected and applied must be based upon sufficient evidence and be satisfactorily explained.[30]

If a comparable sale has subdivision potential equal to that of the property under appraisal, no additional adjustment for that factor is required.

There is conflicting case law as to the admissibility of the actual costs of subdivision development such as the engineering and platting fees incurred by the owner of the property. Some jurisdictions allow the admission of such evidence, but only to better estimate the incremental value present in the property under appraisal, not as a separate value or damage item.[31] In other words, only the contributory value, not the actual cost of such items, may be considered.

27. *Dover Housing Authority v. George*, 220 A.2d 156 (N.H. 1966).
28. *Santa Clara County Flood Control, etc., Dist. v. Freitas*, 2 Cal. Rep. 129, 131 (Cal. 1960).
29. *County of Suffolk v. Firester*, 339 N.E.2d 154, 156 (N.Y. 1975).
30. *Ridgeway Associates, Inc. v. State*, 300 N.Y.S.2d 944, 946–947 (N.Y. 1969).
31. *State v. Chang*, 436 P.2d 3 (Haw. 1967).

The courts' resistance to admitting the development approach stems from a fear that testimony in regard to the approach may mislead the trier of fact into determining just compensation based on a fully developed subdivision, rather than the land as it existed on the date of taking. Before attempting to present a case or testify to a value based on the development approach, extensive review of applicable law in the jurisdiction is required. This review must consider the specific circumstances surrounding the property under appraisal.

Extensive pretrial conferences between the attorney and the appraiser will be required. The admissibility of the development approach may turn on a single question put to the appraiser by the attorney or on the appraiser's response to that question. Because the courts' views on this issue vary, it is difficult to predict the admissibility of development approach evidence. Even the courts can find the absence of definite rules on this issue confusing.

> The line of demarcation between those circumstances in which testimony of specific intended use and lot by lot evaluation is admissible, and those circumstances under which it is not, is too finely drawn for us to follow. We remain uninstructed as to the appropriate method for "properly guarding" such evidence so as to allow its admission.[32]

THE PARTIALLY DEVELOPED PROPERTY

As noted previously, the admissibility of the development approach is less questionable when the property being appraised is either raw acreage or fully subdivided land. Divergent rulings are more prevalent when the property being appraised falls somewhere between these extremes. Factual circumstances, applicable case law, and/or the condemnor's appraisal reporting requirements may necessitate some modification of the traditional development approach to value. Only the written and/or verbal presentation of the approach may be modified, or the factual situation may require modification of the application of the approach.

To illustrate the application of the development approach in a before and after situation, consider the following set of circumstances. The tract of land depicted in Figure 12.2 contains 25 acres and was acquired 10 years ago by a broker/developer. A preliminary plat, or master development plan, of the land was submitted to the planning commission three years ago. This plan is shown in Figure 12.3. While the planning commission was considering the master plan, it was learned that the state planned to widen the freeway right-of-way to the north, which would have a direct effect on the property. For this reason, the property owner requested only preliminary approval of the master plan (Figure 12.3) and final approval of the development of the northerly portion of the property (the 14 lots depicted in Figure 12.4). The preliminary master plan (Figure 12.3) and the final plat of the northerly portion of the property (Figure 12.4) were both approved.

32. *City of Lafayette v. Beeler*, 381 N.E.2d 1287, 1294 (Ind. 1978).

The property is located in a rural area, about 10 miles from a small city with a population of 40,000. There are no public water or sanitary sewer facilities in the area. Consequently, in developing the 14 northerly lots, the property owner drilled a well and constructed a community water system adequate to supply domestic water to all 32 lots proposed in the original master plan. Then the 14 northerly lots were developed and sold. About one year later, the state's right-of-way plans were made public and the owner made no attempt to develop the tract further. The state's right-of-way plan is superimposed over the original master plan in Figure 12.5. Because the original 14 lots were sold, the larger parcel is the unplatted portion of the tract, which consists of 15.21 acres.

FIGURE 12.2 PLOT PLAN - RAW LAND

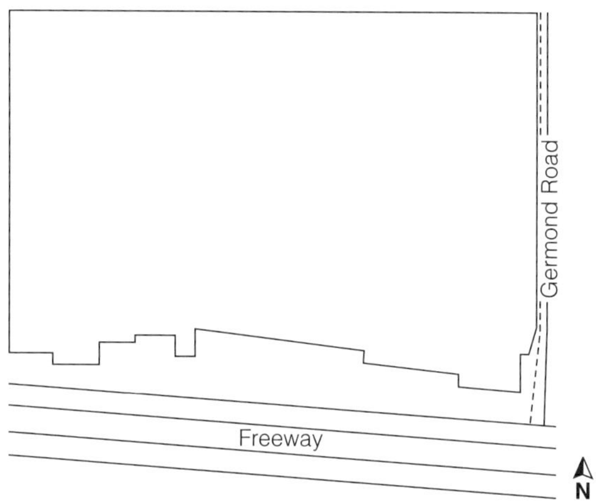

FIGURE 12.3 MASTER DEVELOPMENT PLAN

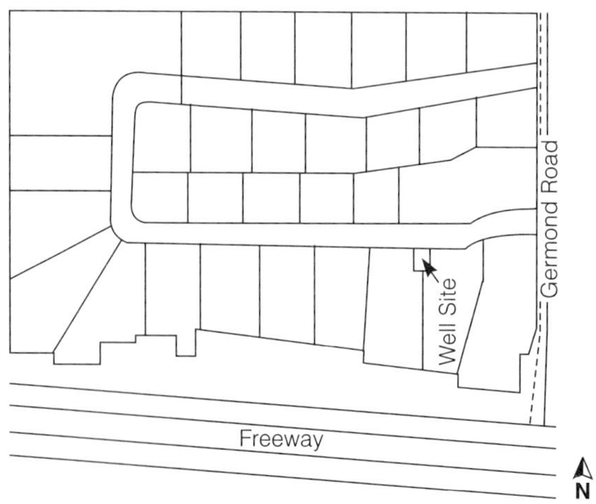

FIGURE 12.4 FINAL PLAT

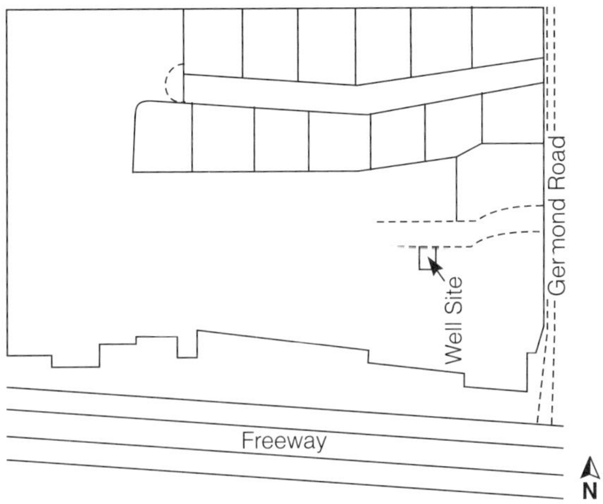

FIGURE 12.5 LARGER PARCEL

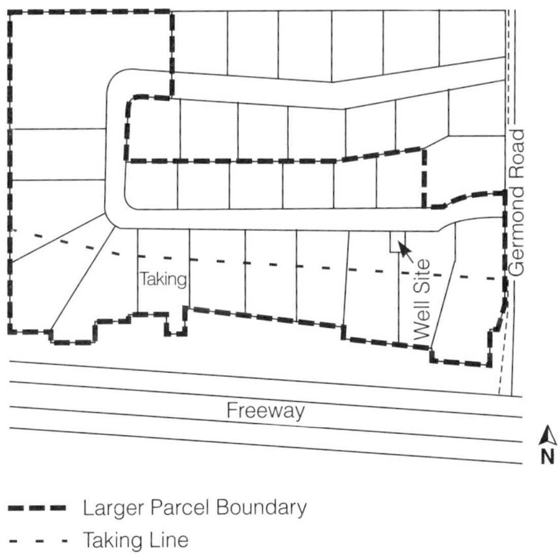

In the before situation, the tract is quite unique for several reasons:

- It abuts a successful existing subdivision.
- A community water system is available to it.
- It is suitable for development with septic tanks.
- It has "preliminary master plan" approval.
- Preliminary engineering on the tract is complete.
- Proposed streets have been roughed in.

Due to the unique features of the tract, a market search uncovered no comparable sales. Analysis of the site indicates that the highest and best use of the tract in the before situation is completion of the subdivision improvements in conformity with the original master plan. Based on the foregoing factors, the development approach to value is deemed appropriate.

The appraiser's research indicates that all lots in the original subdivision sold for $12,500, regardless of their size, and that lot prices at a more recently completed subdivision across the freeway were $12,750, regardless of size. Based upon these data, a developed lot price of $12,750 is considered reasonable. With information from an engineering consultant, cost indexes, an analysis of comparable subdivisions, and the appraiser's data files, the following development costs were estimated.

Direct costs:	
(Final plat and construction engineering, grading, clearing, streets and water lines)	$55,000
Indirect costs:	
Overhead and sales expense	15% of gross sales
Management and supervision	10% of direct costs
Taxes during sellout	$1,000

A two-year sellout period has been estimated based on the historical experience of the subdivision across the freeway.

From these data, the estimated before value of the property can be computed. These calculations are shown in Table 12.3. Analyzing the remainder in the after situation leads to the conclusion that the highest and best use of the remainder tract is for a residential subdivision and that the best method of development would follow the plan shown in Figure 12.6. To analyze the property in the after situation, the following factors must be considered:

- Only nine lots can be developed, so nine lots have been lost.
- The property contains 9.85 acres in the after situation.
- The community water system becomes an overimprovement.

TABLE 12.3 BEFORE SITUATION - VALUE COMPUTATIONS

Gross sales (18 lots @ $12,750)		$229,500
Direct costs:		
Final platting and engineering, grading, clearing, street improvements, water lines		55,000
Subtotal		$174,500
Indirect costs:		
Sales and overhead ($229,500 x 0.15)	$34,425	
Management and supervision ($55,000 x 0.10)	5,500	
Taxes	1,000	
Total indirect costs		$ 40,925
Net income before return on capital and profit		$133,575
Discount income stream for two years @ 10% ($133,575 ÷ 2) x 1.735537*		$115,912
Less profit ($229,500 x 0.10)		22,950
Indicated value of land "as is"		$ 92,962
($92,962 ÷ 15.21 acres) $6,111.90 per acre, say, $6,100 per acre		

* Present worth of $1 per year for two years @ 10%

- All previous master plan approvals are void and all historical engineering data are of little or no value.
- The average lot size will be larger than it was in the before situation.
- The tract will have 1,300 linear feet of frontage on the new frontage road and few interior streets will need to be constructed.
- The new frontage road will carry a fairly high volume of traffic.

FIGURE 12.6 PLOT PLAN—AFTER SITUATION

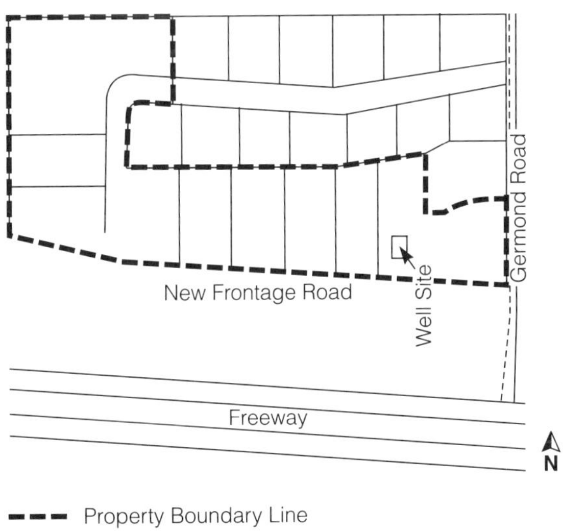

Investigation indicates that lots fronting on arterial streets or frontage roads are typically larger than interior lots, but this advantage is offset by the disadvantage of fronting on a highly traveled street.

Based on these data, discussions with a consulting engineer, reference to cost indexes, and the actual costs of comparable subdivisions, an indication of the after value of the property could be computed (see Table 12.4). In the after situation, the cost of street improvements per linear foot increased because part of the new street had not previously been roughed in. Also, water costs per linear foot increased because the water line could not be extended across the street. Engineering expenses per lot increased because preliminary engineering plans were invalidated by the taking.

TABLE 12.4 AFTER SITUATION—VALUE COMPUTATIONS

Gross sales (9 lots @ $12,750)		$114,750
Less direct costs:		
Engineering, grading, street improvements, water lines		40,900
Subtotal		$ 73,850
Less indirect costs:		
Sales and overhead ($114,750 x 0.15)	$17,213	
Management and supervision ($40,900 x 0.10)	4,090	
Taxes	400	
Total indirect costs		21,703
Net income before profit		$ 52,147
Less profit ($114,750 x 0.10)		11,475
Indicated land value		$ 40,672
or ($40,672 ÷ 9.85 acres) $4,129 per acre, say $4,100 per acre		

Under the federal (before and after) rule the appraiser's conclusion would be:

Before value (15.21 acres @ $6,100)	$ 92,800*
After value (9.85 acres @ $4,100)	40,400*
Difference	$ 52,400

* Rounded

Under the state (taking plus damages) rule, the appraiser's conclusion would be:

Value before taking	$ 92,800*
Less value of part taken (5.36 acres @ $6,100)	32,696
Remainder (before)	$60,104
Less remainder after taking	40,400*
Damage	$ 19,704
Less special benefits	0
Net damage	$ 19,704
Plus value of part taken	32,696
Total difference	$ 52,400

* Rounded

The foregoing example demonstrates a relatively simple application of the traditional development approach to value in a partial taking case. As the complexity of the application increases, the chances of the approach being approved by either the court or the condemnor's review appraiser decrease. As mentioned earlier, it may be necessary to modify the development approach or its presentation to ensure its acceptance.

For example, in analyzing the before situation of the tract (Figure 12.3), the appraiser must first investigate and verify sales of vacant land comparable to the parcel under appraisal but without development improvements. The costs to develop each comparable are then estimated just as the costs to develop the property under appraisal were estimated. For comparison purposes, it is often convenient to convert these cost factors into a cost per lot or a cost per acre. This process is demonstrated in Table 12.5 using the 15.21-acre larger parcel as the subject and a hypothetical comparable sale of 20.2 acres which sold for $79,000. In actual practice, the appraiser may want to break this adjustment down for individual items of dissimilarity such as "comparable's lack of water system," or "comparable's lack of preliminary engineering."

TABLE 12.5 DEVELOPMENT LAND—COMPARATIVE ANALYSIS

	Comparable	Subject
Size	20.2 acres	15.21 acres
Number of potential lots	26	18
Sale price per lot	$12,750	$12,750
Less direct costs per lot*	5,079	3,056
Less indirect costs per lot*	2,731	2,274
Net before capital and profit	$ 4,940	$ 7,420
Discount		
$4,940/2 x 1.735537	$ 4,287	
$7,420/2 x 1.735537		$ 6,439
Less profit 10%	1,275	1,275
Indicated value per lot "as is"	$ 3,012	$ 5,164
Lots per acre	1.287	1.183
Indicated value per acre "as is"		
$3,012 x 1.287	$ 3,876	
$5,164 x 1.183		$ 6,109
Indicated per-acre adjustment for subject's well, physical developments, and greater development potential ($6,109 – $3,876)		$ 2,233
		$ 2,200†
Comparable price		$79,000
Comparable price per acre ($79,000/20.2)		$ 3,911
Adjustment for subject's lesser development cost		2,200
Indicated value for subject per acre		$ 6,111
		$ 6,100†

* Cost figures from Table 12.3

† Rounded

From an appraisal standpoint, the comparative analysis shown in Table 12.5 is nothing more than a slightly modified application of the development approach to value. However, in this case the development approach has not been used to estimate the value of the property under appraisal; rather, it has been used to help the appraiser estimate and support a proper adjustment for the physical and economic differences between the comparable property and the property under appraisal. This adjustment factor is subsequently used in the sales comparison approach to value.

Although this methodology may seem a bit devious (and perhaps it is), appraisers must sometimes resort to such procedures to ensure the acceptance of standard appraisal practices, which are widely recognized in the industry as valuable appraisal tools. This process is much like giving your dog his medication rolled up in a piece of hamburger; it's good for him — he just doesn't know it. The use of this methodology is valid and can mean the difference between the acceptance or rejection of an appraisal report by the condemnor's review appraiser. It can also mean the difference between the *admissibility* or *inadmissibility* of valuation testimony.

If an adjustment methodology has been used, the appraiser may want to meet with legal counsel to consider how much detail about the specific elements of the adjustment factor counsel will want or be allowed to present under direct examination. The appraiser may choose only to testify about the differences between the comparable and the property under appraisal or about the gross adjustment called for. The appraiser may state:

> I considered the fact that the sale property has no water system and the property under appraisal has a water system. I also considered the fact that the preliminary master plan has been approved for the subject, but none exists for the comparable. After considering these differences, the indicated adjustment factor would be +$2,200 per acre, which would indicate a value for the property being appraised in the before situation of $6,100 per acre, or approximately $92,800.

Further explanation of the adjustment factor could meet with objection and be ruled inadmissible. If in cross-examination, however, opposing counsel is so bold as to ask, "And how, Mr. Appraiser, can you justify this outrageous adjustment of $2,200 per acre?" the appraiser should be prepared to explain the adjustment down to the smallest detail.

ADVANCED PROBLEMS

TIME LAG AND THE RISK OF DEVELOPMENT

At one time an appraiser or engineer could walk into a local planning office, pick up a copy of the local zoning ordinance and subdivision ordinance, and determine from these documents how many lots a tract could be subdivided into and the amount of time required to obtain the necessary approvals. This is no longer possible. Zoning and subdivision ordinances are now written in such a way that the local government agency can alter development requirements on a project-by-project basis, which places unique, and sometimes outrageous, demands on developers.[33] Two common demands are development fees and exactions of land or easements for public use. Dedications of road rights-of-way or access easements are common, as are exactions of land for parks, schools, and other public purposes.

In addition to zoning and subdivision land use controls, there are a myriad of new land use regulations. Wetlands, open space, shoreline, water detention (or run-off), and low-income housing ordinances are just a few of these additional ordinances. (See Chapter 7 for more information on land use regulations.) A regulation that required a developer to comply with a city-established wage rate to obtain a building permit was ruled not to be a taking.[34]

The flexibility of land use regulations, the introduction of new regulations, and the practice of exacting money and land from developers have substantially increased the risks of land development. The participation of citizen and environmental groups in the development approval process has also increased the risks, as has the time required to obtain development permits. "Resistance from local residents and the general public has stopped many real estate developments."[35] For these reasons, most sales of land acquired for development purposes are subject to the condition that the purchaser obtain necessary development permits prior to closing. This takes considerable risk out of the development process. If the development approach is applied to a tract of land and development permits have not been issued for its development on the date of valuation, the risks and time lag associated with procuring such permits remain present.

The appraiser must take these factors into consideration in projecting the sellout period for a development and in estimating the appropriate entrepreneurial profit factor to be applied in the development approach to value. It is not unusual for two or three years to be spent obtaining all the permits necessary for the subdivision of land, especially if development approvals are appealed.

The sample application illustrated in Table 12.1 assumed no delay was involved in obtaining permit approvals. If there had been a two-year delay in obtaining such approvals, and the lot prices and costs remained constant, the indicated value of the land would have been reduced from $14,819 per acre to $11,813 per acre. The equation is

$$([3.604776 - 1.690051]^{*} \times \$122{,}777) \div 19.90 \text{ acres}$$

* Present worth of $1 per period factor for 5 years discounted at 12% (3.604776) minus present worth of $1 per period factor for 2 years discounted 12% (1.690051) = present worth of $1 per period factor for three years, deferred for two years.

This reduction in the indicated value of the property by more than 20% highlights the importance of considering permit processing time. It is also probable that a developer who anticipates a delay of two years before development can

33. When these demands become outrageous, the courts have, on occasion, found them to be takings, requiring the payment of just compensation. See Chapter 17.

34. *Associated Builders & Contractors v. Baca*, 769 F.Supp. 1537 (N.D. Cal. 1991).

35. *The Appraisal of Real Estate*, 10th ed., 281.

begin would want a higher percentage of profit than is shown in Table 12.1. Moreover, the cost of holding the land for two years while permits are processed would have to be accounted for, further reducing the present value of the land.

The increased speculation brought about by new development ordinances and more land use regulations will probably make the courts even more reluctant to accept development approach evidence, especially in the appraisal of raw land when no meaningful steps toward development have actually been made.

DEVELOPMENT APPROACH AND DCF ANALYSIS

The development approach lends itself to discounted cash flow analysis and some form of DCF analysis is often employed by market participants in making various development decisions. From a practical standpoint, a development seldom produces level cash flows over its development and sellout period. Returning to the example shown in Table 12.1, such a development would probably not produce level cash flows of $122,777 per year. Because the development is small, all the development costs would probably be incurred during the first year. To attempt to develop this land in three phases would likely increase actual construction costs beyond the amount that could be saved by not incurring all of the direct costs in the first year of development. A more accurate picture of the actual cash flows of such a development is shown in the DCF analysis in Table 12.6.

TABLE 12.6 DEVELOPMENT APPROACH—DEVELOPMENT COSTS IN YEAR 1

	Year 1	Year 2	Year 3
Lot inventory—beginning of year	60	40	20
Sales (20 lots @ $17,500)	$350,000	$350,000	$350,000
Less: Direct costs	318,169	0	0
Overhead and sales costs	35,000	35,000	35,000
Management and supervision	12,000	12,000	12,000
Taxes and insurance	6,250	4,166	2,083
Profit and raw land value	($ 21,419)	$298,834	$300,917
Less profit	– 70,000	– 70,000	– 70,000
Net before cost of capital	($ 91,419)	$228,834	$230,917
Times present value factor at 12%	0.892857	0.797194	0.711780
Present value of income streams	($ 81,624)	$182,425	$164,362

Indicated raw land value: $265,163
Indicated value per acre: $13,325

The projected cash flows in Table 12.6 show that all of the development costs are anticipated to be incurred during the first year. The only other difference in the computations made in Tables 12.1 and 12.6 is the assumption that taxes and insurance costs will decrease each year as the lot inventory is reduced. By comparing the tables, it can be seen that the indicated value of the land under appraisal has been reduced from $14,819 per acre in Table 12.1 to $13,325 per acre in Table 12.6. This 10% reduction was computed after the income stream was revised to reflect more realistic expectations.

An appraiser who applies the development approach using DCF analysis has the advantage of being able to test various development schemes to determine which one will produce the highest residual value to the land. For instance, assume that direct development costs of the subject tract would increase by 15% if the physical development of the land were accomplished over three years rather than one. As demonstrated in Table 12.7, the indicated value of the property under appraisal would then be $12,880 per acre. Thus the optimum development plan would be to complete the development in a single year.

TABLE 12.7 DEVELOPMENT APPROACH—3-YEAR DEVELOPMENT COSTS

	Year 1	Year 2	Year 3
Lot inventory—beginning of year	60	40	20
Sales (20 lots @ $17,500)	$350,000	$350,000	$350,000
Less: Direct costs (per Table 12.1)	121,965	121,965	121,965
Overhead and sales costs	35,000	35,000	35,000
Management and supervision	12,000	12,000	12,000
Taxes and insurance	6,250	4,166	2,083
Profit and raw land value	$174,785	$176,869	$178,952
Less profit	–70,000	–70,000	–70,000
Net before cost of capital	$104,785	$106,869	$108,952
Present value factor at 12%	0.892857	0.797194	0.711780
Present value of income streams	$93,558	$85,195	$77,550

Indicated raw land value: $256,303
Indicated value per acre: $12,880

DCF analysis is particularly useful when the development approach is being applied to a relatively large development that will take several years to sell out. It also is helpful when development financing is being contemplated. Within the DCF framework, appraisers can project different numbers of lot sales in the various years of the development process, use different projection periods (e.g., quarterly rather than annual), and build in anticipated increases or decreases in lot prices and/or expenses. However, appraisers should keep in mind that as the complexity of the development approach and the number of different projections increase, it becomes less likely that the court will find the approach to value admissible and that the trier of fact will understand it.

SUMMARY

The development approach to value can be used to estimate the market value of a tract of land that has a highest and best use for subdivision purposes. The approach is simply the land residual technique applied to undeveloped land. There are many ways to apply the development approach and selecting the correct methodology often depends on the specific facts and circumstances surrounding the property under appraisal. Various applications of the development approach are discussed in detail in other publications.[36]

The best evidence of the value of raw subdivision land is derived from comparable sales. Although the use of comparable sales, when available, is the preferred approach to value, the development approach can, and often should, be used to support the value of the property indicated by the sales comparison approach. If an appraiser testifies that the highest and best use of a property is for subdivision purposes and estimates its value using comparable sales only, with no reference to the development approach on direct examination, the appraiser may still be subject to cross-examination concerning development cost factors. An Illinois court stated,

> The appellants' theory was that the highest and best use for the tract was for subdivision. This being a question in issue, there was no error, based on the record in this case, in allowing cross-examination of their witnesses regarding the cost of improving the property for the sale of lots for dwelling purposes.
>
> The same reasoning applied to the rebuttal testimony offered by the appellee. It being proper to examine the appellants' witnesses as to the basis of their opinions on costs of subdividing, it was proper for the appellee to introduce evidence on its side as to such costs.[37]

The procedural steps in applying the development approach to value are:

1. Prepare a subdivision layout to determine the number, typical size, and shape of all potential lots.
2. Estimate retail value of the lots.
3. Estimate direct development costs.
4. Estimate indirect development costs.
5. Compute the income residual attributable to developer's profit and land value (Step 2 minus Steps 3 and 4).
6. Deduct developer's profit.
7. Estimate the amount of time required to develop and sell out the subdivision.
8. Discount the anticipated income stream into an indication of the current raw land value.

The most difficult items for an appraiser to support with market data are the estimated sellout, or absorption, rate (including the time required to procure nec-

36. *Subdivision Analysis* (1978).

37. *Forest Preserve Dist. of Cook County v. Krol*, 145 N.E.2d 599, 603 (Ill. 1957).

essary development permits) and the appropriate amount of developer's profit to be deducted from the retail sale price of the lots.

In estimating developer's profit, the appraiser must remember that this amount should reflect what a developer would consider a reasonable profit going into a proposed development project, not the amount of profit that a particular developer actually received at the conclusion of a similar project. Analyzing the actual profits received by various developers on completed subdivision projects can help the appraiser select an appropriate profit factor to use in the development approach, but it is not a conclusive test. The appraiser must be certain that the estimate of developer's profit reflects the risk, time, and costs associated with obtaining all necessary development permits as well as the risks associated with the physical development and sellout of the lots.

As a general rule, the courts will not allow the development approach to be admitted into evidence when it is applied to raw subdivision land. On the other hand, when the land under appraisal is fully developed, or nearly so, most jurisdictions will allow use of the development approach and admit evidence in this regard. Case law pertaining to the admissibility of the development approach varies from jurisdiction to jurisdiction, primarily because circumstances differ in each specific case. Some courts are reluctant to admit development approach testimony because they fear it will be misconstrued or misused by the trier of fact. It is imperative that case law in the applicable jurisdiction be extensively investigated before any attempt is made to use or testify to the development approach to value.

The development approach to value is most often applied to tracts that fall between the two extremes of raw acreage and fully subdivided land. Therefore, modification of the procedural steps in the development approach is sometimes warranted. Complex applications of the development approach are less likely to be approved by the condemnor's review appraiser or by the court. Although use of DCF analysis tends to increase the complexity of the development approach, market conditions and the nature of the anticipated cash flows sometimes require the flexibility DCF analysis offers. If the appraiser chooses to apply DCF analysis, care must be taken to ensure that the analysis undertaken conforms with the The Appraisal Foundation's requirements with regard to DCF analysis.[38]

The methodology of the development approach to value can help the appraiser in analyzing the differences between a property in the before situation and the after situation. The methodology can also be modified and applied to the comparative analysis of sales in the sales comparison approach to value.

Because the development approach to value is complex and case law concerning its admissibility is conflicting, the appraiser should not attempt to use this approach, or testify to it, without the assistance of legal counsel, a consulting engineer, and other technical advisors. It follows, therefore, that an uninitiated appraiser should not attempt to apply this unless he or she is associated with an appraiser who has had experience in its use. Similarly, an attorney with little

38. The Appraisal Foundation, *Uniform Standards of Professional Appraisal Practice*, 1994 ed., Statement on Appraisal Standards No. 2, p. 55–57.

eminent domain trial experience should not attempt to undertake a condemnation case involving the development approach to value without obtaining the assistance of an individual experienced in, and thoroughly familiar with, the legal and appraisal intricacies of this approach.

Applying the development approach to value is generally quite time-consuming and expensive. Preparation for trial and the trial itself are lengthy procedures for both the appraiser and the attorney, and thus expensive for their client. As a general rule, no other type of condemnation case requires as much pretrial conferences and pretrial preparation as a case involving the development approach to value. For these reasons, such a case should not be undertaken by an appraiser or attorney unless the client is fully aware of the potential cost involved and is prepared to pay the price. Under no circumstance should an appraiser or attorney go to trial in a case involving the development approach to value without extensive pretrial preparation.

CHAPTER 13

Construction of the Public Improvement

If the acquisition of a parcel of land is a total taking, as opposed to a partial acquisition, the proposed use of the land taken is of no consequence to the appraiser, nor is it of consequence to the attorney once the question of public use and necessity has been adjudicated by the court. At least theoretically, the proposed use of the land taken in a total taking is of no significance to the trier of fact and should have no bearing on the determination of just compensation. Only in the case of a partial acquisition does the proposed use of the land taken need to be considered.

Although some may argue that not all public construction constitutes the construction of a public *improvement*, discussion of this question is beyond the scope of this work. For purposes of this discussion, it is assumed that all public construction constitutes public improvements. Historically, the value of a remainder property in a partial taking case was estimated assuming the public improvement was complete and operational on the date of valuation.[1] Because the size of public projects and the cost of money have increased, as has the amount of time between land acquisition and the completion of many public projects, it is now more common to estimate the value of a remainder property in its physical condition as it exists on the date of valuation, giving consideration to the proposed public construction and its anticipated effect. "The 'after value' is based on the value of the remainder property assuming that the actual construction of the proposed project will not be completed until an estimated future date."[2] In estimating the remainder property's value, the appraiser must exclude from consideration any diminution in the value of the remainder property attributable to

1. Joseph M. Montano, *Recognition of Benefits to Remainder Property in Highway Valuation Cases,* National Research Program Report No. 88 (Washington, D.C.: Highway Research Board, 1970), 8.

2. Washington State Dept. of Transportation, *Right of Way Manual* (revised August 1991), Chapter 4-1, Part I, §A3, p. I-1.

any temporary inconvenience during or caused by the actual construction of the public improvement. Thus one hypothetical condition (i.e., that the public improvement was complete on the date of value) has been replaced with another hypothetical condition (i.e., that disruption of the remainder property during construction of the public improvement will have no impact on its market value). The significance of this change will be discussed in the next chapter.

Although the appraiser is to view the remainder property as it physically existed on the date of value, he or she must consider the impact of the pending construction on the remainder property. Therefore, the appraiser must be able to visualize the remainder property after the proposed public project is complete to estimate its value and reflect the damages and/or special benefits that will accrue to it.

The appraiser demonstrates a full and accurate understanding of the after situation by describing it in writing, in an appraisal report, and verbally, on the witness stand. The appraiser must understand not only the portion of the public project that will abut the remainder property, but also the entire public improvement.

There is considerable case law indicating that damage to the remainder property is limited to the damage caused by only that portion of the public project that occupies the area taken from the original larger parcel.[3] This theory is based on the fact that "... the just compensation assured by the Fifth Amendment [of the U.S. Constitution] to an owner, a part of whose land is taken for public use, does not include the diminution in value of the remainder caused by the acquisition and use of adjoining lands of others for the same undertaking."[4] This concept, and the difficulty of attempting to apply it in the real world, is discussed in Chapter 14.

Engineering, Property Staking, and Inspection

The first thing the appraiser must do is become familiar with the property being appraised. This is accomplished by performing a site inspection, examining the title to the property, and making a preliminary investigation of the zoning, neighborhood trends, and general economic conditions. Then the appraiser should meet with the condemnor's engineer to learn about the proposed construction. If the appraiser has been employed by the condemnee, it is often necessary for the condemnee's attorney to make arrangements for such a meeting. If the condemnor's attorney or engineer is uncooperative, the required information may be elicited through interrogatories or by deposition.

The amount and quality of information concerning construction plans and specifications that is available for review by the appraiser will generally depend on the specific condemnor and the type of public project proposed. Whenever possible, the site should be inspected by the appraiser and the engineer together. If the appraiser does not understand the proposed construction perfectly, he must

3. *St. Regis Paper Co. v. United States*, 313 F.2d 45 (9th. Cir. 1962).

4. *Campbell v. United States*, 266 U.S. 368, 372 (1924).

continue to question the engineer until full comprehension of the proposed project is achieved.

Some condemnors designate one engineer to act as the condemnor's *court engineer*. The court engineer testifies in condemnation cases whenever engineering testimony is required and is usually available to assist the condemnor's attorney and appraiser in preparing for trial. If the condemnor has a court engineer, it is generally advisable for the appraiser to work with or at least through, that individual regardless of whether the appraiser has been retained by the condemnor or the condemnee. The reasons for this are twofold. First, the court engineer is practiced in explaining complex engineering concepts to lay people because of his experience in testifying before a trier of fact. Second, the court engineer will be explaining the engineering details to the trier of fact and it is important that the appraiser obtain all necessary engineering data from the same source. Juries are not impressed when the condemnor's appraiser describes a feature of the public construction in a manner that conflicts with the description given by the condemnor's engineer.

It is often helpful, and in some instances absolutely necessary, for the appraiser to have the property staked by the condemnor's engineer. Some condemnors resist such a request, but if staking is needed for the appraiser to understand the conditions that will exist in the after situation, the appraiser must insist on it. In some instances, it may be possible for the appraiser to limit the appraisal report and reserve the right to alter it after the property has been staked. However, the appraisal report then becomes a *limited report*, and thus unacceptable for trial purposes until the limiting condition is removed. Also, the appraiser must take care not to limit the report to such a degree that it becomes meaningless or misleading.

The appraiser should make arrangements to be notified as soon as the staking is in place. Survey stakes have a tendency to disappear or move about, so it is prudent for the appraiser to view and photograph the property as soon as possible after the staking is complete. The type and degree of staking required by the appraiser will vary from case to case, depending on the type of public construction proposed and the physical characteristics of the property under appraisal. For instance, in a partial acquisition for construction of a new highway, the appraiser might request that the following items be staked:

- Pertinent property corners
- Taking or right-of-way line
- Edge of shoulder of road
- Edge of pavement
- Centerline of road
- Extent of limited-access line, if any
- Location of new road approaches, if any

The acquisition of a power line easement might require staking of the limits of the easement, the tower locations, and the limits of any danger tree areas. (Danger tree areas are discussed in the next section.)

Often the appraiser is required by law or policy to invite the property owner to the property inspection.[5] Whether or not this is required, it is good appraisal practice. If the property is to be staked, the ideal time for a joint inspection is immediately after staking. This is also the best opportunity for the attorney to inspect the property with the appraiser and/or owner. If the attorney does not take advantage of this opportunity, he will probably not have another chance to view the property with the staking in place until one or two days before trial (if then), when the property is staked once again for inspection by the trier of fact. If the attorney does not understand the circumstances surrounding the remainder property until one or two days before trial, there may not be enough time to prepare adequately.

If the appraiser has been retained by the condemnor and is advised that the property owner is represented by legal counsel, the appraiser *must* only contact the owner with, or through, the owner's legal counsel. Direct contact with the property owner should not be made without the permission of the owner's legal counsel. If the appraiser is given permission to arrange for property inspection directly with the owner, but is instructed by the owner's legal counsel that he is not to ask the owner any questions concerning the property, the appraiser must adhere to these instructions. This does not mean, however, that the appraiser cannot take note of any unsolicited comments made by the property owner and consider them in estimating the value of the property. For this reason, the owner's legal counsel is advised to accompany the owner and the condemnor's appraiser on their joint property inspection.

Figure 13.1 depicts an actual taking for construction of a roadway. It is presented to illustrate why the appraiser and/or the owner's attorney should insist that the property be staked and that a joint inspection of the property be made with the property owner. In this case no evidence of a septic tank, drain field, or well was visible from ground level. The applicable health regulations required a totally clear zone 100 feet in diameter around the well and prohibited a drain field, driveway, or other improvement within this area. When the taking line was determined, the condemnor was not aware of the location of the septic tank drain field. The appraiser and attorney retained by the condemnee were also unaware of the location of the drain field until the owner pointed it out during a joint inspection of the property. The taking line was then staked to verify its location in relation to the drain field.

The local health authority was contacted and it was determined that the drain field could not be relocated on the remainder and still keep the required 100-ft. clear zone around the well. Therefore the remainder property suffered damage of nearly 100%. When the condemnor was informed of these circumstances, it decided that it would be physically possible and more cost-effective to

5. Uniform Relocation Assistance and Real Property Acquisition Policies Act of 1970, P.L. 91-646, as amended, 42 U.S.C. §4601, *et seq.*

FIGURE 13.1 PARTIAL TAKING

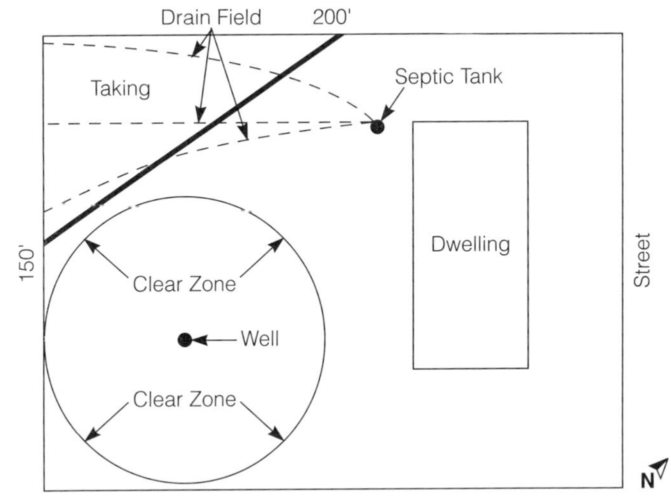

construct a small retaining wall west of the proposed taking line and move the take line enough west to avoid the underground septic tank drain field.

In analyzing the value of a property after a taking, the appraiser must consider the proposed use to which the condemnor will put the land taken.[6] However, the appraiser must remember that the condemnor is generally not limited to the use proposed at the time of the taking unless the condemnor limited or restricted itself to specific plans and specifications submitted at that time. If such a limitation is made by the condemnor, and the condemnor subsequently expands or changes the use of the land, the condemnee may be entitled to additional compensation.[7] If no such limitation is made, however, the condemnor is not restricted in its use of the land taken and the appraiser must consider what the condemnor *is acquiring a right to do*, not what the condemnor *plans to do* as of the date of trial. The appraiser must assume that the condemnor will use the land taken to the fullest legal extent possible.[8]

On the other hand, the appraiser cannot assume that the condemnor will put the land taken to the use that, in the appraiser's opinion, would be the most injurious to the remainder.[9] Any potential uses must be so reasonably probable as to have a detrimental effect on the current market value of the remainder. As one court stated:

> While it is true that a condemnation award must "once and for all" fix the damages, present and prospective, that will accrue reasonably from the construction of the improvement, and in this connection must consider the most injurious use of the property reasonably possible, that does not mean that the jury may speculate on the possibility of damage from some future abandonment of the improve-

6. *United States v. Causby*, 328 U.S. 256 (1946).
7. *McCubbin v. Village of Gretna*, 116 N.W.2d 287 (Neb. 1962).
8. *Western Union Tel. Co. v. Polhemus*, 178 F. 904 (3rd Cir. 1910).
9. *Andrews v. Cox*, 17 A.2d 507 (Conn. 1941).

> ment. Remote, speculative, or conjectural elements of damage cannot be submitted to or considered by the jury.[10] [Citations omitted]

Another court said,

> It has been frequently held that if a portion of a tract is condemned and compensation is paid, the condemnee or his successor in interest cannot recover additional damages because of any subsequent use of the land taken which could reasonably be foreseen at the time of the original condemnation, the theory being that the condemnee was compensated for any use of the condemned property foreseeable at the time of the taking."[11] [Citations omitted]

The most common partial acquisitions are overhead easements (for power lines), surface easements or takings (for roadways), and subsurface easements (for utility lines). The specific engineering data typically available in these cases and the information needed by appraisers to value properties involved in these partial takings are discussed in detail below. Of course, if the taking is of a fee estate rather than an easement, the taking is technically of the entire property including the space above the ground and the area below the ground. Thus references to *overhead, surface* and *subsurface* easements refer to the intended use of the area taken, rather than the form of the taking.

OVERHEAD USE

The most common overhead use easement is acquired for the construction of electrical transmission lines. The installation of long-run, high-capacity lines often requires the services of professional appraisers and can result in condemnation trials. Topographical maps of the easement area are generally available from the condemnor, along with parcel or ownership strip maps.

Figure 13.2 is an example of a strip map. These maps generally show the location of existing buildings, the limits of the proposed easement acquisition, the ownership of the land, the proposed tower locations, and various physical features of the land such as roads, waterways, and fences. Such maps also delineate danger tree areas, labeled "DTA," which are areas outside of the easement proper where the condemnor will have the right to top or completely remove any trees which it perceives as dangerous to the proposed transmission line. Large- and small-scale aerial photographs are also useful and generally available to appraisers involved in valuing larger ownerships.

To value a property subject to an overhead easement, the appraiser will require engineering data on easement widths and areas; danger tree areas, if any; and the types, styles, locations, and heights of towers or poles. The appraiser should also investigate the anticipated initial line capacity, expected increases in line capacity, and whether operation of the line is likely to cause coronas, arcing, TV disturbance, or radio interference. Any and all safety features of the line should also be investigated. Recent cases suggest two elements of damage to be

10. *People ex rel Dept. of Public Works v. Schultz Co.*, 268 P.2d 117, 124 (Cal. 1954).

11. *Texas Electric Service Co. v. Cambell*, 328 S.W.2d 208, 213-214 (Tex. 1959).

FIGURE 13.2 STRIP MAP

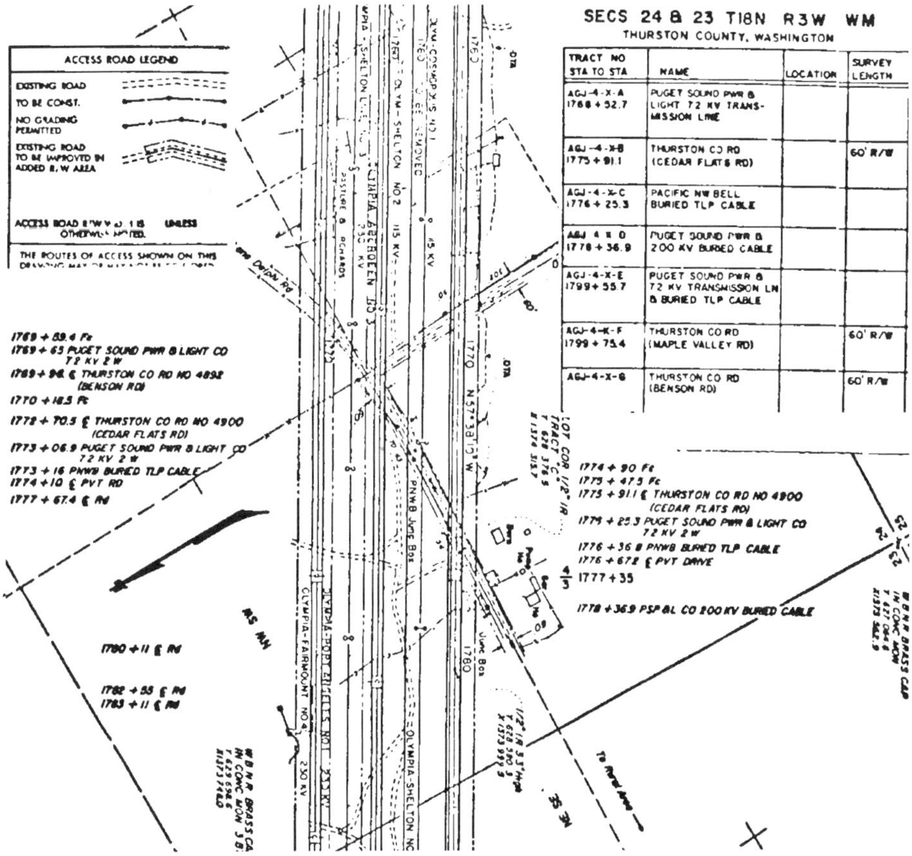

considered by the appraiser: infestation of the property by noxious weeds that are likely to be brought in by the condemnor or its contractors[12] and alleged potential human health hazards from the electromagnetic fields (EMFs) created by the transmission lines.[13] If such elements would have an effect on the current market value of the property, the appraiser should determine what precautions have been, or will be, taken by the condemnor to minimize their effect.

If an easement is to be acquired, its specific terms and conditions must be analyzed to determine which rights will remain with the underlying fee owner and which will be transferred to the condemnor. A standard easement form used by the U.S. Department of Energy is shown in Figure 13.3. Two specific items on this form should be noted. First, the fourth paragraph gives the government the right to designate other trees that are owned by the fee owner but not specified in the easement as "additional danger trees" and to remove them upon payment of their market value to the fee owner. Second, for purposes of this easement, Christ-

12. *United States v. 33.5 Acres, Okanogan Cty., Wash.* 789 F.2d 1396 (9th Cir 1986).

13. *Ryan v. Kansas Power*, 815 P.2d 528 (Kan. 1991).

FIGURE 13.3 STANDARD EASEMENT FORM

CONTRACT AND GRANT OF EASEMENT
Transmission Line and Danger Trees

THIS AGREEMENT, made this_________ day of _________ , 19 ______, between ______________________________the Grantor, whether one or more, and the UNITED STATES OF AMERICA, Department of Energy, Bonneville Power Administration, pursuant to the Bonneville Project Act, Act of August 20, 1937, Ch. 720, 50 Stat. 731, as amended, 16 U.S.C. 832 (1970); the Federal Columbia River Transmission System Act, Act of October 18, 1974, P.L. 93-454, 88 Stat. 1376, 16 U.S.C. 838 (Supp IV); the Department of Energy Organization Act, approved August 4, 1977 (P.L. 95-91); and the Pacific Northwest Electric Power Planning and Conservation Act, Approved December 5, 1980 (P.L. 96-501),

WITNESSETH:

That the parties hereto covenant and agree as follows:

The Grantor, for and in consideration of the sum of __________________________ ($ __________) and the provisions contained in this agreement, hereby grants and conveys to the United States of America a perpetual easement and right-of-way for electric power transmission purposes in, upon, and under the following described land, to-wit:

The grant shall include the right to enter and to locate, construct, operate, maintain, repair, reconstruct, upgrade, remove, and patrol one line of poles or structures and appurtenances thereto, supporting conductors of one or more electric circuits of any voltage together with the present and future right to clear the right-of-way and to keep the same clear of all structures, trees, brush, vegetation, and fire hazards, provided, however, that vegetation and fire hazards shall not include agricultural crops. All such trees, brush, vegetation, structures, and fire hazards presently on the right-of-way shall become the property of the United States on the date of acceptance hereof and may be disposed of by the United States in any manner it deems suitable. Title to trees and merchantable timber hereafter growing within the right-of-way shall be and remain in the United States.

The grantor also hereby grants and conveys to the United States the right to top, limb, or fell, and to remove, sell, burn, or otherwise dispose of those trees and snags (collectively called "danger trees") located within the area of land shown on the attached Exhibit __and which are presently of such height and location that any part thereof could fall within ____ feet of any of the facilities constructed or to be constructed within the adjacent transmission line right-of-way.

The grantor also hereby grants and conveys to the United States the right to enter Grantor's land outside the areas described above at any time prior to _____ and top, limb, or fell, and to remove, sell, burn, or otherwise dispose of those trees and snags, if any, (collectively called "additional danger trees") which could also fall within ____ feet of the above-described facilities; and the United States shall pay the owner of said additional danger trees the prevailing market rate of said trees.

Notice of acceptance of this instrument by the United States shall be given to the Grantor at Grantor's last known address within six months from date of last notarized Grantor's signature or this offer shall be void.

The rights granted herein are subject to easements of record and mineral rights of third parties.

In addition to the consideration recited herein, the United States shall repair or pay for damage to agricultural crops, fences, and irrigation and drainage systems within the easement area that occurs as a result of and during construction, reconstruction, upgrading, removal, or maintenance activities. The United States shall also pay, as damage, for any reduction in market value due to reconstruct or upgrading. Payment under this clause shall be made on the basis of a damage estimate approved by the United States.

The Grantor agrees to satisfy of record such encumbrances, including taxes and assessments, as may be required by the United States and to obtain such curative evidence of title as may be requested by the United States.

The United States shall pay all costs incidental to the preparation and recordation of this instrument and for the procurement of the title evidence.

The Grantor covenants to and with the United States that the Grantor is lawfully seized and possessed of the land aforesaid, with a good and lawful right and power to sell and convey the same; that the land is free and clear of encumbrances, except as herein provided; and that the Grantor will forever warrant and defend the title to the rights granted herein and the quiet possession thereof against the lawful claims and demands of all persons whomsoever.

The provisions hereof shall inure to the benefit of and be binding upon the heirs, executors, administrators, successors, and assigns of the Grantor and upon the assigns of the United States.

No Member of or Delegate to Congress or Resident Commissioner shall be admitted to or share any part of this agreement, or to any benefits that may arise therefrom: but this provision shall not be construed to extend to this agreement if made with a corporation or company for its general benefit.

_______________________   ____
Witness   Grantor
Accepted for the UNITED STATES OF AMERICA __________ ____
By _________ Title _______________ Date   Grantor   BPA 1410 Nov. 1986

mas trees are not considered an agricultural crop and, therefore, the growing of these trees within the easement area is prohibited. Formerly these easements allowed the planting and growing of Christmas trees, but experience showed that the trees were often forgotten by the fee owner and allowed to grow to such heights that they eventually endangered the power lines and had to be removed at the government's expense.

SURFACE USE

The most common land acquisitions for surface use are fee acquisitions for roadway purposes. To appraise a partial acquisition for roadway purposes, the appraiser generally requires substantial engineering data, more than are needed for any other partial taking. Fortunately, most condemnors of road rights-of-way employ competent, full-time engineering staffs so engineering data are plentiful. When the appraiser has been employed by the condemnor, much of this information is furnished at the onset of the appraisal. When the employer is the condemnee, however, the appraiser may have to ask for each specific document or item of data—often several times.

The right-of-way maps prepared by condemnors are generally informative and of good quality. An example of a typical highway right-of-way map was presented in Chapter 5. Centerline profile maps and roadway cross-section maps are also generally available. (See Figure 13.4.) It is important to obtain both centerline and cross-section profile maps of proposed highways (Figure 13.5). Although the centerline elevation map in Figure 13.4 appears to indicate that the taking will cause no loss of view, the cross-section map in Figure 13.5 clearly shows that the property under appraisal will suffer such a loss.

FIGURE 13.4 CENTERLINE PROFILE AND ROADWAY CROSS-SECTION MAPS

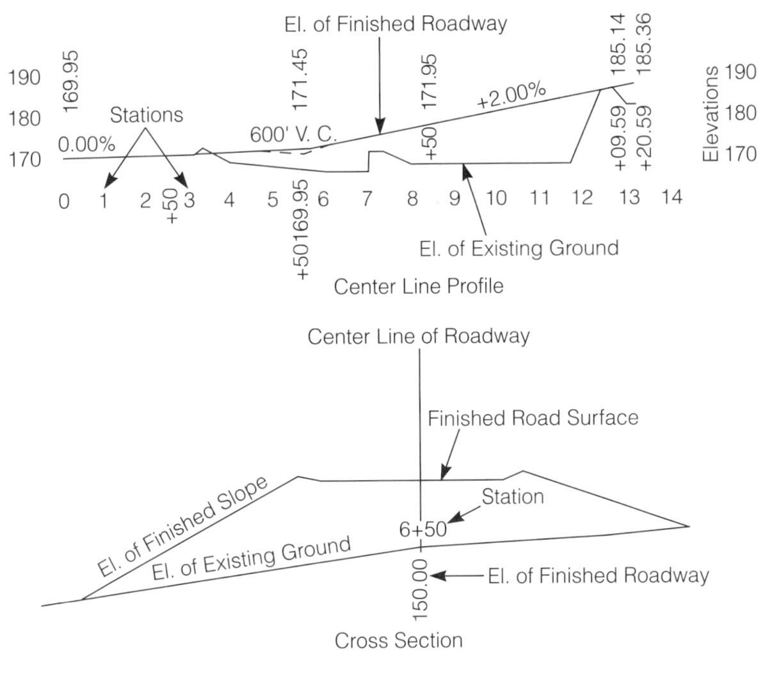

FIGURE 13.5 CENTERLINE AND CROSS-SECTION PROFILE MAPS OF PROPOSED HIGHWAYS

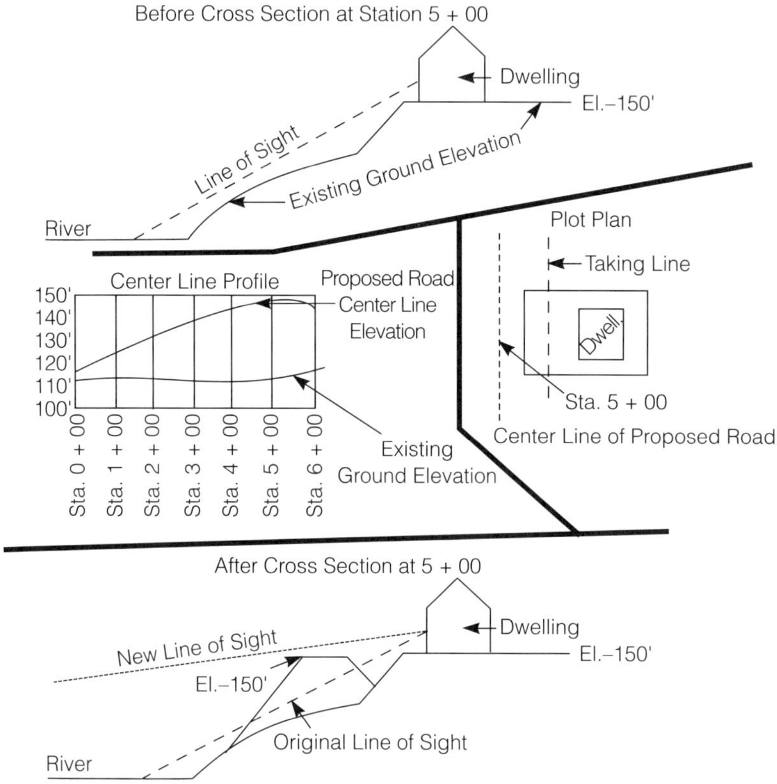

A cross-section map can also help the appraiser determine the feasibility of reconstructing road approaches and driveways. Figures 13.6 and 13.7 demonstrate why this information is necessary. The right-of-way map shown in Figure 13.6 would lead one to assume that damages to the remainder, if any, would be nominal. However, the cross-section map in Figure 13.7 clearly indicates that the garage will be unusable after the taking because an acceptable driveway cannot be constructed. The dwelling may also suffer damage due to the loss of light, view, and air and some drainage problems may result. When a highway right-of-way plan shows that a particular section of the right-of-way is considerably wider than the right-of-way as a whole, it often indicates that the roadway in this section of the right-of-way will be constructed considerably above or below the grade of the existing land.

In addition to showing the areas affected and the location of the improvements, engineering maps can help the appraiser determine whether any ancillary

FIGURE 13.6 PLOT PLANS

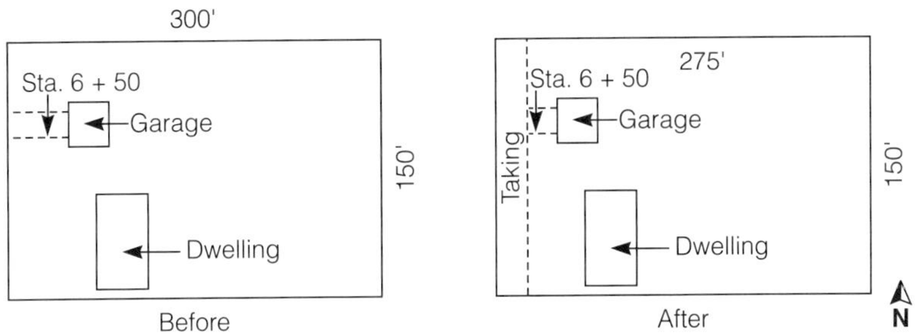

FIGURE 13.7 CROSS SECTIONS AT STATION 6 + 50

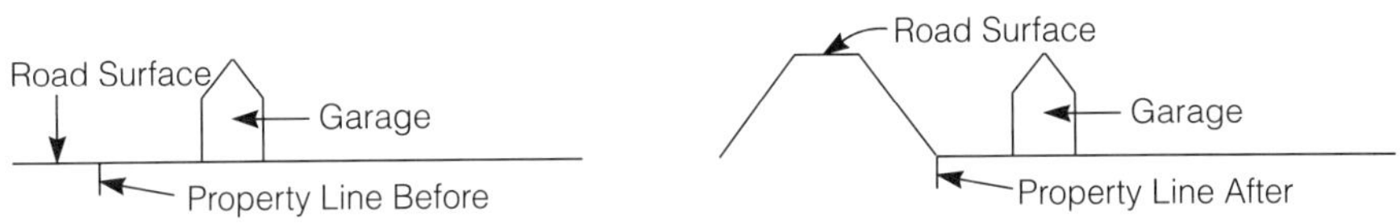

rights are being acquired. Such rights might include slope easements (permanent or temporary); drainage easements; flowage easements (permanent or occasional); construction easements of varying scope; water channel relocations (permanent or temporary); limitations on the right to light, view, and air; and restrictions on road approaches.

The appraiser should obtain detailed plans of drainage, traffic control, and traffic channelization as well as profiles and cross-sections of any frontage road or interchange on/off ramp that could possibly affect the property being appraised. Roadway widths, the number of proposed lanes, and anticipated traffic volume should be investigated along with any plans for the construction of sidewalks and curbs or the installation of streetlights. If fences are to be constructed, the appraiser must know the type of the fence to be built and who will be responsible for its maintenance.

Engineering consultants can help the appraiser estimate the increases or decreases in traffic noise, dust, and headlight glare to be anticipated due to the operation of the proposed improvements. The dust and noise created by *construction* of the improvement are typically noncompensable damage items, but dust and noise created by the *operation* of the completed improvement may be compensable if they diminish the remainder property's market value and the damage is peculiar to the property being appraised. Large- and small-scale aerial photographs of the property are often available and can be particularly helpful if the engineer has identified the boundaries of the property and prepared a clear film overlay depicting the after situation.

Another common type of surface use is a flowage easement in the form of an occasional flowage easement, a permanent flowage easement, or a combination of these two types. Extremely accurate, small-scale topographic maps are absolutely essential in the appraisal of flowage easements. Often the appraiser is responsible for estimating the amount of land area that will be inundated. Using an accurate topographic map, a steady hand, and a planimeter, this estimate can generally be made with relative accuracy. If the easement specifies occasional inundation, the appraiser must determine how frequently the land will be flooded by examining available records and questioning the condemnor's engineer. The appraiser should attempt to discover whether the property to be encumbered by the easement has had a history of flooding.

Two areas are often overlooked in the appraisal of property for flowage easements. The first item is the potential for damage to the unencumbered portion of the property due to the impairment or elimination of physical access from the roadway to the property or from one portion of the property to another. It may be necessary to construct a bridge or roadway with a culvert to rectify this situation.

The second consideration is the potential damage or benefit to the unencumbered remainder from a change in the groundwater elevation caused by the flowage of water to a higher elevation than existed before the acquisition of the flowage easement.[14] The uncumbered remainder can be damaged by more frequent flooding, the killing of crops and trees, or the failure of a septic tank system. On the other hand, increasing the elevation of the water table could benefit arid land, producing natural subirrigation and decreasing or eliminating the need for artificial irrigation of the unencumbered area. If the appraiser is concerned about how a flowage easement will affect surrounding unencumbered land, a hydrology consultant should be employed.

SUBSURFACE USE

An acquisition for subsurface use generally takes the form of an easement for underground utilities such as gas lines, water lines, oil lines, sewer lines, and cables for television, telephone, and electrical service. In appraising a property for the acquisition of a subsurface easement, the appraiser must identify the specific use to which the easement area will be put. If a pipeline carrying a potentially dangerous material is to be installed, the safety features of the pipe must be explored. The cleanup of hazardous waste sites sometimes requires the transportation of hazardous materials by pipeline across neighboring properties. Safety

14. This would not include surface flooding of areas outside the easement taking, however, as such additional surface flooding would be considered an *expansion of the taking* and would be compensable only under a subsequent legal action. See *United States v. 38.60 Acres of Land, More or Less*, 652 F.2d 196, 199 (8th Cir. 1980).

features and the underlying fee owner's liability for cleanup if a leak or spill occurs must be determined by the appraiser.

The depth of the pipe or cable to be laid should be ascertained. Although it will generally require some research, the appraiser should also investigate how often the condemnor will have to go back onto the property to reopen the ground for inspection and/or repair of the pipe or cable. The specific easement form to be used must be examined to answer the following questions:

1. Who is responsible for repairing the surface of the ground?
2. Will any additional temporary construction easements be acquired and, if so, for how long?
3. Can the underlying fee owner build on any part of the easement area?
4. Will the condemnor construct any surface structures within the easement area such as valves, valve houses, pump stations, and manholes?

If unsightly surface structures are to be built, the appraiser can often estimate the damage by calculating the cost of planting sight-obscuring shrubbery around the structures. Of course, this method cannot be used if the cost of buying and planting the shrubbery is greater than the diminution in property value caused by the unsightly structures.

Utility easements can often benefit a property as well as damage it. Figure 13.8 depicts such a situation. Before the easement acquisition and construction of the sewer line, the owner of the property was using a septic tank; all house plumbing was channeled toward the rear of the improvement and connected to the septic tank. In the before situation, connecting the house plumbing to the public sewer would have required running a connection line under the public street, designing the piping system within the house to accommodate the sewer connection, constructing an exit through the front wall of the house, and digging a trench through the front yard of the property. The total cost of these improvements was estimated at $1,900. In the after situation, the owner simply connected the public sewer line running along the north side of the property to the existing piping exiting the dwelling. The total cost of this hookup was $235, so a benefit of $1,665 ($1,900 – $235) seems to have accrued to the property.

Visualizing the After Situation

To ensure complete understanding of the after situation, the appraiser must paint a visual and verbal picture of the property after the taking and after construction of the public improvement. All engineering data used should be verified in writing by the engineer; this document is retained in the appraiser's file for later reference. The appraiser must always identify the plans and specifications used in

FIGURE 13.8 BENEFITS DUE TO PUBLIC PROJECT

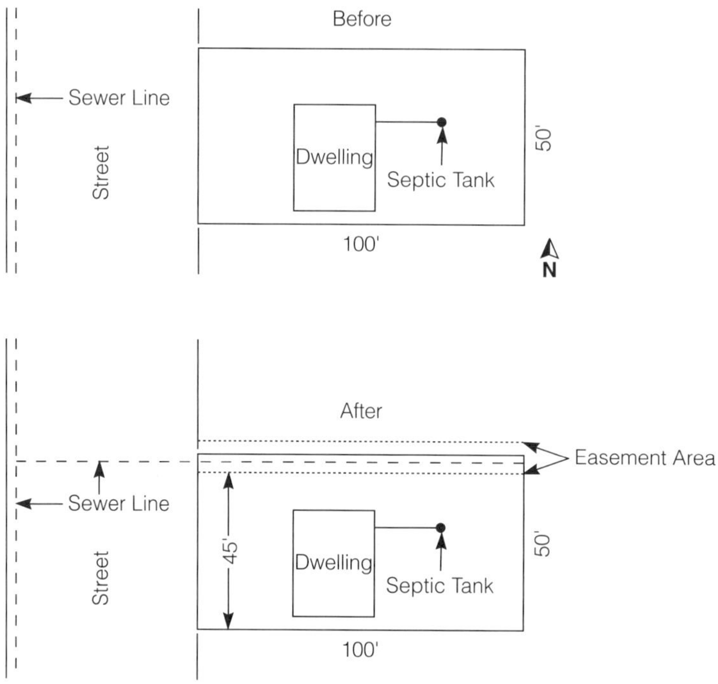

the preparation of the appraisal report and include the date when these plans were last revised. For example, the appraiser might include a statement such as the following in the assumptions and limiting conditions section of the appraisal:

> This appraisal was made under the assumption that the taking and construction of the proposed public improvement will occur as depicted on the Department of Transportation's right-of-way and profile maps for SR 5, MP (mile post) 42.04 to MP 51.66, Rocky Point to Toutle River. Specific reliance has been placed on 1) the right of way plans designated as sheet 19 of 51 sheets having an original date of February 14, 1990 and a last revision date of April 15, 1992 and 2) the profile plan designated as sheet 36 of 51 sheets having an original date of February 14, 1990, with no subsequent revision date. If any modification is made to the above-referenced plans, the appraiser reserves the right to alter the appraisal report to reflect such modifications.

Only with extreme caution should an appraiser rely on an artist's or architect's rendering of an after situation. Those lovely, towering trees that screen the remainder from the offending view and noise of the public improvement will only be 18 inches high when they are planted. The gently sloping, cultivated landward side of the dike or levee may turn out to be quite steep and covered in riprap or large rocks. The appraiser must depend on the engineering plans and specifications, not the fertile imagination of an artist with a flair for drawing aesthetically pleasing pictures.

To guarantee consistency and for self-protection, the appraiser should, if possible, listen to any engineering testimony given at the condemnation trial. If the engineer's testimony and the information furnished to the appraiser by the engineer are not consistent, this discrepancy must be resolved either before the engineer is excused from the witness stand or before the appraiser takes the stand. Although the appraiser may be ready to admit what he does not know on the witness stand, ignorance about basic engineering data that will affect the property under appraisal in the after situation is not acceptable. The appraiser must thoroughly understand the effect the construction may have on the remainder property.

It is imperative that the appraiser and the attorney reach an identical understanding well before the trial of how the engineering plans will affect the property being appraised. If they do not, the attorney may not recognize the inconsistency between the engineer's testimony and the engineering data used by the appraiser until it is too late and the appraiser's description of the property in the after situation is being torn apart under cross-examination.

If the proposed construction is atypical in any manner, the appraiser should try to locate a similarly constructed public improvement, inspect it, and take aerial and/or ground photos of the improvements. The appraiser may also want to inspect previously appraised remainder properties again after the public improvements are complete and operational. By doing so the appraiser can ascertain whether the remainder does, in fact, match the verbal and written picture he prepared before the taking. Interviewing the owners of such properties can also be informative. If the appraiser attempts to inspect a previously appraised property after completion of the public improvements and cannot recognize the remainder property, it is quite possible that the appraiser's visual and written picture of the remainder was somewhat inaccurate.

Visualizing the Before Situation

Sometimes the appraiser is faced with a situation in which the date of value to be estimated is historical and the property to be appraised was physically altered after the date of value and before the appraiser was able to inspect it. The government taking may have already occurred and the public improvement may already have been constructed. In other words, the appraiser may be able to inspect the property in the *after situation*, but not in the *before situation*. This situation typically results when the appraiser is retained by the condemnee, or by the condemnor's legal counsel after negotiations have failed and the case has been turned over for trial.

This is obviously an awkward position for the appraiser, and any cross-examiner who is alert will try to take advantage of it. However, there are a number of things an appraiser can do to determine the condition and physical characteristics of the property in the before situation and dampen the effectiveness of cross-examination. The procedure used to determine the before condition of the property is the same as that used to forecast the after condition of the property under appraisal—only the sources of information are different. The property owner, if available, is a good source of data. Local taxing authorities will often have physical descriptions and photographs of the property. Prior appraisals of the property are also excellent sources of information, as are the appraisers who made them.

Some clients will balk at providing the appraiser with prior appraisals of the property, arguing that they do not want the appraiser to be swayed by prior valuations. This argument seems to be without merit. First, if the appraiser is faced with the problem of appraising a property that he was never able to inspect physically, he should insist on access to *all* information concerning the physical features of the property. Second, the assertion that the appraiser's opinion is going to be unduly swayed by the findings of another appraiser is groundless. If that were the case, the appraiser should not look at the assessed value of the property (which is an estimate of market value), yet most appraisal reporting standards require that the appraiser report this value.[15]

These arguments are, of course, ludicrous. Following such logic one could argue that the appraiser should not become informed as to a recent sale price of the property under appraisal or seek the opinions of local real estate agents familiar with values in the area. This information could also sway the appraiser's opinion. In actual practice, the appraiser should accumulate and consider *all* of the data available on the property under appraisal. The weight given to the data or information accumulated then becomes a matter of judgment for the appraiser. The appraiser must not allow others to screen the information to be considered.

Cross-examiners will often ask the appraiser whether other appraisal reports have been reviewed. However, experience shows that a positive response to this question, rendered in a straightforward, nondefensive manner, has little if any negative impact on the trier of fact.

SUMMARY

When the government exercises its power of eminent domain and takes an entire property, the purpose of the government's acquisition is of no consequence once the court has ruled that there is a public use and necessity for the acquisition. However, if a property owner is left with a portion of the property (often referred

15. *Uniform Appraisal Standards for Federal Land Acquisitions* (Washington, D.C.: U.S. Government Printing Office, 1992), §B-1 13g, p. 71.

to as the *remainder*), the use to which the condemnor will put the land taken becomes important because it may have a significant effect on the remainder property's value. For this reason, the appraiser and the attorney must be thoroughly familiar with the proposed public construction.

The appraiser should be prepared to describe fully, both verbally and in writing, the construction and engineering details of the proposed public improvement. He or she should also determine whether the condemnor is required to put the land taken to the use proposed at the time of the taking, or if the condemnor is also acquiring the right to expand or change the use of the land taken at a later date. In any verbal or written presentation made, the appraiser must clearly identify the specific rights that the condemnor is acquiring and describe, in detail, the proposed public construction. A simple statement such as "The state will build a four-lane freeway." is totally inadequate in describing a proposed government construction. The appraiser should always include in the appraisal report a copy of the easement form and/or a formal description of the estate to be taken from the property under appraisal.

Several courts have held that damage to the remainder property is limited to the damage caused by the portion of the public project located on the property taken. However, in some cases the courts have ruled that it is impossible to separate the damage resulting from the portion of the public project abutting the remainder from the damage caused by the portion of the public project that does not abut the remainder. Therefore, damages to the remainder caused by the entire public project are often considered.

To understand the engineering details of the after situation, the appraiser should obtain written data directly from the condemnor's engineer—preferably the same engineer who will testify before the trier of fact if the case goes to trial. Often it is helpful, if not absolutely necessary, to have the property boundaries and significant construction details staked out on the ground so that the appraiser and the attorney can better visualize the proposed public construction and the remainder property in the after situation. Major cases of a complicated nature may warrant construction of a model of the remainder property.

The amount of construction engineering data required will depend on the use to which the property taken will be put and the complexity of the proposed construction. The quantity and quality of engineering data will often depend on the specific condemnor involved and the nature of the proposed public project. On the witness stand, the appraiser cannot respond "I don't know" to a question regarding the details of the proposed public construction. If the appraiser does not know the construction details of the proposed public improvement, the after value of the remainder property cannot be accurately estimated. Responses such as "I think the property will flood" or "I think the power transmission line will interfere with TV reception" are not acceptable. The appraiser must demonstrate a clear understanding of the after situation. If satisfactory answers cannot be obtained from the condemnor's engineer, the appraiser should either retain another engineering consultant or limit the appraisal report to those engineering or construction details that are clearly understood. However, this is seldom necessary. While condemnors may be reluctant to furnish a condemnee's appraiser with all of the necessary engineering details, they are even more reluctant to give the appraiser the opportunity to respond under direct examination, "I don't know that construction detail. The condemnor's engineer refused to furnish me with that information."

The appraiser should inspect the appraised property again after the public improvement is complete and operational to determine whether the mental picture of the after situation he developed during the initial appraisal process corresponds with the actual, constructed improvement. Such an after-construction inspection can also help the appraiser prepare for future land litigation cases.

In the appraisal report the appraiser must refer to the specific plans and specifications that were relied on in preparing the appraisal. The original date of this material should be noted as well as any dates of revision. The appraiser should reserve the right to alter previous findings if the plans and specifications are changed after the date of the appraisal report.

If the appraiser is retained after the government has taken possession of the property in question and physically altered it, the appraiser will need to determine the physical characteristics of the property as of the date of valuation by investigating all data available. Sources of data will include records of the property owner, tax office records, and prior appraisals of the property.

CHAPTER 14

Damages in Partial Taking Cases

Two definitions of *damages* follow:

> In condemnation, the loss in value to the remainder in a partial taking of a property. Generally, the difference between the value of the whole property before the taking and the value of the remainder after the taking is the measure of the value of the part taken and the damages to the remainder.[1]

> Two types of damages are recognized: consequential and severance.[2]

Of course, damages cannot result when the sovereign acquires the entire ownership because compensation is made for the taking of the total property, and there is no remainder left to damage.

Consequential damages and severance damages are defined as follows:

> **Consequential damages**—A damage to property arising as a consequence of a taking and/or construction on other lands. In many states owners may be compensated for damage as a consequence of a change in grade of a street which adversely affects ingress to and egress from the affected property. In some states property owners are not legally entitled to consequential damages which occur to their real estate. Owners may not be compensated for damage to business, frustration, and loss of goodwill which result as a consequence of a taking or construction by the government.[3]

> **Severance damages**—It is the diminution of the market value of the remainder area, in the case of a partial taking, which arises (a) by reason of the taking (severance), and/or (b) the construction of the improvement in the manner proposed.[4]

1. *The Dictionary of Real Estate Appraisal*, 3d ed. (Chicago: Appraisal Institute, 1993), 87.
2. American Institute of Real Estate Appraisers and the Society of Real Estate Appraisers, *Real Estate Appraisal Terminology*, rev. ed., Byrl N. Boyce, ed. (Cambridge, Mass.: Ballinger Publishing Company, 1981), 69.
3. Ibid., 57.
4. Ibid., 218.

From these definitions it might be concluded that all consequential damages arise from the taking of, or construction on, property other than that consequently damaged, and that this type of damage may or may not be compensable or actionable. Severance damages are generally considered compensable.

The terminology used to describe damages creates confusion between the appraisal and legal professions and within the legal profession itself. According to *Nichols'*, "The term 'consequential damage' has justly been described as ambiguous, irrelevant, equivocal and a deterrent to any hope of a clear understanding of the issue at hand."[5] It "has become a term of art in addressing an issue rather than a term of accurate definition."[6] The first definition of consequential damages given above, which states "[a] damage to property arising as a consequence of a taking and/or construction *on other land*" is, at best, misleading. One example of consequential damage (i.e., noncompensible) cited is "damage to business," but this is generally considered a consequential damage, irrespective of whether it is due to the taking of and/or construction on lands owned by others or is a result of the taking of and/or construction on land that was part of the property in question.

A reading of the various authoritative texts and case law leads to the inescapable conclusion that the use of the term *consequential damages* introduces nothing but confusion to what, from a valuation standpoint, would merely appear be a question of compensability. After a lengthy discussion, *Nichols'* concludes:

> This Treatise deals with issues involved in the exercise of the right of eminent domain. Consequently, all references to "consequential damages" accurately mean damages resulting from acts not amounting to a taking or damages following the taking but caused by intervening and supervening acts of others than the taking authority. If those activities do not amount to a taking, then the damages are a consequence of the taking activities and although they may be addressed on theories of tort, contract, trespass, etc., such activities are not the proper subject of a claim for damage flowing from the exercise of the right of eminent domain by a sovereign.[7]

The general use of the terms *consequential damage* and *severance damage* would appear to be an attempt to differentiate between noncompensable (consequential) damages and compensable (severance) damages in an eminent domain action. It is difficult to understand why these confusing terms continue to be used, particularly in the eastern United States. To avoid confusion here, the terms *consequential damages* and *severance damages* will be replaced with the terms *noncompensable damages* and *compensable damages*. Any further classification of damage is too pedantic for the purposes of this (or most other) discussions.

MEASURE OF DAMAGE

Damages can only result from a partial taking.[8] The taking need not be a physical taking, but may be the taking of a property right. "In this regard, what constitutes

5. *Nichols' The Law of Eminent Domain*, rev. 3d ed. (New York: Mathew Bender Co., Inc., 1992), vol. 4A, §14.01[4].
6. Ibid., §14.01[2].
7. Ibid.
8. *In re Condemnation of 2719,21, 11 E. Berkshire St.*, 343 A.2d 67 (Penn. 1975).

a 'taking' of private property is not susceptible of facile definition, but it is axiomatic that 'it is the character of the invasion [by the sovereign], not the amount of damage which results from it...' which determines the question of whether there has been a taking."[9] For instance " ...a material injury to the easement of view is a taking of property..."[10] as is the placement of cable television facilities (36 feet of cable one-half inch in diameter and two, 4-in. x 4-in. x 4-in. metal boxes occupying one-eighth of a cubic foot) on the roof of a five-story apartment building.[11] It is the damage to that part of the tract not taken which is compensable, in addition to the property or property rights actually taken. This damage arises from the actual taking and/or from the use of the land taken in the manner proposed.

Damages are often dependent on the construction on, or other utilization of, the land acquired by the condemnor. For example, if the acquisition depicted in Figure 14.1 is for public park purposes, any damages to the remainder would be considered differently than if the land were being acquired for construction of a limited-access interstate freeway. Before an appraiser begins to estimate damages to a remainder property, he or she must have a thorough understanding of the proposed use of the portion of the tract being taken by the condemning agency.

FIGURE 14.1 UTILIZATION OF THE AREA TAKEN

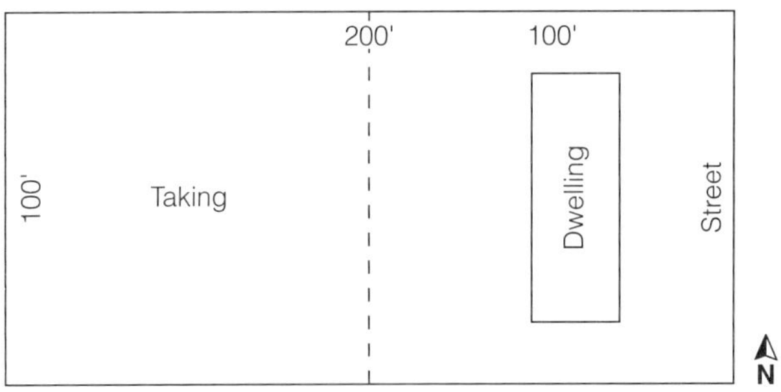

The appraiser must also fully understand what rights are being acquired by the condemnor. The property owner is entitled to consideration for the damage the condemnor has the power to inflict. The appraiser should assume that the condemnor will utilize the rights acquired to their fullest extent.[12]

Nevertheless, it cannot be assumed that the condemnor will put the property taken to the use that is most damaging to the remainder.[13] The appraiser must determine whether the condemnor is required to put the land taken to the specific use proposed on the date of valuation or whether the condemnor has the right to expand or change the use of the land taken at some future date.

9. *Florida East Coast Properties, Inc. v. Metropolitan Dade County*, 572 F.2d 1108, 1111 (5th Cir 1978) *cert. denied*, 439 U.S. 894 (1978).

10. *Bramson v. Berea*, 293 N.E.2d 577 (Ohio 1971).

11. *Loretto v. Teleprompter Manhattan CATV Corp.*, 458 U.S. 419 (1982).

12. *Western Union Tel. Co. v. Polhemus*, 178 F. 904 (3rd Cir. 1910).

13. *United States v. River Rouge Co.*, 269 U.S. 411 (1926).

For example, Figure 14.2 illustrates a proposed taking for a new limited-access highway and shows the proposed plan of construction for the project. The appraiser must consider whether the condemnor is limited in its utilization of the area taken. Could the condemnor at a later date expand or realign the highway facility and bring the traveled roadway to within 20 feet of the dwelling located on the remainder? If this is the case (and it generally is), the damage is not measured as if the planned expansion had or will take place, but rather in recognition of the condemnor's right to expand its use without additional compensation. It is not what the condemnor actually *does* or *plans to do* with the land acquired that determines the amount of damage suffered by the remainder, but rather what the condemning agency *acquires the right to do*.[14]

FIGURE 14.2 PROPOSED UTILIZATION OF THE LAND TAKEN

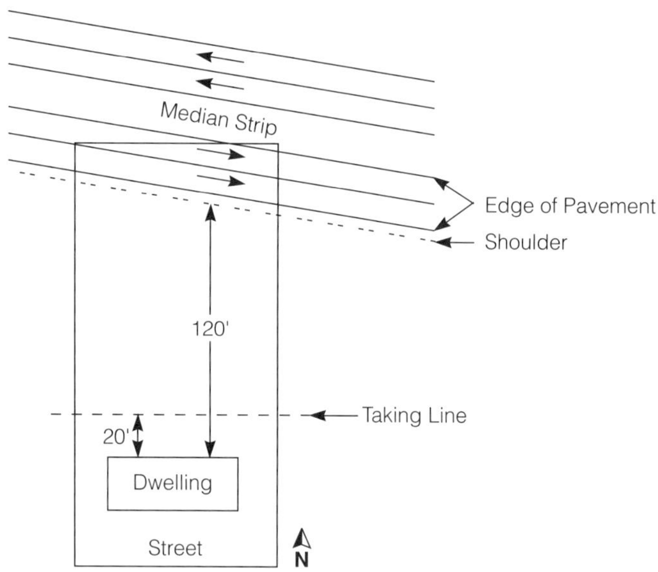

This type of damage is generally measured by analyzing sales of properties that are similar to the property under appraisal in the after situation. Analysis of sales will often show whether buyers and sellers in the market believe that the likelihood of future highway expansion is significant enough to affect the current market value of the property in question.

In analyzing such situations, appraisers must keep this question in mind: If the government does not plan on utilizing all of the rights that it is acquiring, then why is it acquiring them? If a power company is acquiring a transmission line easement for the stated purpose of constructing one 230 kilovolt (kv) power

14. *Manlius Center Road Corp. v. State*, 370 N.Y.S.2d 750 (N.Y. 1975).

line and has no intention of constructing additional lines or increasing the voltage of the line, the rights to be taken should read "an easement for the construction and operation of one 230 kv electrical transmission line," not "an easement for the construction and operation of electrical transmission lines."

> If the State wishes to limit its rights under the easement to the continuance of the presently existing use or to the prospective use envisaged by its expert, it should do so by formal action, by deed, release or otherwise. In the absence of such modification, the damage must be evaluated on the basis of what the State has the right to do under the terms of the easement appropriated.[15]

Another question the appraiser must consider is: Can the condemnor at a future date partially or totally change the use for which the property is being acquired? Can a municipality acquiring land for park purposes later convert the land into a landfill site? Consider Figure 14.3, which depicts an actual situation in which an easement for the construction and maintenance of a drainage canal was acquired. A number of years later, the condemnor devised a plan to use the canal maintenance area as a public bicycle and pedestrian path as well as for canal maintenance. In this case the condemnor's right to put the easement area to this additional use, without acquiring any additional rights or paying additional compensation, hinged on the specific wording of the original easement.[16]

FIGURE 14.3 RIGHTS ACQUIRED

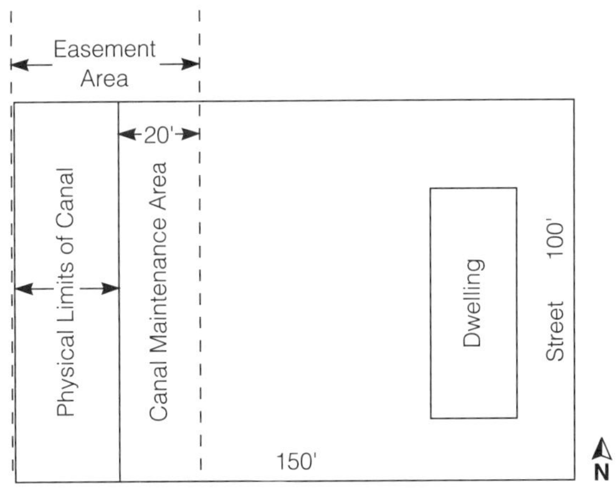

This example highlights the importance of determining exactly what rights are being acquired by the condemnor. If satisfactory clarification cannot be provided by the acquiring agency, the appraiser must obtain legal instructions in regard to the rights being acquired. Whenever possible, a written copy of the

15. *Spinner v. State*, 167 N.Y.S.2d 731, 733 (N.Y. 1957).
16. The agency dropped its plan when it was learned that the expanded use of the easement area would constitute an additional taking and thus require additional compensation.

proposed taking—e.g., the declaration of taking or the easement form—should be obtained by the appraiser and included in the appraisal report. For self-protection the appraiser must always explicitly state the rights that are assumed to be acquired in both the appraisal report and in valuation testimony. This point is further illustrated in Figure 14.4.

FIGURE 14.4 SAMPLE CROSS SECTION OF ALLOWABLE CONSTRUCTION WITHIN EASEMENT

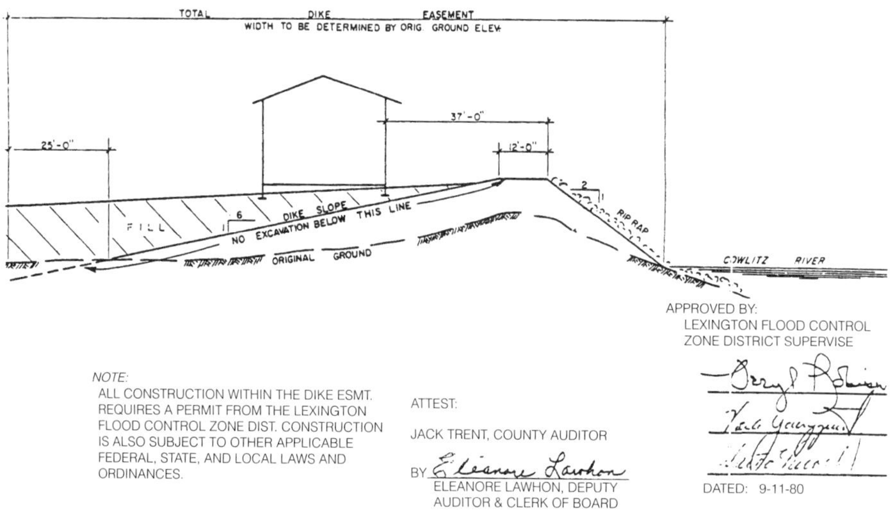

In this case an easement was being acquired for the construction of a levee. The appraiser asked the condemnor to clarify what rights the underlying fee owner would retain in regard to construction within the easement area. When the condemnor's engineer indicated that construction within the easement area would require a permit, the appraiser advised the condemnor that the appraisal would have to be based on the assumption that the condemnor would exercise its rights to the fullest and that no construction within the easement area would be allowed. Discussions with the condemnor and its legal counsel led to the adoption of the drawing shown in Figure 14.4, which was attached to the easement acquired and identified as an illustration of the type of construction that would be allowed within the easement area and for which a permit would be issued. The appraiser included in the appraisal report a copy of the proposed easement and the drawing of "allowable construction."

Two years after construction of the levee, the condemnor found that the elevation of the levee had to be raised, which required an additional easement taking. The condemnor retained the same appraiser to value the property for the second easement taking, which specifically provided that construction within the easement area would not be allowed. The condemnor's legal counsel provided the appraiser with a legal instruction to the effect that construction within the first easement area would require a permit from the condemnor and that the appraiser was to assume that such a permit would be denied. The appraiser refused to accept the legal instruction and, after a review of the appraiser's appraisal report for the first easement taking (which included the drawing of "allowable construction" and the written assumption and limiting condition that such construction would be permitted), the legal instruction was withdrawn. If the appraiser had not insisted upon written clarification of the rights retained by the owner of the land when the first easement was taken and included a comprehensive description of these rights, the owner of the property might well have received substantially less than that to which he was due.

In many jurisdictions appraisers are not technically required to identify specifically or estimate the dollar amount of damages for condemnation trial purposes. They need only estimate the market value of the property before the partial acquisition and the market value of the remainder property immediately after the proposed acquisition. "Notwithstanding the foregoing, appraisals should contain an allocation between the value of the property being acquired and damages to the remainder."[17] Many condemning agencies require this allocation.[18] One reason for this requirement is that payment for the taking and payment for damages to the remainder property are treated differently for income tax purposes. Also, from a practical standpoint, the appraiser must attempt to isolate and identify all elements of damage present in the remainder property. This is not to say that the appraiser must, or even should, estimate a specific dollar amount for each item of damage, only that each should be acknowledged and considered.

Whether the appraiser is working under the *federal rule* or *state rule* of measuring just compensation, the procedural steps of valuation are the same. (See Chapter 3 for a discussion of these two measures of just compensation.) The estimate of damages should be no more conjectural or speculative than the appraiser's estimates of market value before and after the acquisition. Damage estimates must exclude highly improbable damages, but reflect those damages that would be considered significant by prudent buyers and sellers. "[S]trict proof of the loss in market value to the remaining parcel is obligatory."[19] "[T]he extent to which the utility of the property has been destroyed and its market value diminished must necessarily be established by factual data having a rational foundation in support of such a claim."[20]

The appraiser measures damages, not as an end in itself, but to assist in estimating the value of the remainder tract. "Under the Federal rule, compensation is paid for 'takings' not 'damages.'"[21] In other words, the estimate of damages is the basis for arriving at an adjustment that will be applied to various market data in valuing the property in the after situation. One of the most commonly used and reliable methods of estimating damage is by analyzing comparable sales using the matched pairs, or paired data analysis, technique.[22] Damages can also be estimated by capitalizing the net rent loss resulting from the damage.

17. *Uniform Appraisal Standards for Federal Land Acquisitions* (Washington, D.C.: U.S. Government Printing Office, 1992), §A-11, p. 34.
18. U.S. Department of Transportation, Federal Highway Administration, *The Appraisal Guide* (Washington, D.C.: U.S. Government Printing Office, 1990), 9.
19. *United States v. Honolulu Plantation Co.*, 182 F.2d 172, 179 (9th Cir. 1950), *cert. denied*, 340 U.S. 820 (1950).
20. *United States v. 26.07 Acres of Land in Hempstead*, 126 F.Supp. 374, 377 (E.D.N.Y. 1954).
21. *Uniform Appraisal Standards for Federal Land Acquisitions*, §A-11, p. 31.
22. For a description of this analytical technique, see *The Appraisal of Real Estate*, 10th ed. (Chicago: Appraisal Institute, 1992), 394-397.

A third method applied to estimate a proper adjustment for damage is known as the *cost to cure*. This method can be used when the property being appraised has suffered damage that can be physically and economically corrected,[23] e.g., through correction of drainage, replacement of fencing, reestablishment of physical access, or replacement of sewage or water systems. Under no circumstances can the cost to cure measure of damage be applied if the cost to cure exceeds the diminution in value that would result if such a cure were not undertaken.[24] However, if the cost to cure is less than the diminution in the value of the remainder, the cost to cure measure of damage *must* be used.[25]

Although *Nichols'* suggests that the cost to cure measure of damage is an *exception* to the before and after method of valuation and determination of compensation,[26] this measure of damage actually ensures conformance with the rule. If a property with a deficiency is placed on the market, both the buyer and seller will consider the cost to cure the deficiency, if it is physically and economically curable. The price at which the property will sell is the value of the property as deficient or the value of the property without the deficiency minus the cost to cure the deficiency, whichever is higher. If a remainder property lacks a connecting road approach, or driveway, to an abutting road, it would be illogical to estimate the market value of the remainder property as if it would be landlocked in perpetuity. If a road approach could physically and legally be constructed, the value of the property would be its market value with access minus the cost of constructing the access, unless the cost to construct the access exceeded the difference between the value of the property with access less the value of the property as landlocked.

The measure of damages cannot be based on an assumption that adjacent land can be acquired,[27] but the appraiser can consider the general availability of suitable replacement property. This is particularly true when the property in question is a noncontiguous larger parcel.[28] Figure 14.5 illustrates the misuse of such an assumption. In this situation it would be improper to estimate the damage to the remainder of Parcel A as the cost of acquiring Parcel B.

FIGURE 14.5 ACQUISITION OF OTHER LANDS

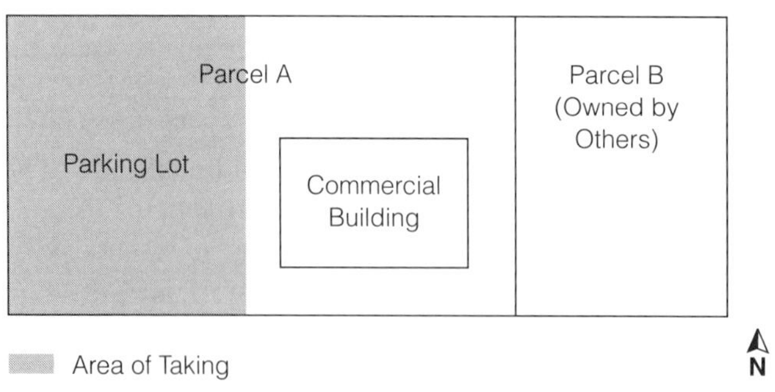

23. *State Highway Comm. v. Speck*, 324 S.W.2d 796 (Ark. 1959).
24. *Arkansas State Hway. Comm. v. Ptak*, 364 S.W.2d 794 (Ark. 1963).
25. *United States v. Dickinson*, 331 U.S. 745 (1947).
26. *Nichols'*, vol. 8A, §16.01[2] (1992).
27. *Utah Dept. of Trans. v. Rayco*, 599 P.2d 481 (Utah 1979); *Jeffery v. Osborne*, 129 N.W. 931 (Wis. 1911).
28. *International Paper Company v. United States*, 227 F.2d 201 (5th Cir. 1955).

By contrast, consider a situation in which 9,500 acres are to be taken from a 25,000-acre tract of timberland. Assume that the timberland is held, along with other lands, as a source of raw material for a paper mill 136 miles away. The mill property and the timberland holdings constitute a unitary use, and are thus a single larger parcel. In an actual case similar to this scenario, the owner's appraiser estimated damages to the mill property "without taking into consideration whether other lands were available for purchase that would in all respects make up the deficiency resulting from the taking." The owner claimed that "the availability of other lands made absolutely no difference in ascertaining that the mill property became worth $46 less for each acre of land that it lost or disposed of." The court found this approach "clearly fallacious," pointing out that "the record show[ed] that [the property owner] actually purchased 100,000 acres of land subsequent to the taking..." of the 9,500 acres.[29] The court found

> [The owner's] contention that it is entitled to receive what amounts to approximately three times the value of the land taken upon the theory discussed above, not only offends the court's sense of justice, but it also offends any rules relating to the awarding of just compensation for property taken for public use. There is no authority for such proposition.[30]

The key to this debate appears to be that the appraiser can consider the availability of replacement land in general, but he or she cannot consider the availability and cost of acquiring any other *specific* parcel in estimating a cost to cure adjustment.

An appraiser who uses the cost to cure method to estimate a proper adjustment must take care to include all the costs that will be incurred. The appraiser must remember that the property is being appraised in its uncured condition. Thus a purchaser of the property in the after situation will acquire it recognizing the need to cure the damage and incur the direct costs of correction. In addition, the typical purchaser will demand an incentive to purchase the damaged parcel. Many appraisers make the mistake of not considering this incentive, or *entrepreneur's profit*, in estimating a cost to cure adjustment.[31]

To illustrate the fallacy of this methodology, consider two identical (or nearly identical) single-family properties (Parcels A and B), each with a before value of $75,000 (see Figure 14.6). An underground utility easement is to be acquired across both parcels. After a detailed analysis of comparable properties, the appraiser concludes that the existence of such an easement, in and of itself, does not result in any diminution in the values of similar properties. However, the septic tank and drain field systems serving Parcel A are located within the easement area and they will have to be relocated. No such condition exists on Parcel B.

The appraiser obtains a firm bid from a local contractor who for $3,500 can replace the septic tank on Parcel A and repair the lawn. The new system can be installed about 30 days after authorization to begin the work is received and

29. Ibid., 207.

30. Ibid.

31. Even when the appraiser does include an entrepreneur's profit in the cost to cure estimate, some condemnors delete this amount from the indicated just compensation before making the property owner an offer of settlement.

FIGURE 14.6 PARTIAL TAKING

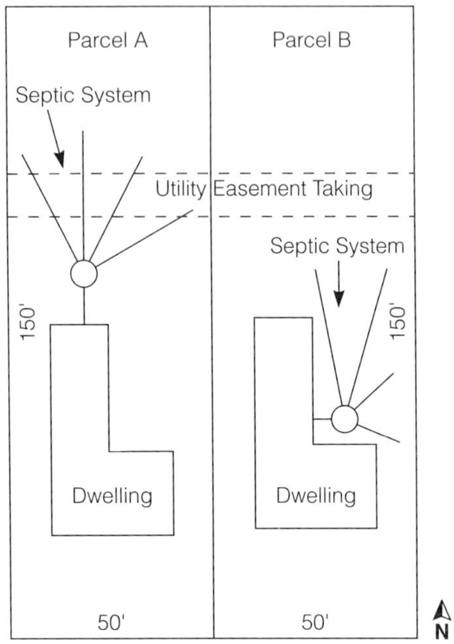

there will be no loss of sewer service during the installation. Using this information the appraiser draws the following conclusions:

Valuation of Parcel A

Before value	$75,000
Minus after value ($75,000 - $3,500 cost to cure)	-71,500
Difference	$ 3,500

Valuation of Parcel B

Before value	$75,000
Minus after value	-75,000
Difference	$ 0

The appraiser must remember that the value of Parcel A in the after situation is estimated in its *as is* condition.

Assume that immediately after the easement taking both Parcel A and Parcel B are placed on the open market for sale; Parcel A is listed at $71,500 and Parcel B at $75,000. Now, a potential purchaser inspects both of the properties and decides to acquire one of them. Which one will it be? Will the purchaser buy Parcel B, which has a functioning septic system, for $75,000, or will he acquire Parcel A for $71,500 knowing that an additional $3,500 will have to be spent to install a new septic system?

Obviously a prudent purchaser would acquire Parcel B to avoid waiting for the installation of a new septic system and the hassle of obtaining the necessary installation permits and dealing with the contractor. This situation is analogous to a situation in which a building contractor offers to sell a potential purchaser a newly completed house or to build an identical house on the lot next door for the same price. All else being equal, the purchaser will take the existing house to avoid the hassle and delay that accompany any construction project.

Returning to the example, it is clear that the damage to Parcel A exceeds the direct cost to cure. The purchaser who acquires Parcel A in its *as is* after condition will need some incentive to undertake the construction project required as a result of the taking. To account for this factor, the appraiser adds an *entrepreneurial profit* to the direct cost to cure, either in the form of a percentage of the contract bid or as a flat dollar amount. To give no consideration whatsoever to entrepreneurial profit in estimating an appropriate cost to cure adjustment is ludicrous.

Consider another scenario in which the cost of replacement fencing is being estimated. In this case care must be taken to recognize all forms of depreciation in the remainder fencing. For example, assume the property shown in Figure 14.7 includes a perimeter chain-link fence 600 feet long in the before situation. The fence has a replacement cost of $10.50 per linear foot and a contributory, or depreciated, value of $8.00 per linear foot, or $4,800. The difference between the contributory value of the fencing and its replacement cost can be attributed to physical deterioration.

FIGURE 14.7 PARTIAL TAKING OF FENCE

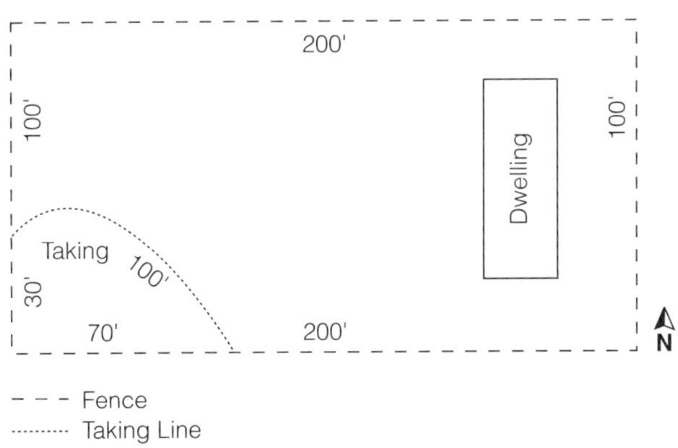

One hundred linear feet of fencing will be taken in partial acquisition. The value of the fencing taken is $800 (100 lin. ft. x $8.00). However, the remaining fencing may suffer from additional functional obsolescence because it has a 100-ft. gap. It will cost $10.50 per linear foot, including entrepreneurial profit, or $1,050, to close the gap. The proper procedure for estimating the contributory value of the fence before and after the taking is shown in Table 14.1.

TABLE 14.1 CONTRIBUTORY VALUE OF FENCE

Before value (600 lin. ft. @ $8.00)			$4,800
After value:			
Replacement cost of fencing (500 lin. ft. @ $10.50)		$5,250	
Less depreciation:			
Physical (500 lin. ft. @ $2.50)	$1,250		
Functional—excess cost over value to reconnect fencing 100 lin. ft. @ $2.50)	+ 250		
Less total depreciation		−1,500	
Total value of fencing—after taking			−3,750
Just compensation for taking and damages to fence			$1,050

The total or partial taking of a private water supply system or sewage disposal system can be analyzed in much the same way. The appraiser must inspect the property closely and interview the property owner to determine whether such underground improvements will be affected by the proposed acquisition. If the system must be replaced, it is imperative that the appraiser determine whether the local health authority will approve the replacement and, if so, under what terms and conditions. Assuming physical replacement can be accomplished, the cost of the replacement should then be established.

It is generally of little consequence how many dollars an appraiser assigns to the value of the portion of the sewage disposal system taken and how much is allocated to damages to the remainder of the system.[32] Normally the value of the part of the system taken plus damages to the remainder property will equal the cost of restoring the remainder system. In some areas, however, it is difficult to estimate the cost of drilling a well so a *well agreement* may be made between the condemnor and the condemnee. Such an agreement stipulates that the condemnor agrees to replace the well taken, at its cost, with one of equal quality on the remainder site. In this situation the appraiser can usually assume that the remainder property includes a domestic water system equal to the one that existed before the taking.

There are literally dozens of reported cases in which appraisers have failed to consider the depreciation in remainder fencing.[33] There are also a number of cases in which an appraiser, applying the state rule, has included the value of the fence in the taking and then estimated a cost to cure damage equal to the cost to replace the fencing.[34] Of course, this methodology results in over-compensation.

32. The amounts allocated do make a difference in situations where the remainder property is specially benefitted and, under applicable law, special benefits can be offset against damages but not against the value of the taking.

33. *State v. McNary*, 664 S.W.2d 589 (Mo. 1984).

34. *United States v. 2.33 Acres*, 704 F.2d 728 (4th Cir. 1983).

Returning to the earlier example and the calculations shown in Table 14.1, the careless appraiser might mistakenly estimate compensation as follows:

Value before taking (600 lin. ft. @ $8.00)	$4,800
Less value of taking (100 lin. ft. @ $8.00)	800
Remainder value before taking	$4,000
Less remainder value after taking (500 lin. ft. @ $8.00 minus cost to cure 100 lin. ft. @ $10.50)	–2,950
Damages	$1,050
Special benefits	0
Net damages	$1,050
Value of part taken	800
Total compensation due	$1,850

These calculations demonstrate how easily the state rule can be misapplied and why many courts and authoritative texts advise against its use. Another common error made by appraisers in regard to fencing is violation of the *consistent use theory*. (See Chapter 6 for a discussion of consistent use.) For example, an appraiser might conclude that the highest and best use of a fenced farm operation is for subdivision purposes and then try to compensate the owner of the property for the fencing within the taking and/or for damages to the remainder fencing. This violates the consistent use theory because, in all probability, the fencing would add no contributory value to the value of the whole property put to its highest and best use as a subdivision. Either the land is farmland, to which a fence contributes value, or it is subdivision land, to which a fence adds no value. The owner cannot have it both ways, and the appraiser cannot appraise it both ways.

CONDEMNOR'S USE OF THE LAND TAKEN

In measuring damages to a remainder property, the appraiser must consider only those elements of damage that are compensable in the applicable jurisdiction and under the specific circumstances of the case. Many jurisdictions use the following rule:

> Allowable "severance [compensable] damages" include diminution in the value of the remainder because of the use to which the [condemnor] will put the part taken; however, diminution in value of the remainder because of the use to which the [condemnor] will put the land taken from others or from use of land it owns cannot be considered.[35]

The foregoing rule has as its genesis *Campbell v. United States* and is commonly referred to as the *Campbell Rule*.[36] This is one of those rules adopted by the courts that appraisers often find impossible to apply in the real world. Figure 14.8 depicts a situation in which the Campbell rule could be applied. Assume that the

35. *Uniform Appraisal Standards for Federal Land Acquisitions*, §A-11, p. 32.

36. *Campbell v. United States*, 266 U.S. 368 (1924).

FIGURE 14.8 USE OF LANDS TAKEN FROM OTHERS

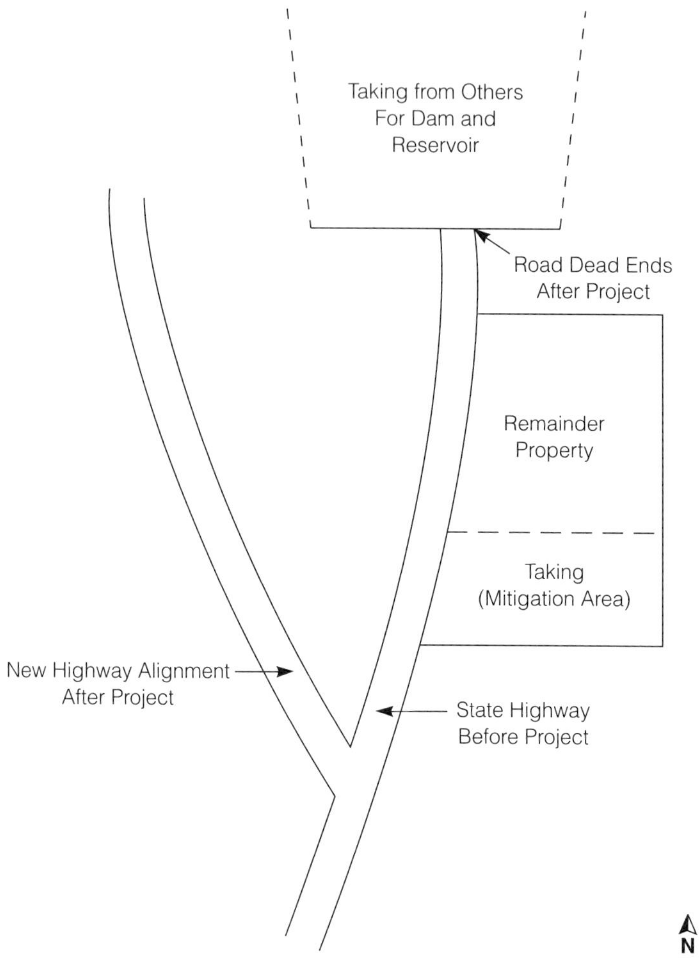

government has taken from others all the lands necessary for the construction of a dam and establishment of a reservoir behind it. The area taken from the property under appraisal is to be used for mitigation of the wetlands destroyed as part of the dam and reservoir project. The area taken will be left in its existing, natural state. In valuing the remainder property under the Campbell rule, the appraiser must exclude from consideration any effect on value caused by the use to which the government has put land taken from others—in this case the entire dam and reservoir. The only damage that can be considered by the appraiser is the diminution in value caused by the taking itself and by the use to which the government will put the land taken, i.e., wetlands mitigation.

Few cases are so straightforward. Refer back to Figure 14.2 and application of the Campbell rule becomes more difficult. Under the rule only damages resulting from the portion of the highway situated on the area taken could be considered. In this case, then, traffic noise might be considered a damaging factor, but only the traffic noise emanating from northbound cars and only when those cars are physically on the portion of the highway located in the area taken. It has been recognized that in such situations "it is difficult, if not impossible to separate one element [of damage] from the other..."[37]

The theory behind the Campbell rule was explained by the Court as follows:

> If the former private owners [of the abutting lands] had devoted their lands to the identical uses for which they were acquired by the United States or to which they probably will be put, as found by the court, they would not have become liable for the resulting diminution in value of plaintiff's property. The liability of the United States is not greater than would be that of the private users.[38]

Of course, this decision was made in 1924, when zoning was almost unheard of in the United States. It also fails to address the fact that few private owners construct dams, highways, or military bases, nor do they operate bombing ranges or nuclear missile sites.

> [O]ne might logically urge that the nine Justices of the Supreme Court in 1924, using their analysis as set forth in Campbell, could not possibly have envisioned 10,000 cars passing a point of land travelling at an average speed of sixty-five miles per hour in one twenty-four hour period. It is equally illogical to presuppose that, had they envisioned such facts, they would have concluded that the damage to Campbell's remainder was separable from the contribution to that damage from the land of others taken for the same project.[39]

Some jurisdictions have taken exception to the Campbell rule, especially when the damages caused by the use of the land taken from the subject parcel are inseparable from the damages caused by the use of the land taken from others. As one court put it:

> For the purpose of determining severance [compensable] damage to the part not taken, the part of the defendant's land taken is to be considered as an integral and inseparable part of a single highway project not limited to the segment of the highway on his land but extending so far as the construction and use of the highway has a reasonable tendency to cause detriment to the part not taken and to reduce the market value of his land not taken from the viewpoint of a ready, able and willing buyer.[40]

The U.S. Court of Appeals for the Ninth Circuit has reviewed the Campbell rule on two occasions—in 1961 and 1982.[41] Commenting on the 1961 case, the court in the 1982 case said:

37. *Commonwealth v. Williams*, 487 S.W.2d 290 (Ky. 1972).

38. *Campbell v. United States*, 266 U.S. 368, 371–372 (1924).

39. *Nichols'*, vol. 4A, §14.01[4] (1992).

40. *State Highway Comm. v. Bloom*, 93 N.W.2d 572, 579 (S.D. 1958).

41. *United States v. Pope & Talbott, Inc.*, 293 F.2d 822 (9th Cir. 1961); *United States v. 15.65 Acres of Land*, 689 F.2d 1329 (9th Cir. 1982), *cert. denied*, 460 U.S. 1041 (1983).

> In [the *Pope & Talbott*] case we noted the existence of three factors that distinguished it from *Campbell*.... (1) the land taken from the condemnee landowner was indispensable to the dam project; (2) the land taken constituted a substantial (not inconsequential) part of the tract devoted to the project; and (3) the damages resulting to the land not taken from the use of the land taken were inseparable from those to the same land flowing from the condemnor government's use of its adjoining land in the dam project. Thus, three elements, indispensability, substantiality, and inseparability, are necessary to negate the application of *Campbell*.
>
> The necessity of these elements is also quite sensible. The element of indispensability assures that the government is being required to pay no more than a private buyer confronted with the same compulsion.... Substantiality tends to assure the existence, in fact, of indispensability, and inseparability tends to assure that the injury to the land not taken does not arise from a use independent of the project with respect to which the property taken was indispensable.[42]

Based on this argument, it appears that the remainder property shown in Figure 14.8 does not have the three elements noted above and would properly fall under the Campbell rule. The area taken was not indispensable to the dam and reservoir project and any damages from the dam and reservoir project would be separable from those caused by the taking and the use to which the government put the land taken.

On the other hand, the property shown in Figure 14.2 might well meet the criteria set down in *Pope & Talbott*. The area taken is obviously indispensable to the project; the project cannot be completed without it. As the test of substantiality is applied to assure indispensability, it would appear that this test has also been met. The third test, inseparability, is also satisfied. Any attempt to separate the damages to the remainder caused by the use to which the property taken was put from the damages caused by the use to which the government put lands taken from others would, from a practical standpoint, be futile.

While strongly advocating application of the Campbell rule, the *Uniform Appraisal Standards for Federal Land Acquisitions* recognizes the conflicting case law on this issue.

> The Ninth Circuit has adopted another rule [in place of the Campbell rule] when the damage may be said to flow from the taking and use of but a portion of the condemnee's property and from the use to which the government puts land taken from a third party neighbor and the damages are inseparable. If confronted with such a situation, it is recommended that you [the appraiser] seek guidance from the agency or Department of Justice attorney.[43]

This is sound advice. If the appraiser has any question whatsoever regarding the compensability of damages that are fully or partially caused by the use to which the government will put land taken from others for the same project, official guidance or legal instructions should be requested. This does not mean, however, that the appraiser must, or even can, accept a legal instruction that is impossible to carry out.

42. *United States v. 15.65 Acres of Land*, 1332.

43. *Uniform Appraisal Standards for Federal Land Acquisitions*, §A-11, pp. 32-33, fn. 95.

For instance, if legal counsel instructed the appraiser who is appraising the remainder depicted in Figure 14.2 that, as a matter of law, the noise damage resulting from cars using the portion of the highway located in the area taken must be separated from the noise damage resulting from cars using the rest of the highway, the appraiser would undoubtedly have to inform legal counsel that such separation is impossible. The law does not require appraisers to guess. If the condemnor thinks it can find an appraiser who is capable of making the separation and convincing a trier of fact of the logic and reasonableness of the separation, the condemnor is free to retain that individual. However, it is the appraiser's professional reputation that is on the line on the witness stand, not the condemnor's.

In the federal courts, it is for the district judge "to decide 'all issues' other than the precise issue of the amount of compensation to be awarded."[44] Therefore, if it is unclear whether the Campbell rule applies to a specific set of circumstances or the *Pope & Talbott* exception is applicable, the best course of action may well be to obtain a court ruling on this matter prior to trial.

VALUATION PROCEDURE

Regardless of the methodology used or the specific rules applied, the estimation of compensable damage in the appraisal must be done thoroughly and in logical steps.

The appraiser's first step is to determine the larger parcel or parcels in the before situation. (See Chapter 5 for more discussion on identifying the larger parcel.) It is important that the appraiser's determination of the larger parcel reflect unity of use, unity of ownership, and physical contiguity. The second step is to estimate the highest and best use of the property in the before situation. (Highest and best use is covered in Chapter 6.) In estimating highest and best use, the appraiser must try to overlook the fact that he will later be considering an after situation. The appraiser should adhere to the principle of *reasonable probability* in estimating both highest and best use and the larger parcel. As a third step in the valuation process, the market value of the property being appraised must be estimated in the before situation, utilizing all applicable approaches to value. In most circumstances, all three approaches will have some applicability. If an approach to value is not applicable, the appraiser must explain why.[45] A client's request or instruction that one or more of the standard approaches to value be excluded is not an acceptable reason to exclude an otherwise applicable approach.

The fourth step starts this procedure all over again, but this time the after situation is studied. The appraiser begins by identifying the larger parcel in the after situation. A property may consist of one larger parcel in the before situation and two in the after situation, or vice versa. As stated by one court:

> It is unfortunate that no witness on either side was asked to express an opinion as to the market value of the two remainder tracts if sold separately.... [I]n the ab-

44. *United States v. Reynolds*, 397 U.S. 14, 20 (1970); Fed. R. Evid. 71A(h).

45. The Appraisal Foundation, *Uniform Standards of Professional Appraisal Practice* (USPAP), 1994 ed., Standards Rule 2-2(j), p. 16; *Uniform Appraisal Standards for Federal Land Acquisitions*, §B-1-8, p. 67.

> sence of evidence to the contrary it may be assumed that the highest and best use of a farm cut in two by a condemnation remains the same after the taking as before, and that its highest value is still as a single unit, [but] this case is different.... The case presents a classic instance in which the remainder tracts should have been evaluated separately.[46]

In the fifth step the appraiser estimates the remainder parcel's highest and best use. In making such a determination in the after situation, the appraiser should specifically consider several factors, including the proximity of the new public improvement to the remainder parcel and the possible existence of special or general benefits resulting from the project. (See Chapter 15 for more information on special and general benefits.) The reduced land area and the change in the shape of the remainder parcel are also important considerations, as are changes in access to the remainder property and the nature of the public improvements to be constructed. The appraiser must not only consider changes in the highest and best use of the property between the before and after situations, but also, "in fairness to the condemnee, consideration should be given to any material change in the intensity of use within a highest and best use."[47] The final step in the valuation process is to estimate the value of the remainder property, again using all applicable approaches to value.

In estimating the value of the remainder tract, it is important that the appraiser consider all observations made in determining the highest and best use of the tract in the after situation and the effect, if any, of the proposed public improvement. It is also important to look beyond the immediate boundaries of the remainder property to identify other forces that could affect the property's after value.

Figure 14.9 illustrates the before and after situations of a single-family dwelling affected by the widening of an interstate highway. In the before situation, the property could be accessed via the frontage road and the interstate or the frontage road and County Roads 1 and 2. In the after situation, the depth of the remainder parcel was only nominally reduced and the traveled lanes of the frontage road were no closer to the dwelling than they were before. However, the highway project called for: 1) the closure of the intersection of the interstate and County Road 1; 2) the closure of the intersection of the interstate and County Road 2; and 3) the construction of a new roadway extending County Road 2 to connect with a new interchange on the interstate. The remainder parcel did suffer from some circuity of travel due to the closure of the two intersections, but this item of damage was ruled noncompensable before the trial.

Based on these facts alone, it would appear that the property in question suffered little, if any, diminution in value by reason of the taking and that there was no compensable damage. However, the appraiser for the property owner testified during the trial that, in the preceding 15 years, County Road 1 had flooded an average of 45 days per year at a point two miles from the remainder property and that during future flooding the only access to the remainder property would

46. *Commonwealth, Dep't of Highways v. Rowland*, 420 S.W.2d 657, 660 (Ky. 1967).

47. *Uniform Appraisal Standards for Federal Land Acquisitions*, §A-3, p. 10.

FIGURE 14.9 DAMAGE - LOSS OF ADEQUATE ACCESS

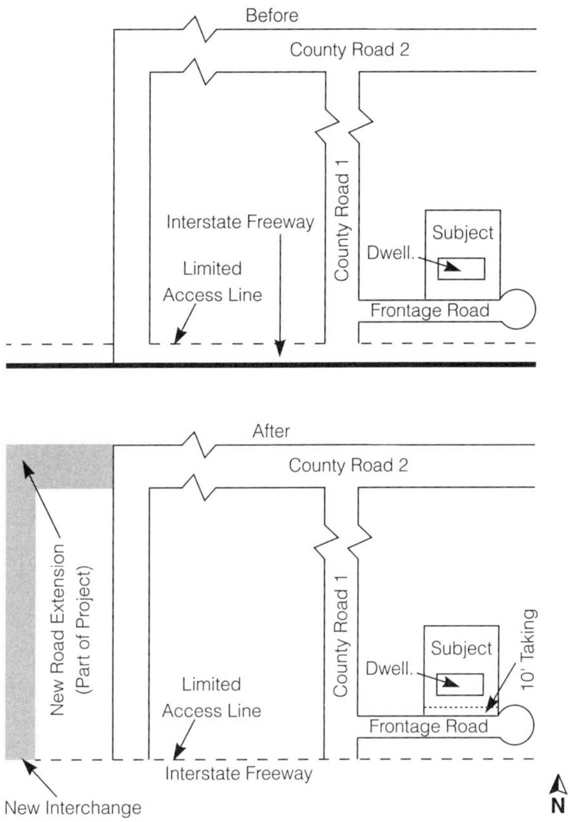

be by rowboat. As there were no plans to alleviate this flooding, the appraiser testified that the subject remainder had suffered extensive damage. After an extended recess of the trial, at the request of the condemning agency, the condemnor stipulated in court that it would expand its project to include elevating County Road 1 to alleviate future flooding.

The difference between the appraiser's estimate of the before value of the property and its after value is the value of the part of the tract taken, as a part of the whole, plus damages to the remainder, if any. Damages reflect the judgment of the appraiser and are based on market analysis, which often requires the use of different comparable sales in the after situation than in the before situation. A damage estimate is not an arbitrary percentage based on the appraiser's "vast years of experience." As L.W. (Pete) Ellwood said:

> I believe experience can teach lessons which may lead to sound judgment. I believe sound judgment is vital in selecting the critical factors for appraisal. But, I also believe the bright 17-year old high school student in elementary astronomy can do a better job estimating the distance to the moon than the old man of the mountains who has looked at the moon for 80 years. So, I find it difficult to accept the notion that dependable valuation of real estate is nothing more than experience and judgment.
>
> I would not give a red cent for an appraisal by the "expert" who beats his breast and shouts; "I don't have to give reasons. I've had 40 years experience in this business. And, this property is worth so much because I say so."
>
> After all, value is expressed as a number. And, no man lives who, through experience, has all numbers so filed in the convolutions of his brain that he can be relied upon to choose the right one without explicable analysis and calculation.[48]

Appraisers must be able to support their conclusions.

> In this connection, unfortunately, appraisers too often use "severance damage" as a catchall. Where their appraisal reports have factual data supporting other conclusions, often so-called severance damages are simply stated as the appraiser's opinion without specification as to the basis for the opinion.[49]

Unsupported damage estimates will be rejected by the courts.[50]

On the other hand, the appraiser must also use common sense. For instance, assume an appraiser is valuing the property depicted in Figure 14.10 in the after situation. After the taking the dwelling is located three feet from the fenced right-

FIGURE 14.10 PROXIMITY DAMAGE

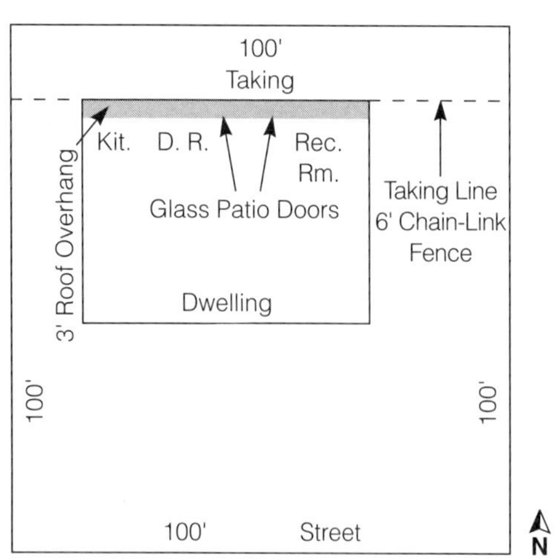

48. L. W. Ellwood, *Ellwood Tables for Real Estate Appraising and Financing* (Ridgewood, N.J.: L. W. Ellwood, 1959), preface p. IX.

49. *Uniform Appraisal Standards for Federal Land Acquisitions*, §A-11, p. 31.

50. *United States v. 26.07 Acres of Land*, 126 F.Supp. 374 (E.D. N.Y. 1954); *United States v. Honolulu Plantation*, 182 F.2d 172 (9th Cir. 1950), *cert. denied*, 340 U.S. 820 (1950).

of-way and its roof overhangs the taking line. The appraiser cannot conclude that the dwelling suffers no proximity damage simply because no comparable sales of dwellings three feet from an interstate highway right-of-way can be found in the market. The appraiser must exercise sound judgment in such matters, whether or not strong market evidence exists.

Some condemnors' right-of-way procedures seem to encourage appraisers to conclude that a remainder property has suffered no damage. A staff appraiser is given a specific amount of time to complete an assignment or a fee appraiser is given a flat fee for the work. If damages (and/or special benefits) are not found, the sales, income, and cost data used in appraising the property in the before situation may still be applicable in the after situation; however, if damages (and/ or special benefits) are found, the appraiser must often collect and analyze a new set of cost, income, and sales data, which is much more time-consuming. Thus the appraiser may be tempted to ignore potential damages. The condemnee's appraiser is often faced with a different dilemma. The condemnee may say, "I don't want you to make an appraisal unless you can come up with damages." The appraiser must guard against all such pressure and be wary of anyone attempting to influence his judgment. (Suggestions for handling these situations are discussed in Chapter 1.)

CAUSES OF DAMAGE

It is simply impossible to develop an all-inclusive list of the potential damages that could accrue to property in a partial taking case. However, some forms of damage do occur regularly.

In considering damages, appraisers must remember that some state constitutions provide for the payment of compensation only when property is taken; others require payment of compensation when a property is taken or *damaged*. Thus in the former case there must be an actual taking of a property right for compensable damages to occur. In the latter case, compensable damages may result even where no actual taking has occurred, but the damage must be specific to the property in question, not a condition suffered in common with the general public.[51]

If the appraiser is uncertain as to the compensability of an item, a properly supported legal instruction should be obtained. If the compensability of the damage is not clearly established under applicable law, the attorney should inform the appraiser of this fact and instruct the appraiser to prepare two after appraisals—one including the questionable item of damage and one excluding it. Then the appraiser will be prepared to testify on this issue regardless of the court's ruling. Sometimes an attorney can submit information on a questionable item of damage to the court and obtain its determination prior to the condemnation trial.

The appraiser must not presume the existence of damages. "'[S]everance damage' should never be assumed merely because there has been a partial taking."[52] "[D]amages are never presumed, and they will not be allowed if based on specu-

51. *Feltz v. Central Nebraska P.P. & I. Dist.*, 124 F.2d 578 (8th Cir. 1942).

52. *Uniform Appraisal Standards for Federal Land Acquisitions*, §A-11, p. 31.

lation or conjecture."[53] Unless the alleged damage has a demonstrable impact on the market value of the remainder property being appraised, it cannot be considered by the appraiser.[54] Some items of damage are considered too remote and speculative to merit consideration. For this reason in a 1911 case a court disregarded an owner's contention that the construction of a railroad across his land would result in tramps using his barn.[55] In a similar 1907 case a court would not consider the argument of a farmer who contended that his laborers would stop work to watch trains go by.[56]

The existence of damages can most easily be discerned when the highest and best use of the property in the after situation is diminished.[57] There may be a complete change in the highest and best use of the property, or the highest and best use that existed in the before situation may have been modified. Generally the most dramatic change in highest and best use occurs when a property is landlocked or left without legal access in the after situation. Technically such a remainder does not have a highest and best use, but merely helps hold the world together. Its only practical use is sale to an abutting owner.

A property without access may actually lack a market value, in the true sense of the word. The number of potential buyers for such property is often so severely limited that the property cannot, for all practical purposes, be placed on the open market. The number of abutting owners to a landlocked remainder property will often have a bearing on its value because these individuals are often the only potential buyers for the property. Another factor to be considered is the value contribution the remainder property would make if it were merged with the various abutting ownerships.

The value of a landlocked property is typically measured by analyzing similarly situated properties which have been sold recently. State departments of transportation often have information on such sales because their highway projects often create landlocked parcels which they must purchase as uneconomic remnants.[58] The agencies then resell the landlocked parcels as excess rights-of-way.

Some appraisers question whether landlocked sales can technically be considered *comparable sales*. These properties are generally not available on the open market and the sellers are under undue compulsion to sell because potential buyers are few and the seller has no legal access to the property.

It is often difficult, if not impossible, to locate sale properties that are physically similar to a landlocked property. In the absence of physically comparable sales, the appraiser must often make a landlock study to estimate the property's loss in value due to the lack of access. This is essentially an application of the paired data technique of sales analysis applied to landlocked properties. Such a study is illustrated in Figure 14.11. Based on the information provided, it might be concluded that the landlocked parcel (Sale 6) would sell for about $1.75 per square foot if it had legal access. In fact, it sold for $0.29 per square foot, indicating an 83% diminution in value due to its landlocked condition ([$1.75 – $0.29]/$1.75).

---

53. *State Dep't of Highways v. Gordy*, 322 So.2d 418, 422 (La. 1975).
54. *United States v. Chandler-Dunbar Water Power Co.*, 229 U.S. 53 (1913).
55. *Louisville, etc. R Co. v. Hall*, 136 S.W. 905 (Ky. 1911).
56. *Yazoo, etc. R Co. v. Jennings*, 43 So. 469 (Miss. 1907).
57. *State, Dep't of Highways v. Beatty*, 288 So.2d 900 (La. 1973).
58. Pub. L. 91-646, Title III §301(9).

FIGURE 14.11 LANDLOCK STUDY

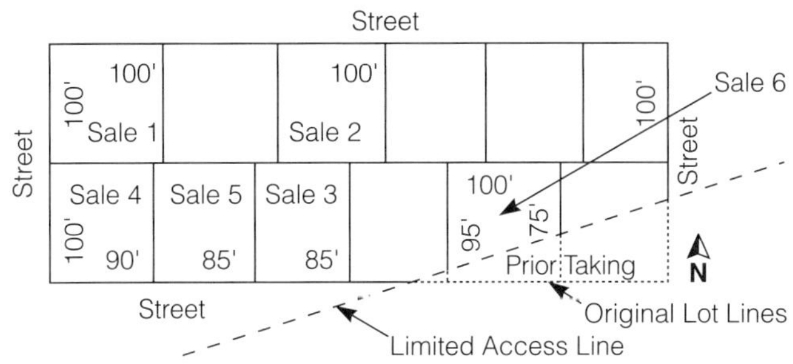

Sale	Price	Size	Price/sq. ft.
1	$18,000	10,000 sq. ft.	$1.80
2	$17,500	10,000 sq. ft.	$1.75
3	$15,000	8,500 sq. ft.	$1.76
4	$16,000	9,000 sq. ft.	$1.78
5	$14,500	8,500 sq. ft.	$1.71
6	$ 2,500	8,500 sq. ft.	$0.29

A number of landlock studies must be made to develop a pattern of value diminution. These studies may show a pattern in the price paid per square foot, total price paid, or percentage of price paid for landlocked parcels as compared to surrounding properties that are not landlocked. It is important that the lands studied are put to the same type of use as the lands surrounding the landlocked parcel under appraisal. If a tract is surrounded by commercial land, which typically sells on a square foot basis, the contribution that the landlocked parcel will make, as a percentage of value, to an abutting parcel with access will tend to be higher. If the surrounding land is residential, the landlocked parcel may only serve to increase the abutting tract's backyard area.

It is quite possible that the details of the appraiser's landlock studies will not be admissible in court, but such studies are often the only basis for estimating the value of a landlocked remainder. Even if the specifics of the studies are not admissible, the appraiser generally can and should testify that he has made the studies and that his conclusion as to the diminution in value of the property appraised (i.e., its after value) is based on these studies.

A change in the shape of a tract due to a partial acquisition can have a damaging effect on the value of the remainder. The change in shape may make it impossible to develop the site with a building as efficient as the building that existed in the before situation. If the property is farmland, inefficiencies may be created by changing the areas of cultivation or irrigation. Generally the effect of an irregular shape on the market value of a property is measured using comparable sales; the capitalized rent loss can also be used in some instances.

Reducing the size of a tract can result in a substantial reduction in the value of the remainder tract, particularly if the reduction transforms the remainder property into a nonconforming use. A taking could reduce the size of a tract below the minimum area required by applicable regulations, or the remaining amount of frontage, depth, or width could fall below the minimum required. If the property in question is improved, a taking could result in inadequate front, side, or rear yard setbacks. A taking could also leave a building with insufficient off-street parking or create a remainder with too high a ratio of building area to land area. If any of these conditions are produced, the effect of the nonconformity must be determined.

Some land use regulations provide that nonconforming properties are automatically considered conforming if the nonconformity resulted from a partial acquisition by a public agency. If no such provision exists, the appraiser must determine if there is a reasonable probability that a variance from the land use regulation could be obtained. The effect of the nonconformity on property maintenance costs, fire insurance rates, and the owner's ability to finance the property must also be ascertained. Depending on the specific effect of the size reduction, the diminution in value can be measured using comparable sales or capitalization of the rent loss. In some instances the appraiser can use the cost to cure—e.g., when the parking facilities taken can be replaced with site improvements on a portion of the remainder not used for such purposes in the before situation.

When the size of a parcel has been reduced by a taking, it is imperative that the appraiser consider the concept of before and after value. Under the state rule (i.e., value of the part taken as a part of the whole plus damages to the remainder), it may be necessary to allocate the total difference between the before and after values to the value of the part taken and damages to the remainder, but it is much safer to do so only after completing the before and after value estimates. If this is not done, the appraiser may be considering the damage to the property twice and thereby duplicating the compensation. A Kentucky case illustrates this potential problem.

> The second basis for damages given by the two witnesses was that, by reason of lack of depth, a portion of the separated parcel had a reduced value for lot purposes. They computed the damages on the basis of percentages of a desirable lot depth. For example, at one end of the separated parcel, where the depth was only 55', one of the witnesses said that the value had been reduced 75%, so he computed that the original potential lot with a value of $1,000 had been damaged to the extent of $750. The trouble with this is that the landowners had already been allowed compensation in the award for the land *taken*, for the land that would have added the necessary depth to the 55' lot. In other words, if the back 75% of the lot is *taken*, and paid for, the landowner should not recover again, in the form of resulting damages, another 75% of the potential lot value. To do so would allow 150% recovery.

> It may be that if 75% of a lot were taken so as to render valueless, because of its smallness, the remaining 25%, the owner should be paid the full value of the lot. But he cannot be paid the value of the part taken and be awarded that value again as damages to the remainder.[59]

If the appraisers involved in this case had used a computational format like the one described in Chapter 3 of this text, or the form shown in Tables 3.1 and 3.2, this error would not have been made.

The taking or alteration of access rights, including changes in grade, physical access, light, view, and air, can also result in damage to the remainder parcel. Because a change in street grade without a physical taking is not compensable in all jurisdictions, compensability must first be determined. A change in street grade can increase the development costs of a remainder property or eliminate existing driveway or road approaches. In the latter case, the physical and economic practicability of replacing the approaches should be considered. In doing so it may be necessary to investigate the use of a curved driveway and retaining walls, the slope of the approach, and the loss of usable site area for driveway fills or cuts. A change in grade can also alter the physical setback required to construct buildings on a site.

For example, consider the before and after situation of the single-family dwelling shown in Figure 14.12. In the before situation, the site was on grade with the street. After the taking, however, the street will be eight feet higher than the site.

FIGURE 14.12 CHANGE IN GRADE

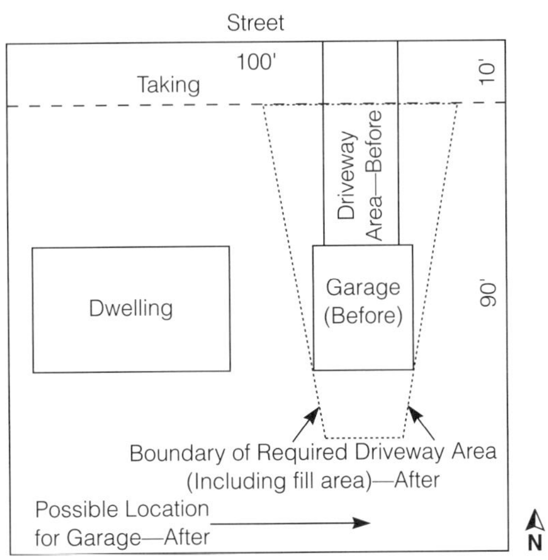

59. *Commonwealth v. Raybourne*, 364 S.W.2d 814, 815 (Ky. 1963).

To establish a new road approach at an acceptable slope, say 12%, the drive must be extended about 67 feet beyond the right-of-way line, which will necessitate removing the garage from its present location. Also, assuming a 2:1 slope of the driveway fill, more than 1,000 square feet of the site must be devoted to fill for the driveway.

The measure of damage in this instance would be the cost to construct the new approach plus either a) the cost to demolish the garage and the diminution in property value due to the lack of garage facilities, or b) the cost of relocating the garage further back on the site to accommodate the new driveway, whichever is less (a or b). Further consideration would, of course, have to be given to the potential value loss due to the greater amount of site area required for fill and driveway purposes and the fact that the site and improvements will be eight feet below street grade. Any loss in value caused by these factors would generally be measured by analyzing comparable sales. If the remainder property were in a market area where a single-family residence without vehicular access would be marketable, the diminution in value caused to the remainder by the lack of vehicular access would have to be compared to the cost to cure items noted above; the lesser amount would be the proper measure of damage.

The severe loss or limitation of access, light, view, and air can alter the highest and best use of a property. Estimating these damages will require the use of different comparable sales in the after situation than in the before situation; thus it can be said that the diminution in value is measured through the analysis of comparable sales.

The term *proximity damage* is defined as "[a]n element of severance [compensable] damages that is caused by the remainder's proximity to the improvement being constructed, e.g., a highway; may also arise from proximity to an objectionable characteristic of a site or improvement, e.g., dirt, dust, noise, vibration."[60] This type of damage is typically measured using comparable sales. Once again, it is often impossible to find recently sold properties that are similar enough to the subject property in the after situation to use for direct comparison. In this case, a *proximity study*, which is similar to the landlock study, should be developed by the appraiser.

The appraiser investigates and analyzes several recently sold comparable properties located near public facilities similar to the proposed public improvement. The appraiser then compares each of these sale properties with other properties that have been sold recently and are comparable except for their proximity to the public improvements. From such a study the appraiser can develop an estimate of the potential damage attributable to proximity of such a public facility.

At times an appraiser may find that there is no price difference between properties near a public facility and similar properties located some distance away. Before the appraiser concludes that no damages are attributable to proximity to the public facility, however, all of the sales utilized in the various proximity studies must be investigated. It may be that the prices paid for the properties reflect no proximity damages, but a much longer time was required to sell these properties.

60. *The Dictionary of Real Estate Appraisal*, 3d ed., 283.

Table 14.2 illustrates a proximity study. If adequate data are available, the appraiser can develop a meaningful statistical analysis of how proximity to a freeway affects the amount of time required to sell similar properties. Assume that the appraiser has studied the data in Table 14.2 and concludes that dwellings close to a freeway can be sold in about 270 days, or nine months. Since the other properties were sold in one to three months, the appraiser should consider the cost of holding the property for an additional six months to be a possible measure of proximity damages. It is highly unlikely that a residential property could be rented while it is actively being marketed so it is unlikely that any income can be generated to offset the holding costs. The appraiser should also consider whether the owner of the property is paying more sales costs (e.g., a higher real estate commission) than the costs paid by owners of property farther from the freeway.

TABLE 14.2 PROXIMITY STUDY

Sale	List Price	Sale Price	Location	Days to Sell
1	$80,000	$79,500	On Freeway	265
2	$82,000	$82,500	No Proximity	64
3	$87,500	$84,000	No Proximity	108
4	$78,000	$78,000	No Proximity	92
5	$67,500	$67,500	On Freeway	272
6	$66,000	$64,000	No Proximity	87
7	$71,000	$70,000	No Proximity	70
8	$65,000	$65,000	No Proximity	91
9	$95,000	$92,500	On Freeway	294
10	$91,000	$90,000	No Proximity	36
11	$92,500	$92,500	No Proximity	102
12	$95,000	$92,500	No Proximity	76
13	$67,000	$66,000	On Freeway	198
14	$60,000	$60,000	No Proximity	94
15	$59,500	$59,000	No Proximity	87
16	$62,500	$62,000	No Proximity	38

It should be noted that all of the property sale prices shown in Table 14.2 are within the same general price range. In any study of marketing time, appraisers must keep in mind that marketing time varies geographically, seasonally, in different price ranges, and in response to the type and amount of financing offered. For these reasons published marketing time studies are notoriously unreliable. They often cover a larger geographical area, include all property sales within a type class (e.g., single-family dwellings), and do not reflect differences in financing. Data on marketing time obtained from a multiple listing service are generally even more skewed. Marketing time is only reported for properties that have been sold; expired listings, which may have been on the market for an extended period, are ignored. Also, once listings have expired, properties are often re-listed and subsequently sold, but only the duration of the second listing is reported as the marketing time for the property. Sometimes sales fall through and the property is placed back on the market under a new listing. This can skew data as can sales that are reported when an earnest money agreement, or sales contract, is signed rather than when a sale actually closes.

If an appraiser is going to use a study of marketing time to estimate an adjustment or an item of damage, the study should be conducted with the specific subject property in mind. Moreover, the appraiser should collect, or at least verify, all the data personally. If he or she does not, the results of the study may be found to be unreliable and inadmissible as hearsay.

It is not always necessary for the appraiser to reach a conclusion as to why the value of a property is diminished by its proximity to a public facility such as a freeway; in fact it is sometimes advisable to avoid this issue. Elements such as noise that one would normally assume to be present in proximity damages have, on occasion, been ruled noncompensable.[61] It is sometimes best for the appraiser to simply demonstrate with market evidence that single-family properties some distance from the freeway sell for *X* dollars, while comparable properties next to the freeway sell for *Z* dollars less. This procedure has been approved by the courts.

> In making the appraisal, it is not only permissible, but necessary to consider all of the facts and circumstances that a prudent and willing buyer and seller, with knowledge of the facts, would take into account in arriving at market value. The testimony of the defendant's expert which is here under attack indicates that he conformed to that formula. He properly and candidly included the facts that the new freeway adjacent to the property, with the attendant increase in traffic and noises, were among the factors considered in making his appraisal. But there was no attempt to segregate and place a separate money value thereon. We think the trial court was well advised in admitting his testimony and that no prejudicial error was committed.[62]

Often a permanent taking is accompanied by a temporary taking in the form of a construction easement. A temporary construction easement, often referred to as a "TCE," accommodates the construction of the public improvement; it is automatically extinguished at the completion of construction and the unencumbered fee interest in the land reverts back to the owner. The fact that a taking is temporary in nature does not relieve the sovereign from the obligation to pay just compensation. Estimating the diminution in value caused by a temporary taking, which can be quite complex, is discussed in Chapter 16.

NONCOMPENSABLE DAMAGES

Some damages are, as a matter of law, noncompensable. However, care must be taken in determining compensability because in some jurisdictions an item of

61. *Fairchild v. Oakland etc., R. Co.*, 169 P. 388 (Cal. 1917).

62. *State Road Comm. v. Rohan*, 487 P.2d 857 (Utah 1971).

damage is compensable only if it is accompanied by a partial acquisition. One example of a noncompensable damage item would be the construction of a median barrier in the center of a street. However, it has been ruled that when a median barrier is placed in the street as a part of a public project for which a portion of the property in question was taken, construction of the median barrier may be considered an element of damage.[63]

Damages that are remote and speculative do not merit consideration.[64] Generally damages resulting from the sovereign's police power are noncompensable.[65] Such actions include changes in traffic patterns that increase or decrease traffic;[66] temporary blockage of a street or highway;[67] and deprivation of access, light, view, and air caused by a newly constructed, limited-access highway.[68] Other items of damage that are generally noncompensable include loss of business,[69] tenant relocation,[70] moving of personal property,[71] and frustration of an owner's plans.[72]

An annoyance or inconvenience[73] such as circuity of travel[74] is often ruled noncompensable because the damage is shared with the public in general and is not peculiar to the remainder property. For the same reason, noise, dust, and fumes from highway traffic are sometimes ruled noncompensable.[75] Because recent inverse condemnation avigation easement suits have been successful, however, there is a trend toward recognizing noise as a compensable item of damage in all types of condemnation so long as the noise has a detrimental effect on the property's market value in the after situation.[76] Moreover, when noise levels reach an unreasonable level, they have been ruled compensable, even when no physical taking has occurred.

> The instant case does not involve a physical taking of respondent's property. This fact does not prevent an award for damages under article 1, section 16, of the Washington Constitution (amendment 9). Generally, compensation is not allowed in such circumstance where the injury or damage is one suffered in common with the general public. On the other hand, where the injury or damage is special or peculiar to the particular property involved and not such as is common to all the property in the neighborhood, compensation may be allowed not as a distinct element of damage, but only as it may affect the market value of the property. The measure of damages is the difference between the fair market value before and after the infliction of the damage....
>
> We believe the [freeway] ramp to be constructed in this case may create an echo chamber for 1-way traffic immediately adjacent to the south end of respondent's warehouse and may thereby materially affect the fair market value

63. *State Department of Highways v. Bagwell*, 255 So.2d 852 (La. 1971).
64. *United States v. Chandler-Dunbar Water Power Co.*, 229 U.S. 53 (1913).
65. *State ex rel. Moore v. Bastian*, 546 P.2d 399 (Idaho 1976).
66. *Commonwealth Dep't of Highways v. Yates*, 383 S.W.2d 340 (Ky. 1964).
67. *Commonwealth, Dep't of Highways v. Fister*, 373 S.W.2d 720 (Ky. 1963).
68. *State v. Calkins*, 314 P.2d 449 (Wash. 1957).
69. *Stipe v. United States*, 337 F.2d 818 (10th Cir. 1964).
70. *Springfield, etc., R. Co. v. Schweitzer*, 158 S.W. 1058 (Mo. 1913).
71. *Pause v. Atlanta*, 26 S.E. 489 (Ga. 1895).
72. *United States v. Easement & Rt. of Way, etc.*, 447 F.2d 1317 (6th Cir. 1971).
73. *Wyoming State Highway Dep't. v. Napolitano*, 578 P.2d 1342 (Wyo. 1978).
74. *Houghs v. Mackie*, 137 N.W.2d 289 (Mich. 1965).
75. *Commonwealth, Dep't of Highways v. Cleveland*, 432 S.W.2d 825 (Ky. 1968).
76. *Roman Catholic Bishop of Springfield v. Commonwealth*, 392 N.E.2d 829 (Mass. 1979).

of respondent's property. This is a special damage differing in kind from the damage sustained by other properties due to the improvement in question. In this situation the jury may consider noise as a factor, if it is a factor, in determining the before and after fair market values of respondent's property. It is not, however, to be singled out separate and apart from all of the other relevant factors in determination of the market values.[77]

ADVANCED PROBLEMS

FEAR

A reasonable fear of danger due to the taking and/or proposed construction and operation of public improvements, if the fear is well-founded, has universally been held to be compensable.[78] However, a fear of danger that is unfounded has met with mixed reaction. Some jurisdictions have ruled that unfounded fear is a compensable item because any factor that has a detrimental effect on the market value of the remainder property is a proper consideration.[79] Other jurisdictions have ruled that unfounded fear is not a proper consideration because the damage was not caused by the condemnor's taking, but rather by "the ignorance, prejudice or folly of those who wrongly conceive and believe that it will cause them damage."[80]

Even if fear of danger is a proper element to be considered in estimating the remainder value of a property, it does not necessarily follow that evidence to prove the reasonableness of the fear will be admissible. For instance, a court in Florida recently ruled that the fear of danger was a proper element of damage, but that evidence to support the reasonableness of the fear (in this case, scientific evidence relating to health hazards) was inadmissible because in Florida such damage is recoverable, irrespective of whether the fear is reasonable.[81]

If the property being appraised is located in a jurisdiction that considers fear of danger an element of damage only if it is determined that the fear is well-founded or reasonable, it is not the obligation of the appraiser to make this determination. This task is generally well beyond the appraiser's expertise and far beyond the scope of the appraiser's assignment. The appraiser's job is merely to estimate the market value of the property under appraisal before and after the taking. If the property reflects a diminution in value because of fear of danger, the appraiser should report this fact to legal counsel, who should, in turn, provide the appraiser with a supported legal instruction as to the proper treatment of the damage item.

Such a legal instruction could take one of several forms. For instance, the instruction could advise the appraiser to consider the fear, whether founded or

77. *City of Yakima v. Dahlin*, 485 P.2d 628, 630–631 (Wash. 1971).

78. *Texas Electric Service Co. v. West*, 560 S.W.2d 769 (Tex. 1977); *United States v. 760.807 Acres of Land*, 731 F.2d 1443 (9th Cir. 1984).

79. *Collins Pipeline Co. v. New Orleans East, Inc.*, 250 So.2d 29 (La. 1971); *United States ex. rel. T.V.A. v. Easement and Right of Way*, 405 F.2d 305 (6th Cir. 1968).

80. *City of Meriden v. Zwalniski*, 91 A. 439, 441 (Conn. 1914).

81. *Florida Power & Light Co. v. Jennings*, 518 So.2d 895 (Fla. 1987).

not, as a damage element if the property is located in a jurisdiction that does not require fear to be reasonable or well-founded. If the jurisdiction requires such fear to be well-founded before it can be considered, the legal instruction could advise the appraiser to conduct a double-premise appraisal in the after situation—one reflecting the diminution in value caused by fear and the other excluding consideration of such damage. As an alternative, the legal instruction could advise the appraiser to assume that the fear was reasonable (or unreasonable) and conduct the appraisal accordingly. However, this latter instruction would have to contain legal and/or scientific support to be accepted by the appraiser.

Much research has recently been conducted concerning the effect on human health of the electromagnetic fields (EMFs) created by electrical transmission lines.[82] There appears to be significant evidence that EMFs may affect human health, but the issue is contested and research is continuing. Market data, however, often reveal that the results of this research are not, at least not yet, affecting the price of property near transmission lines.[83] This may be due to a lack of knowledge on the part of purchasers, a lack of belief in the research results, or a combination of the two.

The appraiser need not decide whether EMFs have an impact on human health or whether EMFs *should* have an effect on real estate values. The appraiser need only determine whether EMFs do, in fact, have an impact on real estate values. The "typical purchasers" referred to in the definition of market value are supposed to be reasonably knowledgeable, but they are not expected to be experts in the field of human health. As additional studies are conducted on the effects of EMFs and the results of these studies become more widely known, it is quite possible that a *measurable effect* on the value of real estate near electrical transmission lines will be identified. For this reason appraisers should not rely on outdated market studies. However, until it can be demonstrated that the proximity of a property to an electrical transmission line has a detrimental effect on its value, appraisers cannot reflect such a diminution in their value estimates.

Some local government agencies have recently begun to adopt land use regulations that require minimum building setback requirements from electrical transmission lines. These regulations have undoubtedly been prompted by the results of some of the health studies conducted. If the property being appraised is subject to such a setback requirement, the appraiser must consider this land use regulation in both the highest and best use estimate and in the estimate of property value. The jurisdictional rules regarding compensability for fear of danger are of no consequence in such circumstances.

ACCESS, CIRCUITY OF TRAVEL, AND DIVERSION OF TRAFFIC

As noted in Chapter 4, a property owner has the right to suitable access and compensation is due if this right is taken. But, as noted earlier in this chapter, an owner is not due compensation for circuity of travel or diversion of traffic. These

82. See Hsiang-te Kung and Charles F. Seagle, "Impact of Power Transmission Lines on Property Values: A Case Study," *The Appraisal Journal* (July 1992), 413–418.

83. Ibid.

seem to be fairly clear rules of law, until the appraiser attempts to apply them in the marketplace and the courts attempt to apply them to factual situations. As one court indicated,

> We do not deal here in absolutes. Circuity of access may be rendered extreme to the point of counting as a substantial impairment of access.... each case consists of assessing a variety of factors, including most notably the existence, availability and feasibility of routes, all in connection with the uses to which the property has been (or may be) put, to determine whether the claimant or his patrons, previously in a reasonable relation to a road system reaching the property, have now been left without such a relation.[84]

One of the problems with applying these rules is that the definition of *suitable access* varies with the current (or highest and best) use of the property in question. What constitutes suitable access for a single-family dwelling may be unsuitable access for commercial purposes. Another problem is that these rules often have harsh results and can lead to an exception to the *before and after rule* wherein all damages are considered.

The harshness of these rules can be illustrated by referring back to Figure 14.8. In this case, property was taken for mitigation of the wetlands destroyed for a dam and reservoir project. The portion of the parcel not taken (the remainder property) was improved with a commercial facility, highly dependent on patronage from those traveling the state highway abutting the property. In the before situation the traffic count on the highway was approximately 10,000 cars per day. Because the new reservoir flooded a portion of the state highway, however, a new highway route was constructed to the east which diverted most of the traffic away from the remainder property. The old highway was closed at a point north of the remainder property. In the after situation the remainder property reverted to a highest and best use for agricultural and residential purposes, reducing its before value by more than 70%.

This diminution in value was not compensable. Access (ingress and egress) to the remainder property had not changed and circuity of travel was minimal. The entire diminution in value resulted from the diversion of the state highway traffic from the old right-of-way to the new highway route. As diversion of traffic is a noncompensable damage, there was no compensation for damages due to the owner of the remainder.

If the government had abandoned the highway right-of-way in front of the remainder property, the owner of the remainder would have been due compensation because the remainder property's access to a public road system would have been unsuitable. Also, in some jurisdictions the owner would have been due compensation if the remainder property had abutted the highway at the point of closure, i.e., if the highway had been closed at the northeast corner of the remainder property.

Often a public project will have a direct impact on the access to a property and, at the same time, will result in some circuity of travel and diversion of traffic.

---

84. *Malone v. Commonwealth*, 389 N.E.2d 975, 979 (Mass. 1979).

It is nearly impossible to segregate the damages to the remainder property due to these individual elements. The rules of compensation for the damages resulting from these combined elements will vary from jurisdiction to jurisdiction and from situation to situation. Often, a court's decision on compensability will hinge on the words the appraiser uses on the witness stand to describe and explain the estimate of damage to the remainder property.

When an appraiser encounters a remainder property that has been affected by a change in access, circuity of travel, and/or diversion of traffic, the best course of action is to request advice on compensability (and supported legal instruction, if necessary) from legal counsel. The worst course of action would be for the appraiser to attempt to classify a damage clearly caused by a diversion of traffic as a damage caused by a change of access. Appraisers do not have the option of bending the rules of compensability to fit their own views of fairness. Appraisers are not in the business of determining what is fair; they are in the business of estimating market value *in accordance with the rules set down by the courts.*

SUMMARY

In condemnation, damage is the loss in the value of a remainder property in a partial taking case brought about by the taking and/or the construction and operation of a proposed public improvement. The appraiser is advised to avoid the terms *consequential damages* and *severance damages* because of the confusion surrounding their precise definitions. In conjunction with the sovereign's right of eminent domain and the act of condemnation, the appraiser need only segregate damages into two categories—compensable damages and noncompensable damages.

A property owner is not compensated for what the sovereign plans to do with the land acquired but, rather, for all damage the condemnor will have the right to inflict on the remainder property. The appraiser must therefore fully understand not only what the condemnor proposes to do with the land taken, but also all of the things it is acquiring the right to do.

Damages are estimated to better estimate the market value of the property being appraised in the after situation. Damages are not individual items of consideration and an owner is not entitled to compensation for each type of damage on an individual basis. Three measures of damage are commonly used: 1) analysis of comparable sales, 2) cost to cure, and 3) capitalized rent loss.

To ensure that all elements that affect property value are considered, the appraiser must perform the appraisal assignment in a logical progression. The steps to be followed by the appraiser in valuing property in a partial taking are:

- Identify the value of larger parcel before acquisition.
- Determine highest and best use before acquisition.
- Estimate market value before acquisition.
- Identify the larger parcel after acquisition.

- Determine highest and best use after acquisition.
- Estimate market value after acquisition.

The damages to a remainder parcel that can result from a partial taking are so varied that an all-inclusive list cannot be prepared. Damages are definitely indicated when the highest and best use of the property in the after situation has been diminished from the highest and best use in the before situation. Not all damages to a remainder property are compensable; remote and speculative damages are universally held to be noncompensable. Many damages have been ruled noncompensable when they are not accompanied by a taking, but are considered compensable when accompanied by a taking. Therefore, the appraiser should not make blanket assumptions regarding the compensability or noncompensability of a particular damage item. Legal counsel should be asked to determine the compensability of any damage item in question.

The major *do's* and *don'ts* of estimating damages are listed below.

Do:

- Follow logical steps in estimating the before and after values of property.
- Consider all the rights being acquired by the condemnor.
- Develop market support for all estimates of damage.
- Use damage estimates to better estimate the market value of the remainder property.
- Use the format shown in Table 3.1 to summarize value conclusions.
- Follow the rules of compensability established by the courts.
- Get supported legal instructions for any damage item of questionable compensability.
- Use common sense.

Don't:

- Assume damages.
- Go on a crusade to find damages.
- Use confusing terminology, e.g., consequential damages, severance damages.
- Consider damage estimates as separate elements of damage to be added together.
- Use the cost to cure measure of damage if the cost to cure exceeds the diminution in market value that would result if the cure were not undertaken.
- Try to disguise noncompensable damages as something else.
- Try to separate elements of damage that are inseparable.

CHAPTER 15

Benefits—General and Special

General and special benefits, like damages, relate only to partial acquisitions. When a total parcel is acquired, there is no remainder to which benefits can accrue. *Benefits*, as used herein, are defined as "the advantageous factors that arise from a public improvement for which private property has been taken in condemnation."[1] There are two classifications of benefits: general benefits and special benefits. Every treatise on eminent domain includes an attempt to define and differentiate between general and special benefits, but none of these attempts has been completely successful. A sampling of definitions follows:

> **special benefits**. Specific, i.e., not general, benefits that accrue to property remaining after a partial taking.
>
> **general benefits**. In eminent domain takings, the benefits that accrue to the community at large, to the area adjacent to the improvement, or to other property situated near the property taken.[2]
>
> **special benefits**. Benefits deductible in ascertaining the amount of damages to be awarded in eminent domain, as resulting from the improvement for which land is taken and peculiar to condemnee's property or interest, not being shared by all the property in the vicinity.
>
> **general benefits**. For purposes of the rule that "general benefits" are not to be deducted from compensation or damages in eminent domain: —those benefits

1. *The Dictionary of Real Estate Appraisal*, 3d ed. (Chicago: Appraisal Institute, 1993), 32.

2. Ibid., 283, 135.

from the improvement which are enjoyed, not only by the property of the condemnee concerned in the litigation, but also by other property.[3]

special benefits. Value accruing to the remainder of a property by reason of acquisition and use by the state of a portion of such property where such value is special to said remainder and not enjoyed by the general public. Benefits may be special although other owners on the facility receive similar benefits.

general benefits. Washington law does not clearly define general benefits. Because of this we have only attempted to explain special benefits and will assume that any benefits which are not "special" may be properly considered to be "general" benefits.[4]

The courts do not seem to have fared any better in their quest to differentiate between special and general benefits. As one court said:

There is probably more judicial discord as to what is or is not a special benefit than in any other area of the law of eminent domain. Where there is an actual physical improvement to the property, such as the draining of a swamp, it is easy to see a special benefit. It is equally easy to recognize, at the other end of the spectrum, a general benefit such as an improved system of highways, since everybody in a community benefits from such an improvement. The difficulty lies in the amorphous grey area between these two extremes.[5]

The *Uniform Appraisal Standards for Federal Land Acquisitions*[6] cites *United States v. 2,477.79 Acres of Land* as its source for the distinction between special and general benefits. That case states:

General and special benefits have been thus distinguished:

"The most satisfactory distinction between general and special benefits is that general benefits are those which arise from the fulfillment of the public object which justified the taking, and special benefits are those which arise from the peculiar relation of the land in question to the public improvement. Ordinarily the foregoing test is a satisfactory one, though sometimes difficult to apply. In other words, the general benefits are those which result from the enjoyment of the facilities provided by the new public work and from the increased general prosperity resulting from such enjoyment. The special benefits are ordinarily merely incidental and may result from physical changes in the land, from proximity to a desirable object, or in various other ways." 3 Nichols on Eminent Domain, 3d Ed., 45, § 8.6203.

It has been held that special benefits are to be differentiated from general benefits where the differences are in kind and not in degree.... We think that special benefits are those which are direct and peculiar to the particular property as distinguished from the incidental benefits enjoyed to a greater or lesser extent by the lands in the area of the improvement. A special benefit is nonetheless such because other lands in like situations are similarly benefitted.[7]

3. *Ballentine's Law Dictionary*, 3d. ed., s.v. "Special Benefits," "General Benefits."

4. Washington State Appraisal Report Guide, Chap. 4-1, p. I-2.

5. *Taylor v. State ex re. Herman*, 467 P.2d 251, 254 (Az. 1970).

6. *Uniform Appraisal Standards for Federal Land Acquisitions* (Washington, D.C.: U.S. Government Printing Office, 1992), §A-12, p. 36.

7. *United States v. 2,477.79 Acres of Land, Etc.*, 259 F.2d 23, 28 (5th Cir. 1958).

In reference to the foregoing argument, another court said,

> This definition of and distinction between general and special benefits, while fundamentally sound, is too general to admit of ready application to specific situations. The difficulty arises not so much from recognition of the basic principles categorizing special and general benefits as in the application of the same to particular factual situations. The application of the distinction between general and special benefits is influenced by the nature of the eminent domain proceedings and the manner in which special benefits are to be utilized.[8]

The current status of special and general benefits was summarized well by Joseph M. Montano:

> Benefits have been classified into two general categories—general and special. The distinction, if indeed one can truly be made, is necessary because in most states it is only special benefits that can be considered as a proper offset against the damages to the residue or value of the land taken, or both. Courts use different terminology to define and distinguish benefits, and for the most part become hopelessly embroiled in an academic discussion of the difference between the two. The Courts appear to have lost sight of the essential thing (i.e., whether the remainder has in fact been benefitted) and rather become preoccupied with a futile attempt to use magic words to distinguish between the two categories.[9]

In light of the various cases and treatises written on the distinction between special and general benefits and attempts to apply that distinction to particular factual situations, the best advice for the appraiser may be to use the same test advocated by Justice Stewart in considering whether a particular motion picture constituted pornography. Justice Stewart said, "I shall not attempt to...define [pornography]...[b]ut I know it when I see it."[10]

Obviously, from the appraiser's standpoint, the best course of action is to prepare a double-premise appraisal in the after situation—with one value estimate reflecting the benefit and the second excluding consideration of the benefit. Then the court can determine whether a special or general benefit is involved.

EXISTENCE OF BENEFITS

The appraiser and the attorney must first determine whether any benefits are present in a specific situation and, if so, whether it makes any difference if the benefits are considered general or special? Because benefits can only accrue to a remainder property in a partial taking case, the appraiser must first carefully consider what constitutes the larger parcel. (See Chapter 5.) Although a parcel may be owned by the same condemnee and may, in fact, be benefitted by the project, benefits cannot accrue unless the parcel is an integral part of the larger parcel. Benefits are not caused by the taking of a portion of a tract of land, but by the use to which the condemnor will put the land taken.[11]

8. *Territory of Hawaii v. Mendonca*, 375 P.2d 6, 13 (Haw. 1962).

9. Joseph M. Montano, *Recognition of Benefits to Remainder Property in Highway Valuation Cases*, National Cooperative Highway Research Program Report No. 88 (Washington, D.C.: Highway Research Board, 1970), 1.

10. *Jacobellis v. Ohio*, 378 U.S. 184, 197 (1964) (Stewart, J., concurring).

11. *Hoyt v. Stamford*, 165 A. 357 (Conn. 1933).

> Confusion has been expressed by some over the seeming inconsistency between the so-called "no project enhancement rule" and the rule that special benefits to the remainder resulting from the project (a kind of project enhancement) are to be offset against compensation. While the confusion can be overcome by a careful analysis of the case law and legal principles involved, a shortcut, rule-of-thumb solution would be to think of the "no project enhancement rule" as the rule to be applied when appraising the property in the "before" position, whether it be a whole or partial taking, and the offsetting of special benefits rule as the rule to be applied when appraising the remainder in a partial taking.[12]

The "no project enhancement rule" is discussed in Chapter 6. It should be noted that project enhancement, which is a proper consideration in the after situation, may be composed of general benefits, special benefits, or a combination of the two. Thus it may be necessary, depending on the jurisdiction, to allocate the beneficial effects of project enhancement between special and general benefits and to consider only the special benefits in estimating the value of the property in the after situation. In considering the presence of benefits, the appraiser must be sure to adhere to the scope of the project rule, which is also covered in Chapter 6.

RULES OF SETOFF

The identification and classification of benefits are important because different jurisdictions have different benefit setoff rules. Five separate benefit setoff rules are currently used by various jurisdictions in the United States. The five basic rules are:

Rule 1. Benefits, whether special or general, cannot be considered.

Rule 2. Special benefits only can be offset against damages to the residue, but not against the value of the land taken.

Rule 3. Special benefits and general benefits can be offset against damages to the residue, but not against the value of the land taken.

Rule 4. Special benefits can be offset against both the damages to the residue and the value of the land taken.

Rule 5. Special and general benefits can be offset against both damages to the residue and the value of the land taken.[13]

Attempts have been made to classify each jurisdiction under one of these five rules. However, there is so much conflicting case law and statute law regarding the offsetting of benefits in some jurisdictions that a precise and totally accurate list cannot be prepared. As the following comments on the federal law of offsetting benefits illustrate, there is much confusion on this subject.

12. *Uniform Appraisal Standards for Federal Land Acquisitions*, §A-12, pp. 38-39.

13. *Recognition of Benefits in Highway Valuation Cases*, 3.

> A controversial setoff question relates to the character of benefits that may be considered. Too frequently it is loosely stated, on the basis of dicta removed from context, that only special benefits may be considered, and general benefits must be excluded. It is the federal view that such position is supportable only if special benefits encompass all real and direct project benefits, and general benefits are equated to nonproject-related value appreciation.[14]
>
> *Federal Rule.*—The federal rule holds that benefits may be offset against the part taken and damages to the remainder. "In arriving at just compensation an offset should be made against the value of the thing taken, and the damage to the remainder, whatever enhancement in value may have resulted from the public work requiring the taking." (*Dick v. United States*, 169 F.Supp. 491).[15]
>
> ...the Supreme Court of the United States...[has] held that only special benefits may be constitutionally setoff.[16]

The 1973 edition of the *Uniform Appraisal Standards for Federal Land Acquisitions* states:

> Under federal law benefits must be considered and they are nonetheless to be offset even though the same benefits are enjoyed by other lands having the same relationship to the project.
>
> While there are cases in which distinctions are attempted to be drawn between "general" and "special" benefits, the Department of Justice has urged in several briefs filed in federal appellate courts that the attempted distinction only obscures rather than clarifies the issue and is of little practical significance.[17]

However, the subsequent edition of this text states:

> It is established Federal law that, in the case of a partial taking, the just compensation payable by the United States should be reduced by *special benefits* to the remainder which are capable of present estimate and reasonable computation.
>
> The law makes a distinction between "general" and "special" benefits, and provides that only "special" benefits may be set off against compensation.[18]

and later, in footnote 107,

> The prior edition of these Standards urged the position that all benefits, without distinction, should be set off against compensation. The courts have not agreed with that position, however, and continue to distinguish between general and special benefits, allowing an offset for the latter only.

With this apparent change in posture on the part of the Justice Department, it now seems clear that only special benefits should be offset against the value of the taking and damages in federal condemnation cases.

---

14. Clyde O. Martz, "The Federal View of Damages and Benefits," *The Appraisal Journal* (April 1969), 206.
15. *Divergences in Right-of-Way Valuations*, National Cooperative Highway Research Program Report No. 126 (Washington, D.C.: Highway Research Board, 1971), 9.
16. *Nichols' The Law of Eminent Domain*, rev. 3d ed. (New York: Mathew Bender Co., Inc., 1992), vol. 3, §8A.05.
17. *Uniform Appraisal Standards for Federal Land Acquisitions* (1973), §A-10, p. 20.
18. Ibid. (1992), §A-12, pp. 35-36 (emphasis added).

Nevertheless, some state jurisdictions still allow the offsetting of general benefits. Thus legal counsel must decide where the weight of authority lies and advise the appraiser as to whether general benefits can or cannot be offset against the taking and/or damages. The Justice Department's new apparent posture in regard to the offsetting of general benefits suggests that no jurisdiction currently follows Rule 5, so it can be said that only the first four rules enumerated above are currently in use.

Table 15.1, which is presented at the end of this section, attempts to classify each jurisdiction by the benefit offset rule that is most prevalent there. Because exceptions and conflicting case law exist in these jurisdictions, it would be unwise to determine the applicable rule based solely on the information in Table 15.1. Applicable case law, statutory law, and constitutional law should be thoroughly researched.

A unique statute relating to condemnation and special benefits was adopted by the state of Washington in 1974.[19] It provided that, if the condemnor is asserting special benefits, the owner of the property has two options: 1) to proceed with the condemnation trial to its conclusion allowing the trier of fact to consider both the value of the taking and damages and to offset these by the special benefits; or 2) to proceed with the trial under the conditions that neither the condemnor nor the condemnee can present evidence in regard to any special benefits and that the trier of fact cannot consider any special benefits.

If the second option is selected, the owner must agree to allow the condemnor to place a lien on the remainder property in the amount of the just compensation found by the trier of fact. Selection of this option "is subject to the consent by the property owner to the creation and recording of a lien against the remainder in the amount of the fair market value of any property taken plus the amount of damages caused by such acquisition to the remainder of the property without offsetting the amount of any special benefits accruing to a remainder of the property, plus interest as it accrues"[20] at the rate of 5% per year. This lien can be removed by several different methods: by mutual agreement between the parties, by payment of the lien by the owner, or by holding a new trial within six years of the date of the condemnation to determine the amount of special benefit, if any, which has actually accrued to the property due to the construction of the public improvement.

The stated purpose of this statute was "to provide procedures whereby more just and equitable results are accomplished when real property has been condemned for a highway, road or street and an award made which is subject to a setoff of benefits inuring to the condemnee's remaining land."[21] What is more likely to happen, however, is that a single condemnation will be expanded from one trial to two trials, six years apart.

The condemnor will undoubtedly take the position that any increase in the value of the property was caused by the special benefit of the public construction; the condemnee will hold that any value increase was caused by natural appreciation or other factors. The complexity of this type of litigation is recog-

19. Laws of 1974, 1st Ex. Sess. Ch. 79 §§1–6; RCW §8.25.210 (Wash).

20. Ibid., §8.25.220(4).

21. Ibid., RCW §8.25.210.

nized by attorneys for both condemnors and condemnees and use of this provision in the state of Washington has been minimal. The Washington State Supreme Court made this statement concerning the statute:

> There is obvious inequity in allowing a present offset of yet-to-be constructed special benefits. Some benefits may eventually accrue to the property while others may not. And, the value of the special benefit is, to a degree, speculative prior to completion of any construction project. It is clear our legislature enacted the above statutes and has allowed condemnees to postpone the determination of special benefits, if any, in order to remedy this inequity and achieve more just results in condemnation cases.[22]

Other jurisdictions have also recognized the speculative nature of special benefits (and damages) to be derived from yet-to-be built public improvements. Colorado provides that "any amount of compensation determined initially shall remain subject to adjustment for one year after the date of the initial determination to provide for additional damages or benefits not reasonably foreseeable at the time of the initial determination."[23] Michigan law provides that "... upon demand of the owner before trial, the court may require the agency to acquire that portion of the remainder of the tract which the agency claims to be enhanced if the agency claims enhancement."[24] A state-by-state discussion of benefit setoff is covered thoroughly in the *American Law Review*[25] and in *Nichols'*.[26]

Because this issue is controversial, several publications have summarized the applicable law in various jurisdictions. One source states:

> *State Rules*.—The state rules as to setoff vary as indicated:
>
> 1. About 14 states follow the federal rule that special benefits can be offset against both damages to the remainder and the value of the part taken. [Rule 4]
> 2. About 20 states follow the rule that special benefits may be set off against damages to the remainder but not against the value of the part taken. [Rule 2]
> 3. In a few states benefits cannot be considered at all. [Rule 1]
> 4. Only a few states follow the rule that both general and special benefits may be set off against both the severance [i.e., compensable] damages and the value of the part taken. [Rule 5].[27]

Table 15.1 indicates the benefit setoff rule followed in each of the 50 states.

22. *State v. Green*, 578 P.2d 855, 56 (Wash. 1978).
23. Colo. Rev. Stat. Ann. §38-1-114(2)(a) (1987).
24. Mich. Stat. Ann. §213.73(3) (1980).
25. 145 A.L.R. 1, "Deductions of Benefits in Determining Compensation"; 13 A.L.R. 1149, "Eminent Domain Deduction of Benefits in Determining Compensation or Damages in Proceedings Involving Opening, Widening, or Otherwise Altering Highways."
26. *Nichols'*, vol. 3, §8A.07 (1992).
27. *Divergences in Right-of-Way Valuation*, 9.

TABLE 15.1 BENEFIT SETOFF RULES

Jurisdiction	Rules 1	2	3	4	Comment
United States				X	
Alabama	X				Offset against damages allowed on highways, water and sewer lines, water conservation districts and water management districts.
Alaska		X			
Arizona		X			Benefit offset not allowed for other than municipal corporations.
Arkansas				X	Benefit offset not allowed for other than municipal corporations.
California		X			See Cal. Civ. Code Tit. 7, § 1263.40
Colorado		X			Limiting rules. See Colo. Rev. Stat. Ann. § 38-1-114 (1987).
Connecticut				X	By special assessment.
Delaware				X	
District of Columbia				X	
Florida		X			Setoff allowed for road right of way, canal, water control facilities, and levies.
Georgia		X			
Hawaii				X	Setoff against damage only when taking is for road widening or realignment.
Idaho		X			
Illinois			X		Special benefits have been defined so broadly that they include general benefits as typically defined.
Indiana		X			Benefit offset not allowed for other than municipal corporations.
Iowa	X				
Kansas				X	Benefit offset not allowed for other than municipal corporations.
Kentucky				X	
Louisiana		X			Courts refuse to draw distinction between general and special benefits—each case determined on own particular facts.
Maine				X	
Maryland		X			
Massachusetts				X	
Michigan				X	
Minnesota				X	
Mississippi	X				Special benefits may be offset against damages when no land is taken.

Jurisdiction	Rules 1	2	3	4	Comment
Missouri				X	
Montana		X			
Nebraska		X			
Nevada		X			
New Hampshire				X	
New Jersey		X			
New Mexico			X		No distinction is made between special and general benefits.
New York			X		No distinction is made between special and general benefits.
North Carolina				X	N.C. Gen. Stat. § 136-112 allows offset of general benefit if taking is for state highway purposes.
North Dakota		X			Benefit offset not allowed for other than municipal corporations.
Ohio	X				Case law conflicts with state constitution.
Oklahoma		X			
Oregon		X			
Pennsylvania				X	
Rhode Island		X			
South Carolina				X	
South Dakota		X			Benefit offset not allowed for other than municipal corporations.
Tennessee		X			
Texas		X			Courts refuse to draw a distinction between general and special benefits—each case determined on own particular facts.
Utah		X			
Vermont		X			
Virginia		X			Both general and special benefits have been offset against damages for at least highways, bridges, and ferries.
Washington				X	Benefit offset not allowed for other than municipal corporations. Optional deferment of benefits provided—see text.
West Virginia			X		
Wisconsin		X			Highway condemnations allow setoff of both special and general benefits.
Wyoming		X			

Rule 1. Benefits, whether special or general, cannot be considered.

Rule 2. Special benefits only can be offset against damages to the residue, but not against the value of the land taken.

Rule 3. Special benefits and general benefits can be offset against damages to the residue, but not against the value of the land taken.

Rule 4. Special benefits can be offset against both the damages to the residue and the value of the land taken.

An article in *Condemnation Appraisal Practice* reaches the following conclusions:[28]

Rule	No. of Jurisdictions
No offset allowed. [Rule 1]	4
Offset allowed against damages only. [Rule 2]	18
Offset allowed against taking and damages. [Rule 4]	10
Offset allowed, but not definite against what element	17

Another text concludes that in two jurisdictions "...neither general nor special benefits can be considered for setoff purposes"; in eight jurisdictions consideration is given to "...both general and special benefits for setoff purposes"; in 16 jurisdictions "...special benefits may be setoff against both the value of the part taken and damages to the remainder"; and "...special benefits may be setoff only against the damages to the remainder" in 29 jurisdictions.[29] The rules applicable in various jurisdictions are summarized in Table 15.1, which indicates that 4 jurisdictions follow Rule 1, 26 follow Rule 2, 4 follow Rule 3, and 18 follow Rule 4. The applicable benefit setoff rule will often dictate the format that the appraiser must use in reporting value conclusions (see Chapter 3).

REASONING FOR RULES

The various setoff rules in existence today have evolved from constitutional law, statute law, and case law. A detailed discussion of why various jurisdictions have adopted one of the five rules is beyond the scope of this work but a general understanding of their reasoning can be useful to the appraiser.

Rule 1. *Benefits, whether special or general, cannot be considered.* This rule originates with provisions in many state constitutions which hold that private property cannot be taken or damaged without the payment of just compensation. In some of these jurisdictions, the courts have historically ruled that just compensation must be paid in money, so the receipt of a benefit by the landowner cannot be substituted. In other jurisdictions, constitutional provisions exclude from consideration, in arriving at just compensation, "any advantage that may result to the owner on account of the improvement for which it is taken."[30]

Rule 2. *Special benefits only can be offset against damages to the residue, but not against the value of the land taken.* Again, this rule exists because many state constitutions require that the sovereign pay just compensation for the taking of property, and case law supports the position that such payment must be made in cash. In many of these jurisdictions, however, there is no special constitutional provision that requires the payment of just compensation for damages. Therefore, it has been established by case law that, although the property owner must be compensated for damages to the remainder property, the compensation may be in the form of benefits rather than cash because the requirement for payment is not a constitutional one.

Rule 2 prohibits the setting off of damages by general benefits. "Arguably, the

28. Clifton W. Enfield and William A. Mansfield, "Special Benefits," *Condemnation Appraisal Practice* (Chicago: American Institute of Real Estate Appraisers, 1961), 207–222.

29. George L. Schmutz, *Condemnation Appraisal Handbook*, rev., Edwin M. Rams, ed. (Englewood Cliffs, N.J.: Prentice-Hall, Inc., 1963), 133–134.

30. Iowa Const., Art. I. §18.

setoff of general benefits denies the condemnee the constitutional guarantee of just compensation since he is singled out and deprived of a share in the increased prosperity of his fellow citizens merely because the public happens to want a portion of his land. The condemnee pays in taxation for his share of general benefits, just as other members of the public, and therefore, is entitled to receive his fair portion of the general advantages brought about by a public improvement."[31]

Rule 3. *Special benefits and general benefits can be offset against damages to the residue, but not against the value of the land taken.* This rule is similar to Rule 2, but it provides that general as well as special benefits may be offset against damages. In jurisdictions that follow this rule it is argued that general benefits do, in fact, reduce the damage suffered by a property owner and, as long as the owner's pecuniary position after the taking is equal to, or better than, the position held before the taking, the constitutional mandate of just compensation has been met.

Rule 4. *Special benefits can be offset against both the damages to the residue and the value of the land taken.* This rule is often referred to as the *before and after rule* or the *federal rule.* (see Chapter 3). The rule exists simply because it ensures that the property owner is in exactly the same monetary position in the after situation as in the before situation. The constitutions of jurisdictions using this rule have generally been interpreted as not necessarily requiring the actual payment of just compensation in cash; rather, they require that the property owner be in as good a position monetarily after the taking as he or she was before. In some states a special benefit assessment may be levied against a remainder property. In such cases great care must be exercised not to offset damages with benefits in the condemnation action and subsequently assess the same property for the same benefit. A Connecticut court has held that if the owner's remaining land has a value greater than its before value, the owner may be liable to the state for the difference.[32]

Rule 5. *Special and general benefits can be offset against both damages to the residue and the value of the land taken.* This rule is similar to Rule 4, but it holds that both general and special benefits may be offset against the taking and damages. As noted previously, this rule does not appear applicable in any jurisdiction. The U.S. Department of Justice is taking the position that general benefits cannot be used as an offset.

GENERAL BENEFITS

A complete list of general benefits cannot be prepared because the specific circumstances of each partial taking will differ. Often a benefit may be ruled as general in one instance and special in another. For example, improved drainage has been ruled both a general benefit and a special benefit.[33] Similarly, Arizona, Vermont, and Missouri have ruled that an increase in traffic is not a special benefit, but a New York court ruled such an increase to be a special benefit.[34] It is

31. *Nichols'*, vol. 3, §8A.05 (1992).

32. *Hanson v. Commissioner of Transp.*, 408 A.2d 8 (Conn. 1979).

33. *Portland, Oregon City Ry. Co. v. Penny*, 158 P. 404 (Ore. 1916); *State v. Cady*, 400 S.W.2d 481 (Mo. 1965).

34. *Phoenix Title and Trust Co. v. State*, 425 P.2d 434 (Ariz. 1967); *Howe v. State Highway Bd.*, 187 A.2d 342 (Vt. 1963); *State Highway Comm'n v. Parker*, 387 S.W.2d 505 (Mo. 1965); and *Vanech v. State*, 270 N.Y.S.2d 357 (N.Y. 1966).

interesting to note that in some cases an increase in traffic that creates a benefit must be considered, but when the increase in traffic has a detrimental effect on property value the damage is generally considered to be noncompensable.[35]

General benefits are those that accrue to an entire neighborhood or community and have a beneficial effect on the value of properties not subject to a taking or damage as well as the properties that have been taken or damaged. A typical example of a general benefit is the construction of an interstate highway. The construction will generally have a beneficial effect on property values in the neighborhood because the highway will improve access to shopping and employment centers. This may, in turn, result in higher land values, new housing starts, and the development of new subdivisions in the area.

Usually, most property owners in the area will contribute no land to the highway project, nor will they be damaged by it; however, they will share in the benefits created by the project. Other property owners will have their lands taken or damaged. It is often argued that because the public improvement is being paid for with tax dollars, the owner whose land is damaged should not have the damage reduced by the amount of general benefit he will receive because the owner has already paid for the benefit by paying taxes. Figure 15.1 illustrates the situation described. In most circumstances, the benefits received by any property owner in the area will be classified as general.

SPECIAL BENEFITS

In the situation depicted in Figure 15.1 none of the properties were specially benefitted, but this is not always the case. Properties that abut the roadway may receive a greater benefit than the community as a whole. This benefit must, of

FIGURE 15.1 GENERAL BENEFITS

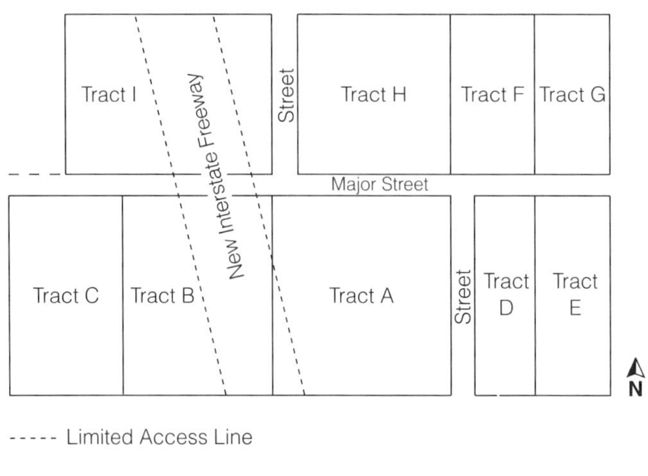

35. *Iowa State Highway Commission v. Smith*, 82 N.W.2d 755 (Iowa 1957).

course, accrue from the construction of the roadway, not from the taking. Special benefits are particularly likely to accrue if an interchange is part of the improvement project, as depicted in Figure 15.2. In this instance, it could be said that

FIGURE 15.2 GENERAL AND SPECIAL BENEFITS

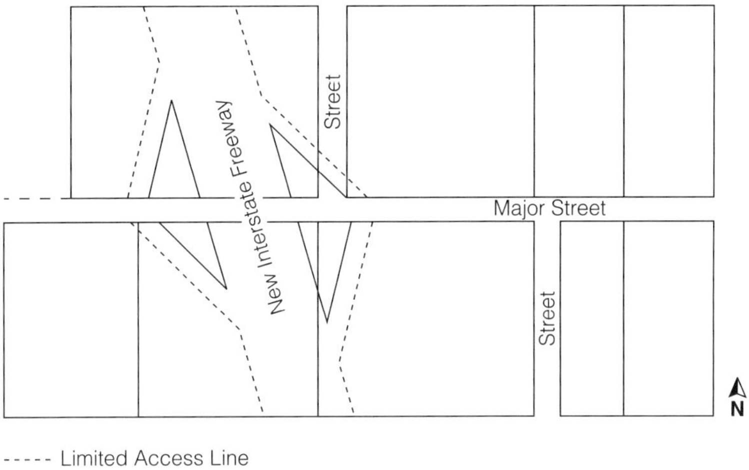

construction of the roadway creates a general benefit, while construction of the interchange ramps results in a special benefit to some of the properties in the immediate vicinity. Thus, these properties may receive both general and special benefits. Situations of this nature illustrate why the courts are reluctant to distinguish between special and general benefits.

Figures 15.3 and 15.4 illustrate special benefits caused by improved drainage. In the before situation, the property in Figure 15.3 might be inundated on occasion by surface water runoff. The remainder parcel to the right of the proposed road construction, however, could be protected from future inundation because the roadway would dam up the water runoff.

FIGURE 15.3 SPECIAL BENEFITS

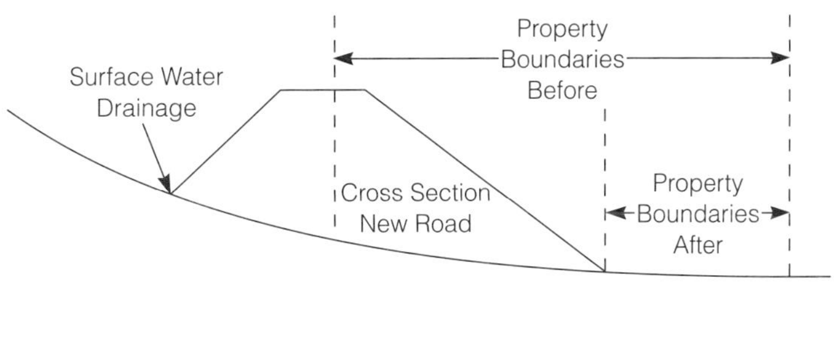

Figure 15.4 Special Benefits

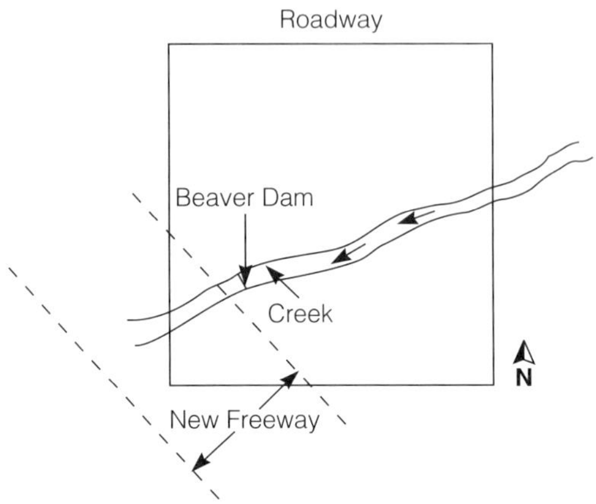

Figure 15.4 depicts an actual situation concerning a property owner who continually removed a beaver dam from his property because it backed up water and caused severe flooding. However, each time the beavers would rebuild the dam and flooding would reoccur. Because of the periodic flooding, the property's highest and best use was for seasonal pasture; if the property did not flood, its highest and best use would have been for subdivision purposes.

As part of state highway construction project, the state was required to place a culvert under the roadway large enough to accommodate maximum water flow from the creek. To accomplish this the state had to remove the beaver dam and to take measures to see that the dam was not reconstructed. The state trapped all of the beavers in the area and relocated them to a different stream some distance away from the existing dam. This action eliminated the flooding of the property in question and changed its highest and best use from seasonal pasture in the before situation to subdivision land in the after situation. The remainder property clearly received a special benefit.

Figure 15.5 depicts another situation with the potential for special benefits. The property will have more than 450 feet of road frontage in the after situation, as compared to 150 feet of road frontage prior to the taking. The increased frontage could increase the utility of the site substantially, depending on its highest and best use.

Figure 15.6 illustrates the taking of a portion of a property for construction of a highway. In this case the property might receive special benefits due to an increase in its marketability and a change in its highest and best use. In the before situation, the property was zoned for low-density residential and farm use, while in the after situation it is, or could be, zoned for multifamily use. This situation is quite similar to the problem appraisers often face when trying to predict the reasonable probability of rezoning in the before situation (see Chapter 7).

FIGURE 15.5 SPECIAL BENEFITS

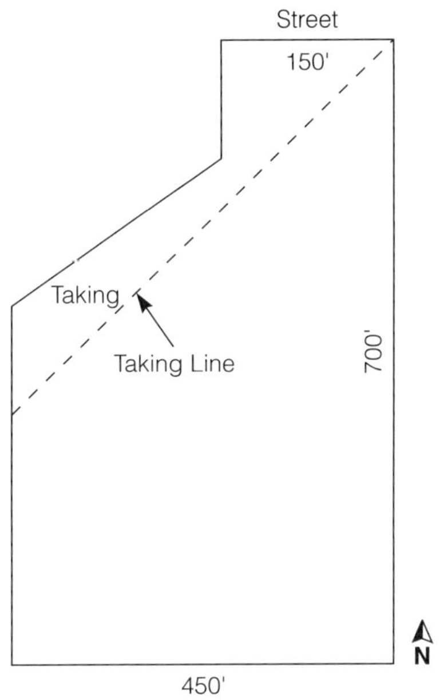

FIGURE 15.6 SPECIAL BENEFITS

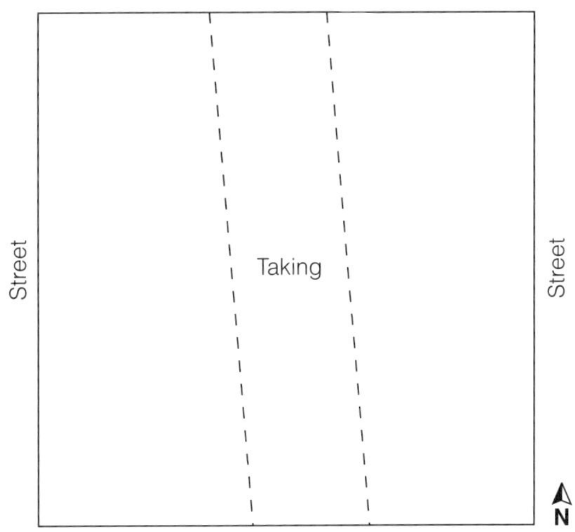

A situation like this one, concerned with the probability of rezoning in the after situation, can often be resolved with greater certainty than the probability of rezoning in the before situation. This is true for two reasons. First, a highway (like most other public projects) has probably been in the planning stages for years and the property in question, although still zoned for low-density residential and farm use, may be designated for multifamily use in the local government's comprehensive plan, which will also designate the location of the long-planned public improvement. Second, a review of the planning commission actions may reveal a definite pattern, indicating that the planning commission tends to zone land abutting an interstate highway or other public facility for multifamily use so the area can be used as a buffer between the highway and surrounding lower-density uses.

A special benefit may also accrue when a taking creates a corner lot from what was originally an inside lot. Consider the before and after situation of a commercial property depicted in Figure 15.7. Under these circumstances, the highest and best use of the site may remain commercial in both the before and after situations, but the site may have greater appeal and utility, and therefore value, in the after situation because of its increased visibility, advertising appeal, and/or accessibility.

FIGURE 15.7 SPECIAL BENEFITS

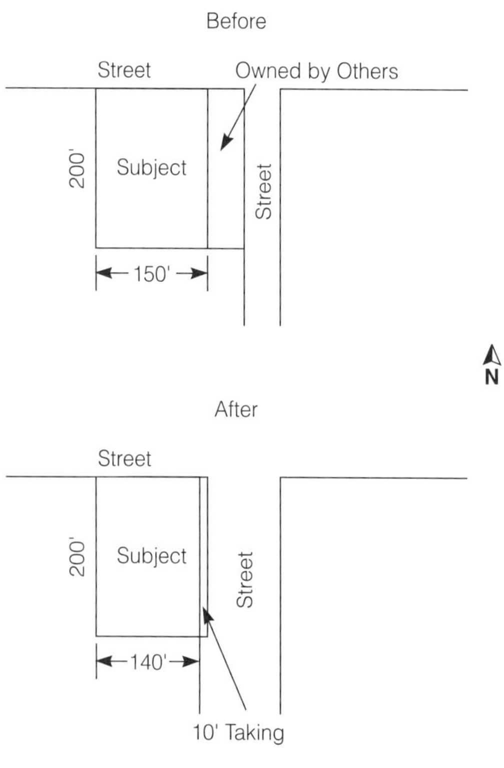

As previously noted, one of the easiest ways to determine that a property has been damaged is when its highest and best use has been diminished in the after situation from that which existed before the taking (see Chapter 14). The opposite is true in discerning special benefits, which may be indicated by a change to a more valuable highest and best use. Figure 15.8 shows the before and after situations of a 20-acre tract. In the before situation, the tract was restricted to one road approach and one single-family dwelling because all other rights of access were previously acquired by the condemnor. Therefore, from a practical standpoint, any highest and best use for the property other than residential use would have to be dismissed as speculative.

FIGURE 15.8 SPECIAL BENEFITS

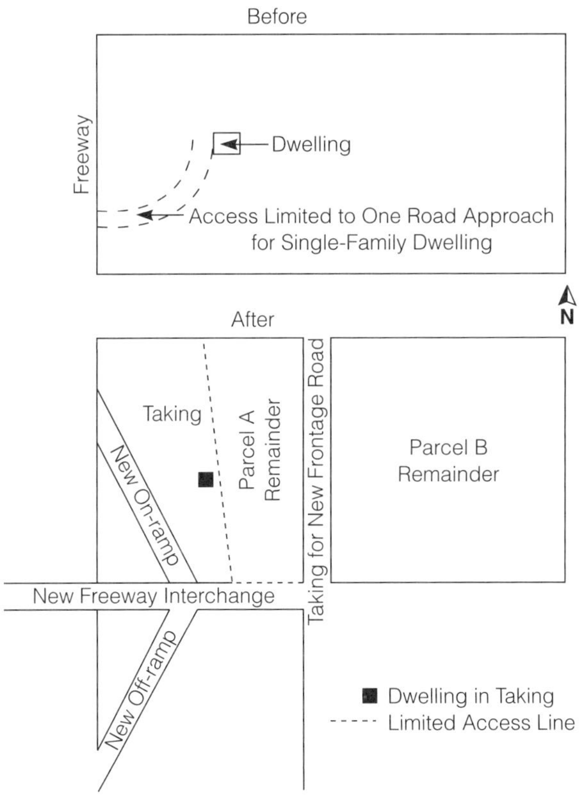

In the after situation, the tract is located on an interchange and is served by a newly constructed frontage road. Five acres of the tract and the single-family dwelling located on the site have been acquired. Parcel A contains five acres and has a highest and best use for commercial purposes; Parcel B contains 10 acres and has a highest and best use for residential subdivision purposes. It is obvious that the property has been specially benefitted. Even under the protest of legal counsel, the appraiser should consider the very real possibility that two larger parcels exist in the after situation—one west of the frontage road and one east of the road.

Now assume that this property is located in a jurisdiction that provides for the offsetting of benefits against both damages and the value of the taking (Rule 4). In such a situation the property owner would likely receive no compensation because the combined values of the commercial land and the subdivision land after the taking will be considerably greater that the property's value before the taking. Market evidence may overwhelmingly support such a conclusion. Difficulties are encountered, however, when the condemnor tries to convince the jury that the property owner, say a little, old widow, should be paid nothing. The condemnor takes her house and five acres of her land and then claims to owe her nothing. What does she want with a potential restaurant/service station site and a potential 30-lot subdivision? *She has no place to live!* In such a case the condemnor's road is all uphill, regardless of the strong market evidence or the predominance of statutory and case law supporting his position.

Figure 15.9 illustrates a special benefit that is often overlooked—the transfer of a financial obligation. The property in question is a farm and, in the before situation, the owner of this farm owns and maintains 10,560 linear feet of fencing. As part of the construction project, the condemnor will be responsible for installing a fence along its easterly right-of-way line and maintaining this fencing in perpetuity. Thus, the landowner has been relieved of the financial responsibility

FIGURE 15.9 SPECIAL BENEFITS

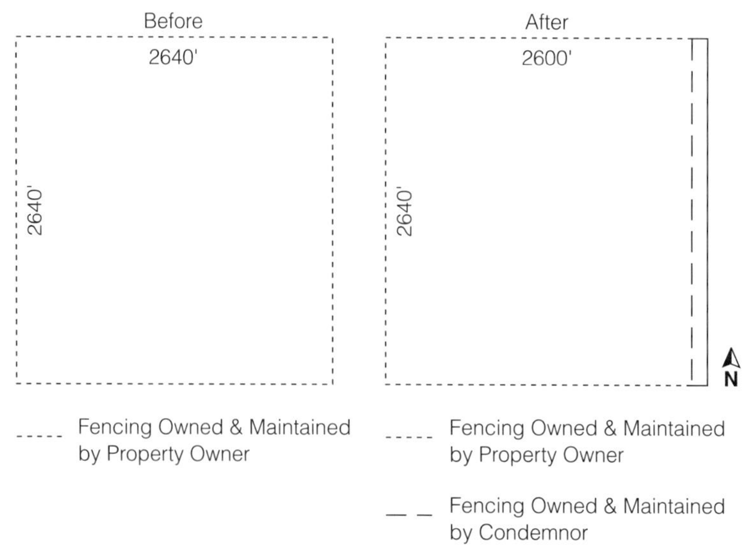

of maintaining 2,720 linear feet of fencing, which could well represent a special benefit. However, it must be remembered that it is not the amount of maintenance assumed by the condemnor that is the benefit; rather, it is the enhancement in the value of the remainder, if any, that has resulted from the condemnor's assumption of the maintenance cost.

The appraiser must also remember that it is not necessary for only one property to receive a special benefit; many properties may be benefitted and the benefit can still be classified as special. As stated by the Arizona court:

> We believe that the following benefits are "special" benefits therefore, offsetable:
>
> 1) The unique benefit—a benefit not shared by any other parcel, and
> 2) The special benefit—a benefit which may be shared by other parcels along the roadway similarly situated.
>
> We would classify as non-offsetable or "general" benefits the following:
>
> 1) The local or neighborhood benefit—a benefit shared with other parcels not abutting the road but in the near vicinity, and
> 2) The general or community benefit—a benefit shared with other parcels in the community arising from the fulfillment of the public object which justified the taking.[36]

A Utah court stated,

> The test is not whether the improvement affects one or more owners by creating special advantages to their property; but whether the benefits are in fact such as add anything to convenience, accessibility, and use of the property as contradistinguished from benefits arising incidentally out of the improvement and enjoyed by the public generally.[37]

For instance, all four quadrants of a highway interchange could receive special benefits.

Figure 15.10 depicts six contiguous ownerships. In the before situation, the street on which these tracts front had no sidewalks. In many jurisdictions, the construction of a sidewalk in front of these dwellings would represent a special

FIGURE 15.10 SPECIAL BENEFITS—TAKING FOR A NEW SIDEWALK

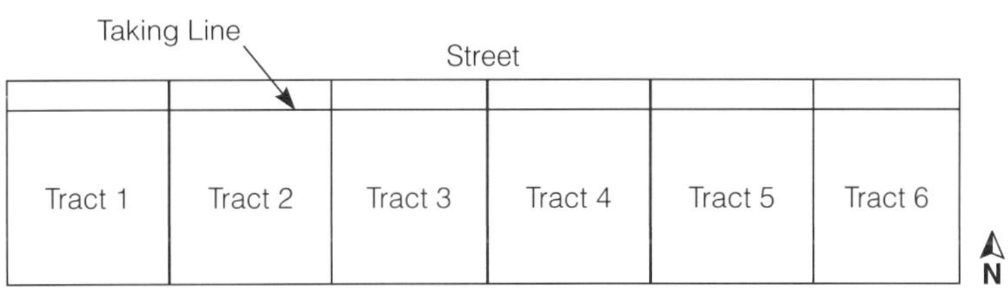

36. *Taylor v. State ex rel. Herman*, 467 P.2d 251, 254 (Az. 1970).

37. *Hempstead v. Salt Lake City*, 90 P. 397, 401 (Utah 1907).

benefit to each of the tracts and, therefore, the sidewalk construction could be offset against the taking and/or damages in some jurisdictions. However, Figure 15.10 could also illustrate another common situation in which a jurisdiction imposes a *special assessment* on each of the affected landowners under the sovereign's power of taxation.

> Special benefits are not offset where the condemning authority has the power to require property owners to pay for the improvements through the levy of special assessments. If the rule were otherwise and damages resulting from condemnation proceedings were offset by special benefits and, either before or after the condemnation proceedings, a special assessment was levied against the same land for such benefits, the landowner would be required to pay twice for the same special benefits. That this denies the landowner the just compensation guaranteed to him by the Federal and State Constitutions has been recognized by an overwhelming majority of the courts in the country.[38]

APPRAISAL PROCEDURES

The procedures used in appraising a property that may be benefitted are no different than the procedures used to value properties that have been damaged by a partial acquisition (see Chapter 14). Here, too, the most common and reliable method of estimating benefits is through the analysis of comparable sales, using the paired data technique. In many cases, the treatment of damages and benefits is quite similar.

If a benefit reduces the expenses of property ownership, and thus increases the net income derived from the operation of the property, the additional income can be capitalized to indicate the value of the benefit received. Also, if a deficiency in a property will be partially or wholly corrected by the construction of a public improvement, a benefit to the remainder would result. Such a situation may occur when the elevation of a roadway is altered, bringing the new, finished roadway closer to the elevation of the tract of land under appraisal. In the after situation, this could benefit the property owner by reducing the cost to construct a road approach into the property.

The units applied to measure damage can also be applied to measure benefits. Like damages, benefits are estimated only to better estimate the market value of the subject property in the after situation. However, in jurisdictions that allow benefits to be offset only against the damages to the remainder, a separate estimate of benefits is needed to ensure that such benefits are not being used to offset any of the value of the part taken.

Some specific points should be addressed by the appraiser and/or the attorney when benefits may be present. First, benefits, like damages, cannot be speculative or conjectural. "A benefit, to be considered at all, must not be so remote or speculative as to be incapable of a reasonably accurate monetary measurement."[39] Second, "the benefit must affect the particular parcel of land from which the

38. *City of St. Louis Park v. Engell*, 168 N.W.2d 3, 7–8 (Minn. 1969).

39. *Nichols'*, vol. 3, §8A.04[1] (1992).

taking was made. Benefits to separate and independent parcels belonging to the same owner cannot be considered."[40] In other words, the trinity of the larger parcel (unity of use, unity of ownership, and contiguity) must be as scrupulously adhered to in a case involving benefits as it is in a case involving damages. In fact, a review of case law on this issue indicates that the courts tend to apply the tests of the larger parcel somewhat more stringently in cases involving benefits than they do in cases involving damages.

While the burden of proof of damages is on the landowner, the burden of proof of benefits is on the condemnor. The condemnor's appraiser must provide market evidence and appraisal report documentation that is extensive and convincing. The landowner and the landowner's attorney will very likely find the appraiser's conclusion of benefits unacceptable and, in some instances, offensive. The appraiser for the condemnor who concludes that benefits exist should also be prepared for resistance from the review appraiser, the negotiator, the condemnor's attorney, and possibly even the head of the condemning agency. In any case, strong market evidence and report documentation will be needed because, if a conclusion of zero compensation is reached, a condemnation trial is sure to follow. When an owner is offered nothing for the taking, he hasn't much to lose by going to trial.

To be considered a benefit, the situation created by the taking must be permanent.[41] Inconvenience during construction is not a compensable damage; similarly, the rerouting of cars in front of a commercial establishment during construction cannot be an offsetting benefit.

The appraiser should remember that project enhancement must be disregarded in the before situation (see Chapter 6) and that, in most jurisdictions, general benefits must be disregarded in the after situation (see Table 15.1). This can be extremely complicated, particularly when special benefits are present and land is appreciating rapidly.

Advanced Problems

The complexity of estimating benefits is illustrated in Figure 15.11. None of the properties shown are restricted in use by a zoning ordinance or any other land use regulation. The properties are located in a rapidly growing residential area. The east-west street shown is the major traffic arterial connecting residential development to the south of these tracts with the central business district and employment center of the city.

The history of real estate activity for the parcels is as follows:

1965	Tract A sold for $5,000 per acre.
1967	Interstate highway plans (shown in Figure 15.12) were announced.
1968	Tract A sold for $10,000 per acre.
1968	Tract E sold for $7,000 per acre.

40. Ibid., §8A.04[1].

41. *Reading, etc., R. Co. v. Balthaser*, 13 A. 294 (Pa. 1888).

1971	Tract A sold for $32,000 per acre.
1972	Tract B (after the taking) sold for $27,500 per acre.
1973	Tract C sold for $28,000 per acre.
1973	Tract E sold for $12,000 per acre.
1973	Tract G sold for $15,000 per acre.

FIGURE 15.11 TRACTS AFFECTED BY PROPOSED FREEWAY

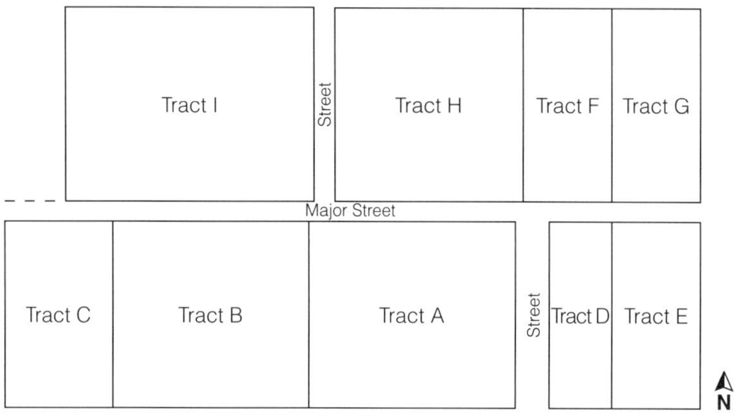

In 1974 several appraisals were obtained relating to Tract H in the before and after situations shown in Figure 15.12. The appraisers were asked to estimate the value of the property as of 1974; they were instructed to disregard any project enhancement in the before situation. Because the property is located in a juris-

FIGURE 15.12 PROPOSED TAKING FOR FREEWAY

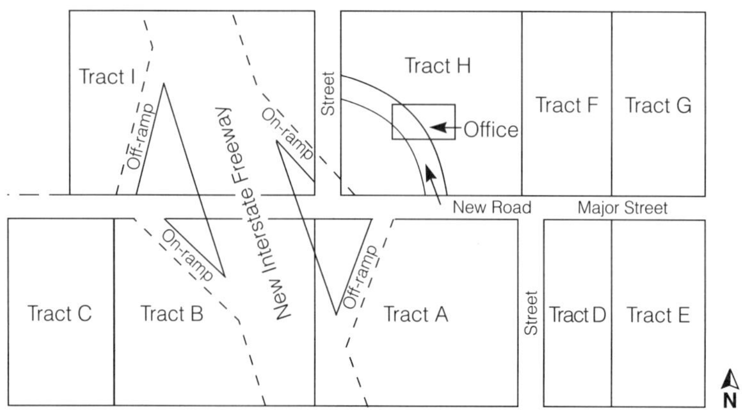

diction that allows special benefits to be offset against both the taking and damages (Rule 4), the appraisers were also instructed to disregard any general or special benefits the property might reflect in the before situation. In the after situation, the appraisers were instructed to disregard general benefits, but to consider any special benefits. The appraisers were further instructed, as was typical at the time, to assume in the after situation that the proposed public improvement had been completed in accordance with plans and specifications.[42]

Using the historical data, careful verification, and price increment studies made in similar neighborhoods with no highway construction pending, each appraiser was asked to estimate the amount of project enhancement, general benefits, and special benefits reflected in each of the sales transactions (involving Tracts A, B, C, E, and G) to assist in arriving at a legally acceptable before and after value estimate for Tract H. Needless to say, the final determination of these questions, and the question of just compensation, was to be made by the trier of fact.

This illustration reveals another problem that is recognized by appraisers and others, but has not been clearly addressed by the courts or covered in most of the appraisal guidelines prepared by various condemning agencies. In appraising property subject to a partial acquisition, the before value of the property is to be estimated as of the date of the taking, as if no proposed public taking or improvement project were contemplated. The after value of the property is also to be estimated as of the date of taking, but many condemnors have historically instructed their appraisers to estimate the value of the remainder property as if the public improvement project were, in fact, complete.

Returning to the illustration, it is apparent that these assumptions conflict. At the time of the trial in 1975, it was anticipated that the entire interstate project, which would convey substantial special benefits to the remainder property, would be completed in 1977. However, in accordance with legal instructions supported by case law, the appraisals in the after situation were made as if the interstate project was actually complete. The interstate project was not actually completed until 1984. Therefore, the benefits that were assessed against the owner in 1975 did not accrue until eight years later.

A situation such as this is probably not so critical when damages are involved because the condemnor is acquiring the right to inflict the damages anytime it desires. Moreover, as previously stated, any inconvenience caused by construction of the public improvement is not a compensable damage.[43] However, timing is particularly important in a benefits case. To illustrate, assume that Tract H in the before situation contained a total of 12 acres and had a value of \$15,000 per acre, or \$180,000. In addition, there was an office building on the portion of the tract taken with a contributory value of \$100,000. The area taken consisted of three acres. The remaining nine acres had a value, assuming the public project was complete, of \$32,500 per acre, or \$292,500. Therefore, *theoretical just compensation* could be computed as follows:

42. *Recognition of Benefits in Highway Valuation Cases*, 8.

43. *Wyoming State Highway Dep't. v. Napolitano*, 578 P.2d 1342 (Wyo. 1978).

Before value:	
Land (12 acres @ $15,000)	$180,000
Office building	100,000
Total before value	$280,000
After value (9 acres @ $32,500)	−292,500
Difference (*just compensation*)	$ 0

Now assume that the remainder property will not receive its benefit until construction of the public improvement is complete, some eight years hence. The benefit that the property will receive at that time is $17,500 per acre ($32,500 – $15,000), or $157.500 (9 acres x $17,500). Thus the owner of the remainder property has the right to receive $17,500 per acre, or $157,500, in eight years. Assuming a 12% discount rate is applicable in this instance, the present value of the right to receive $157,500 in eight years can be computed as $157,500 times the present value of $1 discounted at 12% for eight years, or $157,500 x 0.403883 = $63,612.

So it can be said that the current value of the estimated benefit is $7,068 per acre ($63,612/9 acres), and the after value of the property considering the present value of the benefit to be received in eight years is $22,068 ($15,000 + $7,068), rounded to $22,000 per acre. Based on this premise, *theoretical just compensation* could be computed as:

Before value:	
Land (12 acres @ $15,000)	$180,000
Office building	100,000
Total before value	$280,000
After value (9 acres @ $22,000)	−198,000
Difference (*just compensation*)	$ 82,000

In some circumstances, it could be argued that to take advantage of the benefit that will accrue to his land upon completion of the public improvement, the owner will have to leave his land fallow until the public improvement is complete. This assumes, of course, that there would be no economic interim use to which the land could be put while awaiting project completion. Under this scenario, *theoretical just compensation* would be calculated:

Before value:	
Land (12 acres @ $15,000)	$180,000
Office building	100,000
Total before value	$280,000
After value (9 acres @ $32,500 x 0.403883)	−118,136
Difference (*just compensation*)	$161,864

Under these circumstances it would appear that the benefit is deferred so far into the future that the highest and best use of the remainder is not to hold the property until the benefit is conferred upon it, but rather to utilize it for its highest and best use in the *before situation* assuming this use remains a viable option in the after situation. Assuming its before highest and best use and acreage value, the remainder property would have a value of $135,000 (9 acres @ $15,000). This before use creates a higher value than would be created by holding the property for eight years awaiting the special benefit to be realized.

A time delay has a tremendous effect on benefits and/or damages and this fact is now becoming recognized. For example, the *Uniform Eminent Domain Code* provides:

> *Section 1006. [Compensation to Reflect Project as Planned]*
>
> (a) If there is a partial taking of property, the fair market value of the remainder on the valuation date shall include increases or decreases in value caused by the proposed project including any work to be performed under an agreement between the parties.
>
> (b) The fair market value of the remainder, as of the date of valuation, *shall reflect the time when the damage or benefit caused by the proposed improvement or project will be actually realized.*[44] [emphasis added]

The authors' comment in regard to subsection (b) is particularly enlightening:

> Under subsection (b), the determination of fair market value of the remainder is not based on the often unrealistic view that the improvement has already been completed on the valuation date, but must be computed in a manner that will take into account any anticipated delay before the benefit or damage to the remainder is actually realized. If a subsequent change of plans causes additional damage, the property owner may obtain relief in a proceeding after judgement.[45]

As previously noted, the state of Washington has adopted legislation recognizing that benefits are often deferred.[46] Colorado's eminent domain statutes provide:

> If only a portion of a tract or parcel of land is taken, the damages and special benefits, if any, to the residue of said property shall be determined. When determining damages and special benefits, the appraiser shall take into account a proper discount when the damages and special benefits are forecast beyond one year from the date of appraisal.[47]

The Comment of the Joint State Government Commission on Section 1-606 of Pennsylvania's eminent domain statutes states:

> While the ultimate benefits to be derived from improvements within the part taken may be great, the owner of the remaining property may not enjoy them in some cases for several years. In determining the fair market value of the remaining property, consideration should be given to the necessary time discount, inconvenience and other effects of the construction period, which might materially affect the price which the condemnee would receive if he were to sell the remaining property to a third party immediately after the condemnation, but before completion of the improvement.[48]

---

44. *Uniform Eminent Domain Code*, 1974, §1006, p. 10.11.
45. Ibid., "Comment," p. 10.12.
46. Laws of 1974, 1st Ex. Sess. Ch. 79 §§1-6, RCW §8.25.210 (Wash).
47. Colo. Rev. Stat. Ann. §38-1-114(2)(c) (1987).
48. Comment, Joint State Government Commission, 1964 Report, Pa. Const. Stat. §1-606.

In *Georgia Eminent Domain*, Charles Pursley, Jr. comments:

> In assessing [compensable] damages and [special] benefits, the witness may consider the future damages and benefits from the completed public improvement as they may affect the fair market value of the property on the date of taking. A hypothetical buyer on the date of taking would consider the potential benefit of the public improvement even though he might not pay as much for the future benefit because the improvement was not yet completed. One method for the appraiser to evaluate future benefits would be to determine the expected increase in value in the future and discount that amount to a present value using a discount rate that reflects the risk that the full benefit may not materialize and that the benefit may not be realized for some time. Such an approach recognizes the facts of the real estate market: just after property is acquired for a public improvement, the improvement is one step closer to reality, and a buyer would pay more for the potential benefit although not as much as he would pay after the improvement is completed.[49]

Some condemnors' appraisal guidelines are also recognizing that "[t]he 'after value' is based on the value of the remainder property assuming that the actual construction of the proposed project will not be completed until an estimated future date."[50]

If a considerable time lag is anticipated between the date of valuation and the date an anticipated damage or benefit will actually occur, the appraiser should reflect the time lag in the estimated value of the remainder property unless instructed, as a matter of law, that the remainder property must be valued as if the public construction is complete. If the time interval between the date of valuation and the date of anticipated project completion is some distance in the future, both the appraiser and the attorney should consider whether the estimated benefit or damage is realistic or falls within the realm of speculation and conjecture. If the latter is the case, the benefit or damage should be disregarded. If the benefit or damage is not speculative, the appraiser should apply a discount factor to reflect the time delay before it will be realized, thus considering the current impact of the damage or benefit as opposed to its future impact.

SUMMARY

Remainder properties often receive benefits due to the construction of a public improvement. The appraiser must be aware of any potential benefits and how these benefits are classified and treated in various jurisdictions. There is a considerable amount of disparity among various jurisdictions and, at times, within the same jurisdiction concerning how benefits are treated.

Generally, all jurisdictions fall under one of the following benefit offset rules:

---

49. Charles N. Pursley, Jr., "Georgia Eminent Domain" (Norcross, Georgia: The Harrison Company, 1982), §6-6, 155-156.

50. Washington State Right of Way Manual, Appendix 4-1, "Appraisal Report Guide," p. I-1.

1. No benefits of any type can be considered.
2. Special benefits can be offset against damages to the remainder property, but not against the value of the taking.
3. Both special and general benefits can be offset against damage, but not against the value of the land taken.
4. Special benefits can be utilized to offset both the damages to the remainder and the value of the land taken.

Historically, some condemnors have advocated that both special and general benefits could be used to offset both damages to the remainder property and the value of the property taken. However, it appears that no jurisdiction currently follows such a benefit offset rule.

Both appraisers and attorneys are advised that there are many exceptions to the four rules noted above. For instance, some jurisdictions that appear to allow the offsetting of benefits in one form or another specifically exclude such offset when the condemnor is not a municipal corporation. Appraisers and attorneys *must* determine the benefit setoff rules that apply to the specific factual situation in which they are involved.

Benefits are generally measured by the appraiser through the analysis of market data; this is the same procedure used to identify and measure damages in the after situation.

General benefits are enjoyed by the community at large. These benefits affect the value of properties that have not been taken or damaged as well as the value of properties that are directly involved in the taking. Conversely, special benefits arise because of the particular relationship between the remainder parcel and the public improvement. The fact that more than one property receives the benefit from a public project does not mean that the benefit cannot be classified as special; for example, all four properties on the quadrants of a new interchange may receive special benefits.

The types of benefits that can accrue to a remainder parcel are as numerous as the types of damage that can accrue to a remainder parcel. A clear distinction cannot be made between special and general benefits because the classification of benefits often depends on the circumstances of the specific case. In fact, in several cases, the same benefit has been classified as general in one instance and special in another.

Because many forces affect real estate value, it is often difficult to differentiate between natural real estate appreciation or decline, project enhancement, general benefits, and special benefits. However, because the law in some jurisdictions requires such differentiation, the appraiser may be required to make detailed studies of real estate value trends in areas that are comparable to the area in which the property under appraisal is located, but are not affected by the public project. These studies can be used to develop a sound and supportable basis for the appraiser's value determination.

In estimating the after value of a remainder property that will receive an offsetting benefit, it is important that the appraiser determine that the benefit will accrue within the reasonably foreseeable future. If this cannot be done, the appraiser should reanalyze the anticipated benefit in conjunction with legal counsel. It could ultimately be concluded that the anticipated benefit will be realized so far in the future that to consider it would be speculative. If the future benefit is to be considered, it should be discounted to a present value to reflect its distant date of accrual.

CHAPTER 16

Easements

The ownership of real estate is endowed with a bundle of rights, which may be held by one party or spread among a number of parties. (See the discussion of property rights in Chapter 4.) A right or interest in property is referred to as *an estate*. The most basic property interest is a fee simple estate, the unimpaired ownership of real estate subject only to the governmental limitations of escheat, eminent domain, taxation, and police power. When the bundle of rights is split between two or more parties, lesser estates are created. This is the case when a contractual limitation on a fee simple ownership is created by the establishment of an easement.

An easement is usually the right to perform a specific action on a particular land parcel, or portion of a parcel of land, without owning the underlying fee. In some instances, however, an easement may merely prohibit the underlying fee owner from certain uses of the property in question, without giving the owner of the easement any possessory interest in the real estate (e.g., facade easements, scenic easements). A continuous easement across multiple tracts of land is often referred to as a right-of-way.[1] This term is generally used to refer to easements for roadway or railroad purposes.[2] Such easements are referred to as *easements in gross*, as opposed to appurtenant easements, which are easements used in conjunction with property owned in fee by the owner of the easement.[3] An easement is an estate which may be severed from the bundle of rights and can be defined in terms of time and space.

1. Note that in certain sections of the country, the term *right-of-way* is used whether the right is owned in fee or held through an easement.
2. *The Dictionary of Real Estate Appraisal*, 3d ed. (Chicago: Appraisal Institute, 1993), 311.
3. *Black's Law Dictionary*, abr. 6th ed., s.v. "easement, appurtenant."

EASEMENT DURATION

An easement may be temporary in nature, with either a specific or an indefinite termination date. One common temporary easement with a specific termination date is a temporary construction easement, often referred to as a TCE. This type of easement is necessary when more space is needed to construct a facility than will be needed to operate and maintain the facility after construction is completed. Although such easements generally have a specific termination date, some temporary easements have an indefinite termination date. For example, an easement for ingress and egress through a tract of land for the purpose of harvesting timber on an adjoining tract will often terminate when the harvest is completed.

Some roadway easements terminate upon abandonment of the roadway. However, the courts generally regard such an abandonment clause as having little, if any, bearing on the amount of compensation due a fee owner for the taking of the easement.

> A condemnor cannot demand a perpetual easement with one breath and insist with the next that he be excused from paying full compensation for the perpetual easement on the ground that there is a bare possibility that he may abandon the perpetual easement on some uncertain day before the last lingering echo of Gabriel's horn trembles into ultimate silence. This is true because the law of eminent domain deems the possibility of the abandonment of a perpetual easement by non-user [sic] so remote and improbable it will not allow the contingency to be taken into consideration in determining the value of the easement.[4]

For this same reason, the courts generally rule that a fee ownership encumbered by a perpetual road easement has little or no market value.[5]

Permanent, or perpetual, easements are generally acquired for electrical transmission lines; sewer, water, and other utility lines; highways; and other public facilities. Often an easement will have both temporary and permanent elements, as is the case with many sewer line easements. If an easement width of 40 feet is required for installation of a sewer line, but only 25 feet is required for its maintenance and operation, a 15-ft. temporary construction easement is acquired in addition to a 25-ft. permanent easement.

EASEMENT OCCUPANCY

In terms of space, an easement may be defined as subsurface, surface, or overhead. Subsurface easements are required to install sewer lines, water lines, communication lines, and tunnels; common surface easements allow for drainage, flowage, railroads, and highways. Aviation, air, noise, and line-of-sight easements are overhead easements. Some easements may involve the rights to two or even all three types of space, as is the case with high-power transmission lines. The lines and the upper portion of the towers occupy overhead space, the towers rest on the surface, and the foundation footings for the towers occupy subsurface space.

4. *North Carolina State Highway Dept. v. Black*, 79 S.E.2d 778, 784–785 (N.C. 1954).

5. *Carolina Central Gas Company v. Hyder*, 86 S.E.2d 458 (N.C. 1955).

From a strictly technical point of view, an easement cannot be exclusively a surface easement. An easement for roadway purposes, for example, must include enough subsurface rights for the removal of topsoil and installation of base rock and paving and enough overhead, or above-surface, rights for practical use of the roadway. Although a purely surface easement cannot exist from a practical standpoint, easements for roadways, railroads, and other uses are still commonly referred to as *surface easements*. Only when the encroachment below and/or above the surface of the ground is extreme or excessive for the intended surface use of the easement area is the easement classified as multiple-space occupancy.

SPECIALTY EASEMENTS

Many common easements create no unique problems for appraisers. Properties encumbered by easements for roadway, railroad, power transmission lines, sewer lines, and slopes (or cuts and fills) are common so, with diligence, the appraiser can obtain enough comparable data to make an accurate market analysis of the effect of such easements on a property's market value. In fact, studies have been published on the impact of some common easements such as power transmission line easements.[6] However, because an easement can be created for almost any purpose as long as the right, or estate, to be acquired can be severed from the underlying fee, easements come in many varieties. "Federal acquisitions involve a wide variety of easement types ranging from the traditional to the exotic."[7] These unique, or specialty, easements can create difficult valuation problems for appraisers and, therefore, require individual consideration.

FLOWAGE EASEMENTS

A flowage easement grants the easement owner the right to flood the fee owner's land. Such an easement is often taken in conjunction with a hydroelectric or flood control project. The easement will generally specify whether the easement owner has the right to flood the land occasionally or permanently. If the right is to flood permanently, the fee owner retains only the land under the water; such an easement acquisition can damage the land to nearly 100% of its fee value. The fee owner may retain the right to fill the encumbered land (above the flood stage) and to build structures on it, but these rights often require the specific approval of the easement owner. Also, even the occasional flooding of the land may cause it to be classified as a wetland, thereby requiring state and/or federal[8] development permits.

6. Louis E. Clark, Jr. and E.H. Treadway, Jr., *Impact of Electric Power Transmission Line Easements on Real Estate Values* (Chicago: American Institute of Real Estate Appraisers, 1972). See also the following *Appraisal Journal* articles: Gordon G. Green, "Easement-to-Fee-Simple Value Ratios for Electric Transmission Line Easements: A Common Sense Approach" (July 1992), 399, and Hsiang-te Kung and Charles F. Seagle, "Impact of Power Transmission Lines on Property Values: A Case Study" (July 1992), 413.
7. *Uniform Appraisal Standards for Federal Land Acquisitions* (Washington, D.C.: U.S. Government Printing Office, 1992), §A-20, p. 56.
8. 33 U.S.C. §1251 *et seq.* Clean Water Act 404 permits §1344.

Occasionally a flowage easement gives the easement owner the right to inundate the land only periodically. Such easements are often acquired in addition to permanent flowage easements to allow the easement owner to encroach occasionally on the land above the level of the permanent flowage easement. They also protect the easement owner from damage, or inverse condemnation, suits that might result if the land is eroded by wave action.

A flowage easement is generally described as encumbering all of the fee ownership lying between a low and high elevation mark. Therefore, the appraiser must have access to accurate topographic maps. He or she should investigate whether the land to be encumbered is subject to flooding in the before situation and, if so, to what degree and how frequently. If the acquisition involves an occasional flowage easement, the same information pertaining to flooding will be required for the after situation.

AVIATION EASEMENTS

Aviation easements are divided into two classifications: clearance easements and flight easements. A clearance easement is acquired to ensure that no structure (or natural growth) exceeds a maximum height, if structures are allowed at all. Its purpose is to give aircraft an unobstructed view and provide a safety margin for flights that may have to descend due to pilot error, poor weather conditions, or other circumstances. A flight easement allows the frequent overflight of aircraft over the encumbered land; it is separate and distinct from a clearance easement.[9]

The courts have, on occasion, refused to consider potential damage from overflights when only a clearance easement was being condemned.

> On this record it must be accepted that the claimed right of clearance is merely a provision for assuring that space shall be unoccupied and vision unobstructed above a designated altitude. Unquestionably this is in aid of aviation. But no flight easement is mentioned or to be inferred, much less claimed, in the present pleadings and, therefore, no servitude can be imposed except for the asserted and precisely limited rights of clearance.
>
> It is well established that, absent bad faith which is not argued here, the government's determination and explicit assertion of the nature and extent of the estate to be taken are not judicially reviewable. If any subsequent low flying of aircraft over appellee's land should occur and should be said to invade property rights, the acquisition of the right to keep that space clear will not have conferred any attendant right to fly through it.[10]

In other words, the court in the above case was applying the *expansion of the taking rule*.[11] In a similar situation, the court ruled:

> [S]ince the government has not acquired a right to fly aircraft over the condemnee's land by these proceedings, it follows that, if the government does cause its aircraft to make flights over the lands of these defendants, or has already done so, at such

9. *United States v. 48.10 Acres of Land, etc.*, 144 F.Supp. 258 (S.D. N.Y. 1956).

10. *United States v. 64.88 Acres of Land, etc.*, 244 F.2d 534, 535–536 (3rd Cir. 1957).

11. For a discussion of this rule, see *United States v. 38.60 Acres*, 625 F.2d 196 (8th Cir. 1980). See also *United States v. 101.88 Acres*, 616 F.2d 762 (5th Cir. 1980).

elevation and with such frequency as to result in taking beyond that described in the Declaration of Taking on file in these cases, or in actual physical damages, the landowners would have a right to bring suit against the Government for damages or just compensation.[12]

Because the courts have come to consider overflights as easement takings only since the mid-1940s,[13] minimal case law exists on acceptable methods of measuring damage. For this reason, the federal court[14] has held that a percentage factor applied to the property's before value, based on a mathematical formula,[15] can be used when market data on the property's after value are unavailable. The approved formula considers three factors:

1. The height of the overflight (up to an elevation of 500 feet)
2. The distance the property is located from the center line, extended, of the runway (up to 2,000 feet)
3. The distance between the property and the end of the runway (up to 25,000 feet)

PRESERVATION EASEMENTS

"The term *preservation easement*...includes what are variously called historic, open space, scenic, conservation, and facade easements."[16] Such easements are typically nonpossessory easements—i.e., they restrict the fee owner's use of the land rather than grant some use of the property to the holder of the easement.

FACADE EASEMENTS

Facade easements prohibit the fee owner from altering the facade, or exterior, of an existing improvement on the land in question. Such easements are generally imposed on structures of historic significance and are acquired for the purpose of historic preservation. Facade easements usually apply to a single property and, depending on the specific provisions of the easement or restriction, may constitute a taking. However, if such a restriction is placed on all structures within a geographical area, it is usually accomplished with zoning regulations and, therefore, generally does not constitute a compensable taking.[17]

Often an appraiser will be asked to make a before and after appraisal of a facade easement when the easement has, in fact, been formally donated by the landowner. Such appraisals are often requested for real estate and federal income tax purposes.

One of the most difficult determinations to be made in facade easement cases is whether a taking has actually occurred; the restriction placed on the land may instead fall under the sovereign's police power. Some jurisdictions have ruled that a facade easement may be taken even if the ordinance creating the easement

12. *United States v. 4.43 Acres of Land*, 137 F.Supp. 567, 572 (N.D. Tex. 1956).
13. *United States v. Causby*, 328 U.S. 256 (1946).
14. *Town of East Haven v. Eastern Airlines, Inc.*, 333 F.Supp. 338 *cert. denied*, 411 U.S. 965 (1973).
15. Thomas H. Hall III and William R. Beaton, "A Factor Formula For Valuation of Aviation Easements," *The Appraisal Journal* (January 1965), 29–46.
16. Judith Reynolds, *Historic Properties: Preservation and the Valuation Process* (Chicago: American Institute of Real Estate Appraisers, 1982), 77.
17. *Berman v. Parker*, 348 U.S. 26 (1954).

is directed at only one parcel of land.[18] The appraiser is well advised to obtain legal verification on this point before the appraisal assignment is undertaken. (For further discussion of this issue, consult Chapter 17.)

SCENIC EASEMENTS

Scenic easements became prominent with the adoption of the Highway Beautification Act of 1965. The act provided that 3% of the funds apportioned to each state for federal aid highways in any fiscal year be "used for landscape and roadside development within the highway right-of-way and for acquisition of interests in and improvement of strips of land necessary for the restoration, preservation, and enhancement of scenic beauty adjacent to such highways."[19] The adoption of the Wild and Scenic Rivers Act[20] has also stimulated the proliferation of scenic easements.

Scenic easements generally restrict the underlying fee owner from using the land in question in any manner that would diminish its aesthetic appeal. However, easement forms vary substantially from state to state and from project to project. It is imperative that the appraiser make an exact determination of the rights to be acquired in each instance. Scenic easements are generally acquired on lands parallel to highway rights-of-way or scenic rivers. Studies have been made in an attempt to ascertain how the imposition of a scenic easement affects the market value of a tract of land.[21]

Scenic easements often call for the forced removal of existing advertising signs and prohibit future signs. Compensation for existing signs must be paid to both the landowner and the owner of the sign, in accordance with Title 1 of the Highway Beautification Act.[22] The prohibition against future advertising is almost always accomplished through the sovereign's police power.

With scenic easements, as with facade easements, it is often difficult to determine whether a taking has actually occurred, or whether the sovereign has restricted the use of the land through its police power. Some jurisdictions have ruled that the aesthetic factor alone is a valid basis for police power regulations.[23] Again, the appraiser must clearly distinguish between the rights being acquired by eminent domain and the limitations on rights imposed by the sovereign's police power. Often, this can only be accomplished with the guidance of an attorney who is thoroughly familiar with the applicable law.

ESTATES CREATED

The owner of an easement is said to have a *dominant estate*, while the owner of the underlying fee is said to have a *subservient estate*. A dominant estate is sometimes referred to as an *affirmative easement* and a subservient estate as a *negative easement*.

18. *Mayor, etc., of City of Annapolis v. Anne Arundel County*, 316 A.2d 807 (Md. 1974).
19. Public Law No. 89-285, §301(a), *amending* 23 U.S.C. §319.
20. 16 U.S.C. §1271.
21. Donald T. Sutte, Jr., "Scenic Easements," *The Appraisal Journal* (October 1966), 531–548; Howard L. Williams and W.D. Davis, "Effect of Scenic Easements on the Market Value of Real Property," *The Appraisal Journal* (January 1968), 15–32; and *Scenic Easements—Legal, Administrative, and Valuation Problems and Procedures*, Highway Research Program Report No. 56 (Washington, D.C.: Highway Research Board, 1973).
22. 79 Stat. 1028, *amending* 23 U.S.C. §131.
23. *Berman v. Parker*, 348 U.S. 26 (1954); *Oregon City v. Hartke*, 400 P.2d 255 (Ore. 1965).

The terms are somewhat self-explanatory in that the interest in the land held by the owner of the easement dominates the rights retained by the fee owner. Although the fee owner may retain the right to use the land encumbered by the easement, this use may not interfere in any manner with the easement owner's use of the property for the purposes specified in the written easement. Thus, a fee owner's interest in the easement area is subservient to the interest of the easement owner.

VALUE CONSIDERATIONS

The acquisition of an easement by a condemnor does not give the appraiser a license to guess. The principles and techniques applied in appraising land for easement acquisitions are the same as those applied in other condemnation appraisals. The only difference is that in appraising land for easement acquisitions, only a partial taking may occur. Even if an entire ownership is to be encumbered by an easement, the landowner will retain the underlying fee interest in the form of a subservient estate. In jurisdictions that use the before and after, or federal, rule, the appraiser simply values the property before and after the easement acquisition. As a federal court said in remanding a case for retrial, "...we suggest that the measure of the appellant's detriment should be the difference, if any, between the fair market value of his land immediately before and after the perpetual easements were imposed by the taking."[24]

In jurisdictions using the taking plus damages, or state, rule, the appraiser will be required to estimate the value of the easement interest acquired plus damages to the remainder, if any.[25] When either rule is applied, the measure of damage caused by an easement acquisition is the loss of salable utility both to the area encumbered and to the unencumbered portion of the larger parcel.

Some courts have ruled as a matter of law, that the property's loss in market value is not the proper measure of value in the case of temporary easement acquisitions.[26] It has been held that the proper measure of compensation is the value of the property for the period it is to be held by the condemnor[27] or the diminution in the value of the property by reason of the owner's loss of its use and occupancy during possession by the condemnor.[28] The most common measure of damages accepted by the courts is the rental value of the easement area for the period of occupancy by the condemnor.[29]

Like permanent takings, temporary takings can result in damages. Temporary damages can result when a condemnor acquires a permanent property right, in fee or through an easement, plus a temporary easement beyond the permanent property right for construction of a proposed public improvement. After construction of the public improvement is completed, the construction easement is extinguished and the unencumbered fee interest in the land reverts back to the owner. The fact that a taking is temporary in nature does not relieve the sovereign from paying just compensation.

24. *Calvo v. United States*, 303 F.2d 902, 909 (9th Cir. 1962). See also *United States v. 8.41 Acres of Land, Etc.*, 680 F.2d 388 (5th Cir. 1982).
25. *Illinois Telegraph News Co. v. Meine*, 90 N.E. 230 (Ill. 1909).
26. *City of Norwood v. Sheen*, 186 N.E. 102 (Ohio 1933).
27. *Kimball Laundry Co. v. United States*, 338 U.S. 1 (1949).
28. *City of Norwood v. Sheen*, 186 N.E. 102 (Ohio 1933).
29. *United States v. General Motors Corp.*, 323 U.S. 373 (1945).

Damages that result from temporary construction easements (TCEs) are usually based on the economic rent of the affected area for the term of the temporary easement. If rental data are unavailable, an appropriate rate of return on the land for the term of the easement is customarily estimated. For example, consider a partial taking of a farm as shown in Figure 16.1. Assume that this 80-acre farm has a before value of $1,000 per acre and comparative analysis indicates that land encumbered by a permanent gasline easement is diminished in value by 50%.

FIGURE 16.1 TEMPORARY CONSTRUCTION EASEMENT

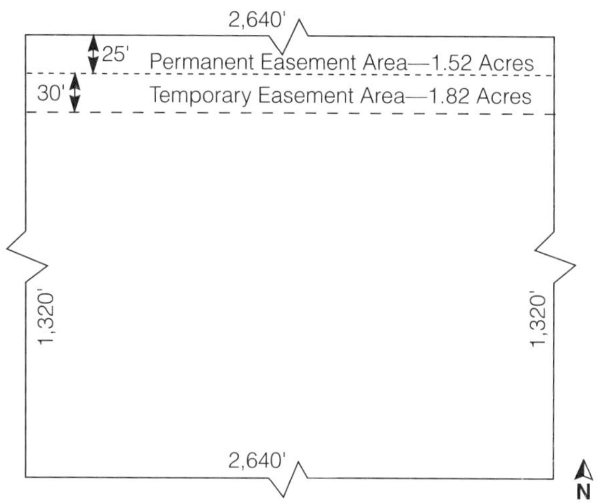

Assume also that the temporary construction easement shown will have a term of 18 months and that comparable farmland would rent for $100 per acre per year. The property's after value could be computed as follows:

76.66 acres @ $1,000		$76,660
1.52 acres permanent easement @ $500		760
Fee value of 1.82-acre temporary easement area @ $1,000	$1,820	
Less rent loss (1.82 acres @ $100 x 1.5 years)	− 273	
Value of temporary easement area		1,547
Total after value		$78,967
Rounded		$79,000

If comparable rental data were not available, the appraiser would have to estimate an appropriate rate of return on the temporary easement area and adjust the value of the area to compensate the owner for losing the beneficial interest in the property for 18 months. If the rate of return was 10% per year, the property value in the after situation would be computed as follows:

76.66 acres @ $1,000		$76,660
1.52 acres permanent easement @ $500		760
Fee value of 1.82-acre temporary easement area @ $1,000	$1,820	
Less return on temporary easement area ($1,820 @ 10%/yr. x 1.5 years)	– 273	
Value of temporary easement area		1,547
Total after value		$78,967
Rounded		$79,000

The rent loss (or appropriate return) is seldom converted into a present value through the application of a discount rate. Usually the land area affected is so small and the term of the temporary easement so short that discounting is unnecessary.[30] Only when the rent loss is substantial and/or the temporary easement is of extended duration does the appraiser need to discount the rent loss, or return on investment, to a present value. "However, if an appraiser elects not to discount the rent loss, it should be noted in the appraisal report that, from a technical standpoint, discounting is required, but in the present instance (because of the minimal amount of rent involved and/or the short duration of the temporary taking) the discount would be insignificant."[31]

It has been suggested that if an economic rent cannot be estimated for the TCE area, the encumbered value of the TCE area can be computed by converting the present unencumbered value of the TCE area into the present value of a reversion at the end of the easement term.[32] This procedure has the advantage of simplicity and would result in the same value indicated in the above examples if the income stream had been discounted to present value.

Of course, if the existence of the TCE will affect the value of the unencumbered land as well as the easement area, this fact must also be considered in estimating the value of the property after the taking.

The examples presented here may suggest a simplicity of estimating the amount of just compensation due for a temporary taking, which will not be borne out in the marketplace. More complex factual situations are discussed in Chapters 17 and 18 of this text.

The damages to land due to the imposition of an easement can range from 0%[33] to 100% of the easement area's fee value.[34] Some courts have ruled, as a matter of law, that under certain circumstances compensation for an easement taking is equal to 100% of the fee value of the land encumbered by the easement. "Under our law it is firmly settled that when a permanent easement is taken by eminent domain, depriving the owner of the use of the property, the compensation must equal the full value of the land, as if a fee were being acquired."[35] Conversely, other courts have ruled, again as a matter of law, that compensation for an easement taking cannot equal 100% of the fee value of the land encumbered. As one court put it "...what the plaintiff took was merely an easement,

30. In the above examples, discounting the income stream at 10% would result in a $30.55 difference in the after value of the easement area.

31. *Uniform Appraisal Standards for Federal Land Acquisitions*, §C-11, p. 98.

32. Ibid.

33. *Fulmer v. State Dep't of Roads*, 134 N.W.2d 798 (Neb. 1965).

34. *Central Louisiana Elec. Co. v. Fontenot*, 159 So.2d 738 (La. 1964).

35. *Chicago Mill and Lumber Co. v. Board of Directors*, 366 S.W.2d 184, 185 (Ark. 1963).

which being in law less than the title, can in law only entail compensation for less than the fee title."[36]

The degree of damage resulting from the same type of easement can vary greatly depending on the highest and best use of the land. For example, a pipeline running 25 feet beneath grazing land may have little or no effect upon the productivity, or market value, of the land encumbered with the easement. If such a pipeline traversed a tract of timberland, however, the loss in salable utility, and thus market value, could be great because the typical pipeline easement agreement precludes the growth of timber within the easement area. Similarly, if the highest and best use of the site were for an office building with underground parking, damages could be substantial.

Another factor that can affect the degree of damage caused by an easement acquisition is the location of the easement in relation to the boundary line of the larger parcel. Consider the situation illustrated in Figure 16.2, which depicts the taking of a 10-ft. water line easement from two, single-family residential lots.

FIGURE 16.2 EASEMENT LOCATION

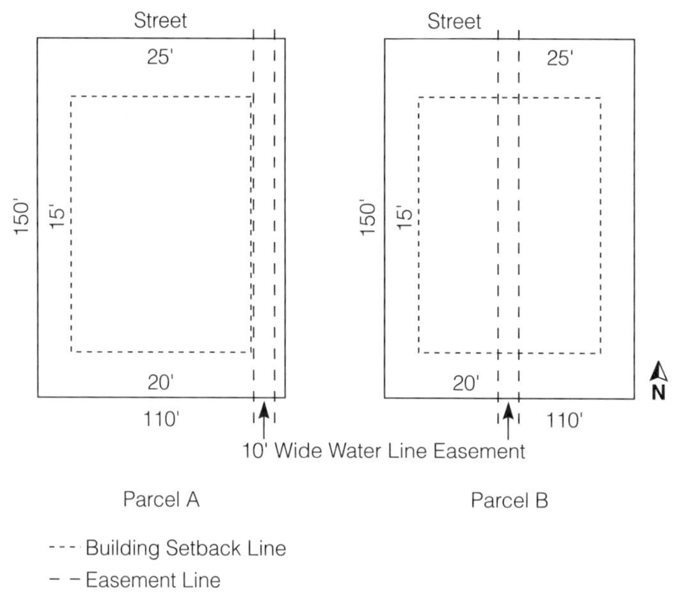

The rights acquired from Parcels A and B are identical, as is the amount of area to be encumbered. However, because the easement is located close to Parcel A's boundary line, the tract has lost little, if any, of its original utility. The tract's highest and best use is for development of a single-family dwelling, both before

36. *Mitchell v. Texas Electric Service Company*, 299 S.W.2d 183 (Tex. 1957).

and after imposition of the easement. Parcel B, on the other hand, has probably suffered severe loss of utility due to the easement acquisition. Before imposition of the easement, the tract's highest and best use was for construction of a single-family dwelling; however, the location of the easement in relation to the tract's boundaries makes such a use impractical in the after situation. The only practical use of Parcel B after the acquisition of the easement would be its sale to an abutting owner, probably at a nominal price.

The location of an easement in relation to improvements on the larger parcel is also important. Figure 16.3 shows two encumbered parcels with identical rights and areas. Due to its location, the easement on Parcel A could severely restrict the future expansion of the industrial building. In addition, the presence of power

FIGURE 16.3 EASEMENT LOCATION

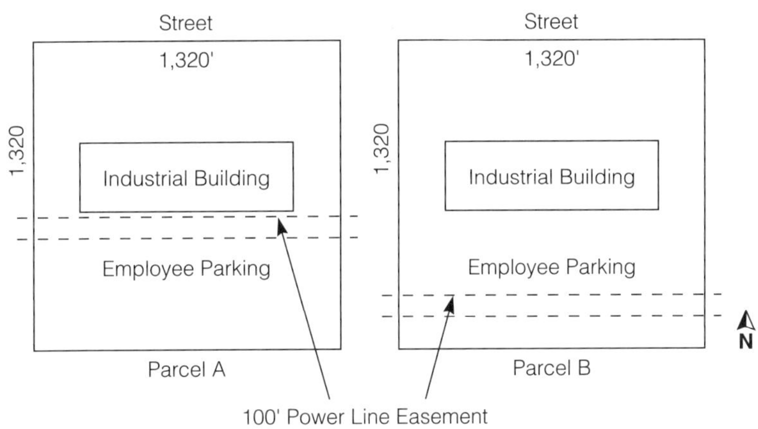

lines could obstruct the use of large industrial machinery around the structure, and the towers could hamper freight loading and/or delivery. Any possible loss in Parcel B's utility by reason of the easement acquisition would be minor. The employee parking area would need to be modified slightly to accommodate the tower locations. In summary, it can be seen that the location of an easement in relation to the larger parcel's boundary lines and to existing improvements can have a substantial effect on the property's market value.

Before the effects of an easement acquisition can be properly evaluated, the appraiser must know exactly how the easement area will be used, what rights are to be acquired, and how responsibilities will be divided between the parties. "There is no such thing, for example, as a generic road easement or a generic scenic easement."[37] The full impact of an easement acquisition cannot be estimated until the appraiser determines: 1) the loss of present utility, 2) the loss of future utility, 3) the accessory rights to be acquired, and 4) the obligations of the parties.

37. *Uniform Appraisal Standards for Federal Land Acquisitions*, §A-20, pp. 56–57.

Accessory rights may include the right to maintain the easement area (including the right to spray power line or pipeline easement areas); the right to enter onto the property for inspection, repair, and/or replacement; and, on occasion, the right to expand the utilization of the easement area for other purposes or to expand the area itself without paying additional compensation or by paying an amount calculated with a predetermined compensation formula. Power line easements, for instance, sometimes include a provision that allows the easement owner to remove danger trees from unencumbered areas of the fee owner's larger parcel perpetually with little or no compensation, or with compensation set by a predetermined formula.

In investigating the obligations of the parties, the appraiser should determine: 1) whether the easement owner will be responsible for returning the land to its original state after the construction, replacement, and/or repairs are completed; 2) who will be responsible for fence repair and maintenance, if any; 3) who is obligated to maintain the easement area, including the control of noxious weeds; and 4) who will be responsible for potential personal injury losses occurring in the easement area.

The following is an actual jury instruction which lists the potential damage items that the appraiser must consider in estimating the diminution in market value caused by an easement acquisition.

> In arriving at this difference [in the market value before and after the easement acquisition], you should take into consideration the actual legal rights taken and also the following items:
>
> (a) depreciation, if any, due to the existence of the pipeline itself; (b) loss of crops, if any, this year and future years; (c) loss, if any, of use of pasture due to the use by the corporation of said fifty foot right-of-way and temporary easements this year and in future years; (d) reasonable expense, if any, to respondents in keeping cattle from said fifty foot right-of-way now and in the future and during periods necessarily required in order to reestablish the crops and pasture on said fifty foot right-of-way; (e) reasonable expense, if any, to respondents in building and maintaining necessary works to insure proper irrigation of the land during such times as said corporation shall have the right to occupy said fifty foot strip under the terms of its easement; (f) reasonable expense, if any, to respondents in keeping water from said fifty foot strip during periods of construction, replacement and repair; (g) reasonable expense, if any, to respondents in leveling and releveling said fifty foot strip and hauling of additional soil to fill settlements; (h) reasonable extra expense, if any, to respondents caused by said fifty foot right-of-way due to the interference thereof with the operation of said dairy herd farm unit and said cattle feeding farm unit; (i) reasonable extra expense, if any, to the respondents in puddling the trench in which said pipeline will be laid in preventing water from seeping along said pipeline, and preventing consequent damage; (j) extra reasonable expense, if any, to the respondents of regrading, replanting and caring for, and seeding said fifty foot right-of-way; (k) reasonable damages, if

> any, to crops and land due to the necessity of keeping water off during periods of occupancy of said right-of-way by said corporation under the terms of its easement; (l) such other reasonable expenses, if any, supported by the evidence, reasonably necessary to restore said premises to normal productivity.[38]

This case was eventually remanded for retrial. In doing so the court said:

> While the listed items may have a bearing on the depreciation in market value which would result from the granting of the easement, they could not be considered as distinct items of damages. It was not proper for the jury to consider them in addition to the legal rights taken, the value of which, the jury had previously been told, was this same difference in market value.[39]

The list of potential damage items that an appraiser must consider is often extensive. In fact, appraising a property subject to an easement may be more complex than valuing a property acquired in a fee taking. Full, detailed appraisal reports are required—i.e., either a full before and after appraisal or an appraisal of the taking plus damages, depending on the applicable rules in the jurisdiction. However, there are occasions when the imposition of an easement will have only a nominal, or even nonexistent, impact on market value as in the case of Parcel A in Figure 16.2.

Nominal Acquisitions

In cases in which damages are nominal or nonexistent, it is often impractical, from an economic standpoint, to have a fully documented appraisal report prepared. The fee for a fully documented appraisal report could amount to considerably more than the estimated loss in property value. The treatment of nominal acquisitions will vary among condemnors. For instance, the Federal Highway Administration's *Appraisal Guide* suggests that a formal appraisal is not required for valuations of less than $2,500 and that only a minimal appraisal is required when the value is less than $5,000.[40] The *Uniform Appraisal Standards for Federal Land Acquisitions* also provides for deviation from its standards based on economic considerations. When the appraisal assignment involves a nominal acquisition, the appraiser should consult with the client to determine the type of appraisal report required. "Under no circumstances, however, may appraisal standards be set at a level below the minimum required under USPAP [The Appraisal Foundation's *Uniform Standards of Professional Appraisal Practice*]."[41]

The above discussion relates only to situations in which minor easements are acquired by voluntary purchase. If the appraisal report is to be used for trial purposes, a fully documented report should be prepared regardless of the diminution in value resulting from the acquisition. An unprepared appraiser will look just as incompetent on the witness stand whether the case involves $500 or $5,000,000.

38. *Pacific Northwest Pipeline Corp. v. Myers*, 311 P.2d 655, 658 (Wash. 1957).

39. Ibid.

40. U.S. Department of Transportation, Federal Highway Administration, *The Appraisal Guide* (Washington, D.C.: U.S. Government Printing Office, 1990), 17 and 18.

41. *Uniform Appraisal Standards for Federal Land Acquisitions*, §B, pp. 63–64.

For large easement acquisition projects (e.g., for the installation of a pipeline through a rural area) some condemnors will analyze land values in the area and make an administrative determination as to the amount of compensation each property owner will be offered. "For some types of easements, such as those acquired by utility companies for electric, telephone, cable lines and pipe lines, there may be an established going rate per pole, per line-mile, per rod, and the like. In appraising a similar type of easement for government acquisition, the appraisal should not be based upon such going rates but should be based upon the usual 'before and after' appraisal method."[42] It therefore goes without saying that sales of easements based on such measures cannot be considered valid comparable sales.

Although appraising is not an exact science, some easement takings have such a minimal effect on value that no discernible difference in market value before and after the taking can be ascertained in the market. Nevertheless, it is generally recognized that no property owner can be expected to convey land or an interest in land without compensation (except in the case of special benefits).

Condemnors' responses to nominal acquisitions differ. If no discernible difference in market value before and after an easement acquisition can be demonstrated, some condemnors will make an administrative determination that the property owner should be offered a nominal amount of compensation, irrespective of the appraisal.[43] For instance, one condemnor states:

> If the market evidence reveals no difference between the value before and the value after the acquisition, the Appraiser reports the facts dictated by the market. The Appraiser is not obligated to report a difference when none exists in fact. The Appraiser is obligated to report only the facts and conclusions based purely on appraisal considerations.[44]

Other condemnors, however, may require an abbreviated appraisal report and attempt to coerce the appraiser into reporting a value differential even when it cannot be supported by market data. This is accomplished with a statement such as "the difference between the value of the property prior to acquisition of the easement and after the acquisition of easement is nominal, say $500." The appraiser may not arrive at specific before and after values or include any sales data in the appraisal report. While this procedure may satisfy the condemnor's requirement that an appraisal be prepared prior to making an offer to a property owner, it transfers a burden that rightfully belongs to the condemnor's administrative staff to the appraiser. Admittedly, nothing ruins a negotiator's day faster that trying to get a property owner to sign an easement that pays him no compensation whatsoever, but it is the condemnor's administration that should determine the amount of compensation.

Nearly all condemnors have the administrative latitude to make such determinations. To force an appraiser to derive a value differential when none, in fact, exists is to corrupt the valuation process. Also, if the easement cannot be ob-

42. *Uniform Appraisal Standards for Federal Land Acquisitions*, §A-20, p. 57, citing *United States v. 8.41 Acres of Land, Etc.*, 680 F.2d 388 (5th Cir. 1982).

43. For instance, U. S. Department of Transportation, Federal Highway Administration, *The Appraisal Guide* (Washington, D.C.: U.S. Government Printing Office, 1990), page 18, provides "a minimum payment of up to $500 may be used even though actual estimated compensation is less."

44. Washington State Dept. of Transportation, *Right of Way Manual*, Appendix 4-1, §C(1)(b), p. I-2.

tained voluntarily, the appraiser who estimated the "nominal, say $500" compensation is usually of no value in a condemnation proceeding because, while the appraiser could have supported a conclusion of no value differential with market data, he will be unable to support his prior $500 compensation estimate. Furthermore, if the appraiser revises the earlier appraisal and reports no differential in value before and after the acquisition, the prior appraisal will undoubtedly be discovered and presented to the trier of fact to impeach the appraiser's testimony.

EXISTING EASEMENTS

The preceding discussion has focused on the appraisal of real estate for easement acquisition purposes. The appraiser must also consider the effects of existing easements on a property's utility and value. Easements can be held *in gross* or as an *appurtenance* to other property that is held in fee, usually by the easement owner. An easement held in gross is one that has utility in and of itself or in conjunction with other continuous easements, such as power line easements, utility easements, etc. An easement held as an appurtenance, however, usually has no independent utility; it is useful only in conjunction with other property. An example of an appurtenant easement is an easement across a tract of land for ingress to and egress from an abutting tract of land that is held in fee by the owner of the easement. This easement would have no material value to its owner if he did not also own the tract of land that the easement serves.

Many jurisdictions require that a tract of land encumbered with an easement be appraised considering the easement's negative effect on the property's market value. "Generally, if property burdened with easements is taken by eminent domain, the property must be valued in its existing condition and not as an unencumbered fee."[45] Therefore, the appraiser must be aware of the effects of all easements encumbering a property under appraisal. It should be recognized that this treatment of easements is an exception to the undivided fee, or unit, rule discussed in Chapter 4 of this text.

The appraiser must also be aware of easements on other lands that may be appurtenant to the parcel under appraisal. Appurtenant easements must be carefully investigated because some jurisdictions do not require that an appurtenant easement be legally described in the condemnor's declaration of taking.[46] When an appurtenant easement exists, the fee parcel is appraised considering the beneficial effect of the easement across the other land. In other words, the larger parcel is the fee ownership plus the easement ownership in the abutting land.[47] Similarly, when only the appurtenant easement is acquired, the interest of the easement owner is considered in light of his abutting fee ownership. In this case, the larger parcel is the easement ownership plus the abutting fee ownership.[48]

> Ordinarily an easement is appurtenant to a parcel of property known as the dominant tenement. Such dominant tenement will naturally be worth more with the appurtenant easement than without it. Thus, if there is a destruction of the ease-

45. *Nichols' The Law of Eminent Domain*, rev. 3d ed. (New York: Mathew Bender Co., Inc., 1990), vol. 4, §12D.03.
46. *State ex rel. Lindemann v. Preston*, 170 N.E.2d 489 (Ohio 1960).
47. *United States v. Welch*, 217 U.S. 333 (1910).
48. *Matter of City of New York (West 10th St.)*, 196 N.E. 30 (N.Y. 1935).

> ment, either by a direct taking of the easement itself, or by a taking of the servient estate, it has been said that the owner of the easement is damaged to the extent that the value of his dominant tenement has been impaired by such taking.[49]
>
> For purposes of valuation an easement is to be considered as appurtenant to the dominant tenement. *Together they constitute a single entity*."[50]

To illustrate this principle, consider the acquisition depicted in Figure 16.4. In appraising Parcel A, the larger parcel is the unencumbered fee of Parcel A plus the dominant estate, or interest, in the access easement across Parcel B. If Parcel A's easement interest across Parcel B were not considered, the tract would be landlocked and could have only a nominal value. However, the existence of the easement gives Parcel A a great deal more utility and value than the tract would have without it. In this instance, Parcel B is not legally affected by the highway acquisition and need not be appraised.

FIGURE 16.4 APPURTENANT EASEMENT

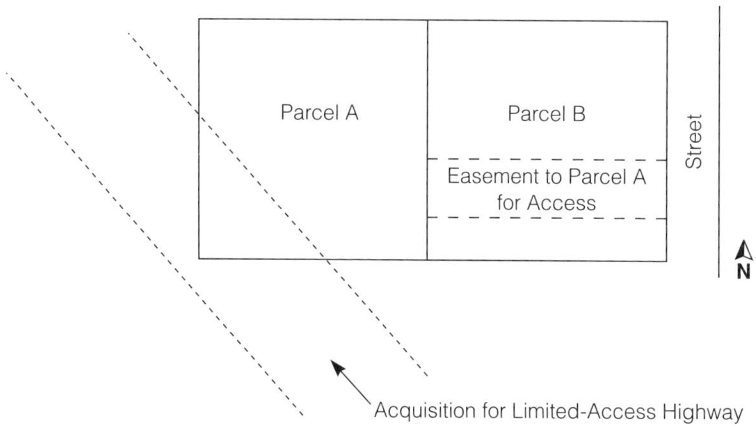

Now, if the acquisition were to follow the course shown in Figure 16.5, Parcel B would be directly affected by the highway acquisition and would need to be appraised. The larger parcel is not the unencumbered fee of the parcel, however, but the fee as encumbered by the easement. In other words, the easement's detrimental effect on Parcel B's value, if any, must be considered by the appraiser in estimating the tract's before and after values.

Although no portion of Parcel A is being acquired in Figure 16.5, an appraisal of the tract is still necessary. As previously stated, the fee and the easement interest are a single entity for purposes of valuation. In Figure 16.4, the larger parcel is the fee estate of Parcel A plus the easement interest in Parcel B. In the situation

49. *Nichols'*, vol. 4, §12D.02 (1990).

50. *Matter of City of New York (West 10th St.)*, 196 N.E. 30, 33 (N.Y. 1935) (emphasis added).

depicted in Figure 16.5, it is quite possible that Parcel A will be more severely damaged by the highway acquisition than Parcel B, even though there is to be no physical invasion of Parcel A.

FIGURE 16.5 TAKING OF AN APPURTENANT EASEMENT

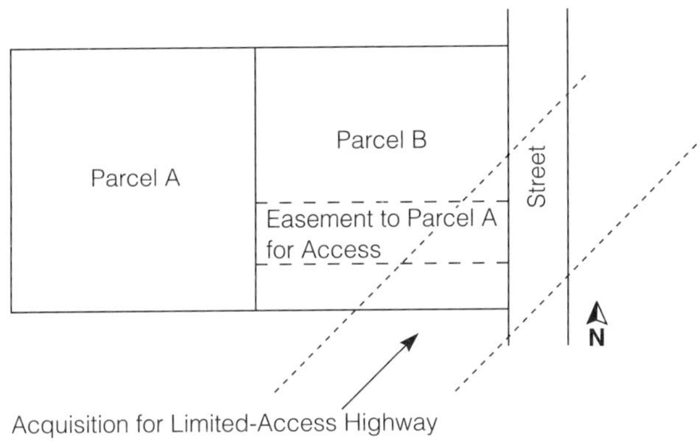

Situations involving appurtenant easements can become much more complex. For instance, consider the situation illustrated in Figure 16.6. The owner of

FIGURE 16.6 APPURTENANT EASEMENTS

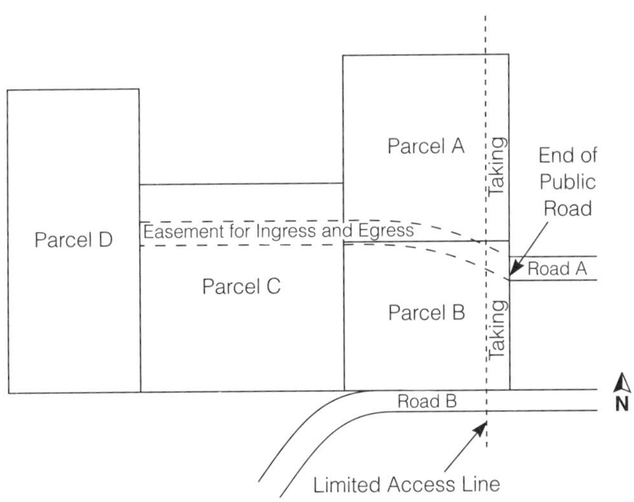

Parcel B has an easement across Parcel A, and the owner of Parcel A has an easement across Parcel B. The owner of Parcel C has an easement across both Parcels A and B, and the owner of Parcel D has an easement across Parcels A, B, and C. Four appraisals would be required by reason of the taking:

1. An appraisal of Parcel A including the appurtenant easement across Parcel B, but subject to the encumbering easement in favor of the owners of Parcels B, C, and D.
2. An appraisal of Parcel B including the appurtenant easement across Parcel A, but subject to the easement across Parcel B in favor of the owners of Parcels A, C, and D.
3. An appraisal of Parcel C including the appurtenant easements across Parcels A and B, but subject to the encumbrance of the easement across Parcel C in favor of the owner of Parcel D.
4. An appraisal of Parcel D together with the appurtenant easements across Parcels A, B, and C.

In such complicated circumstances, it may be advisable for the condemnor to consider constructing a frontage road from Road B across Parcel B to connect the existing easement road to Road B. This could cost far less than the cumulative compensation due the owners of Parcels A, C, and D for the elimination of their only legal access.

When faced with a complex situation like the one shown in Figure 16.6, some condemnors would have a tendency to ignore, intentionally or unintentionally, the interests being taken from Parcels C and D. Condemnors with such tendencies would be wise to read the following chapter, which addresses inverse condemnation.

SUMMARY

An easement is the right to do a specific thing to a particular parcel of land without owning the underlying fee or, in some instances, the right to restrict the use of the land by the underlying fee owner. An easement may be temporary or permanent in nature; it may be classified as subsurface, surface, overhead, or a combination of these types. All easement acquisitions are partial acquisitions because the fee, even if it is raw land of no utility, will remain with the original owner. Damages due to an easement acquisition are measured by the loss of salable utility in both the area encumbered by the easement and the unencumbered portion of the larger tract. Damages to the land area encumbered by the easement range from 0% to 100% of the land's fee value.

While abbreviated appraisal reports are common and acceptable for nominal easement acquisitions that are voluntary, fully documented appraisal reports are required when condemnation of the easement is required. The procedure employed in valuing an easement acquisition is the same as that used for any partial taking: a before and after appraisal or, if the *state rule* is applicable, an estimate of the value of the taking plus damages to the remainder. The amount due for the taking of a temporary easement is usually measured by estimating the rental value of the easement area for the term of the easement. This rental amount is customarily discounted to its present value only when the rental value is significant and/or the term of the easement is long.

The appraiser must consider the effects of an easement under three specific circumstances. First, the effect of a proposed easement must be considered in making appraisals for easement acquisition. In this type of assignment, the appraiser must consider the rights being acquired by the condemnor, the rights remaining with the condemnee, and the obligations and responsibilities of each party. Second, the appraiser must consider the effect of existing easements that encumber the property under appraisal. Third, easements appurtenant to a property under appraisal must also be considered. In this case, the larger parcel consists of the fee simple ownership plus the appurtenant easement attached to it, which are viewed as a single entity.

CHAPTER 17

Inverse Condemnation and Regulatory Takings

> Inverse condemnation should be distinguished from eminent domain. Eminent domain refers to a legal proceeding in which a government asserts its authority to condemn property. Inverse condemnation is "a shorthand description of the manner in which a landowner recovers just compensation for a taking of his property when condemnation proceedings have not been instituted."[1] [Citations omitted].

The concept of inverse condemnation is not new; the U.S. Supreme Court decided an inverse condemnation case in favor of a landowner for the first time in 1872.[2] Inverse condemnation generally occurs for one of two reasons: 1) the physical invasion of private property by the government or by a third party under authority of the government or 2) the overregulation of land use by the government.

As a general rule, a physical invasion is more easily identified as a taking, requiring the payment of just compensation, than is a regulatory taking.[3] The Court has found that a state statute authorizing a cable television company to place cable television facilities on private property was a taking,[4] as was the EPA's placement of monitoring wells on private property.[5] Inverse condemnations can also result from a combination of a physical invasion and an overly burdensome land use regulation. For example, in one case the government attempted to condition the issuance of a building permit on the owner's granting of an easement for public beach access although there was no relationship between the public's ability to access the beach and the proposed construction.[6]

1. *Agins v. Tiburon*, 447 U.S. 255, 258 n.2, (1980).
2. *Pumpelly v. Green Bay & Mississippi Canal Company*, 80 U.S. 166 (1872).
3. *Penn Central Transportation Co. v. New York City*, 438 U.S. 104 (1978).
4. *Loretto v. Teleprompter Manhattan CATV Corp.*, 458 U.S. 419 (1982).
5. *Hendler v. United States*, 952 F.2d 1364 (Fed. Cir. 1991).
6. *Nollan v. California Coastal Comm'n.*, 483 U.S. 825 (1987).

Regulatory takings that do not involve physical invasion are not so easily discernible. In 1922, Justice Holmes said:

> The general rule, at least, is that while property may be regulated to a certain extent, if regulation goes too far it will be recognized as a taking.[7]

The best the Court has been able to do to clarify that general rule is to identify the factors that will be considered in making such a determination. Two sets of factors have been stated:

> [T]he economic impact of the regulation, its interference with reasonable investment backed expectations, and the character of the governmental action . . . have particular significance.[8]

and:

> The application of a general zoning law to particular property effects a taking if the ordinance does not substantially advance legitimate state interests...or denies an owner economically viable use of his land.[9] [Citations omitted]

Even though property owners have had limited success in bringing inverse condemnation actions, this limited success has spawned literally hundreds of inverse condemnation actions. As might be expected, there have been challenges to building permit denials, rezoning denials, denials of permits to fill wetlands, development permit denials, and development permit conditions and exactions. There have also been some rather bizarre alleged takings. For instance, it was ruled that the killing of a farmer's sheep by a bear that was protected by the Endangered Species Act was not a taking of the sheep because the designation of the bear as an endangered species did not make the bear an agent of the government. It has also been ruled that the confiscation of a gun used in a holdup was not a taking requiring compensation, even though the alleged holdup man was found not guilty (by reason of insanity).

When an appraiser is asked to appraise a property in conjunction with an alleged inverse, or regulatory, taking, the appraiser need not form an opinion as to whether a compensable taking has, in fact, taken place. The appraiser need only estimate the value of the property prior to the governmental action that is alleged to have been a taking and estimate the value of the property after the governmental action. The date of value in such cases is generally the date of the alleged taking. As a general rule, just compensation in an inverse condemnation case is measured as it would be in a straight, or direct, condemnation action,[10] but there have been exceptions.[11] Therefore, the appraiser should confirm the proper valuation methodology with legal counsel when an inverse condemnation appraisal is being undertaken.

---

7. *Pennsylvania Coal Co. v. Mahon*, 260 U.S. 393, 415 (1922).
8. *Kaiser Aetna v. United States*, 444 U.S. 164, 175 (1979). See also *Penn Central Transportation Co. v. New York City*, 438 U.S. 104 (1978).
9. *Agins v. Tiburon*, 447 U.S. 255, 260 (1980). See also, *Penn Central Transportation Co. v. New York City*, 438 U.S. 104 (1978); *Nollan v. California Coastal Comm'n.*, 483 U.S. 825 (1987).
10. *Nichols' The Law of Eminent Domain*, rev. 3rd ed. (New York: Matthew Bender Co., Inc., 1992), vol. 3, §8.01[4][c].
11. For example, see *City of Three Forks v. State Highway Comm'n*, 480 P.2d 826 (Mont. 1971); *Game & Fish Comm'n v. Farmers Irrigation Co.*, 426 P.2d 562 (Colo. 1967).

REGULATORY TAKINGS

In 1979 the California Supreme Court ruled that a property owner who claimed a land use ordinance was unconstitutional could not pursue a remedy in inverse condemnation, but was limited to seeking mandamus, or a declaratory judgment, to invalidate the ordinance.[12] The U.S. Supreme Court did not address this issue until 1987, when it found that inverse condemnation is, in fact, a proper remedy for an overly burdensome land use control.[13] At page 321 the Court stated:

> Once a court determines that a taking has occurred, the government retains the whole range of options already available–amendment of the regulation, withdrawal of the invalidated regulation, or exercise of eminent domain. Thus we do not, as the Solicitor General suggests, "permit a court, at the behest of a private person, to require the...Government to exercise the power of eminent domain...." We merely hold that where the government's activities have already worked a taking of all use of property, no subsequent action by the government can relieve it of the duty to provide compensation for the period during which the taking was effective.

In other words, the government may elect to rescind the offending ordinance and pay the owner for the temporary taking of the property from the date the ordinance became effective until the ordinance was rescinded, or it may choose to leave the ordinance in place and pay the property owner for the permanent damage to his property resulting from the ordinance. A "landowner has no right under the Just Compensation Clause to insist that a 'temporary' taking be deemed a permanent taking."[14]

In considering the amount of just compensation due for such temporary takings, the Court indicated that the constitution "requires that the government pay the landowner for the value of the use of the land during this [temporary taking] period" and that "[i]t is the owner's loss, not the taker's gain, which is the measure of the value of the property taken."[15] The Court indicated that substantial guidance could be found in cases where the government temporarily exercised its right to use private property, citing a number of World War II cases in which the government condemned leasehold interests in industrial properties.[16]

But Justice Brennan suggested that "additional rules may need to be developed"[17] and Justice White indicated that "the issue of what constitutes just compensation in this context is a particularly meaty one, which merits substantial reflection and analysis."[18] Chief Justice Rehnquist suggested that "the questions surrounding what compensation . . . is due a property owner in the context of 'interim' takings are multifaceted and difficult [and that he] would not reach these questions without first permitting the courts below to address them."[19]

---

12. *Agins v. Tiburon*, 598 P.2d 25 (Cal. 1979).
13. *First English Evan. Luth. Ch. v. Los Angeles Cty.*, 482 U.S. 304 (1987).
14. Ibid., at 317.
15. Ibid., at 319 citing *United States v. Causby*, 328 U.S. 256, 261 (1946).
16. See *Kimball Laundry Co. v. United States*, 338 U.S. 1 (1949); *United States v. Petty Motor Co.*, 327 U.S. 372 (1946); *United States v. General Motors Corp.*, 323 U.S. 373 (1945).
17. *San Diego Gas & Electric Co. v. San Diego*, 450 U.S. 621, 659 (1981) (Brennan, J., dissenting).
18. *McDonald, Sommer & Frates v. Yolo County*, 477 U.S. 340, 363 (1986) (White, J., dissenting).
19. Ibid., at 364 (Rehnquist, C.J., dissenting).

COMPENSATION FOR TEMPORARY TAKINGS

The foregoing comments by the various Supreme Court Justices have given lawyers practicing in the field of inverse condemnations an opportunity to encourage the lower courts to use methods of determining just compensation in regulatory taking cases that have historically been rejected in direct condemnation cases in which temporary takings were involved–e.g., the taking of temporary construction easements, the taking of leasehold interests. Appraisers should be familiar with the traditional methods of estimating compensation for temporary takings as well as the more novel approaches that have recently been suggested. Appraisers should also be aware that there are significant differences between estimating compensation for a temporary construction easement (TCE), for instance, and a temporary regulatory taking.

First, compensation for the taking of a TCE is generally estimated at, or near, the time the TCE is actually taken and the term of the taking is known. Compensation is effectively paid to the property owner contemporaneously with the taking. In regard to an alleged regulatory taking, the duration of the taking cannot be established until the court has ruled as to whether a taking has actually occurred. This ruling is often made at the same trial in which compensation is considered and the government determines whether it will retain the offending regulation, thereby making the taking permanent, or choose to rescind or amend it. Thus, appraisers often estimate compensation for a regulatory taking in hindsight. They estimate compensation at the end of the temporary taking, rather than at its beginning, and the courts generally allow appraisers to consider market events that occurred during the taking period.

Note that interest on condemnation awards has not been discussed in this text. This is because interest payments are not considered by the appraiser in estimating value. The appraiser assumes that compensation is paid on the date of taking. When such payments are not made on the date of taking, interest on the delayed payment is generally awarded in accordance with an adopted statute. The interest payment is not within the purview of the appraiser, although occasionally appraisers may be asked to present evidence as to the applicable interest rate.

Because compensation for a temporary regulatory taking is never paid until after the termination of the taking, some appraisers, lawyers, and courts seem to have a difficult time separating the compensation paid to an owner for the taking from the interest due because payment of the compensation was delayed. This has resulted in double compensation in some instances. Appraisers have mistakenly added interest to their estimates of compensation to recognize that the compensation has been delayed and then the courts have added interest to the appraiser's estimate for the same delay. Appraisers *must* assume that compensation was paid contemporaneously with the taking. The court will take care of the additional compensation required for the delay in the payment of such compensation. The confusion could be avoided if appraisers would remember that their function is to estimate value, not just compensation.

Nearly all law relating to compensation for temporary takings stems from the three World War II cases cited previously. All of those cases concerned the taking of leasehold interests in industrial properties from lessees. Application of the valuation methodology adopted in these cases was demonstrated in the previous chapter. As noted, however, estimating just compensation for a temporary taking using the method suggested by these cases often becomes complicated, particularly when the temporary taking is the result of an overly burdensome land use regulation. Although many condemning agencies have attempted to cling to simplistic rules for establishing just compensation in temporary taking cases, some courts are beginning to recognize that the rules do not always work. Various theories of compensation advanced by the legal community are gaining judicial recognition. The Arizona Supreme Court[20] summarized some of these theories. At pages 518 and 519, the court stated:

> There has been extensive legal writing on the subject of how damages should be measured for a temporary taking. See generally Hagman & Misczynski, *Windfalls for Wipeouts* (1978); Johnson, Compensation for Invalid Land-Use Regulations, 15 Ga. L. Rev. 559 (1981); Hagman, Temporary or Interim Damages Awards in Land Use Control Cases; Wright, Damages or Compensation for Unconstitutional Land Use Regulations. From these and many other writings have emerged "five basic rules for measuring damages: rental return, option price, interest on lost profit, before-after valuation (two alternatives), and benefit to the government." Hagman, Temporary or Interim Damages Awards in Land Use Control Cases in 1982 Zoning and Planning Land Handbook at 218-227.
>
> Each of these damage measures works well in some "taking" cases and inequitably, if at all, in others. This is because no one rule adequately fits each of the many factual situations that may be present in a particular case. Such problems as: whether the losses are speculative; when the taking actually occurred; whether it caused any damage; and whether it was an acquisitory or nonacquisitory setting combine to make each measure of damages, in some cases, a "guessing game" between too little compensation on the one hand and providing a windfall on the other.
>
> Recognizing this problem, we feel the best approach is not to require the application of any particular damage rule to all temporary taking cases. Instead we hold that the proper measure of damages in a particular case is an issue to be decided on the facts of each individual case. It is our intent to compensate a person for the loss he has actually suffered by virtue of the taking. Either the parties may agree to an appropriate damage measure or each may present evidence as to the actual damages in the case and its correct method of determination. The damages awarded and the way to measure those damages thus may be adapted to compensate the party whose land has been taken for his actual losses.

20. *Corrigan v. City of Scottsdale*, 720 P.2d 513 (Ariz. 1986).

The important point made in this case, from an appraisal standpoint, is that the method of estimating damages used by the appraiser is the method that will "compensate a person for the loss he has actually suffered by virtue of the taking." This does not mean, however, that the appraiser should abandon the methods of estimating compensation that have been proven acceptable in straight, or direct, condemnation cases.

The diminution in value resulting from a temporary taking is usually based on the economic rent of the affected area for the term of the temporary taking; if rental data are unavailable, an appropriate rate of return on the land for the term of the taking is customarily estimated. The purpose of these estimates is, of course, to measure what the owner has lost. The concept of the *market value* of the property before and after the taking is abandoned not because the lost rent is a better measure of what an owner has lost, but rather because there is usually little or no market data with which to estimate the value of a property that has been subject to a temporary taking. Similarly, with little or no rental data from which to estimate the rent lost during the term of the temporary taking, appraisers must often estimate an appropriate return on the property for the term of the taking in some other way.

This is not as easy as it might appear. The appraiser must first estimate the market value of the property in fee simple as of the date of taking, both before and after the taking. The appraiser next estimates the rate of return typical for the type of property under appraisal in the current real estate market. This can be accomplished by analyzing sales of similar property that were rented at the time of sale. The rate of return selected can then be applied to the market value of the property under appraisal, both before and after the taking (assuming there is a residual value). The difference between the values represents what the owner has lost. The return is treated just as if it were rental income. This methodology has been specifically approved:

> Here, the capitalization method of valuation was not employed by owners' witnesses, apparently because of the lack of market data on short-term ground leases of vacant land with the same characteristics of the subject property.
>
> Instead, owners' witnesses adopted a methodology whereby they examined ground leases in the general area of the subject property to determine the prevailing percentage rate relationship between the value of underlying vacant land and the rent it will bring from a tenant developing the property. The testimony regarding the results of the witnesses' inquiry was thus admitted only to show what the owners of property in the general area expected as a return on their investments, and not to establish any absolute rental values for non-comparable properties. Limited to such purpose, the testimony was properly admitted as shedding some light on the appropriate amount of precondemnation damages.[21]

In applying this methodology, it must be remembered that just compensation is assumed to be paid as of the date of taking in one lump sum, while rent (or an appropriate return) would be paid periodically over the term of the lease (or

21. *People etc. v. Peninsula Enterprises, Inc.*, 153 Cal. Rptr. 895, 904 (Cal. 1979).

taking). Thus the appraiser must convert the rental payments lost due to the temporary taking into a lump sum value as of the date of taking. This requires the estimation of an interest, or discount, rate. The rate selected is often the same as the appropriate rate of return developed through the analysis of sale or rental properties.

As a simple example, assume the following sequence of events.

- An industrial development permit application was filed on January 1, 1988.
- The permit was denied on July 1, 1988.[22]
- On January 1, 1991, it was determined that the permit denial was a taking.
- The development permit was issued on July 1, 1991, thus the duration of the temporary taking was three years – July 1, 1988, to July 1, 1991.
- The market value of the industrial land (based on comparable sales) was estimated to be $100,000 as of July 1, 1988, if the permit had been issued.
- The land had no economically viable use without the permit, thus it had only a nominal value after the permit was denied.
- No lands comparable to the subject (with development permits) were leased in the area, thus market rent could not be determined.
- The market rate of return for industrial land in the area was 10% of market value as of July 1, 1988. Therefore, the market rent for (or appropriate return on) the property with the permit is concluded to be the $100,000 value x 10%, or $10,000 per year.[23]

Thus, the owner lost $10,000 per year for three years, or $30,000. Land rent is paid annually.[24] The government is responsible for the payment of a lump sum award as of July 1, 1988.[25] Therefore, the appraiser must compute a lump sum award that is equal to the right to receive $10,000 per year for three years. That computation can be made, using a 10% discount rate.

Date	Period	Payment	*PV* of $1 Discounted at 10% Factor	Present Value
7/1/89	1	$10,000	0.909091	$ 9,091
7/1/90	2	$10,000	0.826446	8,264
7/1/91	3	$10,000	0.751315	7,513
Total		$30,000		$24,868

22. This example could just as easily relate to a taking of a temporary construction easement or a taking of a leasehold interest by the government.

23. The landowner's costs (taxes, insurance, management, etc.) have been disregarded in this example for simplicity.

24. Ground rent is often paid annually in advance but, for purposes of this example, it is assumed that in this area such rent is typically paid in arrears.

25. Typically interest on the award would be paid from July 1, 1988, until the date of payment. However, this is a court determination and should not be considered by the appraiser.

The present value of the right to receive $10,000 per year over the next three years, discounted at 10%, is $24,868. In making the above calculations, the appraiser must remember that the date of taking, and thus the effective date of the appraisal, was determined to be July 1, 1988. The appraiser must *assume* that the government entity responsible for the taking paid the compensation due on that date.

An even easier way to compute the compensation is to recognize that, in this instance, what the owner retains after the permit denial is simply the right to get the property back, with a permit, at the end of three years. Therefore, it is a simple matter to compute the present value of the right to receive $100,000 (in the form of the property with the permit) in three years. The factor used to convert the July 1, 1991, payment to its present value (0.751315) can be applied as follows:

Amount to be received in 3 years	$100,000
Reversion factor	x 0.751315
Present value of reversion	$ 75,132

Therefore,

Property value before the taking	$100,000
Less property value after the taking	75,132
Difference (just compensation)	$ 24,868

This latter methodology has the advantage of retaining the "before and after" methodology of computing just compensation, which has long been favored in condemnation actions in many jurisdictions.

The example included the assumption that the subject property would have no economically viable use during the temporary taking, which would not be unusual in a regulatory taking case. In arriving at the highest and best use of a property subject to a temporary regulatory taking, the appraiser must adhere to the consistent use theory. For instance, assume that the property in the example would have a highest and best use for industrial purposes with the issuance of the requested permit, but if such a permit could be constitutionally denied without paying compensation, the property would have a highest and best use for residential purposes and a value of $50,000. In the context of a temporary regulatory taking, it would not be permissible to conclude that the highest and best use of the property during the temporary taking was for residential use. Such a conclusion would commit the property to a nonindustrial use for a period well beyond the term of the temporary taking.

The only appropriate highest and best use of a property subject to a temporary regulatory taking during the period of that taking is one which will be relatively short-lived, can be terminated on short notice, and requires no or little capital improvement. Such interim highest and best uses might include a parking lot for urban lands or grazing for rural parcels. The continuation of an existing use of the property during the temporary taking might also be appropriate.

Because the purpose of the methodology described in the example is to put the owner in the same position monetarily that he would have enjoyed had no taking occurred, it is important to determine what that position would have been. In doing this, it is easier to assume that the $100,000 land value is in the form of cash rather than land. Then the following analysis can be made:

Cash on hand as of July 1, 1988	$100,000
Interest (rent or return) for Year 1 @ 10%	10,000
Balance at end of Year 1	$110,000
Interest for Year 2 @ 10% ($110,000 x 10%)	11,000
Balance at end of Year 2	$121,000
Interest for Year 3 @ 10% ($121,000 x 10%)	12,100
Balance (cash on hand) at end of Year 3	$133,100

If the government had issued a permit to the owner of the property on July 1, 1988, instead of denying it, the owner's monetary position as of July 1, 1991, would have been $133,100, as shown above.

Now assume that the court decided to award interest on the $24,868 in compensation at a rate of 10% compounded annually from the date of taking (July 1, 1988) to the date of actual payment and permit issuance (July 1, 1991). The owner's monetary position would then be calculated as follows:

Year		Interest	Balance
1	Government payment		$ 24,868
1	($24,868 x 10%)	$2,487	$ 27,355
2	($27,355 x 10%)	$2,736	$ 30,091
3	($30,091 x 10%)	$3,009	$ 33,100
3	Total award (including court-awarded interest)		$ 33,100
3	Reversion (sale of property)		100,000
	Total cash on hand		$133,100

Thus an award of $24,868 plus court-awarded interest would place the owner in the same position as if a taking had never occurred and a permit had been issued on July 1, 1988.

Although the calculations demonstrated here are relatively simple, appraisers, lawyers, and the courts have apparently become confused in applying this methodology to temporary regulatory takings. This confusion can be demonstrated by comparing the results of the example with three temporary regulatory taking cases decided in the federal courts.

When the federal court attempted to apply this methodology in *Nemmers v. City of Dubuque*,[26] it incorrectly used a *future* value of $1 per period factor to convert the lost income into a present value rather than a present value of $1 per period factor and then awarded additional interest for the delayed payment. The court in

26. *Nemmers v. City of Dubuque*, 764 F.2d 502 (8th Cir. 1985).

the *Front Royal*[27] case picked up the formula used in the *Nemmers* case, but forgot to deduct the principal amount from its interest computation, thereby awarding both the future value of the lost income resulting from the temporary taking plus the market value of the whole property.

In a third case[28] an even more bizarre approach was taken. The court assumed that an apartment building could have been built on the property that was subject to a temporary taking and further assumed that the property owner could have obtained a 75% loan on the apartment project. The court then proceeded to award the owner a return on his hypothetical 25% equity investment (without discounting it to a present value) plus compound interest on the face amount of the lost return. In addition to the technical errors in this approach, it appears that the court awarded this owner for frustration of plans and/or lost profits, factors that are usually noncompensable in direct condemnation cases. (See Chapter 14 for a discussion of noncompensable damages.)

Even if lost profits were determined to be a compensable damage item in a temporary regulatory taking case, it would seem only reasonable to take into account the return that the property owner could have earned by investing his hypothetical equity investment in some other way during the taking period. In other words, if the owner lost a 10% return on his equity investment because he was unable to undertake the real estate project, but he was able to invest this equity in a savings account earning 6% interest, the lost profit would amount to 4% of the equity investment, not the 10% awarded by the court.

Some lawyers have been presenting these federal cases to appraisers and suggesting that they adopt the methodology used by the courts in estimating the amount of compensation due for a temporary regulatory taking. To knowingly adopt a technically incorrect method of valuation is a violation of the appraiser's professional standards and code of ethics and to testify to such a procedure is nothing short of a perpetration of fraud upon the court. A court's adoption of a clearly erroneous method of valuation does not give the appraiser license to perpetuate the error.

One factor that has allowed these errors to occur is the insistence by many government agencies that their land use regulations, no matter how restrictive, cannot result in a compensable taking. Thus, they prepare to defend the regulation as a police power action requiring no compensation and continue to go to trial in these matters without developing any valuation evidence of their own for consideration by the trier of fact.

Some temporary regulatory takings can become extremely complex valuation problems. Since the objective is to place the owner in the same economic position he would have enjoyed had the taking never occurred, the appraiser should consider using discounted cash flow (DCF) analysis to determine the effect of the taking. Applying DCF analysis to the property in question both before and after the temporary taking can often provide excellent insights into the impact of the taking on the owner's economic position.

27. *Front Royal and Warren County Industrial Park v. Town of Front Royal*, 749 F.Supp. 1439 (1990).

28. *Wheeler v. City of Pleasant Grove*, 896 F.2d 1347 (11th Cir. 1990).

MULTIPLE REGULATIONS

One issue that has not been fully addressed by the courts is the effect on the value, and economically viable use, of property produced by multiple land use regulations. A single tract of land can be subject to local, state, regional, and national land use regulations simultaneously. Individually, none of these regulations may result in the land having no economically viable use, but the composite effect of all the applicable regulations may leave the land without any utility. For example, a local zoning ordinance may restrict a land parcel to industrial use (precluding residential use), while a state shorelines, or coastal zone, management regulation may restrict the land to residential use. Neither regulation precludes the economically viable use of the land, but the two regulations together result in the land having little, if any, utility or value. Thus one of the regulations may not result in a compensable taking, but the combined effect of the regulations may entitle the landowner to just compensation. Such a situation becomes even more complex when the regulations involved have been promulgated by government entities at different levels and would require consideration by different court systems (e.g., a local regulation would be a state court matter while a federal regulation would require consideration by the United States Court of Federal Claims). The appraiser must be aware of all these possibilities and consult legal counsel if they are encountered.

SUMMARY

No area of condemnation law and condemnation appraisal is more variable than inverse condemnation. Many questions regarding what constitutes a taking and the measure of damages in inverse taking cases remain unclear. Although the U.S. Supreme Court has ruled that a land use regulation that leaves land without an economically viable use is a taking, the definition of an *economically viable use* is not clear. Furthermore, the Court has not addressed how the test of "investment-backed expectations" relates to the *in rem* nature of eminent domain actions—i.e., takings have historically been actions against property, not the owners of property. If a property owner is constitutionally denied a development permit and chooses to sell the property rather than challenge the permit denial, what is the effect on future buyers? Is the future buyer prevented from challenging a permit denial because his investment-backed expectations of development would be considered unreasonable due to the prior permit denial? Such an interpretation would result in a taking without the payment of just compensation, a situation which would appear to be in violation of the Fifth Amendment to the U.S. Constitution and contrary to past U.S. Supreme Court rulings. This is obviously an issue that the courts will have to address in the near future.

Appraisers are professionally obligated to remain apprised of newly developing areas of law and constitutional interpretations that affect the bundle of rights inherent in the ownership of real estate. This does not mean that an appraiser who values a property subject to an alleged taking has to determine whether a compensable taking has, in fact, occurred. The appraiser merely has to estimate the value of the property before and after the government action alleged to be a taking or, as an alternative, estimate what the owner has lost monetarily by the government's action.

In estimating damages for temporary regulatory takings, appraisers should be aware of the tested and approved methods of estimating such damage as well as those methods being advocated by the legal community.[29] The courts have indicated that significant guidance can be gleaned from historical rulings on the measure of damages in temporary taking cases, thus appraisers should not discard them without serious consideration and substantial justification. On the other hand, an appraiser should not adopt new methods of estimating just compensation in temporary regulatory taking cases without recognizing that many of these methods are merely the untested opinions of individual advocates. The ultimate goal of compensation is to place the owner in the same position pecuniarily that he would have been in had a taking never occurred. It must be remembered that the courts have not ruled that the government is liable for punitive damages for a regulatory taking.

Appraisers must recognize that some courts are floundering in their attempts to address the proper measure of damages in temporary regulatory takings. As a result they have, on occasion, adopted methodologies that are technically incorrect. Appraisers must refrain from adopting methods of measuring damages that are patently erroneous, irrespective of their source.

29. For a discussion of the various methods of estimating damages in such situations, see Gideon Kanner, "Measure of Damages in Nonphysical Inverse Condemnation Cases," *Inverse Condemnation and Related Government Liability* course of study material, American Law Institute – American Bar Association, Philadelphia, November 1–3, 1990, pp. 117–142.

CHAPTER 18

Leasehold Valuations

Real estate carries with it a bundle of rights to which the owner of the real estate is entitled. One of the most important of these rights, or interests, is often referred to as the *beneficial interest* in the real estate – i.e., the right of use and occupancy of the realty. Another ownership right is the right to transfer the beneficial interests in property to another person or entity. This act of transference is often accomplished through a lease, which is defined as a "written document in which the rights to use and occupancy of land or structures are transferred by the owner to another for a specified period of time in return for a specified rent."[1]

When a tract of land is leased, the fee simple estate is divided in two. The owner of the real estate is said to hold a *leased fee estate* while the tenant, or lessee, holds a *leasehold estate*. The owner of the leased fee retains the fee to the property, and the rights of use and occupancy are conveyed by lease to others. The owner of the leased fee has two specific rights in the property: the right to receive rent over the lease period and the right to repossess the property upon termination of the lease. The owner of the leasehold estate has the right to use and occupy the realty for the term of the lease subject to the terms and conditions of the lease, including the payment of rent.[2]

Both the leased fee estate and the leasehold estate can be seen as positive or negative interests. If the rental amount specified in the lease is less than the current economic or market rent, the lessee (tenant) holds a positive leasehold interest and the lessor (landlord) holds a negative leased fee estate. Under such circumstances, the lessee, at least theoretically, can sell his beneficial interest in

1. *The Dictionary of Real Estate Appraisal*, 3d ed. (Chicago: Appraisal Institute, 1993), 203–204.

2. *The Appraisal of Real Estate*, 10th ed. (Chicago: Appraisal Institute, 1992), 123.

the property for a sum of money; the landlord, on the other hand, will not be able to sell the leased fee estate for as much as he could get for the property if it were not subject to the lease.

If the rent specified in the lease, or *contract rent*, is greater than the current economic or market rent, the landlord has a positive leased fee estate and the lessee has a negative leasehold estate. Under these circumstances, the owner of the leased fee estate, again theoretically, could sell his interest in the property for more than the property would bring if it were not under lease; the lessee, however, could not give his leasehold estate away, let alone sell it.

UNDIVIDED FEE RULE

It would be unethical for an appraiser to value a property subject to a lease without considering the effect of that lease on the market value of the property, unless such consideration is specifically precluded by the terms of the appraisal assignment.[3] In most condemnation appraisals, the appraiser is instructed to exclude from consideration existing leases and their effect, if any, on the market value of the property and to appraise the property as if all interests in it were held by one individual or entity. This concept is often referred to as the *undivided fee rule* (see Chapter 4). The rationale behind this rule is that the condemnor is acquiring the fee simple title to the property,[4] not the various, separately held interests in it. The federal courts[5] and many state courts have adopted the undivided fee rule.[6] As stated by the Idaho court:

> It was the State's theory of the case at trial and its theory on appeal that the compensation for the value of the land taken and the damages to the remaining property by reason of severance should be assessed in total and only thereafter should the award be apportioned between the lessor Bastian and the lessee Albertson's. The State sought a jury instruction to that effect, but it was denied. The denial of that instruction was error. The mere fact that ownership of land is divided among different persons and of owners of various interest in the title including leasehold does not in and of itself enhance the value of the property.[7] [Citations omitted]

"In appraising such property the undivided fee rule is generally adhered to..."[8] and apportionment of the total award is considered only after the total award has been established by the trier of fact.[9] To attempt to do otherwise has been compared to trying to divide a cake before it is ready for slicing.[10] For this reason,

3. The Appraisal Foundation, *Uniform Standards of Professional Appraisal Practice* (USPAP), 1994 ed., Standards Rule 1-2(c), p. 10.
4. *Montgomery Ward & Co., Inc. v. City of Sterling*, 523 P.2d 465 (Colo. 1974).
5. *United States v. Dunnington*, 146 U.S. 338, 351 (1892); *Bogart v. United States*, 169 F.2d 210 (10th Cir. 1948); *Nebraska v. United States*, 164 F.2d 866, 868 (8th Cir. 1947), *cert. denied*, 334 U.S. 815 (1948); *United States v. 25.936 Acres of Land in Borough of Edgewater*, 153 F.2d 277, 279 (3rd Cir. 1946); *Meadows v. United States*, 144 F.2d 751, 752 (4th Cir. 1944).
6. *Lambert v. Griffin*, 100 N.E. 496 (Ill. 1912).
7. *State ex rel. Moore v. Bastian*, 546 P.2d 399 (Idaho 1976).
8. *Nichols' The Law of Eminent Domain*, rev. 3d ed. (New York: Matthew Bender Co., Inc., 1990), vol. 4, §12D.04[1].
9. *Nebraska v. United States*, 164 F.2d 866, 868 (8th Cir. 1947), *cert. denied* 334 U.S. 815 (1948).
10. Harry T. Dolan, "Unit Rule of Valuation in Federal Condemnation," *The Appraisal Journal* (January 1965), 26.

"[t]he matter of such apportionment is of no concern to the condemnor and is a problem in which only the claimants are involved."[11] "Having participated in the trial to establish the value of the whole, the government should have no concern with or responsibility for the later allocating of the distributive shares, among those owning or claiming subordinate estates or interests in the improved site."[12]

The jurisdictions that have adopted the undivided fee rule have taken the position that the sum of the various estates in a parcel of real estate cannot, as a matter of law, exceed the value of the real estate as a whole.[13] Experienced appraisers recognize that "[a]lthough the value of the whole may be equal to the sum of the separate estates or parts, it also may be greater than or less than the sum of such estates or parts."[14] However, only a limited number of jurisdictions have acknowledged this fact.[15]

The few jurisdictions that abandon the undivided fee rule generally adopted an alternate rule, referred to as *the aggregate of interests rule*. In adopting this rule, a California court reasoned:

> The question to be answered in this case is, of what does the whole really consist, for which payment is to be made by the condemner in one lump sum under § 1246.1, if it so elects? It seems to us that this whole must be the total of what the various involuntary sellers have to sell and not the undivided fee which the condemner is seeking to acquire. The fact that in this situation, by resorting to § 1246.1, the condemner can force the valuation award against it to be a single sum for the entire fee rather than a summation of the various separate sums awarded to the several owners of interests or estates in the total fee, arrived at independently of each other, does not compel the conclusion as a corollary to this requirement that the total fee so valued must of necessity be valued as if it were owned only by one owner, when in fact it is actually owned jointly by more than one owner. In other words, what § 1246.1 requires in this initial evaluation in the first phase of this type of condemnation trial, is a valuation of the fee as a whole, but not a valuation of that fee in an undivided state. The two should not be confused and equated as they so often have been.
>
> We base this conclusion on the fundamental nature of the constitutional requirement of just compensation. All of condemnation law, (statutory and decisional) procedure and practice is but a means to this end of just compensation. The power of eminent domain is granted to the executive branch of the state government so that private property may be taken expeditiously for public use whenever it is so needed, but only upon payment of just compensation to the property owner. The right to take private property involuntarily for public use is conditioned and based upon the performance by public authorities of this obligation to pay the owner of private property the just compensation due him. This obligation of the state to make just compensation to the property owner for the property taken has long been recognized in the state as concomitant with and inseparable from its right of eminent domain.

11. *Nichols'*, vol. 4, §12D.4[3] (1990).
12. *Dolan*, 24.
13. *Korfhage v. Commonwealth*, 296 S.W.2d 476 (Ky. 1956).
14. USPAP, 1994 ed., Standards Rule 1-4(e), p. 12.
15. *Nichols'*, vol. 4, §12D.04[2] (1990).

> Just compensation under the Fifth Amendment to the United States Constitution, so far as taking damages are concerned, means the full and perfect equivalent in money of the property taken. The owner is to be put in as good a position pecuniarily as he would have occupied if his property had not been taken from him. We believe that the due process clause of the Fourteenth Amendment of the United States Constitution requires this as well.
>
> In our opinion this is likewise a mandate of Article I, § 14 of our State Constitution. The property owner must be made whole for his loss and be recompensed in an amount of money equal to that loss. In short, just compensation is based on the loss the owner suffers rather than the benefit which the taker receives. What is to be valued for that purpose is what the involuntary sellers have to sell rather than what the public buyer seeks to acquire.[16]

There is a basic distinction between those jurisdictions that have adopted the undivided fee rule and the California court ruling stated above. The California court hears a condemnation case, at least for this purpose, as a case *against the owners of the property*, while jurisdictions adhering to the undivided fee rule view a condemnation trial as a case *in rem*—an action against the property itself, not its owner. It is for this reason that federal condemnation cases are filed as "United States v. *X* Acres of Land" rather than "United States v. Smith," for example.

Because there are only about six jurisdictions that have, at one time or another, abandoned the undivided fee rule in favor of the aggregate of interests rule, the appraiser will generally be concerned with the undivided fee rule. Under this rule, a property encumbered by a lease is valued in the same way as a property not so encumbered. In other words, the property is appraised as if its fee simple title were held by one individual or entity. This does not mean, however, that the appraiser should not consider the existing rent level specified in the lease in estimating the current economic rent of the property being appraised; nor does it mean that leases should be ignored in considering questions relating to the larger parcel or highest and best use.

Under the undivided fee rule, an appraiser retained by the condemnor generally has completed the appraisal assignment once the market value of the property as if unencumbered by a lease has been estimated.[17] This is usually not the case, however, when the appraiser has been retained by the property owner or lessee. For this appraiser, estimating the market value of the unencumbered property is only the first step.

ALLOCATION OF AWARD

The actual procedures of a condemnation trial and the subsequent allocation of the condemnation award vary from jurisdiction to jurisdiction. Some jurisdictions provide that the trier of fact who determines just compensation also makes

16. *Department of Public Works v. Lynbar, Inc.*, 62 Cal. Rptr. 320 (Cal. 1967).
17. "However, the appraiser may be required by the agency to furnish separate valuations of the separate estates or interests for negotiation purposes." *Uniform Appraisal Standards for Federal Land Acquisitions* (Washington, D.C.: U.S. Government Printing Office, 1992), §A-13, fn. 115, p. 40.

the determination of the proper allocation of the total award, but only after first determining total just compensation. As stated by the Illinois court:

> Where is becomes necessary for the jury to assess damages for separate interests in condemnation proceedings, it is the duty of the jury to first fix the fair cash market value of the entire property between the petitioner and all of the defendants, and then to divide same according to the respective rights of the defendants.[18]

Other jurisdictions hold a separate hearing on the question of award allocation. "The tenant is given his chance to 'fight it out' with his landlord during allocation proceedings where he can point to 'the period of the unexpired term of the lease, the options, if any, therein to renew or of the landlord to terminate, the characteristics of the demised premises and the amount of rent reserved.'"[19] [Citations omitted]

The federal courts have consistently held that it is improper to present any testimony regarding the allocation of a condemnation award to a jury hearing a condemnation case. "Any contest between persons claiming an interest in the award is heard by the Court and not the jury and only after the award of all interests in the land has been made. Various persons claiming an interest in the land may appear and desire to present proof of fair market value in the first phase of the case, e.g., owners and lessees."[20]

Such two-step condemnation procedures can create strange bedfellows. In the first phase of a trial, the actual condemnation and the determination of total compensation, the landlord and tenant are codefendants; they will often work together to develop and present the strongest case possible to the trier of fact in hopes of receiving a high award. In the second phase of the trial, the allocation of the award between the landlord and the lessee, these parties become adversaries.[21] It is not unknown for the appraiser who testified for the condemnor in the condemnation phase of the trial to subsequently be retained by either the lessor or the lessee to estimate and testify to the proper allocation of the total award.

Generally, the appraiser retained by the condemnor will not be involved in the valuation of leased fee estates or leasehold estates or in the allocation of a condemnation award between these two estates. An appraiser retained by a lessor or a lessee in a condemnation action, however, may also be called upon to estimate the proper allocation of the condemnation award. It is also possible that an appraiser totally unconnected with the original condemnation action may be selected by the lessor or lessee to estimate the apportionment.

The specific methods used to calculate the proper allocation of a condemnation award between the lessor and the lessee will vary substantially depending on the jurisdiction in which the property is located and the specific provisions of the lease.

18. *Lambert v. Griffin*, 100 N.E. 496 (Ill. 1912).

19. *New Jersey Sports and Exposition Authority v. Borough of East Rutherford*, 348 A.2d 825 (N.J. 1975).

20. *United States v. 3,276.21 Acres of Land*, 194 F.Supp. 297, 300 (S.D. Cal. 1961).

21. *Clark v. Erich*, 31 Cal. Rptr. 628 (Cal. 1963).

LEASE PROVISIONS

The provisions of the lease encumbering the tract that is acquired or damaged are of extreme importance to the appraiser charged with estimating the proper allocation of a condemnation award, or settlement, between the lessor and the lessee of the property. The value of the leased fee and leasehold interests can only be estimated after the terms and conditions of the lease are determined. The increasing complexity of commercial real estate ownership, financing, and occupancy has all but eliminated the "standard" lease form. Leases can include a variety of provisions between the parties that effect the quality, quantity, and durability of the income steam. A discussion of all the provisions found in various types of leases is beyond the scope of this work, but this information can be found in other texts.[22] The appraiser must, of course, obtain a complete copy of the lease and analyze it in detail; technical questions regarding lease provisions should be addressed to proper legal counsel. The lease provision that will be of utmost importance to the appraiser is the so-called *condemnation clause*.

A condemnation clause will often dictate the formula to be used in determining how much of the condemnation award should be paid to the lessee, if any. In analyzing the condemnation clause in a lease, the appraiser must answer the following questions:

- Does the lease contain a condemnation clause?
- In a total taking, when does the obligation to pay rent cease?
- Is the lessee to share in the award for a total taking? If so, on what basis?
- How is the award for fixtures and tenant improvements to be apportioned in a total taking?
- In a partial taking, is the lessee to share in the award? If so, on what basis?
- Is the lessor to share in the award for a partial taking of the leased premises with a rent abatement? If so, how is the abatement to be determined?
- If, in a partial taking, the lessor does not share in the award for the loss of rental value, is a trust to be established from the award to ensure future payment of rent to the lessor?
- If the lessee remains in possession after a partial taking, who is responsible for restoration of the property? To whose specifications must the repairs be made? Is a trust to be set up from the award to guarantee the repairs? Must the repairs be made within a specified time?
- Should there be an option to terminate the lease on partial taking? If there is such an option, when must it be exercised? May it be exercised by either party?
- If there is a partial taking where percentage leases are involved, is the flat rate per rental period and sales percentage figure to be revised?
- Does the lease cover the possibility of "inverse condemnation"?
- Does the lease address "substantial impairment or loss of access" or other indirect damage to the premises?

22. *The Appraisal of Real Estate*, 10th ed., 429–435.

- Are the rights of the lessor and lessee spelled out vis-a-vis the mortgage lender? If the leasehold is used as a basis of the lessee's mortgage are the rights of theses [sic] parties provided for?
- Are sufficient provisions made for special situations, such as loss of all or part of the parking lot in a shopping center?
- Is each of the critical dates (such as the date of the taking and time limits on repairs) adequately spelled out? Do the parties understand that "date of taking" is a term of art that may be different from the date of filing of the lawsuit or the transfer of possession to the condemnor?
- Is the tenant's obligation to pay all or part of the real estate taxes and/or utilities modified in the event of a condemnation?
- What are the parties' rights and obligations in the event the condemnor abandons condemnation?[23]

In addition to this list of questions, *Nichols'* contains a number of illustrative condemnation clauses.[24] If the terms of a condemnation clause are to preclude any relief for the lessee, the clause must be drafted carefully. The courts have a tendency to interpret such clauses strictly against the owner of the leased fee estate.

The provisions of the condemnation clause and the other provisions of the lease should point the appraiser to the correct methodology to be applied in estimating the allocation of the award between the lessor and the lessee. The appraiser should keep in mind that often the individual or entity in possession of the property is not the original lessee, but a sublessee. In this case, it is necessary to consider how the total award will be allocated between the lessor, the original lessee, and the sublessee. In such a situation the original lessee is often referred to as the *sandwich man* and the lease is referred to as a *sandwich lease*. "In any event, the damages that should be paid to the tenant are not easy to ascertain."[25]

LEGAL RULES AND METHODOLOGY OF VALUATION

To affect the value of the leased fee estate, a lease must meet two conditions. First, the remaining term of the lease must be long enough so that, if the property were placed on the market, a potential purchaser would recognize the lease and be willing to pay more or less for the property because of its existence. Second, the contract rent specified in the lease must be either higher or lower than the existing market, or economic, rent. Again, the difference between the contract rent and the economic rent must be substantial enough to affect what an able, willing buyer would pay for the property.

Often, but not always, the value of the leased fee estate plus the value of the leasehold estate will tend to equal the market value of the property free and clear of any lease. Experienced appraisers know that this is not always the case but, in

23. *Nichols'*, vol. 7A, §11.05[2] (1991).

24. Ibid., §11.06[3].

25. *Nichols'*, vol. 4, §12D.04[4] (1990).

a large majority of jurisdictions, the courts have adopted this concept absolutely. It has been said that "[w]hatever advantage is secured by one interest must be taken from another, *and the sum of all the parts cannot exceed the whole.*"[26] Therefore, appraisers and attorneys generally must work within the confines of this rule.

Proper appraisal practice would require that the leasehold estate and the leased fee estate be valued separately; the sum of these two estates may or may not equal the market value of the property as if unencumbered. To determine the allocation of a condemnation award, however, a different procedure is required.

> The task of determining the value of the unexpired term of a lease is not without its difficulties. Because of restrictions against assignability, the infrequency with which short term leases are sold on the open market; variations in the duration of unexpired terms; and other considerations too numerous to mention, it is virtually impossible to rely exclusively upon the customary test of market value as to leasehold estates and, at the same time, secure to the condemnee the constitutional guarantee of full or just compensation. The actual value, or value to the owner, is usually the best, if not the only adequate test of such compensation."[27]

The Indiana court has ruled otherwise:

> The State contends that there was no proper foundation established to support the opinion evidence of appellees' witnesses, particularly complaining that the opinions were based on a capitalization of net profits. State argues that the proper method of valuing a leasehold interest is to take "the difference between the contract rent and the fair rental value, if any, capitalized for the unexpired term of the lease and discounted by the factor of present worth." For this proposition the State cites [several New York cases]....
>
> Although decisions from other States, including the New York cases above noted, speak of computing the value of a leasehold by measuring the excess of rental value over the rents to be paid during the remainder of the term, we are unable to find any Indiana authority to this effect.
>
> Indiana case and statutory law converge upon the concept that fair market value is the proper measure of damages where a leasehold interest is condemned.[28]

Some courts have, in effect, treated a leasehold interest as they would a special-use property, referring to a leasehold interest as having an *actual value*, *intrinsic value*, and a *value to the owner*. A Pennsylvania court stated:

> But market value is an unsatisfactory test of the value to a tenant of a leasehold interest. It is really no test at all because a lease rarely has any market value. Generally it is not assignable at the will of the tenant, and he pays in rent all that the right of occupation is worth. The right of which he is deprived, and for which he is entitled to full compensation, is the right to remain in undisturbed possession to the end of the term. The loss resulting from the deprivation of this right is what he is entitled to recover.[29]

26. *Lewis on Eminent Domain*, 3d ed., vol. 2, §7.16 [emphasis added].
27. *Orange State Oil Co. v. Jacksonville Expressway Authority*, 110 So.2d 687, 690 (Fla. 1959).
28. *State v. Nelson*, 296 N.E.2d 908, 910–911 (Ind. 1973).
29. *McMillan Printing Co. v. Pittsburgh, Etc., R. Co.*, 65 A. 1091, 1094 (Pa. 1907).

On the other hand, the Massachusetts court held that, when contract rent and economic rent are equal, the tenant has not been compensably damaged.[30]

Through case law, various courts have established methods and formulas to be used in the valuation of leasehold and leased fee estates so that condemnation awards can be allocated. Unfortunately, there is no uniformity in the methods applied to allocate condemnation awards between lessees and lessors.

A Connecticut case held that the leasehold estate is to be valued and apportioned to the lessee, with the balance of the award being allocated to the lessor. The court stated:

> Generally, a leasehold has a value if a fair market rental value of the property, sometimes called economic rent, is in excess of the rent reserved in the lease. In the case of a total taking of property, the accepted method of assessing damages to the leasehold is to determine the annual difference between the contract rent and the economic rent, to multiply the annual difference by the number of years left under the lease, and then to discount that sum to determine its present value. In a partial taking such as in the present case, the same rule is generally followed except that the value of the leasehold before and after the taking must be determined. The measure of damages is the difference between the before and after values of the leasehold.[31] [Citations omitted]

The Tennessee court put forth a similar rule, but this ruling did not make any mention of discounting the rent differential between economic rent and contract rent. It merely stated that the "[a]pportionment between lessor and lessee is accomplished by determining the value of the latter's interest in the taken property, which in turn is calculated by determining the fair rental value of that property for the unexpired term of the lease and subtracting the rent that would actually have been paid for it by the lessee during that term."[32]

The Florida formula conflicts with the Connecticut rule. The Florida court has stated its apportionment formula as follows:

> This method consists of first determining the fair market value of the property being condemned, free of the leasehold estate. The next step in the process consisted of adding to the reversionary value of the fee at the termination of the lease the reserved rent payable during the remainder of the term, and reducing the total to its present value by application of the appropriate annuity tables. The last figure thus reached represented the witnesses's opinion as to what constituted the present market value of the fee subject to the lease which, when deducted from the present value of the unencumbered fee, left a remainder which represented the value of the leasehold.[33]

There appears to be considerable confusion on the part of the courts as to whether it is appropriate to apply a discount factor to the difference between the contract rent and the economic rent to arrive at the value of a leasehold estate. A Missouri court stated:

30. *Uhland Club v. Shupbach*, 47 N.E. 113 (Mass. 1897).
31. *Gigliotti v. Wood*, 397 A.2d 1342, 1344 (Conn. 1978).
32. *State ex. rel. Dep't of Transportation v. Gee*, 565 S.W.2d 498,502 (Tenn. 1977).
33. *Orange State Oil Co. v. Jacksonville Expressway Authority*, 110 So.2d 687, 689 (Fla. 1959).

> Lessors' next point is that the judgment is excessive for failure to reduce the judgment to present cash value. Lessors' argument is that the leasehold bonus would not have been realized in one lump sum, but in a series of annual installments or accruals of $1250 over the next 7 1/2 (we have concluded 17 1/2) years, but for the condemnations proceedings, and that the court should not commute these future benefits and award them presently in one lump sum at their full value, but should "apply a discount factor to arrive at the present value of the market value as a lump sum payable *in praesenti.*"
>
> We are of the opinion that the discount factor should be applied under the particular facts of this case; that this lessee is entitled only to the capitalized value of the bonus. The principle is that of an annuity. The method is the commutation to a lump sum of the series of periodic benefits which but for the condemnation proceedings would have accrued in the future, the enjoyment of which would have been delayed and withheld until by the passage of time the future dates of accrual arrived. The discounted sum, presently to be awarded in one lump sum, with a given rate of interest compounded, will equal the amounts which would have come due annually by the expiration of time under the operation of the lease.[34]

Nichols' cites an Ohio appellate case for the proposition that such rental advantage should not be discounted.[35] The Ohio appellate court ruled:

> Discounting is the determination of the present value of future income or benefits. Appellant's theory of discounting leasehold value is that if there is value to the lease, the lessee will receive this value or benefit ratably over eight years and eight months, and if the lessee receives cash for this benefit at one time, the total amount should be discounted because the benefit will come to the lessee all at once and he does not have to wait for it. Some courts have recognized discounting in determining the value of a leasehold.
>
> However, a majority of courts have ruled that the fair and reasonable market value of a leasehold interest is the full amount of the difference between the fair market rental value of the leased premises for the unexpired term and the rent paid under the terms of the lease.
>
> Ohio also has not recognized the discount theory in determining fair market value of the leasehold interest in apportionment proceedings between the lessor and lessee in an appropriation case. The value of a leasehold interest is the difference between the lease rent and the fair market rent for the term of the lease and option period. There is no Ohio statute or reported case requiring discounting in determining value of a leasehold in an appropriation case.[36] [Citations omitted]

It is unclear why *Nichols'* has continued for more than 10 years to cite this Ohio case proposing that discounting is improper when the Ohio Supreme Court reversed this case in 1974 on the grounds that a discount should have been applied to the rental advantage.[37]

34. *Land Clearance for Redevelopment Corp. v. Doernhoefer*, 389 S.W.2d 780, 788 (Mo. 1965).
35. *Nichols'*, vol. 4, §12D.04[4] (1990).
36. *Pokorny v. Local 310, Int. Hod Carriers*, 300 N.E.2d 464 (Ohio 1973).
37. *Pokorny v. Local No. 310, Int. HOD Carriers B. & C.L.U.*, 311 N.E.2d 866 (Ohio 1974).

The confusion between the two positions held by various courts and others appears to stem from comparing cases involving long-term leaseholds with cases involving short-term leaseholds. For example, if a leasehold advantage of $1,000 per year has only three years until expiration, the total value to be received over the remaining term of the lease will be $1,000 x 3 years, or $3,000. If this three-year income stream is discounted at 10%, the present value of the income stream will be $1,000 x 2.486852 (*PV* of $1 per year for three years discounted at 10%), or $2,486.85. The difference between the results produced with these two methods is only 17%. Now assume that the remaining term of the lease is 23 years instead of three. The total value received over the remaining term of the lease would be $1,000 x 23 years, or $23,000. When this $1,000 per year income stream is discounted at 10%, the present value of the income stream is $1,000 x 8.883218 (*PV* of $1 per year for 23 years discounted at 10%), or $8,883.22. Thus, there is a 61% differential in the results when the two methods are applied to the long-term (23-year) income stream.

In the latter example, the rental advantage was discounted at an appropriate rate to convert it into a present value. This is a standard valuation procedure that is well recognized in the appraisal profession and would be applicable in nearly all instances. Discounting may not be required, however, when minimal rental advantage is to be enjoyed for an extremely short term; the application of a discount factor would have only a nominal effect on the results of the computation.

The absurdity of valuing a leasehold estate simply by multiplying the lessee's annual rental advantage by the remaining term of the lease becomes obvious when long-term, positive leasehold estates are considered.

Presumably, states that have retained the rule that the leasehold interest is simply the aggregate of the rental advantage over the remaining term of the lease have not, as yet, considered the consequences if such a rule is applied to a substantial lease advantage over a remaining term of several years. It must be concluded that when such cases are reviewed by higher state courts in the future, the method of discounting rental advantages described here will become the most prevalent, and indeed the only acceptable, rule.

The Kentucky court took the opportunity to review its previously adopted rulings in regard to the valuation of leasehold interests. The court used an example in its ruling, which clearly illustrated the absurdity of its previous formula for computing the value of a leasehold estate. The court said:

> While we are reversing the judgment because of failure of the trial court to observe the existing rules of law in this jurisdiction applicable to eminent domain cases, we have decided to reexamine those rules, abolish some of them, and state new rules that will govern in the event of another trial of this case, and will have application in other cases as stated at the end of this opinion.

Determination and Allocation of Damages for Leased Property

As related to the leased parcel, and the determination of the respective damages of the landowners and the lessees, the evidence in this case was directed in a loose way towards application of the method outlined in *City of Ashland v. Price*, Ky., 318 S.W.2d 861. The key to this method is "to ascertain the present fair rental value, compare it with the rent stipulated in the contract and allow the aggregate difference for the period of the unexpired term of the lease."

Aside from the fact that the foregoing method furnishes no criterion or basis for determining the lessee's damages where only *part* and *not all* of the leased property is taken, we have come to the conclusion after thorough reconsideration that the method is completely unsound, unfair and unworkable.

Let us use an illustration that is not far afield from the actual facts of this case: The property as a whole, if sold free and clear of the lease, would have a value of $100,000. The fair rental value would be $12,000 per year (there is testimony in this case that 12% rent is fair for commercial property). The lessees have contracted to pay only $6,000 per year. Their lease has 20 years to run. The state condemns the entire tract. By applying the method outlined in the Ashland case, the lessees would be damaged $120,000 ($6,000 per year for 20 years) or $20,000 more than the whole property was worth. This is so patently absurd as to establish beyond any question the fallaciousness of the method. The foregoing illustration is not at all inappropriate because in the instant case the lessees were paying $7,200 a year rent; they said the fair rental was $14,400 a year; their lease had 15 years to run; therefore their damage was $108,000. Yet they testified that the leased property as a whole was worth only $120,000 (one said is was worth only $105,000) and the state took less than one-fourth of the area and none of the structures.[38]

At page 850 the court went on to establish specific rules to be applied in all future leasehold valuation cases tried in the state:

After thorough deliberation we have worked out what we consider to be the most reasonably fair and workable method for determining compensation in cases of condemnation of property that is under lease. Under this method the proof should be directed towards showing, and the instructions should require the jury to find, only the following three values:

A. The fair market value of the leased tract as a whole immediately before the taking, giving consideration to the fact that it has rental value but *evaluating it as if free and clear of the lease*. (This will be factor *A*.)

B. The fair market value of the leased tract as a whole, immediately before the taking, *if sold subject to the existing lease*. (This will be factor *B*.)

C. The fair market value of so much of the leased tract as remains immediately after the taking, giving consideration to the fact that it has rental value but evaluating it as if free and clear of the lease. (This will be factor *C*.) (Of course, if the entire tract is taken by the condemnation, this value will be zero and need not be

38. *Commonwealth Dept. of H'ways. v. Sherrod*, 367 S.W.2d 844, 848 (Ky. 1963).

found by the jury, but for the purpose of the following computations *C* will be considered to be zero.)

After the jury has fixed the foregoing three values the *judge* will compute and apportion the damages as follows:

(1) Subtract *C* from *A*. The result is the total damages payable by the condemnor.

(2) If *B* is the *same* as or *more* than *A*, ignore *B*. In this situation *all* of the damages will go [to] the *landowner*, because the leasehold had no value, by reason of the fact that the existence of the lease has not impaired the market value of the tract.

(3) If *B* is *less* than *A*, subtract *B* from *A* and then *divide* the difference by *A*. The result is the *percentage of ownership interest* the *lessee* is deemed to have had in the leased tract before the condemnation.

(4) *Multiply* the total damages, found under (1) above, by the percentage found under (3) above. The result will be the *lessee's* share of the total damages. Subtracting his share from the total damages will leave the *landowner's* share.

It is proper for the foregoing computations to be made by the judge because they involve only mathematical computations and not a determination of disputed facts. It would confuse the jury to require them to make the computations.

Julius Sackman summarized the rules applicable in New York State, as developed in the landmark *Great Atlantic & Pacific Tea Company* case[39]:

(1) *As to valuation of leased property.*—The property should be valued as if there were no lease and as if single ownership in unencumbered fee simple absolute prevailed. All appropriate methods of valuation can be utilized—the market data approach, the income approach, and the cost approach. However, if the income approach is used, it must be remembered that "rental value," not the reserved rent, should be capitalized.

(2) *Leasehold value.*—Leasehold value exists only if there is a so-called "bonus value" to the lease—i.e., that the rental value, or economic rental as it is sometimes called, is in excess of the reserved rental. The leasehold value is, of course, computed by applying the appropriate Inwood coefficients to the annual bonus values for each year of the remainder of the lease term and aggregating the results so obtained.

(3) *Complete taking.*—It [sic] there is a complete taking the award is apportioned as follows:

    (a) Leasehold value is paid to the lessee.

    (b) Unencumbered fee value minus leasehold value equals the amount to be paid to the lessor.

(4) *Partial taking.*—If there is a partial taking the award is apportioned as follows:

    (a) Leasehold value prior to the taking minus leasehold value of the remainder after the taking equals the amount to be paid to the lessee. The

39. *Great Atlantic & Pacific Tea Co. v. State*, 238 N.E.2d 705 (N.Y. 1968).

leasehold value of the remainder is computed by subtracting the reserved rent, as abated, from the rental value of the remainder area.

(b) The damages computed on the basis of the undivided fee rule, minus the amount found under "(a)" immediately above equals the amount due to the lessor.

(5) *Temporary easement or taking of the entire demised premises.*—If there is a temporary taking of the *entire* premises for a period *shorter* that the balance of the leased term, the entire award belongs to the lessee. If, however, the period of the taking is *longer* than the balance of the leased term and if the taking affects the *entire* property, the award is apportioned as follows:

(a) Leasehold value is paid to the lessee.

(b) The award for the temporary taking, computed under the undivided fee rule, minus the leasehold value equals the amount to be paid to the lessor.

(6) *Temporary easement or taking of part of the demised premises.*—If there is a temporary taking of *part* of the premises for a period which is *shorter* than the balance of the leased term, the entire award belongs to the lessee. In such case, of course, the tenant continues to pay the full rent in unabated amount. If however, as a result of such temporary partial taking, there is an abatement in the rent, the award should be allocated as follows:

(a) If the rent reserved, as abated, is *equal* to or *greater* than the fair rental value of the property either as a temporary remainder area or as the property subject to a temporary easement, then only the landlord is injured by the temporary taking and he should receive the entire award.

(b) If the rent reserved, as abated, is *less* than the fair rental value of the property either as a temporary remainder area or as property subject to a temporary easement, then the award should be apportioned as follows:

1. The present value of the amount of the rental which has been abated should be paid to the lessor.
2. The balance of the award should be paid to the lessee because this represents the decline in the bonus value of the lease.

If the temporary taking of *part* of the demised premises extends *beyond* the balance of the leased term, the award should be broken down into two parts, the first part being allocable to the leased term and the second part being allocable to the reversionary period. The latter part would be paid to the lessor. The first part would be paid to the lessee or the lessor, or apportioned between them, as set forth with respect to takings which expire prior to the end of the leased term.[40]

The foregoing discussion relates to the allocation of a condemnation award when a positive leasehold estate exists and the total condemnation award must be allocated between the lessor and the lessee. The other side of the coin, however, is a situation in which a positive leased fee estate and a negative leasehold

40. Julius L. Sackman, "Apportionment of Award Between Lessor and Lessee," *The Appraisal Journal* (October 1970), 550–551.

estate exist because the contract rent is greater than the economic rent. As previously noted, nearly all courts hold that the aggregate value of the various interests in the real estate cannot exceed the value of the real estate as a whole.[41] The only reasoning in support of this conclusion, other than the fact than a condemnation case is viewed as a case *in rem*, is that any rent received by the lessor in excess of economic rent "...must be considered as a *profit* for which [the landowner] is not entitled to be compensated in condemnation proceedings."[42] This position, however, appears to conflict with the majority rule that "...the government may neither confiscate the owner's bargain, nor be required to assume his loss."[43]

APPRAISAL RULES AND METHODS OF VALUATION[44]

Again, the following discussion relates only to situations involving a positive leasehold estate. If no positive leasehold exists, there is no need to allocate the condemnation award because the entire amount will go to the owner of the leased fee estate.

Before attempting to value a leasehold or allocate a condemnation award, the appraiser must fully understand all the terms and conditions of the lease and be familiar with the condemnation laws applicable in the jurisdiction, specifically the laws relating to a lessee's liability when a leased property is partially or totally acquired. In all instances, the provisions of a condemnation clause within a lease will prevail over statutory and decisional law.[45] Statutory law is generally intended to be applied only when no condemnation clause has been included in the lease. In many jurisdictions, statutory law requires that the tenant continue to pay full contract rent as specified in the lease when a partial taking has occurred.[46] However, some jurisdictions do provide for rent abatement in the event of a partial acquisition.[47]

In analyzing the terms of a lease, the appraiser should note its expiration date and whether there are any provisions for renewal. If the lease can be renewed at the same rent or at another specified rent, and the renewal provision is obligatory on the part of the lessor, the appraiser may assume that the lease will be renewed if the contract rent specified is less than economic rent.[48] This assumption is based on the premise that, by contract, the lessor must renew the lease, and any prudent lessee would choose to renew a lease if the rent specified is below existing economic rent.

41. *Korfhage v. Commonwealth*, 296 S.W.2d 476 (Ky. 1956); *Lewis on Eminent Domain*, 3rd ed., §7.16.
42. *Commonwealth Dept. of H'ways. v. Sherrod*, 367 S.W.2d 844, 849 (Ky. 1963).
43. *Ballentine's Law Dictionary*, 3d ed., s.v. "just compensation"; *Kintner v. United States*, 156 F.2d 5 (3rd Cir., 1946).
44. For a detailed explanation of the mathematics used in the following discussion, see *The Appraisal of Real Estate*, 10th ed., Chapters 20 (Direct Capitalization), 21 (Yield Capitalization–Theory and Basic Applications), 22 (Yield Capitalization–Advanced Applications), Appendix B (Mathematics in Appraising) and Appendix C (Financial Tables).
45. *Savin Hill Yacht Club Ass'n v. Savin Hill Yacht Club*, 140 N.E. 299 (Mass. 1923).
46. *Gluck v. Baltimore*, 32 A. 515 (Md. 1895).
47. *Hinrieks v. New Orleans*, 24 So. 224 (La. 1898).
48. *Matter of City of New York*, 118 App. Div. 865 (1907), *aff'd* 189 N.Y. 508 (N.Y. 1907).

If the lease contains a provision for renewal at a new, arbitrated rent, it is generally assumed that the arbitrated rent will equal economic rent at the time of renewal and the positive leasehold estate will no longer exist.[49] A lessee's unexercised option to purchase the leased property generally has no additional value and should not be considered by the appraiser.[50] Also, if the lessee is restricted to a specific use by the lease agreement, the property's estimated economic rent for condemnation award allocation must be based on the use of the property specified in the lease, not on the highest and best use of the property.[51]

Appraisers must report their allocation conclusions in accordance with the rules applicable in the jurisdiction where the property is located. However, appraisers have much more latitude than the legal rules discussed above may imply.

If the appraiser concludes that the market value of a property subject to a total taking approximates the sum of the values of the various interests that make up the fee simple estate, each interest need not be evaluated individually. If the appraiser was not involved in the condemnation phase of the action, the market value of the property as if free and clear must be estimated. To adopt the value determined by the trier of fact or a stipulated settlement between the condemnor and the condemnee is not appropriate for the same reason that an appraiser cannot adopt a local taxing authority's assessed value as market value. An estimate of the property's market value as if unencumbered by a lease gives the appraiser a basis from which to work. If the property is leased, it must be income-producing; therefore, as a part of the appraisal process, the appraiser will use the income approach to estimate the value of the fee simple estate. In doing so, the appraiser will arrive at conclusions as to the economic rent of the property and the capitalization rate that would be applied to the property if it were free and clear of the lease.

The appraiser compares the economic rent arrived at in valuing the unencumbered property with the contract rent specified in the lease, giving consideration to the remaining term of the lease. This comparison will often tell the appraiser whether the lessor or the lessee has the major interest in the fee simple value of the property. If it appears that the leased fee estate represents 75% to 85% of the value of the fee simple estate, the value of the leasehold estate should be estimated first and deducted from the value of the whole; the remainder will represent the value of the leased fee estate.

For example, consider the total taking of a property with the economic characteristics shown in Table 18.1. First, the value of the unencumbered fee is estimated and the overall capitalization is extracted from market data. Then the lessee's annual rent advantage is calculated at $4,000 and an 11% discount factor, or risk rate, is selected as applicable to the lease advantage. This rate is seldom available directly from market data, but the risk rate selected is generally higher than the overall rate applicable to the property as unencumbered for two reasons:

49. *Kernochan v. Manhattan R.R. Co.*, 55 N.E. 906 (N.Y. 1900).

50. *Haney v. Denny*, 193 N.E.2d 648 (Ind. 1963).

51. *North Coast R. Co. v. Kraft Co.*, 115 P. 97 (Wash. 1911).

TABLE 18.1 VALUATION OF LEASED FEE AND LEASEHOLD ESTATES

Valuation of unencumbered property:	
Net annual economic rent	$ 31,500
Overall capitalization rate (from market)	10%
Indicated fee simple value ($31,500 ÷ 0.10)	$315,000
Valuation of leasehold interest:	
Net annual contract rent	$ 27,500
Remaining lease term	25 years
Annual leasehold advantage ($31,500 – $27,500)	$ 4,000
Lessee's risk rate	11%
Present value of $1 per period for 25 years @ 11%	8.421745*
Indicated value of leasehold estate ($4,000 x 8.421745)	$ 33,687
Valuation of leased fee estate:	
Value of unencumbered fee	$315,000
Value of leasehold estate	– 33,687
Indicated value of leased fee estate	$281,313
Indicated rate applicable to leased fee estate:	
Leased fee dividend rate (27,500 ÷ $281,313)	9.7756%
Leased fee internal rate of return	9.8992%*

* Computed using a financial calculator.

Note. The rates applied in this and subsequent tables are carried out to six decimal points for purposes of illustration. In practice, rates would typically be rounded to four or fewer decimal points.

1. The contract rent is less than the economic rent, so a prudent lessor would void the lease at the first opportunity, i.e., because of a direct violation of the lease provisions or on some small technicality.
2. The lessee's position is analogous to the equity owner's position in a mortgage-equity situation. Any decline in market value, or market rent in this situation, is suffered by the lessee, not the lessor, so the lessee's position carries with it greater risk than that of the lessor.

The calculations in Table 18.1 show that the indicated dividend rate for the lessor's interest is approximately 9.78%, nearly one-quarter of 1% below the 10% overall rate applicable to the unencumbered fee. In this situation, the owner of the leased fee estate is exposed to less risk than he would be if the property were leased at economic rent. It is unlikely that a tenant with an annual lease advantage of $4,000 would default on the lease, so the owner of the leased fee estate will generally settle for a lower return than would be required if the property were leased at economic rent and no positive leasehold estate existed. The example also shows the development of an internal rate of return applicable to the leased fee estate. This rate is slightly higher than the dividend rate because the reversion to the lessor is assumed to be $315,000, as opposed to the $281,313 value of the existing leased fee estate.[52]

52. It could be argued that the discount rate applicable to the reversion would be different from the rate applied to the income stream. For purposes of illustration, however, a single rate has been utilized in this and subsequent examples.

To allocate a condemnation award or stipulated judgment, the values developed in Table 18.1 can be converted into percentages of the unencumbered fee value of the property. For example, if a condemnation award of $345,000 were made, the computations for apportionment would be:

Lessee's interest in fee simple estate ($33,687 ÷ $315,000)	10.69%
Lessor's interest in fee simple estate ($281,313 ÷ $315,000)	89.31%
Total	100.00%
Allocation of award:	
Lessee ($345,000 x 0.1069)	$ 36,881
Lessor ($345,000 x 0.8931)	308,119
Total award	$345,000

If the jurisdiction where the property is located requires that the value of the leased fee estate be deducted from the value of the unencumbered fee, the same methodology can be employed by the appraiser but simply presented in reverse. The computations developed under this rule are shown in Table 18.2.

TABLE 18.2 ALLOCATION OF FEE VALUE OF PROPERTY

Valuation of unencumbered property:	
Net annual economic rent	$ 31,500
Overall capitalization rate (from market)	10%
Indicated fee simple value ($31,500 ÷ 0.10)	$315,000
Valuation of leased fee estate:	
Net annual contract rent	$ 27,500
Remaining lease term	25 years
Amount of reversion	$315,000
Value of income stream ($27,500 x 9.147852*)	$251,566
Value of reversion ($315,000 x 0.094436†)	29,747
Indicated value of leased fee estate	$281,313
Valuation of leasehold estate:	
Value of unencumbered fee	$315,000
Value of leased fee estate	–281,313
Indicated value of leasehold estate	$ 33,687
Indicated rate applicable to leasehold estate	11.00% ‡

* Present value of $1 per period for 25 years @ 9.8992%.
† Present value of $1 for 25 years @ 9.8992%
‡ Computed using a financial calculator.

The computations for apportionment, again assuming an award of $345,000, would be:

Lessor's interest in fee simple estate ($281,313 ÷ $315,000)	89.31%
Lessee's interest in fee simple estate ($33,687 ÷ $315,000)	10.69%
Total	100.00%

Allocation of award:	
Lessor ($345,000 x 0.8931)	$308,119
Lessee ($345,000 x 0.1069)	36,881
Total award	$345,000

There is a very good reason for computing the value of the smaller interest in the fee simple estate and deducting it from the unencumbered fee value to arrive at the indicated value of the remainder interest. If the appraiser's conclusion as to the risk rate applicable to the leasehold is incorrect, valuing the leasehold first minimizes the error. For instance, if the leasehold risk rate should have been 10% instead of 11%, the error in allocating the $345,000 award would be only $2,898, or less than 1%. This computation is shown in Table 18.3.

TABLE 18.3 ANALYSIS OF VALUE ALLOCATION

Indicated fee simple value of property	$315,000
Value of leasehold estate ($4,000 x 9.077040*)	– 36,308
Indicated value of leased fee estate	$278,692
Apportionment computations:	
Lessee ($36,308 ÷ $315,000)	11.53%
Lessor ($278,692 ÷ $315,000)	88.47%
Allocation of award	
Lessee ($345,000 x 0.1153)	$ 39,779
Lessor ($345,000 x 0.8847)	305,221
Total award	$345,000

	Lessee	Lessor
Award assuming 11% lessee risk rate	$36,881	$308,119
Award assuming 10% lessee risk rate	– 39,779	–305,221
Difference	–$ 2,898	$ 2,898
Error in allocation of total award ($2,898 ÷ $345,000)		0.84%

*Present value of $1 per period for 25 years @ 10%.

Now assume that the lessor's interest was computed first, using a rate of 8.9% instead of 9.9%. The resulting error in allocating the $345,000 award would be $31,120, or about 10% of the total award. These computations are shown in Table 18.4. Computing the leased fee interest first at 8.9% would reduce the lessee's portion of the total allocation by $31,120; a loss of nearly 85% of the lessee's award would result from this procedure.

The foregoing discussion relates to a total taking. Other problems arise when a partial taking occurs. In a partial taking case, the lease condemnation clause becomes critical. Consider a partial taking with the following before and after values:

TABLE 18.4 ALLOCATION OF AWARD COMPUTATIONS

Indicated fee simple value of property		$315,000
Value of leased fee interest:		
Income stream ($27,500 x 9.903346*)	$272,342	
Reversion ($315,000 x 0.118681†)	37,385	
Total value of leased fee estate		–309,727
Indicated value of leasehold estate		$ 5,273
Apportionment computations:		
Lessor ($309,727 ÷ $315,000)		98.33%
Lessee ($5,273 ÷ $315,000)		1.67%
Total		100.00%
Allocation of award:		
Lessor ($345,000 x 0.9833)		$339,239
Lessee ($345,000 x 0.0167)		5,761
Total		$345,000

	Lessor	Lessee
Award assuming 9.9% lessor rate	$308,119	$ 36,881
Award assuming 8.9% lessor rate	– 339,239	– 5,761
Difference	–$ 31,120	$ 31,120

* Present value of $1 per period for 25 years @ 8.8992%.

† Present value of $1 for 25 years @ 8.8992%

	Land	Building	Total
Before	$60,000	$70,000	$130,000
After	–40,000	–60,000	–100,000
Difference	$20,000	$10,000	$ 30,000

Assume the property was unimproved when the lease was written and the lessee constructed the improvements. According to the lease, the lessee has the right to remove the improvements at the end of the lease term, which is 25 years from the date of taking. The lease requires a net land lease payment of $4,500 per year to the lessor and has no lease abatement provisions in the event of a partial condemnation. Applicable rates of return on land are currently about 10.5%

As the before and after values indicate, the taking and damages equal $30,000. The appraiser should recognize that a leased fee estate has only two components: the right to receive the rental payments during the term of the lease and the right to occupy and use the property at the termination of the lease. It is evident, therefore, that the only lessor right that is affected by the condemnation is the right to the reversion of the land at the expiration of the lease; the lease payments will remain the same after the taking. Therefore, allocating the taking and damages is simply a matter of estimating the present value of the loss of the lessor's reversionary interest in the property; the balance of the taking and damages will be attributed to the lessee. The calculations follow:

Total taking and damage			$30,000
Lessor's reversion before taking ($60,000 x 0.082403)*		$4,944	
Lessor's reversion after taking ($40,000 x 0.082403)		–3,296	
Lessor's interest in award			– 1,648
Lessee's interest in award			$28,352

* Present value of $1 factor for 25 years discounted at 10.5%.

If, in the example, the lessor were to take possession of the building at the end of the lease term, the right of that reversion would also have be considered. Assuming the improvements would be valued at 50% of their current value at the end of the lease term, the allocation of the total award would be:

Total award			$30,000
Reversion before taking:			
Land	$ 60,000		
Building ($70,000 x 0.50)	35,000		
Total reversion	$ 95,000		
Discount factor	x 0.082403		
Present value of reversion before taking		$7,828	
Reversion after taking:			
Land	$ 40,000		
Building ($60,000 x 0.50)	30,000		
Total reversion	$ 70,000		
Discount factor	x 0.082403		
Present value of reversion after taking		–5,768	
Lessor's interest in award			– 2,060
Lessee's interest in award			$ 27,940

This problem would take another form if, for example, the taking included 25% of the total leased land area and the lease provided for rent abatement, in the event of a partial acquisition, in direct proportion to the land acquired. The lessor's interest in the award could then be computed as follows:

Total award			$30,000
Decrease in lessor's reversion			
(from preceding computations)		$2,060	
Current value of lessor's rent loss:			
Annual rent loss ($4,500 x 0.25)	$1,125		
Discount factor	x 8.739019 *		
Value of lessor's rent loss		9,831	
Lessor's interest in award			–11,891
Lessee's interest in award			$18,109

* Present value of $1 per period for 25 years discounted at 10.5%.

The allocation procedure can become even more complex. Assume that the lessee who originally constructed the improvements has sublet them to a third party. The economic rent for the property as a whole is $14,950 per year. The net lease payments from the sublessee to the original lessee are $12,000, out of which $4,500 is paid by the original lessee (the sandwich man) to the lessor for ground rent. Assume also that the lessor will receive the total reversion of the land and the reversion of the building, which will have an estimated value of 50% of its current value, upon termination of the lease.

The various interests in the fee simple title can be valued with the calculations shown in Table 18.5.

TABLE 18.5 ALLOCATION OF VALUE WITH SUBLESSEE

Property value			$130,000
Annual net economic rent			$ 14,950
Indicated overall capitalization rate ($14,950 ÷ $130,000)			11.5%
Existing land lease			$4,500 per year for 25 years
Indicated risk rate applicable to leased fee estate			10.5%
Existing sublease			$12,000 per year for 25 years
Indicated risk rate applicable to sublease			12.75%
Indicated risk rate applicable to original leasehold estate			11.5%±
Reversion to lessor ($60,000 land value + $35,000 building value)			$ 95,000
Computations			
Total property value			$130,000
Value of lessor's interest:			
$4,500 income x 8.739019*	$39,326		
Reversion $95,000 x 0.082403†	7,828		
Total value of lessor's interest		$47,154	
Value of sublessee's interest:			
Economic rent $14,950			
Contract rent −12,000			
Rent advantage $ 2,950			
Present value of rent advantage ($2,950 x 7.452678‡)		21,985	
Subtotal			− 69,139
Indicated value of sandwich (original lessee) position			$ 60,861
Indicated risk rate to the sandwich man			11.52%§

* Present value of $1 per period for 25 years @ 10.5%.

† Present value of $1 for 25 years @ 10.5%.

‡ Present value of $1 per period for 25 years @ 12.75%.

§ Risk rate computed using a financial calculator.

In this illustration, the estimated risk rate applicable to the original lessee's position is approximately 11.5%. After the lessor's interest and the sublessee's interest are deducted from the value of the fee simple estate, the value of the original lessee's position is found to be $60,861. This value indicates a rate of return of 11.52%, which approximates the estimated, acceptable range of 11.5%±.

Now assume that a partial taking with damage has occurred, as previously described. The after value is $100,000 ($40,000 land value plus $60,000 building value) and the difference between the before and after values of the property is $30,000. The sublease specifies that there will be no rent abatement in the event of a partial taking, but a rent abatement provision remains in the original ground lease on a pro rata basis of the area acquired, in this instance 25%. The economic rent of the property is $100,000 x 0.115, or $11,500. Thus the sublessee's rent loss is $14,950 – $11,500, or $3,450 per year.

Initial analysis indicates that the sandwich man (the original lessee) will not be adversely affected by the taking and/or damage; in fact, the sandwich man's annual net income will actually increase, as shown below:

	Before	After
Contract rent received	$12,000	$12,000
Contract rent paid	– 4,500	– 3,375
Net income to the sandwich man	$ 7,500	$ 8,625

Because his net income increased after the partial taking, it is clear that the original lessee can hold no claim to any portion of the condemnation award. The loss suffered by the owner of the leased fee estate can be computed as:

Present value of lost rent ($1,125 x 8.739019)*	$ 9,831
Present value of lost reversion ($25,000 x 0.082403)†	2,060
Total loss in present value by lessor	$11,891

* Present value of $1 per period for 25 years discounted at 10.5%.

† Present value of $1 in 25 years discounted at 10.5%.

The loss suffered by the sublessee can be calculated:

$3,450 rent loss x 7.452678*	25,712

Thus the total loss incurred by both parties is

Total loss by lessor and sublessee	$37,603

* Present value of $1 per period for 25 years discounted at 12.75%

The losses borne by the lessor and the sublessee can be converted to percentages as follows:

Lessor's loss ($11,891 ÷ $37,603)	31.62%
Sublessee's loss ($25,712 ÷ $37,603)	68.38%
Total loss	100.00%

Now the appraiser can allocate the total award of $30,000 using simple mathematics:

Lessors's allocation	($30,000 award x 0.3162)	$ 9,486
Lessee's allocation	($30,000 award x 0.0000)	0
Sublessee's allocation	($30,000 award x 0.6838)	20,514
Total award	1.0000	$30,000

The number of possible combinations of property interests is almost endless. There are two important items for the appraiser and the attorney to remember. First, each interest in a property must be reviewed to determine whether that interest has been reduced by the taking and damage and, if so, how that loss can be most accurately estimated. Second, the appraiser must always work from his or her own before and after value estimates and estimate of the amount due for the taking and damages. The appraiser seldom, if ever, knows the circumstances and reasoning which led to the determination of the award or settlement. Consequently, an appraiser usually cannot make an accurate and equitable allocation of an award if he begins with the assumption that someone else's estimates of before value, after value, and/or award are correct and were determined in the same manner the appraiser himself would have applied.

The Washington State Appeals Court issued an opinion on this very issue:

> Although the state as condemnor and the owners as condemnees agreed that $363,000 was just compensation, the owners did not agree that the fair market value of their respective interests would be determined by reference to that figure, which was not necessarily the fair market value. Rather, it was the best bargain the owners could strike with the State in the condemnation proceedings. The price paid by the State may have been too high or too low. If it was too high, the owners who made the bargain should reap the benefit of it, if it was too low, the owners should share the disappointment. The only way for the court to equitably apportion the proceeds of the condemnation is to ascertain the fair market value of each interest in the property and give each owner his proportionate share.[53]

The above decision was affirmed by the Washington State Supreme Court, which stated:

> We granted a petition for discretionary review in order to consider the propriety of equitable apportionment of a lump-sum condemnation award; that is, a proportional distribution of a lump-sum award based upon the ratio each separately valued condemned interest bears to the total of all separately valued interests. The trial court refused to apportion the award. The Court of Appeals reversed the trial court and ordered equitable apportionment.[54]

LEASE TYPES

So far, this discussion has only dealt with the type of lease that specifies a rental amount which remains constant over the term of the lease. However, this type of lease is becoming less and less common. Continually increasing costs and the

53. *State v. Spencer*, 559 P.2d 1360, 1362–1363 (Wash. 1977).

54. *State v. Spencer*, 583 P.2d 1201, 1202 (Wash. 1978).

general inflation of the past several years, coupled with significant shifts in property values, have made lessors extremely reluctant to agree to flat rental leases of any length. Many attempts have been made to include various provisions in long-term leases that will address changing conditions and obviate the arbitration of new rental rates and, at the same time, be equitable to both the lessor and the lessee.

Leases that call for an automatic, periodic increase or decrease in rent to a predetermined amount, referred to as *graduated*, or *step-up* and *step-down, leases*, present no real difficulty for the appraiser; they simply call for some additional calculations in the property analysis. Leases that call for unspecified, periodic rent adjustments, on the other hand, do cause problems for the appraiser, the attorney, and the trier of fact in their attempts to evaluate leased fee and leasehold estates and to allocate condemnation awards equitably between the lessor and the lessee.

Percentage leases on commercial properties can also be problematic. Such leases generally, but not always, specify a minimum rent plus an additional sum based on a percentage of sales made by the lessee operating a business on the premises. These leases generally apply to retail businesses; they are quite common for restaurants, grocery stores, service stations, and similar enterprises.

Another type of variable-rent lease is the *revaluation lease*, which typically provides for the periodic revaluation of the property. This revaluation can be an estimate of the market value of the leased property, with a predetermined rate of return to the lessor, or it can be a direct estimate of the economic rent for the property. Under either system, revaluation leases generally provide that the lessee and the lessor each select an appraiser to reevaluate the property. If the two appraisers cannot agree, the two appraisers select a third appraiser. Then, either the opinion of the third appraiser prevails or the majority rules.

A third type of variable lease is the *index lease*. Index leases usually start at a specified rental, which is adjusted periodically based on the increase or decrease in a specific index. Two commonly used indexes are the value of the dollar index and the Consumer Price Index. Some index leases require a rent adjustment as frequently as every year. Many leases also include *expense stops*, which provide that the lessee is responsible for any increases in property expenses above the level established when the lease was executed.

Variable rent leases pose a problem for the appraiser because there is no specific income stream to evaluate. The income stream will fluctuate over the term of the lease, and no one can predict with confidence if the income will increase or decrease, when changes will occur, or how much fluctuation can be expected. Nevertheless, reasonable parameters can usually be determined by the appraiser through the use of discounted cash flow analysis.

Appraisers must be very careful in attempting to project future increases in rent levels based on future retail sales, price indexes, and other variable factors. If risk rates for leasehold estates and leased fee estates can be developed from actual sales of similar interests that are subject to the same potential rental fluctuation as the property being appraised, they would generally be the best and safest data to use. These data indicate that fluctuations in rental rates are being anticipated by buyers and sellers in the marketplace and are reflected in the prices paid and the risk rates indicated by the sales.

One thing the appraiser must not do is develop a risk rate from the sale of a comparable leased fee or leasehold estate using existing rent levels and then apply this risk rate to a projected, escalating income stream for the property being appraised. Attorneys should also be on guard against this practice. For example, assume a leased fee interest in a comparable property was sold for $250,000. The sale property's lease provided for a reserved rent of $20,000 per year at the time of the sale and an annual rental adjustment, based on the cost of living index, over the remaining 10-year term of the lease. A reversion of $250,000 was considered reasonable for this comparable property. The leased fee interest in the property being appraised, on the other hand, has the following characteristics:

- The remaining term is 10 years
- Rent is $12,500 per year with annual adjustments based on the consumer price index
- Current value represents a reasonable reversion

The obvious analysis of these data is:

Sale property:	$20,000 rent ÷ $250,000 price = 8% rate
Subject property:	$12,500 rent ÷ 0.08 rate = $156,250 value

This is the obvious analysis, but the fuzzy thinking described below is often applied in such a situation. First, the appraiser concludes that the Consumer Price Index will increase at the rate of about 5% per year, based on its past performance. Then the rent forecast shown below is made.

Year		Rent Amount
1		$12,500
2	$12,500 x 1.05	$13,125
3	$13,125 x 1.05	$13,781
4	$13,781 x 1.05	$14,470
5	$14,470 x 1.05	$15,194
6	$15,194 x 1.05	$15,954
7	$15,954 x 1.05	$16,752
8	$16,752 x 1.05	$17,590
9	$17,590 x 1.05	$18,470
10	$18,470 x 1.05	$19,394

Next the appraiser uses discounted cash flow (DCF) analysis to convert this projected annual income into a present value by multiplying each year's income by the appropriate discount factor of 8% for that year. The calculations are shown in the following table.

Year	Rent	Factor	Current Value
1	$12,500	0.925926	$ 11,574
2	$13,125	0.857339	11,253
3	$15,125	0.793832	12,007
4	$16,638	0.735030	12,229
5	$18,302	0.680583	12,456
6	$20,132	0.630170	12,687
7	$22,145	0.583490	12,921
8	$24,360	0.540269	13,161
9	$26,796	0.500249	13,405
10	$29,476	0.463193	13,653
Total current value of income stream			$125,346
Value of property at time of reversion:			
Rent level at time divided by rate ($29,476 ÷ 0.08 = $368,450)			
Present value of reversion (368,450 x 0.463193)			170,663
Total present value of leased fee estate			$296,009
Rounded			$296,000

This type of analysis and valuation procedure, or another equally ludicrous analysis, may be undertaken by appraisers for various reasons, including:

1. Improper verification of sale and lease data on comparables, which may cause the appraiser to overlook an index clause in the comparable lease
2. The inability to recognize that the 8% rate indicated by the sale property reflects the potential increase in rents resulting from the index clause in the lease as well as the potential increase in the reversionary value of the property
3. General incompetence
4. Dishonesty, including, at times, advocacy

It is imperative that the appraiser analyze market data carefully. Detailed data are often difficult to obtain; usually, there are not enough data available to allow the appraiser to analyze even a single transaction properly. In the example, the potential rent escalation and reversionary value increase or decrease are identical for the sale property and the property under appraisal. The appraiser does not need to go through extensive mathematical gyrations to apply the market data correctly or to impress the client, the attorney, or the trier of fact.

If the comparable sale described had a flat rental rate with no rent adjustments, the risk rate indicated would have undoubtedly been higher than 8% to reflect the likelihood that the established rent would have less value during the later years of the lease due to the decreasing value of the dollar. In such an instance, comparing these data to the leased fee under appraisal would require more detailed analysis and some adjustment. The appraiser should consider using discounted cash flow analysis not to develop an indication of value, but rather to develop a proper adjustment for the risk rate that is to be applied to the present income stream. It is easier to convince the trier of fact of a single adjustment to the risk rate than it is to justify the accuracy of predicting what the Consumer Price Index will do over the next 10 years.

LEASEHOLD TAKINGS

Sometimes the government will condemn the right of use and occupancy of a property for a limited term. This is often referred to as the "taking of a leasehold interest." This is somewhat of a misnomer because a typical lessee holds the right of use and occupancy of a property subject to the conditions of a lease, including the payment of rent. The owner of the leased fee interest in the property generally retains the right to receive the rental payments and the right to take possession of the premises at the end of the lease term. When the government condemns the right of use and occupancy, however, there is no lease and the government will pay no rent. Instead, it will pay just compensation for the taking. Thus the government's "taking of a leasehold" is merely a shorthand way of describing the government's condemnation of the right of use and occupancy of a property for a specified term.

The government's taking of a leasehold usually occurs under one of two circumstances. Either the government, as the lessee, and the property owner cannot agree on a fair rental or other terms of a lease or the property owner, for one reason or another, does not want to rent the property to the government. This may be because the owner wants to occupy the space himself or has other plans for the property. For example, the owner may want to sell the property to an owner-user or convert the property to an alternative use.

"When the government acquires a leasehold estate, whether by voluntary lease or condemnation, the proper measure of value is the fair market rental value of the occupied premises for the term specified."[55] This statement suggests that the appraiser merely has to estimate the economic, or market, rent for the space to be occupied by the government for the term of its occupation. However, the statement is deceptively simple. Innumerable problems can be encountered in appraising a property subject to a leasehold taking by the government.

Many government agencies measure "net rentable area" like no one else in the world.

> When the lease involves office space, it is imperative that the appraiser use the proper method of determining the rentable area of the given space. There are several methods in use in the private sector across the country, and the [United States] General Services Administration (which leases millions of square feet of space throughout the country) has its own method that differs from the others. Since square feet is the basis for comparison in a leasehold appraisal, it is of

55. *Uniform Appraisal Standards for Federal Land Acquisitions* (Washington, D.C.: U.S. Government Printing Office, 1992), §A-19, p. 52, citing *Kimball Laundry Co. v. United States*, 338 U.S. 1, 7 (1949); *United States v. General Motors Corp.*, 323 U.S. 373 (1945); *United States v. Petty Motor Co.*, 327 U.S. 372 (1946); *United States v. Right to Use, etc., Land, Alexandria, Va.*, 484 F.2d 1140 (4th Cir. 1973).

> paramount importance to use the same common denominator and method of measurement in relating the comparable leases to the subject. If the government's standard of measurement varies from that of the local market, the latter must be used when the leasehold is being acquired by condemnation because just compensation is to be determined with regard to what the owner/lessor could have received for the space on the open market."[56]

When given the task of estimating market rent, an appraiser will generally determine the lease terms and conditions typical in the market for the space under consideration and base the estimate of rent on those terms and condition. For instance, an appraiser estimating the market rent for office space in a multistory, multitenant office building might find that the typical lease terms for such space in the market area are as follows:

Term:	5 years
Base rent:	Dollars per square foot of rentable area, payable monthly in advance
Expenses:	Fully serviced with expense stop (i.e., the lessee pays expense increases over the expense level at the inception of the lease)
Rent adjustments:	Midterm CPI adjustment
Parking:	One parking space for every X square feet of leased space
Tenant improvements:	Landlord allows a certain dollar amount per square foot for tenant improvements
Rent concessions:	One month's free rent for each year of the lease term
Renewal options:	Lessee may renew at negotiated renewal terms

The appraiser would usually estimate market rent assuming that a lease for the space under consideration would contain these provisions. However, if the government condemns a leasehold estate in the space there would be no lease. The rights condemned, which are specified in the government's declaration of taking, may or may not bear a relationship to the lease terms and conditions that are typical in the marketplace. The typical declaration of taking might conflict with typical lease terms in the following ways:

Term:	The term may be shorter or longer than the typical lease term. This difference may require an adjustment to the typical square foot rent.
Base rent:	Rent will not be paid. Just compensation will be paid in a lump sum at the time of the taking. (If payment is not made at the time of the taking, interest will be paid to compensate for the delay in payment.) An adjustment to

56. *Uniform Appraisal Standards for Federal Land Acquisitions*, p. 53, citing *United States v. Bedford Associates*, 548 F.Supp. 732, 743 (S.D. N.Y., 1982), *modified in other respects*, 713 F.2d 895 (2d Cir. 1983).

market rent will be required to reflect the lump-sum payment in advance.

Expenses: The treatment of expenses may vary. Expense stops are not included nor are personal services typically included in market leases such as janitorial services. (The taking of such services would constitute involuntary servitude, i.e., slavery, and would be unconstitutional.) An adjustment to base rent will be required.

Rent adjustments: No rent will be paid, so rent adjustments are not applicable. As noted above, an adjustment to base rent will be required.

Parking: Parking may or may not be included in the declaration of taking. If parking is taken, it may reflect a different ratio than allowed in typical market leases, requiring an adjustment to base rent.

Tenant improvements: The lessor/owner will make no tenant improvements. The government cannot force the landlord to make improvements. An adjustment to the base rent will be required.

Rent concessions: There will be no rent concessions, thus an adjustment to the base rent may be required.

Renewal options: The government may condemn a renewal option, which may require an adjustment to the base rent.

Estimating the amount that the government should pay for use and occupancy of space is not a simple matter of estimating the economic rent for the space. The terms and conditions of the government's occupancy, as specified in the declaration of taking, must be carefully compared to typical lease terms. Adjustments must be made for all significant differences.

When the government condemns a leasehold estate in a portion of a property, such as a part of a multitenant office building, additional appraisal problems may be encountered. The configuration of the space taken by the government may make it difficult to lease other space in the building. Or the taking may include a greater proportion of parking spaces, leaving the remaining space in the building with inadequate parking. As in the taking of a fee interest in a portion of a property, the taking of a leasehold estate in a portion of a property requires that the government pay not only for the value of the part taken, but also for damages to the remainder property. "The taking of a leasehold estate can give rise to compensable severance damages."[57] This form of damage claim appears to be a developing area of the law. Therefore, "[i]n those instances where severance damages may be significant, appraisers should consult with . . . legal counsel before proceeding with the appraisal assignment to ensure that the appraisal will be prepared in accordance with current applicable law."[58]

57. *Uniform Appraisal Standards for Federal Land Acquisitions*, §A-19, p. 54, citing *United States v. 1735 N. Lynn St.*, 676 F.Supp. 693, 698–699 (E.D. Va. 1987).

58. *Uniform Appraisal Standards for Federal Land Acquisitions*, §C-12, p. 100.

This issue is particularly important if the appraiser concludes that a government leasehold taking will preclude the property owner from putting the property to its highest and best use during the term of the government's leasehold. A before and after appraisal is the only way to measure the diminution in the value of the property under such circumstances.

Historically, the federal government has had a nasty habit of "holding over." That is, the government has leased space and, at the end of the lease term, simply refuses to vacate the premises. This usually occurs when the government has been unable to procure alternative space or when lease renewal negotiations have broken down at the last minute. Holding over can lead to inverse condemnation action since the property owner does not have the option of evicting the government, as he would a private tenant. This situation can create some especially difficult problems for the appraiser.

First, because the government's occupation of the space would typically be considered short and indefinite, the appraiser must estimate the economic, or market, rent for such occupancy. Generally little direct market evidence will be available. Some appraisers have attempted to relate the rent estimate to the rents paid by short-term occupants of space that would otherwise be vacant such as the space leased by a candidate running for political office. Such space is often rented at rates below the rent levels paid for comparable space under the terms of a typical lease. Other appraisers have compared this situation to the different rents paid for an apartment under a lease and a motel room of equal size, attempting to demonstrate the "bonus" rent paid for short and indefinite occupancies. While there is no simple answer to this problem, neither of these approaches has met with much success.

Ultimately, appraisers must rely on their judgment to estimate the rents that would be demanded in the marketplace under the circumstances. The estimate should reflect the unusual risks incurred by a landlord who enters into such an arrangement. Some guidance may be found in arrangements made between lessors and lessees when tenants who have planned to move into new space upon the termination of their lease find that they must stay because the new space is not ready on the lease termination date. Thus the tenant must try to negotiate a continuing short and indefinite occupancy with the current landlord. Although this situation will reflect the actions of a lessee who is under some compulsion to lease the space, the government's unilateral holdover is not truly analogous to any open-market situation.

Fortunately, at least for the appraiser, by the time an appraisal is required or the case goes to trial, the term of the occupancy is known. Generally the government will have vacated the premises, signed a lease with the property owner, or filed a leasehold condemnation action that specifies the length of the occupancy.

Nevertheless, the government's subsequent action does not totally eliminate the problem of the short and indefinite term between the expiration of the first lease and resolution of the dispute (by termination of occupancy, lease execution, or condemnation). Even if the government files a leasehold condemnation action, it cannot backdate the date of taking to the original date of lease termination unless permission to do so is obtained from the property owner. Therefore, two appraisals may be required: one for the short and indefinite inverse taking and a second for the leasehold estate taking.

Some of the more complex leasehold taking problems cannot be solved merely by estimating the market rent for the duration of the government's occupancy. It has been said that "the value of the property for the period during which it is held by the condemnor, or the diminution in value of the use of occupancy of the property for such period, has been held to be the measure of compensation. Thus, . . . the condemnee must be paid the fair market value of possession of the property for this period. Such fair market value is calculated as the difference between the fair market value of the property immediately before the taking (and prior to the public use) and the fair market value of the property after the taking."[59] [Citations omitted]

Discounted cash flow analysis is exceptionally valuable in determining the market value of a property before and after a leasehold estate taking. More specifically, it is useful in determining the *difference* in the market value of a property before and after a leasehold estate taking. Many of the disadvantages of DCF analysis are eliminated when it is used for this purpose. Many of the somewhat speculative projections that the appraiser must make in DCF analysis (e.g., ownership term, sales costs on termination of ownership, terminal capitalization rate, rental and expense increases/decreases over the projection term, appropriate discount rate) can have a significant bearing on both the before and after values of the property. However, the important estimate in an appraisal assignment of this nature is the *difference* between the before and after values of the property, which will not be significantly affected by imperfect projections as long as the same projections are used in the before and after situations.

SUMMARY

Many leased properties are acquired by the sovereign, in whole or in part, by exercising its power of eminent domain. The interests in many of these properties are not held by a single individual or entity, but by two or more individuals or entities. The individual values of these separate interests are seldom the concern of the condemnor or the appraiser employed by the condemnor. Most condemning agencies have adopted the undivided fee rule, which holds that the value of a property is to be determined as if all of the interests in the property are owned by one individual or entity. The majority rule clearly indicates that, as a matter of law, the aggregate value of the various interests held in the real estate cannot exceed the value of the property if it were held by one individual.

When a condemned property is subject to a lease, the trial or settlement negotiations are usually separated into two distinct phases. The first phase is the determination of the value of the fee simple estate or, in a partial taking, the determination of *just compensation*. The second phase of the trial or negotiations is

59. *Nichols'*, vol. 4, §12E.01 (1990).

the allocation of the award determined in the first phase between the various interests—e.g., the leased fee estate and the leasehold estate. The condemnor has no part in this second phase; it is up to the lessor and the lessee to fight it out.

The allocation of an award is never undertaken until the amount of the award has been determined. The allocation may be made by the same trier of fact that set the total award, by the court, or by a totally different tribunal at a later date. The procedure will vary from jurisdiction to jurisdiction.

In allocating an award, both the appraiser and the attorney must be thoroughly familiar with the provisions of the lease, especially those provisions that have a direct bearing on the value of the leased fee and leasehold estates. If there is a condemnation clause in the lease, this clause will materially affect, or totally control, the allocation of the condemnation award. If the lease has no such clause, statutory and decisional law will impact the award allocation.

Some courts have ruled that the value of a leased fee estate is determined by computing the value of the leasehold estate and deducting this amount from the total award. Other courts have approved an opposite procedure: the value of the leasehold estate is determined by computing the value of the leased fee estate and deducting that value from the total award. The appraiser must present all valuation and allocation testimony in accordance with the applicable legal rules. However, in arriving at his conclusions, the appraiser need not compute the various estate values in strict compliance with the legal rules. In general, the appraiser can allocate a condemnation award more accurately if the value of the smaller interest is computed first and deducted from the total award, with the residual representing the greater interest.

Many courts have ruled that the value of the leasehold estate is the annual economic rent of the property, minus the annual contract rent, multiplied by the number of years remaining in the lease. In other words, the income stream is not converted into a present value. Recently courts have begun to recognize the absurdity of such a procedure and to adopt new rules, which provide for proper discounting of future income streams. It is in everyone's best interests for the courts to adopt rules that provide for discounting to avoid inequities to the owners of leased fee estates.

In developing an estimate for the proper allocation of a condemnation award, appraisers must work from their own before values and, in partial acquisitions, their own after values. There is no certainty that the total compensation award was made correctly or that it was determined as the appraiser assigned to estimate the allocation would have developed it. The appraiser need only convert his or her own dollar estimates of the damages to the various estates into percentages of the total damages and apply these percentages to the previously determined award.

There are, of course, various types of leases. Those that provide for renewal have given the courts some trouble. But if the lease is favorable to the lessee and the renewal is obligatory on the part of the lessor at the same rent level, or at a rent level that would retain a lessee's advantage, it has generally been held that the renewal of such a lease may be assumed in valuing the leasehold and leased fee estates. Leases that call for a fluctuating income stream are generally more difficult to analyze and evaluate. The most accurate method of valuing the leasehold and leased fee estates in such circumstances is to investigate sale and lease data on properties that are economically and physically comparable and to compare these data to the interests held in the property under appraisal. If adjustments for economic differences are necessary, it is often best to adjust the applicable risk or discount rate, rather than attempt to estimate what the fluctuating income will be for the remaining term of the lease.

The government will sometimes acquire only the right of use and occupancy of a property or a portion of a property for a specified term, rather than acquiring the fee simple interest in the property. This is often referred to as the taking of a leasehold estate. In its simplest form, compensation for such a taking will be equal to the market, or economic, rent of the premises to be occupied for the term of the government's occupation.

When estimating market rent in these situations, however, the appraiser must adjust base rents for differences between the lease terms applicable to the comparables and the terms and conditions of the government's taking, as specified in the declaration of taking. The market rent estimate must also reflect the differences between the characteristics of the income stream under a typical lease and the government's method of paying compensation when a leasehold estate is acquired, which is generally a lump sum payment in advance. Adjusting for this difference can generally be accomplished by applying a present value of $1 per period factor to the periodic market rent, if the estimated market rent will remain stable throughout the lease term. If a fluctuating market rent is projected, discounted cash flow analysis is typically applied.

If only a portion of a property is subject to a government taking of the leasehold estate, the appraiser must consider damages to the remainder property. If damages to the remainder property are present, it is often advisable for the appraiser to use DCF analysis to value the property before and after the taking to estimate the diminution in value caused by the government's action.

CHAPTER 19

Writing the Report

> Condemnation proceedings to acquire private land for public use require a high degree of appraisal skill and considerable judgement by the appraiser. Such problems as estimating the highest and best use for relatively underdeveloped or unimproved property and appraising the value of remaining property in a partial acquisition leave the appraiser open to involvement in court proceedings. The thoroughness with which the appraisal is made and reported is the appraiser's greatest protection against professional embarrassment.[1]

From the moment an appraiser accepts an appraisal assignment, his or her chief thought must be that the culmination of the assignment will be the delivery of a written appraisal report to the client. In appraising for eminent domain, the *purpose* of the appraisal must be clearly understood by the appraiser, the client, and the client's legal counsel. The specific *function*, or *use*, of the appraisal is also important to the appraiser and, while this is not absolutely necessary, it should be understood by the appraiser.

The *purpose* of the appraisal defines "[t]he type of value being sought."[2] "The purpose of an appraisal is the stated reason for an appraisal assignment, i.e., to estimate a defined value of any real property interest, or to conduct an evaluation study pertaining to real property decisions."[3] For eminent domain valuation, the purpose of the appraisal, and the value sought, is generally market value. This must be stated in the appraisal report and the term *market value* must be defined. The appraiser should use the definition of market value that has been approved

1. William C. Himstreet, *Writing Appraisal Reports* (Chicago: American Institute of Real Estate Appraisers, 1971), 28.
2. American Institute of Real Estate Appraisers and the Society of Real Estate Appraisers, *Real Estate Appraisal Terminology*, rev. ed., Byrl N. Boyce, ed. (Cambridge, Mass.: Ballinger Publishing Company, 1981), 195.
3. *The Appraisal of Real Estate*, 10th ed. (Chicago: Appraisal Institute, 1992), 10.

by the courts in the jurisdiction where the property under appraisal is located. The source of the definition should be cited in the appraisal report.

The *purpose* of an appraisal report is not the same as its function. The *function* or *use* of an appraisal is the manner in which a client employs the information contained in the appraisal report. The use or function of an appraisal "[r]elates to the character of the decision to be based on the appraisal, e.g., price at which to buy or sell, amount of mortgage to be made. Not the same as purpose."[4] The purpose and function (use) of an appraisal involving a total taking might be stated in the report as follows:

> The purpose of this appraisal is to estimate the market value of the property being appraised. Market value "is defined as the amount in cash, or on terms reasonably equivalent to cash, for which in all probability the property would be sold by a knowledgeable owner willing but not obligated to sell to a knowledgeable purchaser who desired but is not obligated to buy." Source: *Uniform Appraisal Standards for Federal Land Acquisitions* (Washington, D.C.: U.S. Government Printing Office, 1992) §A-2, pp. 3-4.
>
> The function of this appraisal is to assist the client in *its* determination of just compensation due for the taking of the property being appraised.

In an appraisal involving a partial acquisition, the definition of market value will remain unchanged, but the purpose and function of the report might be described as follows:

> [T]he purpose of the appraisal is to first estimate the market value of the entire ownership and second to estimate the market value of the remainder. The difference between the two values is then to be analyzed (by the Appraiser) as to the allocation of the value differential to the real property acquired and damages or special benefits to the remaining real property and property rights.[5]
>
> The function of this appraisal is to assist the client in *its* determination of the just compensation due for the partial taking of the property being appraised.

The use, or function, of an appraisal for condemnation proceedings has been described as:

- To estimate the market value of a property as a whole—i.e., before the taking
- To estimate the market value of the remainder after the taking
- To estimate the damages to the property[6]

Note that the function of an appraisal made in connection with an eminent domain action is *not* to estimate just compensation; it is to estimate market value. Nonetheless, many appraisers inexplicably believe that they must call their estimate of market value (in whole property takings) or the difference between their before and after value estimates (in partial takings) *just compensation*—often without even defining the term. Appraisers who prepare appraisal reports for mortgage lenders do not include an opinion regarding the amount of the mortgage

4. *Real Estate Appraisal Terminology*, rev. ed., 115.
5. Washington State Dept. of Transportation, *Right of Way Manual*, Chapter 4, Appendix 4-1, Appraisal Report Guide, Part II, tab C, p. 9, Item 5 (revised 8/91).
6. *The Appraisal of Real Estate*, 10th ed., 12.

that should be made on the property. Similarly, an appraiser should not include an opinion of just compensation in an appraisal made in a condemnation action. That determination is for the client to make. Just as factors other than market value are considered by mortgage lenders in determining mortgage loan amounts, factors other than market value are considered by condemnors and condemnees in their determinations of just compensation.

REPORT FORMAT

Much has been written on the proper methodology and format for writing appraisal reports. Most condemning agencies have their own report writing guidelines; these instructions may be similar, but no two sets are identical. Appraisal reporting is discussed in a variety of appraisal publications.[7] Specific report writing guidelines for condemnation appraisals may be found in the *Uniform Appraisal Standards For Federal Land Acquisition*[8] and in the guidelines of various condemning agencies.

Some condemnors' appraisal report guidelines are just that—guidelines—while others are mandatory appraisal report formats. The appraiser must read the appraisal contract and the condemnor's appraisal guidelines to determine whether they are mandatory. The titles of condemnors' documents can be misleading; guidelines are often referred to as *standards* and requirements are often referred to as *guidelines*.[9]

There appears to be a trend toward relaxing the requirements for appraisal report formats. For instance, the 1973 edition of the federal reporting standards were rigid standards providing that "[t]he text of the appraisal report *shall* be divided into four parts as outlined below."[10] The 1992 edition provides that "[t]he text of the appraisal report *should* be divided into four parts..." and includes the following introductory comment:

> These appraisal standards are not intended to establish a required appraisal report format. While the following should be considered a standard for appraisal report content and documentation,...it should be considered only as a *recommended guideline* in regard to report format.[11]

The rationale for relaxing report formatting has been explained as follows:

> It should be recognized that the government's needs for private property for public purposes are quite varied and have a tendency to create unique valuation problems. There has been no attempt in these standards to cover all of the valuation problems that might be encountered in the appraisal of property for gov-

7. See *Communicating the Appraisal: A Guide to Report Writing* (Chicago: American Institute of Real Estate Appraisers, 1982); George L. Schmutz, *Condemnation Appraisal Handbook*, rev., Edwin M. Rams, ed. (Englewood Cliffs, N.J.: Prentice-Hall, Inc., 1963); and *The Appraisal of Real Estate*, 10th ed.
8. *Uniform Appraisal Standards for Federal Land Acquisitions* (Washington, D.C.: U.S. Government Printing Office, 1992), §B-1, pp. 64–83.
9. For example, the *Uniform Appraisal Standards for Federal Land Acquisitions* are guidelines, but the Washington State Department of Transportation's *Appraisal Guidelines* are required standards.
10. *Uniform Appraisal Standards for Federal Land Acquisitions* (Washington, D.C.: U.S. Government Printing Office, 1973), §B-1, p. 35 (Emphasis added).
11. *Uniform Appraisal Standards for Federal Land Acquisitions* (1992), §B, p. 64 (emphasis added).

> ernment acquisition. Therefore, these standards should not be considered as rigid rules which must be applied, without modification, in every instance.
>
> Unique appraisal problems sometimes require modification of the appraisal process and the appraisal report by the appraiser to ensure that the specific appraisal problem is adequately addressed and that the appraiser's final conclusion of value is accurate. Appraisers should feel free to deviate from these standards in those unique cases in which deviation is required to properly solve the appraisal problem, and such deviation can be adequately justified.[12]

Each state department of transportation has its own formatting requirements. A typical reporting format for a state highway department is presented in the addenda. Many states have similar formatting requirements because they are all striving to meet the requirements of the Federal Highway Administration. Nevertheless, state requirements will vary due to variations in state statutory and decisional laws. The recommended format for an appraisal report prepared in conjunction with a federal condemnation can also be found in the addenda.

Although an appraiser must write the appraisal report in the required format when the condemning agency is the client, these regimented reporting requirements must not dictate the appraiser's thinking. In preparing a report for an agency that has only a recommended format or a report for a condemnee, the appraiser generally has a freer hand in determining the format and content of the appraisal report. However, every appraisal report must be tailored to the specific client.

The inclusion of boilerplate is generally unacceptable. Preliminary matter should be limited to the appraiser's qualifications, general assumptions and limiting conditions, and the appraiser's certificate. Even these basic items should be reviewed before they are included in an appraisal report. If the appraiser's client is the condemnee, and the appraiser has made appraisals for the condemnor in the past, this should be noted in the appraiser's qualifications. If the appraiser has made other appraisals in the geographic vicinity of the property being appraised, this too should be mentioned.

The assumptions and limiting conditions of the appraisal must be reviewed carefully. If the appraisal is of vacant land, and the assumptions and limiting conditions state that the appraiser has assumed that the improvements on the site are free from hazardous materials or that they conform to existing zoning and building codes, the client will see the entire report as sloppy boilerplate and the appraisal reviewer may agree. In a partial taking case, the assumptions and limiting conditions must state that the appraiser has assumed that the proposed public improvement will be constructed in a specified amount of time and that the improvements will be constructed in accordance with the plans and specifications available at the time of the valuation. The plans and specifications relied on by the appraiser should be specifically identified by name, page number, original date, and last revision date. The assumptions must also be reviewed carefully to ensure that they do not include an assumption or limiting condition that might

12. Ibid., at 63.

be construed to result in a *limited appraisal assignment* or a *limited appraisal report.*[13] "The adoption of an assumption or instruction that results in a 'limited appraisal assignment' or 'limited appraisal report' will, as a general rule, invalidate the appraisal for eminent domain purposes."[14]

REPORT TIMING

Figure 19.1 illustrates the appraisal, or valuation, process in graphic form. A simpler version of this figure is presented in Chapter 20. Whatever version of the appraisal process is applied, it is extremely important to recognize that the last step in the process is to make a *final estimate* of value and then to prepare a *report of defined value.* When the appraiser sits down to write the appraisal report, he or she should have all of the necessary data at hand; by this time, all data should have been analyzed, applied, and compiled into a final estimate of value.

Some appraisers may ask: Why can't I write each section of my report as I come to it? First, I include regional and neighborhood data, then I make my property inspection and write my site and improvement descriptions, and finally I develop each approach to value and write it up. Then, I'm ready to make my final value estimate and write a conclusion. All too many appraisal reports read as if this was the procedure used to write them. This method is unacceptable, however, because the appraiser wants to set the reader up throughout the report, leading him or her through the reasoning that results in the final value estimate. The appraiser cannot, for instance, establish a basis for land value adjustments, unit costs, and depreciation in the property description section of the report if these factors were not known when this portion of the report was written. The best reports are those that allow the reader to reach a conclusion of value that approximates the appraiser's opinion *before* he or she reads the appraiser's final value estimate.

At times, the attorney for a client will try to dictate the completion date of the appraisal—sometimes with just cause and sometimes without. If the effective date of value in the applicable jurisdiction is the date of trial, it may be wise to delay preparing a fully documented appraisal report until just before trial to avoid the expense of preparing two fully documented reports.

If, however, the attorney has instructed the appraiser not to finish the appraisal report to circumvent applicable discovery rules, the appraiser should not cooperate. In this case, the appraiser should either furnish the appraisal in a timely manner or suggest that the client retain the services of another appraiser.

Another potential problem arises when the attorney for the client tells the appraiser that no written appraisal report will be needed ever. This may be a misguided attempt on the part of the attorney to keep the appraiser's fee down, but it is more likely a ploy to circumvent discovery and/or to give the unscrupulous appraiser the greatest amount of latitude, or *wiggle room,* on the witness stand. What the attorney, and the appraiser, must understand is that the preparation of

13. See The Appraisal Foundation, *Uniform Standards of Professional Appraisal Practice* (USPAP), 1994 ed., "Departure Provisions," 5.

14. *Uniform Appraisal Standards for Federal Land Acquisitions* (1992), §B-1 7, p. 67.

FIGURE 19.1 APPRAISAL PROCESS

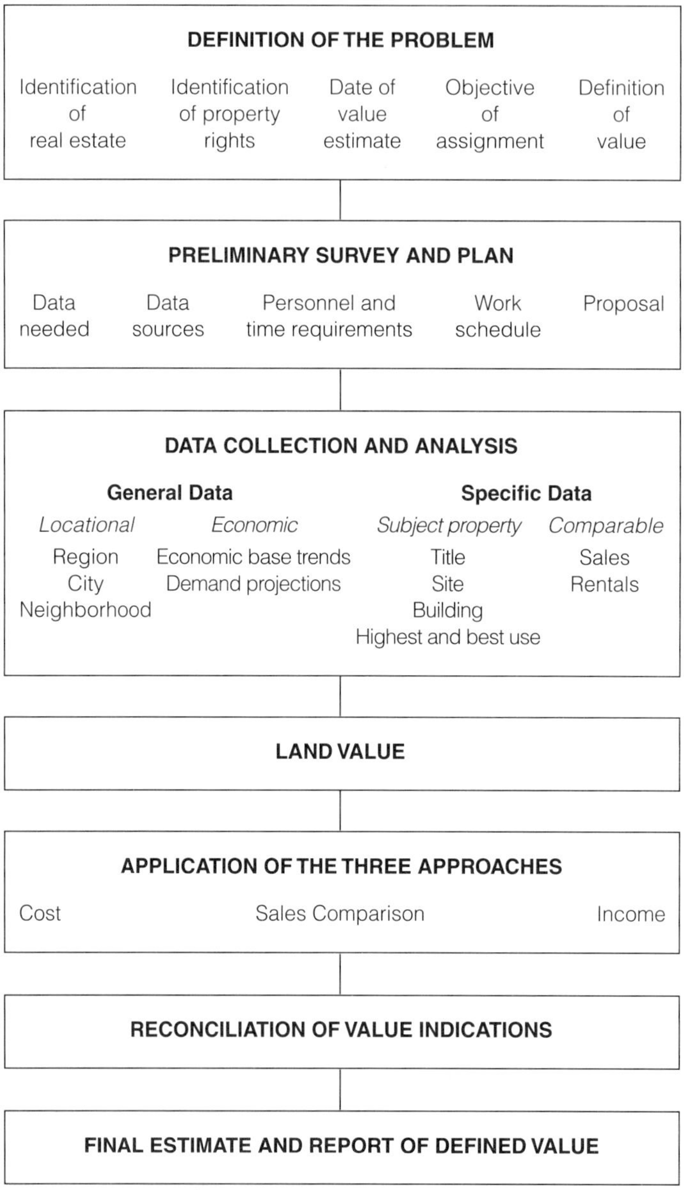

a documented appraisal report is a form of *trial preparation* for the appraiser. Writing down the facts, analyses, and conclusions reached in arriving at a final estimate of value prepares the appraiser to explain his reasoning clearly to the trier of fact. Moreover, many of the graphics included in the appraisal report form the basis for the demonstrative evidence to be used during the trial. Attempting to avoid the cost of a written appraisal report is, without question, a false and foolish economy. If the client cannot afford to pay for a fully documented appraisal report, the case has no business going to trial.

If an appraiser testifies in regard to a property valuation, the appraisal report or file memorandum may become the subject of an audit or review by the state appraiser licensing/certification agency to ensure its compliance with the Uniform Standards of Professional Appraisal Practice. Appraisal reports can also be reviewed by the professional appraisal organizations with which the appraiser is affiliated. Appraisers who agree to testify without a written report or memorandum may very well find themselves writing the report or memorandum after giving testimony on their own time and at their own expense.

The Uniform Standards do not specifically require that an appraiser prepare a written report prior to giving testimony. This is probably because The Appraisal Foundation emphasizes appraisals made for lending purposes. Perhaps when the Foundation has time to direct its attention to appraisals for other than financial institutions, this severe deficiency in its professional standards requirements will be recognized and rectified.

REPORT CONTENT

"Currently the *Uniform Standards of Professional Appraisal Practice* (USPAP) are recognized throughout the United States as the generally accepted minimum standards of appraisal practice."[15] The Uniform Standards have been adopted by the states as a part of their licensing/certification laws. Therefore, any discussion of appraisal report content must, of necessity, begin with these requirements. Standard 2 of the Uniform Standards, which relates to real property appraisal reporting, provides as follows:

> In reporting the results of a real property appraisal an appraiser must communicate each analysis, opinion, and conclusion in a manner that is not misleading.
>
> **Standards Rule 2-1**
>
> Each written or oral real property appraisal report must:
>
> (a) clearly and accurately set forth the appraisal in a manner that will not be misleading;
>
> (b) contain sufficient information to enable the person(s) who are expected to receive or rely on the report to understand it properly;
>
> (c) clearly and accurately disclose any extraordinary assumptions or limiting condition that directly affects the appraisal and indicate its impact on value.

Standard 1 of the Uniform Standards allows for two types of appraisals to be made: the *complete report* and the *limited report*. The limited report, by definition,

15. *Uniform Appraisal Standards for Federal Land Acquisitions* (1992), §B, p. 63.

invokes the Departure Provision of the Uniform Standards. The Appraisal Foundation's Statement on Appraisal Standards No. 7 states, "[W]hile no appraisal conclusion is a guarantee, USPAP allows for different levels of reliability in real property appraisals. The highest level of reliability is a Complete Appraisal performed without invoking the Departure Provision." It is for this reason that, as noted previously, limited appraisals are not acceptable for eminent domain purposes. When an individual's property is taken for a public use, the individual deserves nothing less than the highest level of reliability in the estimation of market value, or just compensation.

Standards Rule 2-2 provides, "[E]ach written real property appraisal report must be prepared under one of the following three options and prominently state which option is used: Self-Contained Appraisal Report, Summary Appraisal Report or Restricted Appraisal Report." Only a self-contained appraisal report is suitable for appraisals made for eminent domain purposes.

The restricted report is unacceptable for condemnation appraisals because, according to The Appraisal Foundation's Advisory Opinion G-12, the restricted report is applicable when "only the client is expected to receive or rely on the report [and]...the intended use of the appraisal warrants restricted disclosure of the steps in and information considered in the appraisal process." Obviously, the client will ask others (i.e., the condemnor or condemnee and/or the trier of fact) to rely on the appraisal report.

A summary report is also unacceptable. Again, Advisory Opinion G-12 specifies that the intended use of the report must be considered and the intended use of a condemnation report requires the "comprehensive . . . disclosure of the steps in and information considered in the appraisal process." The probability that an individual who is unsophisticated in the techniques of appraisal will be asked to rely on a condemnation appraisal report is so great that nothing short of a self-contained report will suffice. Also, if the appraiser's client is a condemnor, a summary report will generally not meet the client's reporting guidelines.

The Appraisal Foundation's Standards Rule 2-2(a), which relates to self-contained appraisal reports, provides as follows:

(a) The Self-Contained Appraisal Report must:
  - (i) identify and describe the real estate being appraised;
  - (ii) state the real property interest being appraised;
  - (iii) state the purpose and intended use of the appraisal;
  - (iv) define the value to be estimated;
  - (v) state the effective date of the appraisal and the date of the report;
  - (vi) state the extent of the process of collecting, confirming, and reporting data;
  - (vii) state all assumptions and limiting conditions that affect the analyses, opinions, and conclusions;
  - (viii) describe the information considered, the appraisal procedures followed,

and the reasoning that supports the analyses, opinions, and conclusions;

(ix) describe the appraiser's opinion of the highest and best use of the real estate, when such an opinion is necessary and appropriate;

(x) explain and support the exclusion of any of the usual valuation approaches;

(xi) describe any additional information that may be appropriate to show compliance with, or clearly identify and explain permitted departures from the specific guidelines of Standard 1;

(xii) include a signed certification in accordance with Standards Rule 2-3.

Standards Rules 2-3, 2-4, and 2-5 follow.

Standards Rule 2-3

Each written real property appraisal report must contain a certification that is similar in content to the following form:

I certify that, to the best of my knowledge and belief:

— the statements of fact contained in this report are true and correct.

— the reported analyses, opinions, and conclusions are limited only by the reported assumptions and limiting conditions, and are my personal, unbiased professional analyses, opinions, and conclusions.

— I have no (or the specified) present or prospective interest in the property that is the subject of this report, and I have no (or the specified) personal interest or bias with respect to the parties involved.

— my compensation is not contingent upon the reporting of a predetermined value or direction in value that favors the cause of the client, the amount of the value estimate, the attainment of a stipulated result, or the occurrence of a subsequent event.

— my analyses, opinions, and conclusions were developed, and this report has been prepared, in conformity with the Uniform Standards of Professional Appraisal Practice.

— I have (or have not) made a personal inspection of the property that is the subject of this report. (If more than one person signs the report, this certification must clearly specify which individuals did and which individuals did not make a personal inspection of the appraised property.)

— no one provided significant professional assistance to the person signing this report. (If there are exceptions, the name of each individual providing significant professional assistance must be stated.)

Standards Rule 2-4

To the extent that it is both possible and appropriate, each oral real property appraisal (including expert testimony) must address the substantive matters set forth in Standards Rule 2-2(b).

Standards Rule 2-5

An appraiser who signs a real property appraisal report prepared by another in any capacity accepts full responsibility for the appraisal and the contents of the appraisal report.[16]

The standards rules quoted above include "comments" which explain the rules in detail. Appraisers should refer to the full standards document published by The Appraisal Foundation.[17]

Various professional appraisal organizations, state licensing/certification agencies, and appraisal clients require that the appraiser's certificate include certifications in addition to those required by The Appraisal Foundation. These may include certifications that the appraisal report has been prepared in accordance with the client's appraisal reporting guidelines, the professional organization's reporting guidelines, or applicable law; that the appraiser is a certified (or licensed) appraiser in the state in which the property is located; or that the appraiser has met the continuing education requirements of the professional organization of which he or she is a member.

The minimum content of an appraisal report is now almost universally dictated by the Uniform Standards. These minimum standards have been adopted, and in some instances augmented by various professional appraisal organizations and condemning agencies. For instance, one set of federal standards states,

> Appraisal preparation, documentation and reporting shall be in conformity with the standards and practices of the industry. Currently the *Uniform Standards of Professional Appraisal Practice* (USPAP) are recognized throughout the United States as the generally accepted minimum standards of appraisal practice. The USPAP should be considered as a supplement to this document....
>
> Under no circumstances...may appraisal standards be set at a level below the minimum required under USPAP.[18]

The Appraisal Institute specifies,

> [W]hen the Appraisal Institute adopted the Uniform Standards [USPAP], it also adopted...Supplemental Standards of Professional Appraisal Practice...
>
> The Uniform Standards [USPAP] and Supplemental Standards are collectively referred to as the "Standards of Professional Appraisal Practice." There can be no conflict between these two components of the Standards of Professional Practice because the Supplemental Standards add to, but do not subtract from, the Uniform Standards.[19]

Appraisers should be aware that, in addition to the Uniform Standards, the Appraisal Standards Board of The Appraisal Foundation has, from time to time,

16. USPAP, 1994 ed.

17. The *Uniform Standards of Professional Appraisal Practice*, which include various "statements on appraisal standards" and "advisory opinions," are published annually by The Appraisal Foundation. Copies may be ordered directly from the Foundation at 1029 Vermont Avenue, N.W., Suite 900, Washington, D.C. 20005-3517. Phone (202)347-7722. Fax (202) 347-7727.

18. *Uniform Appraisal Standards for Federal Land Acquisitions* (1992), §B, pp. 63-64.

19. Appraisal Institute, "Supplemental Standards of Professional Appraisal Practice," Preamble, 1991.

adopted "statements on appraisal standards" and issued "advisory opinions." "Statements on appraisal standards are authorized by the bylaws of The Appraisal Foundation and are specifically for the purpose of clarification, interpretation, explanation or elaboration of the Uniform Standards of Professional Appraisal Practice (USPAP). Statements have the full weight of a Standards Rule..."[20] "Advisory Opinions issued by the Appraisal Standards Board (ASB) do not establish new standards or interpret existing standards. Advisory Opinions are issued to illustrate the applicability of appraisal standards in specific situations and to offer advice from the ASB for the resolution of appraisal issues and problems."[21]

Similarly, the Appraisal Institute periodically adopts "guide notes" to its Standards of Professional Appraisal Practice, which interpret the standards for its members and address specific appraisal problems. "Statements on appraisal standards," "advisory opinions," and "guide notes" can be especially helpful to appraisers who must resolve the unique valuation problems encountered in eminent domain appraisal.

Note that some appraisal organizations require special conduct of their members before testifying in a judicial proceeding. For instance, the Code of Professional Ethics of the Appraisal Institute provides:

> *To Ensure the Highest Level of Competence, a Member or an Affiliate Must Take Certain Steps Prior to Testifying in a Judicial Proceeding.*

> As noted above in Comment E.R. 2-5, membership in the Appraisal Institute has come to be recognized by the Courts and the public as evidence that an appraiser not only has the appropriate educational background but also the knowledge, experience, and integrity required to arrive at and communicate competent, unbiased estimates of market value and other analyses and opinions concerning real property. To maintain this recognition, it is essential that each Member and Affiliate gather and analyze the appropriate data relating to an appraisal assignment prior to appearing as an expert witness in a judicial proceeding and testifying concerning the real property that is the subject of the appraisal assignment.

> If a Member or an Affiliate fails to gather and analyze the appropriate data prior to giving appraisal testimony, each appraisal analysis or opinion expressed will be little more than a guess, and the Member or Affiliate will have improperly used the credibility that the Courts and the public impute to the work product of Members and Affiliates of the Appraisal Institute. This action perpetrates a fraud upon the Court and the public and cannot be tolerated; therefore, the Appraisal Institute requires its Members and Affiliates to prepare a written appraisal report (or complete memoranda) containing the data, reasoning, and conclusions upon which the testimony is to be based before testifying as an appraiser in a judicial proceeding or deposition, or hearing before a quasi-judicial public body, board, or commission.

> Members and Affiliates must use their best efforts to ensure that their appraisal report (or complete memoranda) containing data, reasoning, and conclusions is preserved intact. If an appraisal report (or complete memoranda) is delivered

20. USPAP, 1994 ed., p. 51.

21. Ibid., 67.

> to a client and the client removes portions of such appraisal report (or complete memoranda) prior to delivery to the opposing party, the credibility given to the work product of Members and Affiliates is being used to mislead the opposing party and the Court.[22]

The Uniform Standards permit limited exceptions to the reporting requirements.[23] Departure from the reporting requirements under Standards 2-1, 2-2, 2-3, and 2-5, however, are not allowed. Any departure from the Uniform Standards results in a limited appraisal report and is not acceptable for an appraisal conducted in connection with the sovereign's power of eminent domain.[24]

The foregoing discussion relates to minimum reporting requirements. The additional content of an appraisal report for eminent domain purposes will depend on the property type, the nature of the taking, and the requirements of the client or the client's legal counsel. The condemnor-client may be very specific as to report content and the methodology to be used in writing the report. For instance, one condemnor describes the application of the sales comparison approach as follows:

> B. APPROACHES TO VALUE, WHOLE PROPERTY
>
> RULES: ....
>
> PROCEDURES:
>
> 1. Comparative [sales comparison] Approach
>   a. General Discussion
>   1) Here the Appraiser lays the groundwork for the comparative analysis by a statement of the extent of his search, the sufficiency and comparability of existing data and the general value bracket within which subject will fall.
>   2) Sales that are comparable are listed identifying each by the sale number on the pertinent Market Data Form (WSDOT Form 261-010) in the Addenda. A format similar to the following is used at the present point in the report:
>
> | SALE NO. | GRANTOR/ GRANTEE | LAND AREA | SALE DATE | SALE PRICE |
> |---|---|---|---|---|
>
>   b. Comparative Analysis
>   Ideally, sales used are so closely comparable as to make adjustments unnecessary when equating them to the property being appraised. However, because such close comparability rarely exists, a narrative comparative analysis of each comparable sale is made explaining how the sale relates to subject with regard to those features which tend to influence market

22. *Code of Professional Ethics of the Appraisal Institute*, 1994 ed., Comment E.R. 2-6, p. 17.

23. USPAP, 1994 ed., "Departure Provision," 5.

24. *Uniform Appraisal Standards for Federal Land Acquisitions* (1992), §B-1 7, p. 67.

> value. It is recognized that within comparable properties there may exist many items of dissimilarity to which the market does not react and for which adjustments are not attempted. If market investigation shows adjustment to be necessary, then each significant element of difference between the comparable and the subject is explained separately on its own particular merits, with an indication as to its value differential made either on a dollar or percentage basis. When there is a lack of market support for adjustments, sound and consistent reasoning in the comparison of each item of difference may be acceptable. In this latter instance, a greater number of sales should be used in order to broaden the scope of value evidence. When adjustments are made:
>
> (1) As the number of adjustments or size of any single adjustment increases, the validity of the sale as a "comparable" is reduced.
>
> (2) A comparative analysis chart or "grid" may be an aid to the Appraiser and a help to the reader.
>
> c. Correlation and Conclusion by Comparative [sales comparison] Approach
>
> Here the Appraiser explains how he has weighed the various indications of value, what conclusion of value has been reached, and why the evidence supports such conclusion.[25]

At the other end of the spectrum, another condemnation appraisal report guide states:

> All comparable sales used shall be confirmed by the buyer, seller, broker or other person having knowledge of the price, terms and condition of sale. A narrative comparative analysis of each comparable sale shall be made explaining how the sale relates to the property under appraisal in respect to those features which have an effect on market value. The comparative weight given to each comparable sale by the appraiser in developing a final value estimate by this approach will be explained. A comparative adjustment chart, or grid, may assist the appraiser in explaining his or her analysis in this regard.[26]

These appraisal report guidelines represent two extremes. The first condemnor requires that specific dollar or percentage adjustments be made for each factor affecting market value, while the second merely requires a narrative discussion of such factors and allows the appraiser to decide how the adjustments for the factors will be made and presented in the appraisal report. Figure 19.2 shows a format for presenting comparable sales data and analysis that will ensure a thorough analysis of each sale and meet nearly all reporting guidelines.

Because the appraisal reporting requirements of clients vary widely, an appraiser should never accept an assignment without first reviewing the applicable guidelines. The appraiser who attempts to apply rigid, detailed guidelines for the first time should anticipate some difficulty. A staff appraiser should expect to spend considerably more time on such a report than his superior originally an-

25. *Right of Way Manual*, Chapter 4-1, tab C, item B, p. C-13.

26. *Uniform Appraisal Standards for Federal Land Acquisitions* (1992), §B-1 17, p. 76.

FIGURE 19.2 COMPARATIVE SALES ANALYSIS FORM

MARKET DATA

(1) ADDRESS or LOCATION:

(2) PHOTOGRAPH & PLOT PLAN:

Taken by: __________ Date: _____

(3) a. Access:
b. Present use:
c. H. & B. use:
d. Zoning:
e. Dimensions:
f. Area:
g. Sale date:
h. Price: $
i. Instrument:
j. Terms:
k. Tax #:
l. Grantor:
m. Grantee:
n. Confirmed with (names/dates)
_______________/_______________
_______________/_______________
o. Date inspected

(4) LEGAL DESCRIPTION:

(5) PROPERTY DESCRIPTION:

(6) SALES ANALYSIS:
a. Extraction Data:

Land: (give area or front feet for each type)	$ _______	$ _______
	$ _______	$ _______
Improvements: (give type and area for each)	$ _______	$ _______
	$ _______	$ _______
Land improvements: (itemize)	$ _______	$ _______
	$ _______	$ _______
Total sale price	$ _______	

(7) COST AND DEPRECIATION ANALYSIS:

a. Estimated reproduction cost new of main structure (___ sq. ft. @ $ ___)			$ _______
b. Confirmed sale price		$ _______	
Estimated land value	$ _________		
Estimated value of miscellaneous improvements	$ _________		
Total deductions		$ _______	
Contributory value of main structure			$ _______
c. Accrued depreciation reflected by sale			$ _______
d. Average annual depreciation ($ ____ accrued dep. ÷ age of structure ____ years)			$ _______
e. Annual dep. percent ($ ___ average annual dep. ÷ $ _______ reproduction cost)			_______ %

FIGURE 19.2 COMPARATIVE SALES ANALYSIS FORM—CONTINUED

(8) INCOME DATA ANALYSIS:

a. Gross income analysis from market

Confirmed sale price $ ____ ÷ Annual gross income $ ______
= Gross annual rent multiplier ________

Confirmed sale price $ ____ ÷ Monthly gross income $ ______
= Gross monthly rent multiplier ______

b. Income data from market

Annual gross income		$ ______
Vacancy and credit loss		$ ______
Effective gross income		$ ______
Expenses (itemized)		
Taxes	$ ______	
Insurance	$ ______	
Management	$ ______	
Maintenance	$ ______	
Utilities	$ ______	
Reserves for replacements	$ ______	
Other	$ ______	
Total expenses		$ ______
Net annual income		$ ______

Indicated overall capitalization rate
(Annual net income $_____ ÷ $_____ Sale price) ______ %

(9) DEBT/EQUITY ANALYSIS:

a. Equity analysis

Confirmed sale price	$ ______
Mortgage amount	$ ______
Equity amount	$ ______
Net annual income	$ ______
Annual debt service	$ ______
Net cash flow to equity	$ ______

Equity dividend rate (Net cash flow $_____ ÷ Equity amount $____) ______ %

b. Debt coverage ratio
(Net annual income $ ____ ÷ Annual debt service $ ______) ______

(10) COMPARATIVE ANALYSIS/COMMENTS:

ticipated or allocated; a fee appraiser who is applying such a guide for the first time will consume more time than he anticipated and may consequently suffer an economic loss. The appraiser should view this experience pragmatically and be prepared to write off the loss as an educational experience—no different from the cost of attending a seminar.

Once the appraiser has written his first report using this type of guideline and has received review approval for his effort, future reports become easier. He may want to use the approved report as a guide for writing future reports, rather than referring to the original guide for each new report. However, the appraiser should be aware that some review appraisers will overlook minor deficiencies in an appraisal report and permit some deviation from the written guidelines if the report is generally sound and well presented. The written review will often mention these deficiencies, but conclude that they are unimportant and have no bearing on the factual data reported or the conclusions presented by the appraiser. Unfortunately, the appraiser rarely sees the written review. Thus, if the first report is used as a model for the second report, and the second report is used to write a third, the guideline deficiencies in reports tend to increase geometrically until a report is rejected and returned with a lengthy request (i.e., demand) for revision. It is therefore advisable for the appraiser to refer to the original guidelines periodically and write a report that follows them strictly. Another option is to have each and every report read by an experienced individual who simultaneously compares the report and the guidelines to ensure compliance.

The stated purpose of many appraisal report writing guidelines is 1) to ensure that the appraiser has considered all the required elements of value in arriving at the value conclusion and 2) to maintain a uniform method of narrative appraisal report writing that will facilitate the appraisal review function. Although this first purpose is legitimate, the second is questionable. The purpose of any appraisal reporting guidelines for eminent domain appraisals should be to encourage uniform approaches to appraisal problems that consistently lead to accurate estimates of value and result in equitable treatment of the individual whose property is taken and the public that must pay for it. If this makes the work of the review appraiser more difficult, so be it.

A uniform report format might ensure that a review appraiser can look up Section II, Item 4, Subsection B, ¶1.b in any report reviewed and be confident that he will find the analysis of the sales comparison approach to value in the before situation. Furthermore, because the appraiser is required to specify exact dollar adjustments in the comparative analysis and to analyze the comparable sale in the specific manner shown in Figure 19.2, the review appraiser can plug the appraiser's stated dollar adjustments and dollar allocations into the form and determine, with mathematical precision, the consistency of the appraiser's analysis. This procedure, which is sometimes referred to as the *pluginski syndrome*, negates, to a great extent, the necessity of *thinking* on the part of some review appraisers.

To illustrate, assume that an appraiser has made the following analysis of a comparable sale:

ANALYSIS:	**Total Value**	**Unit Value**
a. Extraction data		
Land:		
8,000 sq. ft.	$14,000	$ 1.75
Improvements:		
Dwelling 1,530 sq. ft.	$39,200	$25.62
Garage 540 sq. ft.	$ 2,000	$ 3.70
Land improvements:		
Drive, lawn, plantings	$ 1,800	Contributory
Total sale price	$57,000	

The appraiser then makes the following comparative analysis:

> The comparable property's site is 1,000 sq. ft. larger than the subject's, thus a downward adjustment is required for this factor. The subject improvement is somewhat larger than the comparable, containing 1,620 sq. ft. The subject's 500 sq. ft. garage is slightly smaller than the comparable's, thus a downward adjustment is required for this factor. All other factors, including on-site improvements, would appear to be equal between the subject and the comparable.

For the review appraiser, the amount of adjustment becomes a matter of mathematics:

Price		$57,000
Adjustments:		
Land (1,000 sq. ft. @ $1.75)	$ −1,750	
Size of improvement (90 sq. ft. @ $25.62)	+2,306	
Garage (40 sq. ft. @ $3.70)	− 148	
Net adjustments		+ 408
Indicated value of subject		$57,408
Rounded		$57,400

Woe to the poor appraiser whose mathematics do not work out with such precision. If the size adjustment were not made at the rate of $25.62 per square foot, the reviewer who suffers from the pluginski syndrome would probably have a seizure. However, as noted previously, the appraiser must not let this regimented appraisal procedure and review process constrain his thinking and limit his professional judgment.

One method that may appease the review appraiser is for the appraiser to include an extensive analysis as to why the mathematics of a specific adjustment do not work out precisely. At times, just using the proper words will mollify the reviewer. Some appraisers have difficulty communicating their findings in a clear and convincing manner. Report writing is an acquired art. Great effort is required to convert the mental processes that went into the appraiser's conclusion into written narrative that can be easily understood by the client and the reviewer.

For example, assume that, in the appraiser's judgment, the size difference between the two properties compared requires an adjustment of $1,000 rather than $2,306 (90 sq. ft. @ $25.62). If the appraiser writes, "Market evidence would indicate that the size differential between these two properties would require an upward adjustment of about $1,000," the review appraiser might go scurrying for a rejection form. The appraiser might try this statement instead, "Considering the larger size of the subject and its utility in relation to its size, as compared to the size and relative utility of the sale property, an upward adjustment of $1,000 is indicated."

This second statement may be approved by the review appraiser for one of three reasons. The reviewer may feel that the appraiser has taken away the reviewer's mathematical crutch, but cannot quite find anything specific to object to. Or the reviewer may determine that, mathematically, the size adjustment should have been $2,306 (90 sq. ft. @ $25.62), but the appraiser used an adjustment of only $1,000 because the subject property was inferior in utility to the comparable property in the amount of $1,306 ($2,305–$1,000). The third possibility is that the review appraiser will accept the adjustment because he is a good reviewer and recognizes from the explanation given that the appraiser has applied reasonable professional judgment. Like report writing, report reading is an acquired art and one that the reviewer must strive to develop.

As previously illustrated, presenting a detailed adjustment process in the appraisal report can pose a problem in jurisdictions that require full discovery or exchange of appraisal reports. The condemnor's legal counsel may turn pale when such an exchange is ordered. The appraiser should be prepared to justify why each dollar adjustment was made and the precise the amount of each adjustment reported.

Although the appraiser may use specific dollar adjustments when comparing properties, presenting these precise adjustments in an appraisal report can mislead the reader. Using finite adjustments suggests that the appraisal of real estate is an exact science, rather than an art. After analyzing comparable sales, some appraisers state that "after analysis, this sale property indicates a value for subject of about *X* dollars," or "in the neighborhood of *X* dollars," or "greater (or less) than *X* dollars." This type of phrasing can also be used in stating the value indications derived by the various approaches to value. Then the final estimate of value can be stated as a precise figure if a single, specific amount is required by law and/or the client.

An appraiser retained by the condemnee is generally given a freer hand in determining the content of the appraisal report. However, it is always advisable to include a thorough explanation of the premises on which the various approaches to value are based and the methodology applied. It is also advisable to state the legal premise of just compensation briefly and to explain that the appraiser is generally bound by the applicable jurisdiction's concept of just compensation, i.e., market value. The appraiser should indicate that the owner's unwillingness to sell or sentimental attachment to the property has no bearing on market value and, therefore, cannot be considered in the appraisal process.

The appraiser should consult with the client's legal counsel as to the content of the appraisal report. This discussion will give the appraiser an indication of the attorney's understanding of the appraisal process, which may, in itself, help the appraiser determine the appropriate report content. During this consultation the appraiser and the attorney can review the applicable rules of discovery in the jurisdiction and discuss how these rules may or may not affect the desired report content. Under no circumstances, however, can the report's content fall below the minimum content required by the Uniform Standards.

Discovery rules are becoming increasingly liberal. Some federal courts require the exchange of appraisal reports, in total, prior to trial. On occasion, this has led to an unequal exchange of information. The condemnor's appraisal report may be written in accordance with detailed reporting guidelines, while the report commissioned by the property owner consists of a one- or two-page letter communicating an unsupported opinion of value. With the adoption of nationally recognized minimum appraisal reporting requirements (i.e., USPAP), it is hoped that court orders for the exchange of appraisal reports will begin to include the provision that the exchanged reports be prepared in accordance with the Uniform Standards for a self-contained report and that the Departure Provision to the standards not be invoked by either party.

Because nationally recognized appraisal reporting standards were lacking in the past, some courts have adopted their own set of standards for appraisal reports that are to be exchanged. These courts may well replace their reporting requirements with the Uniform Standards, but until they do appraisers should be aware of these other report requirements that must be met. Before preparing an appraisal report, the appraiser should ask legal counsel to determine whether there are any reporting requirements unique to the jurisdiction in which the case will be heard.

Graphics, photos, and other exhibits are an important part of an appraisal report. Appraisers do not always agree as to which exhibits should be included in the body of a report and which should be left for the addenda. Each appraiser must make his or her own decision in this regard, keeping in mind the client's reporting requirements.

For example, the body of an appraisal report on a medical office complex might include:

- An aerial photograph of the subject (following the letter of transmittal)
- A graph depicting the ratio of doctors to the trade area population over the past 20 years
- A list of nursing homes in the city, including the class of each home and the number of beds it contains
- A neighborhood occupancy map (on a page facing the neighborhood data section of the report)
- A list of comparable land sales, showing the sale number, grantor/grantee, sale date, land size, price, and price per square foot (or price per square foot of allowable floor area) of each comparable
- A detailed reproduction cost estimate
- A list of rental comparables, showing the rental number, lessor/lessee, location, size, rent, and rent per square foot of each
- A reconstructed operating statement
- A graphic analysis of the capitalization rate selected
- A list of comparable improved sales, showing the sale number, grantor/grantee, sale date, building size, and price of each

The addenda of this report might include the following items:

- A city or regional map
- A neighborhood map
- An aerial photograph of the neighborhood
- A legal description of the property (If the legal description is short, it would typically be included in the body of the report.)
- A plot plan
- Subject photographs (with the location and direction of each photo shown on the preceding plot plan)
- A comparable land sales map
- Comparable land sales data and photographs
- Executed leases on the subject property
- A comparable rental map
- Comparable rental data and photographs
- A comparable improved sales map
- Comparable improved sales data and photographs
- A detailed discounted cash flow analysis for the subject property

When an economic or geographic peculiarity has, or may have, affected property values over a large area, a detailed discussion of this factor would more properly be included in the addenda than in the body of the report.

In writing appraisal reports and preparing exhibits for appraisals made for eminent domain purposes, appraisers should keep in mind that their reports are often read and reviewed by individuals who have never seen the property. They may never have been in the city or state where the property is located and may have little, if any, knowledge of the government project for which the property is being acquired. For this reason, plot plans, neighborhood maps, and comparable sales maps should be prepared carefully, assuming the reader of the report is unfamiliar with the property, the neighborhood, the region, and the project necessitating the condemnation.

While the local review appraiser might skip over the appraiser's neighborhood description and the local project engineer might find reading the section on the government's project tedious, the regional or national reviewer and/or attorney who has been assigned the case will find this information most helpful. Finding basic information up front may put the reader in a receptive frame of mind and facilitate reviewing the important valuation sections of the appraisal report later on. Remember, the city map provided in the report may be the only information the attorney assigned to the case has to find his hotel from the airport.

REPORT APPEARANCE

The quality of an appraisal report will be judged on its appearance as often, if not more often, than on its content. Often the appraiser and the client never meet face to face; the only way the client can judge the appraiser is through the written appraisal report. Most appraisers consider themselves professionals, so their product—the appraisal report—must look professional. One way to emphasize the importance of the report's appearance is to divide the appraisal fee by the number of pages in the finished report. An appraisal report can cost the client more than $100 per page, and the client who pays that much money deserves more than smeared typing, typographical errors, and hand-sketched exhibits stuffed into a 25¢ binder. Appraisers should be aware that many regional and national review appraisers must respond to one important question after they review an appraisal report: Would you recommend this appraiser for future assignments?

With the availability and low cost of word processors, spreadsheet and graphic programs, and high-quality printers and copiers, there is absolutely no excuse for submitting anything less than a professional-looking appraisal report. However, both writers and users of appraisal reports should be warned that boxed-in charts and fancy graphics will not make up for other deficiencies. Clients deserve clearly written appraisal reports that contain adequate documentation and support for a well-reasoned estimate of value. An appraisal report that expresses an unsupported opinion of value developed by fuzzy thinking and presents its conclusions in a little box with fancy borders is still a lousy appraisal report.

THE PROJECT APPRAISAL REPORT

At times an appraiser will be asked to appraise several properties for the same public project. Such an assignment sometimes lends itself to the preparation of a *project report*. Project reports are often requested for reasons of economy. "Project appraisal reports are *not* appraisal shortcuts; they are clerical shortcuts."[27] They are intended to eliminate the repetition of standard sections of the appraisal report such as the city or neighborhood description, the scope of the appraisal, appraiser qualifications, and assumptions and limiting conditions. If the same comparable sales are used in the appraisal of all, or most, of the parcels, base information and photographs concerning these sales need only be included in the addenda of the project report.

The assignments suitable for project reports are those in which a group of parcels are being taken in whole, all parcels are vacant or similarly improved, all have the same or a similar highest and best use, and the same market data will be used in the valuations. A project appraisal report may include extensive market studies such as time (market condition) studies, damage studies, and benefit studies, which may not be justified in the appraisal of a single parcel.

---

27. Ibid., §C-13, p. 100.

Some condemnors have specific guidelines for the preparation of project appraisal reports, while others develop them on an ad hoc basis. It is important that the project report and the appraisal of each parcel within the project report meet the requirements of the Uniform Standards. Note that project reports may be acceptable to the condemning agency for purposes of negotiation, but they may not be acceptable to the agency's legal counsel if one or more of the parcels has to be condemned.

Project reports do not lend themselves to discovery or exchange. There may be information in the project report that is not applicable to the property being condemned and that the agency or its legal counsel does not want to divulge to opposing counsel. In such a case, the appraiser should be prepared to develop a self-contained appraisal report that covers only the parcel that is the subject of the condemnation action.

One thing is essential in the preparation of a project appraisal report — consistency in the analysis of the various comparable sales and the various subject properties. For instance, consider the following analysis comparing the location of Subject Property A with the locations of Comparable Sales 1, 2, and 3.

Sale 1	Sale 2	Sale 3
+10%	+5%	Equal

Now assume that these same sales were compared to Subject Property B with the following results:

Sale 1	Sale 2	Sale 3
+10%	+5%	-5%

The inconsistency in these analyses is obvious. If the location of Sale 1 was 10% inferior to Subject A and Subject B and Sale 2 was 5% inferior to both subject properties, the locations of Subject A and Subject B must be equal. Thus the location adjustment made to Sale 3 when it is compared to Subject B must be the same as the location adjustment made to Sale 3 when it is compared to Subject A. Making disparate adjustments such as this in individual appraisal reports of Subject A and Subject B is just as inconsistent as they are when made in a single project report. It is just that the inconsistency is not so glaring.

Because there is great potential for inconsistent adjustments in project reports, and in multiple appraisals of properties in the same area, appraisers should avoid reporting their value conclusions about individual parcels on a piecemeal basis. A wiser strategy is to reach conclusions as to the value of all the parcels being appraised and verify the consistency of the adjustments before any of the value conclusions are conveyed to the client.

THE REVIEW PROCESS

The foregoing discussion may suggest that the appraiser and the review appraiser are adversaries; nothing could be (or at least should be) further from the truth. There are good reviewers and poor reviewers. In fact, the review appraiser can be the appraiser's best friend, pointing out gross errors or foggy reasoning before they are exposed to the light of day. The review appraiser can be most helpful in counseling the appraiser during the valuation process, before the appraisal report is completed. The appraiser should use the review appraiser as a sounding board. This can be particularly beneficial when the appraiser cannot discuss specific appraisal problems with other knowledgeable appraisers on the same staff or in the same office.

When an appraiser questions a reviewer about applying a proposed appraisal methodology to a specific appraisal problem and the reviewer responds by tearing the methodology to shreds, the reviewer has shown his greatest worth to the appraiser. It is much better to hear criticism early on than to have it revealed after the appraisal report is complete or, worse yet, during cross-examination on the witness stand. Because a good review appraiser can be invaluable to the appraiser and the client, it seems incredible that some condemning agencies have adopted rules that prohibit any communication between the appraiser and the reviewer.

One condemning agency, for instance, historically prohibited all communication between the appraiser and the reviewer. When the reviewer found a report that needed correction, he did not contact the appraiser directly, but sent an interdepartmental communication (IDC) to the senior appraiser.

> Upon receipt of notice from the Review Appraiser that corrective action is needed ...the Senior Appraiser:
>
> A. Confers with the Appraisal Review Section Supervisor and/or the Review Appraiser as needed.
>
> B. *Does not reveal the Review Appraiser's IDC...to the Fee Appraiser under any circumstances.*
>
> C. Takes action to obtain the necessary corrections, including recommending that payment for contracted services be withheld pending contract fulfillment.[28]

This type of regulation is time-consuming and leads to misunderstanding, promoting adversarial, stubborn postures in all the parties involved. Eliminating such rules would greatly diminish the animosity that has developed between some appraisers and review appraisers.

Improved relations also might result if appraisers would try to develop a better understanding of the reviewer's duties and function. In the past, informa-

28. *Right of Way Manual*, Part IIC, Chapter 4, §4-5.09 (1976).

tion on the review function has been fragmented and difficult to obtain. Recently, however, a number of articles on the subject have been published and various seminars on review appraising are now being presented. Much interest has been generated by the increased review activity in the lending industry, which was mandated under FIRREA[29] and has substantially increased the interaction between appraisers and review appraisers. Even an appraiser who has no inclination to review an appraisal report should be familiar with the reviewer's function and how it is achieved. Such knowledge is invaluable in preparing appraisal reports for eminent domain purposes.

Both the appraiser and the reviewer must remember that it is not the reviewer's job to reappraise the property. This fact is sometimes forgotten by reviewers and by those who write job descriptions for review appraisers. If a review appraiser concludes a value estimate that is different than that of the appraiser and reports it, the reviewer must prepare his own appraisal report.[30] "It is the review appraiser's responsibility to determine whether the appraisal is adequately supported, whether it complies with recognized appraisal principles and practices, [whether it meets the reporting standards of the client], and whether it conforms to governing legal premises as prescribed by legal counsel."[31]

In the past, some reviewers for condemning agencies have been required to make a determination of value (DV) based on their review of one or more appraisals. Because the new appraisal review standards of USPAP require that a reviewer who determines a value different than that of the appraiser and reports it must prepare his own appraisal report, this practice will have to be modified.

One of the greatest compliments a reviewer can give an appraiser is to approve the appraisal report, but reject the appraiser's final estimate of value. Although the reviewer has historically substituted his own judgment for the appraiser's in writing a DV, the fact that the reviewer approves the report is evidence that the appraiser has written it in accordance with the applicable guidelines, has met all the conditions of the appraisal contract, and has adequately substantiated and justified the value conclusion reached. It is only natural for the reviewer to try to find fault with the procedure and analysis used when he disagrees with the final conclusion. Thus, it is a good sign when the reviewer cannot fault the appraiser's work or conclusions although he concludes a different opinion of value.

Appraisers may be subjected to more than one level of review, particularly when they appraise for condemnors. The first level of review, which has already been discussed, is usually conducted by a staff reviewer of the condemning agency. The staff reviewer's primary concerns are that the appraisal report conforms to the provisions of the appraiser's contract with the agency, including its reporting guidelines; that the report is free of mathematical errors; and that it presents a reasonable value estimate that is minimally supported. Once the appraiser has received report approval from the agency, his initial contract obligations are complete.[32]

29. Pub. L. No. 101-73, Title XI, Financial Institutions Reform, Recovery and Enforcement Act (FIRREA), 1989.

30. USPAP, 1994 ed., Standards Rule 3-1.

31. *Uniform Appraisal Standards for Federal Land Acquisitions*, §C-8, p. 94.

32. The contract may provide for additional services such as appraisal report updating or testimony at trial, for which the appraiser receives an additional fee.

If the agency is unsuccessful in its negotiations with the property owner, however, the case may be turned over to the agency's legal counsel for condemnation. The package turned over to counsel typically includes the appraiser's original report, or the appraiser may be asked to update the appraisal report for trial purposes. If such a request is made, the appraiser should bear in mind, both in quoting his fee for the update and in preparing the updated report, that this report will probably be reviewed at a different level and more critically than the original. Moreover, the updated report will probably end up in the hands of the property owner's lawyer as a part of the discovery or exchange process.

An appraisal report updated for trial purposes should generally be a completely new, self-contained appraisal report. Some agencies provide for updating an appraisal report by letter, often stating that new sales data that do not indicate a change in the subject property's value need not be included, or allowing report changes to be made by inserting "revised pages" into the original report. Such directives should be ignored. It is the appraiser who must defend the appraisal report on the witness stand, not the agency.

A pre-trial reviewer, who can be an appraiser or an attorney, will often have a different focus than the agency reviewer. The pre-trial reviewer is not concerned about whether the report meets the provisions of the appraiser's contract or the agency's precise formatting guidelines. Instead, the pre-trial reviewer will concentrate on whether the value estimate, and the data and analysis on which it was based, can stand up to the rigors of trial. The agency reviewer wants to approve the report and, therefore, may overlook technical errors that have no influence on the final value estimate. The pre-trial reviewer views the report as he believes legal counsel for the property owner will view it. Thus, attention is focused on the weaknesses and technical errors in the report.

For example, assume an appraiser stated in a report that it was his observation that the market was appreciating at the rate of 10% per year and adjusted the comparable sales accordingly. The agency reviewer may have approved this appraisal report because he knew from his own experience that the conclusion was reasonable. The pre-trial reviewer, on the other hand, may insist that the appraiser prepare a market-supported time-increment study, using paired sales or sales-resales, to support the propriety of the time adjustment. The reviewer does not make this demand because the adjustment is unreasonable, but because he wants the appraiser to be able to demonstrate the propriety of the adjustment to the trier of fact.

The appraiser and/or agency reviewer may feel that the time adjustment has little impact on the final value estimate and, therefore, does not justify the additional research and analysis. The pre-trial reviewer has another motivation, however; he wants to avoid a long, drawn-out cross-examination. Also, the pre-trial reviewer may have information that is not available to the appraiser or the agency reviewer—e.g., a copy of the agency negotiator's report or correspondence from owner's legal counsel asserting that property values in the area have been increasing at the rate of 30%, not 10%, per year.

The pre-trial reviewer may make other demands as well. He may ask that the appraiser remeasure the improvements on the subject property or reconfirm a sale if these items have been questioned by the owner during negotiations.

The pre-trial reviewer may also insist that the appraisal report be modified to correct a minor technical violation of USPAP, not to harass the appraiser, but to avoid cross-examination of the appraiser about the technical violation and the suggestion that the appraiser routinely acts in an unprofessional manner. The pre-trial reviewer is essentially a surrogate cross-examiner. Unlike cross-examination by the owner's counsel, the pre-trial reviewer's cross-examination is conducted in private and gives the appraiser an opportunity to conduct additional market research and think of better ways to explain his conclusions before the questions are asked again in a public trial.

The appraiser should take advantage of the pre-trial review process, which provides an opportunity to bolster weaknesses in the appraiser's analysis and conclusions. However, it is important for the agency, the pre-trial reviewer, and the agency's legal counsel to recognize that any appraisal work conducted after the initial approval of the appraisal report by the agency is beyond the scope of the appraiser's initial assignment and contract, and thus the appraiser should receive additional compensation for the additional work. Even if the pre-trial reviewer believes that the agency erred in approving the initial appraisal report, it is of no consequence. The appraisal report *was* approved, so additional appraisal work entitles the appraiser to additional compensation.

SUMMARY

"The thoroughness with which the appraisal is made and *reported* is the appraiser's greatest protection against professional embarrassment."[33] The appraiser must know the purpose of the appraisal and clearly define the value sought, e.g., market value, in terms that are legally acceptable in the applicable jurisdiction. It is not absolutely necessary for the appraiser to know the function of the appraisal, but this knowledge can help the appraiser determine the content and format of the appraisal report.

Some clients will specify the format required for an appraisal report, while others will leave report presentation totally in the hands of the appraiser. Whatever the client's instructions, an appraisal report must be developed in a logical, sequential manner which leads the reader to the same conclusion reached by the appraiser and meets the minimum reporting requirements of USPAP. A report prepared for eminent domain purposes must be a self-contained report and cannot invoke the Departure Provision. In all cases appraisers must avoid the tendency to regiment their thinking to conform to their clients' format and content requirements.

The appraiser should not begin writing the appraisal report until he or she has completed all necessary investigation, analysis, and computations and has

33. *Writing Appraisal Reports*, 28.

arrived at all the conclusions necessary to complete the report. It is also useful for the appraiser to prepare all graphic materials and photographs that will appear in the report before the actual report writing is begun. If this is done, the appraiser will have all these materials at hand and can avoid conflicts between the narrative and graphic portions of the report.

The content of an appraisal report will depend on the nature of the property, the nature of the taking, and the requirements of the client and/or the client's legal counsel. Regardless of the client's requirements, the appraiser should use a report outline or checklist to ensure that no important factors have been overlooked. In writing an appraisal report for a condemnee, it is often advisable to use the condemnor's appraisal report guidelines as a checklist. If the condemnor wants a specific factor covered by its own appraiser, the condemnor's attorney will probably want to know whether this factor has also been considered by the condemnee's appraiser.[34]

A single outline cannot be developed for an appraisal report's format and content because different types of properties will require different reports. Many publications contain demonstration, or illustrative, appraisal reports for different types of properties, but these formats will not be acceptable to all clients or suitable for all property types in all jurisdictions. In fact, it cannot even be assumed that the samples presented are well-written reports applicable to the type of property appraised in the particular jurisdiction. Many should be viewed only as reports that *were* submitted in a particular case, not reports that *should have been* submitted.

Regardless of the property type or the client's instructions, the appraiser should be certain that any report written meets the minimum requirements of USPAP for a self-contained report, without invocation of the Departure Provision, and the standards set down by professional appraisal organizations. These requirements should be met whether or not the appraiser is a member of one of these organizations; this is simply good professional appraisal practice.

Appraisal report content should be discussed with the client's legal counsel, particularly when report content may relate to applicable rules of discovery. The appraiser must not, however, bow to the wishes of the client's legal counsel and exclude pertinent data from an appraisal report just because it is detrimental to the client's interest. If a dwelling has termites, it has termites. It is not enough to reflect the presence of the termites in the value estimate; the appraiser must clearly state, "This house has termites." in the appraisal report, regardless of the wishes of the client.

The typical appraisal client may judge the quality of an appraisal report as much by its appearance as by its content. Therefore, appraisers should strive to produce only professional quality reports. Professional-looking reports do not, however, replace the need to produce professional, high-quality value estimates.

34. The condemnee's appraisal is also often turned over to the condemnor during negotiations. Reviewers for condemnors have a habit of rejecting such a report for not meeting their report content requirements, even though the report was not written to do so. When the condemnee's appraisal conforms to the condemnor's content requirements, the reviewer is forced to accept or reject the value estimate, rather than reject the report for technical deficiencies.

CHAPTER 20

Preparation for Trial

The appraiser should begin preparing for trial the moment the appraisal assignment is received. The attorney, of course, will obtain a general understanding of the case and the basis of the dispute when he or she is retained by the client.

Some condemnors' legal counsel hold the opinion that any appraisal report prepared for a government acquisition should be adequate for condemnation trial purposes. Thus, modification of the appraisal report should not be an essential part of trial preparation. While this is admirable in theory, experience and economics suggest that it is often not practical. Condemning agencies often award appraisal contracts to the lowest qualified bidder, recognizing that the vast majority of parcels are acquired without the necessity of a trial. Agency reviewers are more concerned with the reasonableness of the final estimate of value than they are with the appraiser's ability to support the estimate at a trial. Therefore, modification of initial appraisal reports, sometimes major modification, in preparation for trial is generally the rule rather than the exception.

The preparations for trial will vary somewhat depending on whether the client is a condemnor or condemnee. A client that is an active condemnor generally has one or more staff attorneys or an attorney on retainer. An active condemnor will also have an approved appraiser list and/or a staff of appraisers.

An appraiser who is given an assignment by a condemnor often knows the attorney who will handle the case. On the other hand, the attorney usually does not have any input into the selection of the appraiser. In fact, the attorney is often unaware of the case until the staff or fee negotiators have failed to settle the dispute. When the case is turned over to the attorney, he generally has the choice of keeping the original appraiser or choosing a new appraiser to replace or assist the first one.

Many condemnor's attorneys, as a matter of policy, refuse to go to trial with a staff appraiser, particularly when the compensation at stake is substantial. The reason for this practice is that many attorneys do not feel that they can convince a trier of fact that the staff appraiser is not an advocate in favor of the condemnor who employs him. While this policy is reasonable and probably well founded, it has the unfortunate consequence of eliminating from the trial the appraisers who, in many instances, are most familiar with the market data in the area and have more experience in the appraisal of neighborhood properties than any fee appraiser who might be retained for trial purposes.

When the client is the condemnee, the situation is different. The client may approach either the attorney or the appraiser first. If the appraiser is contacted first, he should encourage the client to retain legal counsel immediately. If the attorney is contacted before an appraiser has been retained, one of his primary functions will be to counsel the client to retain the services of an appraiser. "If at all possible, trial counsel should participate in the selection of the valuation expert."[1] "Trial strategy begins with the selection of the expert valuation witness."[2] The sooner the appraiser/attorney team is determined, the better.

Some attorneys wait until the last possible moment to retain the services of an appraiser. This may be because the attorney believes he can settle the case without the services of an appraiser or because he is too busy to worry about it until the date of trial is very near. Some attorneys falsely believe that hiring the appraiser late in the game can save the client appraisal fees because the appraiser will not be able to spend as much time on the appraisal and the preparation for trial. Whatever the reason for procrastination, the attorney should retain the services of an appraiser at the outset; the appraiser should decline to accept any assignment if there is not adequate time to complete the appraisal properly and prepare for trial.

> Many good appraisers are in too much of a hurry to try to turn out their appraisal reports for clients who waited too long to hire them. Many mistakes in arithmetic are made. Many items are overlooked in the physical inspection. If the cross-examining attorney can find one mistake, his favorite questions are: And what else did you overlook? And what else did you do wrong? Small details which are missed are blown way out of proportion because [the appraiser is] an expert.[3]

> Successful resolution of a condemnation proceeding, whether from the viewpoint of the condemnor or condemnee, depends upon teamwork between attorney and appraiser and other experts. The value of any parcel being condemned is difficult to determine. Determination of the property's value, however, is the object of the condemnation proceeding. A smoothly functioning appraiser-attorney team represents the client's best, indeed only, chance of obtaining just compensation.[4]

---

1. *Nichols' The Law of Eminent Domain*, rev. 3d ed. (New York: Matthew Bender Co., Inc., 1992), vol. 7A, §13.03.
2. Ibid.
3. *Nichols'*, vol. 9, §App. C-2(b) (1980).
4. *Nichols'*, vol. 7, §4.03 (1992).

The team sometimes breaks down, however, because "... the appraiser probably thinks that the lawyer is an unadulterated idiot, because the attorney is unable to tell the appraiser what the law is which will probably control the case. In turn, the lawyer thinks the appraiser is an unadulterated idiot because the appraiser—as is true of all nonlawyers—always knows what the law is."[5] This attitude can be overcome only by recognizing that "[f]or optimum effectiveness, the lawyer should be familiar with appraisal methods and problems, and the appraiser should have an understanding of court procedures and rules of evidence governing admissibility of appraisal information. To this end, attorneys and experts should help each other understand those matters necessary to the condemnation proceeding."[6]

References to the *appraiser/attorney team* should not be misconstrued to imply that the objectives of the appraiser and the attorney are the same. The appraiser and the attorney act as a team not because their goals are the same, but because they may be compatible. The attorney is an advocate for his client's interest. He strives to obtain the most favorable award for his client—i.e., as high as possible for the condemnee-client and as low as possible for the condemnor-client. The appraiser, on the other hand, is an advocate only for his opinion of value.

Only when the appraiser's opinion of value supports the proper amount of compensation as conceived by the client and his attorney can the appraiser and attorney form a team and function effectively. Therefore, until the appraiser has reached an opinion of value, it cannot be determined that a team relationship actually exists. If the appraiser's opinion of value does not support the client's position, there is no team; if the appraiser's opinion of value does support the client's position, the appraiser and the attorney can work together because their goals are compatible.

Experience has shown that triers of fact have an uncanny knack for distinguishing between the expert witness who is an advocate for his client and is testifying to a false value and the expert who is testifying to his unbiased opinion of value. Experienced condemnation lawyers know this and will dump, without hesitation, any appraiser who taints his value estimate to satisfy the interest of his client. An attorney was overheard to say that he would never again use the appraiser who testified on his client's behalf in a recent condemnation trial won by the attorney because the appraiser accepted, and testified to, every valuation theory, whether valid or not, put forward by the attorney during trial preparation. The appraiser who cannot ignore the interests of the client and develop an objective, supportable opinion of value will have a short professional career.

SELECTION OF THE APPRAISER

The selection of an appraiser by the attorney, generally in consort with the client, may be one of the most important steps in preparing for trial. All states now have appraiser licensing or certification laws which incorporate the Uniform Standards

5. Fred M. Winner, "The Expert Witness from a Lawyer's Viewpoint," *Condemnation Appraisal Practice* (Chicago: American Institute of Real Estate Appraisers, 1961), 445–452.

6. *Nichols'*, vol. 7, §4.03 (1992).

of Professional Appraisal Practice developed by The Appraisal Foundation. However, not all states require appraisals conducted for all purposes to be prepared by licensed or certified appraisers. Because the impetus for the licensing or certification of appraisers was federal legislation in response to the savings and loan crisis, some states applied the federally mandated licensing/certification requirements only to appraisals made for lending purposes in which the lender is a federal agency or a federally insured institution. Therefore, in some states appraisers do not need to be state licensed or certified to make appraisals for eminent domain purposes.

Nevertheless, many condemning agencies have adopted the policy that all fee appraisers retained to prepare appraisals for the agency must be licensed or certified. Federal regulations now require that all federal agencies that employ contract appraisers must hire only state certified appraisers[7] and "only those contract appraisals prepared by certified appraisers will be acceptable for federal condemnation purposes."[8] Many state condemning agencies have also adopted requirements that all contract appraisers employed be licensed or certified.

Although in some states a condemnee may have the option of retaining an appraiser who is not licensed or certified, there is no advantage in exercising this option and many potential disadvantages. All state licensing/certification laws require uniform minimum experience and continuing education[9] as well as adherence to the Uniform Standards, which dictate minimum appraisal report content. These requirements safeguard clients. Although possession of a state license or certificate does not guarantee an appraiser's competence to perform an eminent domain appraisal assignment, the client is assured of some minimum qualifications.

If the attorney is not personally familiar with any appraisers, referrals can generally be obtained from other attorneys, real estate agents, bankers, and various condemnors. When relying on a referral, the attorney should be careful to avoid enlisting the services of an unscrupulous appraiser. There are appraisers who work only one side of the street—i.e., only for condemnors or for condemnees. This in and of itself is no reason to reject a referral, but if the referred appraiser only works for condemnees, it is advisable to ask some attorneys who represent condemnors about the appraiser. Similarly, if the appraiser in question works only for condemnors, it is advisable to obtain the opinions of attorneys who specialize in representing condemnees. Experience has shown that attorneys have respect for well-qualified, honest appraisers, even if they only work the other side of the street. If, however, the appraiser sees every condemned parcel as a potential shopping center site or, at the other end of the spectrum, only sees the potential for use as pastureland, attorneys are not likely to keep silent on the matter.

Hiring an unscrupulous appraiser (or an appraiser who is continually overoptimistic or overpessimistic) may initially appear to be in the best interest of the client. However, this practice can have serious, adverse results. First, opposing counsel may take the position that "If the other side is going to use that unscru-

7. 49 C.F.R. 24.103(d).

8. *Uniform Appraisal Standards for Federal Land Acquisitions* (Washington, D.C.: U.S. Government Printing Office, 1992), §C-6, pp. 92-93.

9. As developed and adopted by The Appraisal Foundation.

pulous appraiser then we are going to hire our own." This is the "fight fire with fire" approach. Second, hiring a disreputable appraiser will all but eliminate the possibility of a negotiated settlement. Third, the client may draw false hope if the appraiser reaches an outlandish conclusion. When the condemnation award does not even approach the appraiser's value estimate, the attorney will be partially to blame, at least in the eyes of the client. Finally, if the appraiser testifies to a value that the trier of fact finds totally unbelievable, the trier of fact's only alternative is to base the award solely on the evidence presented by the opposing party to the dispute.

For example, if the condemnor's appraiser testifies to a value of $300,000 and the condemnee's appraiser testifies to a value of $400,000, the odds are strong that the trier of fact will split the difference and set the award at $350,000. This would be highly improbable if the condemnee's appraiser testifies to a value of $800,000. When the valuation testimony diverges greatly, the trier of fact will generally adopt the premise presented by one party to the suit and exclude the other; therefore, the award will likely be based on a single premise and value estimate. There is another reason to avoid presenting excessively high or low estimates of compensation. In some jurisdictions, the decision as to whether a condemnee is awarded trial costs is based on the relationship between the compensation award and the valuation testimony of the witnesses.

If the appraiser selected has a reputation for competency and objectivity as well as a professional demeanor on the witness stand, just retaining the appraiser may assist in reaching a negotiated settlement. This is particularly true if the appraiser selected has worked with opposing counsel in the past. Opposing counsel will then know that the case presented will be creditable, well-prepared, and believable.

There is debate within both the legal and appraisal professions as to whether appraisers should accept assignments from both condemnors and condemnees, particularly in cases that relate to the same public improvement project. Some condemnors have gone so far as to include a clause in their appraisal contracts that prohibits the appraiser from making appraisals for any condemnee involved with the same project. Of course, each individual appraiser engaged in such work and each attorney who retains appraisers on behalf of clients must determine whether or not to agree to this clause. There are a couple of factors to be considered in making this decision.

First, appraisers might not want to restrict themselves because appraisers who have worked for both condemnors and condemnees can include this information in testifying to their qualifications. It is particularly effective when an appraiser testifying on behalf of a condemnee can state that he has appraised for the condemnor on the same public project. This infers that the condemnor finds the appraiser competent, unbiased, and honest. In this situation, the condemnor can only suggest to the trier of fact that, although the appraiser is well-qualified, this time he has made a mistake. Thus, it has been said that "[u]se of an appraiser who specializes in representing only condemnors or condemnees...should be avoided."[10]

10. *Nichols'*, vol. 7, §4.02[2][b] (1992).

If an appraiser has been offered an appraisal contract by a condemnor, but has declined the assignment because of a restriction against conducting appraisals for condemnees, this fact can also be effective under direct examination. For this reason, condemnors should carefully consider the consequences of adopting such a restrictive policy.

Appraisers should also be wary of the condemnee's attorney who wants to put the appraiser on a small "retainer," allegedly because the client is not quite ready to have the appraiser prepare a fully documented appraisal report. Some attorneys have used this technique as a means of ensuring that a particular appraiser will not be available to the opposing party although they have no intention of actually contracting for the appraiser's services.

The appraiser who works for both condemnors and condemnees is, of necessity if not inclination, kept honest. The appraiser's analysis of a sale property simply cannot change from assignment to assignment; once the analysis is made and reported, the appraiser is stuck with it. For instance, in analyzing the *Coulter* case,[11] George C. Handley explained:

> It happened that in the present proceeding the condemnee's two expert witnesses had been previously employed by the state in a similar capacity. Moreover, each of the witnesses had made studies, appraisal reports, and in one or more instances had testified in court as a state witness in relation to the value of property in the immediate area. It was developed on cross-examination that one of their appraisals concerned the property adjoining the [property under appraisal], and that another appraisal was in relation to an entire block of property directly across [the street from the property in dispute]. Further cross-examination with respect to sales data (upon which the state's experts were to rely in large measure) disclosed that while these two witnesses had each previously considered the same data helpful in their appraisals of property in this vicinity when appearing for the state, they now chose to disavow the comparability of such transactions.[12]

In selecting an appraiser, the attorney must determine the appraiser's competency and review his general qualifications. Any sensible attorney will consider only state licensed or certified appraisers and thus be assured of at least minimum qualifications. An appraiser who holds a designation from a professional appraisal organization will have specific additional qualifications and is subject to a strict code of ethics. The attorney should take care to ensure that the appraiser's designation has been granted by a reputable appraisal organization, not by one of the mail-order designation mills that have popped up over the past few years. As a minimum, the attorney should only give credence to designations granted by appraisal organizations that are appraisal sponsors of The Appraisal Foundation.[13] The designation requirements, standards of professional appraisal practice, and codes of ethics of many of these organizations go far beyond the require-

11. *B. F. Coulter Co. et al.*, Superior Court, Los Angeles, Case No. 574469.
12. George C. Handley, "Presentation of the Case," *Condemnation Appraisal Practice* (Chicago: American Institute of Real Estate Appraisers, 1961), 492–512.
13. Appraisal sponsors include the American Association of Certified Appraisers, American Society of Appraisers, American Society of Farm Managers and Rural Appraisers, Appraisal Institute, International Association of Assessing Officers, International Right of Way Association, National Association of Independent Fee Appraisers, National Association of Master Appraisers, and the National Society of Real Estate Appraisers.

ments of the Uniform Standards and state licensing and certification requirements. The reputation of the appraiser should also be investigated; this is especially important in small communities.

The attorney should determine whether the appraiser will need any special qualifications or experience for the assignment. For instance, an appraiser who is qualified to cruise timber may be helpful in a case involving timberland. Experience in litigation valuation and as an expert witness is advantageous as is an appraiser's attendance at educational offerings that emphasize the appraisal of property for condemnation and other litigation purposes. The appraiser selected should be able to assist the attorney in the preparation of exhibits, preparations for negotiations and the trial, and, of course, testimony during the trial. It is, perhaps, unfortunate that the attorney must put so much emphasis on the appraiser's demeanor on the witness stand. However, if the appraiser falls apart under cross-examination, or under direct examination for that matter, he becomes a liability rather than an asset to the attorney.

Once the appraiser has been selected, a contract for appraisal services should be prepared and signed. A condemnor-client will generally have a standard form appraisal contract. These form contracts would probably never be signed if appraisers read them carefully and fully understood their terms. Condemnor contracts generally provide that payment for the appraiser's work does not have to be made until the appraisal is reviewed and approved, but there is often no time limit on how long the condemnor has to complete such a review. Another typical provision of such a contract states that any disputes relating to the quality or acceptability of the report furnished by the appraiser will be decided by the condemnor. Most condemnors apply these contract provisions reasonably and many appraisers take the position that they will continue to sign them as long as the terms are not applied unreasonably.

Some appraisal contracts provide for hourly or daily compensation for pretrial and trial work, while other contracts specify that the appraiser agrees to remain available to the client's legal counsel for such work, with compensation to be negotiated between the appraiser and legal counsel. Because the time required for trial preparation and testimony varies, a flat-fee contract for such appraisal services is uncommon and very dangerous. Appraisers who are asked to estimate a maximum fee for such services are well advised to make the estimate quite liberal.

A contract between the condemnee and the appraiser is generally much more informal than a condemnor's contract. Some of these contracts specify a flat fee for appraisal services, while others specify a daily fee (sometimes with an agreed maximum). Provisions are generally made for pretrial and trial work. Such contracts are generally made directly between the appraiser and the client. Many condemnees cannot pay the appraisal fee until the condemnation award has been received, so provisions must be made for subsequent payment. Often the attorney will agree to pay the appraisal fee directly out of the condemnation award. In this way, the appraiser is guaranteed the appraisal fee and payment of a retainer or prepayment of the fee is obviated. Appraisers should make provisions to ensure the payment of appraisal fees by clients who may otherwise refuse to pay because they object to the appraiser's final estimate of value.

Selection of the Attorney

Sometimes the tables are turned, and it is the appraiser who counsels the client in selecting an attorney, rather than the attorney who helps select the appraiser. If the appraiser is active in condemnation work, he may be familiar with local attorneys who specialize in condemnation or, at least, have some experience in the field. The first thing the appraiser should determine is whether the client has an attorney who handles most of his legal affairs; if so, the appraiser should advise the client to seek advice from his regular attorney, if the appraiser can make such a recommendation in good conscience.

The type of property and potential values involved will have some bearing on the selection of an appropriate attorney. Of course, the appraiser's ability to work with the selected attorney is also important. Some attorneys are trial lawyers and others are not. If the client's regular attorney is not a trial lawyer, the appraiser should try to determine who in the attorney's law firm would probably try the case if it went to trial. The client's regular attorney may not have enough trial experience, but another attorney in the same firm may be qualified. If asked to recommend an attorney, the appraiser should consider giving the client the names of several attorneys and discussing the strengths and weaknesses of each.

In the end, of course, the client will actually select the appraiser and the attorney. If the individuals chosen do not feel they can work together effectively, it is best that they refuse the assignment. Nothing is worse that a three-party condemnation trial: e.g., condemnor vs. condemnee's attorney and condemnee's appraiser; condemnee's attorney vs. condemnor, condemnor's appraiser, and condemnee's appraiser; or condemnee's appraiser vs. everybody.

In that same vein, the appraiser should reach a preliminary understanding with the client's legal counsel, whether the client is the condemnor or the condemnee, in regard to what other experts the attorney plans to call upon in the case. In some instances an attorney will use one well-qualified, objective appraiser and one unscrupulous appraiser or expert swearer. If the professional appraiser does not want to work on the same side of the case as the disreputable appraiser and thereby have his name associated with him, the professional must immediately either refuse the appraisal assignment or advise legal counsel of his unwillingness to work with the other appraiser. Then the attorney must make the choice as to which of the potential witnesses will be most valuable to his case.

THE APPRAISAL REPORT

There is considerable disagreement in legal circles as to how much legal instruction the attorney should initially give the appraiser. If the appraiser is experienced in condemnation appraising, the only instruction needed, at least initially, will be "Appraise the property." Experienced appraisers know the rules of determining just compensation, which damage items are compensable and which are not, and the rules regarding the offsetting of benefits in the applicable jurisdiction. More importantly, the experienced appraiser will recognize a questionable point of law and will ask for assistance from legal counsel. The appraiser can usually do a much better job if the attorney is not continually looking over his shoulder.

If the appraiser has been retained by the condemnor or its legal counsel after initial acquisition negotiations have failed, at least one appraisal report on the property already exists. A hotly contested question immediately arises: Should the newly retained appraiser be furnished any or all of the information in the initial appraisal report? Those who are against providing such information argue that they do not want the new appraiser's opinion swayed or corrupted by the analysis or opinion of the first appraiser. They also question what impact the fact that the appraiser was furnished a prior appraisal will have during cross-examination.

These arguments may have some validity, but not much. First, a professional appraiser is (or should be) retained for his objectivity. Nearly all condemnors' appraisal guidelines require that the appraiser investigate and report the subject property's assessed value and tax burden. A property's assessed value is nothing more than the assessor's opinion of the property's market value, yet condemnors are not concerned that the assessor's opinion will corrupt the opinion of the appraiser. Furthermore, in the collection and analysis of market data, appraisers are advised to seek information and opinions from Realtors®, appraisers, managers, and bankers.[14] Again, there is no suggestion that an appraiser's objectivity will be destroyed by this information.

Refusal to furnish the appraiser with information from a prior appraisal is akin to the historical practice of many appraisers who did not want to know the recent sale price of a property under appraisal, its pending sale price, or its listed price because they wanted to remain objective. The absurdity of this practice has now been recognized.

> In developing a real property appraisal, an appraiser must:
>
> (a) consider and analyze any current Agreement of Sale, option, or listing of the property being appraised, if such information is available to the appraiser in the normal course of business;
>
> (b) consider and analyze any prior sales of the property being appraised that occurred within the following time periods:

14. *The Appraisal of Real Estate*, 10th ed. (Chicago: Appraisal Institute, 1992), 155.

(i) one year for one- to four-family residential property; and

(ii) three years for all other property types.[15]

The appraiser should request, and the condemnor-client should furnish, a copy of all prior appraisals of the subject property. If the appraiser's objectivity can be corrupted by merely reading someone else's appraisal of the property, the appraiser should not have been hired in the first place. Concern about cross-examination questions is unnecessary; the appraiser should testify on direct examination that the prior report was one of the items of information furnished to him by his client. If the question does come up on cross-examination, the appraiser should respond, "Of course I reviewed the prior appraisal of the property. I reviewed every bit of information I could get my hands on regarding the property that I was asked to appraise."

If the appraiser is employed by the condemnee, he should be apprised of the initial offer made by the condemnor and furnished with any information submitted to the property owner by the condemnor in support of the offer, including any comparable sales information and appraisal reports. With knowledge of the condemnor's offer, the appraiser may be able to save the client thousands of dollars in appraisal fees. If the appraiser is familiar with the area where the property is located, he will generally be able to arrive at a range of values within which the final estimate of value will fall.

Whether or not the appraiser has knowledge of the condemnor's offer, the work should cease after a range of values is developed. At this point the appraiser should provide the client and the client's legal counsel with the following information:

- Appraisal fees due to date
- Anticipated appraisal fees required to complete the appraisal report (if not previously determined)
- Range of values anticipated upon completion of the appraisal report
- Estimate of time and charges that may be required for court preparation, pretrial conferences, depositions, and participation in the trial

With this information, the client and legal counsel can determine their best strategy. The appraiser who completes a fully documented appraisal report, knowing it will be of no financial benefit to the client, may (and probably should) have difficulty collecting his appraisal fee. It is certain that future referrals from the attorney involved in the case will be few and far between.

If the appraiser's preliminary estimate of value is unsatisfactory to the condemnee-client and the attorney, the attorney will usually try to reemphasize the advantageous aspects of the property and/or the potential damages that may accrue to the property due to the taking and construction of the public improvement. It is only natural, of course, that the attorney will want to confirm that the appraiser has considered the important factors affecting the property. However,

15. The Appraisal Foundation, *Uniform Standards of Professional Appraisal Practice* (USPAP), 1994 ed., Standards Rule 1-5, p. 13.

under no circumstances should the attorney attempt to coerce the appraiser into altering a valid estimate of value (although the appraiser should not be surprised at such an attempt). Even if the attorney were successful in his persuasion, the appraiser would not be able to testify to the value estimate with conviction and total honesty.

If the value estimate is unfavorable, the attorney must counsel his client as to the available alternatives. The condemnee can accept the condemnor's offer or attempt to negotiate a higher settlement figure without an appraisal. Another option is to hire another appraiser. If this alternative is chosen, the costs of hiring an additional appraiser should be discussed. At this point, the attorney has the opportunity to stay in the good graces of the client and, at the same time, lead the client to the conclusion that is in his best interest. The attorney need not, and should not, express to the client his own opinion of value or just compensation.

The most advantageous posture for the attorney to take is to inform the client that serious negotiations cannot begin until the client obtains an appraisal. If the results of the appraisal commissioned are unfavorable to the client, the next move is the client's. The attorney should maintain that without a valid appraisal, he cannot take the case to trial. Does the client want to incur the expense of another appraisal, and another, and another? By taking this position, the attorney remains a friend and counselor to the client while the appraiser is the bad guy, a position which appraisers have grown accustomed to in condemnation actions. Clients have a tendency to become more realistic about just compensation when they have to shell out money time after time just to be told that their expectations are unrealistic.

If the range of values reported by the appraiser is found to be acceptable and the client wishes to proceed, the appraiser can begin to develop a well-documented appraisal report that includes photographs, sketches, and charts. The appraiser determines the actual content of the report in conjunction with the attorney and in light of applicable court rules, the rules of discovery, and the minimum requirements for a self-contained report set forth by the Uniform Standards and by any professional appraisal organization to which the appraiser belongs.

At this point the appraiser should consider the legal date of the taking and the legal date of valuation. In many federal condemnations, the declaration of taking is the date of valuation, but the date of taking actually precedes the preparation of the appraisal report. Therefore, the appraiser should bear in mind that whatever is included in the appraisal report must be supported during the trial. There are no second chances in such a situation.

On the other hand, many jurisdictions require that the date of valuation be the date of the trial. Similarly, when the federal government files a complaint in condemnation rather than a declaration of taking, the date of value is usually the date of the trial. In this case, the appraiser may be required to update the appraisal report just before the trial. This sometimes gives the appraiser a second chance to verify all the factual data in the report and to strengthen and augment the conclusions reached. However, the appraiser should be aware that any prior appraisal may become the subject of discovery by opposing counsel. Thus the appraiser may be subjected to cross-examination regarding errors in an outdated report, even though they have been corrected in the updated report, and inconsistencies between various reports.

APPRAISAL REVIEW

The attorney, or the attorney's review appraiser, should be given ample time to review the appraisal report carefully. In this review the attorney should look for data, methods, or approaches that may be inadmissible. He should keep in mind that the inadmissibility of a piece of data does not necessarily mean that the appraiser should not have considered or even relied on it. For instance, an offer to sell is usually inadmissible. Therefore, it would be improper for the appraiser to testify that he considered the fact that a property abutting the property under appraisal was listed at $5.00 per square foot. It would not be improper, however, for the appraiser to testify that he considered the present listing price of a property abutting the property being appraised. It is the actual *asking price* that is inadmissible, not the fact that it was considered.

In reviewing an appraisal report, the attorney should use a checklist to verify that the appraiser has included all pertinent data. The condemnor's published appraisal guidelines are useful for this purpose. *Nichols'* also contains an excellent "pretrial checklist" for use by attorneys.[16] A checklist designed for use in conjunction with an appraisal report prepared under the *Uniform Appraisal Standards for Federal Land Acquisitions*[17] can be found in the addenda.

If the appraiser has been retained by the condemnor, the attorney's review of the report is at least the second, and more likely the third or fourth, review of the appraisal report conducted. Neither the appraiser nor the attorney should assume the report is error-free just because it has withstood a number of reviews. For example, the following excerpt is quoted from an actual appraisal that was reviewed and approved by three government agencies, including one at the federal level.

> Even in the before situation water and sewer connections are some distance from the site, something in the nature of 200' to 300' and bringing these facilities onto the site would be rather more expensive than is typical. In the after situation, the circumstance is greatly compounded by the fact that, having brought the utility lines to the toe of the dike at the southwest aspect of the [state highway/county road] intersection, a tunnel would have to be dug under the dike in a northeasterly direction in order to bring those utility connections on the Subject remainder. The distance involved in that tunneling project would be a minimum of 180'. In an effort to grasp the magnitude of this tunneling project, I have interviewed several convicts who have tunneled out of [the state prison]. They uniformly report that it takes several days for two men to plan such a tunnel and it takes two

16. *Nichols'*, vol. 7, §4.04[7] (1992).

17. *Uniform Appraisal Standards for Federal Land Acquisitions* (Washington, D.C.: U.S. Government Printing Office, 1992).

> men several days to dig one.... For the reasons discussed just above, I am of the opinion that the highest and best use of the Subject Property in the after situation if for recreational river access.

In addition to reviewing the appraisal report, the attorney should look over any prior reviews of the appraisal report and any notes in the case file concerning past negotiations. A negotiator's report can be useful in anticipating the claims made by opposing parties and the direction that cross-examination of the attorney's expert may take.

After reviewing an appraisal report, the attorney should consider two alternatives. First, the attorney must decide if a second appraiser should be employed. The answer to this question generally depends on the number of appraisers retained by opposing counsel and, more important, the amount of money at stake. The condemnee's attorney should consider whether there are any provisions for the condemnor to pay the condemnee's expert witness fees in the jurisdiction where the case will be heard. Also to be considered are the local rules of the court; some court rules limit the number of appraisal witnesses who may testify at a trial.

The attorney should acknowledge that it is unlikely that two appraisers will approach a valuation problem the same way or arrive at exactly the same value. Therefore, using two or more appraisers will generally result in the presentation of two or more different approaches and conclusions to the trier of fact. If the trier of fact is a jury, the submission of two or more approaches and conclusions by the same party may adversely affect the outcome of the trial. "The outcome of the trial of a case involving the value of real estate depends upon the presence of well-qualified and thoroughly competent expert witnesses. The trial pattern and the success or failure of the case is in direct ratio to the *quality*, not quantity of the witnesses testifying in the proceedings."[18]

The second alternative the attorney may want to consider is whether to employ a consulting appraiser. The appraiser who values the property and will testify in court is an advocate only for his own value estimate. The consulting appraiser, on the other hand, is retained strictly as a consultant. He never appraises the property. The consulting appraiser can, and should, be an advocate for his client's interest. He is available to the attorney throughout the preparations for trial and, if necessary, during the trial itself. The consultant can often find technical flaws in the appraisal that would not be noticed by the attorney. Moreover, the consultant can usually see the weaknesses of the appraisal approaches used more objectively than the appraiser who applied them.

Some condemnors and many large private law firms that specialize in real estate litigation have appraisal consultants on staff. Such a consultant may be called an appraiser, a review appraiser, or an appraisal consultant, but his primary function is to help the attorney and the appraisal witness prepare for trial. The purpose of the typical appraisal review has been described as follows:

18. Theodore J. Labrecque, "The Court and the Expert Witness," *The Appraisal Journal* (January 1961), 87–93.

- Ascertain whether the appraisal report contains the pertinent data available;
- Determine whether the factual information logically relates to the conclusions made by the appraiser;
- Determine whether the appraisal conforms with acceptable appraisal practices and techniques; and
- Decide whether the reasoning and logic applied to the data in the appraisal process result in a logical conclusion.

An appraisal review must be an impartial analysis of the total work of [the] appraiser.[19]

It has also been said that "[t]he reviewer must not approach the report as a headhunter or nitpicker for his own reasons or those of his employer."[20] Unlike the typical review appraiser, however, the consulting appraiser's review function is to act as a headhunter and nitpicker. The consulting appraiser reviews the appraisal report as he believes it will be reviewed by the opposing party's legal counsel. So, the purpose of the consulting appraiser's review is twofold. While it is intended to ensure technical conformance with The Appraisal Foundation's Uniform Standards of Professional Appraisal Practice (and specific agency guidelines, if applicable), its primary purpose is to assist the client's legal counsel in preparing for trial (and preparing the appraiser for trial). The consultant's review identifies areas within the appraisal report that may not be technically incorrect, but are weak or insufficient to meet the special demands of a condemnation trial.

Because of the dual purpose of consulting reviews, they are used only as a trial preparation tool by legal counsel and often are not shown to the appraiser who prepared the value estimate. If some appraisers were to read these reviews and realize how vulnerable they will be on cross-examination, they might refuse to take the witness stand.

The purpose of a consulting review is not to belittle or degrade the appraiser. There are weaknesses in all appraisal reports and in the appraisal process itself; every approach to value has its inherent weaknesses. The appraiser must recognize these weaknesses and be prepared to respond to questions and criticism on the witness stand.

For example, if an appraiser has relied on the cost approach to value because market data with which to develop a reliable value indication by sales comparison are lacking, he must be prepared to defend his methodology. The appraiser may have used cost service data in estimating the reproduction cost of improvements and employed a modified age-life method in estimating depreciation. The consulting appraiser may acknowledge the acceptability of this procedure, but must also recognize the following potential problems:

1. The use of published cost service data may be challenged as hearsay or as the use of averages not applicable to the particular property.

19. Max J. Derbes, "Appraisal Review Ethics," *The Appraisal Journal* (April 1990), 161.

20. *Nichols'*, vol. 7, §4.07[2][e] (1992).

2. The use of an age-life method of estimating depreciation is mechanical in nature and not supported by market data.
3. The courts have, on literally hundreds of occasions, stated that the cost approach results in a "summation appraisal," which may have little relationship to the market value of the property as a whole.

To address these concerns, the consulting appraiser may recommend that the appraiser be asked to obtain the services of a contractor or cost estimator to assist in the development of a reproduction cost estimate of the improvements and, if necessary, to testify to that estimate. A further recommendation might be that the appraiser attempt to develop applicable depreciation rates using the sales comparison approach, even if the sale properties are not sufficiently comparable for direct use in the sales comparison approach and substantial adjustment is required. A third suggestion might be for the attorney to discuss with the appraiser the court's attitude toward the cost approach. Then the appraiser can formulate a reasonable response to the court's likely criticism of the appraiser's application of the approach, which will surely be raised at the trial. The whole purpose of trial preparation, from the appraiser's perspective, is to ensure that the appraiser will not be asked a question he did not expect and one for which he has no acceptable answer.

Attorneys should consider retaining a consultant under four circumstances. First, if the attorney has very little condemnation experience, the consultant can be of invaluable assistance. Second, a consultant may be useful in a complex case because the appraiser who is preparing for his own portion of the trial may not have enough time to assist the attorney in preparing other portions or elements of the trial. Third, if the case involves very technical appraisal methodology, even a seasoned condemnation lawyer may need assistance in preparing for and conducting the trial. The attorney may need clarification if the appraisal problem involves the use of statistics or the application of a newer, more technical aspect of the income capitalization approach to value. Finally, a consulting appraiser can be very useful in jurisdictions in which *the rule* is typically invoked. (*The rule* is a court order which excludes witnesses from the courtroom so they cannot hear the testimony of other witnesses.) In this situation, the consulting appraiser may be the only appraisal expert available to the attorney who is allowed to remain in the courtroom throughout the trial. (*The rule* is discussed further in the next chapter.)

Consulting appraisers can also assist by discussing technical appraisal matters directly with the appraiser. Attorneys have a tendency to talk in *legalese*, while appraisers may hear in *appraisalese*. Consulting appraisers can act as interpreters between them. Consulting appraisers can also advise attorneys when they are overstepping their bounds by asking the appraiser to do something that may jeopardize his objectivity or violate professional appraisal standards.

ATTORNEY/APPRAISER CONFERENCE

Once the attorney (and the consulting appraiser if one is used) has completed the appraisal review, he should confer with the appraiser. Again, a "pretrial checklist" can be used for such a conference.[21] The first matter to be covered in this conference is any deficiencies in the appraisal report that may require corrective action. The strengths and weaknesses of the appraiser's approach to the valuation problem should be discussed in detail. The appraiser should acknowledge the inherent weaknesses in the approach to value and discuss them with the attorney.

If the appraiser has relied heavily on the income capitalization approach to value and the market data used to justify the capitalization rate is weak, this fact should be pointed out to the attorney and both individuals should decide how best to present the available capitalization data to the trier of fact. Probable cross-examination and redirect examination on this matter should also be discussed. The appraiser should inform the attorney of all market data that were considered, but eventually rejected, because these data may be addressed on cross-examination. The appraiser should be able to explain clearly why the data were rejected. If the appraiser is unable to do this, the trier of fact may get the impression, with the assistance of opposing legal counsel, that the appraiser has utilized only those data that support a dictated or preconceived value estimate.

> The appraisal report should contain only those comparable sales actually relied upon (not only considered) by the appraiser in arriving at the estimate of market value. All comparable sales data and verification sheets, deeds, and site, locational and/or plat maps, including those used in the report, should be contained in a separate indexed data book or file together with all other information reviewed and considered by the appraiser.[22]

The appraiser must convey this secondary information to the attorney.

Making rejected data available to the attorney has another advantage in that it makes the attorney aware of these data and why they were not comparable. This information can be invaluable to the attorney in cross-examination if the opposing party uses these data in his value estimate. Because the discovery process has become more liberal, the appraiser should exclude data on noncomparable sales from the appraisal report itself; the appraiser will have enough trouble handling cross-examination without providing opposing counsel with ammunition.

During their initial conference, the attorney and the appraiser should determine what exhibits will be required for trial and who will be responsible for their preparation. If an exhibit is directly connected with the appraiser's testimony, the appraiser should have the responsibility of preparing it or having it prepared. An appraiser can become confused, disoriented, and vulnerable to attack by opposing counsel if the exhibit presented does not conform to his report or testimony. Also, by taking responsibility for the preparation of his own exhibits, the ap-

21. William H. Crouch, "Pretrial Conference Checklist of Factors Affecting Valuation," *The Appraisal Journal* (October 1964), 523-530.

22. *Nichols'*, vol. 7A, §13.04 (1992).

praiser can ensure that he will not be presented with an exhibit just before or during the trial which distorts his analysis or findings.

THE DISCOVERY PROCESS

Discovery is an integral part of the trial preparation process. Through this process the attorney and the appraiser learn the theory of the opposing party's case and the facts and opinions on which it is based. Eminent domain cases are a battle of experts.

> In cases of this character, a prohibition against discovery of information held by expert witnesses produces in acute form the very evils that discovery has been created to prevent. Effective cross-examination of an expert witness requires advance preparation. The lawyer even with the help of his own experts frequently cannot anticipate the particular approach his adversary's expert will take or the data on which he will base his judgement on the stand. A California study of discovery and pretrial in condemnation cases notes that the only substitute for discovery of experts' valuation materials is "lengthy—and often fruitless—cross-examination during trial," and recommends pretrial exchange of such material.[23]

A significant change in the Federal Rules of Civil Procedure relating to discovery of experts took effect in December of 1993. Rule 26 provides:

> (2) Disclosure of Expert Testimony.
>
> (A) ...a party shall disclose to other parties the identity of any person who may be used at trial to present evidence under Rules [relating to expert testimony].
>
> (B) Except as otherwise stipulated or directed by the court, this disclosure shall, with respect to a witness who is retained or specially employed to provide expert testimony in the case or whose duties as an employee of the party regularly involve giving expert testimony, be accompanied by a written report prepared and signed by the witness. The report shall contain a complete statement of all opinions to be expressed and the basis and reasons therefor; the data or other information considered by the witness in forming the opinions; any exhibits to be used as a summary of or support for the opinions; the qualifications of the witness, including a list of all publications authored by the witness within the preceding ten years; the compensation to be paid for the study and testimony; and a listing of any other cases in which the witness has testified as an expert at trial or by deposition within the preceding four years.
>
> (C) These disclosures shall be made at the times and in the sequence directed by the court. In the absence of other directions from the court or stipulation by the parties, the disclosures shall be made at least 90 days before the trial date or the date the case is to be ready for trial.[24]

---

23. Federal Rule of Civil Procedure 26 (Notes of Advisory Committee on Rules 1970 amendment).

24. Ibid., pp. 29–30.

The new rule also provides that "[a] party may depose any person who has been identified as an expert whose opinions may be presented at trial. If a report from the expert is required under subdivision (a)(2)(B), the deposition shall not be conducted until after the report is provided."[25]

This rule should put a stop to the practice of some appraisers who subvert the discovery process, often with the encouragement of attorneys, by not preparing a written appraisal report or by preparing a one-page document expressing an opinion of value without any reasoning or data to support the opinion. When preparing their appraisal reports, appraisers should keep in mind that, under this rule, opposing counsel will have at least 90 days to scrutinize their appraisal reports and prepare questions for cross-examination. Appraisers should not assume that misstatements of facts or omissions, however small, will go unnoticed.

The attorney should inform the appraiser that many depositions are taken under a *subpoena duces tecum*, which means that the appraiser must bring to the deposition all papers and materials in his possession that have any bearing on the case. Essentially the appraiser must submit his entire appraisal file to opposing counsel for inspection, and for copying if counsel so wishes. Thus it is essential that the appraiser be aware of what is in his file and what is not.

Draft copies of appraisal reports should be discarded once they have been revised. Computations and notes that were not used in the final value estimate should be removed from the file. For instance, if the appraiser, early on in the appraisal process, found that the property under appraisal was being leased for $100,000 per year and that capitalization rates were approximately 9.5% to 11%, he might jot down the following calculations:

Indicated value range for subject:

	High	Low
Gross rent	$100,000	$100,000
Vacancy (5% to 10%)	– 5,000	– 10,000
Effective gross income	$ 95,000	$ 90,000
Expenses (20% to 30%)	– 19,000	– 28,500
Net income	$ 76,000	$ 61,500
Indicated value (at 9.5% and 11%)	$800,000	$559,091

The appraiser may have made such computations to determine selection parameters for comparable sales or to evaluate the reasonableness of an offer of settlement made by either party. Whatever the reason for the calculations, if opposing counsel finds the figures in the appraiser's file he will have a field day with them, if not in the trial at least in deposition, whatever the appraiser's final estimate of value. Once the appraiser arrives at his final opinion of value, the note has no validity and should be removed from the file. All superfluous notes, memos, calculations, and phone messages should be discarded. The appraiser must be aware of, and able to explain, every scrap of paper in any file taken to the deposition.

25. Ibid., p. 34.

If legal counsel has submitted anything in writing to the appraiser that is marked "attorney's work product" or "confidential," this material should be removed from the file. If the file contains any correspondence from legal counsel that is not so marked, but may be considered to be the "attorney's work product," the appraiser should ask legal counsel whether it should be left in the file. If the appraiser being deposed is asked whether he has removed anything from the file, or has any other papers concerning the case that he did not bring to the deposition with him, he should answer in the affirmative and explain, if asked, that the papers were considered "attorney's work product." If opposing counsel wishes to challenge that classification, he can ask the court for a ruling on the matter and it is up to the attorneys to fight it out.

Initial discovery is generally accomplished through interrogatories.[26] A standard set of interrogatories taken from a law book should not be used because each condemnation case has its own peculiarities. Under no circumstances should an attorney send out a set of interrogatories without asking his client's appraiser, "Is there anything you need to know to make your job easier or to better prepare you for trial?" Although the answer to a seemingly trivial question suggested by the appraiser may mean nothing to the attorney, it may reveal to the appraiser the entire valuation approach that the opposing party's appraiser is going to use.

One crucial item of information is, of course, the list of sales that the opposing party's appraiser has used, and will probably testify to, in arriving at the value conclusion. If a request for information on these sales is made by interrogatory, it must be worded carefully. The interrogatory should not ask about all the sales *considered* by the opposing party's appraiser because appraisers *consider* a great number of sales. They may unconsciously consider all the sales known to them, although most are immediately rejected as noncomparable. The interrogatory should request a list of all sales that were *relied on* and to which the appraiser will testify. Otherwise, the list of *considered* sales could run several pages and contain much more sales data than could be analyzed or verified effectively.

Once the list of sales is obtained by counsel, a copy should be sent to the appraiser immediately. The appraiser and the attorney work as a team, and it is the appraiser's responsibility to verify and analyze the sales submitted as comparable by the opposing party to the litigation. The appraiser should furnish all pertinent data relating to these sales to the attorney, including the following information:

- Verification that the sale did, in fact, occur
- Date of sale
- Price
- Terms
- Detailed property description
- Photo of property

26. For a definition, see *The Dictionary of Real Estate Appraisal*, 3d ed. (Chicago: Appraisal Institute, 1993), 188.

- Determination of comparability
  If it is not comparable, why not?
  If it is, why wasn't it used in the appraiser's own analysis?

The importance of this type of investigation is illustrated by the following findings, which concern actual sales data submitted in the discovery process:

- A sale reported as 600 acres of dry wheat land was found to contain an additional 600 acres of irrigated wheat land.
- A sale reported was found to have never occurred.
- A sale reported to be dry wheat land was found to have been timberland with more than one million board feet of merchantable timber on it.
- An office building reported to contain 12,000 square feet of rentable area was found to be a three-story structure with 12,000 square feet of rentable area on each floor.

All of these findings were presented to the trier of fact during the trial and the credibility of the appraisal witness who relied on the faulty data was seriously eroded, if not destroyed.

A consulting appraiser's notes or appraisal review are not generally subject to discovery and the consultant's deposition cannot be taken. The consultant's appraisal review is prepared in anticipation of the trial and is generally considered privileged as trial preparation material.

> A party may, through interrogatories or by deposition, discover facts known or opinions held by an expert who has been retained or specially employed by another party in anticipation of litigation or preparation for trial and who is not expected to be called as a witness at trial only . . . upon a showing of exceptional circumstances under which it is impracticable for the party seeking discovery to obtain facts or opinions on the same subject by other means.[27]

"Consequently, a defense against such discovery is the showing that exceptional circumstances do not exist and discovery should thus be restricted.... The Rule recognizes that with nontestifying experts, there is no need to obtain discovery for effective cross-examination. The party seeking disclosure under this Rule carries a heavy burden of proving exceptional circumstances under which it is impracticable to obtain the facts or opinion by other means."[28]

DEMONSTRATIVE EVIDENCE

When the term *demonstrative evidence* is used, many people think in terms of formal exhibits. However, demonstrative evidence is, "That evidence addressed directly to the senses without intervention of testimony. Such evidence is concerned with real objects which illustrate some verbal testimony and has no probative value in itself."[29]

27. Federal Rules of Civil Procedure, pp. 34–35.
28. *Nichols'*, vol. 7, §7.03[3][b] (1993).
29. *Black's Law Dictionary*, abr. 6th ed., s.v. "Demonstrative evidence."

Demonstrative evidence may take many forms, including

- Blackboards
- Charts
- Graphs
- Diagrams
- Renderings
- Document enlargements
- Color coding
- Photographs
- Projection slides
- Motion pictures
- Videotapes
- Models
- Actual objects
- Computer analyses and representations.[30]

The identification and preparation of formal exhibits are essential to proper trial preparation. The complexity of the case and the amount of money involved will affect both the number and quality of the exhibits required. The attorney and the appraiser must determine the exhibits that will be required early on because preparing exhibits can be time-consuming and a hastily prepared exhibit is much more likely to contain errors than one prepared well in advance. If a witness has to correct an erroneous exhibit during testimony, the correction will be obvious and, each time the trier of fact views the exhibit, the witness's error will be reinforced. It makes no difference to the trier of fact whether the exhibit was prepared by the witness or by someone else; the trier of fact will view it as the witness's error.

The new Federal Rules of Civil Procedure make the early identification and preparation of exhibits even more critical. As noted earlier, the expert's report must be provided to opposing counsel at least 90 days before trial and this report must include "any exhibits to be used as a summary of or support for the opinions" of the expert. The attorney and the appraiser must reach an agreement as to what exhibits will be used at trial so these exhibits can be included in the appraisal report.

One of the first exhibits that should be considered is a simplified diagram of the appraisal process similar to Figure 20.1. This is particularly necessary for the party that has the burden of proof because that party's appraiser will generally be the first appraisal witness. In testifying, the appraiser can use such an exhibit to explain the steps taken to arrive at the estimate of value. The exhibit can serve as a road map for the appraiser's forthcoming testimony and facilitate the trier of fact's understanding of all the appraisal testimony given in the trial.

30. *Nichols'*, vol. 7, §3.11 (1992).

Figure 20.1 Appraisal Process

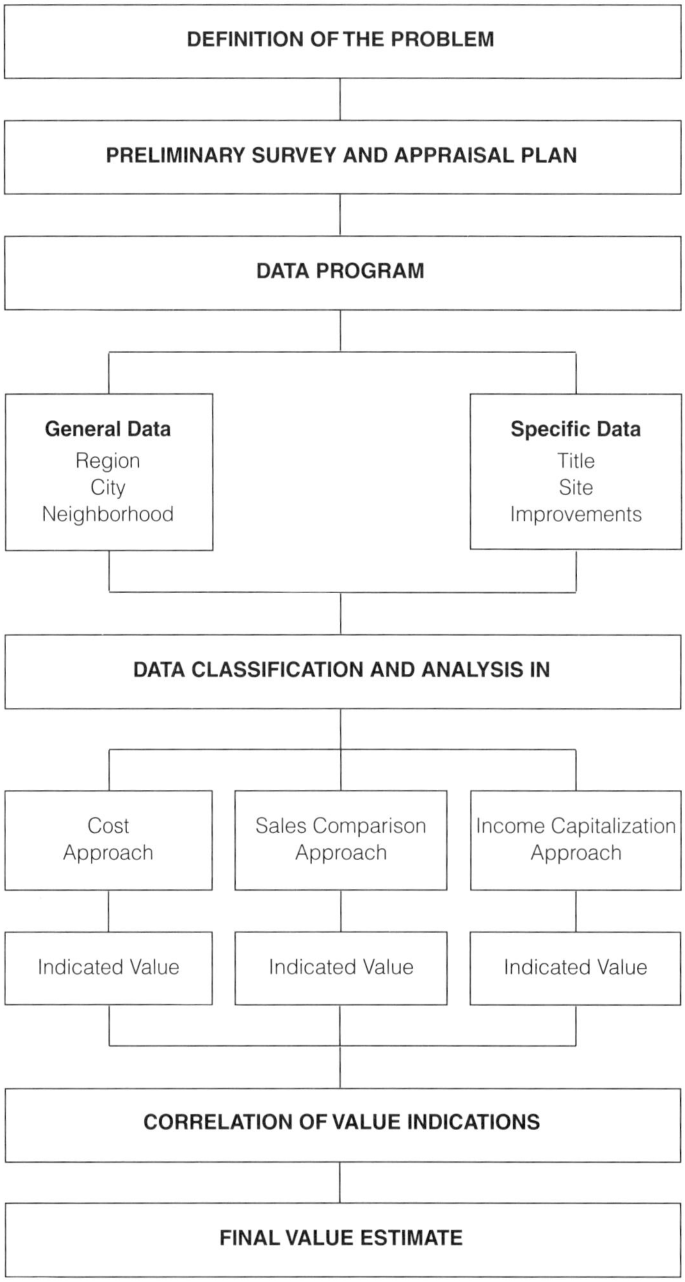

The appraisal report and any addenda to the report are excellent sources of possible exhibits. Cost approach computations and data supporting depreciation estimates, income capitalization approach data and computations, and market data charts should always be viewed as potential exhibits. (For specific examples, see Chapter 8; Tables 9.1 through 9.7 in Chapter 9; and Tables 10.1, 10.2 and 10.5 in Chapter 10.) Photographs should almost always be considered required exhibits—e.g., photographs of the property being appraised, photographs of comparable land sales, photographs of comparable rentals, photographs of comparable improved sales. All photographs submitted as exhibits should be in color and large, at least 8 inches by 10 inches. Each photograph should be clearly identified with the appraiser's name, the date the photo was taken, and the property depicted (e.g., Comparable Rental 5). Comparable sales or rental maps sometimes make good illustrations, as do detailed before and after plot plans, sketches, and small-scale aerial photographs of the property being appraised and the neighborhood.

Information uncovered in the discovery process will often suggest exhibits that may be helpful in the presentation of rebuttal evidence. For example, the condemnor in one case learned through interrogatories that the condemnee's expert would testify that the dwelling being condemned was in a neighborhood where property values had, since 1990, been adversely affected by the pendency of the government's project. The condemnee's appraiser then used "comparable sales" from an entirely different neighborhood in the city.

In light of this knowledge, the condemnor's attorney and appraiser concluded that a detailed presentation of historical sales data from the subject neighborhood and from other neighborhoods in the city was essential. The condemnor's appraiser surveyed residential sale prices in four different neighborhoods in the city, including both the subject neighborhood and the neighborhood from which the condemnee's expert has selected his "comparable sales." Figure 20.2 depicts the results of that survey. The figures demonstrate that sale prices per square foot for dwellings in the subject neighborhood (Neighborhood 1) increased from 1989 through 1992 by a greater percentage than did sale prices in the alleged "comparable" neighborhood (Neighborhood 4) and in the city as whole.

Figure 20.3 depicts the average sale price per square foot for dwellings in each neighborhood for each year from 1987 through 1992. It clearly shows that dwellings in the neighborhood from which the condemnee's appraiser selected his comparables have historically sold for higher prices per square foot than the dwellings in the subject neighborhood. In fact, the prices per square foot in this neighborhood are far above the average prices paid in the other neighborhoods studied and in the city as a whole.

Figures 20.2 and 20.3 prove their point and demonstrate the effectiveness of presenting large amounts of data graphically. Actual court exhibits of such graphs are typically prepared in a multicolor format, which makes them easy to read and presents the results of the analysis dramatically. The significance of the data pre-

Figure 20.2 Comparison of Neighborhood Price Changes

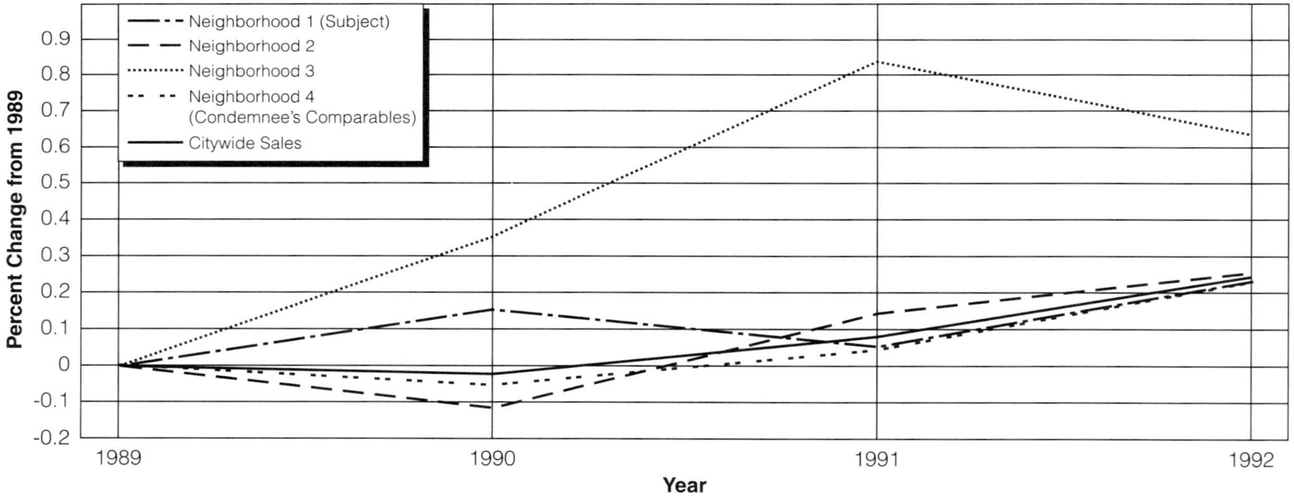

Prices in City & Percent Change From 1989

Year	Neighborhood 1 Price/ Sq. Ft	Neighborhood 1 % of 1989	Neighborhood 2 Price/ Sq. Ft.	Neighborhood 2 % of 1989	Neighborhood 3 Price/ Sq. Ft.	Neighborhood 3 % of 1989	Neighborhood 4 Price/ Sq. Ft.	Neighborhood 4 % of 1989	Citywide Price/ Sq. Ft.	Citywide % of 1989
1989	$24.82	0.0%	$22.64	0.0%	$18.80	0.0%	$46.71	0.0%	$27.57	0.0%
1990	$27.83	12.1%	$20.08	-11.3%	$25.73	36.9%	$43.70	-6.4%	$26.94	-2.3%
1991	$26.34	5.5%	$25.97	16.6%	$34.35	60.4%	$49.24	5.8%	$30.27	10.0%
1992	$30.65	22.1%	$28.45	22.4%	$30.99	35.5%	$56.85	20.6%	$33.83	20.7%

Figure 20.3 Comparison of Neighborhood Prices

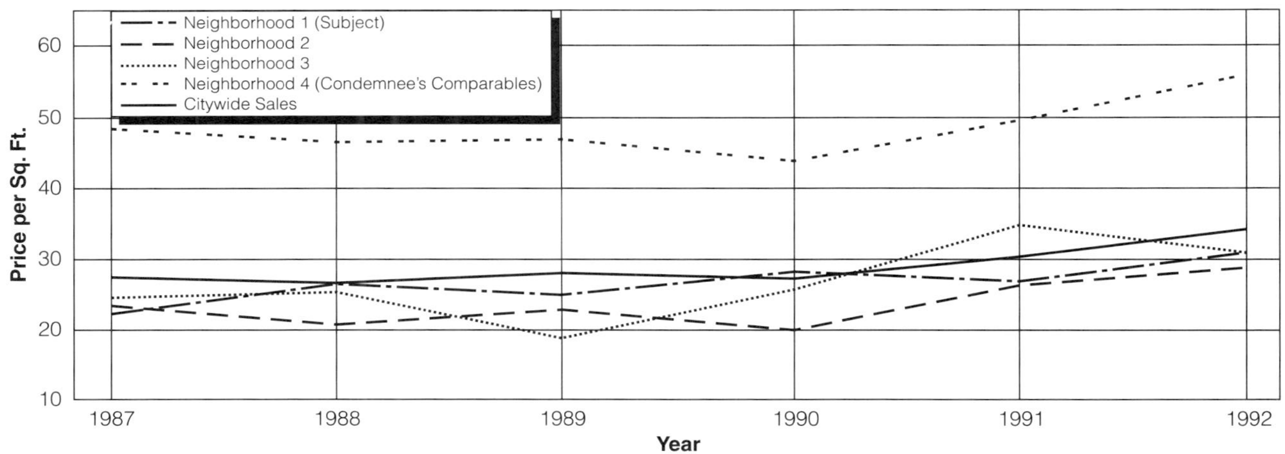

Sales Activity and Prices in City

Year	Neighborhood 1		Neighborhood 2		Neighborhood 3		Neighborhood 4		Citywide	
	Price/ Sq. Ft.	No. of Sales	Price/ Sq. Ft.	No. of Sales	Price/ Sq. Ft.	No. of Sales	Price/ Sq. Ft.	No. of Sales	Price/ Sq. Ft.	No. of Sales
1987	$21.77	21	$23.00	28	$24.17	20	$48.08	10	$27.15	317
1988	$26.00	24	$20.37	25	$25.26	14	$46.21	13	$25.99	378
1989	$24.82	32	$22.64	28	$18.80	14	$46.71	19	$27.57	402
1990	$27.83	20	$20.08	35	$25.73	24	$43.70	8	$26.94	474
1991	$26.34	16	$25.97	22	$34.35	17	$49.24	13	$30.27	424
1992	$30.65	17	$28.45	31	$30.99	19	$56.85	14	$33.83	442

sented in Figure 20.3 is much more easily discerned from the graph than from the figures presented in tabular form.

Even the simplest data can sometimes be presented more effectively in a graphic format. For instance, assume that the appraiser has included in his appraisal report the following figures relating to the income and expenses of the property under appraisal:

	3 Years Ago	2 Years Ago	1 Year Ago	Average	Projected
Gross income	$31,097	$32,100	$34,708	$32,635	$34,208
Expenses	-11,373	-10,750	-14,148	-12,090	-14,077
Net income	$19,724	$21,350	$20,560	$20,545	$20,131
Net/gross ratio	63.4%	66.5%	59.2%	63.0%	58.8%

Rather than present this information to the trier of fact in table form, the appraiser may find it more effective to present it in graphic form as shown in Figure 20.4.

FIGURE 20.4. HISTORICAL AND PROJECTED INCOME AND EXPENSES

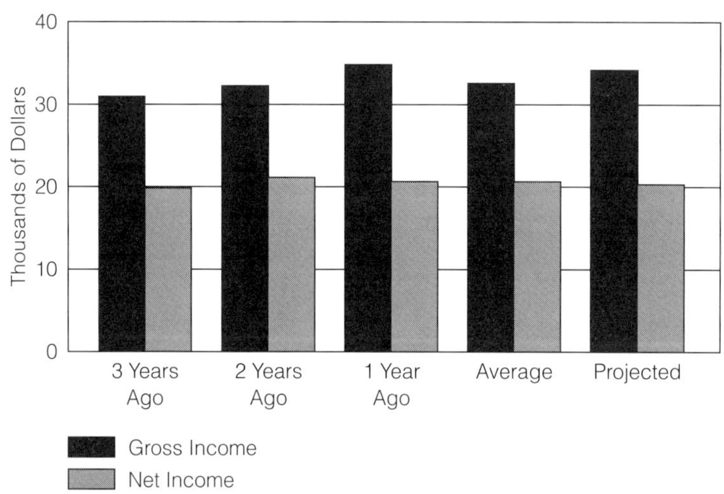

Statistical analysis can also be more effectively presented in graphic form. For instance, one statistical technique often used by appraisal reviewers, and sometimes by appraisers, is to consider the indicated adjustments for differences in land size between the property under appraisal and the comparable sales after first making all the other necessary adjustments to the prices of the comparables and then applying an airframe learning curve to the indicated unit prices (e.g., prices per square foot or per acre).[31] The results of such an analysis might be presented to the trier of fact using the graph shown in Figure 20.5. The statistical analysis presented in this figure indicates greater market sensitivity to size than

FIGURE 20.5 SIZE ADJUSTMENT ANALYSIS

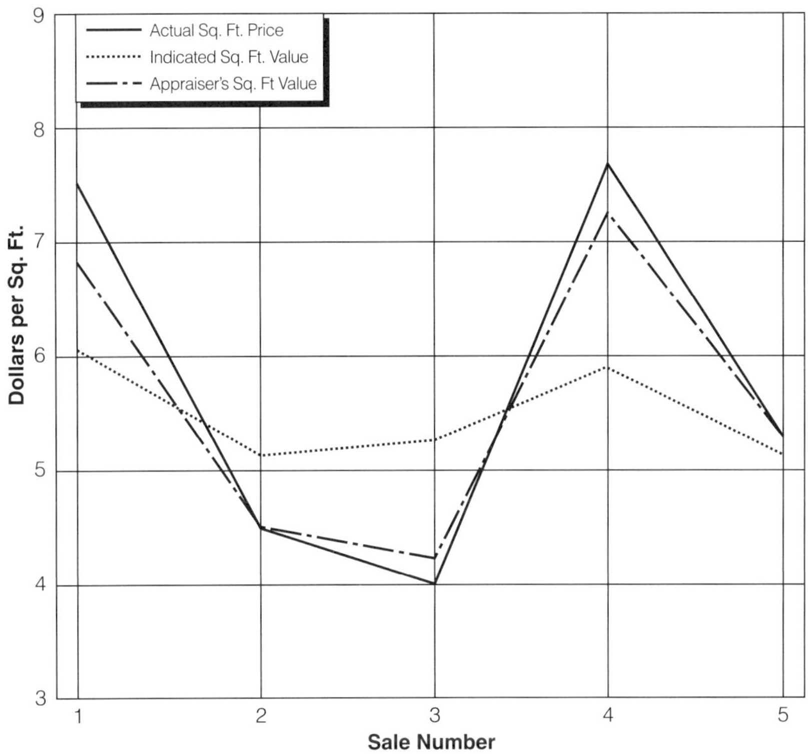

PARCEL #35–858 (35,000 SQUARE FEET) COMPARISON OF SIZE ADJUSTMENTS

Sale No.	Sq. Ft. Size	Price/ Sq. Ft.	Indicated % Adj.	Appraiser's % Adj.	Indicated Sq. Ft. Value	Appraiser's Sq. Ft. Value
1	22,858	$7.18	0.84	0.95	$6.03	$6.82
2	47,800	$4.47	1.14	1.00	$5.10	$4.47
3	66,247	$4.02	1.30	1.05	$5.23	$4.22
4	18,445	$7.65	0.77	0.95	$5.89	$7.27
5	32,622	$5.25	0.97	1.00	$5.09	$5.25
Mean		$5.71			$5.47	$5.61
Standard deviation		1.62248			0.44479	1.37667
Coefficient of variation		0.284147			0.081447	0.245396

31. For a discussion of this method of statistical analysis, see Gene Dilmore, "Size Adjustment Tables," *The Real Estate Appraiser* (May–June 1976), 23–27 and Dilmore, "A Program to Generate, Test, and Select Land Size Adjustment Factors," *The Appraisal Journal* (April 1981), 290–295.

do the estimates made by the appraiser. While the appraiser made size adjustments ranging from -5% to +5%, the statistical analysis suggests adjustments of -23% to +30%. The data also demonstrate that the appraiser's adjustments resulted in little change in the standard deviation and coefficient of variation from the unadjusted prices, but both the standard deviation and coefficient of variation were significantly reduced when the statistically developed size adjustments were applied to the unit prices of the comparables.

This analysis could be used to support the appraiser's final value estimate if it approximates $5.50 per square foot. However, it could also be used to cast doubt on the appraiser's conclusion if the appraiser has selected a final value at the low end ($4.22 to $4.47) or the high end ($6.82 to $7.27) of the range of indicated values developed after applying size adjustments.

ARITHMETIC AND VERIFICATION

All computations used in the appraisal report that will be included in the appraiser's testimony should be checked, double-checked, and triple-checked. When an attorney asks, "Would you step down to the board and show us just how you calculated that?" most appraisers tend to become uneasy, no matter how many times they have rechecked their mathematics. Their stomachs begin to churn as they try to remember whether net income is divided or multiplied by the capitalization rate. While such apprehension can never be eliminated, the appraiser should take all steps to minimize the panic that arises when asked to demonstrate a calculation on the witness stand.

All computations in an appraisal report should be checked at least three times before trial by three different people. If an appraiser is asked to demonstrate a computation made in the appraisal and an error was made, he will invariably copy the erroneous figures from his notes. Since the advent of calculators and computers, many people have difficulty doing mathematics in their heads. With 12 jurors and a judge waiting for the appraiser to complete his calculations, and an attorney ready to pounce on the smallest of errors, a difficult task becomes impossible.

To avoid other potential problems, the appraiser should verify all of his sales again before trial. Although the initial verification may have been done very carefully, the process should be repeated, preferably by interviewing a different party to the transaction. In one instance the condemnor's appraiser testified that he did not use a particular sale as a comparable because the purchaser told him that the property was purchased sight unseen. The condemnee's appraiser did use the sale as a comparable and, when cross-examined in regard to the purchaser's knowledge of the sale property, stated that the purchaser had seen the property before purchase. In fact, the appraiser had shown the purchaser the property prior to the sale. He even produced a photograph of the property that showed the purchaser in the foreground and, in the background, construction activity that was completed before the date of the sale. This experience should remind appraisers that they may occasionally be misled by buyers and sellers who, for one reason or another, have their own agenda.

Mock Examination

When all information has been gathered and all exhibits are prepared, the attorney and appraiser should stage a mock examination. There is no law against rehearsing the appraiser's direct examination and cross-examination. It is, in fact, a vital step in the trial preparation process. The attorney should ask the appraiser every question he expects to ask on the witness stand, and the appraiser should answer the questions as if he were in court. This rehearsal should be repeated until the attorney is satisfied. Then the attorney, or preferably an associate attorney, should take the position of opposing counsel and cross-examine the appraiser. This rehearsal will uncover any weak points in the appraiser's presentation and give the appraiser and the attorney time to strengthen the testimony.

It has been said that "[b]y rehearsing with the expert, counsel can determine the expert's reaction under the stress of trial. In addition, counsel can suggest ways that the expert might refine the testimony."[32] Appraisers and attorneys must remember, however, that refinement is one thing, but corruption is another. If the appraiser's answer to a question cannot be ethically and objectively refined by the appraiser to the satisfaction of the attorney, there is a very simple solution: The attorney should not ask the question.

After a few rehearsals between the appraiser and the attorney, the process can be abbreviated. In fact, the entire process of preparing for trial will be expedited if each member of the team is aware of what is expected of him and both have enough confidence in each other to know that they will perform as required.

Summary

The foregoing discussion presumes that the appraiser's opinion of value supports the client's contention of just compensation. If this is not the case, the appraiser will not be preparing for trial and the information in this chapter will not be applicable. Most condemnation cases never go to trial and the appraiser's trial preparations are curtailed. This may happen early on, as soon as the appraiser reaches a preliminary value range for the property being condemned, or later if the condemnor and the condemnee reach a negotiated settlement just before trial.

The attorney and the appraiser must function as a team so that the attorney can properly represent the client's interest. The composition of this team should be determined as soon as possible. If the client is an active condemnor, the appraiser and the attorney are often thrown together only after the appraiser has

32. *Nichols'*, vol. 7, §8.04[4] (1992).

completed the appraisal report. Still, the condemnor's attorney will generally have the option of retaining the services of another appraiser.

The only totally safe assumption to make is that every parcel of land that is the subject of an eminent domain action will result in a trial to determine the compensation due for the taking and/or damage to the property. A common ploy, and one that continues to work for some inexplicable reason, is for one party to a lawsuit to assure the opposing party that settlement is close at hand (while at the same time continuing to prepare for trial feverishly). This leads the opposing party to delay trial preparation until it is too late. The cautious appraiser will begin preparing for trial as soon as he receives the appraisal assignment; the attorney should start his preparations immediately after he is retained by the client. Trial preparation should not be forestalled in hopes of a settlement until a settlement has, in fact, formally been reached.

Preparing a condemnation case involves the following steps:

1. The appraiser/attorney team is formed.
2. The appraiser develops a range of value (or compensation).
3. A preliminary conference is held between the attorney and the appraiser.
4. A conference is held between the attorney and the client to develop future strategy.
5. The appraiser completes the research.
6. A conference between the attorney and the appraiser is held to determine the content of the appraisal report.
7. The appraiser completes the appraisal report.
8. The attorney (and the attorney's appraisal consultant, if used) reviews the appraisal report.
9. An appraiser/attorney conference is held to determine trial strategy, necessary exhibits, any additional information required, and the data to be requested from the opposing party through discovery.
10. The exhibits are prepared.
11. The appraiser investigates and verifies the market data used by the opposing party's appraiser as revealed through the discovery process.
12. The attorney and the appraiser determine the line of direct testimony.
13. The attorney develops a specific list of questions to ask the appraiser.
14. The attorney and the appraiser hold a mock direct examination session.
15. The attorney and the appraiser hold a mock cross-examination session.

CHAPTER 21

The Expert Witness

An *expert* is "[o]ne who is so qualified, either by actual experience or by careful study, as to enable him to form a definite opinion of his own respecting a division of science, branch of art, or department or trade about which persons having no particular training or special study are incapable of forming accurate opinions or deducing correct conclusions."[1] An *expert witness* is "[a] witness who has been qualified as an expert and who thereby will be allowed (through his/her answers to questions posed) to assist the jury in understanding complicated and technical subjects not within the understanding of the average lay person."[2]

Appraisers, as expert witnesses, are not always regarded favorably by the courts.[3] Some members of the legal profession have also been critical of individual real estate appraisers and the appraisal profession.

> Is there any hope that the jury system and the expert witness can live in an honest and peaceful co-existence? The chance is slim, but it is still there. Hope here will rest upon an immediate and drastic house and soul cleaning job by reputable appraisal organizations and societies and, what is even more vital, a complete and objective self-analysis by every individual who henceforth will take the stand and qualify as an expert.[4]

In response to such criticism, one appraiser has pointed out that the attorney is an advocate for his client and "...instructions by an attorney/client to make an improper appraisal, although a reflection of his personal ethics, in no way violate formal pledges of conduct. Accepting and acting on such instructions, however,

1. *Ballentine's Law Dictionary*, 3d ed., s.v. "expert."
2. *Black's Law Dictionary*, abr. 6th ed., s.v. "Expert witness."
3. See Chapter 9, "Income Capitalization Approach to Value," footnotes 39 and 40 and the quoted text to which they refer.
4. John P. Hogan, "Ten Court Room Commandments for Appraisers," *Right-of-Way* (October 1959), 21–25.

do constitute a breach of ethics for the appraiser."[5] However, when an appraiser includes in his testimony a statement such as "I must state that I was legally instructed to appraise the property as though it had potential for industrial use, and that assumption was made in making this appraisal," it makes one wonder about the intelligence of the appraiser and the attorney, let alone their ethics.

The finger-pointing will probably continue in the future. Any appraiser or attorney who doesn't have his head in the sand knows that there are unethical individuals in both professions, and these individuals seem to have an uncanny knack for finding each other.

> [G]roups of self-styled "appraisers" make their living by giving "made to order" appraisal testimony. They are primarily professional witnesses and should be distinguished from professional appraisers. These witnesses are supported by some legal firms who handle condemnation cases in the same manner as personal injury litigation in which distorted claims for damages commonly occur.
>
> Such situations are the probable cause of many major divergences in court testimony between appraisers. They are and will remain the most difficult to cure.
>
> Some courts contribute to "legalizing" divergency by permitting the uninformed political appointee and the known "actor" to function as an expert witness when a more strict enforcement of qualifying standards would do much to discourage erroneous valuations and unjust awards.
>
> Under present circumstances virtually anyone can qualify as an expert witness. The resultant testimony is often afforded as much credence by the judge, jury, or commission as is the testimony of a competent and qualified appraiser.[6]

Because of these circumstances, some trial tacticians continue to suggest that the "description of an expert valuation witness is subject to revision depending on the jurisdiction where the trial will be held. For example, a... 'good ole boy'...in a small rural area where the state was building a turnpike, may be the best... expert witness for whichever party retains that witness first."[7]

There is, however, some hope of eradicating unethical practices. The Tennessee appellate court has said:

> [T]he facts in this case at bar point up the need for a change in the rules of evidence pertaining to the qualifications of a witness who is permitted to give an opinion as to the value of real estate involved in litigation. Until recent years there were only a limited few people trained in the science of real estate appraising, but it has now reached a professional status that should be recognized by the courts. The American Institute of Real Estate Appraisers has developed real estate appraising to almost an exact science.
>
> Something is wrong with our rules of evidence when a verdict can be predicated on the opinion of a person completely ignorant of real estate values and the opinions of skilled, knowledgeable, professional experts ignored. It is likened to taking the opinion of a midwife over that of an obstetrician....

5. Seymour Simon, "Responsibilities of the Appraiser Accepting Legal Instructions," *The Appraisal Journal* (April 1974), 181.
6. *Divergences in Right-of-Way Valuations*, National Cooperative Highway Research Program Report No. 126 (Washington, D.C.: Highway Research Board, 1971), 2.
7. *Nichols' The Law of Eminent Domain*, rev. 3rd ed. (New York: Matthew Bender Co., Inc., 1992), vol. 7A, §13.03.

> [W]e are not satisfied that justice has been done. We have seen a number of cases in this court where we think the ends of justice would have been more nearly met had only qualified expert witnesses been permitted to express an opinion as to real estate values. . . . But until such time as our ancient rules of opinion evidence relating to real estate values have been modernized these injustices will continue.[8]

The time is ripe to made the necessary changes. Each state now has a real estate licensing/certification law which incorporates The Appraisal Foundation's Uniform Standards of Professional Appraisal Practice. The Uniform Standards have become the standard of the profession and the minimum standard of practice required by the vast majority of appraisal clients. The courts should take this opportunity to establish rules that only appraisers licensed or certified in the jurisdiction in which the property in question is located may qualify as expert witnesses. They should also require that each expert witness prepare a self-contained written report available for discovery in accordance with the Uniform Standards, without invoking the Departure Provision.

Burden of Proof

The term *burden of proof* is defined as follows: "In the law of evidence, the necessity or duty of affirmatively proving a fact or facts in dispute on an issue raised between the parties in a cause. The obligation of a party to establish by evidence a requisite degree of belief concerning a fact in the mind of the trier of fact or the court."[9] The courts in the United States have employed all three possible rules with respect to the burden of proof in condemnation cases:

> (1) The taking agency has the burden of proving just compensation. It is the moving party and seeks to change the status quo. The condemnor therefore must prove all parts of its case. (Followed in Georgia, Mississippi, and Washington. Illinois and Kentucky also may be placed in this group for want of a further subdivision to fit their somewhat unusual procedural practices.)
>
> (2) Neither party has the burden of proof. The measurement of just compensation involves a question of fact to be determined *in rem* and without adversary pleadings. This rule is based on the theory that the parties are not adversaries, therefore neither should have a greater burden of proof than the other. (Ohio)
>
> (3) When the taking agency is a governmental subdivision, it is presumed to have made a fair offer, and accordingly, the landowner has the burden of proof that just compensation requires a sum greater than the amount conceded by the government. (So-called majority rule, followed in at least 24 states [and in federal courts].)[10] [Citations omitted]

The party that has the burden of proof is generally given the right to open and close the trial proceedings—i.e., makes its opening remarks first and has the

8. *Newport Housing Authority, Inc. v. Harsell*, 533 S.W.2d 317, 322 (Tenn. 1975).

9. *Black's*, s.v. "Burden of proof."

10. *State v. Nelson*, 353 P.2d 616, 617 (Ore. 1960).

last closing argument. The party with the burden of proof usually will present its case in chief first. (The *case in chief* is "that part of a trial in which the party with the initial burden of proof presents his evidence after which he rests.")[11] The appraiser called by the party with the burden of proof can generally expect to spend more time on the witness stand than other appraisers because the first appraisal witness usually must educate the trier of fact as to the property involved, the appraisal process, appraisal terminology, and other technical matters. Many times, however, some engineering testimony has already been presented or the trier of fact may have viewed the property before the first appraiser testifies. These preliminaries will assist the appraiser in describing the property and/or the public improvement project which necessitates the taking.

THE VIEW

The trier of fact is often given the opportunity the view the property in question. Some jurisdictions do not provide for a view of the premises by statute, so the court may decide whether or not to view the property.[12] On occasion, a view is denied because the property in question has been altered so much between the date of valuation and the date of trial that such a view might mislead the trier of fact. A view could also be denied if the property in question is far away from the location of the trial and a view of the property would therefore be extremely time-consuming.

Depending on the circumstances, a view can be advantageous or disadvantageous to the parties. In one instance, the owner's claim that the land in question had a highest and best use as a recreational subdivision was somewhat defused when the federal marshall who accompanied the jurors to the property refused to allow them to exit the bus, explaining that he was fearful that someone would be bitten by a rattlesnake. In another instance, a judge accompanied the jury to view a recreational island being acquired by the government. While traveling to the property by pleasure boat on an unusually beautiful spring day, the judge was overheard telling the government's legal counsel, "It looks like a million dollar day to me."

Those permitted to accompany the trier of fact to view a condemned property will vary with the jurisdiction and the circumstances. The judge will often, but not always, accompany a jury. A bailiff, or federal marshall, will always accompany a jury and legal counsel for both parties will nearly always go too. On occasion, an engineer or other factual witness familiar with the property and the government project will accompany the jury on the view. If a juror has a question while on the view, it may be presented to the judge who, in turn, may ask the engineer to answer it. Otherwise, those accompanying a jury on a view are not allowed to speak to the jurors. Appraisers seldom, if ever, participate in a view of the property, nor do owners, except when the property involved is the owner's personal residence. In this case the owner is generally allowed to be present at the residence during the view.

11. *Black's*, s.v. "Case in chief."

12. *Justice v. United States*, 145 F.2d 110 (9th Cir. 1944).

A view of the property in question by the trier of fact can be considered in two ways. Some jurisdictions allow the trier of fact to consider what he or she has seen on the view as evidence; other jurisdictions instruct the trier of fact that this information is not evidence, but only background to facilitate a better understanding of the testimony. Realistically, however, the trier of fact is going to consider what it saw on the view, regardless of the court's instructions. In any case, if the jury has viewed the property in question, presentation of the case is easier for both parties to the suit.

Appraiser's Attendance in Court

The appraiser's appearance is important, whether the appraiser is on the witness stand or simply an observer in the courtroom. Unless the appraiser is excluded from the courtroom, he or she should be present throughout the trial, except during closing arguments. The attorney/appraiser team falls apart if half the team is missing or does not follow what is going on. The appraiser should take notes on the testimony of other witnesses, so he can discuss this testimony with legal counsel. The appraiser can be especially helpful to the attorney by explaining the technical elements of the other appraiser's testimony.

An attorney who wants the appraiser in the courtroom only when he is to testify is foolish, unless the attorney has retained a consultant to assist during the trial. The attorney who dismisses an appraiser because he feels he does not need any assistance may find out otherwise. If the appraiser is dismissed to save money, this is probably a false economy; if two or three extra days of appraisal fees are that critical, the case probably never should have gone to trial in the first place. Sidney Z. Searles advises fellow attorneys that "[b]efore undertaking a cross-examination you should consult your own experts; I have found such consultation of considerable assistance, and I would recommend that your expert be present in court to listen, not only to the direct examination of the expert of the adverse party, but the cross-examination as well."[13]

The Rule

As mentioned earlier, the appraisal witness may be excluded from the courtroom if "the rule" is imposed. "A trial judge may, under certain circumstances, sequester witnesses and require that they be kept apart from other witnesses until they are called to testify."[14] Thus, from the time an appraisal witness is placed under the rule of exclusion:

13. Sidney Z. Searles, "Examination and Cross-Examination of Appraisers in Eminent Domain," *Institute on Planning, Zoning and Eminent Domain*, Southwestern Legal Foundation (New York: Matthew Bender & Co., Inc., 1973).

14. *Black's*, s.v. "Exclusion–witness."

> until the trial is over, no fact or detail of the case should be discussed with anyone. Otherwise, testimony may be disqualified. In jurisdictions that base their evidence and procedure rules on the federal model, and in all federal courts, the requirement that no witness discuss the case with jurors, other witnesses, or the opposing party is so strong it is known among attorneys merely as "The Rule"; it is the only rule, of several hundred rules of evidence and procedure, that is so referenced. If the court places a witness "under the Rule," the witness will be required to wait outside the courtroom to testify, and will not be permitted to hear the testimony of other witnesses. What a layperson might consider casual conversation in the hall with jurors, other witnesses, or the judge can result in extremely serious consequences. The expert may not be allowed to testify, previous testimony may be disregarded, or a mistrial may be called; in extreme cases contempt of court might be cited.[15]

"At the request of a party the court shall order witnesses excluded so that they cannot hear the testimony of other witnesses and it may make the order of its own motion."[16] "The efficacy of excluding or sequestering witnesses has long been recognized as a means of discouraging and exposing fabrication, inaccuracy, and collusion."[17]

The practice of imposing the rule in condemnation cases appears to be regional in nature. In some parts of the country, invocation of the rule is standard operating procedure, while in others it is all but unheard of. Both the attorney and the appraiser must know the custom in regard to imposition of the rule in the jurisdiction where their case will be heard. The unexpected imposition of the rule can turn a well-prepared case into a disaster. For this reason, it is wise to assume that the rule will be invoked, even in those jurisdictions in which it is seldom imposed.

As discussed in Chapter 20, some attorneys retain the services of a consulting appraiser. When such a consultant is retained, the appraiser's continual presence in the courtroom is not necessary and the imposition of the rule is less problematic. Some condemnors assign a staff appraiser to assist legal counsel. This appraiser should be aware of the contents of the condemnor's appraisal report and be familiar with all the circumstances surrounding the case. With a staff appraiser or consulting appraiser to assist, the appraisal witness can be released without disbanding the appraiser/attorney team. Of course, the condemnor and legal counsel must agree on the concept of using a staff or consulting appraiser. The ultimate decision as to whether a consultant should be used and, if so, who will be retained, must be left to trial counsel. Although it is permissible, and sometimes advisable, for a staff appraiser-consultant or an independent consultant to sit at the counsel table with the attorney, it is not advisable, and has historically been regarded as unethical,[18] for an appraisal witness to be seated at the counsel table.

15. John S. Bean, Theresa H. Waller, and Neil G. Walker, "Real Estate Professionals as Expert Witnesses," *The Appraisal Journal* (January 1988), 87.
16. Federal Rule of Evidence 615.
17. Ibid., Notes of Advisory Committee on 1972 Proposed Rules.
18. American Institute of Real Estate Appraisers, Regulation No. 10, *Code of Professional Ethics and Standards of Professional Conduct*, Canon 1, p. 3 (adopted Nov. 13, 1981).

PREPARING TO TESTIFY

When the appraiser takes the witness stand, he should take along any notes or materials that he may need under direct examination and cross-examination. The appraiser should always take a calculator to the stand because he invariably will be asked to make some calculations. All calculators work a little differently, and the witness stand is not the place to try out a new one, especially if it is one offered by opposing counsel. A jury will not be impressed with an appraiser who does not know how to operate a calculator.

The appraiser should take his entire file, including a copy of the appraisal report, to the witness stand. This material should be carried in a briefcase and, if at all possible, left in the briefcase. Opposing counsel has the absolute right to inspect any paper referred to by the appraiser on the witness stand. Therefore, while on the witness stand, the appraiser must not refer to any document that could embarrass the appraiser or be detrimental to the client's case.

The appraiser should prepare a set of notes for use on the stand which will not be detrimental to him or to his client if they fall into the hands of opposing counsel. Notes written in the appraiser's personal form of shorthand are often useful for this purpose. Some attorneys like to take the appraiser's notes and continue to ask the appraiser questions which the appraiser needs the notes to answer. The appraiser can, of course, ask for his notes back, but it is more effective for the appraiser to produce a second (or even a third) copy of the notes that he has prepared prior to trial. This lets the cross-examiner know that the appraiser is well-prepared for most cross-examination tricks.

It is extremely important that the appraiser have his notes and his file in order. The appraiser should know all the questions that he will be asked on direct examination and be able to answer them without referring to his notes or, at least, have the answer in the notes at hand. The appraiser should also be able to anticipate nearly all the questions he will be asked on cross-examination and have the notes needed to answer these questions readily.

"The witness must be able to respond to questions in a timely, professional manner, and should not be constantly searching or fumbling through large stacks of paper or documents for answers."[19] In preparing notes for the witness stand, the appraiser must be very thorough and organized. The cross-examining attorney will often ask trivial questions, in the hope that the appraiser will have to fumble through his papers for the answers. A few seconds of silence in the courtroom, while a witness looks through papers for an answer, can seem like hours. Responding in a timely manner to any such questions will ensure that this line of questioning is short-lived.

The trier of fact in an eminent domain trial can be the court (i.e., the judge), a commission, or a jury. The nature and extent of an appraiser's testimony will depend to a certain degree on the forum in which it will be heard. If a trial will be heard only by the court, and the judge has considerable experience in hearing (or, in a past life, trying) condemnation cases, a detailed explanation of the appraisal

19. *Nichols'*, vol. 7A, §13.03 (1992).

process will not be required. Similarly, an experienced commission will not need a short course in appraisal. If the parcel is one of several being condemned for a large government project, it is quite possible that the commission will have heard a number of cases relating to similar properties in the same area; thus the neighborhood description can be abbreviated and local land use regulations and the comparable sales may already be known to the commission.

The attorney will know whether a trial will be heard by the court, a commission, or a jury. The attorney will (or should) structure his case and the appraiser's testimony accordingly. He will also know, or should find out, the background and experience of the court or the members of the commission. With this information, a determination can be made as to the amount of basic appraisal methodology and terminology that will have to be presented.

The following discussion assumes that the condemnation trial will be heard by a jury. In that instance more elementary and detailed appraisal testimony is required. It is also under these circumstances that some attorneys feel they must put on a show for the jury, becoming belligerent or attempting to trap witnesses with trick questions. An attorney may even cut off the bottom of his tie in giving his final argument to demonstrate the effects of a partial taking. Actions like this are typically not appreciated, and sometimes not tolerated, by experienced judges and commissions.

DIRECT EXAMINATION

The appraiser's direct examination can be logically broken down into specific steps, probably presented in this order:

1. Qualification as an expert
2. Description of the appraisal process
3. Appraiser's description of the work undertaken in appraising the property that is the subject of the trial
4. Description of the property
5. Highest and best use
6. Application of the cost approach
7. Application of the income capitalization approach
8. Application of the sales comparison approach
9. Final reconciliation of value

If the trial concerns the partial taking of a property, Steps 4 through 9 will be presented as they apply to the property in the before situation and then be repeated for the property in the after situation.

As noted in the previous chapter, the attorney and the appraiser should rehearse the appraiser's testimony in preparation for trial. Some practitioners suggest that the attorney write out all the questions that the appraiser will be asked on direct examination.[20] Others believe that only an outline should be prepared because "[u]se of written questions detracts from the spontaneity of counsel's presentation...[and] both counsel and the witness may find it difficult to vary from the script as the process of the trial may require."[21] If the trial date is approaching and the attorney has not furnished the appraiser with a list or outline of the questions he plans to ask the appraiser, the appraiser should prepare his own list or outline of questions he believes the attorney should ask him and furnish it to the attorney. Perhaps the appraiser's questions will spark the attorney's inquisitiveness and encourage the attorney to prepare for trial properly.

In responding to questions, the appraiser must speak loudly enough to be heard by the trier of fact, the attorneys, and the court reporter. The appraiser should address the jury, not the questioner; if the attorney did not already know the answer to the question, it would not have been asked. The appraiser must not talk down to the jury or answer questions in a monotone. He should behave as naturally as possible on the witness stand and not try to project a false image. Cross-examining attorneys will often stand on the opposite side of the room from the jury when asking their questions to make it awkward for the witness to address to the jury. In such a situation, the appraiser should face the jury, turn his head to face the cross-examiner only while the question is being asked, and turn back to address his response to the jury. If, on direct examination, counsel moves to a spot behind or beside the jury to ask his questions, this is probably a subtle reminder to the witness that he is forgetting to face the jury when responding to questions.

QUALIFYING AS AN EXPERT

> The first object of the direct examination of the expert is to establish qualifications. Because it is best to try and impress the jury with the qualifications and experience of the appraiser, counsel should not accept a stipulation to the appraiser's qualifications [unless, of course, opposing counsel is willing to stipulate that the appraiser is the best qualified and the most experienced appraiser that will appear as a witness in the trial]. Establishing the appraiser's qualifications may be an awkward phase of the trial, however, because it may appear immodest for the expert to recite qualifications.[22]

The specific methodology for eliciting such testimony should be determined well before the trial. Qualification testimony is usually best presented by the appraiser responding to the attorney's leading questions.[23] For instance, the question, "Who have you made appraisals for?" puts the appraiser in an awkward position. He can reply "Government agencies, lending institutions, industrial clients, and a number of individuals" or he may recite specific clients; listing individual clients, however, can be quite time-consuming and may make the appraiser look like a braggart in the eyes of the jury. This type of open-ended question is asked only by an attorney who is unprepared, lazy, or incompetent.

---

20. McCarthy, *How to Make Appraisal Testimony More Effective*, 4 Prac. Real Estate Law. 51 (March 1988).

21. *Nichols'*, vol. 7, §8.04[4] (1992).

22. Ibid.

23. Ibid.

To present the appraiser's credentials to the jury most effectively, the question should be broken down into several segments. The exchange might proceed as follows:

Attorney: Mr. Appraiser, have you ever made any appraisals for the federal government?

Appraiser: Yes.

Attorney: And could you tell the jury for which agencies of the federal government you have made appraisals?

Appraiser: The United States Corps of Engineers, U.S. Fish and Wildlife Service, etc.

The attorney can continue asking questions in the same form to present the appraiser's experience working for state governmental agencies, local governmental agencies, industrial clients, commercial clients, etc. If the appraiser has made appraisals for the condemnor, this should always be mentioned when testifying for the condemnee. Similarly, in testifying for a condemnor, the appraiser should note any appraisals he has made for condemnees where the opposing party was this same condemnor. The appraiser should also reveal if he has made any appraisals for the county or city in which most of the jurors reside, or if he has made appraisals for the employers of one or more of the jurors or their spouses. The specific clientele cited will depend on the type of property being appraised, the location of the property, the location of the trial, the makeup of the jury, and other factors.

Testimony on the appraiser's qualifications will generally cover historical employment experience, current employment, general educational background, specialized training in appraising, any teaching experience, professional affiliations and designations and any offices held, articles or papers published, typical clientele, types of property appraised, expert testimony and experience, and the geographical area of experience.

"The trial of an eminent domain case is aptly called a battle of experts."[24] All else being equal, the trier of fact will rely on the expert who is best qualified and most experienced. For that reason it is important that the appraiser's qualifications are adequately presented before the trier of fact. Even if opposing counsel is willing to stipulate that the appraiser is an expert, and therefore qualified to express an opinion, the court is required to allow counsel to present the expert's qualifications to the jury.[25] As one court put it:

> It was error not to permit appellants' expert to state his qualifications. The fact that the commonwealth "accepted" his qualifications went only to whether the court should permit him to testify. It did not meet the further question of what weight the jury might wish to give his opinion, which might well be governed by its appraisal of his background and experience.[26]

24. Ibid.

25. *Trowbridge v. Abrasive Co. of Philadelphia*, 190 F.2d 825 (3rd Cir. 1951).

26. *Wolf v. Commonwealth of Puerto Rico*, 341 F.2d 945 (1st Cir. 1965).

DESCRIPTION OF THE APPRAISAL PROCESS

After the appraiser's qualifications are established, the appraiser will describe the appraisal process. An exhibit like the chart shown in the preceding chapter (Figure 20.1) can assist in presenting this testimony. Emphasis should be placed on those parts of the process that were most significant in the appraisal of the property being acquired. In other words, the appraiser can skim over the cost and income capitalization approaches if a nonincome-producing tract of land with no improvements is being appraised. In this instance the description of the appraisal process will focus on the sales comparison approach. In the overview of the appraisal process, only a brief description of the approaches to value is needed; a detailed description of the applicable approaches is best left until the appraiser begins to testify on how each approach was applied to the property being appraised. Because it generally falls to the first appraiser to educate the jury as to the appraisal process, subsequent witnesses need not explain the process in detail.

The description of the appraisal process provides an opportunity for the appraiser to define some appraisal terms which will be used throughout the trial. These terms might include *market value, highest and best use, the subject property,* and *capitalization rate.* The appraiser and the attorney should decide which terms will be used and at what points in the description of the appraisal process the attorney will interrupt the appraiser to ask for the definition of a term. The attorney may say, "A moment ago you mentioned the term *highest and best use.* Could you explain to us what appraisers mean when they use this term?" In this way, the terminology is explained to the jury without the appraiser lecturing or talking down to them. Also, by using the term "us" in the question, the attorney lets the jury know that they are not expected to be familiar with the term. This helps to establish rapport between the attorney and the jury. The attorney should only interrupt the appraiser's description of the appraisal process at a natural breaking point, so as not to destroy the continuity of the description.

DESCRIPTION OF THE WORK PROCESS

The appraiser explains the work process to show the jury that he has made a thorough investigation and that an appraisal consists of more than looking at a property and estimating its value. The explanation of the work process should essentially be a narrative description of the "scope of the appraisal" section of the appraisal report.[27] The description should be thorough, following the appraisal process step by step. It is often helpful to refer back to the appraisal process at certain points. For instance, in describing the growth or lack of growth in a neighborhood, the appraiser may state that growth factors are developed as part of the general neighborhood data to indicate demand in the foreseeable future, which will influence property values.

27. A required element of the appraisal report under The Appraisal Foundation's *Uniform Standards of Professional Appraisal Practice,* 1994 ed., Standard Rule 2-2(a)(vi)).

PROPERTY DESCRIPTION

In verbally describing the property to the jury, as in the written appraisal report, the appraiser should attempt to set the audience up to accept the final conclusion. If the property suffers from functional obsolescence, this fact should be stated in describing the property, so the jury is not surprised when the appraiser makes a deduction for functional obsolescence in the cost approach. The appraiser is also advised to include a detailed property description among the reference notes he brings to the witness stand. These notes are most useful when prepared in outline form. In preparing these notes, the appraiser should be extremely thorough. The cross-examiner may well attempt to demonstrate to the jury that there is some physical feature about the property that the appraiser does not know. All features should be noted even if they have no bearing on the market value of the property.

Here again, the attorney can help the appraiser present a full description of the property to the jury by asking specific questions such as "Would you describe the land?" "Would you describe the dwelling?" "Would you describe the on-site improvements?" and "Are there any other improvements on the land?" These questions usually lead to a more detailed property description than a question such as "Would you describe the property?" The attorney may want to prepare a list of the important physical features of the property so that he can mark them off as they are described by the appraiser. Then the attorney can ask about a specific feature of the property if it is important to the case and has not been mentioned. Again, the first appraiser will generally be expected to give the most detailed description of the property.

Photographs are, of course, helpful in describing a property and their use can shorten the appraiser's testimony. In describing the property, the appraiser should consider whether the jury has viewed the property. If so, obvious property features can be noted without details. In describing specific property elements, the appraiser may preface his remarks by saying, "As I am sure the jurors saw when they viewed the property,..."

HIGHEST AND BEST USE

The extent of the appraiser's testimony regarding highest and best use will depend on whether the parties agree or disagree on the subject. If the highest and best use of the property under appraisal is its existing use and the opposing party agrees with that position, little evidence on the subject is needed. Testimony can generally be limited to the definition of highest and best use and a statement that the subject's existing use conforms to its highest and best use. In defining highest and best use, the appraiser should always emphasize that the use must be physically possible, legally permissible, financially feasible, and result in maximum profitability.

If the highest and best use of the property is different from its current use, greater explanation is required, even if there is no dispute between the parties concerning the property's highest and best use. The appraiser must explain the steps taken in arriving at the opinion of highest and best use and the data and analysis on which it was based. If the existing improvements are not compatible with the property's highest and best use, and will add little or nothing to the value of the property as a whole, a careful explanation of the consistent use theory, with clear examples, will be needed. The trier of fact must not be surprised when the appraiser later testifies that the improvements have no value.

A difference of opinion regarding highest and best use is generally recognized as the leading cause of divergence in market value estimates in eminent domain cases. The appraiser and the attorney must recognize this fact and be prepared to convince the jury that the appraiser's conclusion of highest and best use is correct. If this is done, the case is no longer about whose comparable sales are better or whose adjustments are right. Instead, it boils down to the single question of highest and best use, and the party that presents the most convincing evidence in this regard will win the case. For that reason, this portion of the appraiser's testimony may well be the most important part to be presented. Therefore, it must be planned with precision and presented with utmost clarity. If circumstances warrant, it may be advisable to have subsidiary witnesses, such as marketing experts, contractors, or developers, available to support the appraiser's analysis and conclusion.

COST APPROACH

If the cost approach was not used in valuing the property, the jury should be told why. If it was applied, the appraiser should explain in detail how an estimate of value is developed by this approach. The appraiser should keep in mind that the jury was briefly exposed to the cost approach during the description of the appraisal process. It is important to emphasize that the value estimate developed by the cost approach is an estimate of *market value*, not some ill-defined *sound value* or *physical value*, but *market value*. The advantages and disadvantages of the various methods of estimating cost and depreciation in the cost approach and the likelihood of these methods being understood by the trier of fact were discussed in Chapter 8.

First the appraiser presents to the trier of fact the data used in developing the estimate of land value. The verbal presentation should be augmented with photographs of the comparable site sales and some form of sales comparison chart (see Chapter 10). Because the cost approach is rather mechanical, it lends itself to graphics. Each step in the cost approach should be presented to the jury in chart form as well as verbally. Even if the appraiser has not estimated physical deterioration, functional obsolescence, and external obsolescence separately, he should define these terms and emphasize that each form of depreciation was considered in arriving at the total depreciation estimate. If they were not estimated independently, he should explain that they were estimated as a lump sum, perhaps using the abstraction, or market, method of estimating depreciation.

INCOME CAPITALIZATION APPROACH

The mechanics of the income capitalization approach can be very difficult for a jury to understand. If the income capitalization approach is integral to the appraiser's value estimate, it is worthwhile to present the intricacies of the approach in detail. The appraiser should first describe the basic steps in the income capitalization approach and then go back and carefully explain and illustrate the capitalization process and the derivation of a capitalization rate. (The presentation of these data is covered extensively in Chapter 9.) The methodology used by the appraiser to select an appropriate capitalization rate will have a major bearing on the extent of explanation needed to make the jury understand. If the capitalization rate was developed by direct comparison, the explanation can be rather simple; if the mortgage-equity method of rate selection was used, however, extensive explanation may be required.

When a complex method of rate selection must be explained, some appraiser/attorney teams prefer to have the appraiser testify on rate development in a rather general manner on direct examination. For instance, the appraiser might explain that he used the mortgage-equity method of rate selection, which necessitates the consideration of available financing, the equity rates required by investors, potential appreciation or depreciation, and the typical ownership term. If opposing counsel wants to delve further into the development of the capitalization rate, the appraiser should be prepared to explain the process under cross-examination. One advantage of waiting until cross-examination to describe the mortgage-equity rate is that, if the jurors get confused (as they surely will) and cannot follow the testimony, they will often blame the attorney rather than the witness. If asked to explain a complex capitalization rate, the appraiser should attempt to demonstrate its derivation in writing as well as verbally. If, on cross-examination, an appraiser starts to explain the derivation of a capitalization rate by writing out the Ellwood formula

$$R_O = \frac{Y_E - M(Y_E + P1/S_n - R_m) - \Delta_O 1/S_n}{1 + \Delta_I J}$$

the attorney will generally wish he never asked the question.

The attorney and the appraiser must be absolutely certain that the jury understands the concept and mathematics of the income capitalization approach before they attempt to present the approach as it relates to the property being condemned. The development of the property's economic rent and stabilized annual net income should be presented to the jury both verbally and in chart form. Mathematical computations should be presented in a chart or the appraiser can actually work the calculations while testifying. If the appraiser states, "Based on the subject's net income and the capitalization rate, the value of the property is $150,000," the jury will wonder where the $150,000 came from. The jurors usually cannot take notes nor do they have calculators, so the best way for an appraiser to present a final estimate of value by the income capitalization approach is to write the computations while explaining them. As the appraiser writes the computations on a board, he might say: "Now that the net income from the property has been estimated and a proper capitalization rate has been selected, a simple mathematical calculation is used to develop the indicated market value of the property. The basic *IRV* formula, which I explained earlier, is used. The income is known and the rate is known, thus the unknown factor is value; the formula is Income ÷ Rate = Value. The net income previously developed was $18,000 and the proper capitalization rate is 12%. Dividing the $18,000 income by the 12%, or 0.12, capitalization rate results in a value indication of $150,000."

Explaining such a simple calculation in detail may seem unnecessary, but bear in mind that the mere concept of valuing property by the income capitalization approach is completely new to the jury. While the appraiser and the attorney are constantly exposed to the concepts and mechanics of the income capitalization approach, the jury is not. Furthermore, the appraiser and attorney have spent hours preparing for trial (or they should have). They have analyzed the concepts and mathematics of the income capitalization approach in relation to the specific property in question, but the jury has not had this opportunity.

It is extremely discouraging to watch an appraiser spend several hours on the witness stand carefully explaining the concept and mathematics of the income capitalization approach, developing in minute detail the estimate of economic rent, and convincingly explaining the derivation of the capitalization rate to the jurors only to ruin the presentation at the last minute by neglecting to show the final computation. Once again, it is extremely important to stress that the value indication developed by the income capitalization approach is *market value*.

SALES COMPARISON APPROACH

The sales comparison approach to value is most often relied on by the trier of fact. Therefore, it is important that the appraiser/attorney team present this approach to value in a detailed, believable, and accurate manner. Photographs of comparable sales are almost always essential. These photographs should be admitted into evidence so that the jury can look at them while the appraiser is describing each comparable sale. This procedure is very effective. The photographs will also be available to the jury during their deliberations, so the appraiser should note the specifics of the sale on the back of each photograph. This information might include the sale number, the location of the property, the date of the photograph, and the appraiser's name.

Graphics for presenting comparable sales data and analysis to the trier of fact were discussed in Chapter 10. It is generally advisable to have such graphics prepared before the trial by professionals to ensure that they can be easily read by the trier of fact. Both the appraiser and the attorney must remember that the sale price of a property is generally not admissible until the property's comparability has been established. Establishing the comparability of sales may be handled in two ways.

First, the sales chart may be prepared without the comparable sale prices and indicated value of the property being appraised. As the appraiser testifies to the comparability of each sale property and explains his analysis, he can testify to the price of each comparable and then write the price on the sales chart. As the comparative analysis is further developed, the appraiser can fill in the prices of all the comparables and, ultimately, write the value of the subject property as indicated by the comparable sales analysis.

A second, and perhaps cleaner, method of admitting into evidence the comparable sales chart, which includes the price of each comparable and the value of the property being appraised as indicated by the analysis of the sales, is for the appraiser first to give an adequate amount of testimony on each sale property to establish its comparability to the satisfaction of the court. This testimony will generally include the date of the sale, the location of the sale property, and a general description of its physical characteristics. Once the attorney feels that the appraiser has provided enough information for the court to rule on the admissibility of the sale price of the comparable property, the attorney should ask the appraiser the sale price of the property and move on to the next comparable sale. If opposing counsel objects to the admissibility of the sale price of a property on the grounds that comparability has not been established and the court sustains this objection, the attorney must then elicit more information on the sale property and its comparability from the appraiser until the court is satisfied that the sale is comparable and allows testimony as to the price of the property to be admitted.

After the appraiser has testified to all the comparable sales on the sales chart in the manner indicated, the attorney can have the sales chart identified by the court. The appraiser can then refer to the chart in giving detailed testimony as to the similarities and dissimilarities of each sale property. Thus, the jury is led through the comparative analysis and adjustment process applied by the appraiser to each comparable sale. Once the appraiser has testified to all the sales on the chart in the manner described, the attorney may confidently move for the chart to be admitted into evidence. After the chart is admitted, the jurors will have the opportunity to study the chart during their deliberations. If the chart were not so admitted, the jury would have to try to remember its contents.

This second method of securing the admission of a comparable sales chart has an added advantage in that it reduces the possibility that opposing counsel will raise numerous objections as to comparability during a critical part of the appraiser's testimony. With this procedure, the court will have ruled that each sale property has sufficient similarity to be admitted as a comparable before the appraiser even begins testifying to the details of the comparable analysis. If numerous objections are made during the appraiser's presentation of the comparable analysis, the continuity and effectiveness of the testimony can be destroyed. Such interruptions can also confuse the trier of fact or, worse yet, the appraiser.

Extreme care must be exercised in selecting the comparable sales relied on by the appraiser and shown on the comparable sales chart. If, on cross-examination, opposing counsel is able to establish that one of the sales used by the appraiser is not a valid comparable, as a matter of law, the cross-examiner will relish striking the sale from the chart with a bold marker. Later, when the jurors are contemplating the chart during their deliberations, it is debatable whether they will be thinking about the detailed, professional analysis the appraiser has made or about the fact that the court has ruled that a part of the data upon which the appraiser has relied in reaching his conclusion is invalid.

FINAL RECONCILIATION OF VALUE ESTIMATE

In final reconciliation, the appraiser has the opportunity to review with the trier of fact the indicated market value of the property as developed by the various approaches to value. To begin this portion of the trial, the appraiser should testify to his final estimate of market value. This allows a chart similar to Table 21.1 to be placed before the jury or other trier of fact early in this portion of the appraiser's testimony. This chart will help the appraiser review and summarize his testimony and, at the same time, provide the trier of fact with visual exposure to the appraiser's conclusion. When the direct examination is over, opposing counsel will usually remove from view all charts and diagrams presented as part of the appraiser's direct testimony. Because the attorney does not want the trier of fact exposed to the appraiser's conclusions any longer than necessary, he will usually remove any visual evidence under the pretext that the exhibit space will soon be needed for other purposes.

TABLE 21.1 CORRELATION OF APPRAISER'S ESTIMATE OF MARKET VALUE

Approach to Market Value	Indicated Market Value
Cost approach	$123,500
Income capitalization approach	$117,000
Sales comparison approach	$120,000
Final estimate of market value	$120,000

Once a chart such as Table 21.1 has been placed before the trier of fact, the appraiser should briefly review how each indication of market value was developed. Note that Table 21.1 refers to *indicated market value*, not *indicated value* or simply *value*. The fact that all three approaches to value result in an indication of *market value* should be continually emphasized. The appraiser should describe in detail the reasoning he applied to arrive at the final opinion of value and how the results of each approach to value were weighed in that opinion.

The reliability of each approach to value and its applicability in solving the particular appraisal problem should be explained. If one approach to value was emphasized, the reasons for this should be given. The appraiser's testimony should highlight the strengths of the approach that was given primary weight in the final conclusion. It is also important to explain the weaknesses of the other approaches under the particular circumstances of the case. The testimony of other appraisers, whether it is presented earlier or anticipated in the future, will have a bearing on the appraiser's presentation. If all the appraisers agree that a particular approach to value is the most reliable in the instant case, detailed testimony on the weaknesses of the other approaches to value is not needed. Instead, the importance of properly analyzing the integral elements of the most applicable approach to value should be emphasized.

The foregoing discussion assumes that the appraiser has applied, and will testify to, all three approaches to value. There are times when an appraiser gives primary weight to one approach to value, usually the sales comparison approach, and uses the other approaches to check, or test, the indicated value derived by sales comparison. The attorney may elect to have the appraiser testify only to the sales comparison approach. This is the attorney's decision and the appraiser must abide by it. To fulfill his professional obligations, the appraiser need only testify that he did apply the other approaches to value and that they supported the opinion of value derived by the sales comparison approach.

There are valid reasons why an attorney may want to present only the sales comparison approach. First, it is the approach preferred by the courts. Second, presenting all three approaches to value in detail is time-consuming, and thus may bore a jury and irritate the court. Also, the more testimony that is given in direct examination, the more opportunity there is for effective cross-examination. If an appraiser has relied on the sales comparison approach to value, there is no reason to subject him to cross-examination concerning his selected capitalization rate (the income capitalization approach) or his estimate of incurable functional obsolescence caused by a superadequacy (the cost approach). Finally, the presentation of three indications of market value developed with three approaches to value, or six indications of value in a partial taking case, can be confusing to the trier of fact.

AFTER VALUE

If the case involves a partial taking, the appraiser repeats Steps 4 through 9 of the direct examination (i.e., property description; highest and best use; application of the cost, income, and sales comparison approaches; and final reconciliation), but this time in the after situation. The procedure followed to value the property in the before situation should be repeated with equal clarity and detail in the after situation. It is useless to convince the trier of fact of the accuracy of the before value if the trier does not accept the after value estimate. Awards in partial taking cases are not based on before value alone.

If jurisdictional rules require that the state, or taking plus damages, rule be applied, the after value testimony must be framed to comply with the applicable rules. If benefits are not present in the after situation, little alteration will generally be required and the results will, or at least usually should, be identical to the results produced using the federal, or before and after, rule.

Under the federal rule, the indicated market value of the property in the after situation should be presented to the trier of fact in the manner shown in Table 21.1; the remainder value after the taking should be presented in the same way under the state rule. However, the final mathematical calculation under the federal rule might be presented as shown in Table 21.2, while the mathematical computations under the state rule, assuming no benefits, might be presented as shown in Table 21.3. If special benefits are present, the appraiser's conclusions under the state rule would be presented as shown in Table 21.4, assuming special benefits are to be offset against damages.

TABLE 21.2 APPRAISER'S FINAL CONCLUSIONS UNDER FEDERAL RULE

Before value	$120,000
After value	– 86,000
Difference	$ 34,000

TABLE 21.3 APPRAISER'S FINAL CONCLUSIONS UNDER STATE RULE

Value before taking	$120,000
Value of part taken	– 22,000
Remainder value before taking	$ 98,000
Remainder value after taking	– 86,000
Damages	$ 12,000
Value of part taken	22,000
Total difference	$ 34,000

TABLE 21.4 APPRAISER'S FINAL CONCLUSIONS UNDER STATE RULE ASSUMING SPECIAL BENEFITS

Value before taking	$120,000
Value of part taken	– 22,000
Remainder value before taking	$ 98,000
Remainder value after taking	– 90,000
Damages	$ 8,000
Special benefits	– 6,000
Net damages	$ 2,000
Value of part taken	22,000
Total difference	$ 24,000

CROSS-EXAMINATION

How do the attorney and the appraiser prepare for cross-examination? First, they try to identify the points on which the appraiser will be most closely cross-examined. In other words, what are the weaknesses in the appraiser's approach to value and, thus, the weakest points in the appraiser's testimony? How can the appraiser best defend himself against cross-examination on these points? The appraiser/attorney team should not assume that the appraisal is without weak points or hope that opposing counsel will overlook them. They must view their case objectively, identify problem areas, and prepare to defend them against attack. Sometimes appraisers have trouble identifying weak points in their own appraisals. This is only natural. The appraiser has completed a thorough and professional appraisal, perhaps over several months, and he is confident in the accuracy of his value estimate. For this reason, some attorneys prefer to have an appraisal consultant identify technical weaknesses in the appraisal rather than rely on the appraisal witness. This practice has the added advantage of not making the appraisal witness identify the weaknesses in his own conclusion. If there is one thing the attorney does not need just prior to trial, it is an appraiser who has begun to doubt the accuracy of his conclusions.

With proper preparation, opposing counsel should never be able to bring out a weakness of the appraiser's direct testimony that has not been recognized as a weakness by the appraiser/attorney team prior to trial. For instance, in one case the value estimate developed by the condemnor's appraiser was 30% below the price actually paid for the property two months prior to the date of the taking. Thanks to proper preparation before the trial, the appraiser was able to defend his value estimate on cross-examination so successfully that the trier of fact completely disregarded the prior sale price of the property and found the property's market value to be the value testified to by the condemnor's appraiser.

It has been said that "cross-examination takes the place in our legal system that torture occupied in the medieval systems of civilization."[28] From the attorney's point of view, the ultimate goal of cross-examination is to destroy the witness's direct testimony completely. If as a by-product the witness's professional reputation is tarnished or destroyed, so be it. This is, after all, an adversarial proceeding. Appraisers have wisely been advised that "[c]ross-examination is the anvil of truth and you must be prepared for the thorough hammering."[29] It is with these thoughts in mind that the appraiser should prepare for cross-examination.

Some believe that "[b]eing an expert witness can be a profitable avenue of income,"[30] but others have found it can also be an avenue to ulcers, stress headaches, and hypertension. Cross-examination can lead to ridicule and humiliation for the unprepared. It has been suggested that appraisers should actually solicit assignments as expert witnesses;[31] needless to say, this suggestion came from lawyers. The appraiser who has experienced 16 hours of cross-examination knows that there are much less stressful "avenues of income" than to subject oneself to public questioning by someone bent on your professional destruction.

28. 5 *Wigmore on Evidence* 29 (1940).

29. *Right-of-Way*, 21–25.

30. John S. Bean, Theresa H. Walter, and Neil G. Waller, "Real Estate Professionals as Expert Witnesses," *The Appraisal Journal* (January 1988), 80–88.

31. Ibid.

It can be either a great insult or a great compliment for a cross-examiner to stand up after the appraiser's direct testimony and say, "No questions." If the appraiser has presented a strong and detailed case for his opinion of value during direct examination, cross-examination may be declined because opposing counsel feels the appraiser is so well-prepared and confident on the witness stand that any cross-examination would only strengthen his direct testimony. Under such circumstances, it is best for opposing counsel to try to give the trier of fact the impression that the appraiser's approach to the valuation problem is so ill-conceived that cross-examination would be a waste of time. Cross-examining a very strong witness can do more harm than good, and the cross-examiner's best strategy is to get the appraiser out of sight, and hopefully out of mind, as quickly as possible. Even in these circumstances, some attorneys cannot overcome the temptation to ask a couple of "nonquestions" such as: "Isn't it true, Mr. Appraiser, that appraisal is not an exact science?" and "Isn't a fact, Ms. Appraiser, that two professionally trained appraisers can reach different opinions of value for the same property?" The answers to these questions do not tell the jury anything new, but the questions tell opposing counsel that the cross-examiner thinks his case is in trouble.

On the other hand, a cross-examiner may forego cross-examination if the appraiser's direct testimony is not particularly strong or does not materially damage the cross-examiner's case in chief. For example, if the appraiser testifies to a value estimate under direct examination without providing the facts on which the opinion is based, it is often wise to forego cross-examination. The cross-examiner might ask, "Do you have any sales to back up your totally unsupported opinion?" to point out to the trier of fact that the opinion is unsupported. However, this strategy could backfire if the witness answers the question well. The opinion might be much better supported than the cross-examiner wanted it to be and, even worse, the question will allow opposing counsel to delve into the question of comparable sales on redirect examination. Often it is best for the cross-examiner to forego cross-examination and emphasize during closing arguments that the appraiser's opinion is without basis.

It is most important for the cross-examiner to ask the appraiser the assumptions, limiting conditions, and legal instructions under which the appraisal was made, if this information is not covered in direct examination. Too often the question is left unasked. Regardless of the answer, this question should not be injurious to the cross-examiner's case. The trier of fact is seldom aware of the standard assumptions and limiting conditions under which a typical appraisal is made. For instance, a typical list of assumptions and limiting conditions for an appraisal involving a partial acquisition might reveal any of the following flaws:

- A definition of market value that conflicts with the definition used in the jurisdiction in which the trial is being held
- Reference to government plans for the construction of the public improvement that have been modified since the appraisal report was prepared

- A statement that the appraisal was made assuming that the appraised property was a fee simple estate, when in fact the property was encumbered by one or more easements
- An assumption that the property is free from infestation by termites, dry rot, or toxic contamination when the facts of the case suggest otherwise
- An assumption that the property has been operated in conformance with applicable land use laws or is not in violation of the Americans with Disabilities Act,[32] when these assumptions have been shown to be questionable
- The assumption that a subsidiary report (e.g., engineering report, feasibility study, environmental report, mineral appraisal, timber cruise, fixture appraisal) adopted by the appraiser is correct, especially when the subsidiary report has been shown to be flawed
- The adoption of an appraisal instruction that has questionable legal foundation

While a recitation of the appraiser's assumptions and limiting conditions will not be particularly harmful to the appraiser, the cross-examiner may try to convince the trier of fact in his final argument that the appraiser seems to have assumed everything and knows nothing.

The real advantage of asking for a recitation of the appraisal's assumptions is the possibility that one of the assumptions, limiting conditions, or legal instructions applied is contrary to eminent domain and valuation law in the jurisdiction or results in a "limited appraisal" under the Uniform Standards.[33] For example, one appraisal report made for a condemnee was prepared under the following limiting condition and instruction:

> Zoning has been completely disregarded. The appraiser has been instructed to value the property based upon the Highest and Best Use of the site, irrespective of present zoning or use.

Another report prepared for a condemnee, which involved a warehouse constructed in 1903, was made under the following assumptions:

Assumptions

> That the owners have a legal right of ingress and egress by deed or prescription. [The property was legally landlocked]
>
> That, *as limited investigation has revealed,* there are no valid, comparable sales of property and buildings. [Emphasis added]
>
> That there are no land and buildings in the area currently being rented to provide income data. [This might be a proper conclusion to reach after market investigation, but it should not be an assumption.]
>
> That the replacement [of the property] is necessary to the business and the loss of the subject facility would cause economic harm far in excess of the cost of replacement. [The appraiser estimated the value of the business, not the value of the realty.]

32. Pub. L. No. 101-336, Americans with Disabilities Act of 1990.

33. *Uniform Standards of Professional Appraisal Practice,* 1994 ed., Departure Provision.

It may surprise attorneys who do not specialize in eminent domain litigation to know that very often real estate appraisals are made under assumptions, limiting conditions, and/or attorney instructions that are unacceptable to the court. When this flaw is exposed, it can substantially weaken the effectiveness of the witness and, at times, the court may rule that all testimony given by the appraiser/witness should be disregarded by the trier of fact.

Before acting as expert witnesses, appraisers should read "One Hundred Questions on Cross-Examination" by Walstein Smith, Jr. Other articles of interest by the same author include "One Hundred Questions on Direct Examination" and "One Hundred Questions Which Will Worry Weak Witnesses."[34] In this last article, Smith states:

> It does not take 100 questions to upset an expert witness. Sometimes it takes only one question asked at the right moment with the proper voice inflection. However, sometimes it takes a selection of two or three hundred questions to get the right one.

The 100 questions to worry weak witnesses are divided into ten categories of questions designed to demonstrate

1. Bias—factual or inferred
2. Collusion and advocacy
3. Lack of real estate experience on special property types
4. Lack of appraisal education, training, and professional recognition
5. Personal incompetence–factual or inferred
6. Dishonesty
7. Lack of local experience
8. Lack of preparation and carelessness
9. Imperfections of appraisal techniques
10. Trick questions

Smith summarizes his observations by stating, "[N]ow, after reading these 100 questions, you know why many appraisers refuse to do condemnation appraisals."

Appraisers who lack experience in cross-examination and do not know quite what to expect should go to the source—the lawyers. They are advised to read articles written by and for lawyers about how to cross-examine appraisal experts.[35]

Although the appraiser is an advocate for his opinion, there must be nothing in his testimony or demeanor to suggest advocacy for his client's interest. This position is particularly difficult to maintain under cross-examination because the cross-examiner is intent on convincing the trier of fact of the appraiser's advo-

34. Walstein Smith, Jr., "One Hundred Questions on Cross-Examination," *Real Estate Appraiser* (May 1963), 8–13; "One Hundred Questions on DirectExamination," *Residential Appraiser* (June 1962), 3–6; "One Hundred Questions Which Will Worry Weak Witnesses," *Real Estate Appraiser* (February 1967), 11–16.

35. See West, *Preparation and Trial of a Condemnation Case,* 1962 Institute on Eminent Domain 67, 100; Long, *Basic Considerations in Cross-Examination in Valuation For Eminent Domain*, 459 (1973); and Lupardus, *Cross Examination of an Expert Appraisal Witness*, 1959 Inst. on Eminent Domain 185.

cacy, whether it exists or not. The appraiser must remain calm on the witness stand and think before answering each question. He should respond to each question as briefly as possible, but avoid a long series of "yes" and "no" answers. Many appraisers answer too quickly, without considering the full ramifications of the question and/or the answer.

The appraiser should not be lulled into a feeling of false security on the witness stand. He must be on the lookout, at all times, for trick and hypothetical questions. The question, "Did you consider the sale of 1234 X Street for $50,000?" is improper if no proof of this sale has been submitted. Opposing counsel should object to such a question. Hypothetical questions such as "If a sale of 1234 X Street occurred two months ago for $50,000, would that affect your opinion?" are acceptable and should be answered. Only with proper preparation can the appraiser respond to this question; he must know that there was, in fact, no sale of 1234 X Street two months ago. The appraiser should not try to argue whether such a sale did or did not occur. It is opposing counsel's job to point out to the trier of fact, one way or the other, that no proof of such a sale was presented.

The appraiser should always be prepared to testify regarding the sales used by the opposing party's appraiser. When questioned about such a sale during cross-examination, the appraiser may answer, "Yes, I considered that sale, but felt it was not comparable." Or "Yes, I considered that sale, but disregarded it in my final analysis because it occurred more than two years ago, the property was twice the size of the subject property, it did not have sewer service like the subject, it has flooded three out of the last five years, and it is subject to a different zone classification than the property being appraised." The first response will generally prompt the cross-examiner to ask the same question about each and every comparable sale used by the other appraiser; the second, more complete response will generally lead to an entirely new field of inquiry and shorten the cross-examination process.

Generally, appraisers will be allowed to respond to questions on cross-examination by stating "Yes, because..." and go on to explain their reasoning. However, there are times when the court, usually at the request of the cross-examiner, will instruct the witness to answer the question simply, without any explanation. The appraiser must heed this instruction scrupulously.

Humor is a wonderful thing and it is not necessarily out of place in the courtroom, particularly near the end of a four-day condemnation trial. Nevertheless, the appraiser should leave humorous remarks to the court and the attorneys. Although appraisers must keep a sense of humor on the witness stand, which is sometimes difficult when their professional credibility is being attacked, appraisers are not hired as comedians and should never, under any imaginable circumstances, attempt humor from the witness stand.

REDIRECT

Redirect examination of an appraisal witness could more descriptively be called *reconstruction*. Redirect examination gives the attorney/appraiser team a chance to repair any damage done during cross-examination and to clarify any points that were made confusing, intentionally or not, by opposing counsel. In redirect examination the attorney can, through his questions to the witness, clarify that there was no sale of 1234 X Street two months ago as suggested by opposing counsel. In addition, the appraiser can explain more fully the simple "yes" and "no" responses given in cross-examination, if further explanation is desirable.

Final Argument

Final arguments are totally within the purview of the attorneys. This is not the time to explain appraisal techniques to the jury. If the jurors do not understand the case by this time, the attorney may as well save his breath—the case is lost.

There is some debate as to whether the appraiser should stay in the courtroom during the final arguments. The appraiser must abide by the wishes of legal counsel, but will generally encourage counsel to allow him to be excused. If the appraiser is going to stay in the courtroom, how should he react? Each time the appraiser's name is mentioned, every member of the jury will turn to watch the appraiser's reaction. When his client's attorney extols his virtues, should the appraiser blush or shuffle his feet? Does he watch the attorney or stare the jurors square in the eye? During final arguments, opposing counsel may well imply that the appraiser is an advocate, a nonprofessional, an incompetent, or worse. Again, how does the appraiser, sitting there in the spectator's gallery in full view of the jury, react—with a noncommittal look on his face? staring straight ahead with a threatening glare at the cross-examiner? or with a smile on his lips? Does he look at the jury or thumb his nose at opposing counsel? If the appraiser is a masochist, he should, by all means, stay. If not, the appraiser should request, and plead with legal counsel if necessary, to be excused from the courtroom.

Summary

Appraisers are allowed to testify as to their opinions of value only because they are classified as experts in the field of real estate valuation. "The role of the client advocate is exclusively reserved to the attorney. The appraiser is employed to express an opinion of value, which, to warrant being accorded weight must be supported by factual data. While it is important that an appraiser testify with sincerity in support of his views, it is also important that he bear in mind that it is neither his property nor his money and his only function is to testify to his impartial opinion of value."[36] Although appraisers are not always regarded favorably by courts and attorneys, it is generally recognized that their testimony is necessary in a condemnation trial. There always have been, and there probably

36. *Uniform Appraisal Standards for Federal Land Acquisitions* (Washington, D.C.: U.S. Government Printing Office, 1992), §C-3, p. 91.

always will be, individuals who call themselves professional appraisers, but arrive at made-to-order opinions of value. By the same token, there are an ample number of attorneys to place the order.

The specific procedures of a condemnation trial will vary from jurisdiction to jurisdiction. Some jurisdictions provide that the condemnor has the burden of proof, while others place that burden on the condemnee. Still other jurisdictions hold that neither party has the burden of proof.

It is advisable for the appraiser to be present throughout the condemnation trial, except during final arguments. In this way the appraiser can assist legal counsel in preparing appropriate questions for both direct examination and cross-examination. When the condemnation case is unusually complex or when "the rule" has been imposed, legal counsel is well advised to retain the services of an appraisal consultant to assist at the trial.

The appraiser should prepare detailed, but abbreviated, notes for use on the witness stand. Appraisers should always keep in mind that any notes they use on the stand are subject to inspection by opposing counsel. During testimony, the appraiser should speak clearly and loudly enough to be heard by everyone in the courtroom. He should not speak so quickly as to confuse the trier of fact and/or the court reporter. The appraiser should avoid using a monotone and should always direct his remarks to the jury when answering questions. If the appraiser will be on the witness stand for any length of time, a glass of water should be provided within easy reach. Staring at the pitcher of ice water on the counsel's table can cause the appraiser to lose his train of thought.

The appraiser's direct examination can be broken down into nine logical steps:

1. Qualification as an expert
2. Description of the appraisal process
3. Specific description of work undertaken
4. Property description
5. Highest and best use
6. Cost approach
7. Income capitalization approach
8. Sales comparison approach
9. Final value estimate

In a partial taking case, Steps 4 through 9 will be repeated for the property in the after situation. The steps must be modified in the after situation if the jurisdiction requires use of the state, or taking plus damages, rule. The appraiser should use as many visual aids (e.g., charts, graphs, photos) as possible to help the trier of fact understand the appraiser's testimony.

An objective analysis of the appraiser's data and methodology will reveal the weak points in the appraiser's presentation. Recognition of these weaknesses will give the appraiser/attorney team the opportunity to plan its rebuttal or defense of these points, which will undoubtedly be brought out in cross-examination. The purpose of cross-examination is to weaken the appraiser's direct testimony. An attorney who undertakes cross-examination and does not weaken the appraiser's direct testimony has not prepared properly or should never have chosen to cross-examine the witness.

Every appraisal methodology and approach has its weaknesses. If the attorney cannot bring them out in cross-examination, he is unprepared. It is not a question of whether an appraiser's direct testimony can be weakened by cross-examination, but rather how much it can be weakened. Redirect examination is an attempt to patch up the weak points brought out in cross-examination; it provides the appraiser with an opportunity to explain the "yes" and "no" answers he was limited to under cross-examination. The degree to which the appraiser's direct testimony was weakened by cross-examination will dictate the amount of redirect examination required.

The appraiser should not remain in the courtroom during final arguments, unless he is specifically instructed to do so by counsel. Some attorneys do instruct the appraisers to remain, but most recognize the disadvantage of having the jury's attention drawn to the appraiser, rather than the attorney's argument. The content of the attorney's argument will depend on the circumstances of the case. In almost every case, the attorney will point out to the trier of fact: 1) the superb qualifications of his expert witness; 2) the lack of qualifications of the opposing party's expert, 3) the objectivity of his expert; 4) the bias or advocacy of the opposing party's expert; 5) the thoroughness of his expert's work and the reasonableness of the expert's opinion; and 6) the slipshod work of the opposing counsel's expert and the absurdity of this expert's opinion. The attorney will also highlight those little items that make each case unique, such as the fact that the property owner was born and raised on the property or the allegation that the condemnor's appraiser cannot possibly know the value of the property because he does not live in the community.

CHAPTER 22

Appraisals for Other Litigation

It is not possible to develop a list of all the different types of litigation that could require real estate appraisals and testimony by real estate valuation experts. The possibilities are endless; they are as varied as the imaginations of buyers, sellers, and users of real estate and their legal counsel. There are, however, several types of real estate litigation which appear frequently on civil court dockets. A review of these cases reveals that the rules of evidence and the appraisal procedures applied are surprisingly similar, if not identical, to the rules and procedures used in condemnation trials. The appraiser who is knowledgeable and experienced in the area of condemnation appraisal will find his experience applicable to the appraisal of real estate for most civil litigation.

The common forms of civil litigation discussed in this chapter require real estate valuations but are not related to the sovereign's power of eminent domain. Some forms of civil litigation create no unique valuation problems, while others may create technical problems which the appraiser can solve only with outside assistance.

In many civil litigation cases, there is an irreconcilable conflict between the attorney and the appraiser. If both parties recognize the conflict and why it is incurable, they will generally have a better understanding of each other's needs. A civil litigation action such as a divorce case need not lead to conflict between the attorney and the appraiser. In many litigation cases, the difference of opinion in regard to the value of real estate is comparatively minimal. However, the attorney has an obligation to attempt to procure the services of the best (and often most expensive) appraiser available while, at the same time, considering the small amount of money at issue.

The appraiser, on the other hand, must assume that he will be required to testify to his opinion of the value of the real estate. To do otherwise will almost ensure that the appraiser will find himself on the witness stand. Therefore, the appraiser will generally quote a substantial appraisal fee, assuming that he must be prepared to testify as to his value conclusion. This may cause the attorney to comment, "This is a divorce case, not a million dollar condemnation." or "I didn't ask you to buy the property—just appraise it."

The appraiser must realize that the attorney cannot economically justify a high appraisal fee if the amount of money involved in the case is not large. Nevertheless, the attorney must also understand the appraiser's circumstances. The unprepared appraiser will be made to look incompetent under cross-examination whether the case involves $10,000 or $10,000,000. The integrity and reputation of the appraiser are at stake every time he takes the witness stand. If an appraiser is unprepared on the witness stand, the members of the legal community will not be so forgiving as to say, "It doesn't matter because he was only testifying in a divorce case."

The appraiser who is tempted to take the witness stand without thorough preparation because the amount of money at stake is small should keep in mind that the judge who sits on the case may well be the trier of fact in the next major condemnation case in which the appraiser testifies. Once a bad impression of the appraiser is implanted in the mind of the judge, it will be difficult, if not impossible, to eradicate it. Thus the appraiser will not only weaken his own credibility as a professional by testifying when he is unprepared, but he will also be doing a disservice to his future clients.

If the appraiser and the attorney cannot reach a compromise, and the conflict between their positions cannot be resolved, they should part company on good terms. The appraiser may be able to recommend an associate appraiser who is competent to do the work, or he may refer the attorney to an appraiser in another firm. On occasion, the appraiser can provide consulting services to the attorney or help the attorney develop evidence in support of his position without presenting formal appraisal testimony. The appraiser's assistance will not be forgotten by the attorney.

DIVORCE

When the attorney tells the appraiser, "This is only a divorce case, so you won't be called to testify." the appraiser generally can double the odds of winding up on the witness stand. The appraiser may also be able to guess whether the attorney represents the husband or the wife and who is likely to keep what property. In describing the real estate, the attorney may say, "The only real estate involved is a rundown house and a high-quality office building from which the husband is operating a highly successful professional business." This attorney probably represents the wife, who will be keeping the house while the husband retains the office building. The valuation problems resulting from a divorce, or the dissolution of a marriage, might include estimating the market value of a single-family dwelling; valuing complex, special-purpose properties; valuing a leased fee and/or leasehold interest; valuing a partial interest in real property; or estimating an equitable partitionment of real property.

The purpose of an appraisal in a divorce action is to estimate the market value of any real estate or interest in the real estate involved. The appraisal methodology used to estimate the market value of property in such a case is no different than that employed to estimate the before market value of a parcel in condemnation except, of course, that there is no need to disregard condemnation blight or project enhancement if the property being appraised happens to be affected by either of these factors. Also, the appraiser may be required to estimate the value of partial interests in real estate or the value of real estate encumbered by existing financing; these factors are generally not encountered in the typical condemnation assignment.

In addition to valuing real estate in divorce cases, an appraiser is sometimes asked to value, or at least testify as to the correct procedure for valuing, a deferred annuity. In some jurisdictions, the current value of a spouse's retirement plan has been ruled to belong to the community—i.e., the husband and the wife each have an undivided half interest in the current value of the retirement plan. Some attorneys do not fully understand the mathematics involved in valuing a deferred annuity, and they prefer to have a witness present the procedure to the court rather than trying to present it themselves through argument.

For example, assume the husband in a divorce action is 55 years of age and will be eligible for retirement at age 62. At that time, his retirement benefits will be $1,500 per month until his death. Assume also that a proper discount factor is 8% and that mortality tables show that a 55-year-old male has a remaining life expectancy of approximately 20 years. Thus the current value of the deferred annuity is the present value of the 20-year annuity deferred seven years (until the husband reaches retirement age). The computations would be:

Factor for 240-month (20-year) annuity	119.554292
Factor for 84-month (7-year) annuity	(64.159261)
Factor for 156-month (13-year) annuity deferred 84 months (7 years)	55.395031
Monthly annuity payment	x $1,500
Present value of annuity (or interest in retirement fund)	$ 80,093

If asked to prepare a written report or to testify, the appraiser is well advised to make his computations using various interest, or discount, rates at 1% increments and to let the attorneys argue as to the applicable rates.

INSURANCE CLAIMS

Appraisals are made for insurance claim purposes when the insurance company and the insured cannot agree on the amount of property damage sustained. Most losses result from fire, wind damage, earthquakes, flooding and other water damage, and soil slippage, but sometimes unique occurrences such as tidal waves and volcanic eruptions are involved. Appraisals for insurance claim litigation generally take the same form as appraisals for federal condemnation. That is, the appraiser estimates the market value of the property before the damage and the market value of the property after the damage has occurred.

Often the appraiser must use public records and available photographs of the property to establish its before condition. If this is the case, it is important that the appraiser limit his appraisal report and testimony in this regard by clearly specifying the assumptions made about the condition of the property prior to the damage. This type of situation will not be new to an appraiser who makes condemnation appraisals. In many partial takings, the appraiser must base his understanding of a property's after condition on the government entity's plans for construction of the public improvement. Moreover, appraisers are often asked to make appraisals of properties being condemned well after the actual date of taking, and thus the effective date of value. They must therefore determine the condition of a property on some historical date and, in some instances, at a time when the improvements on the property had already been removed.

It is important for appraisers to understand which items of damage are recoverable and which are not. A property may suffer a diminution in value that exceeds the cost to restore it to its original condition. For instance, assume a property is damaged by a landslide in the area. The cost to restore the property to its original physical condition may be $5,000, but the difference between the market value of the property before and after the landslide may be $25,000. The extra $20,000 reflects the market's reaction to the potential for landslides in the future. If the appraisal assignment is performed in conjunction with a claim by a property owner against his insurance company, the recoverable loss is only $5,000, which would typically cover only direct, out-of-pocket expenses. The recoverable costs would not include an entrepreneurial profit factor, as they would (or should) in cost-to-cure estimates made in partial taking condemnation appraisals. However, if the claim is made against an abutting property owner (and his insurance company) who caused the landslide by removing a lateral support, the recoverable loss is $25,000, assuming it can be proven that the actions of the abutting owner were the proximate cause of the landslide.

Another form of insurance claim is a title insurance loss. This type of loss occurs when a purchaser (or sometimes a mortgagee) of property purchases title insurance and the title insurance company insures the fee title of the property, subject only to the specific exceptions in the policy. If a defect, or encumbrance, in the title to the property that is not specified in the insurance policy exceptions is later found, the title insurance company may be liable for the loss. There are typically three types of title loss in which an appraiser may be involved: the existence of an undisclosed easement, the encroachment onto or by the subject property, and an incorrect legal description. In each case the loss is generally measured using a before and after methodology identical to that applied in federal condemnation valuations.

For example, assume a property is encumbered by a water-line easement, but was insured as free and clear of easements. The proper valuation procedure would be to estimate the market value of the property as if no easement existed and then to estimate the market value of the property as encumbered by the easement; the difference between these values, from a legal standpoint, represents the insurable loss up to the maximum coverage of the policy. Often the title insurance company will bring the original seller of the property into the suit, as a third-party defendant, if this individual transferred the property to the purchaser by way of a warranty deed and did not expressly except the easement on the face of the deed.

GUARDIANSHIP/TRUSTEE MATTERS

An individual who is under legal age or has been ruled incompetent is a *ward*, and a guardian is responsible for handling a ward's affairs. If the ward is under legal age, the ward's parents are usually his legal guardians. If the individual is an incompetent adult, the court will appoint a guardian for the ward. The powers of a guardian and a trustee vary from jurisdiction to jurisdiction. However, the actions taken by a guardian are subject to review by the court and, in many instances, the guardian must get court approval before taking any material action.

When a guardian acts on behalf of a ward in a real estate transaction, an appraiser is often retained to value the property involved so that the guardian has documentation that the transaction contemplated is in the best interest of the ward. In such a case, the appraiser may be called to the witness stand to testify to the value of the property so the court can make a prudent decision on the guardian's motion to take action. Because a guardian has legal and financial responsibilities to his ward, decisions regarding real estate are generally more carefully investigated, analyzed, and documented than they would be if the guardian were acting on his own behalf. In reviewing the prudence of a real estate action taken by a guardian, the court often has the advantage of hindsight. Therefore, if a real estate decision made by a guardian ultimately results in an unfavorable conclusion, the guardian wants to have documentation that he made the decision only after conducting an appropriate investigation and procuring a competent appraisal of the property.

Appraisal assignments performed in conjunction with guardianship matters can call for any number of real estate appraisal and consulting services. Most assignments will involve estimates of market value or economic rent and can be handled with the same procedures used to estimate the before value of a property in a condemnation action.

FRAUD AND MISREPRESENTATION

Fraud and misrepresentation actions are generally brought by a disgruntled buyer (or lessee) of real estate against the seller (or lessor) and/or the seller's agent. In some cases the buyer requests that the sale of the property be rescinded and that the seller return all of the buyer's money. An appraiser may or may not be involved in such a case. For instance, one case involved a general contractor who had just been awarded a substantial contract to construct a portion of an interstate highway. To do the work, the contractor was in immediate need of a large quantity of gravel for fill material. A nearby property owner offered his property to the contractor, who confirmed the quantity and quality of the gravel on the site by drilling test holes. The contractor purchased the property, but only after the seller allegedly advised him that a shorelines management permit would not be required to remove the gravel. The seller allegedly told the buyer that this fact had been confirmed by the local planning agency.

After closing of the sale, however, the purchaser was advised by the local planning agency that a shorelines management permit would be required before any material could be taken from the site and that obtaining such a permit could take several months. To meet construction deadlines and complete the project in a timely manner, the contractor had to acquire another site to obtain the gravel. The buyer brought suit against the seller and asked for rescission of the sale.

The market value of the property was not in question. The issue was whether the seller misrepresented the property to the buyer and whether the buyer relied on this misinformation. The buyer was not interested in the market value of the property; he was unable to use it for his intended purpose in a timely manner and, therefore, did not want it at any price. Even though the seller retained an appraiser who testified that the market value of the property was equal to its sale price, the court found that the seller did, in fact, misrepresent the property to the buyer and that the buyer relied on this misrepresentation. The court therefore ruled that the value of the property was not at issue and ordered that the sale be rescinded.

Another case in which an appraiser's services were required is described as follows. In anticipation of selling his property, an owner obtained a survey of the property and had a legal description drawn by an engineering firm. The topography of the site was quite irregular and the land was covered with trees and brush. The engineering firm described the property as "containing 42.6 acres, more or less." The property was placed on the market and sold for $100,000 to a purchaser who intended to develop the property into a mobile home park. The buyer immediately began drawing up plans for a mobile home park to be submitted to the local land use agency. The applicable land use ordinance allowed a maximum of eight mobile homes per acre. In preparing the mobile home park plans, the buyer found that he had only 35.4 acres of land and, thus, could develop the site with only 283 (35.4 x 8) mobile home pads, not 340 (42.6 x 8) pads as he anticipated at the time of purchase.

The purchaser brought suit against the seller asking that the sale price of the property be reduced. The seller brought the engineering firm into the suit as a third-party defendant. The seller alleged that he never represented the property as being any specific size and that the lump-sum price paid was in no way based on the number of acres in the tract or the number of mobile home pads that could be developed on the tract. The buyer testified that he purchased the property with the understanding that it contained approximately 42.6 acres and purchased it because he felt $2,350 per acre was a fair price.

The buyer retained an appraiser who was legally instructed to appraise the property as if it contained 42.6 acres and then to appraise it again assuming the tract had the same boundary lines but contained only 35.4 acres. The appraiser testified that similar tracts were typically offered, sold, and bought on a price-per-acre basis. Under the first premise, the appraiser's estimate of the tract's market value was $100,000 (42.6 acres x $2,350, rounded); under the second premise, his estimate of the market value of the tract was $83,000 (35.4 acres x $2,350, rounded).

The court found no intentional fraud or misrepresentation, but ordered the seller to refund $17,000 to the purchaser because the term *more or less* does not excuse an error of nearly 17%, and because similar tracts generally sold on a per-acre basis. It also ordered that the engineering firm pay both the purchaser's and the seller's attorneys' fees. The court reasoned that, had it not been for the engineer's error in calculating the size of the tract, there would have been no trial and no fees would have been incurred.

Appraisal assignments involving fraud and misrepresentation are usually similar to assignments to appraise a partial taking in a condemnation case using the before and after rule. The market value of the property in the before situation is based on how it was allegedly misrepresented and the after value is based on the actual circumstances. The difference, if any, represents the effect of the alleged misrepresentation on the value of the property. It is of no concern to the appraiser whether or not actual fraud or misrepresentation occurred. The appraiser must, however, obtain clear, written instructions from legal counsel as to what special elements are to be assumed in both the before and after situations. These instructions must be included in the appraisal report and should be noted in any testimony the appraiser may give regarding to the property.

BANKRUPTCY

In an involuntary bankruptcy case, the services of an appraiser may be required both to value the real estate and to testify to its market value in court. Such an appraisal assignment is identical in nature to the before value estimate made in a condemnation assignment. An appraisal assignment associated with bankruptcy often comes about when a creditor attempts to force a debtor into bankruptcy, claiming that the debtor is insolvent, i.e., the debtor owes more than the total value of his assets. If the debtor contests the bankruptcy, the value of the real estate he owns becomes quite important because it may determine the debtor's solvency.

REMOVAL OF LATERAL SUPPORT

Another situation requiring the services of an appraiser may arise when an abutting, downhill property owner removes the lateral support necessary to stabilize the abutting, uphill property of another, thereby causing the uphill property to slide and damaging the uphill land and/or the improvements. Figure 22.1 depicts the before and after situations in such a case. An excavation on the downhill ownership has caused a portion of the uphill ownership to become unstable and

FIGURE 22.1 CROSS SECTION
BEFORE EXCAVATION AND AFTER EXCAVATION

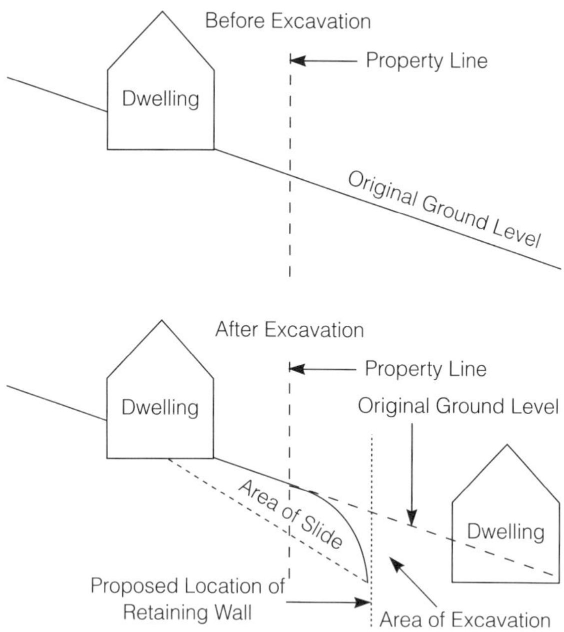

begin to slide, damaging the uphill land and buildings. In this situation the appraiser's function would be to appraise the uphill ownership before the excavation and after the excavation and subsequent slide; the difference between the two values is the amount of damage suffered by the uphill owner.

Often the appraiser will need to retain a consulting engineer to determine whether the area of the slide can be stabilized and, if so, at what cost. From the illustration shown in Figure 22.1, a soil engineer and a structural engineer concluded that constructing a properly designed, concrete retaining wall at the toe of the excavation would restabilize the area. Estimates of the cost to construct the retaining wall and repair the damage to the uphill land and dwelling were obtained by the appraiser. It was concluded that these costs were less than the diminution in the value of the uphill property that would result if the corrective work were not undertaken. Therefore, the appraiser was correct in using a cost-to-cure adjustment to estimate the property's after value. The computations might be presented as follows:

Before value		$100,000
Less cost of retaining wall	20,000	
cost to repair landscaping	1,000	
cost to repair dwelling	5,000	
After value		74,000
Difference between before and after values		$ 26,000

Two factors must be considered in appraising a property that has become subject to movement. First, the appraiser must be sure that the cost-to-cure adjustment includes all cost-to-cure items as well as an entrepreneurial profit. (Entrepreneurial profit was described in Chapter 8.) The other factor to be considered is whether the fact that the property once had a sliding problem will affect the property's value after the slide condition is physically corrected. This market reaction to an adverse condition has been dubbed "stigma."

The appraiser must keep in mind that there can be considerable divergence between the opinions of different soil engineers. One might say that a slide can be stabilized for $1,000, while another believes that the cost to stabilize the area is greater than the appraiser's estimate of the property's before value. The appraiser should not accept either opinion blindly, even if one of the opinions was developed by a consulting engineer retained by the opposing party. The appraiser should review all consulting reports, regardless of their origin, in accordance with applicable professional standards,[1] and give each the consideration it deserves in arriving at a final value estimate. It is improper for the appraiser to assume that a consultant hired by the appraiser's client is always right and that consultants hired by the client's adversary are always wrong or biased.

Often a diligent search of sales records will reveal the sale of a property similar to the one under appraisal that also has a propensity for sliding. The sale property can then be compared with comparable properties not subject to slides, using the paired data technique of analysis, to arrive at the diminution in value attributable to the possibility of sliding in the future. Even if the properties studied are not very similar to the one being appraised or are not in the same geographical area, their analysis may help the appraiser make a proper adjustment for the sliding potential of the property being appraised.

1. See *Standards of Professional Appraisal Practice of the Appraisal Institute*, Guide Note 6, "Reliance on Reports Prepared By Others."

In the situation shown in Figure 22.1, the corrective retaining wall is to be constructed on the downhill property. In this case the downhill owner was the defendant in the case because his excavating action caused the slide; thus the downhill owner offered the uphill owner an easement to construct and maintain the wall as a means of mitigating the damages to the uphill owner's property. This is a unique situation. In most cases the appraiser cannot assume a stabilization project that would involve construction work on any property other than the parcel being appraised. If the slide condition cannot physically be corrected by measures conducted wholly within the boundaries of the subject property, it must be assumed that the property cannot be stabilized.

A slide condition can be caused by factors other than the removal of lateral support. For instance, the construction activity of an uphill owner, such as the paving of previously vegetated ground for a parking lot, can increase the amount or velocity of rainwater running onto the downhill owner's property, thereby oversaturating the soil and causing a slide. The unintentional diversion of a natural water course can have the same result. Of course, the intentional diversion of a water course can cause damage to the land of a downhill owner. Although the intentional diversion of water is construed as intentional trespass and is therefore a criminal act, the uphill owner remains liable to the downhill owner for any resulting property damage caused.

Whatever the reason for the slide, the damage caused by a slide or by the increase or diversion of a water course is generally measured as the difference between the market value of the property before and after the damage. Therefore, the appraisal methodology applied in federal partial taking condemnation actions would apply in these instances.

FORECLOSURES

Under normal circumstances an appraiser will not be asked to testify in a foreclosure action. Generally the appraiser will only be asked to appraise the property for a lien holder so that the holder can determine the advisability of starting a foreclosure action. However, some jurisdictions provide for the establishment of an upset bid price in a judicial foreclosure. An *upset bid price* is the minimum amount for which a property can be sold in a foreclosure sale. This price is established to protect any junior lien holders and/or the underlying fee owner.

For example, consider a property with a market value of $50,000 that is encumbered by a first mortgage of $10,000 and a second mortgage of $2,000; this leaves the underlying fee owner with $38,000 in equity. If no upset bid price has been established, the first-position lien holder could foreclose its lien and bid in the property at $10,000, leaving the junior lien holder and the underlying fee owner out in the cold.

When a junior lien holder or the underlying fee owner asks the court to set an upset bid price, the appraiser may be required to testify. The appraiser will estimate the market value of the property and testify to it. This testimony gives the court a foundation on which to base an upset bid price; in this example, the upset bid price might be approximately $35,000.

PRIVATE WAY OF NECESSITY

Many jurisdictions recognize a *private way of necessity* lawsuit, which may arise in a situation like the one illustrated in Figure 22.2. Parcel B is legally landlocked and the only practical access to Parcel B is through Parcel A. If the owner of Parcel A refuses to give or sell an easement for ingress and egress to the owner of Parcel B at a reasonable price, the owner of Parcel B may bring a suit against the owner of Parcel A to force an access easement across Parcel A to Parcel B. In effect, the owner of Parcel B is given the limited right of eminent domain in this situation.

FIGURE 22.2 PRIVATE WAY OF NECESSITY

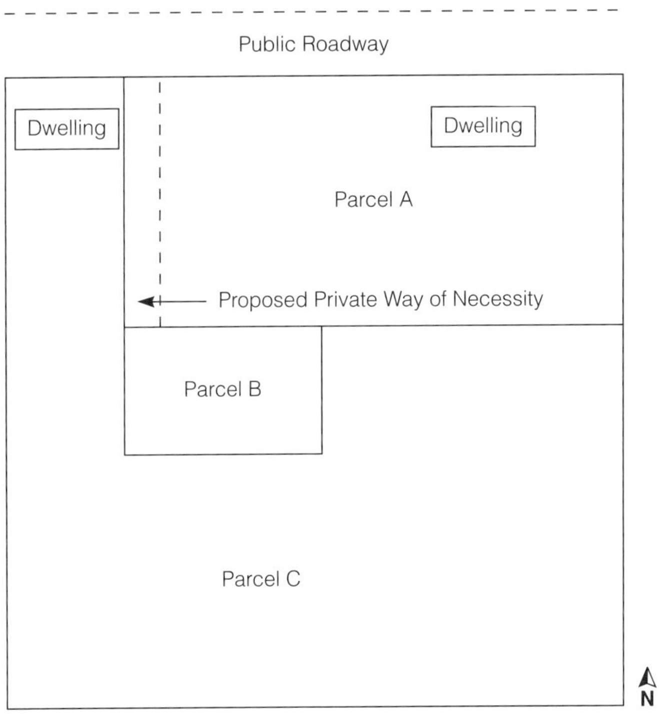

Along with this right, the owner of Parcel B acquires the obligation to pay the owner of Parcel A for the taking of the easement area and for any damages to the remainder of Parcel A caused by the taking and the proposed use of the easement.

In appraising a property for a private way of necessity, the appraiser proceeds as he would in a typical condemnation action. In this example, the owner of Parcel B is acting as the condemnor and the owner of Parcel A is the condemnee. The appraiser must consider three important factors: the estimate of the market value of Parcel A before the taking, the estimate of the market value of Parcel A after the taking, and the difference between the two estimates. The amount by which the new easement enhances the value of Parcel B is of no consequence.

Generally a private way of necessity is limited in use. For instance, it may be limited to use for ingress and egress to a single-family dwelling on Parcel B or, if Parcel B is wooded, it may be limited to use for the ingress and egress of logging equipment to harvest the timber on Parcel B. In the latter case, the easement for the private way may be extinguished once the harvesting is complete.

The key difference between an appraisal for a private way of necessity and an appraisal prepared for a regular condemnation action is that the party obtaining the private way of necessity will not have all the facts when he first contacts the appraiser. He will not know exactly where the easement will go across the neighboring tract; the width, surface, or finished grade of the proposed private way; or whether any drainage problems will be caused by the proposed construction. If there is a drainage problem, he will not know how it will be corrected. The amount of detail needed by the appraiser will vary from case to case. In each case the appraiser should develop a complete list of the data needed to complete the appraisal so that these data can be developed by or through the individual obtaining the private way.

PARTITIONMENT

Litigation to partition a parcel of property is generally necessitated by the termination of a partnership, a divorce, or the division of property in an estate. In a partitionment case, the appraiser's assignment is often twofold in nature. First, the appraiser must estimate the value of the whole property as a single entity, as he would for the before valuation in a condemnation case. Then, the appraiser should make a hypothetical division of the property into two parcels of equal value or into several parcels representing specified percentages of the aggregate value of the total property.

For instance, if the property being appraised is held by a two-person partnership and each partner has a 50% interest in the partnership, the appraiser will determine how the property could be physically split into two independent parcels of equal value. If a number of individuals hold interests in the property to be partitioned and/or their interests are unequal, the appraiser's task of economically partitioning the property becomes more complex. For example, consider the appraisal of a property owned by a four-person partnership or estate in which the partners, or heirs, hold interests of 36%, 26%, 26%, and 12%. Once the appraiser has completed the hypothetical partitionment, he must estimate the market value of each of the partitioned segments of the whole property as a separate entity.

Each step in the appraiser's partitionment procedure will furnish the court with information needed to make a logical and equitable ruling. Sometimes it is physically and/or legally impossible to partition a property in direct proportion to the various interests held. If the interests in a property are 36%, 26%, 26%, and 12%, as previously stipulated, and the property is a large tract of timberland, a partitionment that is both physically and legally equitable can probably be made. However, if the property is a single commercial building, partitionment will not be possible. In such an instance, the court will generally use the appraiser's estimate of the market value of the whole property and order the property to be sold, with the proceeds of the sale divided among the partners according to their various interests in the property.

At first glance it may seem unnecessary to estimate the actual market value of each partitioned portion of the total parcel so long as the partitionment can physically and legally be made, and the market values of the various partitioned parcels coincide with the partners' percentage of interest in the whole parcel. However, in some instances an economic hardship can arise from partitionment, even though the partitionment can legally and physically be made. For instance, consider again the large tract of timberland with ownership interests of 36%, 26%, 26%, and 12% and assume that the tract contains 200 acres and has a value of $600,000 before partitionment. It is quite possible, under such circumstances, that the aggregate value of the partitioned parcels would be considerably less than the value of the whole property before partitionment.

If there is a direct relationship between the value of each acre of the tract and the total value of the tract (i.e., each and every acre is worth $3,000), the partitionment will result in four independent ownerships of 72 acres, 52 acres, 52 acres, and 24 acres. It is quite possible that the value of these four parcels will not equal the value of the whole property before partitionment. The cost of moving logging equipment into an area and setting up a logging operation is the same, whether 24 acres, 72 acres, or 200 acres are to be logged. After partitionment, the setup costs will have to be incurred to log each parcel rather than the original 200-acre tract. It is quite possible that it would not be economically feasible to log the 24-acre parcel as a separate entity at all.

The court must know the aggregate market value of all the partitioned tracts so it can compare this value with the value of the whole property and determine whether the partitionment creates an unreasonable economic hardship for one or more of the partners holding interests in the property. If an economic hardship is created, the court will often reject the partitionment and order that the property be sold as a single entity, with the proceeds of sale split among the various owners in proportion to their ownership interests.

Deciding exactly how to partition a property is probably the most difficult part of the appraiser's assignment. The appraiser often uses trial and error, drawing different lines of partitionment and appraising the resulting parcels as if they were remainder parcels in a condemnation proceeding. The appraiser must adjust the line or lines of partitionment until the proper interest-to-property-value ratio is achieved. The specific location of the dividing line or lines finally selected by the appraiser is often the subject of intense cross-examination. The appraiser should be prepared for such cross-examination and readily admit that, as a general rule, the property in question could be partitioned in a number of different ways and still maintain the proper ratio of property interest to value.

CONSTRUCTION FAULTS

On occasion, an appraiser is asked to appraise a property recently improved with a building that was not constructed in accordance with the building specifications and/or applicable building codes. Often this type of assignment will require the assistance of a structural engineer, a mechanical engineer, or an electrical engineer, depending on the specific deficiency in the construction.

Such an appraisal assignment is identical in nature to a partial taking in a condemnation case. The before value of the property is estimated assuming the improvement was constructed in strict adherence to the building specifications and all applicable building codes. The after value of the property is then estimated with the improvements in their *as is* condition. The difference between the before and after values is the damage suffered by the property owner. In many instances, the loss of value caused by a construction deficiency can be measured by the cost to cure the deficiency. If this is so, the appraiser's assignment is comparatively easy. When a construction deficiency cannot be cured economically, however, the appraisal assignment becomes more complex.

The *cost to cure* a deficiency plays a major role in the appraisal assignment depicted in Figure 22.3. This plot plan shows a single-family dwelling which was constructed under contract. In locating the dwelling and the attached garage on the site, the contractor measured the minimum required front yard setback incorrectly and situated the 20-ft.-by-24 ft. garage only 18 feet from the front lot line instead of the required 24 feet. The building inspector did not notice the error until construction was completed and an occupancy permit was requested. The permit was denied and the contractor applied to the local board of adjustment for a variance to the front yard setback. The variance was also denied and the owner was ordered to correct the 6-ft. encroachment of the garage.

The four options available in this case involved cost-to-cure versus diminution-in-value issues. The options included:

1. Remove six feet of garage leaving an 18-ft. deep garage (which will not have much market appeal).
2. Remove six feet from the front of the garage but extend the rear by six feet, eliminating the patio and relocating or removing the sliding glass doors.
3. Remove the garage entirely.
4. Convert the remaining 18-ft. garage into a recreation room.

FIGURE 22.3 NONCONFORMING SETBACK

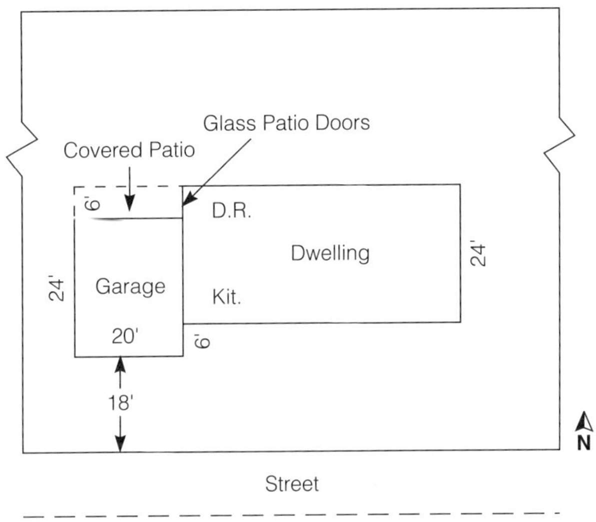

Each of these options was analyzed by the appraiser in terms of its cost and its impact on the market value of the property. As Figure 22.4 illustrates, Option 2 was selected. The garage was to be extended to the rear, the patio was to be uncovered, and the sliding glass doors were to be relocated. This option was selected because it could be completed for the least dollar amount, considering

FIGURE 22.4 CONFORMING SETBACK

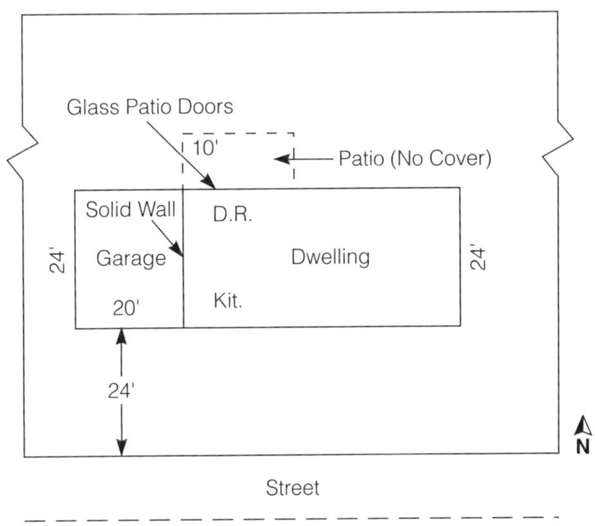

both the cost to make the construction alterations and the difference between the before value of the property and its value after alteration. In selecting among several options, the appraiser must remember that the option that is most cost-effective (taking into consideration both the cost to cure and the residual diminution in value), is the measure of damage, not the option favored by the client. In the situation described, the case was settled on the basis of the appraiser's selected option, but the property owner preferred and actually undertook Option 4.

Now consider another example, which presents a more complex problem for the appraiser. A two-story, single-family dwelling was constructed on contract at a cost of about $200,000. As is too often the case, the plans and specifications for the dwelling were quite sketchy, but the house was constructed in an area with standard building codes. After construction was completed, an occupancy permit was granted and the owners began to move in. While attempting to move a large dresser into the master bedroom upstairs, the new owners learned that the stairway was exceptionally narrow. Upon further investigation it was learned that the stairway was six inches narrower than the minimum width specified in the applicable building code.

After the appraiser inspected the property and discussed the problem with several contractors, it became obvious that the stairway could not economically be widened to the minimum acceptable width. Therefore, the appraiser concluded than the diminution in the property's market value due to the narrow stairway would have to be measured using market data. The before value of the property was estimated as if the stairway met the minimum required width, and the after value estimate of the property was made in its *as is* condition. The appraiser was able to find a number of comparable sales of properties with stairways of adequate width, so the before value of the property was easily estimated.

However, being quite familiar with the market area, the appraiser knew that he would not be able to find many recent sales of comparable, newer, two-story houses in the $200,000 price range with stairways six inches narrower than required by the building code. The appraiser found the contractor's opinion that no damage was caused by the narrow stairway to be a bit unrealistic; he also found the owner's contention that the property was damaged in the amount of $50,000 to be a bit of an overstatement. Therefore, the appraiser resorted to the classic paired data technique to arrive at a proper, supportable adjustment for the narrow stairway.

Sales of older, two-story dwellings were investigated. Many of these structures were built before the building code was adopted and some had stairways narrower than the minimum width required by the current building code. Recent sales of older dwellings with narrow stairways were compared to sales of similar older dwellings with wider stairways. From this paired data analysis, the appraiser was able to develop a percentage to represent the diminution in the value of second-floor space caused by narrow stairways. For example, second-floor space may sell for the same price per square foot as first-floor space if the second-floor space is served by a stairway of adequate width; second-floor space served by a narrow stairway, however, might sell for only 85% of the square foot price of first-floor space.

By using the paired data technique, an appraiser can often develop a measurable, supportable adjustment for an unusual or unique property feature. It would, of course, be preferable to make a direct comparison between a sale property and the property under appraisal, but in valuations for litigation appraisers often encounter situations that are simply one of a kind. In these cases the appraiser must apply ingenuity and common sense to develop measurable, supportable, and appropriate adjustment factors.

APPRAISER'S NEGLIGENCE

"As happens in any profession, the conduct or performance of an appraiser occasionally falls short of the standards established by the profession or the expectations of society at large. When such a situation is discovered, it normally is policed satisfactorily within the 'fraternity.' Now and then, however, an appraiser will find himself/herself unhappily defending a lawsuit brought by an equally unhappy employer, client, or other seemingly aggrieved person."[2] This type of litigation is becoming increasingly prevalent. Historically, appraisers have been defended successfully on the grounds that appraising was not a true profession, that there was no universal standard of conduct for appraisers, and that the appraisal of property is merely an opinion.

Times have changed. The appraisal of real estate is becoming recognized as a true profession. With the required incorporation of the Uniform Standards[3] into every state's appraisal licensing/certification law, a minimum standard of professional conduct now exists and the courts have a standard with which to measure the conduct of individual appraisers. No longer can appraisers hide behind statements such as, "You paid for my opinion and that's what you got." Nor can they avoid liability by including unreasonable assumptions or limiting conditions in their appraisal reports. The inclusion of the recommended disclaimer in an appraisal report concerning the assumed absence of property contamination is not going to save the appraiser who ignored obvious signs of contamination during the property inspection.[4]

A discussion of appraisers' liability for errors in their work product is beyond the scope of this work.[5] It is the measure of liability that is important here. In some liability cases, appraisers are not required as expert witnesses because the measure of liability is not based on the diminution or difference in value. For instance, in one case an appraiser was retained to furnish the client with an appraisal for mortgage loan purposes. The appraiser made a computational error,

2. Stanley J. Fineman, "Law and the Appraiser," *The Appraisal Journal* (October 1981), 603.

3. The Appraisal Foundation, *Uniform Standards of Professional Appraisal Practice.*

4. *Standards of Professional Appraisal Practice of the Appraisal Institute*, Guide Note 8, "The Consideration of Hazardous Substances in the Appraisal Process." See also, The Appraisal Foundation, *Uniform Standards of Professional Appraisal Practice*, Advisory Opinion G-9.

5. For a discussion of appraiser liability, see Fineman, 603–611 and John F. Shampton, Theresa H. Waller, and Neil G. Waller, "Appraiser Malpractice: Sources of Liability and Damage," *The Appraisal Journal* (July 1988), 399–405. See also, Bibliography and Suggested Reading sections of "The Appraiser's Legal Liabilities," seminar workbook, Appraisal Institute, 1992.

which was discovered several months later before the loan was closed. The court ruled that the appraiser was liable for the costs incurred by the client, in reference to the appraised property, between the date of the first report and the date of the corrected report; these costs amounted to $256,250.01[6].

Many appraiser liability cases do require appraisal services because the measure of damage is the difference between the market value of the property as described (and/or certified) by the appraiser and the market value of the property in its *as is* condition. It has been ruled that the cost to cure is admissible as some evidence of diminished value, but this cost is not the controlling factor.[7] In liability cases, as in condemnation trials, the cost to cure is a proper measure of damage when it does not exceed the diminution in market value.

Like many appraisals made in conjunction with pending litigation, appraisals made for appraiser negligence cases are identical to appraisals made for condemnation trials using the federal, or before and after, rule. The appraiser assumes the property existed in the before situation as it was described by the defendant-appraiser in his appraisal report. The after appraisal estimates the value of the property in its actual, as is, condition.

An appraiser may also be asked to estimate the market value of a property with, and without, knowledge of allegedly critical market data which the defendant-appraiser negligently overlooked. Appraisers may also be asked to testify to the proper application of a particular appraisal technique or the proper application of the Uniform Standards and to the effect, if any, that misapplication of the technique or standard may have on a property value estimate.

AD VALOREM TAXATION

As stated previously, the ownership of real estate carries with it certain rights, commonly referred to as the *bundle of rights*. The bundle of rights is limited because some rights are retained by the sovereign, including the sovereign's right of taxation.

Over the years, the ownership of real estate has, at least in the eyes of many, become synonymous with wealth and, of course, there is no more fertile area to collect taxes than from the wealthy. Ad valorem (i.e., according to value) real estate taxation is a natural extension of this philosophy. Appraisers are often asked by assessing authorities, and by property owners, to appraise property and to testify to its value for ad valorem tax purposes. All ad valorem taxing authorities work from a base figure identified as market value. In some jurisdictions a property's assessed value is 100% of market value, while in others the assessed value is "...a statutorily determined percentage of market value."[8]

The procedure a property owner follows to appeal the assessor's determination of value varies from jurisdiction to jurisdiction. Generally, however, an appraiser who has completed an appraisal for the property owner should ask for a conference with the assessor. If an informal conference can be held before the

6. *Breckenridge Hotels Corp. v. Real Estate Research Corp.*, 452 F.Supp. 529 (E.D. Mo. 1978), *vacated at request of parties upon settlement*, 465 F.Supp. 385 (F.D. Mo. 1978).

7. *Alva v. Cloninger*, 277 S.E.2d 535 (N.C. 1981).

8. American Institute of Real Estate Appraisers and the Society of Real Estate Appraisers, *Real Estate Appraisal Terminology*, rev. ed., Byrl N. Boyce, ed. (Cambridge, Mass.: Ballinger Publishing Co., 1981), 19.

assessment roll is closed, the appraiser may be able to convince the assessor that his value estimate is correct and that the prior assessed value of the property should be abandoned or modified to conform to this new value estimate.

One reason such a conference can be effective is that the assessed value of property is usually arrived at using mass appraisal procedures, which give considerable weight to the cost approach, sometimes to the complete exclusion of the sales comparison and income capitalization approaches. The appraiser's estimate of value, on the other hand, is specific to the individual property, is based on all the approaches to value, and is probably much better documented than the assessed value. Another reason an informal conference can produce results is that the assessor, like all appraisers, is more likely to admit and correct an error in the privacy of his own office than he would be if he were called upon to defend the assessed value before a hearing board.

Even if the assessment roll has been closed, and the assessor cannot change the roll unless ordered to do so by the hearing board or board of equalization, a prehearing conference can still be effective. If the assessor is convinced that the appraiser's value estimate is correct, the assessor can join in the owner's request to the board of equalization and the assessed value can be altered to coincide with the appraiser's estimate of value.

For an appraiser/assessor conference to be effective, the appraiser must, of course, have a good working relationship with the local assessor. To develop and maintain such a relationship, the appraiser must never be an advocate for anyone or anything other than his opinion of value. The appraiser must always treat the assessor with professional courtesy and realize that the assessor, like himself, only wants to find the right answer. If someone is going to allege incompetence on the part of the assessor, let the attorney do it during the hearing process. In fact, it is generally best that the attorney not discuss the matter with the assessor until the hearing or at least not until shortly before the hearing. It is usually more effective to keep the discussion on a nonadversarial, appraiser-to-appraiser basis, at least until all hope of convincing the assessor is extinguished.

The appraisal of real estate for ad valorem tax purposes calls for a straightforward estimate of market value. The only change in procedure required of the appraiser is in the application of the income capitalization approach. The stabilized net income derived from the operation of the property in question cannot be estimated because one major expense of owning property is real estate taxes, and these taxes cannot be known so long as the assessed value of the property is being contested. Consequently, the appraiser must estimate the net income of the property before the payment of real estate taxes and then add the real estate tax factor to the overall capitalization rate to arrive at the indicated value of the property by the income capitalization approach.

For example, assume that the appraiser's analysis indicates that an overall rate of return of 11% is appropriate for properties similar to the one being appraised. Further assume that real estate taxes on these properties are approximately $18.50 per $1,000 of market value. If the property being appraised is producing a net income before real estate taxes of $15,000 per year, the indicated value of the property will be approximately $116,700, computed as follows:

Overall capitalization rate	0.1100
Tax rate ($18.50 ÷ $1,000)	0.0185
Total rate to be applied to net income before real estate taxes	0.1285
Indicated property value ($15,000 net income before taxes ÷ 0.1285)	$116,732
Rounded	$116,700

These calculations can be checked by deducting the real estate tax expense from the net income before payment of real estate taxes to arrive at the true net income; this net income is then capitalized at the 11% overall rate indicated by market data. The computations follow.

Net income before real estate taxes	$15,000.00
Real estate taxes ($116.732 thousand x $18.50)	2,159.54
Net income	$12,840.46
Indicated property value ($12,840.46 ÷ 0.11)	$ 116,732
Rounded	$ 116,700

Hearing and appeal procedures vary, but usually an initial hearing is held before a local hearing board or board of equalization. The decision of this board can generally be appealed by either party to a state hearing examiner or a state tax appeals board. The final appeal is made to the court.

LOCAL IMPROVEMENT DISTRICTS

Local government agencies have also found the taxation of real estate to be an effective method of financing local improvement projects. This type of real estate tax is often referred to as a *special assessment* and is limited to property within a specifically created taxing district, known as a *local improvement district* (LID).

Through a local improvement district, a public agency finances an improvement project by assessing the property owners directly affected by the project. This type of assessment falls within the government's power of taxation, not the power of eminent domain.[9] In some states the amount of the assessment cannot exceed the benefit accruing to the property.[10] In other states the only criterion appears to be that the cost of the project must be assessed on all of the parcels in the local improvement district in proportion to some equitable ratio, e.g., based on the number of square feet, acres, or front feet; zone and termini; or assessed value. Some jurisdictions specify by statute the methods of cost proportionment that are equitable and/or defensible.

9. *Fallbrook Irr. Dist. v. Bradley*, 164 U.S. 112 (1896).

10. *Waitaker & Co. v. Sewer Improvement District No. 1*, 221 F.2d 649 (8th Cir. 1955).

For instance, in specifying the zone and termini method of assessment, a Washington statute requires "the cost and expenses shall be assessed upon all the property in accordance with the special benefits conferred thereon in proportion to area and distance back from the marginal line of the public way or area improved."[11] The area within the district is divided into zones radiating from the improvements and each zone is assessed at a different rate. For example, consider three parcels in the LID shown in Figure 22.5. Assume that the outermost boundary of the LID is 200 feet from the street and four zones within the district are designated by the municipality. The assessment is to be computed at $1.00 per square foot for Zone 1, $0.75 per square foot for Zone 2, $0.50 per square foot for Zone 3, and $0.25 per square foot for Zone 4.

FIGURE 22.5 LOCAL IMPROVEMENT DISTRICT ASSESSMENT ZONE AND TERMINI METHOD

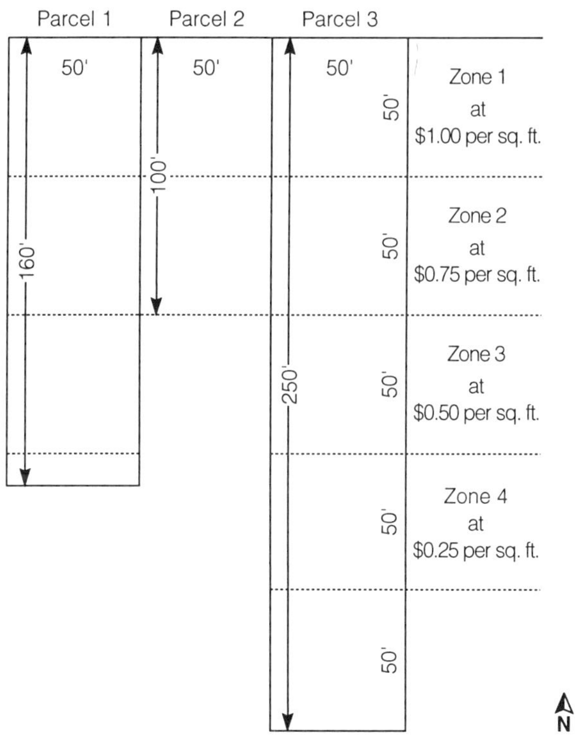

The results of this assessment plan are calculated in the following table.

11. R.C.W. 35.44.010 (Wash.).

Zone	Parcel 1	Parcel 2	Parcel 3
1	$2,500	$2,500	$2,500
2	1,875	1,875	1,875
3	1,250	0	1,250
4	125	0	625
Total assessments	$5,750	$4,375	$6,250

This formula is similar to the outdated 4-3-2-1 rule formerly used by tax assessors.

Appraisers are most likely to be involved in this type of situation in jurisdictions which require that the special benefit to a property equal or exceed the special assessment placed on the property. Because we are a litigation-oriented society and LID laws have been abused by local governments in the past, LID assessments and whole LID projects are frequently challenged. This has caused some local agencies to request before and after appraisals of all properties within a proposed LID taxing district so that the agency will be prepared to defend assessments when they are challenged. Again, benefits are measured using the before and after valuation procedures applied in federal condemnation.

INCOME, GIFT, AND ESTATE TAXES

In addition to the ad valorem taxes assessed directly against real estate, any income generated by real estate is subject to taxation through the real estate owner's income tax. Therefore, real estate valuation decisions are also needed in conjunction with income tax regulations. Because federal income tax regulations are complex and in a constant state of flux, real estate appraisers are advised not to make appraisals in conjunction with income tax matters without the assistance of a tax accountant or tax lawyer. A tax advisor may be retained by the client or by the appraiser.

In regard to income tax matters, the appraiser's function is generally in the area of cost allocation rather than market value estimation. The allocation of land and improvement value or fixture and equipment value is sometimes needed for depreciation purposes. Or an appraiser may be asked to allocate property value among various parts of the larger parcel when an owner purchases a parcel of real estate and then resells a portion of it. Such an allocation is used to determine the owner's cost basis in the portion of the tract sold.

An appraiser might also be retained to estimate the casualty loss suffered by a property owner. Casualty losses generally result from damage caused by fire, flood, wind, or other natural phenomena. If the property owner is not reimbursed for such a loss by an insurance company, the loss can be taken as a deduction for income tax purposes. The appraiser's assignment is to estimate the market value of the property before and after the loss. The procedure is identical to a before and after appraisal made for federal condemnation proceedings.

An appraiser may also be retained in a dispute between a taxpayer and the Internal Revenue Service. For example, assume a taxpayer purchased a tract of swampland for speculation. After two years of land use hearings, the taxpayer was given a permit to use the site for dumping solid waste. The land was about 25 feet below grade and had considerable capacity for such material. The taxpayer then entered into a contract with a local logging firm to pick up its solid wood waste and dispose of it on the land.

The taxpayer deducted the depreciation and maintenance of equipment, the wages paid to truck drivers and equipment operators, and other costs as business expenses on his federal income tax return. During a routine audit, the Internal Revenue Service ruled that not all of these expenses could be deducted; they considered half of the expenses to be capital improvements to the land being filled with wood waste. The taxpayer was unable to sway the Internal Revenue Service so he retained an appraiser and asked that two appraisals of the property be made: 1) an estimate of the market value of the site as if no wood waste had been placed on it and 2) an estimate of the market value of the site in its *as is* condition, filled with about 12 feet of wood waste.

The procedure applied by the appraiser was identical to the procedure used in a before and after appraisal for a federal condemnation case. The appraiser found that local land use authorities would not allow any construction on the site once it was filled because of the nature of the fill material, which has a tendency to produce methane gas as it decays. The appraiser's analysis of market sales of similar disposal sites indicated that the site would not increase in value as it was filled, as the Internal Revenue Service contended, but would decline in value. Based on these findings, the Internal Revenue Service reversed its ruling. In fact, the taxpayer was able to amend his past tax returns to reflect the declining value of the waste site as it was being filled.

When property is given as a gift, it may become subject to federal gift taxes. If a gift is given to a charitable organization, the current value of the gift may be deductible by the grantor for federal tax purposes. Historically, some taxpayers have abused the gift tax laws by ascribing excessive values to property given to charitable organizations. In response, the Internal Revenue Service has adopted strict requirements regarding the documentation of the value of such gifts.[12] An appraiser who conducts an appraisal for gift tax purposes must be totally familiar with this regulation.

Some of the more important requirements of the regulation, from the appraiser's standpoint, are:

1. The value of any gift of property claimed to have a value in excess of $5,000 must be substantiated by a "qualified appraisal."
2. A "qualified appraisal" is an appraisal that was prepared within certain time parameters, is signed by a "qualified appraiser," and contains an adequate description of the property and its physical condition.

12. Treas. Reg. §1.170A-1.

3. The appraisal must include the date (or expected date) of the donation, any restrictions to be placed on the property by the donor, the qualifications of the appraiser, a statement that the appraisal was prepared for income tax purposes, the date of the appraisal, the estimate of fair market value (as defined in the regulation), and the method of valuation used to determine the value of the property, including the specific basis for the valuation such as comparable sales transactions.
4. The appraiser must certify that the fee for the appraisal was not a contingent fee.

Although the taxpayer does not have to submit an appraisal of the donated property to the IRS with his tax return, he must submit an appraisal summary signed by the appraiser. The appraiser must certify a number of items in this summary, including the fact that an intentional false or fraudulent overstatement of the value of the property may subject the appraiser to a civil penalty for aiding and abetting an understatement of tax liability and an acknowledgment that the appraiser may have future appraisals "disregarded pursuant to 31 USC §330(c)."

The estate or wealth of a deceased person is also taxed according to value; such taxes are commonly referred to as *death taxes*. Real estate is, of course, included in the assets of many estates.

Estate, or death, taxes are computed as a percentage of the market value of the assets of an estate. Therefore, the appraiser's assignment is generally a straightforward estimation of market value. It is critical that the appraiser determine the desired effective date of the appraisal. The heirs have the option of having the assets of the estate valued as of the date of death or as of a date six months after the date of death. Although the value of most real property will not change materially over a six-month period, there are exceptions. For instance, in one case the value of 600 acres of harvestable timberland declined more than 20% between the owner's death and six months thereafter due to a rapid decline in the stumpage value of the timber on the tract.

In making appraisals for estate tax purposes, the IRS has recognized that, under certain circumstances, liquidation value can be a valid indicator. In other circumstances, the real estate holdings of an estate and their historical method of operation may qualify them to be viewed as an active trade or business. In this case it might be proper to view all of the properties held by the estate as a single integrated entity, which may have a "market value" less than the sum of the values of the individual properties if viewed independently. Partial interests in real estate held by an estate should be valued at the price at which the interest could be sold on the open market. Thus, a 50% interest in a parcel of real estate may not have a market value equal to one-half of the value of the property.

Condemnors often complain that they are at a disadvantage in many instances because condemnees often have access to the condemnor's full appraisal report before the condemnee's appraisal is even begun. The condemnee's appraiser has the advantage of knowing the conclusions of the condemnor's valuation expert and the data and analysis upon which the condemnor's valuation is based. This complaint has some justification. In the case of income tax disputes, however, it is the government agency (the IRS) that has the advantage because it has the taxpayer's appraisal before it takes a position or orders an appraisal. In fact, the IRS position is especially advantageous because the taxpayer's initial return, and thus his appraisal report, are treated as an admission against interest.

In a typical condemnation action, the government has the option of abandoning its initial appraisal, and its initial appraiser, in favor of another appraiser. The initial appraisal is not admissible in court unless the condemnee wants to call the first appraiser as its own witness. Even if the condemnee does so, he is generally not allowed to inform the trier of fact that the appraiser was initially retained to appraise the property by the government. In a tax appeal case, the taxpayer is essentially precluded from this course of action. The IRS can use the property owner's initial return and appraisal as an admission by the taxpayer that the property in question has the minimum value represented in the initial appraisal.

Experience suggests that the IRS uses its advantage to the fullest extent. In many instances the taxpayer's appraisal is reviewed by an IRS staff appraiser whose intent is to find fault with the methodology and analysis of the appraiser, but only if rejecting the appraiser's methodology and analysis will result in a higher property value. In some instances an IRS appraisal is a rebuttal to the taxpayer's appraisal, rejecting the elements of the taxpayer's appraisal that support a lower value in favor of the elements of the appraisal that suggest a higher value. Therefore, appraisers who make appraisals for taxpayers should assume that their reports will be reviewed not by an objective appraisal professional, but rather by an advocate who is bent on extracting the highest possible value from the data available. The IRS is not likely to inform taxpayers that they have overvalued their real estate on their estate tax returns.

Because of the complexity of the tax laws and the adversarial manner in which taxpayers' appraisal reports are viewed, appraisers who make appraisals for taxpayers should use extreme care in preparing their appraisal reports and *never* prepare such a report without first obtaining guidance from a professional tax accountant or lawyer.

LAND USE HEARINGS

Included in the bundle of rights inherent in the ownership of real estate is the owner's right of use and occupancy. However, through the use of its police power, the sovereign has reserved the right to control how the owner of a parcel of real estate uses it. The government's control of land use is generally exercised by the adoption of land use regulations intended to protect the public's health, safety, and general welfare. In other words, land use regulations effectively place the owner's right to use land in a subservient position to the interests of the general public. Public land use regulations can have an immediate and dramatic impact on real estate values.

Land use regulations are intended, at least in theory, to maintain and protect real estate values. This is in the public interest because higher real estate values mean more taxes can be collected. However, because land use regulations are written by people, they do not always produce the desired effect. Appraisers are sometimes called upon to appraise individual properties that have been affected by a land use regulation or may be affected by a proposed land use regulation in the future. An appraiser may also be asked to analyze and estimate the probable impact of a proposed land use regulation on a specific property and to testify to his conclusions before the decision-making body, an appeal board, or even a court.

Appraisers are increasingly requested to become involved in land use matters and to testify at land use hearings. These requests can come from proponents of a proposed land use regulation, from opponents of a proposed land use regulation, or from the individuals or agencies empowered to act on such matters.

Appraisers are more often asked to make a general analysis of the impact of a proposed land use regulation on real estate values than to estimate the market value of a specific parcel of real estate before and after the adoption of a specific ordinance. For example, a planning commission might request an analysis of how a funeral home would affect the value of abutting or nearby single-family dwellings in a residential neighborhood. The results of such an analysis might help the commission determine whether it should allow funeral homes to locate in residential areas without any special permit, by special-use permit only, or not at all. Generalized appraisal studies may be requested in connection with zoning decisions, shoreline management or wetlands permits, board of adjustment decisions, comprehensive land use planning decisions, and forest practices decisions.

Many divisions of government now require that both economic impact statements and environmental impact statements be prepared for major real estate projects. In preparing an economic impact statement, the appraiser may be asked to estimate the market value of the real estate project as if complete. This information will be used to determine increases in the area's real estate tax base and, thus, the increase in the amount of ad valorem tax collected. The appraiser might also be asked to analyze similar projects to determine their impact on surrounding land values. Appraisers are sometimes requested to assist in estimating the potential gross sales of a proposed commercial project to assess possible increases in sales, business and occupation, income, or other applicable taxes.

Most land use actions require public hearings. Whether or not the appraiser has submitted a written report to the client, he will generally be asked to make an oral presentation of his findings at the public hearing, assuming, of course, that these findings and conclusions support the client's position.

Public awareness of the impact land use can have on our environment has increased and the number of land use and environmental lawsuits has skyrocketed. This trend has been strengthened by a number of factors: the advent of site-specific or project-specific land use controls; the litigious attitude prevalent in our society; the "not in my backyard" syndrome; the "I've got mine—the hell with you" perspective; and the formation of politically active "tree-hugger societies." The lawsuits will continue until the courts lay down some definitive rules identifying where the rights of special interest groups stop and the property rights of the individual begin. Until that time, appraisers will continue to play an active role in analyzing the economic impact of land use decisions.

It is important for appraisers to remember that, when they act as unbiased professionals, they must set their personal beliefs on social issues aside and focus their attention on the *economic* impact of the land use decisions.

SUMMARY

It would be impossible to list all the different types of civil litigation in which real estate appraisal services might be required. Those discussed in this chapter represent a mere sampling of the situations in which an appraiser might be asked to make an appraisal and to testify at a hearing or civil proceeding. Even when a court is hearing a case relating to appraiser negligence and liability, real estate appraisers are needed to make appraisals and testify.

The foregoing discussion reveals a pattern as to how damage is measured in litigation cases. In nearly all cases, the market value of the property before the damage less the market value of the property after the damage represents the award due the complainants.

Because some civil litigation cases involving real estate are unique in nature, all the answers cannot be found in this, or any other, text. Occasionally appraisers encounter appraisal problems for which there are no written rules of procedure. This is when they must use their imagination, ingenuity, and common sense to face the challenge and earn their fees. Before applying any new or imaginative methodology, however, an appraiser should discuss his plans with another qualified appraiser. In this way he can test the validity of his approach before it sees the light of day, or the dark corridors of the courthouse.

CHAPTER 23

Standards of Practice

Two important statements appear in the Preamble to the Uniform Standards of Professional Appraisal Practice: "It is essential that a professional appraiser arrive at and communicate his or her analyses, opinions, and advice in a manner that will be meaningful to the client and will not be misleading in the marketplace....The importance of the role of the appraiser places ethical obligations on those who serve in this capacity."[1]

In the past codes of ethics for appraisers were developed by various professional appraisal organizations. These codes and their enforcement varied to some degree and only those appraisers who were members of these professional organizations were subject to their codes. However, with the creation of The Appraisal Foundation and the adoption of its Uniform Standards of Professional Appraisal Practice (USPAP), the ethical obligations of appraisers have become somewhat standardized. Because the states have incorporated the Uniform Standards into their appraiser licensing/certification laws, most professional appraisers are required to abide by the same standards.[2]

Nearly all of the major professional appraisal organizations have adopted the Uniform Standards. Some, such as the Appraisal Institute, have supplemented these standards to ensure that their members comply with the organization's unique requirements.

The Ethics Provision of the Uniform Standards is short and to the point. It covers four major areas: conduct, management, confidentiality, and record keeping. It provides that an appraiser must perform appraisal services competently, must not accept contingent fees for appraisal services, must not advertise falsely,

1. The Appraisal Foundation, *Uniform Standards of Professional Appraisal Practice* (USPAP), 1994 ed., Preamble.
2. Some states do not require licensing or certification of all appraisers, but appraisers who do not become licensed or certified are not eligible to make many types of appraisals. As a practical matter, these appraisers should not be retained to perform litigation appraisals.

must protect the confidential nature of the appraiser–client relationship, and must retain written records of all appraisals and other assignments for at least five years after completion of the assignment or two years after final disposition of any judicial proceeding in which testimony was given.[3] The Competency Provision sets forth the actual standards of practice to which an appraiser must adhere in performing appraisal services.

"Ethics, by definition, are standards imposed on persons presumed from the outset to be honest."[4] A code of ethics "cannot make an honest appraiser out of a dishonest one. But codes of ethics...never were intended for that purpose."[5] All standards of appraisal practice, whether promulgated by The Appraisal Foundation or a professional appraisal organization, define the minimum level of appraisal performance required. They are in a continual state of change due to the development of new appraisal theory and techniques.

Codes of ethics and written standards of practice are not established to restrict a professional's activities, but to help professionals understand the minimum standards expected of them by society as a whole and by other members of the profession. In the final analysis, however, the most effective incentive to a true professional is a personal desire for individual excellence, the respect of one's peers, and the confidence of society.

The codes of ethics established by major appraisal organizations are generally much more detailed than those of The Appraisal Foundation. The Code of Professional Ethics of the Appraisal Institute is shown in Table 23.1. The code itself is brief, but it is supplemented with ethical rules and explanatory comments. The

TABLE 23.1 APPRAISAL INSTITUTE CODE OF PROFESSIONAL ETHICS

CANON 1
A Member or an Affiliate must refrain from conduct that is detrimental to the Appraisal Institute, the real estate appraisal profession and the public.

CANON 2
A Member or an Affiliate must assist the Appraisal Institute in carrying out its responsibilities to the users of appraisal services and the public.

CANON 3
In the performance of an appraisal assignment, a Member or an Affiliate must develop and communicate each analysis and opinion without bias for the client's interest and without accommodation of his or her own interests.

CANON 4
A Member or an Affiliate must not violate the confidential nature of the appraiser-client relationship.

CANON 5
In promoting an appraisal practice and soliciting appraisal services, a Member or an Affiliate must use care to avoid advertising or solicitations that are misleading or otherwise contrary to the public interest.

CANON 6
A Member or an Affiliate must comply with the requirements of the Standards of Professional Appraisal Practice.

3. USPAP, 1994 ed., Ethics Provision.
4. J. B. Featherston, "Ethics: A Matter of Trust," *The Appraisal Journal* (July 1975), 328.
5. Ibid., 330.

Appraisal Institute also has its own Standards of Professional Appraisal Practice, which consist of the Uniform Standards plus supplemental standards with explanatory comments and guide notes. Table 23.2 shows the six standards of The Appraisal Foundation's Uniform Standards of Professional Appraisal Practice that relate to real estate appraisals. Again, these standards are supplemented with specific rules and considerable explanation.

TABLE 23.2 THE APPRAISAL FOUNDATION'S UNIFORM STANDARDS OF PROFESSIONAL APPRAISAL PRACTICE RELATING TO REAL ESTATE APPRAISALS

Standard 1
In developing a real property appraisal, an appraiser must be aware of, understand, and correctly employ those recognized methods and techniques that are necessary to produce a credible appraisal.

Standard 2
In reporting the results of a real property appraisal an appraiser must communicate each analysis, opinion, and conclusion in a manner that is not misleading.

Standard 3
In reviewing an appraisal and reporting the results of that review, an appraiser must form an opinion as to the adequacy and appropriateness of the report being reviewed and must clearly disclose the nature of the review process undertaken.

Standard 4
In performing real estate or real property consulting services, an appraiser must be aware of, understand, and correctly employ those recognized methods and techniques that are necessary to produce a credible result.

Standard 5
In reporting the results of a real estate or real property consulting service, an appraiser must communicate each analysis, opinion, and conclusion in a manner that is not misleading.

Standard 6
In developing a mass appraisal, an appraiser must be aware of, understand, and correctly employ those generally accepted methods and techniques necessary to produce and communicate credible appraisals.

Including a detailed discussion of codes of professional ethics and standards of professional appraisal practice in this text would not alter the conduct of certain individuals—the "professional actors" and "expert swearers" who have become familiar to courts and members of the legal profession. Therefore, this chapter will explore personal standards of practice, which go beyond the written standards set down by The Appraisal Foundation and various professional organizations.

THE WRITTEN REPORT

There is an ethical rule of the Appraisal Institute that relates to litigation appraisal work and therefore must be discussed. Ethical Rule 2-6 states:

> It is unethical to give testimony as to an appraisal opinion in a deposition or affidavit, or before any board, commission, tribunal or court, unless a written appraisal report or file memoranda is prepared prior to giving such testimony.[6]

Any written appraisal report must, of course, meet the content requirements of the Standards of Professional Appraisal Practice of The Appraisal Foundation and the Appraisal Institute. For purposes of the above ethical rule, a *file memoranda*:

> shall include in statement, outline or reference form, with work sheets, data sheets and related material, sufficient information to demonstrate substantial compliance with the Standards of Professional Appraisal Practice. In most cases sufficient information should include: identification/brief description of real estate; real property interest being appraised; purpose of the appraisal; definition of value being estimated; effective date of the appraisal; scope of the appraisal; all assumptions and limiting conditions; information considered, procedures followed, and reasoning in support of analyses, opinions and conclusions; highest and best use; rationale for exclusion of any of the valuation approaches; and any additional information required to demonstrate compliance with the Standards of Professional Appraisal Practice; and appraisal conclusions.[7]

Because of this rule, an appraiser *cannot* accept an appraisal assignment if the client, or the client's legal counsel, asks for a letter of opinion only or requests that the appraiser not prepare a written report or written file memoranda. This is as it should be. Such requests are not made to minimize appraisal fees; they are an attempt to circumvent the court's established rules of discovery. An appraiser should not cooperate in such attempts because "a prohibition against discovery of information held by expert witnesses produces in acute form the very evils that discovery has been created to prevent."[8]

When appraisers recognize that they will probably be subjected to a *subpoena duces tecum*, which will require them to appear for a deposition *and bring their appraisal file* and all other documents pertinent to the case with them for inspection by opposing counsel, they will come to realize that preparing a file memoranda instead of a formal appraisal report will cause them nothing but grief. An appraiser might as well do it right in the first place and prepare a proper appraisal report.

If legal counsel asks the appraiser to include or exclude a specific piece of information, analysis, or conclusion from the appraisal report, this request must be considered in light of the appraiser's ethical obligation to prepare a report that meets the Standards of Professional Appraisal Practice and the code of ethics and will not be misleading to the client or a third party reading the report. Unless the appraiser can answer "no" to the question, "Would I be embarrassed if this omission (or insertion) came to light during my cross-examination or in a peer review of my report?" the appraiser is well advised to refuse the attorney's request.

6. *Code of Professional Ethics of the Appraisal Institute*, Ethical Rule 2-6, 1994 ed.
7. Ibid., Definitions.
8. Federal Rule Civil Procedure 26 (Notes of Advisory Committee on Rules 1970 amendment).

ADVOCACY

It has been said that, as appraisers, "we don't win or lose."[9] In fact, some suggest that appraisers should not use the words "win" or "lose" in discussing a court proceeding because to do so indicates advocacy for the client's interest. The mere use of these words, however, does not mean the appraiser is the client's advocate. Appraisers must take particular care to ensure that their analyses, opinions, and conclusions concerning real estate are arrived at without bias in favor of the client or the accommodation of their personal interests. But, after arriving at an unbiased analysis, opinion, or conclusion, the appraiser may defend or advocate the correctness of his or her value estimate.

Like it or not, the statement "No, Mr. Appraiser, in court you don't win, nor do you lose"[10] is not necessarily correct. Every appraiser who testifies in court has a job to do and he is assisted in this job by legal counsel. The appraiser must convince the trier of fact that his estimate of value is correct; in so doing, the incorrectness, or error, of the other appraiser's estimate becomes apparent. If the appraiser does not believe his estimate of value is correct and the other appraiser's estimate is incorrect, he should not be on the witness stand. When an appraiser says, "We won our case." he is not admitting advocacy; rather, he is saying "I prevailed in proving the correctness of my appraisal analyses, opinions, and conclusions and thereby convinced the trier of fact that the other appraiser's estimate of value was wrong. My attorney teammate and I won."

Admittedly, the terms "win" and "lose" should be used with great care when discussing the outcome of a trial with the uninitiated. No explanation of the terms is necessary, however, for the condemnation appraiser or the attorney who specializes in condemnation. In discussions with others, the terms either should not be used or they should explained as they relate to the appraiser. Appraisers must not only avoid advocacy, they must avoid the *appearance* of advocacy. For instance, to avoid the appearance of advocacy when none exists, appraisers who appear as expert witnesses in a trial are advised not to join the attorney at the counsel table, either before or after the testimony, because the trier of fact or the spectators may construe this as an indication of advocacy on the part of the appraiser.

Appraisers must understand that they may be put under considerable pressure to become advocates for their clients' interests. After all, the appraiser is working for two very strong advocates—the client and the client's legal counsel. "Advocacy on the part of the appraiser is a common cause of divergency [in valuation testimony]. It is understandable when one considers the economic and social atmosphere in which the appraiser functions."[11] The appraiser must make it

9. C. Robert Boucher, "We Don't Win or Lose," *The Appraisal Journal* (October 1963), 501.

10. Ibid.

11. *Divergences in Right-of-Way Valuations*, National Cooperative Highway Research Program Report No. 126 (Washington, D.C.: Highway Research Board, 1971), 12.

clear when he accepts the assignment that his employment and/or the appraisal fee are in no way contingent on his conclusions or on any settlement or award. For this reason, and many others, the appraiser should insist on a written contract with the client.

The appraiser must also be careful to avoid what may be termed *reverse advocacy*. Appraisers who prepare appraisal reports for condemnors often respond to questions about a specific adjustment, analysis, or conclusion by saying, "I gave the property owner the benefit of the doubt." The next question put to the appraiser should be "*Why?*" An appraiser is not apt to say "I was making the appraisal for the seller so I gave the purchaser the benefit of the doubt." or "I was appraising for the bank so I gave the borrower the benefit of the doubt." or "I was appraising for the taxpayer so I gave the IRS the benefit of the doubt." Bankers, the IRS, and property owners (and their attorneys) can look after themselves. They need no help from appraisers.

An appraiser's estimate of market value should be exactly the same irrespective of the function of the appraisal or the parties involved. Similarly, market value does not change because a property is being condemned for a park rather than for a solid waste disposal site. If an appraiser gives the benefit of the doubt to either party to a transaction when developing adjustments, analyses, or conclusions, the resulting value estimate will be distorted and not representative of market value. When a question concerning a specific adjustment is asked, it deserves a response that relates to supporting market data, not one that suggests advocacy or bias.

Cross-Examination of the Opposing Party's Appraiser

As mentioned in Chapters 20 and 21, the appraiser should be prepared to assist counsel in preparing to cross-examine the opposing party's appraiser. Some appraisers refuse to do this because they believe that, with their help, counsel could cross-examine the opposing party's appraiser so effectively as to cast doubt on the real estate appraisal profession as a whole. If the appraiser holds this belief, this must be conveyed to the prospective client and to the client's legal counsel before the appraiser accepts the assignment. The client and his counsel must decide whether to retain the appraiser under these circumstances.

Appraisers who do assist counsel in preparing to cross-examine the opposing party's appraiser generally feel that, if this appraiser is honest and well-prepared, an effective cross-examination will only demonstrate that two qualified experts can have a difference of opinion. This fact, in and of itself, will not discredit the profession as a whole. Also, the appraiser generally takes the position that the analyses, opinions, and conclusions he has developed are well-supported and correct and, in view of the available data and the use of proper techniques, the other appraiser must be wrong. If there were no difference of opinion, there would be no trial. These appraisers feel obligated to assist counsel in showing the trier of fact that it is the other appraiser who is wrong. After all, if he is wrong, he deserves whatever he gets.

APPRAISAL FEE

Most appraisal contracts will provide for a flat appraisal fee or a per diem charge for the actual appraisal and the preparation of a written appraisal report. The contracts also provide for an additional per diem charge for appraisal updating, if necessary, pretrial conferences, preparation for trial, and trial time. Some appraisers specify a higher per diem rate for court testimony than they do for other appraisal services. Admittedly, court testimony is a nerve-wracking experience, but many believe that there is little, if any, justification for charging more for this appraisal service than for others.

Appraisers who charge a higher per diem rate for court work attempt to justify the practice by pointing out that trial work interrupts the appraiser's schedule and last-minute continuances are often encountered; thus, a higher rate is reasonable. They may also argue that in other appraisal work they usually have some control over the timing of their tasks, while in a trial the appraiser is at the mercy of the attorney and the court. Nevertheless, it must be recognized that paying the appraiser more than his regular rate may be viewed as a means to ensure that his opinion is a favorable one.

Opposing counsel will often try to make this practice appear suspect. He may ask, "Isn't it a fact, Mr. Appraiser, that if you were in your office or out in the field doing appraisal work you would be earning $150 per hour, but here on the witness stand you are charging $250 per hour?" From this question, which will be reinforced by opposing counsel during closing argument, the trier of fact may infer that the appraiser had a personal, monetary interest in creating a disparity in value between the parties to ensure that a trial would ensue.

If an appraiser is retained by a condemnee after the condemnor has made an offer of settlement to the condemnee, the appraiser should be made aware of the offer. The appraiser should be certain that the terms of the appraisal contract permit him initially to perform only the work necessary to determine if the results of the appraisal will be of value to the client. Although it is not actually a violation of professional standards to develop a complete appraisal report knowing it will be of no value to the client, it certainly should be a violation of the appraiser's personal ethics. Once the appraiser has completed enough work to develop a range of value, he should confer with the client and the client's attorney before proceeding with the assignment. Even if the appraisal will result in a value estimate higher than the condemnor's offer, it may not be economically wise for the client to spend the funds necessary to have the appraisal completed. Considering anticipated attorney and appraisal fees, as well as other trial costs, and the impact on any relocation allowances, it may be impractical for the client to proceed with the appraisal.

In light of these factors, it is sometimes advisable for an appraiser hired by a condemnee initially to enter into a contract for an evaluation of the offer tendered by the condemnor, rather than a full appraisal. The appraiser first evaluates the reasonableness of the offer; if the offer is unreasonable, he should indicate how unreasonable it is. He can then estimate how much it will cost to complete a documented appraisal report of the property in question and, perhaps, recommend further steps to be taken by the client. The appraiser may suggest that the client retain legal counsel, continue negotiations without a written appraisal report, or ask that the condemnor reconsider its original appraisal. The appraiser may also help the client gather additional market data which will be submitted to the condemnor for its consideration.

The above procedure should not be confused with an appraiser's acceptance of a contingency assignment or a contingency fee.

The Appraisal Institute's Code of Professional Ethics addresses employment in phases with the following comment:

> To illustrate the point involved, let us assume the following facts: A is the owner of Blackacre on X-date and on that date the state highway department files a condemnation proceeding to take a right-of-way running diagonally across the parcel. The highway department then offers to pay A the sum of $100,000 for the taking and $300,000 for damage to the remainder. In support of this offer, the highway department delivers to A an appraisal report indicating that the value of the taking was $100,000 and that the damage to the remainder was $300,000. A believes that the value of the taking and the damage to the remainder was much greater; however, it is a very complicated issue and A does not have the expertise needed to evaluate the highway department's offer. A then contacts B, a professional real estate appraiser, and offers to hire B on the following basis: B is to review the appraisal submitted by the highway department and also make a preliminary appraisal of Blackacre on X-date for a fee computed on an hourly basis. If, on the basis of this preliminary appraisal, B arrives at an unbiased opinion that the value of the taking plus the damage to the remainder was substantially in excess of the offer of the highway department, A will retain B to prepare a complete appraisal for a fixed fee of $10,000. If, however, on the basis of this preliminary appraisal B arrives at an unbiased opinion that the value of the taking plus the damage to the remainder was not substantially different from the offer of the highway department, then B will not be retained to prepare a complete appraisal.
>
> If B accepts the proposal of A, B will not be in violation of the rule that prohibits the acceptance and performance of an assignment if such assignment "is contingent upon reporting a predetermined analysis or opinion." The assumed facts state that B must arrive at an unbiased opinion and communicate this opinion to A in an unbiased manner; therefore, despite the contingency, both the preliminary appraisal (a limited assignment) and the complete appraisal are required to be performed in strict accord with the Appraisal Institute rules that prohibit bias

in favor of the client. In this connection, however, it should be noted that there may be other rules applicable to the assumed facts and B would have to carefully consider and comply with all such rules before accepting the assignment.[12]

The appraiser seldom knows what the total appraisal fees will be until all testimony is complete and the attorneys begin final argument. However, it is strongly advised that the appraiser compute the total fees due as soon as he is excused by the court and make sure that a statement is hand delivered or faxed to the attorney's office as promptly as possible. If this is done, the appraiser's bill will be received in the attorney's office before the verdict is announced by the court. This prevents anyone from claiming that the appraisal fees were in any way contingent on the outcome of the trial. It also lessens the possibility that the client or his attorney will approach the appraiser and request a reduction of the fees because the verdict was unfavorable.

In accepting an appraisal assignment from a property owner in a condemnation case, the appraiser should recognize that the condemnee may not be able to pay the entire appraisal fee until the case is settled, either by negotiation or by trial. In such a situation, a schedule for the payment of appraisal fees should be drawn up before any appraisal work is done; this schedule should be included in the appraisal contract. Some appraisers feel it is their ethical obligation to make arrangements for appraisal fee payments that do not unduly burden the condemnee to ensure that the condemnee has the same access to professional appraisal services as the condemnor.

QUALIFICATIONS AND EXPERIENCE

It is, of course, unethical for appraisers to accept appraisal assignments for which they are not qualified by experience and/or training or to misrepresent their professional qualifications to imply nonexistent experience. If an appraiser is not qualified to accept an appraisal assignment, he may associate himself with a more qualified individual, assuming the client approves of this plan before entering into the appraisal contract. The appraiser must disclose any such professional assistance in the appraisal report, so as not to mislead the public. However, it is better for the appraiser to refuse the litigation assignment and acquire his experience and/or training in an assignment that will not involve litigation. It is often possible for an unqualified appraiser to associate himself with another appraiser with the required expertise in the specific area, but the unqualified appraiser cannot confer with the associated appraiser while under cross-examination on the witness stand.

When offered a litigation assignment, the appraiser should analyze his qualifications from two points of view. First, is the appraiser qualified by experience and/or training to make an appraisal of the property in dispute? Second, is the appraiser qualified to testify in court? Often appraisers will accept assignments

12. *Code of Professional Ethics of the Appraisal Institute*, Explanatory Comments Relating to Ethical Rule 3-3.

involving partial takings without knowing the jurisdictional rules of valuation to be applied. In other words, the appraiser might appraise only the portion of the property to be taken, neglecting to consider the larger parcel, remainder damages or benefits, or the impact of the specific public improvement for which the property is being taken.

Although an appraiser may be qualified to appraise a specific property, it does not necessarily follow that he is qualified to testify as an expert witness. Of course, an appraiser cannot gain experience as an expert witness without actually testifying. However, the appraiser can get valuable training by attending seminars on the subject or, better yet, by attending several civil litigation cases in which appraisers testify as expert witnesses. In this way the appraiser can learn court procedures before approaching the witness stand himself. He will know what to expect on direct examination and cross-examination and the different methodologies employed by expert valuation witnesses and attorneys. Knowledge acquired in this way is as valuable as any that could be gained at a seminar, and there is no tuition.

After the appraiser has attended a number of trials and feels confident that he has enough training to take the witness stand and testify effectively, he would be wise to start off slowly. Testifying to the market value of a single-family dwelling in a divorce proceeding is a good beginning. It is not advisable for the appraiser to start off by testifying in a partial taking condemnation case that involves complex legal and valuation matters and a great deal of money. The appraiser may be technically competent to take the stand but, without actual trial experience, he can be made to look (and feel) totally incompetent by a cross-examiner who is skilled, and perhaps ruthless.

In a simpler case involving real estate values such as a divorce proceeding, the cross-examiner may be as inexperienced in questioning a real estate valuation expert as the appraiser is in testifying. This situation provides a mutual learning experience for the appraiser and the attorney, and the experience will not be particularly painful for either.

LEGAL INSTRUCTIONS

"Instructions by the attorney to the appraiser on a matter of law are certainly a proper element to be expressed in the attorney-appraiser relationship, but instructions to the appraiser on valuation are another matter. The appraiser has the choice of accepting or rejecting the attorney's premise. *Once accepted without reservation, the premise becomes the appraiser's responsibility*."[13] Sometimes attorneys try to instruct an appraiser in regard to a valuation determination "under the guise of legal instructions as to a point of law."[14] For instance, an attorney may go beyond legal instruction by telling an appraiser to assume the boundaries of the larger parcel are as specified in the instruction.

As stated in Chapter 5, the determination of the larger parcel depends on three factors: unity of title, unity of use, and contiguity. Unity of title is a legal

13. *Divergences in Right-of-Way Valuations*, 10 (emphasis added).

14. Ibid.

matter and may properly be addressed through legal instructions. The attorney may also address the question of legal contiguity. However, unity of use or, more properly, unity of highest and best use is not a legal question for the attorney; questions of highest and best use are to be analyzed and determined by the appraiser.

"Some attorneys want appraisers they can influence. This is perhaps understandable [due to the attorney's position as an advocate], but the instructed appraiser is the antithesis of ethical requirements of the profession."[15] The appraiser who states, "I did it this way because the attorney told me to. It was a legal instruction." is often being evasive to avoid fulfilling the requirements of the professional standards of practice. Such a response does not let the appraiser off the hook. Both The Appraisal Foundation and the Appraisal Institute have ethical rules concerning the appraisal of property under hypothetical conditions.[16] The explanatory comment to the Appraisal Institute's Ethical Rule 3-5 states:

> *In the Performance of an Appraisal Assignment, Members and Affiliates Must Observe Certain Rules Relating to Hypothetical Conditions.*
>
> A Member or an Affiliate of the Appraisal Institute is permitted to accept an appraisal assignment that is based upon a hypothetical condition posited by a client or required by *a legal instruction from the client's attorney, only if*
>
> (a) the Member or Affiliate makes a careful investigation of the relevant economic, *legal*, and physical factors and concludes that such hypothetical condition is likely to be realized in the foreseeable future, and reasonable persons, given the same information, could reach the same conclusion;
>
> (b) the appraisal report or file memoranda setting forth the results of such appraisal clearly and accurately describes the investigation made and explains the basis for such conclusion; and
>
> (c) the appraisal report or file memoranda setting forth the results of such appraisal clearly explains the hypothetical condition and its effect upon the analyses and opinions in the report or file memoranda. In such case, the Member or Affiliate must use great care to make certain that the report or file memoranda is designed to prevent any misunderstanding by the users of the report or the public.[17]

Thus, a legal instruction falls under the definition of a hypothetical condition. Throughout this work, appraisers have been advised to obtain legal instruction from appropriate legal counsel. In each case, the reference has specified legal instruction "*with supporting case law*," or "*with supporting citations*." Legal "instructions must be valid and well-founded. *Opinions expressed by an attorney that are not valid and are without foundation should be disregarded by an appraiser*."[18]

15. *Divergences in Right-of-Way Valuations*, 10.
16. USPAP, 1994 ed., Ethics Provision, Conduct; *Code of Professional Ethics of the Appraisal Institute*, Ethical Rule 3-5, 1994 ed.
17. *Code of Professional Ethics of the Appraisal Institute*, Explanatory Comments Relating to Ethical Rule 3-5 (emphasis added).
18. *Divergences in Right-or-Way Valuations*, 16 (emphasis added).

The foregoing discussion is not intended to preclude the appraiser from accepting a legal instruction from counsel which is contrary to existing law if legal counsel is attempting to create *new law*. (It certainly cannot be denied that innovation is needed in certain areas of condemnation law.) However, if this is the case, the circumstances must be fully discussed by the attorney and the appraiser. The legal instructions from the attorney to the appraiser should be very specific, including a thorough dissertation on the existing law, with supporting citations, and a detailed explanation of what specific point of law the attorney wishes to challenge and how the legal instruction to the appraiser specifically relates to this challenge. "An appraiser accepting such an assignment, under conditions specifically outlined in writing by counsel, must also be prepared to give an estimate of market value under existing law should the court rule against the 'new' legal premise."[19]

The appraiser need not agree with the attorney's interpretation of the law, as long as the attorney's interpretation of the law is reasonable. If "reasonable persons, given the same information, *could* reach the same conclusion," the appraiser is free to accept the instruction even if it conflicts with his own interpretation.

The adoption of any legal instruction must, of course, be conspicuously noted in the appraiser's written appraisal report. Similarly, the instruction must be revealed on direct examination by the appraiser testifying in connection with the appraisal. The appraiser should make it clear to the attorney that the court will be informed of the instruction; this information may be solicited by the attorney or opposing counsel at the trial or the appraiser may inform the court of the instruction on his own initiative. Both The Appraisal Foundation and the Appraisal Institute define court testimony by an appraiser as an oral appraisal report. Therefore, the appraiser must address the substantive matters set forth in the Standards of Professional Appraisal Practice,[20] including the disclosure of assumptions, limiting conditions, and hypothetical conditions.

SUMMARY

Professional standards are based on professional ethics and personal ethics. A dishonest person who will not generally abide by the standards of professional practice and an individual who does not competently meet the standards of professional practice both must have questionable personal ethics. An appraiser with high personal ethics will generally insist on performing well above the minimum rules set forth in the written standards and ethical codes of The Appraisal Foundation and the major appraisal institutes and societies.

There are many legal and ethical reasons why an appraiser should prepare a well-documented appraisal report before testifying to an opinion of market value. There are few, if any, legitimate reasons for not preparing such a report. Therefore, appraisers are well advised to reject any appraisal assignment that does not call for the preparation of a fully documented appraisal report before the appraiser is required to testify.

19. Ibid.

20. USPAP, 1994 ed., Standards Rule 2-4, pp. 17-18.

The appraiser must not only avoid becoming an advocate for his client's interest, he must also avoid *reverse advocacy* and the appearance of advocating his own interest. The appraiser should make no reference to "winning" or "losing" a condemnation trial, or should use these words with great care. Nevertheless, the appraiser's use of these terms should not automatically brand him as an advocate for his client's interest. An appraiser who has an intense interest in the outcome of a legal proceeding is not necessarily an advocate for his client's interest; the appraiser may be motivated by a strong desire to know how effectively he has accomplished his assigned task. The trier of fact's verdict in a civil litigation dealing with real estate values may be an indication of the appraiser's effectiveness as an expert witness, but it does not necessarily prove or disprove the competence with which the appraiser has performed his assignment.

Legal counsel will expect the appraiser to assist in preparing for the cross-examination of the opposing party's appraiser or appraisers. If this violates the appraiser's personal ethics, this fact must be revealed to the client and the client's legal counsel before the appraisal assignment is begun.

If the appraiser concludes that the results of his preliminary analysis will not be of use to the client, a conference should be held between the client, the client's attorney, and the appraiser before additional appraisal work is undertaken and additional expense is incurred. To complete an appraisal assignment knowing that the results of the appraisal will be of no benefit to the client is, without a doubt, not in the client's best interest and, therefore, should be contrary to the appraiser's personal ethics.

In appraising for a condemnee, the appraiser must recognize that the client may not be able to pay the appraisal fee until a settlement is reached or the trial is concluded. Therefore, an understanding in regard to the payment of the appraisal fee must be reached before any appraisal work begins. Often a condemnee's appraiser must wait for payment until the award is received by the condemnee. Some appraisers feel a personal, ethical responsibility to accept such assignments to ensure that the condemnee has the same access to professional appraisal services as the condemnor.

It is, of course, unethical for appraisers to undertake appraisal assignments for which they are not qualified by experience and/or training. This is doubly important in litigation appraising. There are two areas of expertise and/or training which the appraiser should possess before accepting such an assignment. First, the appraiser must have the technical experience and/or training to make the actual appraisal and, second, he must have the experience and/or training to act as an expert valuation witness. If the appraiser has not had trial experience, he can educate himself by attending several civil litigation cases involving expert witnesses and real estate valuations. Once the appraiser has gotten some exposure in this way, he should feel confident enough to testify in a simple civil litigation case involving real estate valuation.

At times the appraiser needs legal instructions on matters of law to guide him in arriving at value conclusions using methodologies that will be acceptable to the courts. However, the appraiser should never accept an attorney's instruction in regard to valuation blindly, even if it is in the guise of a legal instruction. Any legal instruction accepted must be received in writing, included within the appraisal report, and stated by the appraiser on the witness stand.

There is a severe shortage of qualified real estate appraisers who make competent expert witnesses. Thus there is absolutely no reason for an appraiser to compromise his ethics and jeopardize his professional standing by becoming an advocate for his client's interest. Any appraiser who becomes an advocate for his client's interest can be presumed incompetent. One of these days, lawyers are going to realize that *there is no one worse on the witness stand than an incompetent advocate.*

Addenda

Eminent Domain Constitutional and Statutory Provisions

Jurisdiction	Constitutional Provisions		Statutory Provisions
	Year	Provision	
United States	1791	5th Amend.	40 USCA §§ 257, 258, 25 Stat. 357 40 USCA § 258a-258e, 46 Stat. 1421
Alabama	1901	Art. 1, § 23	Ala. Code § 18-1A-1 *et seq.*
Alaska	1959	Art. 1, § 18	Alaska Stat. § 09.55.240 *et seq.*
Arizona	1912	Art. 2, § 17	Ariz. Rev. Stat. Ann. § 12-1111 *et seq.*
Arkansas	1874	Art. 2, § 22	Ark. Code Ann. § 18-15-101 *et seq.*
California	1879	Art. 1, § 19	Cal. Civ. Code § 1230.010 *et seq.* Cal. Gov't. Code Ann. §§ 25350.5, 25431, 37350.5 Cal. Pub. Util. Code § 600 § 610 *et seq.*
Colorado	1876	Art. 2, §§ 14, 15	Colo. Rev. Stat. Ann. § 38-1-101 *et seq.*
Connecticut	1965	Art. 1, § 11	Conn. Rev. Gen. Stat. Ann. § 48-1 *et seq.*
Delaware	1897	Art. 1, § 8	Del. Code Ann. tit. 10, § 6101 *et seq.*
District of Columbia			D.C. Code Ann. § 16-1301 *et seq.*
Florida	1968	Art. 10, § 6	Fla. Stat. Ann. § 73.012 *et seq.*; § 74.011 *et seq.*
Georgia	1976	Art. 1, § 3, ¶ 1	Ga. Code Ann. § 36-101 *et seq.*
Hawaii	1959	Art. 1, § 18	Hawaii Rev. Stat. § 516-21 *et seq.*
Idaho	1890	Art. 1, § 14	Idaho Code § 7-701 *et seq.*
Illinois	1970	Art. 1, § 15	Ill. Ann. Stat. ch. 110, § 7-101 *et seq.*
Indiana	1851	Art. 1, § 21	Ind. Stat. Ann. § 32-11-1-1 *et seq.*
Iowa	1857	Art. 1, § 18	Iowa Code Ann. § 471.1 *et seq.*; § 472.1 *et seq.*
Kansas	1861	Art. 12, § 4	Kan. Stat. Ann. § 26-101 *et seq.*
Kentucky	1891	§ 13	Ky. Rev. Stat. Ann. § 416.010 *et seq.*

Jurisdiction	Constitutional Provisions		Statutory Provisions
	Year	Provision	
Louisiana	1974	Art. 1, §§ 2, 4	La. Stat. Ann. ch. 11, § 2626 *et seq.* La. Rev. Stat. Ann. § 19:1 *et seq.*
Maine	1876 (Amend. 1965)	Art. 1, § 21	Me. Rev. State. Ann. tit. 30, § 4001 *et seq.*
Maryland	1867	Art. 3, §§ 40, 40A	Md. Real Prop. Code Ann. § 12-101 *et seq.*
Massachusetts	1780	Part the First, Art. 10	Mass. Gen. Laws Ann. ch. 79, § 1 *et seq.*; ch. 80A, § 1 *et seq.*
Michigan	1963	Art. 10, § 2	Mich. Stat. Ann. § 8.1 *et seq.*
Minnesota	1857 (As Amend. 1974)	Art. 1, § 13	Minn. Stat. Ann. § 117.001 *et seq.*
Mississippi	1890	Art. 3, § 17	Miss. Code Ann. § 11-27-1 *et seq.*
Missouri	1945	Art. 1, §§ 26, 27, 28	Mo. Stat. Ann. § 523.010 *et seq.*
Montana	1972	Art. 3, § 14	Mont. Code Ann. § 70-30-101 *et seq.*
Nebraska	1875	Art. 1, § 21	Neb. Rev. Stat. § 76-701 *et seq.*; § 25-2501 *et seq.*
Nevada	1864	Art. 1, § 8	Nev. Rev. Stat. Ann. § 37.009 *et seq.*; § 340.010 *et seq.*
New Hampshire	1792	Part the First, 12th	N.H. Rev. Stat. Ann. § 498-A:1 *et seq.*
New Jersey	1947	Art. 1, § 20	N.J. Stat. Ann. § 20:3-1 *et seq.*
New Mexico	1912	Art. 2, § 20	N.M. Stat. Ann. § 42A-1-1 *et seq.*; § 42-2-1 *et seq.*
New York	1939	Art. 1, § 7	N.Y. Em. Dom. Proc. L. § 101 *et seq.*
North Carolina	1970	Art. 1, § 19	N.C. Gen. Stat. § 40A-1 *et seq.*
North Dakota	1889	Art. 1, § 14	N.D. Cent. Code Ann. § 32-15-01 *et seq.*
Ohio	1851	Art. 1, § 19	Ohio Rev. Code Ann. § 163.01 *et seq.*

Jurisdiction	Constitutional Provisions		Statutory Provisions
	Year	Provision	
Oklahoma	1907	Art. 2, §§ 23, 24	Okla. Stat. Ann. tit. 27, § 1 *et seq.*; tit. 66, § 53 *et seq.*
Oregon	1859	Art. 1, § 18	Ore. Rev. Stat. § 35.205 *et seq.*
Pennsylvania	1874	Art. 1, § 10	Pa. Stat. Ann. tit. 26, § 1-101 *et seq.*
Puerto Rico			P.R. Laws Ann. tit. 32, § 2901 *et seq.*
Rhode Island	1843	Art. 1, § 16	R.I. Gen. Laws Ann. § 37-6-1 *et seq.*; § 37-6.1-1 *et seq.*; § 37-6.2-1 *et seq.*
South Carolina	1895	Art. 1, § 13	S.C. Code Ann. § 28-1-10 *et seq.*
South Dakota	1889	Art. 6, § 13	S.D. Rev. Codified Laws § 21-35-1 *et seq.*
Tennessee	1870	Art. 1, § 21	Tenn. Code Ann. § 29-16-101 *et seq.*
Texas	1876	Art. 1, § 17	Tex. Prop. Code Ann. § 21.001 *et seq.*
Utah	1895	Art. 1, § 22	Utah Code Ann. § 78-34-1 *et seq.*
Vermont	1793	Chap. 1, Art. 2nd	Vt. Stat. Ann. tit. 24, § 2805 *et seq.*; § 3602 *et seq.*; § 3210 *et seq.*
Virgin Islands			V.I. Code Ann. tit. 28, § 411 *et seq.*
Virginia	1971	Art. 1, §§ 6, 11	Va. Code Ann. § 25-46.1 *et seq.*
Washington	1889	Art. 1, § 16	Wash. Rev. Code Ann. § 8.04.010 *et seq.*
West Virginia	1872	Art. 3, § 9	W. Va. Code § 54-1-1 *et seq.*
Wisconsin	1848	Art. 1, § 13	Wis. Stat. Ann. § 32.01 *et seq.*
Wyoming	1889	Art. 1, §§ 32, 33	Wyo. Stat. Ann. § 1-26-501 *et seq.*

Source: *Nichols' The Law of Eminent Domain*, rev. 3rd ed. (New York: Mathew Bender Co., Inc., 1990), vol. 2.

State Highway Standard Narrative Appraisal Report

SECTION I—IDENTIFICATION AND SUMMARY
- Page 1, Certificate of Appraiser (WSDOT Form 261-015)
- Page 2, Summary of Conclusions (WSDOT Form 261-016)
- Page 3, Photographs of all Principal Improvements and/or Features Affecting Value (WSDOT Form 261-017)
- Page 4, et seq., Narrative Report:
  - Item 1—Owner
  - Item 2—Address (or location) of subject property
  - Item 3—Legal description
  - Item 4—Delineation of title
  - Item 5—Purpose of appraisal
  - Item 6—Summation of appraisal problems

SECTION II—EVALUATION OF TOTAL OWNERSHIP
- Item 1—Assumptions and limiting conditions
- Item 2—Neighborhood location and description
- Item 3—Description of subject property
  - A. Present use
  - B. Accessibility and road frontages
  - C. Land contour and elevations
  - D. Land area
  - E. Land shape
  - F. Utilities
  - G. Present zoning
  - H. Highest and best use of land if vacant
  - I. Improvements
  - J. Specialty items
  - K. Real estate taxes
  - L. Assessments
  - M. Existing lease or rental data
  - N. Highest and best use of property as improved
- Item 4—Valuation of property
  - A. Site analysis and evaluation
    - 1. Comparative approach, site evaluation
      - a. General discussion
        - (1) Data search area, time frame, market units
        - (2) Sales that are comparable
      - b. Comparative analysis
      - c. Correlation and conclusion by comparative approach
    - 2. Income approach, site evaluation
      - a. Data
      - b. Analysis
      - c. Correlation and conclusion by income approach
    - 3. Correlation and final conclusion, land value
  - B. Approaches to value, whole property
    - 1. Comparative approach
      - a. General discussion
        - (1) Data search area, time frame, market units
        - (2) Sales that are comparable
      - b. Comparative analysis
        - (1) Whole property comparisons
        - (2) Comparative units
      - c. Correlation and conclusion, comparative approach
    - 2. Income approach (when necessary or appropriate)
      - a. Data
      - b. Analysis
      - c. Correlation and conclusion, income approach
    - 3. Cost approach (when necessary or appropriate)
      - a. Cost new
      - b. Accrued depreciation
      - c. Land value
      - d. Indicated value by cost approach
  - C. Correlation of value indications from all approaches

SECTION III—REMAINDER EVALUATION
- Item 1—Assumptions and limiting conditions
- Item 2—Neighborhood factors
- Item 3—Description of subject remainder as an entity
  - A. Accessibility and road frontages
  - B. Land contour and elevation
  - C. Land area
  - D. Land shape

- E. Utilities
  - 1. Utilities actually remaining
  - 2. Utilities lost and possible corrective potentials
- F. Probable remainder zoning
- G. Highest and best use of remainder land if vacant
- H. Improvements
  - 1. Improvements remaining in whole
  - 2. Improvements remaining in part
    - a. Descriptions
    - b. Rehabilitation specification, if rehabilitation feasible
- I. Remainder specially item considerations
- J. Estimated real estate taxes
- K. Possible remainder assessments
- L. Lease or rental potential
- M. Highest and best use of remainder as improved

Item 4—Valuation of property remaining

- A. Site analysis and evaluation
  - 1. Comparative approach, site evaluation
    - a. General discussion
      - (1) Data search area, time frame, market units
      - (2) Sales that are comparable
    - b. Comparative analysis
    - c. Correlation and conclusions by comparative approach
  - 2. Income approach, site evaluation
    - a. Data
    - b. Analysis
    - c. Correlation and conclusion by income approach
  - 3. Correlation and final conclusion, land value
- B. Approaches to value, remainder whole property
  - 1. Comparative approach
    - a. General discussion
      - (1) Data search area, time frame, market units
      - (2) Sales that are comparable
    - b. Comparative analysis
      - (1) Whole property comparisons
      - (2) Comparative units
    - c. Correlation and conclusion, comparative approach
  - 2. Income approach (when necessary or appropriate)
    - a. Data
    - b. Analysis
    - c. Correlation and conclusion, income approach
  - 3. Cost approach
    - a. Cost new
    - b. Accrued depreciation (including analysis and explanations)
    - c. Land value
    - d. Indicated value by cost approach
- C. Correlation of remainder value indications from all approaches

SECTION IV—ACQUISITION ANALYSIS

Item 1—Recapitulation

- A. Value of property before acquisition
- B. Value of property after acquisition
- C. Difference between "before" and "after" values

Item 2—Explanation of damages

Item 3—Explanation of special benefits

SECTION V—ADDENDA

- A. *Market Data* (WSDOT Forms 261-020 and 261-020A)
- B. Market data map
- C. Special instructions, charts and illustrations
- D. *Report of Contact with Owner* (WSDOT Form 261-013)
- E. Title report

Source: Washington State Department of Transportation, *Right of Way Manual*, §C-1 (1991).

Recommended Format for Federal Appraisal Reports

PART I—INTRODUCTION

1. Title page
2. Letter of transmittal
3. Table of contents
4. Appraiser's certification
5. Summary of salient facts and conclusions
6. Photographs of subject property
7. Statement of assumptions and limiting conditions
8. Scope of the appraisal
9. Purpose of the appraisal
10. Summary of appraisal problems

PART II—FACTUAL DATA—BEFORE TAKING

11. Legal description
12. Area, city and neighborhood data
13. Property data:
    a. Site
    b. Improvements
    c. Equipment
    d. Use history
    e. Sales history
    f. Rental history
    g. Assessed value and annual tax load
    h. Zoning and other land use regulations

PART III—DATA ANALYSIS AND CONCLUSIONS—BEFORE TAKING

14. Analysis of highest and best use
15. Land valuation
16. Value estimate by cost approach
17. Value estimate by sales comparison (market) approach
18. Value estimate by income capitalization approach
19. Correlation and final value estimate

PART IV—FACTUAL DATA—AFTER TAKING

20. Legal description
21. Neighborhood factors
22. Property data
    a. Site
    b. Improvements
    c. Equipment
    d. History
    e. Assessed value and annual tax load
    f. Zoning and other land use regulations

PART V—DATA ANALYSIS AND CONCLUSIONS—AFTER TAKING

23. Analysis of highest and best use
24. Land valuation
25. Value estimate by cost approach
26. Value estimate by sales comparison (market) approach
27. Value estimate by income capitalization approach
28. Correlation and final value estimate

PART VI—ACQUISITION ANALYSIS

29. Recapitulation
30. Allocation and explanation of damages
31. Explanation of special benefits

PART VII—EXHIBITS AND ADDENDA

32. Location map
33. Comparable data maps
34. Detail of comparative data
35. Plot plan
36. Floor plan
37. Title evidence report
38. Other pertinent exhibits
39. Qualifications of appraiser

Source: *Uniform Appraisal Standards for Federal Land Acquisitions* (Washington, D.C.: U.S. Government Printing Office, 1992), §B-1.

Uniform Appraisal Standards for Federal Land Acquisitions: Appraisal Report Documentation Checklist

TITLE PAGE

Agency name______________ Property address____________
Agency tract no.____________ Appraiser's name(s)_________
Appraiser's address_________ Effective date of value________

LETTER OF TRANSMITTAL

Date of letter_______________ Identification of property______
Prop. rights appraised_______ Effective date of value________
Special assumptions________ Special instructions__________
Estimate of before value_____ Estimate of after value________
Appraiser signature_________

TABLE OF CONTENTS Omitted_____ Adequate_____ Inadequate_____

APPRAISER'S CERTIFICATION

Facts true & correct_________ Limited only by assump.______
No interest in property_______ No contingent fee___________
Conforms to USPAP_________ Conforms to Yellow Book_____
Property inspection_________ Offered owner accomp.______
Professional assistance_____ Before value_______________
After value_________________ Effective date of value_______

SUMMARY OF SALIENT FACTS AND CONCLUSIONS

Ident. of property__________ Effective date of value________
H & B use—before__________ H & B use—after___________
Description before_________ Description after___________
Value before: Value after:
Cost_________________ Cost___________________
Market_______________ Market_________________
Income_______________ Income_________________
Final est.______________ Final est.______________

PHOTOGRAPHS OF SUBJECT Omitted_____ Adequate_____ Inadequate_____

ASSUMPTIONS & LIMITING CONDITIONS

Appropriate_________________ Suitable for trial____________
Extraneous assumptions_____ Limited appraisal____________

SCOPE OF APPRAISAL Omitted_____ Adequate_____ Inadequate_____

PURPOSE OF APPRAISAL

Defin. of market value_______ Defin. of property rights____________

SUM. OF APPRAISAL PROB. Omitted_____ Adequate_____ Inadequate_____

LEGAL DESC.—BEFORE Omitted_____ Adequate_____ Inadequate_____

AREA DATA—BEFORE Omitted_____ Adequate_____ Inadequate_____

SITE DATA—BEFORE (Overall) Adequate_____ Inadequate_____

Present use_____ Access______ Topog._____ Soils___________
Vegetation______ Land area____ Land shape___
Utilities_________ Minerals______ Easements____ Hazards________

IMPROVEMENT DATA—BEFORE (Overall)		Adequate____	Inadequate____
Type__________	Size________	Actual age____	Effective age___
Condition______	Quality______	Occupancy___	On-site imp.____

EQUIPMENT—BEFORE	Omitted____	Adequate____	Inadequate____

HISTORY—BEFORE			
Use	Omitted____	Adequate____	Inadequate____
Sales	Omitted____	Adequate____	Inadequate____
Rental	Omitted____	Adequate____	Inadequate____

ASSESSED VALUE & TAX LOAD—BEFORE			
Assessed value	Omitted____	Adequate____	Inadequate____
Tax load	Omitted____	Adequate____	Inadequate____

ZONING & LAND USE REGULATIONS—BEFORE			
Description	Omitted____	Adequate____	Inadequate____
Rezone probability	Omitted____	Adequate____	Inadequate____
Land use regs.	Omitted____	Adequate____	Inadequate____

HIGHEST AND BEST USE—BEFORE			
Vacant	Omitted____	Adequate____	Inadequate____
Improved	Omitted____	Adequate____	Inadequate____
L.P. considered	Omitted____	Adequate____	Inadequate____
Reasonable conclusion		Yes__________	No__________

LAND VALUATION—BEFORE			
Comparables:			
Description		Adequate____	Inadequate____
Photos	Omitted____	Adequate____	Inadequate____
Analysis	Omitted____	Adequate____	Inadequate____
Suitable for trial		Yes__________	No__________
Final value analysis		Adequate____	Inadequate____

COST APPROACH—BEFORE			
Justified omission	Yes________	No__________	N/A__________
Reproduction cost		Adequate____	Inadequate____
Depreciation:			
Market supported		Yes__________	No__________
Analysis	Omitted____	Adequate____	Inadequate____
Final estimate		Adequate____	Inadequate____

SALES COMPARISON APPROACH—BEFORE			
Comparables:			
Description		Adequate____	Inadequate____
Photos	Omitted____	Adequate____	Inadequate____
Analysis	Omitted____	Adequate____	Inadequate____
Suitable for trial		Yes__________	No__________
Final value analysis		Adequate____	Inadequate____

INCOME CAPITALIZATION APPROACH—BEFORE

Justified omission Yes________ No__________ N/A___________
Gross income estimate Adequate_____ Inadequate_____
Vacancy Omitted_____ Adequate_____ Inadequate_____
Expenses:
Fixed Omitted_____ Adequate_____ Inadequate_____
Operating Omitted_____ Adequate_____ Inadequate_____
Reserves Omitted_____ Adequate_____ Inadequate_____
Capitalization rate:
Market supported Yes__________ No___________
Selection method Adequate_____ Inadequate_____
Suitable for trial Yes__________ No___________

FINAL VALUE ESTIMATE—BEFORE

Reasoned analysis Omitted_____ Adequate_____ Inadequate_____
Avoided summation appraisal Yes__________ No___________
Suitable for trial Yes__________ No___________

LEGAL DESCRIPTION—AFTER (OR DESCRIPTION OF TAKING)

Omitted_____ Adequate_____ Inadequate_____

NEIGHBORHOOD FACTORS—AFTER

Project desc. Omitted_____ Adequate_____ Inadequate_____
Project impact Omitted_____ Adequate_____ Inadequate_____

SITE DATA

Shape_____ Size_____ Utilities_____ Access_____ Easements_____
Relationship to Project Adequate_____ Inadequate_____

IMPROVEMENTS—AFTER

Description Omitted_____ Adequate_____ Inadequate_____

EQUIPMENT—AFTER Omitted_____ Adequate_____ Inadequate_____

HISTORY—AFTER

Use/rental since take:
Omitted_____ Adequate_____ Inadequate_____

ASSESSED VALUE—TAX LOAD—AFTER

Estimated A.V. Omitted_____ Adequate_____ Inadequate_____
Estimated tax load Omitted_____ Adequate_____ Inadequate_____

ZONING & LAND USE REGULATIONS—AFTER

Rezone considered Omitted_____ Adequate_____ Inadequate_____

HIGHEST & BEST USE—AFTER

Change considered Omitted_____ Adequate_____ Inadequate_____
Intensity considered Omitted_____ Adequate_____ Inadequate_____
Restoration considered Yes________ No__________ N/A___________
Effects of TCE's Yes________ No__________ N/A___________
Reasonable conclusion Yes__________ No___________

Non-conformity Omitted_____ Adequate_____ Inadequate_____

LAND VALUATION—AFTER

Comparables:			
Same comparables as before		Yes_________	No___________
Description		Adequate____	Inadequate____
Photos	Omitted_____	Adequate____	Inadequate____
Analysis	Omitted_____	Adequate____	Inadequate____
Suitable for trial		Yes_________	No___________
Final value analysis		Adequate____	Inadequate____

COST APPROACH—AFTER

Justified omission	Yes________	No__________	N/A__________
Reproduction cost		Adequate____	Inadequate____
Depreciation:			
Market supported		Yes_________	No___________
Analysis	Omitted_____	Adequate____	Inadequate____
Final estimate		Adequate____	Inadequate____

SALES COMPARISON APPROACH—AFTER

Comparables:			
Same comparables as before		Yes_________	No___________
Description		Adequate____	Inadequate____
Photos	Omitted_____	Adequate____	Inadequate____
Analysis	Omitted_____	Adequate____	Inadequate____
Suitable for trial		Yes_________	No___________
Final value analysis		Adequate____	Inadequate____

INCOME CAPITALIZATION APPROACH—AFTER

Justified omission	Yes________	No__________	N/A__________
Gross income estimate		Adequate____	Inadequate____
Vacancy	Omitted_____	Adequate____	Inadequate____
Expenses:			
Fixed	Omitted_____	Adequate____	Inadequate____
Operating	Omitted_____	Adequate____	Inadequate____
Reserves	Omitted_____	Adequate____	Inadequate____
Capitalization rate:			
Market supported		Yes_________	No___________
Selection method		Adequate____	Inadequate____
Suitable for trial		Yes_________	No___________

FINAL VALUE ESTIMATE—AFTER

Reasoned analysis	Omitted_____	Adequate____	Inadequate____
Avoided summation appraisal		Yes_________	No___________
Suitable for trial		Yes_________	No___________

ACQUISITION ANALYSIS

Avoided valuing take		Yes_________	No___________
Shown in proper form		Yes_________	No___________

ALLOCATION & EXPLANATION OF DAMAGES

Value of take/damages properly allocated		Yes________	No________
Damage explanation	Omitted____	Adequate____	Inadequate____
Noted accounting tabulation		Yes________	No________
Cost to cure damage estimated		Yes________	No________
Cost justified	Omitted____	Adequate____	Inadequate____
Profit	Omitted____	Adequate____	Inadequate____
Cost v. diminution in market value considered:	Omitted____	Adequate____	Inadequate____

SPECIAL BENEFITS

Adequately explained	Yes________	No________	N/A________

LOCATION MAP	Omitted____	Adequate____	Inadequate____

COMPARABLE DATA MAPS

All comps on map	Yes________	No________
Subject shown on map	Yes________	No________

COMPARABLE DATA SHEETS

Confirmed	Yes____	No____	Terms reported	Yes____	No____
Buyer/seller	Yes____	No____	Date of sale	Yes____	No____
Recording info	Yes____	No____	Location	Yes____	No____
Present use	Yes____	No____	H&B Use	Yes____	No____
Zoning	Yes____	No____	Legal	Yes____	No____

Physical description	Adequate____	Inadequate____

PLOT PLAN

Property boundaries shown	Yes________	No________
Dimensions before	Yes________	No________
Dimensions after	Yes________	No________
Street frontage before	Yes________	No________
Street frontage after	Yes________	No________
Photo locations	Yes________	No________
Improvement locations	Yes________	No________

FLOOR PLAN	Adequate___	Inadequate___	N/A________
TITLE REPORT	Omitted____	Adequate____	Inadequate____
OTHER EXHIBITS	Adequate___	Inadequate___	N/A________
QUALIFICATIONS	Omitted____	Adequate____	Inadequate____

Source: *Uniform Appraisal Standards for Federal Land Acquisitions* (Washinton, D.C.: U.S. Government Printing Office, 1992.)

TABLE OF CASES ALPHABETICALLY

	Chapter	Footnote
Calvo v. United States, 303 F.2d 902 (9th Cir. 1962).	16	24
Campbell v. United States, 266 U.S. 368 (1924).	13	4
	14	36
	14	38
Carmichall v. United States, 273 F.2d 392 (5th Cir. 1960).	4	69
Carolina Central Gas Company v. Hyder, 86 S.E.2d 458 (N.C. 1955).	16	5
Central Louisiana Elec. Co. v. Fontenot, 159 So.2d 738 (La. 1964).	16	34
Chicago, etc., R. Co. v. Dresel, 110 Ill. 89 (Ill. 1884).	5	30
Chicago Mill and Lumber Co. v. Board of Directors, 366 S.W.2d 184 (Ark. 1963).	16	35
Chicago v. Harbecke, 100 N.E.2d 616 (Ill. 1951).	10	62
Chicago v. Taylor, 125 U.S. 161 (1888).	4	22
City of Beaumont v. Marks, 443 S.W.2d 253 (Tex. 1969).	4	46
City of Buffalo v. Goldman, 406 N.Y.S.2d 407 (N.Y. 1978).	5	46
City of Chester v. Commonwealth Dept. of Transp., 434 A.2d 695 (Pa. 1981).	11	38
City of Chicago v. Giedraitis, 150 N.E.2d 577 (Ill. 1958).	9	13
City of Chicago v. Vaccaro, 97 N.E.2d 766 (Ill. 1951).	10	38
City of Evanston v. Piotrowiez, 170 N.E.2d 569 (Ill. 1960).	10	53
City of Fenton v. Lutz, 250 N.W.2d 579 (Mich. 1977).	4	75
City of Fresno v. Cloud, 102 Cal. Rptr 874 (Cal. 1972).	3	19
	7	23
City of Gilroy v. Filice, 34 Cal. Rptr. 368 (Cal. 1963).	10	87
City of Houston v. Fox, 429 S.W.2d 201 (Tex. 1968).	4	26
City of Lafayette v. Beeler, 381 N.E.2d 1287 (Ind. 1978).	12	23
	12	32
City of Los Angeles v. Allen, 36 P.2d 611 (Cal. 1934).	3	18
	4	98
City of Los Angeles v. Retlaw Enterprises, Inc., 546 P.2d 1380 (Cal. 1976).	10	58
City of Meriden v. Zwalniski, 91 A. 439 (Conn. 1914).	14	80
City of New York v. Nelkin, 415 N.E.2d 970 (N.Y. 1980).	7	22
City of Norwood v. Sheen, 186 N.E. 102 (Ohio 1933).	16	26
	16	28
City of St. Louis Park v. Engell, 168 N.W.2d 3 (Minn. 1969).	15	38
City of St. Louis v. Vasquez, 341 S.W.2d 839 (Mo. 1960).	10	57
City of Three Forks v. State Highway Comm'n, 480 P.2d 826 (Mont. 1971).	17	11
City of Tucson v. Ruelas, 508 P.2d 1174 (Ariz. 1973).	10	60
City of Washington v. Koch, 456 S.W.2d 628 (Mo. 1970).	5	35
City of Winston-Salem v. Davis, 296 S.E.2d 21 (N.C. 1982).	10	34
City of Yakima v. Dahlin, 485 P.2d 628 (Wash. 1971).	14	77
Clark v. Erich, 31 Cal. Rptr. 628 (Cal. 1963).	18	21
Cloverport Sand & Gravel Co. v. United States, 6 Cl.Ct. 178 (1984).	4	60
Cole Investment Co. v. United States, 258 F.2d 203 (9th Cir. 1958).	5	34
Collins Pipeline Co. v. New Orleans East, Inc., 250 So.2d 29 (La. 1971)	14	79
Commonwealth, Dep't of Highways v. Cleveland, 432 S.W.2d 825 (Ky. 1968).	14	75
Commonwealth, Dep't of Highways v. Fister, 373 S.W.2d 720 (Ky. 1963).	14	67
Commonwealth, Dep't of Highways v. Gibson, 523 S.W.2d 885 (Ky. 1975).	8	17
Commonwealth, Dep't of Highways v. Rowland, 420 S.W.2d 657 (Ky. 1967).	14	46
Commonwealth Dep't of Highways v. Yates, 383 S.W.2d 340 (Ky. 1964).	14	66
Commonwealth Dept. of H'ways v. Sherrod, 367 S.W.2d 844 (Ky. 1963).	4	44
	18	38
	18	42

	Chapter	Footnote
Commonwealth, Dept. of Highways v. Dennis, 409 S.W.2d 292 (Ky. 1966).	5	17
Commonwealth of Kentucky, Dept. of Highways v. Whitledge, 406 S.W.2d 833 (Ky. 1966).	10	28
Commonwealth v. Raybourne, 364 S.W.2d 814 (Ky. 1963).	14	59
Commonwealth v. Williams, 487 S.W.2d 290 (Ky. 1972).	14	37
Conness v. Commonwealth, 69 N.E. 341 (Mass. 1904).	6	21
Correia v. New Bedford Redevelopment Authority, 377 N.E.2d 909 (Mass. 1978).	8	4
Corrigan v. City of Scottsdale, 720 P.2d 513 (Ariz. 1986).	17	20
County of San Luis Obispo v. Bailey, 483 P.2d 27 (Cal. 1971).	10	64
County of Santa Clara v. Curtner, 54 Cal. Rptr. 257 (Cal. 1966).	5	25
County of Smith v. Labore, 15 P. 577 (Kan. 1887).	5	18
County of Suffolk v. Firester, 339 N.E.2d 154 (N.Y. 1975).	12	29
Dash v. State, 491 P.2d 1069 (Ak. 1971).	12	19
Davidson County Bd. of Ed. v. First American Nat. Bank, 301 S.W.2d 905 (Tenn. 1957).	6	20
De Kalb County v. Cowan, 261 S.E.2d 478 (Ga. 1979).	9	19
De Salvo v. Arkansas Louisiana Gas Co., 239 F.Supp. 312 (E.D. Ark. 1965).	2	20
Debruhl v. State Highway & Public Works Comm., 102 S.E.2d 229 (N.C. 1958).	2	22
Denver Urban Renewal Authority v. Hayutin, 583 P.2d 296 (Colo. 1978).	10	44
Dep't of Transportation v. Great Southern Enterprises, 225 S.E.2d 80 (Ga. 1976).	6	12
Dep't. of Public Works & Buildings v. Exchange Nat. Bank, 356 N.E.2d 376 (Ill. 1976).	10	52
Department of Public Works & Buildings v. Hubbard, 1 N.E.2d 383 (Ill. 1936).	4	43
Department of Public Works & Buildings v. Oberlaender, 235 N.E.2d 3 (Ill. 1968).	3	13
	5	57
Department of Public Works v. Lynbar, Inc., 62 Cal. Rptr. 320 (Cal. 1967).	18	16
Dept. of Public Works & Bldgs. v. Exchange Nat'l Bank, 334 N.E.2d 810 (Ill. 1975).	7	9
	7	24
Dept. of Transportation v. Janssen, 339 N.E.2d 359 (Ill. 1975).	6	11
Dover Housing Authority v. George, 220 A.2d 156 (N.H. 1966).	12	27
East Pennsylvania R. Co. v. Hiester, 40 Pa. 53 (Pa. 1861).	10	11
Eikelberger v. State, Dep't of Highways, 429 P.2d 555 (Nev. 1967).	9	34
Fairchild v. Oakland etc., R. Co., 169 P. 388 (Cal. 1917).	14	61
Fallbrook Irr. Dist. v. Bradley, 164 U.S. 112 (1896).	22	9
Feltz v. Central Nebraska P.P. & I. Dist., 124 F.2d 578 (8th Cir. 1942).	14	51
First English Evan. Luth. Ch. v. Los Angeles Cty., 482 U.S. 304 (1987).	17	13
	17	14
	17	15
Flair Corp. v. City of Brecksville, 359 N.E.2d 459 (Ohio 1976).	7	1
Florida East Coast Properties, Inc. v. Metropolitan Dade County, 572 F.2d 1108 (5th Cir 1978).	14	9
Florida Power & Light Co. v. Jennings, 518 So.2d 895 (Fla. 1987).	14	81
Florida Rock Industries, Inc. v. United States, 21 Cl. Ct. 161 (1990).	7	19
Florida Rock Industries, Inc. v. United States, 18 F.3d 1560 (Fed. Cir. 1994).	7	20
Forest Preserve Dist. of Cook County v. Krol, 145 N.E.2d 599 (Ill. 1957).	12	37
Foster v. Sanders, 557 S.W.2d 205 (Ky. 1977).	5	55
Front Royal and Warren County Industrial Park v. Town of Front Royal, 749 F.Supp. 1439 (1990).	17	27

	Chapter	Footnote
Fulmer v. State Dep't of Roads, 134 N.W.2d 798 (Neb. 1965).	16	33
Gains v. City of Calhoun, 42 Ga.App. 89 (Ga. 1931).	5	54
Game & Fish Comm'n v. Farmers Irrigation Co., 426 P.2d 562 (Colo. 1967).	17	11
Gebrian v. Bristol Redev. Agency, 370 A.2d 1055 (Conn. 1976).	7	5
	7	7
Geffen Motors, Inc. v. State, 307 N.Y.S.2d 389 (N.Y. 1970).	10	80
Gigliotti v. Wood, 397 A.2d 1342 (Conn. 1978).	18	31
Glendenning v. Stahley, 91 N.E. 234 (Ind. 1910).	5	19
Gluck v. Baltimore, 32 A. 515 (Md. 1895).	18	46
Goldblatt v. Town of Hempstead, 369 U.S. 590 (1962).	4	20
Great Atlantic & Pacific Tea Co. v. State, 238 N.E.2d 705 (N.Y. 1968).	18	39
Haney v. Denny, 193 N.E.2d 648 (Ind. 1963).	18	50
Hannan v. United States 131 F.2d 441 (D.C. Cir. 1942).	10	49
Hanson v. Commissioner of Transp., 408 A.2d 8 (Conn. 1979).	15	32
Harvey School v. State of New York, 180 N.Y.S.2d 724 (N.Y. 1958).	8	18
Harwell v. United States, 316 F.2d 791 (10th Cir. 1963).	2	29
Hawaii Housing Authority v. Midkiff, 467 U.S. 229 (1984).	2	14
	2	15
	2	16
	4	13
Hays v. State, 342 S.W.2d 167 (Tex. 1960).	10	10
	10	63
Hempstead v. Salt Lake City, 90 P. 397 (Utah 1907).	15	37
Hendler v. United States, 952 F.2d 1364 (Fed. Cir. 1991).	17	5
Hickey v. United States, 208 F.2d 269 (3rd Cir. 1953).	8	17
	10	36
Hinrieks v. New Orleans, 24 So. 224 (La. 1898).	18	47
Houghs v. Mackie, 137 N.W.2d 289 (Mich. 1965).	14	74
Howe v. State Highway Bd., 187 A.2d 342 (Vt. 1963).	15	34
Hoyt v. Stamford, 165 A. 357 (Conn. 1933).	15	11
Hunt v. Director of Pub. Works, 206 A.2d 91 (R.I. 1965).	10	78
Illinois Telegraph News Co. v. Meine, 90 N.E. 230 (Ill. 1909).	16	25
In re Allen St. & 1st Ave., Borough of Manhattan, City of New York, 176 N.E. 377 (N.Y. 1931).	4	74
In re Appropriation For Highway Purposes, 239 N.E.2d 110 (Ohio 1968).	5	43
In re Condemnation of 2719,21, 11 E. Berkshire St., 343 A.2d 67 (Penn. 1975).	14	8
In re Elgart's Appeal, 149 A.2d 641 (Pa. 1959).	5	46
In re Lincoln Square Slum Clearance Project, 222 N.Y.S.2d 786 (N.Y. 1961).	9	23
	11	3
In re Park Street, Vicinity of Bay Land, 325 N.Y.S.2d 555 (N.Y. 1971).	8	6
In re Washington Market Co. Prop., 295 F. 950 (D.C. Cir. 1924).	8	18
	11	29
Ink v. City of Canton, 212 N.E.2d 574 (Ohio 1965).	4	94
International Paper Company v. United States, 227 F.2d 201 (5th Cir. 1955).	14	28
	14	29
	14	30
Iowa State Highway Comm. v. Smith, 82 N.W.2d 755 (Iowa 1957).	4	28
	4	30
	15	35
Ives v. Kansas Tpke. Authority, 334 P.2d 399 (Kan. 1959).	5	36
Jacobellis v. Ohio, 378 U.S. 184 (1964).	15	10

	Chapter	Footnote
Jeffery v. Osborne, 129 N.W. 931 (Wis. 1911).	14	27
Jockheck v. Shawnee Cty., 37 P. 621 (Kan. 1894).	2	10
Jones v. United States, 258 U.S. 40 (1922).	10	18
Justice v. United States, 145 F.2d 110 (9th Cir. 1944).	21	12
Kaiser Aetna v. United States, 444 U.S. 164 (1979).	4	18
	17	8
Kayo Oil Co. v. State, 340 So.2d 756 (Ala. 1976).	9	14
Kernochan v. Manhattan R.R. Co., 55 N.E. 906 (N.Y. 1900).	18	49
Kerr v. South Park Commissioners, 117 U.S. 379 (1886).	2	33
Kimball Laundry Co. v. United States, 338 U.S. 1 (1949).	9	20
	16	27
	17	16
	18	55
Kinter v. United States, 156 F.2d 5 (3rd Cir. 1946).	2	45
	18	43
Kohl v. United States, 91 U.S. 367 (1876).	2	4
	2	9
	2	18
Korfhage v. Commonwealth, 296 S.W.2d 476 (Ky. 1956).	18	13
	18	41
Lake County Forest Preserve Dist. v. Petersen, 417 N.E.2d 862 (Ill. 1981).	7	31
Lake County Forest Preserve District v. Reliance Standard Life Ins. Co., 329 N.E.2d 344 (Ill. 1975).	7	28
Lambert v. Griffin, 100 N.E. 496 (Ill. 1912).	18	6
	18	18
Lamm v. Volpe, 449 F.2d 1202 (10th Cir. 1971).	4	10
Land Clearance for Redevelopment Corp. v. Doernhoefer, 389 S.W.2d 780 (Mo. 1965).	18	34
Lataille v. Housing Authority of City of Woonsocket, 280 A.2d 98 (R.I. 1971).	10	5
Latham Holding Co. v. State of New York, 209 N.E.2d 542 (N.Y. 1965).	10	88
Laurel, Inc. v. State, 362 A.2d 1383 (Conn. 1975).	7	30
Lawrence v. Greenwood, 90 N.E.2d 53 (N.Y. 1949).	10	15
Legislative Route 1094, Appeal of Commonwealth, Dept. of Transp., 352 A.2d 244 (Pa. 1976).	4	89
Lembo v. Town of Farmingham, 115 N.E.2d 370 (Mass. 1953).	10	29
Levitin v. State of New York, 207 N.Y.S.2d 798 (N.Y. 1960).	8	27
Linkins-Foster Monterey Corp. v. United States, 308 F.2d 595 (9th Cir. 1962).	9	36
Loretto v. Teleprompter Manhattan CATV Corp., 458 U.S. 419 (1982).	14	11
	17	4
Los Angeles County Flood Control Dist. v. McNulty, 379 P.2d 493 (Cal. 1963).	3	16
Louisville, etc. R. Co. v. Hall, 136 S.W. 905 (Ky. 1911).	14	55
M & R Invest. Co. v. Nevada DOT, 744 P.2d 531 (Nev. 1987).	5	5
M.T.M. Realty Corp. v. State, 261 N.Y.S.2d 815 (N.Y. 1965).	5	28
Mabe v. State, 360 P.2d 799 (Idaho 1961).	4	36
Malone v. Commonwealth, 389 N.E.2d 975 (Mass. 1979).	14	84
Manlius Center Road Corp. v. State, 370 N.Y.S.2d 750 (N.Y. 1975).	14	14
Martens v. State, 554 P.2d 407 (Alaska, 1976).	7	13
	7	27
Matter of City of New York (Blackwell's Island Bridge), 103 N.Y.S. 441 (N.Y. 1907).	6	15
Matter of City of New York (West 10th St.), 196 N.E. 30 (N.Y. 1935).	16	48
	16	50

	Chapter	Footnote
Park Dist. of Highland Park v. Becher, 208 N.E.2d 621 (Ill. 1965).	7	26
Pause v. Atlanta, 26 S.E. 489 (Ga. 1895).	14	71
Penn Central Transportation Co. v. New York City, 438 U.S. 104 (1978).	17	3
	17	8
	17	9
Pennsylvania Coal Co. v. Mahon, 260 U.S. 393 (1922).	4	17
	17	7
People, Dep't of Public Works v. Southern Pacific Transp. Co., 109 Cal. Rptr. 525 (Cal. 1973).	7	12
People etc. v. Peninsula Enterprises, Inc., 153 Cal. Rptr. 895 (Cal. 1979).	17	21
People ex rel Dept. of Public Works v. Schultz Co., 268 P.2d 117 (Cal. 1954).	13	10
People ex rel. Dept. of Pub. Works v. Corp. of Pres. of Church of Latter Day Saints, 91 Cal. Rptr. 532 (Cal. 1970).	3	14
People v. Alexander, 27 Cal. Rptr. 720 (Cal. 1963).	6	18
People v. City of Fresno, 26 Cal. Rptr. 853 (Cal. 1962).	4	92
People v. Hemmerling, 58 Cal. Rptr. 203 (Cal. 1967).	5	26
People v. Murata, 326 P.2d 947 (Cal. 1958).	10	17
People v. Ocean Shore R.R., 196 P.2d 570 (Cal. 1948).	5	5
People v. Sayig, 226 P.2d 702 (Cal. 1951).	4	37
Petition of Michigan State Highway Comm. v. McGuire, 185 N.W.2d 187 (Mich. 1970).	10	32
Petition of Omaha Public Power Dist., 95 N.W.2d 209 (Neb. 1959).	6	23
Phillips Petroleum Co. v. City of Omaha, 106 N.W.2d 727 (Neb. 1960).	10	41
Phoenix Title and Trust Co. v. State, 425 P.2d 434 (Ariz. 1967).	15	34
Pipeline v. O'Brian, 418 F.2d 15 (5th Cir. 1969).	10	13
Pokorny v. Local 310, Int. Hod Carriers, 300 N.E.2d 464 (Ohio 1973).	18	36
Pokorny v. Local No. 310, Int. HOD Carriers B. & C.L.U., 311 N.E.2d 866 (Ohio 1974).	18	37
Portland, Oregon City Ry. Co. v. Penny, 158 P. 404 (Ore. 1916).	15	33
Priestly v. State, 242 N.E.2d 827 (N.Y. 1968).	4	27
	4	39
Prudential Insurance v. Central Neb. Pub. P.&I. Dist., 296 N.W. 752 (Neb. 1941).	6	39
Pumpelly v. Green Bay & Mississippi Canal Company, 80 U.S. 166 (1872).	17	2
Reading, etc., R. Co. v. Balthaser, 13 A. 294 (Pa. 1888).	15	41
Redevelopment Agency v. Contra Costa Theatre, 185 Cal. Rptr. 159 (Cal. 1982).	7	29
Redevelopment Auth. of City of Chester v. Swagger, 316 A.2d 136 (Pa. 1974).	9	19
Redevelopment Comm. of Greenville v. Capehart, 150 S.E.2d 62 (N.C. 1966).	4	56
Ridgeway Associates, Inc. v. State, 300 N.Y.S.2d 944 (N.Y. 1969).	12	9
	12	30
Riley v. District of Columbia Redevelop. Land Agency, 246 F.2d 641 (D.C. Cir. 1957).	8	16
	10	82
Roberts v. New York El. R. Co., 128 N.Y. 455, 28 N.E. 486 (N.Y. 1891).	9	40
Robinson v. Commonwealth, 141 N.E.2d 727 (Mass. 1957).	7	2
Roman Catholic Bishop of Springfield v. Commonwealth, 392 N.E.2d 829 (Mass. 1979).	14	76
Ryan v. Kansas Power, 815 P.2d 528 (Kan. 1991).	13	13
Sacramento Southern R. Co. v. Heilbron, 104 P. 979 (Cal. 1909).	6	22

	Chapter	Footnote
Sams v. Redevelopment Authority, 244 A.2d 779 (Pa. 1968).	5	29
San Diego Gas & Electric Co. v. San Diego, 450 U.S. 621 (1981).	17	17
Sanitary Dist. of Chicago v. Pittsburgh, Ft. W. and C. Ry. Co., 75 N.E. 248 (Ill. 1905).	11	16
Santa Clara County Flood Control, etc., Dist. v. Freitas, 2 Cal. Rep. 129 (Cal. 1960).	12	28
Sasso v. Housing Authority of the City of Providence, 111 A.2d 226 (R.I. 1955).	5	41
Savin Hill Yacht Club Ass'n v. Savin Hill Yacht Club, 140 N.E. 299 (Mass. 1923).	18	45
Sharp v. United States, 191 U.S. 341 (1903).	5	12
Shelby County R-IV School District v. Herman, 392 S.W.2d 609 (Mo. 1965).	11	14
Shillito v. Metropolitan Edison Co., 252 A.2d 650 (Pa. 1969).	12	7
Shoemaker v. United States, 147 U.S. 282 (1893).	2	10
Shrader v. Horton, 471 F.Supp. 1236 (W.D. Va. 1979).	4	16
Sill Corp. v. United States, 343 F.2d 411 (10th Cir. 1965).	9	30
So. Calif. Fisherman's Assn. v. United States, 174 F.2d 739 (9th Cir. 1949).	4	90
Southern Indiana Gas and Electric Co. v. Riley, 299 N.E.2d 173 (Ind. 1973).	12	22
Spano v. State of New York, 253 N.Y.S.2d 730 (N.Y. 1964).	6	31
Spinner v. State, 167 N.Y.S.2d 731 (N.Y. 1957).	14	15
Springfield, etc., R. Co. v. Schweitzer, 158 S.W. 1058 (Mo. 1913).	14	70
St. Louis Housing Authority v. Bainter, 297 S.W.2d 529 (Mo. 1957).	9	17
St. Regis Paper Co. v. United States, 313 F.2d 45 (9th. Cir. 1962).	13	3
State, Commissioner of Transportation v. Charles Investment Corp., 363 A.2d 944 (N.J. 1976).	4	34
State Commissioner of Transportation v. Township of South Hackensack, 322 A.2d 818 (N.J. 1974).	11	22
State, Dep't of Highways v. Beatty, 288 So.2d 900 (La. 1973).	14	57
State Dep't of Highways v. Gordy, 322 So.2d 418 (La. 1975).	14	53
State, Dep't. of Highways v. Luster, 277 So.2d 181 (La. 1973).	6	32
State Department of Highways v. Bagwell, 255 So.2d 852 (La. 1971).	14	63
State, Dept. of H'ways v. LeDoux, La., 184 So.2d 604 (La. 1966).	3	20
State Dept. of H'wys. v. Stegemann, La., 269 So.2d 480 (La. 1973).	3	15
	4	99
State, Dept. of Highways v. Terrace Land Co. Inc., 298 So.2d 859 (La. 1974).	5	49
	5	50
State ex rel. Lindemann v. Preston, 170 N.E.2d 489 (Ohio 1960).	16	46
State, ex rel. Merritt v. Linzell, 126 N.E.2d 53. (Ohio 1955).	4	38
State ex rel. Moore v. Bastian, 546 P.2d 389 (Idaho 1976).	14	65
	18	7
State ex. rel. Dep't of Transportation v. Gee, 565 S.W.2d 498 (Tenn. 1977).	18	32
State H'way Comm. v. Callahan, 410 P.2d 818 (Ore. 1966).	10	77
State Highway Comm. v. Bloom, 93 N.W.2d 572 (S.D. 1958).	14	40
State Highway Comm. v. Chatham, 161 So. 674 (Miss. 1935).	4	35
State Highway Comm. v. Miller, 155 N.W.2d 780 (S.D. 1968).	5	24
State Highway Comm. v. Speck, 324 S.W.2d 796 (Ark. 1959).	14	23
State Highway Comm'n v. Parker, 387 S.W.2d 505 (Mo. 1965).	15	34
State of California v. United States, 169 F.2d 914 (9th Cir. 1948).	11	35
State Road Comm. v. Rohan, 487 P.2d 857 (Utah 1971).	14	62
State Roads Commission v. Novosel, 102 A.2d 563 (Md. 1954).	11	17

	Chapter	Footnote
State, through Department of Highways v. Hoyt, La., 284 So.2d 763 (La. 1973).	3	17
State v. Arnold, 341 P.2d 1089 (Ore. 1959).	6	29
State v. Bowling, 414 S.W.2d 551 (Mo. 1967).	10	39
State v. Cady, 400 S.W.2d 481 (Mo. 1965).	15	33
State v. Calkins, 314 P.2d 449 (Wash. 1957).	14	68
State v. Chang, 436 P.2d 3 (Haw. 1967).	12	31
State v. Dillon, 121 N.W.2d 798 (Neb. 1953).	4	63
State v. Fonburg, 328 P.2d 60 (Idaho 1958).	4	31
State v. Gorga, 138 A.2d 833 (N.J. 1958).	7	21
State v. Green, 578 P.2d 855 (Wash. 1978).	15	22
State v. Greenfield, 399 P.2d 989 (Mont. 1964).	10	20
State v. Hoblitt, 288 P. 181 (Mont. 1930).	5	38
State v. Johnson, 191 S.E.2d 641 (N.C. 1972).	10	13
State v. Lavasek, 385 P.2d 361 (N.M. 1963).	4	24
State v. Maplewood Heights Corp., 302 N.E.2d 782 (Ind. 1973).	12	21
State v. McNary, 664 S.W.2d 589 (Mo. 1984).	14	33
State v. Nelson, 296 N.E.2d 908 (Ind. 1973).	18	28
State v. Nelson, 353 P.2d 616 (Ore. 1960).	21	10
State v. Spencer, 559 P.2d 1360 (Wash. 1977).	18	53
State v. Spencer, 583 P.2d 1201 (Wash. 1978).	18	54
State v. Vorhof-Duenke Co., 366 S.W.2d 329 (Mo. 1963).	9	39
State v. Whitlow, 52 Cal. Rptr. 336 (Cal. 1966).	6	10
State v. Widen, 128 N.W.2d 755 (Minn. 1964).	4	45
State v. Wilson, 420 P.2d 992 (Ariz. 1966).	4	32
State v. Wilson, 493 P.2d 1252 (Wash. 1972).	8	3
State v. Wineberg, 444 P.2d 787 (Wash. 1968).	4	40
Stipe v. United States, 337 F.2d 818 (10th Cir. 1964).	14	69
Stubbs v. United States, 21 F.Supp. 1007 (D. N.C. 1938).	4	53
Surfside of Brevard, Inc. v. United States, 414 F.2d 915 (5th Cir. 1969).	10	82
Symonds v. Bucklin, 197 F.Supp. 682 (D. Md. 1961).	7	10
Taylor v. State ex re. Herman, 467 P.2d 251 (Az. 1970).	15	5
	15	36
Tennessee Gas Transmission Co. v. Violet Trapping Co., 200 So.2d 428 (La. 1967).	2	5
Territory of Hawaii v. Adelmeyer, 363 P.2d 979 (Haw. 1961).	5	56
Territory of Hawaii v. Mendonca, 375 P.2d 6 (Haw. 1962).	15	8
Texas Electric Service Co. v. Cambell, 328 S.W.2d 208 (Tex. 1959).	13	11
Texas Electric Service Co. v. West, 560 S.W.2d 769 (Tex. 1977).	14	78
Tlingit and Haida Indians of Alaska v. United States, 389 F.2d 778 (Ct. Cl. 1968).	11	7
Town of East Haven v. Eastern Airlines, Inc., 333 F.Supp. 338 (D. Conn. 1971).	16	14
Trowbridge v. Abrasive Co. of Philadelphia, 190 F.2d 825 (3rd Cir. 1951).	21	25
Tucker v. Massachusetts C.R. Co., 118 Mass. 546 (Mass. 1875).	5	38
Uhland Club v. Shupbach, 47 N.E. 113 (Mass. 1897).	18	30
United Artists Theatre Circuit, Inc. v. State, 384 N.Y.S.2d 543 (N.Y. 1976).	12	10
United States ex rel. T.V.A. v. Bailey, 115 F.2d 433 (5th Cir. 1940).	10	47
United States ex. rel. T.V.A. v. Easement and Right of Way, 405 F.2d 305 (6th Cir. 1968).	14	79

	Chapter	Footnote
United States v. 50 Acres of Land, 469 U.S. 24 (1984).	11	26
	11	27
	11	37
United States v. 564.54 Acres of Land, 441 U.S. 506 (1979).	11	24
	11	25
United States v. 57.09 Acres of Land, 706 F.2d 280 (9th Cir 1983).	5	22
United States v. 64.88 Acres of Land, etc., 244 F.2d 534 (3rd Cir. 1957).	16	10
United States v. 70.39 Acres of Land, 164 F.Supp. 451 (S.D. Cal. 1958).	6	47
	6	48
	8	7
United States v. 75.13 Acres of Land, etc., 693 F.2d 813 (8th Cir. 1982).	8	29
United States v. 760.807 Acres of Land, 731 F.2d 1443 (9th Cir. 1984).	14	78
United States v. 765.56 Acres of Land, 174 F.Supp. 1 (E.D. N.Y. 1959).	10	30
United States v. 7936.6 Acres of Land, 69 F.Supp. 328 (P.R. 1947).	5	11
United States v. 8.41 Acres, 680 F.2d 388 (5th Cir. 1982).	3	8
	6	7
	6	8
	16	24
	16	42
United States v. 8.41 Acres of Land, 783 F.2d 1256 (5th Cir. 1986).	5	4
United States v. 84.4 Acres of Land, 224 F.Supp. 1017 (W.D. Pa. 1963).	11	12
United States v. 97.19 Acres, 582 F.2d 878 (4th Cir. 1977).	3	9
United States v. Becktold, 129 F.2d 473 (8th Cir. 1942).	4	71
	10	31
United States v. Bedford Associates, 548 F.Supp. 732 (S.D. N.Y. 1982).	18	56
United States v. Benning Housing Corp., 276 F.2d 248 (5th Cir. 1960).	11	30
United States v. Causby, 328 U.S. 256 (1946).	13	6
	16	13
	17	15
United States v. Certain Interest in Prop., 271 F.2d 379 (7th Cir. 1959).	9	4
United States v. Certain Interest in Property, 239 F.Supp. 822 (D. Colo. 1965).	9	36
United States v. Certain Interest in Property in the Borough of Brooklyn (Fort Hamilton), 326 F.2d 109 (2d Cir. 1964).	8	32
United States v. Certain Lands, 69 F.Supp. 815 (S.D. N.Y. 1947).	4	68
United States v. Certain Property, 306 F.2d 439 (2nd Cir. 1962).	2	37
United States v. Chandler-Dunbar Water Power Co., 229 U.S. 53 (1913).	14	54
	14	64
United States v. Cors, 337 U.S. 325 (1949).	2	40
	2	41
United States v. Delano Park Homes, 146 F.2d 473 (2d Cir. 1944).	10	85
United States v. Dickinson, 331 U.S. 745 (1947).	14	25
United States v. Dunnington, 146 U.S. 338 (1892).	4	47
	18	5
United States v. Easement & Rt. of Way, etc., 447 F.2d 1317 (6th Cir. 1971).	14	72
United States v. General Motors Corp., 323 U.S. 373 (1945).	9	15
	16	29
	17	16
	18	55
United States v. Honolulu Plantation, 182 F.2d 172 (9th Cir. 1950).	5	21
	14	19
	14	50

Table of Cases by Jurisdiction

	Chapter	Footnote
United States Supreme Court:		
Agins v. Tiburon, 447 U.S. 255 (1980).	17	1
	17	9
	17	12
Andrus v. Allard, 444 U.S. 51 (1979).	4	19
Bauman v. Ross, 167 U.S. 548 (1897).	2	25
	3	21
Berman v. Parker, 348 U.S. 26 (1954).	4	9
	16	17
	16	23
Brown v. United States, 263 U.S. 78 (1923).	11	23
Campbell v. United States, 266 U.S. 368 (1924).	13	4
	14	36
	14	38
Chicago v. Taylor, 125 U.S. 161 (1888).	4	22
Fallbrook Irr. Dist. v. Bradley, 164 U.S. 112 (1896).	22	9
First English Evan. Luth. Ch. v. Los Angeles Cty., 482 U.S. 304 (1987).	17	13
	17	14
	17	15
Goldblatt v. Town of Hempstead, 369 U.S. 590 (1962).	4	20
Hawaii Housing Authority v. Midkiff, 467 U.S. 229 (1984).	2	14
	2	15
	2	16
	4	13
Jacobellis v. Ohio, 378 U.S. 184 (1964).	15	10
Jones v. United States, 258 U.S. 40 (1922).	10	18
Kaiser Aetna v. United States, 444 U.S. 164 (1979).	4	18
	17	8
Kerr v. South Park Commissioners, 117 U.S. 379 (1886).	2	33
Kimball Laundry Co. v. United States, 338 U.S. 1 (1949).	9	20
	16	27
	17	16
	18	55
Kohl v. United States, 91 U.S. 367 (1876).	2	4
	2	9
	2	18
Loretto v. Teleprompter Manhattan CATV Corp., 458 U.S. 419 (1982).	14	11
	17	4
McDonald, Sommer & Frates v. Yolo County, 477 U.S. 340 (1986).	17	18
	17	19
Mississippi and Rum River Boom Co. v. Patterson, 98 U.S. 403 (1879).	6	2
Nollan v. California Coastal Comm'n., 483 U.S. 825 (1987).	17	6
	17	9
Olson v. United States, 292 U.S. 246 (1934).	6	9
	6	25
	11	8
Penn Central Transportation Co. v. New York City, 438 U.S. 104 (1978).	17	3
	17	8
	17	9
Pennsylvania Coal Co. v. Mahon, 260 U.S. 393 (1922).	4	17
	17	7

	Chapter	Footnote
Pumpelly v. Green Bay & Mississippi Canal Company, 80 U.S. 166 (1872).	17	2
San Diego Gas & Electric Co. v. San Diego, 450 U.S. 621 (1981).	17	17
Sharp v. United States, 191 U.S. 341 (1903).	5	12
Shoemaker v. United States, 147 U.S. 282 (1893).	2	10
United States v. 50 Acres of Land, 469 U.S. 24 (1984).	11	26
	11	27
	11	37
United States v. 564.54 Acres of Land, 441 U.S. 506 (1979).	11	24
	11	25
United States v. Causby, 328 U.S. 256 (1946).	13	6
	16	13
	17	15
United States v. Chandler-Dunbar Water Power Co., 229 U.S. 53 (1913).	14	54
	14	64
United States v. Cors, 337 U.S. 325 (1949).	2	40
	2	41
United States v. Dickinson, 331 U.S. 745 (1947).	14	25
United States v. Dunnington, 146 U.S. 338 (1892).	4	47
	18	5
United States v. General Motors Corp., 323 U.S. 373 (1945).	9	15
	16	29
	17	16
	18	55
United States v. Miller, 317 U.S. 369 (1943).	2	29
	6	41
	6	42
United States v. Petty Motor Co., 327 U.S. 372 (1946).	17	16
	18	55
United States v. Reynolds, 397 U.S. 14 (1970).	5	14
	6	43
	14	44
United States v. River Rouge Co., 269 U.S. 411 (1926).	14	13
United States v. Welch, 217 U.S. 333 (1910).	16	47
Village of Euclid v. Ambler Realty Company, 272 U.S. 365 (1926).	4	15
United States Circuit Courts:		
Adaman Mutual Water Co. v. United States, 278 F.2d 842 (9th Cir. 1960).	4	96
Baetjer v. United States, 143 F.2d 391 (1st Cir. 1944).	5	10
	5	27
	5	32
	5	39
Bogart v. United States, 169 F.2d 210 (10th Cir. 1948).	4	47
	4	88
	18	5
Calvo v. United States, 303 F.2d 902 (9th Cir. 1962).	16	24
Carmichall v. United States, 273 F.2d 392 (5th Cir. 1960).	4	69
Cloverport Sand & Gravel Co. v. United States, 6 Cl.Ct. 178 (1984).	4	60
Cole Investment Co. v. United States, 258 F.2d 203 (9th Cir. 1958).	5	34
Feltz v. Central Nebraska P.P. & I. Dist., 124 F.2d 578 (8th Cir. 1942).	14	51
Florida East Coast Properties, Inc. v. Metropolitan Dade County, 572 F.2d 1108 (5th Cir 1978).	14	9
Florida Rock Industries, Inc. v. United States, 21 Cl. Ct. 161 (1990).	7	19
Florida Rock Industries, Inc. v. United States, 18 F.3d 1560 (Fed. Cir. 1994).	7	20

	Chapter	Footnote
Hannan v. United States 131 F.2d 441 (D.C. Cir. 1942).	10	49
Harwell v. United States, 316 F.2d 791 (10th Cir. 1963).	2	29
Hendler v. United States, 952 F.2d 1364 (Fed. Cir. 1991).	17	5
Hickey v. United States, 208 F.2d 269 (3rd Cir. 1953).	8	17
	10	36
In re Washington Market Co. Prop., 295 F. 950 (D.C. Cir. 1924).	8	18
	11	29
International Paper Company v. United States, 227 F.2d 201 (5th Cir. 1955).	14	28
	14	29
	14	30
Justice v. United States, 145 F.2d 110 (9th Cir. 1944).	21	12
Kinter v. United States, 156 F.2d 5 (3rd Cir. 1946).	2	45
	18	43
Lamm v. Volpe, 449 F.2d 1202 (10th Cir. 1971).	4	10
Linkins-Foster Monterey Corp. v. United States, 308 F.2d 595 (9th Cir. 1962).	9	36
Mayor and City Council of Baltimore v. United States, 147 F.2d 786 (4th. Cir. 1945).	11	36
McGinsey v. Central Neb. P.P. & Irr. Dist., 124 F.2d 692 (8th Cir. 1942).	4	53
Meadows v. United States, 144 F.2d 751 (4th Cir. 1944).	18	5
Midkiff v. Tom, 702 F.2d 788 (9th Cir. 1983).	2	13
Nebraska v. United States, 164 F.2d 866 (8th Cir. 1947).	4	72
	18	5
	18	9
Nemmers v. City of Dubuque, 764 F.2d 502 (8th Cir. 1985).	17	26
Onego Corporation v. United States, 295 F.2d 461 (10th Cir. 1961).	10	37
Pipeline v. O'Brian, 418 F.2d 15 (5th Cir. 1969).	10	13
Riley v. District of Columbia Redevelop. Land Agency, 246 F.2d 641 (D.C. Cir. 1957).	8	16
	10	82
Sill Corp. v. United States, 343 F.2d 411 (10th Cir. 1965).	9	30
So. Calif. Fisherman's Assn. v. United States, 174 F.2d 739 (9th Cir. 1949).	4	90
St. Regis Paper Co. v. United States, 313 F.2d 45 (9th. Cir. 1962).	13	3
State of California v. United States, 169 F.2d 914 (9th Cir. 1948).	11	35
Stipe v. United States, 337 F.2d 818 (10th Cir. 1964).	14	69
Surfside of Brevard, Inc. v. United States, 414 F.2d 915 (5th Cir. 1969).	10	82
Tlingit and Haida Indians of Alaska v. United States, 389 F.2d 778 (Ct. Cl. 1968).	11	7
Trowbridge v. Abrasive Co. of Philadelphia, 190 F.2d 825 (3rd Cir. 1951).	21	25
United States ex rel. T.V.A. v. Bailey, 115 F.2d 433 (5th Cir. 1940).	10	47
United States ex. rel. T.V.A. v. Easement and Right of Way, 405 F.2d 305 (6th Cir. 1968).	14	79
United States v. 10.48 Acres of Land, 621 F.2d 338 (9th Cir. 1980).	10	48
United States v. 100 Acres in Marin County, 468 F.2d 1261 (9th Cir. 1972).	5	15
	10	4
	12	15
	12	25
United States v. 101.88 Acres, 616 F.2d 762 (5th Cir. 1980).	16	11
United States v. 103.38 Acres of Land, 660 F.2d 208 (6th Cir. 1981).	4	61
United States v. 1,053.27 Acres of Land in Osage Co., Kan., 446 F.2d 1234 (10th Cir. 1971).	10	74
United States v. 125.07 Acres of Land, 667 F.2d 243 (1st. Cir. 1981).	12	25

	Chapter	Footnote
United States v. 15.65 Acres of Land, 689 F.2d 1329 (9th Cir. 1982).	14	41
	14	42
United States v. 158.76 Acres of Land, etc., 298 F.2d 559 (2nd Cir. 1962)	9	37
United States v. 18.46 Acres of Land, 312 F.2d 287 (2d Cir. 1963).	10	19
United States v. 2.33 Acres, 704 F.2d 728 (4th Cir. 1983).	3	32
	3	34
	14	34
United States v. 24.48 Acres, 812 F.2d 216 (5th Cir. 1987).	10	4
United States v. 2,477.79 Acres of Land, Etc., 259 F.2d 23 (5th Cir. 1958).	15	7
United States v. 25.936 Acres of Land in Borough of Edgewater, 153 F.2d 277 (3rd Cir. 1946).	18	5
United States v. 312.50 Acres, Prince William County, Va., 812 F.2d 156 (4th Cir. 1987).	10	59
United States v. 320.0 Acres of Land, More or Less in Cty., 605 F.2d 762 (5th Cir. 1979).	5	15
	10	59
United States v. 33.5 Acres, Okanogan Cty., Wash., 789 F.2d 1396 (9th Cir. 1986).	13	12
United States v. 341.45 Acres of Land, 633 F.2d 108 (8th Cir. 1980).	5	15
United States v. 38.60 Acres, 625 F.2d 196 (8th Cir. 1980).	13	14
	16	11
United States v. 429.59 Acres of Land, 612 F.2d 459 (9th. Cir. 1980).	5	17
	5	23
	5	28
United States v. 47.14 Acres, 674 F.2d 722 (8th Cir. 1982).	9	4
	9	48
United States v. 47.3096 Acres, etc., 583 F.2d 270 (6th Cir. 1978).	12	3
	12	20
	12	25
United States v. 57.09 Acres of Land, 706 F.2d 280 (9th Cir 1983).	5	22
United States v. 64.88 Acres of Land, etc., 244 F.2d 534 (3rd Cir. 1957).	16	10
United States v. 75.13 Acres of Land, etc., 693 F.2d 813 (8th Cir. 1982).	8	29
United States v. 760.807 Acres of Land, 731 F.2d 1443 (9th Cir. 1984).	14	78
United States v. 8.41 Acres, 680 F.2d 388 (5th Cir. 1982).	3	8
	6	7
	6	8
	16	24
	16	42
United States v. 8.41 Acres of Land, 783 F.2d 1256 (5th Cir. 1986).	5	4
United States v. 97.19 Acres, 582 F.2d 878 (4th Cir. 1977).	3	9
United States v. Becktold, 129 F.2d 473 (8th Cir. 1942).	4	71
	10	31
United States v. Benning Housing Corp., 276 F.2d 248 (5th Cir. 1960).	11	30
United States v. Certain Interest in Prop., 271 F.2d 379 (7th Cir. 1959).	9	4
United States v. Certain Interest in Property in the Borough of Brooklyn (Fort Hamilton), 326 F.2d 109 (2d Cir. 1964).	8	32
United States v. Certain Property, 306 F.2d 439 (2nd Cir. 1962).	2	37
United States v. Delano Park Homes, 146 F.2d 473 (2d Cir. 1944).	10	85
United States v. Easement & Rt. of Way, etc., 447 F.2d 1317 (6th Cir. 1971).	14	72
United States v. Honolulu Plantation, 182 F.2d 172 (9th Cir. 1950).	5	21
	14	19
	14	50

	Chapter	Footnote
United States v. Mattox, 375 F.2d 461 (4th Cir. 1967).	5	9
	5	33
United States v. Pope & Talbott, Inc., 293 F.2d 822 (9th Cir. 1961).	14	41
United States v. Right to Use, etc., Land, Alexandria, Va., 484 F.2d 1140 (4th Cir. 1973).	18	55
United States v. Tampa Bay Garden Apartments, Inc., 294 F.2d 598 (5th Cir. 1961).	9	32
United States v. Whitehurst, 337 F.2d 765 (4th Cir. 1964).	4	58
	4	59
	9	33
Waitaker & Co. v. Sewer Improvement District No. 1, 221 F.2d 649 (8th Cir. 1955).	22	10
Washington Metropolitan Area v. One Parcel of Land, 691 F.2d 702 (4th Cir. 1982).	6	45
Western Union Tel. Co. v. Polhemus, 178 F. 904 (3rd Cir. 1910).	13	8
	14	12
Wheeler v. City of Pleasant Grove, 896 F.2d 1347 (11th Cir. 1990).	17	28
Wolf v. Commonwealth of Puerto Rico, 341 F.2d 945 (1st Cir. 1965).	21	26
United States District Courts:		
Associated Builders & Contractors v. Baca, 769 F.Supp. 1537 (N.D. Cal. 1991).	12	34
Breckenridge Hotels Corp. v. Real Estate Research Corp., 452 F.Supp. 529 (E.D. Mo. 1978).	22	6
De Salvo v. Arkansas Louisiana Gas Co., 239 F.Supp. 312 (E.D. Ark. 1965).	2	20
Front Royal and Warren County Industrial Park v. Town of Front Royal, 749 F.Supp. 1439 (1990).	17	27
Midkiff v. Tom, 483 F.Supp. 62 (Haw. 1979).	2	12
Shrader v. Horton, 471 F.Supp. 1236 (W.D. Va. 1979).	4	16
Stubbs v. United States, 21 F.Supp. 1007 (D. N.C. 1938).	4	53
Symonds v. Bucklin, 197 F.Supp. 682 (D. Md. 1961).	7	10
Town of East Haven v. Eastern Airlines, Inc., 333 F.Supp. 338 (D. Conn. 1971).	16	14
United States v. 0.88 Acres of Land, 670 F.Supp. 210 (W.D. Mich. 1987).	9	21
United States v. 147.47 Acres of Land, 352 F.Supp. 1055 (M.D. Pa. 1972).	12	4
	12	24
United States v. 1735 N. Lynn St., 676 F.Supp. 693 (E.D. Va. 1987).	18	57
United States v. 2184.81 Acres of Land, 45 F.Supp. 681 (W.D. Ark. 1942).	4	93
United States v. 26.07 Acres of Land, 126 F.Supp. 374 (E.D. N.Y. 1954).	14	20
	14	50
United States v. 27,223.21 Acres of Land, Las Animas County, 589 F.Supp. 1121 (Colo. 1984).	6	50
United States v. 3,276.21 Acres of Land, 194 F.Supp. 297 (S.D. Cal. 1961).	18	20
United States v. 4.43 Acres of Land, 137 F.Supp. 567 (N.D. Tex. 1956).	16	12
United States v. 48.10 Acres of Land, etc., 144 F.Supp. 258 (S.D. N.Y. 1956).	16	9
United States v. 49,375 Square Feet of Land in Borough of Manhattan, 92 F.Supp. 384 (S.D. N.Y. 1950).	8	5
United States v. 70.39 Acres of Land, 164 F.Supp. 451 (S.D. Cal. 1958).	6	47
	6	48
	8	7
United States v. 765.56 Acres of Land, 174 F.Supp. 1 (E.D. N.Y. 1959).	10	30
United States v. 7936.6 Acres of Land, 69 F.Supp. 328 (P.R. 1947).	5	11
United States v. 84.4 Acres of Land, 224 F.Supp. 1017 (W.D. Pa. 1963).	11	12

	Chapter	Footnote
United States v. Bedford Associates, 548 F.Supp. 732 (S.D. N.Y. 1982).	18	56
United States v. Certain Interest in Property, 239 F.Supp. 822 (D. Colo. 1965).	9	36
United States v. Certain Lands, 69 F.Supp. 815 (S.D. N.Y. 1947).	4	68
United States v. Land in Dry Bed of Rosamond Lake, 143 F.Supp. 314 (S.D. Cal. 1956).	4	57
Virgin Islands Housing Authority v. 15.5521 Acres of Land, 230 F.Supp. 845 (D. V.I. 1964).	10	33
Washington Metropolitan Area Transit Authority v. One Parcel of Land, 413 F.Supp. 102 (D. Md. 1976).	7	11
Alabama:		
Kayo Oil Co. v. State, 340 So.2d 756 (Ala. 1976).	9	14
Alaska:		
Dash v. State, 491 P.2d 1069 (Alaska 1971).	12	19
Martens v. State, 554 P.2d 407 (Alaska, 1976).	7	13
	7	27
Arizona:		
City of Tucson v. Ruelas, 508 P.2d 1174 (Ariz. 1973).	10	60
Corrigan v. City of Scottsdale, 720 P.2d 513 (Ariz. 1986).	17	20
Moschetti v. City of Tucson, 449 P.2d 945 (Ariz. 1969).	7	16
Phoenix Title and Trust Co. v. State, 425 P.2d 434 (Ariz. 1967).	15	34
State v. Wilson, 420 P.2d 992 (Ariz. 1966).	4	32
Taylor v. State ex re. Herman, 467 P.2d 251 (Ariz. 1970).	15	5
	15	36
Arkansas:		
Arkansas State H'way Comm. v. Arkansas Real Estate Co., 471 S.W.2d 340 (Ark. 1971).	5	12
Arkansas State H'way Comm. v. Hartsfield, 454 S.W.2d 82 (Ark. 1970).	10	75
Arkansas State Highway Comm. v. Wallace, 459 S.W.2d 812 (Ark. 1970).	6	34
Arkansas State Hway. Comm. v. Ptak, 364 S.W.2d 794 (Ark. 1963).	14	24
Arkansas State Hwy. Comm. v. Wilmans, 370 S.W.2d 802 (Ark. 1963).	9	15
Baucum v. Arkansas Power & Light Co., 15 S.W.2d 399 (Ark. 1929).	2	33
Chicago Mill and Lumber Co. v. Board of Directors, 366 S.W.2d 184 (Ark. 1963).	16	35
State Highway Comm. v. Speck, 324 S.W.2d 796 (Ark. 1959).	14	23
Yonts v. Public Service Co., 17 S.W.2d 886 (Ark. 1929).	10	50
California:		
B. F. Coulter Co. et al., Superior Court, Los Angeles, Case No. 574469.	20	11
City of Fresno v. Cloud, 102 Cal. Rptr 874 (Cal. 1972).	3	19
	7	23
City of Gilroy v. Filice, 34 Cal. Rptr. 368 (Cal. 1963).	10	87
City of Los Angeles v. Allen, 36 P.2d 611 (Cal. 1934).	3	18
	4	98
City of Los Angeles v. Retlaw Enterprises, Inc., 546 P.2d 1380 (Cal. 1976).	10	58
Clark v. Erich, 31 Cal. Rptr. 628 (Cal. 1963).	18	21
County of San Luis Obispo v. Bailey, 483 P.2d 27 (Cal. 1971).	10	64
County of Santa Clara v. Curtner, 54 Cal. Rptr. 257 (Cal. 1966).	5	25
Department of Public Works v. Lynbar, Inc., 62 Cal. Rptr. 320 (Cal. 1967).	18	16
Fairchild v. Oakland etc., R. Co., 169 P. 388 (Cal. 1917).	14	61

	Chapter	Footnote
Los Angeles County Flood Control Dist. v. McNulty, 379 P.2d 493 (Cal. 1963).	3	16
People, Dep't of Public Works v. Southern Pacific Transp. Co., 109 Cal. Rptr. 525 (Cal. 1973).	7	12
People etc. v. Peninsula Enterprises, Inc., 153 Cal. Rptr. 895 (Cal. 1979).	17	21
People ex rel Dept. of Public Works v. Schultz Co., 268 P.2d 117 (Cal. 1954).	13	10
People ex rel. Dept. of Pub. Works v. Corp. of Pres. of Church of Latter Day Saints, 91 Cal. Rptr. 532 (Cal. 1970).	3	14
People v. Alexander, 27 Cal. Rptr. 720 (Cal. 1963).	6	18
People v. City of Fresno, 26 Cal. Rptr. 853 (Cal. 1962).	4	92
People v. Hemmerling, 58 Cal. Rptr. 203 (Cal. 1967).	5	26
People v. Murata, 326 P.2d 947 (Cal. 1958).	10	17
People v. Ocean Shore R.R., 196 P.2d 570 (Cal. 1948).	5	5
People v. Sayig, 226 P.2d 702 (Cal. 1951).	4	37
Redevelopment Agency v. Contra Costa Theatre, 185 Cal. Rptr. 159 (Cal. 1982).	7	29
Sacramento Southern R. Co. v. Heilbron, 104 P. 979 (Cal. 1909).	6	22
Santa Clara County Flood Control, etc., Dist. v. Freitas, 2 Cal. Rep. 129 (Cal. 1960).	12	28
State v. Whitlow, 52 Cal. Rptr. 336 (Cal. 1966).	6	10
Colorado:		
Denver Urban Renewal Authority v. Hayutin, 583 P.2d 296 (Colo. 1978).	10	44
Game & Fish Comm'n v. Farmers Irrigation Co., 426 P.2d 562 (Colo. 1967).	17	11
Montgomery Ward & Co., Inc. v. City of Sterling, 523 P.2d 465 (Colo. 1974).	18	4
Connecticut:		
Andrews v. Cox, 17 A.2d 507 (Conn. 1941).	13	9
Burritt Mutual Savings Bank v. City of New Briton, 140 A.2d 324 (Conn. 1958).	9 9	29 31
City of Meriden v. Zwalniski, 91 A. 439 (Conn. 1914).	14	80
Gebrian v. Bristol Redev. Agency, 370 A.2d 1055 (Conn. 1976).	7 7	5 7
Gigliotti v. Wood, 397 A.2d 1342 (Conn. 1978).	18	31
Hanson v. Commissioner of Transp., 408 A.2d 8 (Conn. 1979).	15	32
Hoyt v. Stamford, 165 A. 357 (Conn. 1933).	15	11
Laurel, Inc. v. State, 362 A.2d 1383 (Conn. 1975).	7	30
Florida:		
Anderson v. State Road Dept., 204 So.2d 899 (Fla. 1967).	6	39
Florida Power & Light Co. v. Jennings, 518 So.2d 895 (Fla. 1987).	14	81
Orange State Oil Co. v. Jacksonville Expressway Authority, 110 So.2d 687 (Fla. 1959).	18	27
Georgia:		
Bowers v. Fulton County, 176 S.E.2d 219 (Ga. 1970).	10	23
Calhoun v. State Hwy. Dep't., 153 S.E.2d 418 (Ga. 1967).	1	20
De Kalb County v. Cowan, 261 S.E.2d 478 (Ga. 1979).	9	19
Dep't of Transportation v. Great Southern Enterprises, 225 S.E.2d 80 (Ga. 1976).	6	12
Gains v. City of Calhoun, 42 Ga.App. 89 (Ga. 1931).	5	54
Pause v. Atlanta, 26 S.E. 489 (Ga. 1895).	14	71

	Chapter	Footnote
Kansas:		
County of Smith v. Labore, 15 P. 577 (Kan. 1887).	5	18
Ives v. Kansas Tpke. Authority, 334 P.2d 399 (Kan. 1959).	5	36
Jockheck v. Shawnee Cty., 37 P. 621 (Kan. 1894).	2	10
Ryan v. Kansas Power, 815 P.2d 528 (Kan. 1991).	13	13
Kentucky:		
Commonwealth, Dep't of Highways v. Cleveland, 432 S.W.2d 825 (Ky. 1968).	14	75
Commonwealth, Dep't of Highways v. Fister, 373 S.W.2d 720 (Ky. 1963).	14	67
Commonwealth, Dep't of Highways v. Gibson, 523 S.W.2d 885 (Ky. 1975).	8	17
Commonwealth, Dep't of Highways v. Rowland, 420 S.W.2d 657 (Ky. 1967).	14	46
Commonwealth Dep't of Highways v. Yates, 383 S.W.2d 340 (Ky. 1964).	14	66
Commonwealth Dept. of H'ways v. Sherrod, 367 S.W.2d 844 (Ky. 1963).	4	44
	18	38
	18	42
Commonwealth, Dept. of Highways v. Dennis, 409 S.W.2d 292 (Ky. 1966).	5	17
Commonwealth of Kentucky, Dept. of Highways v. Whitledge, 406 S.W.2d 833 (Ky. 1966).	10	28
Commonwealth v. Raybourne, 364 S.W.2d 814 (Ky. 1963).	14	59
Commonwealth v. Williams, 487 S.W.2d 290 (Ky. 1972).	14	37
Foster v. Sanders, 557 S.W.2d 205 (Ky. 1977).	5	55
Korfhage v. Commonwealth, 296 S.W.2d 476 (Ky. 1956).	18	13
	18	41
Louisville, etc. R. Co. v. Hall, 136 S.W. 905 (Ky. 1911).	14	55
West Kentucky Coal Co. v. Commonwealth, 368 S.W.2d 738 (Ky. 1963).	10	22
	10	76
Louisiana:		
Central Louisiana Elec. Co. v. Fontenot, 159 So.2d 738 (La. 1964).	16	34
Collins Pipeline Co. v. New Orleans East, Inc., 250 So.2d 29 (La. 1971)	14	79
Hinrieks v. New Orleans, 24 So. 224 (La. 1898).	18	47
State, Dep't of Highways v. Beatty, 288 So.2d 900 (La. 1973).	14	57
State Dep't of Highways v. Gordy, 322 So.2d 418 (La. 1975).	14	53
State, Dep't. of Highways v. Luster, 277 So.2d 181 (La. 1973).	6	32
State Department of Highways v. Bagwell, 255 So.2d 852 (La. 1971).	14	63
State, Dept. of H'ways v. LeDoux, La., 184 So.2d 604 (La. 1966).	3	20
State Dept. of H'wys. v. Stegemann, La., 269 So.2d 480 (La. 1973).	3	15
	4	99
State, Dept. of Highways v. Terrace Land Co. Inc., 298 So.2d 859 (La. 1974).	5	49
	5	50
State, through Department of Highways v. Hoyt, La., 284 So.2d 763 (La. 1973).	3	17
Tennessee Gas Transmission Co. v. Violet Trapping Co., 200 So.2d 428 (La. 1967).	2	5
Maryland:		
Andrews v. City of Greenbelt, 441 A.2d 1064 (Md. 1982).	4	83
	4	84
	4	85
Gluck v. Baltimore, 32 A. 515 (Md. 1895).	18	46
Mayor, etc., of City of Annapolis v. Anne Arundel County, 316 A.2d 807 (Md. 1974).	16	18
State Roads Commission v. Novosel, 102 A.2d 563 (Md. 1954).	11	17

	Chapter	Footnote
Massachusetts:		
Boston Chamber of Commerce v. City of Boston, 81 N.E. 244 (Mass. 1907).	4	90
Conness v. Commonwealth, 69 N.E. 341 (Mass. 1904).	6	21
Correia v. New Bedford Redevelopment Authority, 377 N.E.2d 909 (Mass. 1978).	8	4
Lembo v. Town of Farmingham, 115 N.E.2d 370 (Mass. 1953).	10	29
Malone v. Commonwealth, 389 N.E.2d 975 (Mass. 1979).	14	84
National Bank of Commerce v. City of New Bedford, 56 N.E. 288 (Mass. 1900).	10	12
	10	86
Robinson v. Commonwealth, 141 N.E.2d 727 (Mass. 1957).	7	2
Roman Catholic Bishop of Springfield v. Commonwealth, 392 N.E.2d 829 (Mass. 1979).	14	76
Savin Hill Yacht Club Ass'n v. Savin Hill Yacht Club, 140 N.E. 299 (Mass. 1923).	18	45
Tucker v. Massachusetts C.R. Co., 118 Mass. 546 (Mass. 1875).	5	38
Uhland Club v. Shupbach, 47 N.E. 113 (Mass. 1897).	18	30
Michigan:		
City of Fenton v. Lutz, 250 N.W.2d 579 (Mich. 1977)	4	75
Houghs v. Mackie, 137 N.W.2d 289 (Mich. 1965).	14	74
Petition of Michigan State Highway Comm. v. McGuire, 185 N.W.2d 187 (Mich. 1970).	10	32
Minnesota:		
City of St. Louis Park v. Engell, 168 N.W.2d 3 (Minn. 1969).	15	38
State v. Widen, 128 N.W.2d 755 (Minn. 1964).	4	45
Mississippi:		
State Highway Comm. v. Chatham, 161 So. 674 (Miss. 1935).	4	35
Yazoo, etc. R. Co. v. Jennings, 43 So. 469 (Miss. 1907).	14	56
Missouri:		
City of St. Louis v. Vasquez, 341 S.W.2d 839 (Mo. 1960).	10	57
City of Washington v. Koch, 456 S.W.2d 628 (Mo. 1970).	5	35
Land Clearance for Redevelopment Corp. v. Doernhoefer, 389 S.W.2d 780 (Mo. 1965).	18	34
Shelby County R-IV School District v. Herman, 392 S.W.2d 609 (Mo. 1965).	11	14
Springfield, etc., R. Co. v. Schweitzer, 158 S.W. 1058 (Mo. 1913).	14	70
St. Louis Housing Authority v. Bainter, 297 S.W.2d 529 (Mo. 1957).	9	17
State Highway Comm'n v. Parker, 387 S.W.2d 505 (Mo. 1965).	15	34
State v. Bowling, 414 S.W.2d 551 (Mo. 1967).	10	39
State v. Cady, 400 S.W.2d 481 (Mo. 1965).	15	33
State v. McNary, 664 S.W.2d 589 (Mo. 1984).	14	33
State v. Vorhof-Duenke Co., 366 S.W.2d 329 (Mo. 1963).	9	39
Montana:		
City of Three Forks v. State Highway Comm'n, 480 P.2d 826 (Mont. 1971).	17	11
State v. Greenfield, 399 P.2d 989 (Mont. 1964).	10	20
State v. Hoblitt, 288 P. 181 (Mont. 1930).	5	38

	Chapter	Footnote
Nebraska:		
Balog v. State, Dep't of Roads, 131 N.W.2d 402 (Neb. 1964).	4	33
Fulmer v. State Dep't of Roads, 134 N.W.2d 798 (Neb. 1965).	16	33
McCubbin v. Village of Gretna, 116 N.W.2d 287 (Neb. 1962).	13	7
Northeastern, etc., v. Frazier, 40 N.W. 604 (Neb. 1888).	5	37
Petition of Omaha Public Power Dist., 95 N.W.2d 209 (Neb. 1959).	6	23
Phillips Petroleum Co. v. City of Omaha, 106 N.W.2d 727 (Neb. 1960).	10	41
Prudential Insurance v. Central Neb. Pub. P.&I. Dist., 296 N.W. 752 (Neb. 1941).	6	39
State v. Dillon, 121 N.W.2d 798 (Neb. 1953).	4	63
Nevada:		
Eikelberger v. State, Dep't of Highways, 429 P.2d 555 (Nev. 1967).	9	34
M & R Invest. Co. v. Nevada DOT, 744 P.2d 531 (Nev. 1987).	5	5
New Hampshire:		
Dover Housing Authority v. George, 220 A.2d 156 (N.H. 1966).	12	27
New Jersey:		
New Jersey Sports and Exposition Authority v. Borough of East Rutherford, 348 A.2d 825 (N.J. 1975).	10	46
	18	19
State, Commissioner of Transportation v. Charles Investment Corp., 363 A.2d 944 (N.J. 1976).	4	34
State Commissioner of Transportation v. Township of South Hackensack, 322 A.2d 818 (N.J. 1974).	11	22
State v. Gorga, 138 A.2d 833 (N.J. 1958).	7	21
New Mexico:		
State v. Lavasek, 385 P.2d 361 (N.M. 1963).	4	24
New York:		
Application of Huie, 202 N.Y.S.2d 954 (N.Y. 1960).	9	19
Beaux Arts Prop., Inc. v. United Nations Dev. Corp., 328 N.Y.S.2d 16 (N.Y. 1972).	6	40
City of Buffalo v. Goldman, 406 N.Y.S.2d 407 (N.Y. 1978).	5	46
City of New York v. Nelkin, 415 N.E.2d 970 (N.Y. 1980).	7	22
County of Suffolk v. Firester, 339 N.E.2d 154 (N.Y. 1975).	12	29
Geffen Motors, Inc. v. State, 307 N.Y.S.2d 389 (N.Y. 1970).	10	80
Great Atlantic & Pacific Tea Co. v. State, 238 N.E.2d 705 (N.Y. 1968).	18	39
Harvey School v. State of New York, 180 N.Y.S.2d 724 (N.Y. 1958).	8	18
In re Allen St. & 1st Ave., Borough of Manhattan, City of New York, 176 N.E. 377 (N.Y. 1931).	4	74
In re Lincoln Square Slum Clearance Project, 222 N.Y.S.2d 786 (N.Y. 1961).	9	23
	11	3
In re Park Street, Vicinity of Bay Land, 325 N.Y.S.2d 555 (N.Y. 1971).	8	6
Kernochan v. Manhattan R.R. Co., 55 N.E. 906 (N.Y. 1900).	18	49
Latham Holding Co. v. State of New York, 209 N.E.2d 542 (N.Y. 1965).	10	88
Lawrence v. Greenwood, 90 N.E.2d 53 (N.Y. 1949).	10	15
Levitin v. State of New York, 207 N.Y.S.2d 798 (N.Y. 1960).	8	27
M.T.M. Realty Corp. v. State, 261 N.Y.S.2d 815 (N.Y. 1965).	5	28
Manlius Center Road Corp. v. State, 370 N.Y.S.2d 750 (N.Y. 1975).	14	14

	Chapter	Footnote
Matter of City of New York (Blackwell's Island Bridge), 103 N.Y.S. 441 (N.Y. 1907).	6	15
Matter of City of New York (West 10th St.), 196 N.E. 30 (N.Y. 1935).	16	48
	16	50
Matter of City of New York, 118 App. Div. 865, (N.Y. 1907).	18	48
Matter of City of New York, 82 N.Y.S.2d 55 (N.Y. 1948).	9	12
	9	22
O'brien v. City of New York, 32 A.D.2d 1059 (N.Y. 1969).	5	8
Priestly v. State, 242 N.E.2d 827 (N.Y. 1968).	4	27
	4	39
Ridgeway Associates, Inc. v. State, 300 N.Y.S.2d 944 (N.Y. 1969).	12	9
	12	30
Roberts v. New York El. R. Co., 128 N.Y. 455, 28 N.E. 486 (N.Y. 1891).	9	40
Spano v. State of New York, 253 N.Y.S.2d 730 (N.Y. 1964).	6	31
Spinner v. State, 167 N.Y.S.2d 731 (N.Y. 1957).	14	15
United Artists Theatre Circuit, Inc. v. State, 384 N.Y.S.2d 543 (N.Y. 1976).	12	10
Vanech v. State, 270 N.Y.S.2d 357 (N.Y. 1966).	15	34
North Carolina:		
Alva v. Cloninger, 277 S.E.2d 535 (N.C. 1981).	22	7
Barnes v. North Carolina State Highway Comm., 109 S.E.2d 219 (N.C. 1959).	5	39
Carolina Central Gas Company v. Hyder, 86 S.E.2d 458 (N.C. 1955).	16	5
City of Winston-Salem v. Davis, 296 S.E.2d 21 (N.C. 1982).	10	34
Debruhl v. State Highway & Public Works Comm., 102 S.E.2d 229 (N.C. 1958).	2	22
North Carolina State Highway Dept. v. Black, 79 S.E.2d 778 (N.C. 1954).	16	4
Redevelopment Comm. of Greenville v. Capehart, 150 S.E.2d 62 (N.C. 1966).	4	56
State v. Johnson, 191 S.E.2d 641 (N.C. 1972).	10	13
Ohio:		
Bramson v. Berea, 293 N.E.2d 577 (Ohio 1971).	14	10
City of Norwood v. Sheen, 186 N.E. 102 (Ohio 1933).	16	26
	16	28
Flair Corp. v. City of Brecksville, 359 N.E.2d 459 (Ohio 1976).	7	1
In re Appropriation For Highway Purposes, 239 N.E.2d 110 (Ohio 1968).	5	43
Ink v. City of Canton, 212 N.E.2d 574 (Ohio 1965).	4	94
Pokorny v. Local 310, Int. Hod Carriers, 300 N.E.2d 464 (Ohio 1973).	18	36
Pokorny v. Local No. 310, Int. HOD Carriers B. & C.L.U., 311 N.E.2d 866 (Ohio 1974).	18	37
State ex rel. Lindemann v. Preston, 170 N.E.2d 489 (Ohio 1960).	16	46
State, ex rel. Merritt v. Linzell, 126 N.E.2d 53. (Ohio 1955).	4	38
Oregon:		
Oregon City v. Hartke, 400 P.2d 255 (Or. 1965).	16	23
Portland, Oregon City Ry. Co. v. Penny, 158 P. 404 (Or. 1916).	15	33
State H'way Comm. v. Callahan, 410 P.2d 818 (Or. 1966).	10	77
State v. Arnold, 341 P.2d 1089 (Or. 1959).	6	29
State v. Nelson, 353 P.2d 616 (Or. 1960).	21	10
Pennsylvania:		
Berman v. Urban Redevelopment Authority of Pittsburgh, 324 A.2d 811 (Pa. 1974).	5	31

	Chapter	Footnote
Brown &. Vaughn Dev. Co. v. Commonwealth, 143 A.2d 815 (Pa. 1958).	9	41
City of Chester v. Commonwealth Dept. of Transp., 434 A.2d 695 (Pa. 1981).	11	38
East Pennsylvania R. Co. v. Hiester, 40 Pa. 53 (Pa. 1861).	10	11
In re Condemnation of 2719,21, 11 E. Berkshire St., 343 A.2d 67 (Pa. 1975).	14	8
In re Elgart's Appeal, 149 A.2d 641 (Pa. 1959).	5	46
Legislative Route 1094, Appeal of Commonwealth,Dept. of Transp., 352 A.2d 244 (Pa. 1976).	4	89
McGarrity v. Commonwealth, 166 A. 895 (Pa. 1933).	4	21
McMillan Printing Co. v. Pittsburgh, Etc., R. Co., 65 A. 1091 (Pa. 1907).	18	29
Reading, etc., R. Co. v. Balthaser, 13 A. 294 (Pa. 1888).	15	41
Redevelopment Auth. of City of Chester v. Swagger, 316 A.2d 136 (Pa. 1974).	9	19
Sams v. Redevelopment Authority, 244 A.2d 779 (Pa. 1968).	5	29
Shillito v. Metropolitan Edison Co., 252 A.2d 650 (Pa. 1969).	12	7
Rhode Island:		
Hunt v. Director of Pub. Works, 206 A.2d 91 (R.I. 1965).	10	78
Lataille v. Housing Authority of City of Woonsocket, 280 A.2d 98 (R.I. 1971).	10	5
Nasco, Inc. v. Director of Public Works, 360 A.2d 871 (R.I. 1976).	10	79
Palazzolo v. Rayhill, 394 A.2d 690 (R.I. 1978).	8	15
Sasso v. Housing Authority of the City of Providence, 111 A.2d 226 (R.I. 1955).	5	41
Wolfe v. City of Providence, 74 A.2d 843 (R.I. 1950).	4	42
South Dakota:		
State Highway Comm. v. Bloom, 93 N.W.2d 572 (S.D. 1958).	14	40
State Highway Comm. v. Miller, 155 N.W.2d 780 (S.D. 1968).	5	24
Tennessee:		
Davidson County Bd. of Ed. v. First American Nat. Bank, 301 S.W.2d 905 (Tenn. 1957).	6	20
Nashville Housing Authority v. Cohen, 541 S.W.2d 947 (Tenn. 1976).	7	18
Newport Housing Authority, Inc. v. Harsell, 533 S.W.2d 317 (Tenn. 1975).	21	8
State ex. rel. Dep't of Transportation v. Gee, 565 S.W.2d 498 (Tenn. 1977).	18	32
Texas:		
City of Beaumont v. Marks, 443 S.W.2d 253 (Tex. 1969).	4	46
City of Houston v. Fox, 429 S.W.2d 201 (Tex. 1968).	4	26
Hays v. State, 342 S.W.2d 167 (Tex. 1960).	10	10
	10	63
Mitchell v. Texas Electric Service Company, 299 S.W.2d 183 (Tex. 1957).	16	36
Texas Electric Service Co. v. Cambell, 328 S.W.2d 208 (Tex. 1959).	13	11
Texas Electric Service Co. v. West, 560 S.W.2d 769 (Tex. 1977).	14	78
Utah:		
Hempstead v. Salt Lake City, 90 P. 397 (Utah 1907).	15	37
State Road Comm. v. Rohan, 487 P.2d 857 (Utah 1971).	14	62
Utah Dept. of Trans. v. Rayco, 599 P.2d 481 (Utah 1979).	14	27
Vermont:		
Howe v. State Highway Bd., 187 A.2d 342 (Vt. 1963).	15	34

	Chapter	Footnote
Washington:		
City of Yakima v. Dahlin, 485 P.2d 628 (Wash. 1971).	14	77
North Coast R. Co. v. Kraft Co., 115 P. 97 (Wash. 1911).	18	51
Pacific Northwest Pipeline Corp. v. Myers, 311 P.2d 655 (Wash. 1957).	16	38
	16	39
State v. Calkins, 314 P.2d 449 (Wash. 1957).	14	68
State v. Green, 578 P.2d 855 (Wash. 1978).	15	22
State v. Spencer, 559 P.2d 1360 (Wash. 1977).	18	53
State v. Spencer, 583 P.2d 1201 (Wash. 1978).	18	54
State v. Wilson, 493 P.2d 1252 (Wash. 1972).	8	3
State v. Wineberg, 444 P.2d 787 (Wash. 1968).	4	40
Wisconsin:		
Jeffery v. Osborne, 129 N.W. 931 (Wis. 1911).	14	27
Vobrecht v. State Highway Comm., 143 N.W.2d 429 (Wis. 1966).	4	58
Wyoming:		
Wyoming State Highway Dep't. v. Napolitano, 578 P.2d 1342 (Wyo. 1978).	14	73
	15	43

Index